An Introduction to English Legal History

An Introduction to English Legal History

Second edition

By J. H. Baker MA, LLB, PHD
of the Inner Temple and Gray's Inn, barrister;
Fellow of St Catharine's College and
University Lecturer in Law, Cambridge

London
BUTTERWORTHS
1979

England	Butterworth & Co (Publishers) Ltd
London	88 Kingsway, WC2B 6AB
Australia	Butterworths Pty Ltd
Sydney	586 Pacific Highway, Chatswood, NSW 2067
	Also at Melbourne, Brisbane, Adelaide and Perth
Canada	Butterworth & Co (Canada) Ltd
Toronto	2265 Midland Avenue, Scarborough M1P 4S1
New Zealand	Butterworths of New Zealand Ltd
Wellington	77–85 Customhouse Quay
South Africa	Butterworth & Co (South Africa) (Pty) Ltd
Durban	152–154 Gale Street
USA	Butterworth (Publishers) Inc
Boston	19 Cummings Park, Woburn, Mass 01801

ISBN Casebound 0 406 55502 8
Limp 0 406 55503 6

Filmset in 10/12 point Baskerville
Printed and bound in Great Britain
by Mackays of Chatham Ltd

Reprinted 1981
Reprinted 1983

The cover of the limp edition shows a detail from *The Court of Chancery in the reign of George I*, c. 1720–25, by B. Ferrers, in the National Portrait Gallery, London

Preface

Some might think a second edition of a textbook on legal history more in need of justification than a new edition of a textbook on some rapidly developing branch of modern law. Surely, they will ask, legal history does not go out of date? The straight answer to their question is that all history, meaning history as we see it rather than the bare facts of the past, is subject to change; and in the last eight years original research has revealed so many new facts that our interpretations of English legal history are having to change as fast as the modern law does. The more honest answer to the question is, alas, more subjective. When the first edition was written the author saw things with a clarity given only to those who have not come fully to appreciate the extent of their own ignorance. No doubt that defect gave the book an illusory strength from the point of view of the groping student, but equally it must have caused widespread irritation among the more discerning readers. Many shortcomings, ranging from undue compression to manifest error, became apparent as the years passed, through further reading and research, and through trying to make sense of the subject to successive generations of students. In the optimistic belief that slightly more comprehensiveness is not incompatible with comprehensibility, I have made numerous additions throughout and have rewritten most of the first part. No doubt in eradicating the more obvious shortcomings I have introduced others. I have, nevertheless, tried hard not to alter the character of the book as an elementary historical introduction to English law, through which the reader may find his way to more substantial works. Perhaps the most formative influence on the shape and content of this edition has been the experience of lecturing on the history of English law to the inns of court, a yearly task which I was pleased to attempt six times; and I wish to record my gratitude to the Council of Legal Education for providing me with the opportunity of reconstruction. Among the many influences on the substantive rethinking behind this edition the foremost have been my Cambridge colleagues;

to them, and indeed to all who have helped me, knowingly or otherwise, my gratitude knows no bounds.

J.H.B.
Cambridge,
December, 1978

Preface to the first edition

"A law student in the present day," said Professor Amos in an unpublished lecture in 1831, "should be like the ancient God Janus. He should have two faces, looking forwards and backwards on his profession; or he may perchance find the choicest stores of his industry suddenly converted into useless and cumbersome rubbish." He was addressing his law class at University College London, at the dawning of the age of law reform; and his words are particularly meaningful today, as practitioners and students face another period of rapid legal change. The modern student, like his predecessor of 1831, has to come to terms with the fact that much of the law he learns, perhaps even some of what he is taught to consider axiomatic, will become obsolete in the course of his professional career. The academic discipline of law, therefore, if it is to have any lasting value, cannot confine itself to the mere learning of rules. It must impart some understanding of the rules, and a dynamic sense of legal evolution. To this end, some knowledge of the historical development of the law will always be indispensable. History alone reveals the reasons—though it does not provide any justifications—for the present shape of the law and legal concepts.

Legal history is a fascinating and intricate study in itself, and it continues to attract the attentions of researchers and scholars. But perhaps by its seeming to fall between the two disciplines of law and history, its basic relevance to both is sometimes overlooked. The present book is not designed for the student specialising in legal history, but for the student who requires a short history, in brief outline, of the principal English legal institutions and doctrines. Anyone who wishes to understand the history of English law at a deeper level must read Professor Milsom's stimulating *Historical Foundations of the Common Law* (1969).

This book is based on a course of lectures delivered to the first year law students at University College London, in the progress of which I first felt the need for an elementary textbook of this kind. I wish to acknowledge, with deep thanks, the debt I owe to Professor Milsom

vii

and his work, and the help I have received directly and indirectly, from all my colleagues at University College. I am particularly indebted to Mr Daniel Prentice for his patient criticism of the manuscript and his numerous valuable suggestions for improvement.

J. H. Baker
March 1971

Contents

Part two

Appendix A

Appendix B

Table of Statutes

In the following Table references to '*Statutes*' are to Halsbury's Statutes of England (Third Edition) showing the volume and page where the annotated text of the Act will be found.

Table of Cases

Kings and queens of England since 1066

with the dates of their accession

House of Normandy
William I, *25 Dec 1066–1087*
William II, *26 Sept 1087–1100*
Henry I, *5 Aug 1100–1135*
Stephen, *26 Dec 1135–1154*

Angevins *(House of Plantagenet)*
Henry II, *19 Dec 1154–1189*
Richard I, *3 Sept 1189–1199*
John, *27 May 1199–1216*

House of Plantagenet *(continued)*
Henry III, *28 Oct 1216–1272*
Edward I, *20 Nov 1272–1307*
Edward II, *8 July 1307–1327*
Edward III, *25 Jan 1327–1377*
Richard II, *22 June 1377–1399*

House of Lancaster
Henry IV, *30 Sept 1399–1413*
Henry V, *21 Mar 1413–1422*
Henry VI, *1 Sept 1422–1461*

House of York
Edward IV, *4 Mar 1461–1483*
Edward V, *9 April 1483*
Richard III, *26 June 1483–1485*

House of Tudor
Henry VII, *22 Aug 1485–1509*
Henry VIII, *22 April 1509–1547*
Edward VI, *28 Jan 1547–1553*
Mary I, *19 July 1553–1554*

Philip & Mary, *25 July 1554–1558*
Elizabeth I, *17 Nov 1558–1603*

House of Stuart
James I, *24 Mar 1603–1625*
Charles I, *27 Mar 1625–1649*
[Interregnum *1649–60*]
Charles II, *30 Jan 1649 (de jure)*; restored *29 May 1660–1685*
James II, *6 Feb 1685–1688*
William & Mary, *13 Feb 1689–1694*
William III, *28 Dec 1694–1702*
Anne, *8 Mar 1702–1714*

House of Hanover
George I, *1 Aug 1714–1727*
George II, *11 June 1727–1760*
George III, *25 Oct 1760–1820*
George IV, *29 Jan 1820–1830*
William IV, *26 June 1830–1837*
Victoria, *20 June 1837–1901*

House of Saxe-Coburg and Gotha
Edward VII, *22 Jan 1901–1910*

House of Windsor
George V, *6 May 1910–1936*
Edward VIII, *20 Jan 1936*
George VI, *11 Dec 1936–1952*
Elizabeth II, *6 Feb 1952–*

Table of Abbreviations

LQR	Law Quarterly Review
Legal History Studies 1972	D. Jenkins ed *Legal History Studies 1972* (1975)
Legal Records and the Historian	J. H. Baker ed *Legal Records and the Historian* (1978)
Milsom HFCL	S. F. C. Milsom *Historical Foundations of the Common Law* (1969)
Plucknett CHCL	T. F. T. Plucknett *Concise History of the Common Law* (5th edn., 1956)
Pollock & Maitland	F. Pollock and F. W. Maitland *History of English Law before the time of Edward I* (2nd edn., 1898; reissued 1968)
Potter HIEL	H. Potter *Historical Introduction to English Law* (4th edn., by A. K. R. Kiralfy, 1958)
Radcliffe & Cross	Lord Cross and G. R. Y. Radcliffe *The English Legal System* (6th edn., by G. J. Hand and D. J. Bentley, 1977)
Rolle Abr	H. Rolle *Un Abridgement des Plusieurs Cases* (1668), in two volumes
Rot Parl	*Rotuli Parliamentorum* (1783), in six volumes
SS	Selden Society, annual volumes
Simpson IHLL	A. W. B. Simpson *Introduction to the History of Land Law* (1961)
Stat	Statute; references are to the *Statutes at Large* unless otherwise stated
TRHS	Transactions of the Royal Historical Society
YB	Year book; references are given by term, regnal year, folio, and placitum

Printed law reports are cited by the references currently in use. They may also be found in the *English Reports* reprint.

Part one
1. Law and Custom in Early Britain

When, in 1470, an English serjeant-at-law maintained that the common law had been in existence since the creation of the world,[1] it is not improbable that he believed it literally. There was even a veneer of truth upon the notion, inasmuch as English law represented an unbroken development from prehistoric time. There had been no conscious invention, or introduction from outside. What the serjeant did not perceive was that there had been a time, not so many centuries before his own, when there was no law at all as he understood it. For him, as for ourselves, law consists in rules laid down by judicial or legislative authority; and the common law embodies a particular system of rules, with their own rational coherence. But four centuries before 1470, at the time of the Norman conquest, England had neither legislature nor judicature in any developed sense. There were decision-making bodies, from the king's council down to the village meeting; but tribunals do not necessarily follow or make binding rules, and in these ancient assemblies no distinction could have been made between the processes of adjudication, administration and legislation. Decisions settled the matter in hand and were not expected to do more; they were neither constrained by the past nor constraining upon the future. That is not to suggest that there was widespread despotism or anarchy. Decisions were doubtless guided by custom and wise counsel. Even so, good order, custom and due deliberation are not quite the same as 'law'.

VARIETY OF CUSTOMS IN EARLY BRITAIN

One feature of 'custom' which distinguishes it from the later common law tradition is its variability from one people to another and from one area to another. Uniformity was hardly to be expected when social habits and attitudes varied from place to place and from one family to another. It follows from this, given the many vicissitudes of the tribes and races which inhabited this island before the Normans, that any search for the laws or customs of England before the centralisation of

1. *Wallyng v Meger* (1470) 47 SS 38 per Catesby Sjt.

the nation itself are bound to fail. To the extent that common features may be discerned in the customs of different people and places, the unifying force is not law but the general social and moral assumptions of the age, or even the natural instincts of mankind at particular stages of development; the parallels often transcend national and geographic boundaries.

Our first glimpses of ancient British customs are through Roman eyes, because the learned men among the Britons preferred to pass on their traditions by mouth rather than commit them to writing. Julius Caesar described the native priest-judges, called druids, who preserved and enforced the Celtic religion and customs; but of those customs he related very little, save that they involved human sacrifice. The Romans themselves had a sophisticated jurisprudence, and to them the usages of the British had little more than anthropological interest. Whether their colonisation of Britain made any lasting impact on native traditions is doubtful. Roman law certainly operated, at least on Roman citizens, and the famous jurist Papinian is known to have heard cases in the forum at York. Yet, in the confusion which followed the Roman withdrawal at the beginning of the fifth century, the Celts were left to pursue their tribal customs without impediment. The chief enduring survival was the Christian Church, which lingered on to vie with the druidical order for spiritual authority and ultimately to prevail. During the next two centuries the British mainland was subject to continuous invasion from across the North Sea. The conquering Angles and Saxons pushed the Celtic people back into the west of the island, into Wales, Cornwall and south-west Scotland. The invading races differed from the Celts in religion, language and physical appearance; and they brought with them Teutonic customs which even the Romans had noticed as being different from those of Britain and Gaul.

The Anglo-Saxons are the first inhabitants of whose customs anything is known, because they were the first to introduce written laws. The first surviving English legislation, that of King Aethelberht I of Kent, appeared in about 600 A.D. and has traditionally been associated with the supposed conversion of that king to Christianity by St Augustine. The early Christian kings relied upon the counsel of their bishops in temporal as in spiritual affairs, and the clergy had the literary skill to initiate the technique of government through the written word. Bede wrote, two centuries later, that the new laws had been made 'according to the Roman example', and many were taken up with ecclesiastical matters; the laws of Wihtred (c. 700 A.D.) were, indeed, expressly stated to be the outcome of a clerical assembly.

Recent research has raised the contrary possibility that Aethelberht's laws were those of the last pagan king. They were written in Anglo-Saxon, not in clerical Latin, and it is likely that Bede retrospectively overemphasised Augustine's influence. Whatever the truth may be, it is clear that the Anglo-Saxon codes did not 'codify' existing customs, let alone make new law. They were directed at those who could be presumed to know the customs, and offered fixed rules to govern situations which must previously have rested on discretion. Prominent in them, as in foreign codes of similar type, was the fixing of the blood-money payable in lieu of feuding. It is easy to imagine how arbitration failed to assuage the passion for retribution. The definite pre-ordained scales of penalties which peace and pride required seem closely associated with the disciplinary codes (called 'penitentials') which the northern Church devised to facilitate exact spiritual emendation for sins.[2]

The Danish invasions in the ninth century subjected the eastern parts of the country to new Scandinavian influences. Where the Danes conquered, their 'Danelaw' prevailed. The very word 'law' is believed to have been a Danish importation. The struggle between the Anglo-Saxon peoples and their common enemy gave King Alfred of Wessex (d. 899 A.D.) his opportunity to begin the unification of the former into the single kingdom of England. King Alfred is reputed to have taken a deep interest in justice, and to have taken on himself the occasional review of decisions made by subjects. In the prologue to the code which he promulgated for the West Saxons he claimed that he and his advisers had studied the laws of Aethelberht of Kent, Ine of Wessex, and Offa of Mercia, together with the Bible and the penitentials of the Church, before embarking upon their task. This may have been the first attempt to compare the miscellaneous customs of the English. But Alfred's written laws were still far removed from anything like comprehensive common law. They were an attempt to impose uniformity in certain limited fields, and as such set a constitutional precedent for legislation by kings of England. The precedent was followed by nearly all of Alfred's successors, including the Danish King Cnut (1016–35). The laws of Cnut and of King Edward the Confessor (1042–66) were the main sources of old English usages for writers after the Norman conquest. Nevertheless, despite all this legislative activity, England was still governed rather by custom than by universal legal principles; and the customs of English and Danish

2. See T. P. Oakley *English Penitential Discipline and Anglo-Saxon Law* (1923). For the reappraisal of Aethelberht's laws, see Richardson & Sayles *Law and Legislation*, pp. 1–10, 157–169.

people alike remained for the greater part unwritten. The principal reason for the absence of common law at this stage was the absence of any judicial machinery to require or produce it.

'Communal' Justice

Societies are slow to recognise legal authority as now understood. Custom and religion are forces in the community to be upheld and maintained as a matter of tradition and social obligation, or to earn eternal salvation; but legal sanctions necessitate the imposition of forces which the early community is unready or even unable to wield. Force belongs in the state of nature to individuals, and the suppression of private force by investing the 'community' at large with a greater force required a degree of social organisation which it must have taken countless dark and forgotten centuries to achieve. If one man takes something from another, the most obvious remedy is for the victim to try to take it back; when it was also the only remedy, no man had any rights beyond what he had the physical power to protect for himself. Thus, in the absence of strong government or judicial control, people administered their own justice by self-help: by forcible entries, reprisals and family feuds. One of the first causes of a legal system is the desire to prevent, or discourage, feuding; and this was best achieved by offering some peaceful alternative. Here the community could assist, as a body in public meeting, by encouraging the parties to settle their differences or to submit them to arbitration. Feuding parties were given the opportunity to air their grievances before their fellows, and with communal guidance to reach an honourable compromise. If the parties could not agree, the community did not decide between them, but might press upon them, or one of them, a supernatural test which could not be disputed. Procedures of this kind did not yet reflect a notion of judicial authority or coercion; but parties who would not co-operate might be cut off from the community by what would later become outlawry.

Very little is known of the growth of communal organisation in England. The 'moot' or folk-assembly, first mentioned in the Kentish laws of the eighth century, was of prehistoric origin. It would be unrealistic to regard it, even when the dim rays of history first fall upon its outlines, as a court of law. It was an open-air meeting of the population to discuss local affairs. It had no judge; the principal men of the locality met under the presidency of a 'doomsman' or 'shire-man', but acted as a community. It issued no writs and kept no records; consequently very little is known about it. Maitland described what could be seen as 'thoroughly characteristic of archaic legal systems in general. Nothing in it is peculiarly English, not much is peculiarly German'.[3] The procedure in contentious matters was calculated to avoid decision-making. If the parties could not be persuaded to make a 'love-day'—to settle amicably—then the dispute was referred to a supernatural test. Sometimes the test took physical form as an 'ordeal', which involved an appeal to God for His miraculous intervention in human disputes. Doubtless pre-Christian in their inception, several forms of ordeal were consecrated by the early Christian Church. In the ordeal of hot iron, a piece of iron was put in the fire and then, briefly, in the party's hand; the hand was then bound, and inspected a few days later; if the burn had festered, God was taken to have decided against the party. The ordeal of hot water followed a similar method. The ordeal of cold water required the party to be trussed and lowered into a pond; if he sank, the water was deemed to have 'received him' with God's blessing, and so he was quickly rescued. Perhaps more widespread as a test, after the advent of Christianity, was the oath. One or other of the parties would be required to swear to the truth of his case on the holy evangels, and usually he would have to bring with him a number of neighbours as 'oath-helpers' to back up his word.

There is some evidence that in historic times men lost faith in the ordeal, and that priests began to feel some moral responsibility to arrange the result they considered right. In any case, it was tempting Providence to seek miracles as a matter of routine, and in 1215 the Lateran Council prohibited further clerical participation and thereby stifled them. The oath, on the other hand, remained reliable, final and inscrutable.[4] There was no question of deciding whether the oath was true, and no investigation of the facts of any individual case. The oath, like the ordeal, was intended to preclude human judgment on the merits of the case. It is commonly said that judgment preceded proof, because once it was adjudged that one of the parties should perform the test there was no further decision to make. The wise men of each community needed to know how to regulate disputes, when and how tests should be imposed on disputing parties, and what should be done when the result was known. Here was room for argument and human discretion. But the essence of the dispute, and any principles

3. Pollock & Maitland, vol. I, p. 43.
4. It passed into the common law as 'wager of law', not formally abolished until 1833: p. 65, post. Trial by battle was not affected in 1215, but it was probably a Norman innovation.

on which it was determinable, were for God, not man, to discover and apply. Accordingly, the 'law' of the early English, if so it may be called, had little sophisticated content. Rights and liabilities could not be worked out in detail. Early law stopped short at what we now call procedure.

THE OLD ENGLISH ASSEMBLIES

The primeval moot or local folk-assembly was constrained by no jurisdictional boundaries other than those inherent in the natural variety of customs and peoples in different places. Each meeting was in that sense sovereign. Of the organisation and distribution of separate communities in the Dark Ages we have but a faint picture, dependent chiefly on archaeology. 'An English kingdom in the sixth century was not very far removed from the little kingdoms of Märchenland, rude and pastoral, where a journey of a day or two or even less might take a traveller from the heart of one king's dominion to the heart of another.'[5] The same was probably true even of villages; we need not suppose that the average Englishman thought of himself as English or had much consciousness of anything beyond the little closed world of his own village.

By the tenth century a more homogenous scheme of local government was being imposed by an increasingly effective monarchy, in order both to delimit the geographical authority of existing institutions and to locate some personal responsibility for their working. The laws of Athelstan (d. 939 A.D.) and his successors mention 'hundreds' as administrative units under the responsibility of a hundredman, with monthly meetings. The hundreds were divided into ten 'tithings', which were notionally groups of ten families under the responsibility of a tithingman. The sorting of the population into tithings and hundreds was a means of maintaining good order and of raising taxes to support the king. At the monthly assemblies of the hundred was transacted the ordinary judicial business of the community; and twice a year, at what was later called the 'view of frankpledge', the tithings were reviewed to make sure that every free man was 'in borh' (pledged to good behaviour) and that all crimes were being duly presented.

At about the same time as the appearance of hundreds,[6] the whole country was divided into the larger units called 'shires' (counties). Apart from some tinkering with boundaries, particularly in 1972,

---

5. Richardson & Sayles *Law and Legislation*, p. 6.
6. The word 'shire' was used in Wessex as early as the 7th century, but there is no evidence of wider use at that date.

these have remained substantially the same in name and shape to the present day. Some of the shires south of the Thames, and also Essex and Middlesex, correspond to old Saxon kingdoms, while names such as Norfolk and Suffolk suggest ancient tribal communities. But most of our shires derive their name from a borough at or near their centre, and it is likely that these represent a northward extension of the shiring system from Wessex for military purposes. The boroughs themselves had been established as royal strongholds against invasion, and in some cases by capture had become the stronghold of invaders; they were therefore suitable centres of a defensive system under which, in the tenth and eleventh centuries, the shires surrounding them were assigned to royal provincial commanders called 'ealdormen'. The shire had an assembly, which by the time of King Edgar (959–975 A.D.) met twice a year, attended by the ealdorman and bishop, to discuss the more important affairs of the region. The laws of Ine of Wessex (c. 690 A.D.) refer to justice (*riht*) being demanded before the *scirmen* or shire-man—perhaps the ealdorman's deputy—and it seems the shire moot, like all other assemblies of people, combined judicial and administrative functions. Although most hundreds fell exactly within the bounds of one shire, there was no hierarchic relationship between the two institutions; both, within their geographical limits, were sovereign, though it is likely that only the more important or troublesome disputes were reserved for the infrequent and solemn shire moots.

The boroughs also had assemblies of like nature, called burgh moots, portmanmoots or (when held indoors) hustings. In medieval times these would develop into busy courts for merchants, and despite the ancient character of their procedural customs[7] they managed to adapt to the needs of the mercantile community and flourished until Tudor times, in some cases beyond. The borough performed similar functions for town people, both administratively and judicially, as the hundred performed for country folk; borough and hundred were therefore reckoned to be mutually exclusive. In London, however, the husting was really equivalent to a shire and came to displace the old shire moot; the London equivalent of the hundred was the 'ward', and the division into wards has continued largely unchanged to the present.

The smallest assembly was that of the village. Although it may often have coincided with a tithing, it was not a subdivision of any of the other units but simply a conglomeration of dwellings correspond-

---

7. Many of these customs were in medieval times codified: see M. Bateson *Borough Customs* (18 and 21 SS, 1904–06).

ing roughly to the later parish (an ecclesiastical unit). The settlement of a group of families in a village, with open-field farming, must have necessitated at least a communal agricultural policy, and it is possible that village meetings had been the place to settle it. Of the early village moot, however, we find little or no trace in history. When we first hear of it, it has become the court of a 'manor', the hall moot of a feudal lord in which the free men of the village had a voice and in many places could make byelaws and punish minor crimes in addition to considering agricultural and feudal business. The community of the vill continued to exercise police functions, independently of manorial feudalism, into the common law era.

FROM COMMUNAL TO PERSONAL AUTHORITY

The earliest form of justice was not conceived of as emanating from a ruler or from learned judges. We do not hear of the king's law, or of a lord's law, but only of communal justice or the custom of the people (*folcriht*), a term frequently encountered even in the royal legislation of the Anglo-Saxon period. In the various assemblies of manor, borough, hundred and shire, there was no 'judge' as such. The business was transacted by those attending as 'suitors', under the chairmanship of the lord or ealdorman or his deputy. Yet such is the dependency of good administration and effective justice upon the energy of the elders or leaders of a community that, almost as soon as these institutions are noticed in written sources, jurisdiction seems to be a duty vested in persons rather than in the community at large. The origins of this aspect of lordship are difficult to trace. Eventually it would merge with feudal lordship, but it seems to be present before any feudal characteristics can be identified. Some ealdormen probably represented ancient royal families. In some cases lordship may have developed from prehistoric notions of chieftainship, in others by delegation from the king; its roots were not in legal theory, for there was none, but in the fact of power and personal leadership. What may seem to us to be a shift of authority from the community to lordship was probably in reality no more than a failure to conceptualise the 'community': authority was associated with people, not with constitutional theories. The way of thinking is most apparent in the sphere of public order, where what is protected is not the safety of the community but the peace (*grith*) of particular persons. In this concept, what we regard as public and private rights are merged; the peace of a churl was simply his right to compensation for wrongs done to him and his family, but the peace of a lord included the protection of his vassals and was a right more akin to jurisdiction than a cause of action.

By far the most important consequence of this personalisation of authority was the constitutional ascendancy of the king. The king had been responsible for establishing the borough, hundred and shire, and in all of them he placed his own officials called 'reeves' to watch over their operation. The laws of Edward the Elder (d. 925 A.D.) and Athelstan (d. 939 A.D.) make plain the duty of the king's reeves in borough and hundred to see that all men received the benefit of the *folcriht* and the 'doom-book' (presumably Alfred's code) in those assemblies. Some hundreds were allowed to fall under the control of lords, and some parcels of hundredal jurisdiction came to belong to lords of manors; in such cases, the lords were said to possess *sake* and *soke*, the right to hold court and to compel suitors to attend it. Even in these situations, however, the king retained some supervisory control and might claim to deprive a lord who abused his authority. The shire remained more closely in the king's control; and the shire-reeve or sheriff, whose duties extended to visiting the hundreds twice yearly for the view of frankpledge, was soon to become one of the most important officials in the country.

Before the Norman conquest of 1066, therefore, the constitutional notion that justice is a prerogative of the Crown was beginning to have some foundation in fact, though it was not yet expressed in words. The king's peace was a concept capable of bringing many disputes within the purview of the king's own court, his council of wise men or *witan*. Kings had already undertaken on occasion to look into legal disputes if parties alleged a failure of justice elsewhere. And kings were using written instruments to confer or define jurisdiction: codes containing general directions to reeves and lords, charters granting *sake* and *soke*, criminal jurisdiction,[8] or borough status, and writs referring disputes or declaring rights to meetings of the shire. Still, be it noted, there was no king's law. But the seeds of the common law system which flowered in the twelfth century had begun to grow.

Further reading

Pollock & Maitland, vol. I, pp. 1–63
Holdsworth HEL, vol. II, pp. 1–118
Plucknett CHCL, pp. 3–10, 83–100
Milsom HFCL, pp. 1–13
D. Whitelock, *English Historical Documents 500–1042* (1955),
   pp. 327–459

8. Each crime seems to have needed a separate grant: e.g. *grithbreche* (breach of the peace), *hamsocn* (housebreaking), *infangthief* and *utfangthief* (theft), *forsteal* (ambush), etc.

J. E. A. Jolliffe, *The Constitutional History of Medieval England* (4th edn, 1961), pp. 1–138

H. G. Richardson and G. O. Sayles, *Law and Legislation from Aethelberht to Magna Carta* (1966), pp. 1–29

THE OLD ASSEMBLIES

Pollock & Maitland, vol. I, pp. 527–688; F. W. Maitland, *Domesday Book and Beyond* (1897)

S. B. Chrimes in Holdsworth HEL, vol. I, (7th edn), pp. 1*–24*, 5–24

W. A. Morris, *The Frankpledge System* (1910); *The Early English County Court* (1926)

W. O. Ault, *Private Jurisdiction in England* (1923)

H. M. Cam, *The Hundred and the Hundred Rolls* (1930); *Law-finders and Law-makers in Medieval England* (1962), chaps. I, III–V; *Liberties and Communities in Medieval England* (1963)

J. P. Dawson, *A History of Lay Judges* (1960), pp. 178–286

H. M. Jewell, *English Local Administration in the Middle Ages* (1972)

A. Harding, *The Law Courts of Medieval England* (1973), pp. 13–31

2. Origins of the Common Law

The conquest of England by Duke William of Normandy in 1066 was described by Maitland as a catastrophe which determined the whole future of English law.[1] Yet the changes which are usually attributed to this event did not all occur suddenly. William claimed to be king by lawful right as well as by conquest, and one of his first acts was to promise the English that they could keep their own laws. The Normans were warlike, uncultured and illiterate. Whether they appreciated it or not, they found in England a system of law and government as well developed as anything they had left in Normandy. Certainly they had nothing of refined jurisprudence to transplant. The immediate effects of the conquest were to introduce new racial discriminations—this time between French and English—a new and rather barbaric form of ordeal (trial by battle), the separation of ecclesiastical courts from the shires and hundreds, the subjection of the forests to an alien and oppressive 'forest law' protecting the royal hunt, and a brand of military feudalism which gave seignorial jurisdiction a new basis. None of this helped produce a common law: rather the reverse.

The common law emerged in the twelfth century from the efficient and rapid expansion of institutions which existed in an undeveloped state before 1066. England, unlike Normandy, was already a unified nation with a central government ruling through sheriffs answerable to the king, and it had the beginnings of a bureaucratic administration operating through written instruments under the king's seal. To this the Normans, and their Angevin successors, brought a taste for strong government and a flair for administration, so that within a century the rudimentary court of the Anglo-Saxon kings had grown to produce two great departments of state (the Chancery and the Exchequer) and a judicial system whereby the king's justice was dispensed regularly by members of his household.

The effect of these changes on legal administration can be understood by comparing two twelfth-century law books. The state of things as William I had found them was described in the compilation

1. Pollock & Maitland, vol. I, p. 79.

known as the *Leges Henrici Primi* (c. 1118), which was probably the work of a continental observer in Wessex. There were three distinct systems of law in England: the law of Wessex, the law of Mercia, and the Danelaw. But there were differences of detail, particularly in procedure, in each of the thirty-two counties. There were the courts of shires, hundreds and boroughs, the courts of lords, and the courts of the king. Trial was by oath, ordeal or battle; but the operation of these varied from place to place and according to the status of the parties. Litigation, according to the author, was as uncertain as a game of dice.[2] The uncertainty is well illustrated by the confusion in the book, which collects ill-digested Anglo-Saxon laws with scraps of Canon law and personal observations. The writer did, nevertheless, perceive the paramount position of the king, whose enormous power (*tremendum regiae majestatis imperium*) placed him above all other laws. The king's court, too, enjoyed a special position: 'over and above everything stand the pleas of the royal court, which preserves the use and custom of its law at all times and in all places and with constant uniformity'.[3]

Such was the activity of that royal court during the next seventy years that in the 1180s a treatise could be written on 'the laws and customs of England' which was based solely on its workings. The treatise, traditionally but questionably attributed to Sir Ranulf de Glanvill (justiciar of England 1180–89), gives the impression that the variety of local customs had in no way diminished; and so the book avowedly only presents one aspect of the law of the time. The great step forward was in the author's treatment of the fixed customs of the king's court as constituting *jus et consuetudo regni*, the law and custom of the realm. Whether Glanvill and his contemporaries could actually foresee that the law of the realm would in due course virtually displace local custom does not affect the significance of the twelfth-century jurisprudential advance. Just as the monk Gratian a generation earlier at Bologna had produced from the confusion of canon laws a coherent system of Canon law deriving ultimate authority from the pope, so Glanvill and his fellow judges under King Henry II (1154–89) produced a coherent system of English law deriving ultimate authority from the king. Against that uniform system local custom would thereafter be seen as at best exceptional and at worst exceptionable.

Unlike Gratian, who had to resolve discrepancies in the canonical

---

2. *Leges Henrici Primi*, vi, 6 (Downer edn, p. 98): 'incerta penitus alea placitorum', the utterly uncertain dice of pleas.
3. Ibid., pp. 97, 109.

sources by means of a 'concordance of discordant canons', Glanvill isolated the law of England by focusing on the work of the king's justices to the exclusion of all else. His custom of the realm was a law of writs, of the instruments which initiated lawsuits in the king's courts and of the remedies which they enshrined.[4] Both the organisation of the courts, and the forms of remedy available in them, may have been regulated by royal legislation since lost. Glanvill himself refers to 'assizes' and 'constitutions' of this nature, and also to unwritten laws promulgated by the king's council. Some of these decisions may have been reached in considering actual disputes, so that they resemble case-law; but a distinction between adjudication and legislation would at this period still be unreal. Moreover, few decisions were embodied in authoritative texts or records, and so the means by which the common law of England was brought into being are largely lost to historians. It is possible, nevertheless, to show in broad outline how the institutions of the common law emerged from the bold experiments of the twelfth century.

REGIONAL AND ITINERANT ROYAL JUSTICE

If the main consequence of the spread of royal justice was intellectual, its causes were more mundane. The Crown developed the scope of breach of the king's peace in order to preserve public order. Effective criminal justice is the first prerequisite of good government, and the Normans took up and strengthened the Anglo-Saxon system of communal responsibility, introducing safeguards to counterbalance the growing power of the sheriffs. There was an added financial incentive, in that the pursuit of law and order was profitable. Some pleas of the Crown were purely fiscal, but all criminal justice bore golden fruit in fines and forfeitures. The pipe rolls of the Exchequer testify to the steady revenue from judicature, and in 1301 it was recorded that Edward I 'gained great treasure' to pay for his military campaigns by 'causing justice to be done on malefactors'.[5] The people are said to have groaned under the burden of royal investigations and money-raising judicial expeditions, and yet they apparently flocked to the same judges for the recovery of their possessions and were prepared to pay a price for royal justice. The main attractions for the private litigant were probably the effective process and execution which royal writs authorised, and the availability (after 1200) of a central written record which would end dispute for all time. To squabble about weighty matters in local courts was often to waste time to no purpose,

4. For the history of the writs, see chap. IV, post.
5. *Croniques de London* (Camden Society, 1844), pp. 28–29.

because even if a fair hearing were obtained the judgment might be unenforceable, and there was always the risk that it would be reopened before the king. The king's law was not yet universal; but the king's judgments were judgments which could not be questioned or ignored. Royal justice triumphed because it suited both Crown and litigants that it should do so. Yet it could not have undergone its tremendous expansion if the king had attempted to hear all royal pleas in person. The innovation, or development, which more than any other achievement of the Norman period made possible the common law was the practice of delegation. It is interesting to note that the pope introduced judges-delegate at the same period and for the same reason. The Anglo-Norman equivalent of the judge-delegate was the *justiciarius*.[6]

The justiciar was in a very real sense a viceroy, a deputy of the king empowered to act in royal affairs, and as such was concerned with all affairs of state. The first and greatest justiciars, notably Bishop Roger of Salisbury (d. 1139) and Sir Richard de Lucy (retired 1178), were really prime ministers; and their principal monument was the elaborate revenue system centred on the Exchequer. In addition to these justiciars of England, King Henry I (1100–35) appointed local justiciars to attend to Crown business in particular counties or groups of counties. This enabled an extension of royal justice without extending the powers of sheriffs. But the idea of locally based royal justice was short-lived, probably because viceregal power was politically dangerous if severed from the king's central court. In the troubled reign of King Stephen (1135–54), Geoffrey de Mandeville (d. 1166) provided kings with a warning of the power which subjects could acquire if unchecked; he became not only earl and sheriff of Essex, but also chief justiciar of Essex and other counties. By Glanvill's time, county justiciars had disappeared.

Another method of delegation which appeared at the same time, and was to prove more enduring, was to send justices out on an ad hoc basis from the royal household. The travelling justices would form a nucleus of *justiciarii totius Angliae*, who had no local roots, and who would also belong to the king's council and transact national business when required. Still this did not constitute a regular system of courts, and one litigant who sought royal justice in 1158 has left a detailed picture of the expense and trouble involved in pursuing the king or his justiciars in various parts of the country.[7]

6. The word continued to be used for 'justices' of the superior courts of common law. There is no difference of substance between a justiciar and a justice.
7. See P. M. Barnes 'The Anstey Case' (1960) 36 *Pipe Roll Soc* 1–23.

Following these experiments, Henry II proceeded a step further. In 1166 he appointed Earl Geoffrey de Mandeville and Sir Richard de Lucy as justices to tour the whole of England, with a particular view to enforcing the new assize of Clarendon and the assize concerning disseisin.[8] Mandeville's death in October 1166 ended the exercise, but the experiment was frequently repeated between then and the end of the century with notable success. In 1176 the itinerant justices were organised into six circuits, though the number was to fluctuate before six became the settled number for the assize circuits.[9] The justices assigned to these circuits, who numbered twenty or thirty at a time in the 1180s, were known as *justiciae errantes* (justices in eyre); and the French word 'eyre'[10] became the name of an established, if yet irregular, feature of royal justice. Every so often a 'general eyre' would visit each county in the realm, bringing the king's government with it. Large throngs of people attended, to account for themselves or to seek justice; special regulations were required to control the price of board and lodging during the crowded sessions; the writs were read and the justices' authority publicly proclaimed, local officials delivered up their insignia of office as if to the king in person, and the justices started into their long agenda (the 'chapters of the eyre'), investigating crimes and unexplained deaths, misconduct and negligence by officials, irregularities and shortcomings of all kinds, the feudal and fiscal rights of the Crown, and private disputes. The general eyres were not merely law courts; they were itinerant government. They begat fear and awe in the entire population. We read that the eyre of 1194 reduced the whole kingdom to poverty, and we learn of Cornishmen fleeing to the woods to escape the eyre of 1233.[11] Popular reaction was to kill the general eyre in the mid-fourteenth century. Yet it was the strength, the severity even, of Angevin government which incidentally gave England a body of national law unique in Europe.

Central Royal Justice

The focal point of royal government was the *Curia Regis* (king's court), the body of advisers and courtiers who attended the king and supervised the administration of the realm. It was not a specific court of law, any more than the eyre was, but was the descendant of the

8. See pp. 201–202, 415, post.
9. See p. 20, post.
10. From the Latin *iter*, a journey or circuit.
11. *Annales Monastici* (Rolls ser), vol. III, p. 135.

Anglo-Saxon *witan* and the ancestor of the king's council which later subdivided into parliament and the privy council. The justices in eyre were usually members of the *Curia Regis*, to which they returned when their itinerant duties were performed. But the eyre system did not exhaust the judicial resources of the *Curia Regis*, which continued to attract suitors who could not await the next eyre or who wanted the king's personal attention. To the extent that the king delegated such business, there appeared yet another way of employing justices: instead of sending them round the country, they would remain at the centre to hear suitors from all parts.

When we speak of the *Curia Regis* as the 'centre' of royal administration, we should remember that the centre was not static. The king himself was given to peripatetic rule, for to stay in one place for too long was not sound policy; and the *Curia Regis* followed the king wherever he went. Nevertheless, even in the twelfth century there was a tendency for a corps of administrators to settle in the king's principal palace at Westminster while the king was away. The Exchequer was the first department to be left behind; the king's treasure and the elaborate revenue service which controlled it had become too cumbrous to keep constantly on the move. For the same reason, the Exchequer was the first department to develop a continuous Latin record of its proceedings, the pipe roll. During the long absences from the realm of Henry II and Richard I in the later twelfth century, the 'central' judicial business of the *Curia Regis*—Glanvill's *capitalis curia*—also found a domicile at Westminster.

THE TWO BENCHES

The establishment of a stationary royal court, functioning independently of the king's personal presence, marks the origin of the traditional judicial system of England. It is impossible to say precisely when it happened, because records from that period are scarce. It is known from a chronicle that in 1178, after complaints that people had been vexed by the over-efficient eyres, Henry II ordered that five judges were to remain *in curia regis* and not to depart therefrom, and that they should refer only difficult cases to himself. Controversy has never ceased as to whether this ordinance established the King's Bench or the Common Pleas, as the two principal royal courts were later called. The better view now is that it established neither, but was another of Henry II's experiments with the judicial system. What is clear is that under Henry II a central royal court, called 'the Bench', began to sit regularly at Westminster. Glanvill refers to the justices staying in the Bench (*in banco residentes*) in contrast to those who were wandering about on eyre. In one text of his preface he defines his subject as the laws and customs used *in curia regis ad scaccarium et coram justiciis ubicumque fuerint.* This passage has been read by some to indicate three institutions: 'in the *Curia Regis*, at the Exchequer, and before the justices wheresoever they might be'. But it is far more likely that it refers but to two: 'in the king's court at the Exchequer, and before the justices wheresoever they might be'. The *curia regis ad scaccarium* was the Bench, and the Exchequer was that part of the palace most suitable for its meetings. The Exchequer Chamber, so called from the chequered table used by the revenue department, remained in use for judicial meetings unconnected with revenue until the last century.

Glanvill's distinction between the justices who went on circuit and those who stayed behind is a very simple distinction. It does not imply any difference of jurisdiction, nor even of personnel. It was simply a difference in the manner of employing the king's justices. By about 1200, however, a new distinction is perceptible at the centre. The typical justices of the Bench were no longer politicians, administrators and men of public affairs, but professional judges spending most of their time on the administration of the nascent common law. By way of contrast with this ordinary system, the king and his greater advisers entertained suits which particularly interested the government. Proceedings of the latter kind were described as *coram rege* (before the king), and in 1200 some business *coram rege* was recorded on a separate roll. King John (1199–1216) seems to have been chiefly responsible for encouraging such proceedings before himself, and after the loss of Normandy in 1204 he was able to give more attention to domestic affairs than his predecessors. So far did this trend proceed that in 1209 the Bench at Westminster was completely discontinued.

The brief suspension of the Bench cannot be regarded as the abolition of a court. There was still only one kind of royal judge, and all John did was to rearrange the sittings of his judges so that none remained at Westminster save when he was there himself. Perhaps, in the sense that the moving king was the administrative centre of the kingdom, he saw it as a form of centralisation. The measure was not, however, popular. The static Bench had proved too useful to be done away with. In 1214 it was revived, and by Magna Carta it was given statutory protection by the provision that common pleas should not follow the king but should be kept in some certain place.[12] For the next

---

12. Magna Carta 1215, cl.17; Magna Carta 1225, cl.11. The 'certain place' was not defined. It was usually Westminster, but it could be changed provided process was returnable in some fixed geographical location. See further p. 34, post.

twenty years the Bench was the sole royal court, because the jurisdiction *coram rege* was in abeyance during the minority of Henry III and was not revived until 1234. During that time it acquired a professional bar, the *prolocutores Banci* or countors of the Bench,[13] and before long its business became so important and sophisticated that the very arguments of the judges and countors would be reported in books.[14]

After proceedings *coram rege* recommenced in 1234, it is possible to perceive the origins of the two principal courts of common law, the Bench (or Common Bench) and the court *coram rege* (or King's Bench). From 1234 there were two distinct series of plea rolls, called *coram rege* and *de banco*, and within a generation there were two fully distinct courts, each with its own judges and officials. The later history of these courts, which remained in being for over six centuries, will be traced in the next chapter.

COMMISSIONS AND THE CIRCUIT SYSTEM

The establishment of eyres and the two benches still left a major practical problem. The eyres, which brought royal justice into the county, were far too infrequent to enable routine criminal or civil business to be dealt with on a regular basis. The normal interval between eyres was reckoned to be seven years. The work could quite properly be done in the interim by the old county and hundred assemblies, but to the extent that royal justice was desired in the county on a regular basis the eyres did not provide it; and in the mid-fourteenth century the eyres themselves ground to a halt.[15] Litigation in the central courts, on the other hand, by reason of their separation from the county, could be expensive and inconvenient if not wholly impracticable. The difficulties of personal attendance through the various stages of a lawsuit were solved from around 1200 by the appearance of a class of professional attorneys who were allowed to represent their clients in litigation. The chief difficulty, however, was that both the presentment of crimes and trial by assize or jury—which rapidly became a feature of royal justice[16]—required the presence of twelve or more men from the vicinity where the matter in question occurred. To have required the presence at Westminster, or before the king's person, of juries of presentment or trial would soon have brought the system to the point of collapse. In fact the

13. See p. 135, post.
14. See pp. 151–153, post.
15. They were never abolished. Eyres were occasionally held for specific purposes, such as the Lynn *quo warranto* in 1521: Spelman Rep (93 SS) 99. Chief justices in eyre of the forests north and south of the Trent were appointed until 1817.
16. See pp. 63–65, post.

system was probably never intended to work that way. By a combination of miscellaneous expedients, which were eventually brought together to form another enduring institution of the common law (the 'assizes'), the centralisation of royal justice was reconciled with the need for local investigation and trial.

The means of achieving this compromise was the 'commission', an ad hoc grant of judicial authority by letters patent under the great seal of England. The justices in eyre acted under commissions to try 'all pleas whatsoever', but there was a wide range of more limited commissions developing in the twelfth and thirteenth centuries. The two principal types of commission for hearing pleas of the Crown were those of oyer and terminer (to enquire into, hear and determine the offences specified) and gaol delivery (to try or release the prisoners in the gaol specified). Commissions of oyer and terminer could be general, extending to all or most offences committed within certain named counties, or special, extending only to named persons or particular disorders or to privileged places. On the civil side, among the most popular remedies in the later twelfth century were the 'petty assizes'[17] introduced by Henry II, which required a body of men to be summoned from the vicinity to answer a question put to them. Each assize between two parties required in effect a separate court, constituted by an individual patent; but it was convenient for justices in eyre to take assizes—which they had authority to do without a special patent—and also for justices to be commissioned to take assizes between eyres.

All these commissions were independent of the two benches. The problem of litigation there was solved in a similar way. Juries were summoned to Westminster, or before the king himself, on a certain day 'unless before then (*nisi prius*) the king's justices shall have come' into the county. In truth no one expected the jurors to obey the principal summons, and it was usually arranged that the king's justices would come into the county first, empowered by writs of *nisi prius* to receive jury verdicts there for transmission to the bench on their return. The *nisi prius* system may have begun in the twelfth century; it was placed on a regular footing by legislation beginning in 1285. The theory of the *nisi prius* business always remained different from that of the assizes. Whereas assize commissioners had original jurisdiction to hear the matter from beginning to end, with power to refer difficult questions to the centre, the justices at *nisi prius* had power only to proceed on issues referred to them for convenience out of one of the benches, and had to send the results back to the court for

17. See pp. 201–202, post.

judgment. At first the *nisi prius* function was exercised by a judge of the bench where the matter arose; after 1340 it could be exercised by any justice of assize. Unlike the other powers of circuit judges, it was not conferred by commission: it was a delegated power, which statute extended to judges who happened to be going on circuit under other commissions.

Despite the variety of these activities, they were all welded together in the thirteenth century into a single and regular system known later as the assizes. During the course of that century it became usual for the active members of the commissions to be men of law, often including the justices of the two benches; after 1340 the assize commissioners had to be justices of either bench or serjeants-at-law. In 1293 the commissioners were organised into four circuits, rearranged as six in 1328. By statutes of 1299 and 1328 it was ordained that assize commissioners should stay to deliver the gaols in the counties where they sat; and it became usual for the same commissioners also to be given commissions of general oyer and terminer. All this settled into a routine. Twice a year two judges or serjeants would be assigned to each of the six circuits, through which they would ride with their clerks and records during the vacation. At each county town, or other appointed place, the commissions would be read out in public and the justices would proceed to take the assizes, deliver the gaol, try any other prisoners accused before them, and try the other civil cases at *nisi prius*. The assizes, though moulded into a regular routine, never became a distinct court in the usual sense of the word. The jurisdiction of the judges rested entirely on the commissions which issued for each circuit; so, not only could the judges be interchanged, but it was quite normal (after 1340) for *nisi prius* business from the Common Pleas to be heard before a King's Bench judge, and vice versa. The *nisi prius* proceedings were merely an extension of the work of the benches, and were recorded in the rolls of the latter. The other proceedings were, however, so divorced from the central system that no central record system was devised and many assize and gaol delivery rolls have been lost. For all its oddities, the assize system proved so useful and adaptable that it remained part of the English way of life until its abolition in 1971.[18] Even since 1971, it is a feature of the English legal system that judges from the central courts may be sent to various parts of the country to try important cases; but their disposition is now a matter of administrative discretion.

18. Courts Act 1971 (c.23), s.1(2), which restrains commissions of assize, but not commissions of oyer and terminer or gaol delivery. Since 1914 a composite short-form commission of assize, oyer and terminer, and gaol delivery, had been in use.

Effects on Local Justice

It would be agreeably neat if the progress of royal justice could be regarded as a single-minded campaign to replace the old order of things by the common law of the king's courts. That such was the inevitable consequence was not necessarily intended or foreseen, and it is doubtful whether at any stage in the process kings or their advisers had such a sweeping historical vision. Throughout the period when the greatest advances were made, kings seemed more concerned to impose control on counties and hundreds and feudal lords than to lessen their jurisdiction. Henry I ordained that men should litigate in the shires as they had done before the conquest. The twelfth-century justices in eyre sat in the county court and took over its proceedings in the king's name, so that in furthering the king's power they might also seem to be enhancing the authority of the older institution. The justices of assize, too, were enjoined by Magna Carta to sit on the day and at the place of the county court. Communal justice was too deep-rooted for anyone to think of abolition; it was simply absorbed into the new system. Neither was there any deliberate attack on feudal jurisdiction. Fear that the royal courts were encroaching on lords resulted in another provision of Magna Carta, that no free man should be deprived of his court by any royal writ; the king's court thereafter would only entertain writs of right for land held of subjects if the lord had waived his court or failed to do justice. As late as 1278, the prospect of the royal courts being bothered by too much petty litigation resulted in legislation requiring trespass suits for less than forty shillings to be brought in the counties, as had been accustomed.[19] Whereas we, in looking back, find it so easy to assume that the common law was from the start universal and paramount, contemporaries saw it quite differently: it was in the twelfth and thirteenth centuries relatively new and exceptional, to be called into operation only with the king's consent and for good reason. We shall see later how this attitude resulted in some curious distortions of the common law, particularly in the sphere of contract and tort, when the king's law ceased to be exceptional and had to take on work it had previously excluded.[20]

Although there was no policy of attacking the ancient assemblies, there was a continuing policy under the Normans and their successors of curtailing the powers of sheriffs. 'The Crown's incurable fear of the sheriff'[21] was no doubt well founded, for the potential power

19. Statute of Gloucester 1278, c.8.
20. See pp. 57–59, 271 et seq, post.
21. Plucknett CHCL, p. 105.

of the sheriff—as continental experience of analogous magnates showed—was such as to challenge the king's own authority. The Crown reduced the tenure of office to one year, and subjected sheriffs to stringent financial supervision through the Exchequer. As early as the 1120s we learn of a sheriff, fearsome and mighty in his own county, trembling in his boots when the time came for his reckoning at the chequered table.[22] By reducing the judicial power of sheriffs, however, the Crown indirectly struck at the ancient bodies over which the sheriffs had assumed control. The greatest blow was the removal from sheriffs of pleas of the Crown, a process which began de facto with the eyres and was completed de jure by the absolute prohibition in Magna Carta. The prohibition was taken to exclude from the sheriff's cognisance even civil actions for trespass against the king's peace. The governmental work of the county suffered a similar decline. Where once the king had visited the counties, in person or by his justices in eyre, by the end of the thirteenth century the practice had begun of summoning the county, by its representatives, to the king in parliament.

These changes left the county, the greatest of the local assemblies, bereft of most of its jurisdiction and power. For the remainder of the middle ages it exercised a minor civil jurisdiction in contract and tort. Even in that sphere, the absence of jury trial and the lack of effective final process, coupled with the fifteenth-century interpretation of the Statute of Gloucester 1278 which limited county jurisdiction generally to forty shillings,[23] kept litigation in the county at a low level. The actual decline was slowed by the practice of conferring greater jurisdiction on sheriffs by royal writs called *justicies*; but these were limited to specific cases, and they emphasised that the jurisdiction belonged to the king. The inherent jurisdiction of the community of the county had been taken away. The county survived the medieval period mainly because of its exclusive non-judicial functions, particularly in relation to parliamentary elections and the pronouncement of outlawries. John Wilkes was outlawed at the Middlesex county court held at the Three Tuns in Holborn:[24] a far cry from the old grand assembly of magnates, bishops and leading county figures. Uncertain in its origins, its end was abrupt and ignominious. Shorn of all remaining functions in the nineteenth century, on 17 October 1977 the old county court ceased even in theory to exist.[25]

22. J. H. Round *The Commune of London* (1899), p. 123.
23. 94 SS *51*. That this was not the original position is shown by J. S. Beckerman in *Legal History Studies 1972*, pp. 110–117.
24. *R v Wilkes* (1770) 4 Burr 2527 at 2530.
25. See p. 27, post.

PEACE-KEEPING AT LOCAL LEVEL

The king's eyres and assizes could strike terror into the hearts of malefactors, but they could not police the country; and without an efficient system for bringing crimes to their attention they would have made little impact. The old system of communal responsibility was therefore continued and reinforced. Hundreds remained responsible for presenting crimes, and could be collectively punished for failing to discover the perpetrators of known crimes.[26] The representatives of hundreds and vills who were bound to attend and present crime before the royal judges became the institution known as the grand jury.[27] Twice a year the sheriff visited each hundred to hold the 'sheriff's tourn', to review the frankpledge or tithing system and to deal with pleas of the Crown. But, however neat the system appears in theory, it broke down as a result both of the harnessing of shrieval power and of the fragmentation of jurisdiction in private hands. After Magna Carta the tourn could not hold pleas of the Crown, and was confined to making preliminary enquiries before presentment to the royal judges. Many hundreds fell into private hands, and lords of hundreds often claimed to oust the tourn and to hold their own 'courts leet' in its stead. The view of frankpledge, or oversight of the tithing system, was kept up by lords possessing courts leet as a means of raising a small income from 'head money'; but as a means of preserving order its only lasting consequence seems to have been the election of constables, a practice which was maintained with varying degrees of success until the establishment of a professional police force in the last century.

The problem was solved by yet another innovation. As early as 1200 the practice had begun of appointing a number of knights in each county to 'keep the peace', which seems to have imported a militia or police responsibility rather than one of judicature. As the most reliable section of the county establishment, these conservators of the peace were frequently employed on special commissions of oyer and terminer and gaol delivery, to relieve the load on the justices of assize between eyres; and by a series of statutes in the reign of Edward III (1327–77) the judicial functions of these officials were increased and regularised, so that they became 'justices of the peace'. The principal safeguard against excessive local power, from the king's point of view, lay in the use of commissions; without a commission the justices could not act, and every new commission (whatever changes

---

26. The main provision was the Statute of Winchester 1285, c.2, making the people of the hundred answerable for all robberies.
27. See p. 415, post.

it contained) superseded the last. At intervals a 'commission of the peace' was drawn up for each county, listing the substantial knights and gentry of the country and taking care to include the *sages et apris de la leye*,[28] charging them both to keep the peace and to enquire into, hear and determine a long list of crimes, ranging from felonies to economic offences and sorcery. The first of these charges imposed an individual police responsibility on each justice; justices could arrest criminals and commit them to gaol, and could require anyone to give surety for keeping the peace—a realistic substitute for frankpledge. The second was in effect a general commission of oyer and terminer to any two or more of the justices (with a 'quorum' of lawyers) and empowered the justices to hold their sessions of the peace.[29] Directed by statute to be held at four seasons (Michaelmas, Epiphany, Easter and the Translation of St Thomas), these were known as the general quarter sessions of the peace. The jurisdiction of quarter sessions was in theory virtually coterminous with the assizes, but in practice inferior. For six centuries until their abolition in 1971, the quarter sessions provided a mixed tribunal of lawyers and laymen to deal with the less serious pleas of the Crown which could not be tried by the assize judges. Until the reorganisation of local government in the last century, the justices also administered the public works of the county, such as provision for the poor and orphans and the maintenance of highways and bridges. Some of this administrative business, and the pre-trial police work of the justices, was transacted in private between quarter sessions; the intermediate 'petty sessions', as they were later called, also became minor courts by virtue of legislation giving the justices powers of summary conviction.[30] The petty sessions, alone of all the courts we have mentioned so far, are still in existence.

The rise of the justices of the peace corresponds very closely with the demise of the county and hundred as institutions for the despatch of public judicial and administrative business. Soon after the hearing of pleas of the Crown was taken from sheriffs, it was handed directly to the justices. In 1461 the remaining powers of the sheriff's tourn were mainly given to the justices.[31] Parliament repeatedly ignored the existence of the old county assembly as it heaped new duties of all kinds upon the magistrates. What had happened in reality was that

28. Stat 18 Edw III (sess.ii), c.2.
29. The commission still has two 'assignations', but since 1973 it is addressed generally to such persons as may from time to time hold office as justices; new justices are no longer appointed by adding their names to the commission, but by instrument under the hand of the Lord Chancellor.
30. See p. 419, post.
31. Stat 1 Edw IV, c.2. The tourn was not abolished till 1887.

the Crown had taken the county from the sheriff and put it into commission. The greater men of the shire—the *buzones* (as Bracton called them), on whose nod the decisions turned—still served the shire but in different roles. As knights of the shire they represented the county in parliament, which was itself a triumph of centralisation. And as justices of the peace they continued the judicial and adminis-trative work of the shire, but now under commissions through which alterations in personnel and duties could be made at will. The reality of this continuity was such that the old assembly did not need aboli-tion; the leaders of the county could afford to ignore it. The duty of attendance at the shire moot became an unwelcome burden annexed to certain pieces of land; and a combination of exemptions, powers of attorney, and evasions, enabled the effective withdrawal of those who now wielded their influence at Westminster or in the sessions. The multifarious county customs mentioned almost with despair by the eleventh-century writers had, of course, disappeared in the process. Once again, no one had decreed that the common law should prevail; but a stream of expedients had gradually produced a situation in which the old ways of doing things died a natural death.

LOCAL CIVIL JUSTICE

The communal jurisdictions endured longest at the level of borough and manor, perhaps because at that level they were independent of the sheriff. Ironically, these courts in many cases outlived even the King's Bench and Common Pleas, which were abolished in 1876. But here, too, the continuity concealed another triumph of the common law.

Most city and borough courts continued unabated until Tudor times, and many a good deal longer; a few flourished until the axe of uniformity fell upon them in 1971.[32] For most of this period they were patronised by mercantile litigants, for whom they offered various procedural advantages. In Tudor times merchants transferred much of their business to the King's Bench, and the King's Bench encour-aged them by upsetting judgments of municipal courts on technical grounds. It was possible to challenge a borough record by writ of error, on the grounds that the common law and custom of the realm had not been complied with.[33] Although the King's Bench disting-uished substantive common law from procedural customs, the threat

---

32. Courts Act 1971 (c.23), ss.42–43, abolished the Mayor's and City of London Court, the Norwich Guildhall Court of Record, the Salford Hundred Court of Record, and the Tolzey Court of Bristol.
33. See 94 SS *51–52, 258*, 324–325.

of reversal must have persuaded borough courts to assimilate their practices as far as possible to those of the central courts; and so these valuable small-debt jurisdictions, invariably from the fifteenth century presided over by recorders bred in the inns of court, became urban courts of common law.

The higher feudal courts, those of baronies and honours, disappeared at an early date; but manorial courts flourished well beyond the middle ages. By royal grant, or (more usually) immemorial usage, many manorial courts enjoyed 'franchises' giving them jurisdiction in non-feudal matters; some, as we have seen, claimed to have the 'public' jurisdiction of hundred and tourn within the precincts of their leets. These franchises varied almost infinitely from one manor to another, but they were eaten into by all the trends mentioned in this chapter and were subjected to royal control. Even the feudal jurisdiction over land, the right apparently assured to lords by Magna Carta, was overtaken by the common law. The royal courts assumed jurisdiction over writs of right either through lords failing to claim their courts or by the fiction that they had waived them. A wide range of remedies, notably the assizes of Henry II and the writs of entry,[34] curbed the suzerainty of lords to such an extent that they became free to decide only as the king's law allowed them, with the result that, at a very early date as regards free tenants, the 'feudal' land law became the cornerstone of the common law. Feudal control, subject to manorial custom, clung slightly longer to the unfree or copyhold tenant; but royal justice reached him in the fifteenth and sixteenth centuries,[35] and so by yet another jurisprudential miracle 'tenancy according to the custom of the manor' became a tenancy at common law. Manorial courts retained some importance until 1925 as providing the only means for conveying copyhold land, and a few continued to exercise franchisal jurisdiction until relatively modern times.

By the nineteenth century the accidents of history had left a very uneven pattern of minor civil jurisdiction across the country. In some towns, borough courts or municipal courts leet continued to provide speedy justice; in others all semblance of judicature had ceased. In rural areas the chances that a court leet or franchisal court had survived were slender, and in any case few of them offered civil remedies. A number of statutory experiments with 'courts of requests' had been made in the larger towns in the eighteenth century, with varying success. In 1846 a nationwide system of 'county courts' was established, under which small civil claims could be tried by a profes-

34. See pp. 201–203, post.
35. See pp. 259–260, post.

sional judge. The new county courts bore no relation to the old shire moot, save that their jurisdiction in 1846 was similar to that possessed in theory by the latter. They were the first general courts of common law to have been deliberately introduced by statute, and their jurisdiction has been greatly extended since. The manorial courts, counties, hundreds, leets, courts of pie poudre, and various other obsolete jurisdictions were finally swept away in 1977.[36]

The Isolation of English Law

The common law of England proved remarkably durable. It survived civil wars and changes of dynasty. At various times it was claimed to have superiority over the king, parliament and the Church. Both the Reformation and the growth of constitutional monarchy were assisted by common law ways of thinking. And, with few outward signs of struggle, the common law withstood two waves of Romanism which swept across the Continent. The rediscovery of Justinian's *Digest*, and the consequential explosion of Roman legal studies in the universities of the twelfth and thirteenth centuries, made Roman Civil law the common currency of European lawyers, including the doctors of law at Oxford and Cambridge. Early royal judges were in touch with the new learning, and may have injected some juristic notions into the early chaos; but the effect was prophylactic, and served to immunise English law against fatal infection.[37] Compared with the rest of Europe, England and its common law were precocious. The system of writs described by Glanvill and the attendant procedure and terminology, the developed notion of pleas of the Crown with all the machinery for the discovery and trial of criminals, the existence of central and itinerant royal courts capable of subjecting the whole nation to the king's law and government: all these things were unique to England, and were in being before the importation of foreign ideas became a practical possibility. And so, 'while the other nations of Western Europe were beginning to adopt as their own the ultimate results of Roman legal history, England was unconsciously reproducing that history; it was developing a formulary system which in the ages that were coming would be the strongest bulwark against Romanism and sever our English law from all her sisters'.[38] The second wave of Romanism struck at the end of the middle ages, when

36. Administration of Justice Act 1977 (c.38), s.23, Sch.4; S.I. 1977 No. 1589.
37. Brunner's metaphor: *Essays AALH*, vol. II, p. 42.
38. Pollock & Maitland, vol. II, p. 558.

Renaissance humanism drove out archaic methods of proof and encouraged the application of rational legal principles based on the Civil law. But once again England had anticipated the rest of Europe without recourse to scholastic learning. Through the process called 'pleading' the common lawyers had built their own elaborate and rational system of law around the writs which governed the business of the royal courts.[39] England's lawyers had their own law schools, located not in the universities but between London and Westminster Hall, where the chief study was not classical texts but writs and pleading and feudal land law.[40] Not that England in any way escaped the rapid social and legal changes of the Renaissance period; but the common law system was sufficiently adaptable to accommodate them without foreign assistance.[41]

Having stood its ground in the land of its birth, the English common law became a force to rival the Civil law beyond the seas. The men who sailed for the new world in the seventeenth and eighteenth centuries, and those who built the British empire in the eighteenth and nineteenth centuries, took the common law with them as a matter of course. By a breath-taking twist of fate, the insular and arcane learning of the small band of lawyers who argued cases in the great hall of Westminster became the law by which a third of the people on the earth were governed and protected, the second of the two great systems of jurisprudence known to the world. Within Europe, however, England was and has remained to this day an island in law. There are obvious political and social reasons why this should be so. The common law was initially coextensive with the king's courts. Even its more abstract doctrines were not easily transportable to countries which had different systems of courts and knew nothing of writs or juries. And so English law flourished in noble isolation from Europe, and even from parts of Britain.

WALES AND THE COMMON LAW

The kingdom to which the Normans succeeded in 1066 did not in fact include the Celtic strongholds which have become Wales, Ireland and Scotland. The Celts defiantly preserved the titular kingship of Britain until the death of King Cadwaladr in the seventh century, and of course they preserved their own language, culture and customs once they had been driven back into the western and northern extremities of the island. It is tempting to think that the Welsh bards

39. See pp. 67–71, post.
40. See pp. 138–140, post.
41. See further 94 SS *23–51*.

and Irish 'brehons' who preserved the British customs by memory represent a continuation of the druidical tradition observed by Caesar. The earliest extant texts of the Irish laws date from around 1000 A.D., and those of the Welsh laws from the twelfth century; but both purport to be of much earlier origin, and may provide the link between prehistoric British custom and known civilisation. The Welsh customs which were codified in medieval times as the 'laws of Hywel Dda'[42] superficially resemble the Anglo-Saxon codes in the use of compensation payments to discourage feuding; but they stressed the ties of kinship rather than those of community or feudal homage. Welsh law was not a law of counties, hundreds and feudal lords, but of tribes and families and chieftains. Yet the customs were not static. The codes themselves were agglomerations of matter from different periods, and Welsh kings altered some of the rules within historical memory.

The English affected to regard Celtic custom with contempt, and Archbishop Pecham advised Edward I that the laws of Hywel Dda were irrational and came directly from the Devil. After the conquest of Wales by Edward I an attempt was made to codify some of the basic principles of English law for the use of Welsh royal officials;[43] but there was no attempt to substitute English for Welsh law in general, and the failure to extend the English system of courts into Wales left the Welsh free to pursue their old customs until the sixteenth century.

The English courts refused to hear any dispute arising in Wales, because they had no means of finding the facts; and therefore even the most serious crimes were outside the jurisdiction of the king's courts.[44] The incorporation of Wales into the common law framework was no gradual process of infiltration but was achieved by a sudden act of parliament in 1535. Welsh law had become outmoded and unloved, and there was no great outcry when the 'sinister usages and customs' of the Welsh were abrogated and Welsh subjects were granted the same laws and liberties as the English.[45] A new system of courts, called the Great Sessions of Wales, was introduced. The courts were to sit twice a year in four circuits, each comprising three counties, and to each circuit were appointed justices 'learned in the laws of this realm' and officials. These courts operated alongside

---

42. Hywel 'Dda' (the Good) was king of Wales and died c. 950 A.D. How much of the codification occurred in his time is uncertain.
43. Statute of Rhuddlan [or, of Wales] 1284.
44. E.g. *R v Owain Glyn Dŵr* (1401) 88 SS 114; *Dolbyn v Ap Tudor* (1532–34) Spelman Rep (93 SS) 156, 94 SS 340.
45. Stat 27 Hen VIII, c.26; 34 & 35 Hen VIII, c.26. The effect was not to abolish reasonable local customs, which may be proved as in England: Dyer 363 (1579).

the English courts, and they had the same jurisdiction in Wales as the King's Bench and Common Pleas had in England. Error, and certiorari in criminal cases, lay to the King's Bench at Westminster. The problem of venue continued to prevent a Welsh cause of action being tried by an English jury, but it was always accepted after 1543 that the process of the English Chancery and Exchequer would run into Wales, and eventually after much controversy it was established that King's Bench process would run there also.[46] In 1830 the Great Sessions were abolished, and by procedural assimilation England and Wales became at last one unified jurisdiction, two extra circuits being added to the English assize system.

IRELAND AND THE COMMON LAW

Ireland was never absorbed into the English court system, but it received the common law and administered it in courts closely analogous to their English counterparts. The English settlers in Ireland at first regarded the Irish as being of inferior status, akin to aliens, and left them to their own customs. Then, by means of general charters and specific grants of denization, and by the direct application of English statutes to Ireland, the privilege of English justice was extended to most Irishmen who sought it. By 1300 the king's courts had branched out, as in England, into a 'Chief Place' (before the king's lieutenant or justiciar), a Common Bench, an Exchequer and a Chancery. The jurisdictional boundaries were not as distinct as in England, because the 'common pleas' provision of Magna Carta did not affect the Irish courts; but by 1500 the 'four courts' in Dublin resembled in their workings the four courts at Westminster. Their judges were lawyers who had spent some time in the English inns of court, and occasionally an Englishman was appointed. After 1540 Dublin had its own inn, called the King's Inns, but it offered no educational facilities and Irish barristers continued to resort to England to learn the common law. In 1615 the first volume of Irish law reports was published,[47] and thereafter a slender stream of common law books flowed from Dublin. The establishment of royal courts on the English pattern, presided over by men bred in the common law, resulted in an effective transplantation of English law without the need for statutory intervention. Native Irish customs, or 'brehon law', continued outside the Pale; but, like English local custom or Welsh local custom after 1535, such customs were struck down by the

46. *Whitrong v Blaney* (1677) 2 Mod Rep 10, Vaugh 395; *Lampley v Thomas* (1747) 1 Wils 193; *Penry v Jones* (1779) 1 Dougl 213.
47. J. Davies *Le Primer Report des Cases en Les Courts del Roy en Ireland* (Dublin, 1615). The author was an Englishman.

Dublin courts if they were adjudged 'unreasonable' by common law standards.[48]

The old Dublin courts were never wholly independent; for they were the king's courts and, the king being absent, their decisions were subject to review by the king. Error therefore lay to the English King's Bench, and from thence (at any rate after 1719[49]) to the English House of Lords. The jurisdiction to hear error from Ireland was taken from the King's Bench in 1783, and after the Act of Union appeal lay directly to the House of Lords of the United Kingdom parliament.[50] When Ireland was divided in 1920, new courts for the province of Northern Ireland were set up in Belfast, from which appeal lies to the House of Lords. In 1922 the Four Courts in Dublin were blown up by terrorists and centuries of legal records were destroyed.

THE LAW OF SCOTLAND

Although early Scots customs were Celtic, and therefore closer to those of Ireland and Wales than those of England, the percolation into Scotland of Anglo-Norman feudalism and sheriffs, justiciars, and the writ system, raised the possibility that Scotland might have become the first common law country outside England. Indeed, it seems that Edward I had the same policy of legal revision in Scotland as he pursued in Wales and Ireland. War ended that possibility. Throughout medieval times, the Scots were alien enemies and intellectual contact with England was broken for centuries. Scotsmen who read law did so on the Continent, or in their own universities, where Roman law prevailed. The kind of centralisation and professionalism which produced the common law in England was not achieved in medieval Scotland, and the result was a fragmented confusion of custom and Canon law administered through feudal, shrieval, borough and ecclesiastical courts. A central system emerged when, in the fifteenth century, appeals to the king of Scotland were referred to a council called the Session. In 1532 the Session was refounded as the College of Justice, the members of which sit to this day as the Court of Session. Akin in many ways to the English Star Chamber, the Session knew no distinction between law and equity and was free to devise its own procedure and find its own law. Soon after 1532 the lawyers practising before the Session formed themselves into a Faculty of Advocates, the members of which were trained in Roman law in French and (later) Dutch universities. It was natural that, when

48. *Case of Tanistry* (1608) Dav Ir 78.
49. Stat 6 Geo I, c.5. This was to end a doubt; in a recent case one party had appealed to the Irish House of Lords and the other to the English House.
50. Stat 23 Geo III, c.28, s.2; Act of Union 1800, 39 & 40 Geo III, c.67.

refined procedures began to call for legal doctrine, these men should have followed Continental practice by drawing on the intellectual legacy of Rome. Roman law was never treated as authority in itself, but it was a framework upon which the unwritten customs of Scotland could be systematised. In the two centuries after the foundation of the Court of Session, a body of Scots law was perfected which from the English point of view was wholly foreign. The two classic *Institutes of the Laws of Scotland*, written by Lord Stair (1681) and Sir George Mackenzie (1684), betray no hint of English influence whatever.

The merger of the crowns of Scotland and England in 1603 might have led to a merger of laws. James I said in 1604 that he wished to leave 'one country entirely governed, one uniformity in laws'. But the English lawyers, championed by Sir Edward Coke, were horrified at the prospect of the least Roman infiltration, and the king's scheme for legal union soon foundered.[51] When full political union between England and Scotland took place in 1707, there was no question but that Scots law should be preserved, subject to any alterations made by the parliament of Great Britain.[52] Since 1707 appeals have been allowed from the Court of Session to the House of Lords,[53] but the decisions in such appeals are treated in England as foreign law if the matter is one where Scots and English law differ.

Further reading

Pollock & Maitland, vol. I, pp. 64–110, 136–173

Holdsworth HEL, vol. I, pp. 24–193, 264–298

Plucknett CHCL, pp. 11–26, 101–105, 139–156, 165–169

Milsom HFCL, pp. 15–25

J. E. A. Jolliffe, *The Constitutional History of Medieval England* (4th edn, 1961), esp. pp. 139–331

H. G. Richardson and G. O. Sayles, *Governance of Medieval England* (1963), esp. pp. 173–215; *Law and Legislation from Aethelberht to Magna Carta* (1966), esp. pp. 30–154

D. Stenton, *English Justice between the Norman Conquest and Magna Carta* (1965), esp. pp. 54–114

R. C. Van Caenegem, *The Birth of the English Common Law* (1973)

A. Harding, *The Law Courts of Medieval England* (1973), pp. 32–85

51. See B. P. Levack 'The Proposed Union of English Law and Scots Law' (1975) 20 *Juridical Rev* (NS) 97–115.
52. Act of Union 1706, 6 Annae, c.11, art. 18–19.
53. *Greensfields v Provost of Edinburgh* (1710) Colles 427. This was not provided for in the Act.

ITINERANT JUSTICE

W. C. Bolland, *The General Eyre* (1922)

M. M. Taylor, 'Justices of Assize' in *The English Government at Work 1327–36* (1950), pp. 219–257

R. B. Pugh, *Itinerant Justices in Law and History* (1967)

J. S. Cockburn, *History of the Assizes 1558–1714* (1972)

JUSTICES OF THE PEACE

S. B. Chrimes in Holdsworth HEL, vol. I, (7th edn), pp. 24*–29*, summarising the work of B. H. Putnam

A. Harding, 'The Origins and early History of the Keeper of the Peace' (1960) 10 TRHS (5th ser.) 85–109

WALES

Holdsworth HEL, vol. I, pp. 117–132

R. R. Davies, 'The Twilight of Welsh Law, 1284–1536' (1966) 51 *History* 143–164; 'The Law of the March' (1970) 5 *Welsh History Review* 1–30

IRELAND

G. J. Hand, *English Law in Ireland 1290–1324* (1967), esp. pp. 172–213; 'Aspects of Alien Status' in *Legal History Studies 1972*, pp. 129–135; 'English Law in Ireland 1172–1351' (1972) 23 *N. Ireland Legal Qly* 393–422

F. H. Newark, *Elegantia Juris* (F. J. McIvor, Ed, 1973), pp. 185–228

SCOTLAND

G. C. H. Paton (Ed), *An Introduction to Scottish Legal History* (Stair Society, 1958), esp. pp. 1–43

P. G. Stein, *Roman Law in Scotland* (1968), Ius Romanum Medii Aevi, V, 13b, and works there cited

3. The Superior Courts of Common Law

Westminster Hall, built for William Rufus in about 1099 and enlarged under Richard II around 1395, was the home of the superior English courts until they moved to the Strand in 1882. The hall may still be entered by the great north door. On the far side is a flight of steps which used to divide the Court of King's Bench from the Court of Chancery. On the west side of the hall, near the door, was the Court of Common Pleas. The Exchequer was a large chamber which connected with the hall through a passage. Each court occupied a space marked out by a wooden bar at which counsel stood, and in the centre was a large table covered with green cloth at which the court officials sat and spread their records. Against the wall, on a raised platform or bench beneath tapestries with the royal arms, sat the judges. There were no seats for counsel until about 1700. Each court was scarcely out of earshot of the others, and speakers had to compete with the noise made by the throng of suitors, attorneys and shopkeepers in the body of the hall; until the eighteenth century there were not even any screens to divide the courts from the open thoroughfare. This arrangement, seemingly impracticable to modern eyes, was a feature of English public life for five centuries. It survived two civil wars, and even in times of rebellion the judges and serjeants kept up their attendance, sometimes with armour beneath their robes. The requirement of a 'certain place' in Magna Carta was strictly observed. Only in times of plague or flood did the courts leave Westminster Hall, and then only after a formal adjournment by proclamation. A story, possibly apocryphal, is told of Sir Orlando Bridgman, Chief Justice of the Common Pleas in the 1660s, that he would not have his court moved back a few feet to avoid the draught from the north door, because it would have been against Magna Carta.[1]

The conservative attachment of lawyers to all the old forms gave them the appearance of complete immunity to change. Yet, beneath

---

1. R. North *Life of Lord Guilford* (1819 edn), vol. I, p. 155. In fact the old court was demolished and rebuilt in 1741: E. Wynne *Degree of Serjeant at Law* (1765), p. 124. As to flooding, see *Memorandum* (1629) Hutton 108.

this timeless exterior, there occurred in the sixteenth century a massive redistribution of jurisdiction associated with changes in the common law more far-reaching than anything brought about by either the Norman conquest or the reforms of the nineteenth century.

MAGNA CARTA AND COMMON PLEAS

We have seen that the effect of clause 17 of Magna Carta was the establishment of the two royal benches. The Court of King's Bench was the bench held *coram rege ubicumque fuerit in Anglia*—before the king wheresoever he should be in England—and was therefore excluded by the charter from hearing 'common pleas' because it was not in a fixed place. Common pleas for this purpose were any suits in which the king had no interest. As a corollary, the Common Bench (or Court of Common Pleas)[2] had an exclusive jurisdiction over them; and they included all the real actions, and all personal actions not alleging a breach of the peace. The most important of the latter was the action of debt. There was nothing in Magna Carta to prevent the Common Pleas from also hearing pleas of the Crown, and at an early date it occasionally did entertain appeals of felony; but its traditional jurisdiction as settled by the end of the fourteenth century, though it included trespass (shared with the King's Bench), excluded felony. The Common Pleas also had a supervisory jurisdiction over county courts by *recordari facias loquelam*, and over all other local and feudal courts (other than courts of record) by *accedas ad curiam*.

By the fourteenth century the jurisdiction of the King's Bench was also settled. The Crown side had unlimited criminal jurisdiction throughout the realm; but after the fourteenth century it acted as a court of first instance in Middlesex cases only, and confined itself chiefly to questions of law arising on indictments removed from other courts. The civil or 'plea' side of the King's Bench comprised mainly actions of trespass, appeals of felony, and suits to correct errors in the Common Pleas or borough courts of record. By comparison with the Common Pleas, the jurisdiction of the King's Bench was slender. Its records filled but one or two hundred skins of parchment a year, whereas those of the sister court filled a thousand or two.

The Common Pleas was the court which more than any other made the medieval common law. It had usually four or five judges, a select bar of serjeants-at-law, and a large staff of officers: the *custos brevium* or keeper of the writs, the prothonotaries and filazers (who kept the rolls

---

2. Often called 'the Bench' or 'the Place' in medieval times. The name 'Court of Common Pleas', presumably alluding to Magna Carta, was not used until Tudor times.

and files), and numerous under-clerks. It was the place where the young students attended to learn their law, huddled in a raised wooden box called the 'crib'. What a judge or serjeant said in the Common Pleas he published to the legal world as his opinion on the law, and he might be sure someone would remember it or make a note of it; the year-books were taken up almost exclusively with the debates in this court, and it was not until the sixteenth century that the work of other courts was regularly reported.[3]

This uneven sharing of business made sense while the King's Bench was still peripatetic, since it left that court free to hear the pleas of the Crown for which it was especially designed. The original criminal jurisdiction, however, was virtually superseded by the assize system. The last occasion when the King's Bench went on circuit to try criminal cases was in the fourteenth century. The court therefore settled down in Westminster Hall. Save perhaps on ceremonial occasions, no king sat in it again. It had de facto come to rest in a certain place. The fact of its domicile, however, was one of which the law took no notice whatever. The style of the court remained *coram rege*; the process of the court was returnable 'before the lord king wheresoever he should be in England', and until 1876 the full designation of a judge of the court was 'one of the justices assigned to hold the pleas before the queen herself'. Whatever the reality, therefore, the Court of King's Bench was not in law held in a certain place and was therefore restrained by Magna Carta from hearing common pleas.

THE COMMON LAW COURTS THREATENED

During the fifteenth century the superiority of the ancient common law courts was threatened by the jurisdictions associated with the king's chancellor. Some have seen these rising jurisdictions as threats to the common law itself. The medieval chancellors were doctors of Canon and Civil law, as were many of the masters in Chancery and the later officials of the Council. Could not these courts have done the Romanising which in Germany was carried out by the equivalent Reichskammergericht?[4] Yet the real threat was probably not of a jurisprudential kind. The newer courts were as English as the two benches, and did not administer foreign law. Their attraction lay in their procedure: in its relative informality, the ease with which opponents could be arrested, and in their inquisitorial trial procedure

---

3. See pp. 94, 154, 157, post.
4. F. W. Maitland *English Law and the Renaissance* (1901), where he gives a tentative answer to his own question.

which by-passed the sheriff and the jury. In procedure, Roman influence may well have been felt; but it was embodied in an English form, the bill of complaint and subpoena. The history of these courts must be postponed.[5] The reason for intruding them here is that their initial success had an adverse effect on the business of the common law courts, so that from the middle of the fifteenth century there began a downhill slide in the number of cases taken to the older courts. The judges and officers of the two benches were acutely aware of the challenge; and they recognised that to meet it they would have to devise reforms both in law and procedure which would win back the patronage of the litigants and the lawyers who advised them. The problem was most acute in the King's Bench, which had all to lose; it lacked the staple of debt to support itself, and had lost its proper work to the assizes. It was the King's Bench, therefore, which devoted the most study to the means of reform. As early as 1482, Fairfax J urged pleaders to develop remedies which would maintain the jurisdiction of the court, 'and then the subpoena will not be used as often as it now is'.[6] By 1500 the process of reform was well under way. The King's Bench developed its own bill system, with swift process and procedure to match that of the Chancery, and was also acquiring a jurisdiction over common pleas by ingenious evasions of Magna Carta. Within a generation or two, the tide had turned in favour of the common law, a tide swelled by the flood of central litigation following the rapid decay of local courts in Tudor times. After the mid-Tudor period the common law courts and the newer courts were able to find a more stable and rational division of business between themselves. By the time that happened, however, the Common Pleas was becoming suspicious of the amazing explosion of King's Bench business, and for the rest of the sixteenth century it adopted a reactionary approach to the changes which the King's Bench was trying to introduce into the legal system. The events of the sixteenth century then took on the appearance of an internecine struggle for business between the common law courts themselves, in which Magna Carta became the charter of liberties of the outdone officers of the Chancery and Common Pleas.

BILL PROCEDURE IN THE KING'S BENCH

A bill is a petition addressed directly to a court in order to commence an action. Bill procedure was obviously more convenient for litigants than writ procedure, for the latter required the first complaint to be made in Chancery so that a writ could be sent to the court where proceedings were to be taken.[7] There was nothing particularly new about procedure by bill when it blossomed in Chancery and Council—and parliament—between 1350 and 1450. The bill had an older history as a means of bringing complaints before the justices in eyre. The eyre literally took over the county where it sat, and the sheriff was personally attendant; it was therefore unnecessary to send to the Chancery for a writ addressed to the sheriff in order to initiate a suit from that county. The same was true of the King's Bench, which in the county where it sat was superior even to an eyre, so that local complaints could be made directly to the judges by bill. The extension of this procedure to complaints from other counties required the use of a fiction; but before we come to that we should first notice another case in which bills had always been allowed in the King's Bench.

Each superior court had jurisdiction in all personal actions over its own officers and prisoners, to prevent the inconvenience which would arise if plaintiffs could have them arrested and moved into other courts. A clerk of the King's Bench, or a prisoner in the custody of the marshal of the Marshalsea,[8] could therefore be sued by bill in actions such as debt or covenant, notwithstanding Magna Carta, because his personal presence in court gave that court jurisdictional priority. Wise attorneys kept a careful watch on the marshal's gaol calendar, because they might be able to save their own clients' time and money by taking advantage of process commenced by someone else. Plaintiffs could also combine the procedures themselves. If *A* wished to sue *B* for trespass and a debt, he need only sue a writ of trespass, upon which *B* would be arrested and committed to the marshal; *A* could then prefer a bill of debt against his prisoner, and save the expense of a writ of debt. By the second half of the fifteenth century attorneys had discovered that the same advantage could be obtained even if there was no genuine complaint of trespass. Some encouragement for such a fiction may have been taken from decisions under Fortescue CJ around 1450, that the court would not enquire into the reason why the defendant was in custody;[9] it was enough that the bill was brought

---

7. For original writs, see pp. 49–52, post.
8. The marshal was the gaoler to the court, but was appointed by the earl marshal of England. The Marshalsea prison was in Southwark, but the marshal's attendance in court enabled his prisoners to be deemed to be 'before the king himself'.
9. *Kempe's Case* (1448) YB Mich 27 Hen VI, 5, pl.35 (a bill lies against a prisoner unlawfully arrested); *Selby's Case* (1452) YB Mich 31 Hen VI, 10, pl.5 (a bill lies against a prisoner bailed from the Marshalsea, even though there is no record of his first committal).

against someone 'who is in the custody of the marshal of the lord king's marshalsea before the king himself'.[10] The arrest was secured by an unsworn ex parte complaint in Chancery of an imaginary trespass; once the defendant was in prison and had been impleaded by bill the action of trespass could be quietly discontinued before it came to trial. The falseness of the complaint of trespass was therefore never officially discovered. By 1500 the practice, if slightly unethical, had become common form and had given the King's Bench de facto jurisdiction over common pleas such as debt.

In order to utilise this jurisdictional dodge, the defendant had to be put into the Marshalsea. A writ of trespass would do it, but the King's Bench had the means of short-circuiting the Chancery altogether. If the alleged trespass was fictitious, the plaintiff might as well make it a trespass in Middlesex, the county in which Westminster Hall was situated and in which the King's Bench now invariably sat.[11] The defendant could then be arrested upon the mere presentation of a bill to the court. Thus, by the use of two bills—the bill of Middlesex (for trespass), followed by the true bill—the King's Bench litigant could sue in debt without writ. The second device was coeval with the other, and by the sixteenth century the plea rolls contain a remarkable proportion of bills complaining of trespasses to land in Westminster or Hendon; the plaintiffs, of course, always return within a term or two to pursue bills of debt. It mattered not that the plaintiff and defendant had never in reality set foot in Hendon, or even Middlesex; the mere complaint of a trespass there sufficed to have the defendant arrested. In the usual case where the defendant was not in Middlesex when the bill of Middlesex was presented, the sheriff of Middlesex would duly return that the defendant 'is not found' (*non est inventus*); the plaintiff would then inform the court that the defendant 'lurks and runs about' (*latitat et discurrit*) in, say, Yorkshire; and the court then issued a writ called a *latitat* to the sheriff of Yorkshire, who was able to effect the arrest. The final perfection of the procedure came in the later sixteenth century when, with the connivance of the court staff, it became possible to commence with the *latitat* and simply to pretend that the fictitious bill of Middlesex had been issued.

The new King's Bench bill procedure offered the litigant some of the advantages of Chancery bill procedure, particulary in that the

---

10. This included prisoners on bail: last note. In civil actions a defendant was entitled to 'reasonable bail', and in minor cases the sureties became fictitious (John Doe and Richard Roe); but if the claim exceeded £10, the plaintiff could require 'special bail' with real sureties, in default of which the defendant would remain in custody.

11. When the court adjourned to Hertford or St Alban's in time of plague, a bill of Hertfordshire was used.

latitat (unlike the original writ)[12] did not tie the plaintiff to any particular cause of action, and so defendants could be arrested to answer whatever kind of complaint the plaintiff chose to put into his bill. The advantage of this was that 'money need not be spent upon advice till it appeared upon the arrest that the defendant would stand suit'.[13] As one attorney described it, 'the *latitat* is like to Doctor Gifford's water, which serves for all diseases, and so it holds one form in all cases and actions whatsoever'.[14] Well might a Common Pleas attorney associate the *latitat* with quack medicine, for it had made the King's Bench a more popular tribunal for common pleas than the Common Pleas itself. The Common Pleas litigant still needed an original writ from Chancery, for which he paid a 'fine' proportional to the debt claimed, to get into court; when he got there, he found it took longer to arrest the defendant, that repetitive procedures required more ink and parchment, that technical slips were more likely to upset his suit, and that the whole business cost him more than it would have done in the King's Bench. The King's Bench deliberately wooed litigants with competitive costs, and sometimes even lowered its fees in order to multiply causes. Small wonder, then, that by the end of Elizabeth I's reign the King's Bench had begun to overtake the Common Pleas. From a trickle of *latitats* at the end of the fifteenth century, and a few hundred rolls a year, within a century the court was issuing—according to one estimate—20,000 *latitats* a year and filling 6,000 rolls.

SUBSTANTIVE REFORMS IN THE KING'S BENCH

In conjunction with the procedural campaign to redistribute business in its own favour, the King's Bench also broadened the range of substantive remedies available at common law. This was the technique which Fairfax J had in mind in 1481; and, as he had also suggested, the main vehicle of reform was the action on the case.[15] Actions on the case were extended by 1499 to enable the enforcement of parol promises. Fyneux CJ, in announcing this reform, stressed that it rendered unnecessary a Chancery suit by subpoena.[16] Also in the time of Fyneux CJ were developed an action on the case for not paying debts, which had several advantages over the action of debt,[17]

---

12. In suits by writ, a 'variance' between the writ and the plaintiff's opening claim was fatal, because the writ was the only warrant for the subsequent proceedings and had to be followed precisely.
13. North CJ in Yale *Lord Nottingham's Two Treatises*, p. 171.
14. T. Powell *The Attourneys Academy* (1623), p. 166.
15. For the development of actions on the case, see pp. 58–59, post.
16. Fitz Abr *Accion sur le Case*, pl. 45; p. 279, post.
17. See pp. 282–283, post.

and another for defamation, which had previously been only partially remedied in the ecclesiastical courts.[18] In the 1530s came the action on the case for trover and conversion, which replaced for most purposes the action of detinue.[19] The court even overcame the major limitation of bill procedure, that it could not be used for real actions to try title to land. It achieved this by developing a species of trespass action, called ejectment, in which the land could be recovered. The decision to allow recovery of the land, a fundamental change in the law, was made by Fyneux CJ in 1500; its full exploitation followed the introduction of a fiction in the mid-sixteenth century.[20]

It can hardly be coincidence that so much of the reform was initiated by Sir John Fyneux, who presided over the court from 1495 to 1525 when its fortunes were at their lowest ebb. He appointed his son-in-law John Rooper as chief clerk in 1498, and the Rooper family made its fortune from the office. The Tudors knew what modern society has forgotten, that institutions often work more effectively when upright, inventive men have a direct interest in their success. The cynic might criticise the judges and clerks for making the King's Bench a family business; but they had no monopoly, and they thrived only by satisfying litigants. However we judge the motives of those concerned, it is a fact that most of the innovations they made during the early sixteenth century have been accepted and embedded in our law ever since. Just as the *Curia Regis* in the eleventh century gave England a common law, which was developed and refined by the medieval Common Pleas, so the recovery of the King's Bench in the sixteenth century brought about a recasting of the law into a form which would last until the nineteenth century and beyond.

REACTION BY THE COMMON PLEAS

While the King's Bench saw itself and came to be regarded as a fountain of new legal remedies, the Common Pleas took an increasingly conservative, and in the course of time distinctly jaundiced, view of such novelties. The warmest quarrel over substantive law took place in the context of contract, where after years of dissension the King's Bench won a marginal and unconvincing victory in 1602.[21] Reaction to the *latitat* followed a similar course chronologically, but the dispute did not cease in 1602.

When the *latitat* was first extended by fiction, the Common Pleas had little cause for concern. They had up to ten times the business of

18. See pp. 364–366, post.
19. See p. 332, post.
20. See pp. 253–255, post.
21. *Slade's Case* (1602) 4 Co Rep 92; pp. 285–287, post.

the King's Bench, probably more than they could easily cope with, and could afford to share some of it. In fact they probably did not lose any business, because the decline of local courts was bringing more litigation to Westminster; the diversion of most of the new work to the King's Bench did not diminish the cause-lists of the other court. By the end of the sixteenth century, however, the officers and attorneys of the Common Pleas were becoming worried; and their grumbles, which had begun as early as the 1540s,[22] broke into open hostility. The Common Pleas attorneys could not simply copy the King's Bench tricks, because the court was not comparable to an eyre and could not arrest defendants without the authority of a Chancery writ. They had *latitats*, but could not turn them to advantage because Middlesex writs were no better than any others. The best they could do was to procure fictitious writs of trespass to land, so as to secure the arrest of the defendant on a cause which might be dropped. This gave them the advantage of time and flexibility, and enabled multiple actions to be brought upon a single process; but the Common Pleas could not escape the need for original writs and it failed to make substantial reductions in its scale of costs, allegedly because the three prothonotaries could never reach agreement on any specific proposal for cuts. Given its disadvantages with respect to costs and procedure, it seems remarkable that the Common Pleas survived the competition at all. The chief reason for its doing so was that it continued to have at least ten times as many attorneys as the King's Bench, many of whom practised in the country and brought in clients to whom King's Bench attorneys were inaccessible or unknown.

During the Interregnum the Common Pleas received a welcome boost from the abolition of fines upon original writs; but ironically this was to spark off the final collision of jurisdictions when in 1660 the fines were revived, for 'then the very attorneys of the Common Pleas boggled at them and carried all their finable business to the King's Bench'.[23] The immediate solution was an act of parliament in 1661,[24] designed to discourage *latitats* based on fictions by denying the advantages of special bail in any action where the 'true cause of action' was not expressed in the process.

The King's Bench were shaken by this attack, but within six years they devised an evasion of dubious validity. The writ to arrest a man 'to answer in a plea of trespass' would no longer suffice if the trespass was fictional, and so they extended the phrase: 'to answer in a plea of

22. See 94 SS 59.
23. North CJ in Yale *Lord Nottingham's Two Treatises*, p. 172.
24. Stat 13 Car II (sess. ii), c.2.

trespass and also (*ac etiam*) to answer in a plea of debt'. The true cause of action was then expressed in the process, in addition to the false one, and the statute appeared to be satisfied. The validity of the device could be questioned, however, not merely because it plainly evaded the policy of the statute, but also because the King's Bench had no power to arrest anyone to answer a plea of debt. The *ac etiam* clause, unlike the other fictions, did infringe Magna Carta. But who was to correct the King's Bench?

The obvious solution was for the Common Pleas to enlist the support of the Lord Chancellor, who was losing his share of the fines for writs. There were precedents from as far back as the reign of Elizabeth I for injunctions or writs of *supersedeas* to stay *latitats* on the ground that they were intended to defraud the Crown of the fine payable for a writ. Lord Clarendon C did in the 1660s sanction a general form of *supersedeas* to stay *latitats* with *ac etiam* clauses in delusion of the 1661 statute.[25] But Lord Nottingham C early in the 1670s foresaw that this policy would not work. The King's Bench, to avoid extinction, might ignore the *supersedeas* and punish sheriffs who tried to execute it; even if the *supersedeas* were obeyed, there was no guarantee that the Common Pleas and Exchequer would not develop similar practices; and if all the courts were stayed, ostensibly for the Lord Chancellor's profit, there would be an embarrassing scandal. The Chancery, therefore, decided to remain aloof. As a result, the *ac etiam* threatened the Common Pleas with extinction. There were now twenty *latitat*s issued to every original writ, and the loyalty of the attorneys, the only protection of the Common Pleas, was breaking. Sir Matthew Hale, Chief Justice of the King's Bench from 1672 to 1676, conceded that the Common Pleas would be 'in effect destroyed', and that this would be generally unacceptable. When Sir Francis North became Chief Justice of the Common Pleas in 1675 he found the court unable to occupy more than a quarter of its time of sitting, and he sensed impending disaster. Having failed to persuade Lord Nottingham to help directly, he adopted the only remaining solution and reluctantly sanctioned the use in his own court of *ac etiam*s in conjunctions with fictitious writs of trespass to land; and to this compromise Lord Nottingham, who supervised the issue of all original writs, assented. A century of competition was thus ended. Beneath the legacy of double fictions lay improvements in procedure which might not have otherwise occurred.

---

25. 'Reasons against the Latitat', Hertford Record Office, Verulam MS XII.A.30, from the papers of Sir Harbottle Grimston MR.

THE EXCHEQUER OF PLEAS

Our account of the common law courts has so far omitted the Exchequer, which was the last of the three to achieve the position of a regular court for common pleas. It was, in a sense, the oldest of the three. The author of the twelfth-century *Dialogue of the Exchequer* praised the new department not only for its advanced accounting methods, but also for its power to conduct judicial enquiries when needed. At that date, however, there was no court to be distinguished from the revenue office. By the middle of the thirteenth century the judicial procedures were more developed, and a distinction could be drawn between two 'sides' of the Exchequer. The two sides corresponded to the two chief clerical officers, who kept separate records. The Lord Treasurer's Remembrancer was concerned with the fixed revenue of the Crown and with routine auditing and debt-collecting. This side was called the 'Exchequer of Receipt'. The King's Remembrancer was concerned with casual revenue, and therefore with litigation by the Crown. His work divided into two parts: the purely Crown business, the recovery of debts, enforcement of seizures, and such like, and actions by subjects who enjoyed the privilege of suing in the Exchequer. The latter distinction was sharpened in 1236 by the appearance of a new series of rolls, the plea rolls, for the second class of business, to supplement the memoranda rolls which recorded the Crown business. The judicial side of the Exchequer was called the 'Exchequer of Pleas', and its judges were the 'barons' of the Exchequer. The court was quite independent of the Chancery, and could summon defendants by writs under its own seal, kept by the chancellor of the Exchequer; but its contentious procedure was close to that of the other common law courts.

The attraction of the court to private litigants needs little explanation: the methods used by the king to collect his own revenue must be the best. By 1290 the court styled itself a court for common pleas: *placita communia coram baronibus de scaccario*.[26] But attempts were already being made to stop it hearing common pleas, probably because they were impeding the king's business. Whether anyone in 1215 had thought that clause 17 of Magna Carta would reach the Exchequer is doubtful; it was not then an issue. By 1280, however, appeals were being made to Magna Carta, on the ground that the Exchequer was not in law held in a certain place. In view of the doubts, legislation was passed making it clear that the Exchequer was not for common pleas. As a result, the Exchequer of Pleas throughout the fourteenth, fifteenth and sixteenth centuries was a relatively minor civil jurisdic-

26. E.g. 48 SS 123.

tion limited to actions by or against Exchequer officials, sheriffs, local officials or others who were bound to render accounts at the Exchequer. The latter category included debtors to the Crown, who were entitled to recover their own debts in the Exchequer in order to be able to satisfy the king. The procedure was known as *quominus*, because in both the bill of complaint and the ensuing process the plaintiff alleged that by reason of the debt or damages due to him he was 'so much the less able to satisfy the lord king of the debts which he owes at the Exchequer' (*quo minus domino regi satisfacere valeat de debitis quae debet ad scaccarium*).[27] It is not clear whether the theory was that the Crown had an indirect interest in such a suit, so that it was not a common plea, or that an 'accountant' was constructively present in court and therefore enjoyed the like privilege as an officer or prisoner.

The *quominus* procedure suggested a means of expansion when the jurisdictions at Westminster came under stress in the Tudor period. Suppose a plaintiff wishing to sue in the Exchequer alleged fictitiously that he was a debtor to the king: would this be a refutable assertion, or would the mere allegation give the court jurisdiction? There is evidence that the latter possibility had been contemplated as early as Henry VII's time, chiefly in order to find a remedy against executors for the debts owed by their testators; and there is clear evidence that the fiction was used in Elizabeth I's reign.[28] The development of actions on the case against executors in the King's Bench, from the 1520s, may have eased the pressure. But expansion was held up by the court itself, which unlike the King's Bench long held out against fictions by allowing the defendant to challenge the false allegation.[29] The court also refused, in 1588, to allow a lessee of the queen's lessee to sue there, 'or else by such means all the causes of England might be brought into the Exchequer'.[30] But what was still unthinkable in 1588 became common form at some time in the next century, perhaps in the period 1650–60. Sir Matthew Hale, as Chief Baron in 1665, scrupulously attacked the fiction and also the assumption that a man could recover the whole of his own demand even if it exceeded his liability to the Crown: 'to make the king's prerogative a stale to satisfy other men's debts would be unreasonable, inconvenient and mischievous to the subject'.[31] But by then it was too late, and this

27. For the writ in full, see p. 438, post.
28. 94 SS *63*. Wager of law was not allowed in *quominus*, and so debt lay against executors.
29. The clearest case is *Ragland v Wildgoose* (1581) Sav 11 at 15. But it does not easily square with *Jervas' Case* (1582) Sav 33.
30. *Calton's Case* (1588) Brit Lib MS Hargrave 12, f.238v.
31. *A.-G. v Poultney* (1665) Hard 403 at 404. Cf. *King v Lake* (1668) Hard 470. See also Hargrave *Law Tracts*, p. 278.

particular prerogative had become common property. Against Magna Carta and subsequent legislation, and perhaps against the better judgment of the barons, the Exchequer of Pleas had been turned by litigants into a third court for common pleas. The *quominus* allegation had become mere form, unquestionable and therefore fictitious. Anyone with a claim for liquidated or unliquidated damages could choose to sue in the Exchequer if he wished.

Meanwhile the barons had advanced in status. In 1550 only the chief baron was usually a serjeant, the others being readers in the inns of court. After 1579 the barons were always appointed from the serjeants-at-law, which qualified them to be assize judges and to belong to Serjeants' Inn. From being, in medieval times, experts in the mysterious course of the Exchequer, they had become fully fledged common law judges.

Uniformity and Abolition

The outcome of these developments was that by 1700 the three central courts of law had acquired comparable jurisdictions over common pleas and had developed procedures which, though divergent in outward forms and in costs, worked alike in practice. Each court retained specialist functions. The King's Bench still had its supervisory role, through certiorari on the Crown side and mandamus and error on the civil side, and occasionally entertained criminal trials at bar. The Exchequer continued its proper revenue jurisdiction. The Common Pleas kept a monopoly of the true real actions, because the King's Bench bill procedure was confined to personal actions and the *quominus* was appropriate only for claims to money which could be applied in paying a Crown debt. In reality, however, this restriction had come to mean very little, because the real actions had been replaced for most purposes by ejectment. Even the Exchequer could hear ejectment, although the main object was to recover land, because the damages would support a *quominus* clause. The only actions, therefore, in which the Common Pleas kept a true monopoly were those real actions which lay for types of property not recoverable in ejectment. The most important were *quare impedit* (for an advowson) and the writ of right of dower *unde nihil habet* (for a widow's unassigned third share of her husband's land).

By the eighteenth century it was customary to speak of the 'twelve judges' as a body equal in status and authority and function, and to regard their assignment to three separate tribunals as an accident of

history. The trial of cases, moreover, was shared equally and indiscriminately between the twelve judges as assize commissioners. Only
questions of law arising from the trial would reach one or other of the
courts sitting at Westminster in term time. The prospect of a legal
difficulty might have influenced the choice of court to deal with it; but
probably the choice more often depended on the sphere of practice of
the attorneys, and on subtle differences in costs and procedural
advantages. Nevertheless, despite the parity between the three
courts, business was not equally distributed. The King's Bench had
acquired the lion's share, and the others had become quiet back-
waters. Brougham thought that so long as there were three courts
unevenness was inevitable: 'it is not in the power of the courts, even
were all monopolies and other restrictions done away, to distribute
business equally, as long as the suitors are left free to choose their own
tribunal'; there would always be a favourite court, and the business
would draw the best lawyers and judges, and this would entrench its
favoured position.[32] Upon Brougham's exposure of various defects in
the system, a commission was appointed to enquire into the practice
and procedure of the courts of law. The most immediate reforms were
the abolition of the Welsh courts in 1830, and the introduction of
uniform process, in place of the *latitat* and *quominus* and other writs of
summons, in 1832.[33] By degrees the ancient offices in the courts were
reorganised or suppressed; and then, finally, in 1875, the courts
themselves were abolished and their jurisdiction transferred to a
single High Court.

The High Court of Justice as created in 1875 was split into five
divisions, three of which corresponded to the Queen's Bench, Common Pleas and Exchequer. The reason for continuing the three courts
was to avoid the compulsory retirement or demotion of the Chief
Justice of the Common Pleas (Coleridge) and the Chief Baron
(Kelly), which would have broken the constitutional principle that
judges were irremovable. By chance, Cockburn CJ (of the Queen's
Bench Division) and Kelly CB both died in 1880, and soon afterwards
the Common Pleas and Exchequer Divisions were abolished by
Order in Council. The Queen's Bench Division became the court of
common law, and Lord Coleridge thereupon became Lord Chief
Justice of England.[34] The irony of the resulting situation is preserved
to this day, in that common pleas are tried by the judges of the

32. H. Brougham *Present State of the Law* (1828), p. 10.
33. Uniformity of Process 1832, 2 & 3 Will IV, c.39.
34. This title had been used informally for chief justices of the King's Bench. Since 1875
 it has been the official title of the president of the Queen's Bench Division.

Queen's Bench Division, an irony compounded in 1971 by the creation of a new Crown Court to do the work for which the King's Bench
had been first established. But the irony is superficial. There is, once
more, a single *Curia Regis*.[35]

Further reading
Holdsworth HEL, vol. I, pp. 194–264, 633–650
Milsom HFCL, pp. 42–46, 51–61
A. Harding, *Law Courts in Medieval England* (1973), pp. 86–123;
    'Plaints and Bills in the History of English Law . . . 1250–1350'
    in *Legal History Studies 1972*, pp. 65–86
J. H. Baker, 'English Law and the Renaissance' (1978) 94 SS
    23–51

KING'S BENCH AND COMMON PLEAS
F. North [*Concerning the King's Bench and Common Pleas*] in D. E. C..
    Yale (Ed), *Lord Nottingham's 'Manual of Chancery Practice' and
    'Prolegomena of Chancery and Equity'* (1965), pp. 169–174 (and Lord
    Nottingham's response, pp. 158–159)
[M. Hale?] in F. Hargrave (Ed), *Law Tracts* (1787), vol. I, pp.
    357–376
M. Hastings, *The Court of Common Pleas in 15th Century England*
    (1947)
R. V. Turner, *The King and his Courts . . . 1199–1240* (1968); 'The
    Origins of Common Pleas and King's Bench' (1977) 21 AJLH
    238–254
C. A. F. Meekings, 'King's Bench Bills' in *Legal Records and the
    Historian*, pp. 97–139
J. H. Baker, 'The Court of King's Bench' (1978) 94 SS *53–63*
M. Blatcher, *The Court of King's Bench 1450–1550* (1978)

EXCHEQUER
H. Jenkinson, *Select Cases in the Exchequer of Pleas* (48 SS, 1932),
    introduction
H. Wurzel, 'The Origin and Development of Quominus' (1939) 49
    Yale Law Jo 39–64
D. J. Guth, 'Notes on the early Tudor Exchequer of Pleas' in A. J.
    Slavin (Ed), *Tudor Men and Institutions* (1972), pp. 101–122
W. H. Bryson, *The Equity Side of the Exchequer* (1975), esp. pp. 24–27
J. H. Baker, 'The Exchequer of Pleas' (1978) 94 SS *63–64*

35. *Parliamentary Debates* (HL), ccxiv (3rd ser.), col. 336–337 per Lord Selborne, intro-
    ducing the Judicature Act 1873.

4. The Forms of Action

In the mind of the modern lawyer pleading and procedure are ancillary to the substantive law, and the law student may complete the academic stage of his studies without reading the *Supreme Court Practice* or becoming immersed in precedents of pleading. Law is treated as a body of abstract rules which are applicable to given fact situations. How disputes are initiated and clarified, and what rules have to be followed in bringing them before courts for examination and settlement, are matters of practical importance but limited jurisprudential interest. The law, in other words, has attained an existence independent of the legal system. But much of our legal history will defy comprehension unless this rigid separation of law and procedure is put out of mind. The learning about writs, forms of action and pleading was fundamental to the old common law, not simply because lawyers were more punctilious about forms than they now are, but also because the procedural institutions preceded the substantive law as it is now understood. The principles of the common law were never mapped out in the abstract, but grew around the forms by which justice was centralised and administered by the king's courts. There was a law of writs before there was a law of property, or of contract, or of tort.

Originating an Action

Legal proceedings are commenced, or 'originated', when a plaintiff makes his complaint in due form. In the local courts the plaint itself was enough to set the process of justice in motion. When, in the early days of itinerant royal justice, complaints were laid before the justices in eyre or justices *coram rege* by bill, the royal courts were merely taking over existing procedure. Where, however, a plaintiff wished to originate a suit in the Common Pleas or in the King's Bench (when sitting in another county) or an assize, he had to purchase a royal writ from the king's Chancery to authorise the commencement of proceedings.

The reason is that these royal courts, although they rapidly became the ordinary and regular courts of law, were at first exceptional. The king was not, in his courts, merely taking over a traditional system administering local customs, but was offering a new and separate justice of his own. This royal justice was a favour which had to be specifically granted by the king. The 'original writ', therefore, was a pass admitting suitors to the royal courts, and it usually had to be paid for. By 1200 many types of writ had become common form in the Chancery, and were issued on payment of a standard fee; but the writ remained an indispensable preliminary to litigation at Westminster. *Non potest quis sine brevi agere.*[1]

The original writ did not, as did a commission,[2] confer jurisdiction on the court by direct grant. It was addressed to the sheriff of the county where the action was brought, and authorised him to commence the process against the defendant.[3] The writ was, however, 'returnable' into one of the Westminster courts; or, in the case of an assize, before the justices of assize in the county. This meant that the sheriff had to send it to the justices endorsed with a note of the action he had taken. On receipt of the returned writ, the justices had jurisdiction in the matter and could themselves issue further writs (called 'judicial writs') to secure the attendance of the defendant. It has been suggested that original writs began as writs containing executive commands to sheriffs to do justice between the parties in the county or to take some specified action. Such writs were in use in Anglo-Saxon times. Some writs, such as habeas corpus and mandamus, retained their executive form and became known as 'prerogative writs'.[4] The development which turned other executive writs into original writs was for the command to be coupled with the alternative of coming to the king's court to explain why it was not obeyed. The failure to obey royal writs was itself a plea of the Crown,[5] and so long as there was no limitation on what might be commanded any matter could be made a plea of the Crown by first issuing a writ. This form of original writ, a command with an 'or else' clause, was established in the twelfth century. Another formula, not much later in date, merely ordered the sheriff to take pledges from the defendant to appear in court to explain himself. This appears to represent a further stage in which the option of carrying out a royal command has been removed. Of these two principal species of writ there will be more to say

1. Bracton, f.413b (Thorne edn, vol. IV, p. 286).
2. See p. 19, ante.
3. For specimens of writs, see Appendix A, pp. 435–447, post.
4. See pp. 123–130, post.
5. *Leges Henrici Primi*, c.10, s.1 (Downer edn, p. 108).

presently. A third formula, confined to the petty assizes, was to order the sheriff to summon men of the vicinity to answer a question framed in the writ, and to summon the defendant to be there to hear the answer.[6]

The original writs were designed to regulate justice, not to limit it. Bracton said there were as many writ formulae as there were types of action,[7] and until the mid-thirteenth century new forms could be drafted when need arose by the chancellor and his masters, perhaps in consultation with the king's council and judges. Once a writ had been used it became a precedent for the future, and before Bracton's time there were substantial collections of precedents to guide the Chancery clerks and the legal profession in general. A plaintiff did not, there-fore, concoct his own writ, in the way that he was free to draw his own plaint or bill when approaching a court directly. He had either to find a known formula to fit his case, or apply for a new one to be invented. By the middle of the thirteenth century there were so many writs in being that the uninhibited invention of new ones was seen as some-thing of a grievance, voiced in the Provisions of Oxford 1258 which forbade the Chancery clerks in future to seal unprecedented writs without the permission of the king's council. After this period, although occasional innovations were sanctioned by parliament,[8] the categories became more or less closed. The effect was momentous. Finding a formula was no longer simply a matter of consistency and routine. If the plaintiff could not find a writ in the register of writs he was without remedy as far as the king's courts were concerned. This is not to say he was without remedy at all. The royal courts did not have exclusive or even comprehensive jurisdiction, and the denial of royal justice in particular cases was often a reaction based on fears that the old order of things would break down and the king's courts would be swamped with business they were not equipped to dispatch. Nevertheless, as the common law of the king's courts gradually became the regular law of the land, so the law of the land was dominated by the range and the wording of the original writs. For-mulae which had been drafted for more or less administrative purposes, to authorise the impleading of an adversary before an exceptional royal tribunal, came to provide the immutable intellec-tual framework of English law.

The choice of writ governed the whole course of litigation from

6. See pp. 201, 202, post.
7. Bracton, f.413b (Thorne edn, vol. IV, p. 286).
8. The Statute of Westminster II 1285, c.24 (*in consimili casu*), gave the clerks power to devise new writs on the analogy of existing writs which did not quite fit the case; but it seems to have been little used.

beginning to end, and the plaintiff selected the most appropriate writ at his peril. Procedures and methods of trial available in an action commenced by one kind of writ were not necessarily available in another. The classification of writs was therefore more than just a convenience for reference purposes; it was a classification of all the procedures, and in course of time of the substantive principles, of the common law. Later lawyers referred to the compartments of law and practice associated with particular writs as the 'forms of action'. These forms of action were the first object of legal study. The two earliest treatises on the common law, called Glanvill and Bracton, were essentially books about forms of action. And we know that the first stage in a medieval law student's training was to learn the writs, doubtless by rote, in one of the inns of chancery. The medieval tract *De Natura Brevium* was the student's primer; and when the renowned legal author and judge Sir Anthony Fitzherbert published a new *Natura Brevium* in 1534 he wrote in the preface that the writs were the 'fundamentals on which the whole law depends'.

MESNE PROCESS

Process is the name given to that part of the machinery of justice whereby persons are brought to justice and judgments enforced. The details of the process available in different forms of action are points of practice which have little fascination for posterity; but historians must not forget that such things were of immense importance to litigants, and may often have affected their choice of remedies and the development of the law. Process was governed by writs, but not Chancery writs. When the original writ was returned into the Common Pleas or King's Bench it was taken to an officer of the court called a 'filazer' who thereafter issued all the writs of mesne process: that is, until the appearance of the defendant. Judicial writs, issued under the seal of the court, resembled originals in that they were addressed to the sheriff and were returnable into court. The principal forms were the writ of attachment (under which the defendant had to provide pledges for his appearance), the *distringas* (under which the defendant was to be distrained by seizure of property) and the *capias ad respondendum* (under which the defendant was arrested).

The effectiveness of process depended on the sheriff. Unable as he was to claim expenses, and liable in damages if he made mistakes, the temptation for him to do nothing was considerable. The sheriff could return to a *distringas* that he could find nothing to distrain, or to a *capias* that the defendant was ill or not to be found. Whether he had looked was a question one was not allowed to ask, and so these returns became common fictions for use by sheriffs who could not be persuaded to take positive action. There was, in any case, a succession of judicial writs to be issued before any real sanctions began to operate. If after three writs of *capias* the defendant could not be found, the plaintiff could proceed to outlaw him, another elaborate rigmarole, which required the sheriff to 'exact' the defendant by calling him to come forth at five separate county assemblies. Even outlawries were not so terrible as they sound. They could easily be reversed for technical slips, and technical escape routes seem to have been left almost as a matter of course; if all else failed, an outlawry could be pardoned on payment of a pound or two to various officials.

A contributing cause of delay was the division of the legal year into terms. The original reason may have been the Canon law prohibition of litigation at certain seasons, combined with the need for the king's judges to be at home or with the king at the chief festivals of the Church. All Sundays and certain saints' days were, and still are, *dies non juridici* at common law. In addition, the three religious seasons of Christmas (with Advent and Epiphany), Lent (with Easter) and Trinity (with Whitsun and Corpus Christi) were to be kept free. These three periods were therefore 'vacations' in which no legal process moved at Westminster and the courts closed down. A fourth vacation, the 'Long Vacation', kept the summer months free for home pursuits in weather which made town life unsafe, and for riding circuits. Thus the legal year came to be divided into four terms when business could be transacted in the courts: Michaelmas (in October and November), Hilary (in January and February), Easter (in April and May) and Trinity (in May and June). The total number of working days in the year, in Elizabeth I's time, was only 99;[9] later reforms took away about ten more days, so that for as much as three quarters of the year there were no common law courts sitting at Westminster.

Each term was divided into four or more 'returns', each return day being a week apart. All writs were made returnable at one of these days, and at that stage the plaintiff had to take his next step. There were three days of grace at each return, and a provision for late entries on payment of a fine after the fourth day; but if the plaintiff missed the return altogether, his action was 'discontinued' and he had to give up or start again. If the sheriff or the defendant defaulted at the return, then the next judicial writ issued, returnable at the prescribed return day the next term. It was the function of the attorneys to watch their clients' causes to make sure that the business was transacted at the

9. C. A. F. Meekings in *Legal Records and the Historian*, p. 111, n. 1.

proper days. The chief consequence was again delay. It was not uncommon for a year or two to pass before a defendant appeared. This was one of the reasons why plaintiffs preferred bill procedure, to which the system of return days was inapplicable because the defendant was present in court, and why forms of action were chosen (if choice there were) which needed the fewest writs to procure an appearance.

Types of Original Writ

A writ was a thin strip of parchment containing a letter, in Latin,[10] from the king and sealed with the great seal. That is as much as can be said in general about the form of writs, because the contents of the letters varied from one form of action to another. Today there is only one type of original writ, and the plaintiff fills his own particulars into a stereotyped form. But the common law writs were different in form from each other, and some of the deeper divisions of form may reflect what had once been different approaches to litigation. The classification of original writs begins with the rudimentary distinction between a right and a wrong. The assertion of a right received different treatment from a complaint about a wrong. A right was continuous, even eternal, and it was necessary that its vindication be accomplished with care and caution; the highest solemnities of royal justice were accordingly lent to the protection of rights, especially those of a proprietary nature, for the decision would bind the parties in perpetuity. A wrong was something past, something which was beyond undoing, and which at first concerned the royal courts only in so far as it infringed the king's peace. The consequences of serious wrongs, in terms of life and property, might be just as grave as in actions about rights, but the philosophy with which they were approached was quite different. Enquiries into misdeeds were less perplexing, and less solemn, than enquiries into rights. Minor wrongs were not at first within the ambit of the king's justice at all.

PRAECIPE WRITS

The forms of action for vindicating rights belonged to the category of writs which we suggested may have been the first stage in the development from executive commands to commands originating actions. The sheriff is told to command (*praecipe*) the defendant to do right in some specified manner, or else to come before the king's

10. For the conversion to English, see p. 76, post.

justices to explain why he would not. The king's court is given jurisdiction in default of performance or restitution by the defendant. Writs in this class are known as *praecipe* writs, from the first operative word which is their common feature. Presumably at an early stage the option of performance was real; but by the end of the medieval period, if not long before, it had become fictional.[11] The disappearance of the reality of an option made the *praecipe* writs truly original, in that they were conceived of as originating an action from the time of their issue rather than from the moment of non-compliance.

The classical *praecipe* formula was settled by 1150, and there were numerous species in the register of writs. The principal species, perhaps the prototype, was the writ of right for land; the sheriff was to command the defendant to 'render' (or yield up) to the plaintiff the land which the latter claimed as his right.[12] There were variants of this species for claiming types of inheritable property as diverse as advowsons and easements; and there were variants, such as writs of entry and formedon, to protect various kinds of title.[13] For personal property there was an analogous formula, in which the command was to render the chattel or debt which the defendant unjustly detained; this formula governed the two forms of action called debt and detinue. In the sphere of contract there were two other basic forms. The writ of covenant included a command that the defendant keep the covenant made with the plaintiff, and the writ of account required the defendant to render an account to the plaintiff of money received. The *praecipe* formula was not appropriate for redressing torts, for there was nothing the defendant could be commanded to do. The nearest it came to this was the writ *quod permittat*, in which the defendant was to be ordered to permit the plaintiff to knock down an obstruction or nuisance; but even here the underlying assumption is not that the nuisance is to be abated because it is wrong, but that the plaintiff is seeking to be put back into possession of his right to be free of the nuisance, and this (in the form of an 'easement') was a proprietary interest. All the *praecipe* actions have this in common, that they look not to compensation for misconduct but to the restoration of the plaintiff's right; they are prospective rather than retrospective. Some of them did indeed result in orders to restore the property claimed; these are called real actions. Where, however, the right claimed was to personal services by the defendant (as in covenant or account) or to personal property (as in detinue), the only remedy if the defendant

11. See the Inner Temple moot (c.1485) in Keil 116, pl. 57.
12. This was addressed to the sheriff only where land was held in chief: p. 200, post.
13. See pp. 202–203, 232–233, post.

refused to do his duty was to award damages; these were personal actions.

As these were the oldest and most solemn of actions, the procedure which accompanied them was archaic and solemn and slow. Much parchment and wax was needed to secure the appearance of the defendant, who could safely ignore several initial stages in the process against him, and even at a later stage was allowed various 'essoins', which were recognised excuses for not appearing. In the writ of right, trial was originally by battle, the judgment for God. In debt, and at one time in covenant, trial was by wager of law (oath-taking), the most familiar mode of proof in the old communal courts. The *praecipe* forms of action were therefore close to the old ways of doing things and out of keeping with the confident, rational administration of justice associated in particular with Henry II and Edward I. One course might have been to modify the procedures to make them more rational. In the twelfth century that was still thinkable, and Henry II did indeed introduce trial by the 'grand assize', a form of jury, as an alternative to battle at the option of the defendant. By Edward I's time, however, the conservatism which accompanied the rise of the legal profession and had identified the common law with the forms of action put an end to further radical change. As neither their wording nor the concomitant procedures could be modified, the *praecipe* writs became less and less usable; and their fate was to be gradually replaced by whatever newer and more effective remedies could be found. One solution was found in the bill procedure of the Chancery and conciliar courts. But an alternative existed within the common law forms of action, in that second main category of writs which was concerned more with wrongs than with rights.

TRESPASS WRITS

The second family of writs is called 'trespass'. Trespass, the law-French word for *transgressio* or wrongdoing, was not in the beginning a term of art. In the English translation of the Lord's Prayer—'forgive us our trespasses'—the word is used for both the *peccatum* and the *delictum* of the Vulgate.[14] Trespass was not a single form of action, and the word was not used in the writs; it was a group of forms of action based on a different premise from the *praecipe* actions. Whereas a *praecipe* writ ordered the defendant to do right or else explain himself, a trespass writ summoned the defendant to come and explain why he had done wrong. Trespass writs were not concerned with the vindication of rights, but with punishment and amends for past transgres-

14. Matthew, vi, 14; Luke, xi, 4.

sion. A writ of trespass therefore offered no option of doing right, but required the sheriff forthwith to summon the defendant to show why (*ostensurus quare*) he had done the alleged wrong. In Blackstone's terminology, the *praecipe* writs were 'optional', but the trespass writs were 'peremptory'.[15]

The *ostensurus quare* formula appeared in the decades before 1200, and after some initial uncertainty it was settled that the Chancery clerks would issue such writs only for those trespasses done 'with force and arms and against the king's peace' (*vi et armis et contra pacem regis*), or for wrongs done in opposition to royal franchises, or for deceits of the king's courts. Only such wrongs were suitable for royal justice. Wrongs in general were considered more appropriate for local jurisdictions, and there was a policy of discouraging private disputes about mere wrongs in the royal courts. In 1278 it was enacted that actions of trespass should be brought in the county as in the past, and that no one should have a writ of trespass unless he swore that the goods taken were worth at least forty shillings or (in the case of battery) that the claim was true.[16] Three principal kinds of wrongdoing were encompassed within the idea of forcible trespass: trespass to land by breaking a close (*ostensurus quare clausum fregit*); taking and carrying away goods (*ostensurus quare bona et catalla cepit et asportavit*); and assault and battery (*ostensurus quare in ipsum X insultum fecit et ipsum verberavit, vulneravit et male tractavit*). These could be combined in one writ, with modifications where appropriate, and there were other forms (such as false imprisonment, invariably tacked on to battery); but most wrongs of violence fell into these broad categories.

The limitation of writs of trespass to wrongs *vi et armis* and *contra pacem* did not reflect any narrow understanding of 'trespass'; it was merely a jurisdictional fetter on the royal courts. The desire for remedies at common law soon came into conflict with this limitation, which in the fourteenth century was widely felt to be an inconvenience. Since local courts were not supposed to entertain suits for more than forty shillings without royal sanction,[17] there would have been a failure of justice if non-violent trespasses involving more than that sum were exluded from the king's courts as well. The king's courts therefore modified their attitude to non-violent wrongs. At first the solution was to use the *vi et armis* writ fictitiously, smuggling in actions under the pretence of force in the hope that no exception would be

---

15. Bl Comm, vol. III, p. 274.
16. Statute of Gloucester 1278, c.8.
17. The date of this rule is now uncertain: see J. S. Beckerman in *Legal History Studies 1972*, p. 110.

taken. A group of actions for injuring horses with force and arms, brought against defendants identified as smiths, suggests irresistibly that the complaints were really of shoeing accidents;[18] and doubtless there were other fictions which are no longer capable of detection. The necessity for the phrase *vi et armis* had become an embarrassment, and was the last major limitation on royal justice to be removed.

TRESPASS ON THE CASE

The *vi et armis* restriction was openly abandoned in the third quarter of the fourteenth century, when the Chancery clerks began to make writs of trespass in which the phrase was omitted. It was orthodox teaching from the sixteenth to the present century that the occasion for this innovation was a statute of 1285[19] which empowered the Chancery clerks to draw new writs on the analogy of existing writs. Recent research has exploded this theory. The development did not begin until at least fifty years after 1285, and the fictions resorted to in the interim would have been otiose if the statute had been intended to warrant trespass actions without *vi et armis*. Even if we assume that the Chancery clerks took fifty years to awaken to their new powers, there is a persuasive argument against attributing it to the statute in that the statute was never recited in the new writs of trespass, whereas it was recited in the one writ known to have been drawn *in consimili casu*.

The new writs differed considerably from the vast run of *vi et armis* writs. They embodied the same *ostensurus quare* formula; but whereas the *vi et armis* writs were usually 'general', fitting wide spectra of facts into stereotyped forms,[20] all other writs of trespass had to set out the plaintiff's cause of action with some particularity in what was called his 'special case'. The special facts were recited in a *cum* (whereas) clause which followed immediately after the words *ostensurus quare*.[21] This wider family of non-forcible trespass actions was therefore named trespass on the special case, or 'trespass on the case'.

The difference of form seems to represent nothing more than an accident of history. The general *vi et armis* writ came first, and the plaintiff who could not find one suitable for his use had to have a special one instead. At first any other differences were minimised. For instance, it was arguable that trespass on the case was a common plea and therefore outside the jurisdiction of the King's Bench; but the

18. See S. F. C. Milsom in 74 LQR at 220–221, 586.
19. Statute of Westminster II 1285, c.24 (*in consimili casu*).
20. Thus the battery formula (p. 442, post) would embrace wrongs as diverse as shooting and running down with a horse and cart. See p. 340, post.
21. For early specimens, see pp. 443–444, post.

point was not pressed and had no practical effect.[22] It was also arguable that trespass on the case should not be triable by jury, and should not enjoy the privileged process (by *capias*) available for complaints of breach of the king's peace; but these arguments likewise had little effect, and the last doubt was laid to rest in 1504.[23] Such, however, became the dominance of form over substance that in later centuries lawyers convinced themselves that 'trespass' and 'case' must be conceptually distinct entities. Suing out the wrong writ was fatal; and so different did trespass and case become in the legal mind that they could not even be joined in one action. The nature of the distinction was arbitrary and difficult to appreciate. Eighteenth-century rationalisation made the test one of directness: 'in trespass the plaintiff complains of an immediate wrong, and in case of a wrong that is the consequence of another act'. An action of trespass for fixing a spout so that it directed rainwater onto the plaintiff's house was therefore struck down by the King's Bench on the ground that the proper action was case. Fortescue J put the distinction between a man who threw a log into the highway and hit someone (battery), and a man who left a log in the highway and someone tripped over it (case).[24] The accident of history had been elevated by eighteenth-century misunderstanding into a principle of law, a rule which would require much effort and learning to avoid.[25]

End of the Forms of Action

The introduction of actions on the case was the beginning of the end of the rigid framework of the forms of action. For, although there were specimen actions on the case in the registers of writs, the 'special case' was wholly without limits on form or substance. This flexible action therefore provided the common law with a temporary escape from the formulary system, and an opportunity to melt down the medieval law and recast it in new moulds. Most of the law as we know it was shaped by this process. Trespass on the case brought new areas of jurisdiction to the royal courts, such as defamation; it filled gaps in the *praecipe* actions, by enabling damages to be awarded for breach of parol

---

22. 94 SS *57–59*.
23. Stat 19 Hen VII, c.9 (like process in case as in trespass). The suggestion that defendants in case could wage their law was dismissed as early as 1375: *Stratton v Swanlond* (1375) Kiralfy SB, p. 185, Fifoot HSCL, p. 82.
24. *Reynolds v Clarke* (1725) 1 Stra 634, 2 Ld Raym 1399, Fifoot HSCL, p. 201
25. See further p. 345, post.

contracts, for past nuisances, and for conversion of goods; and finally it enabled the *praecipe* actions themselves to be replaced. The last development was resisted, on the grounds that special actions were only allowed where there was no general action: an axiom which was partly derived from the Tudor interpretation of the statute *In consimili casu*, which only applied where there was no existing writ in the register. The resistance sparked off a raging controversy in Elizabethan times, but was settled in 1602 in favour of actions on the case.[26] After that the only *praecipe* writs commonly used were debt and covenant to enforce contracts under seal. As the law was redistributed into its new forms, the commonest types of trespass and case became the basis of a new scheme of forms of action: *assumpsit* (to enforce parol agreements), trover (to protect personal property) and ejectment (to recover land).[27] But the flexibility inherent in actions on the case prevented any recurrence of the restrictiveness associated with the *praecipe* actions. And the redistribution of so much of the law under one 'form' introduced a good measure of procedural uniformity.

The progression towards uniformity was carried to a conclusion by nineteenth-century legislation. Most of the forms of action were abolished in 1832 and 1833. Actions were thereafter commenced by one form of writ, in which the kind of action was merely inserted in the space provided. After 1852 it became unnecessary even to state the 'form of action' in the uniform writ.[28] The return days were abolished, and eventually the intervention of the sheriff was for most purposes dispensed with, so that parties served their own writs and pleadings within set time-limits. Since 1875 there has been but one type of original writ, which, like the Chancery subpoena, is addressed to the party himself ordering him to appear; the substance of the claim is endorsed on the back, but not in any technical phrases. These changes were procedural, and were not supposed to alter any of the substantive law which was enforced through the forms of action. Yet the law was so inseparable from the writs that the disappearance of the latter left a distinct void. The chief conceptual problem arises from the fact that so many of the writs overlapped. Since 1833 there has been an election between trespass and case, so long as the wrong complained of is not wilful.[29] But what is the substantive distinction, if

26. *Slade's Case* (1602) 4 Co Rep 92; pp. 285–287, post.
27. Ejectment was a form of trespass *vi et armis*: pp. 252–255, 443, post.
28. Uniformity of Process 1832, 2 & 3 Will IV, c.39; Real Property Limitation Act 1833, 3 & 4 Will IV, c.27, s.36; Common Law Procedure Act 1852, 15 & 16 Vict, c.76. For the new form see p. 447, post.
29. *Williams v Holland* (1833) 10 Bing 112; p. 345, post.

any, between trespass and case?[30] The election between conversion
and detinue remained important until a statute of 1977 declared
curtly that 'detinue is abolished'. But what exactly was thereby
abolished?[31] There may still be a similar distinction between *indebitatus assumpsit* and debt, though it has a subtlety which seems to be
appreciated only in the,Antipodes.[32]

'The forms of action we have buried,' said Maitland at the turn of
the century, 'but they still rule us from their graves'.[33] The passage of
years seems not to have greatly diminished their influence. Within the
last decade a learned judge, denying that the ghosts of the forms of
action always stood in the path of justice 'clanking their mediaeval
chains',[34] has gone so far as to claim that 'if one is not unduly timorous
one may find that they are waving one along the path of justice'.[35] Yet
the posthumous rule of the forms of action has tended towards a
tyranny which in life they were never permitted. The categories of
legal thought were closed in 1832, and where once the law might have
developed through the recognition of new writs it is now left at the
mercy of commissions and an overworked parliament. Law reform is
no longer subject to judicial review.

Further reading

Pollock & Maitland, vol. II, pp. 558–597

Milsom HFCL, pp. 22–27, 103–139, 211–213, 244–270

F. W. Maitland, *The Forms of Action at Common Law* (1909, rep.
1962)

A. K. R. Kiralfy, *The Action on the Case* (1957), pp. 1–54

S. F. C. Milsom, 'Trespass from Henry III to Edward III' (1958)
74 LQR 195–224, 407–436, 561–590

R. C. Van Caenegem, *Royal Writs in England from the Conquest to
Glanvill* (77 SS, 1959)

M. J. Prichard, op. cit., at p. 350, post

D. Sutherland, 'Mesne Process upon Personal Actions in the early
Common Law' (1966) LQR 482–496

G. D. G. Hall and E. de Haas, *Early Registers of Writs* (87 SS, 1970)

J. H. Baker, 'Original Writs and Mesne Process' (1978), 94 SS
85–92

30. Until 1959 there was thought to be a remaining procedural distinction: *Fowler v
Lanning* [1959] 1 QB 426, [1959] 1 All ER 290.
31. See p. 335, post.
32. *Young v Queensland Trustees* (1956) 99 CLR 560.
33. *Forms of Action at Common Law* (1962 edn), p. 2.
34. *United Australia Ltd v Barclays Bank Ltd* [1941] AC 1 at 29 per Lord Atkin, referring to
the fictitious promise in *indebitatus assumpsit*: p. 305, post.
35. *Sir Robert McAlpine & Sons Ltd v Minimax Ltd* [1970] 1 Lloyd's Rep 397 at 422 per
Thesiger J.

5. The Jury and Pleading

When a medieval law student had learned the writs in his inn of chancery, he progressed to an inn of court to learn pleading. 'It is one of the most honourable, laudable and profitable things in our law,' Littleton advised his son, 'to have the science of pleading well.'[1] This was an understatement. The common law had developed through the process of pleading, and was embodied in the forms of pleading. The year-books seem to be filled with little else. Pleading was not, as now, a preliminary exercise to be conducted in chambers; it was the core of the lawyer's art, the prime task of the medieval advocate in open court, the end to which all legal training was then directed.

The occasion for the creation of this science, a science taught only in England and used only in Westminster Hall, was the appearance of another English institution, the jury. Systems of justice which depended on general oaths and supernatural tests had no need of pleading in any refined sense, because God could not be interrogated. God would choose between the parties, but He could not be told how or asked to reveal His reasons. Divine intervention stopped short of finding facts or making law. Juries, too, would choose between parties; but they could be asked questions and could raise them. Lawyers had to make sure that questions referred to these 'lay folk' were questions they could not misunderstand; and so questions thought to be outside the competence of the jury had to be raised in advance before the judges. Matters which judges decided without juries became the common law, and discussions which occurred before the jury was summoned helped to refine and clarify the law.

The original writs provided no more than a thin framework for the common law. The wording of the *praecipe* writs showed that a man was entitled to recover his 'right and inheritance', his chattels and his debts, was entitled to have covenants performed, and so on. The trespass writs likewise showed that a man was entitled to redress for being beaten or imprisoned, or for having his goods taken or his land trodden on, and so forth. But the writs did not say, and it was not their

1. *Tenures*, s.534. This was printed in 1481: p. 163, post.

business to say, what an inheritance was, let alone a 'right'; they did not indicate what it was that made a man 'owe' money to another, or what constituted a covenant; they did not hint at whether a man might be beaten or imprisoned lawfully (as, by process of law), whether his goods might be taken lawfully (as by distress for rent), or whether there might be justifications for going on his land (as, to answer an invitation). Unless such questions can be raised and answered, there is no body of law in anything like the modern sense. Yet before the introduction of juries and pleading such questions were unaskable. So long as men suspended rational discussion of disputes and referred them to the Almighty, the words of the writs—words like 'inheritance', 'owe', 'covenant', 'force and arms'—remained innocent of legal meaning and incapable of technical definition. Inheritance can only become a legal concept when the pedigree can be discussed, and someone can be asked whether one descendant or another has the right to succeed. Owing can only become a legal concept when transactions can be looked into, and someone asked whether they result in a debt. And this is true of the whole law. 'Legal development consists in the increasingly detailed consideration of facts.'[2]

From 'Proof' to 'Trial'

The older methods of ending disputes are better referred to as methods of 'proof' than of 'trial', because trial suggests the weighing up of evidence and arguments by an intelligent tribunal. Supernatural proofs were absolute and inscrutable; no questions were asked, no reasons given, no facts found, no rules declared. Human decision stopped once the test was awarded, and in that sense 'judgment preceded proof'. All this explains why early law and custom is so elusive. But decision by proof was not confined to the local courts. The king's judges did not start out with an inspired vision of a new way of doing things; they simply took over and continued what had gone before. The ordeals of fire and water, and wager of law, became part of the procedure of the royal courts, and the Normans added the quasi-ordeal of judicial combat. Nevertheless a different, rational approach began to assert itself at an early stage and to displace older practices.

THE RISE OF THE JURY

A jury was a body of ordinary men sworn to give a true answer (*veredictum*, verdict) to some question. The idea of swearing men to

2. Milsom 'Law and Fact in Legal Development' 17 *Univ Toronto Law Jo* 1.

furnish information was very old and not confined to England. It was the only way of collecting information needed for fiscal and administrative purposes. Magic tests could pick one of two alternatives; but they could not produce suspects or count sheep. The inquest had roots in Scandinavia and in the old Carolingian empire. It may have been used before 1066 in England and Normandy, but not for settling private disputes. Norman kings used sworn inquests to uncover information of use to the Crown, an early instance being the enormous Domesday survey of the country in the 1080s. Much use was made of juries of accusation, sworn to inform the king's judges of suspected criminals without concealment; but the suspects would be tried the old way, by water. Under the Normans the jury might rather have been seen as a technique for relentless government prying than as the bastion of liberty which later theory made it. Yet what was found effective for kings was soon demanded by subjects, and kings were willing to provide it, at a price. Under Henry II the petty assizes and the grand assize each provided escapes from battle, an institution about which Glanvill wrote scathingly in about 1190.[3] The classical form of the jury appeared first in actions of trespass, where its use was warranted by the allegation of breach of the king's peace. When the parties in trespass joined issue, a writ of *venire facias* was sent to the sheriff commanding him to cause twelve men of the neighbourhood, unrelated to the parties, to come before the court to 'make recognition'; that is, to enquire into the matter and state the truth therein. This body of twelve, being sworn to say the truth, was called a jury (*jurata*); and its members were *juratores*, persons who have been sworn.

After years of theological and scientific doubts, the Church stopped ordeals in 1215. Thereafter, in England, juries were used to try the guilt of suspected criminals.[4] Battle became a rare archaism even in medieval times, and it is doubtful whether any judicial battles were fought after 1485; it escaped abolition, by virtue of being totally disused, until a gauntlet was thrown into a startled court of King's Bench in 1818.[5] The one archaic mode of proof which survived to any consequential extent in the royal courts was wager of law, or compurgation, which was regularly used in actions of debt and detinue until about 1600. The defendant swore that he did not owe the money or withhold the goods, and produced eleven oath-helpers to testify to

3. Glanvill, ii, 7. For the assizes of Henry II, see p. 201, post.
4. The presenting jury then becomes the 'grand' jury, because it has more members than the 'petty' or trial jury.
5. *Ashford v Thornton* (1818) 1 B & Ald 405; Stat 59 Geo III, c.46. The last wager of battle in a writ of right was in 1638, but the fight was stopped at the last minute: *Claxton v Lilburn* (1638) Cro Car 522. See also 94 SS *116*.

his credibility. This had worked well in local courts, where a dishonest man would be hard put to find so many character witnesses. At Westminster it was impracticable, because the *nisi prius* system did not extend to compurgation, and it must have been well-nigh impossible to fetch compurgators from the farther parts of the country. By Tudor times, therefore, and perhaps long before, the procedure was partly fictionalised. The defendant was able to hire professional perjurers to help him out, and by 1600 it was part of the official duty of the court porters to provide them. Wager of law thus became, in reality, the single oath of the defendant. It survived until 1833, chiefly because it had been out of use for two centuries.

The triumph of the jury in civil cases was a major consequence—and perhaps a contributory cause—of the triumph of trespass and case, for in trespass no other method of proof or trial was permissible.[6]

TRIAL BY JURY

It was obvious from its inception that the jury operated very differently from an ordeal or compurgation. What was not clear was whether jurors were to speak collectively and inscrutably, or whether they were to be examined separately as witnesses. Bracton was quite clear that, in criminal cases, the judges were to examine the jurors one by one and evaluate their answers.[7] His statement is borne out by records which show judges putting questions to different jurors and even to different juries in the same matter, reserving to themselves the final decision. Those judges did not see a clear distinction between finding the facts and applying the law. And yet jurors were not the same as witnesses; we hear of evidence being given to the jurors, and Bracton himself speaks of jurors as having a judicial function.

By the fourteenth century the collective, judicial character of the jury was obviously going to prevail. Although jurors were allowed, even encouraged, to inform themselves before the trial, it became an irregularity to communicate with them once they were sworn other than by giving evidence in open court.[8] If the jurors were spoken to, or treated to food or drink, by either party, their verdict could be quashed. The sequestration of the jury became a principle of paramount importance as improper influences became rife, and it was enforced with such rigidity that its members became as prisoners to

6. See p. 59, ante.
7. Bracton, f.143 (Thorne edn, vol. II, p. 404). There is a mordant allusion to Pontius Pilate, who accepted a verdict without satisfying himself.
8. See *Pole's Case* (1391) 88 SS 64; *Wantley v White* (1391) ibid. 80; YB Mich 11 Hen IV, 17, pl.41 (motion in arrest of judgment).

the court. After the charge, the jurors were confined 'without meat, drink, fire or candle', or conversation with others, until they were agreed; and if they could not agree they were supposed to be dragged round the circuit in a cart till they did. The merest suspicion of misbehaviour was punishable, and we read of sixteenth-century jurors being fined for eating sweets.[9] So far was the judicial theory of jury trial carried, that by the mid-sixteenth century it was irregular even for jurors to inform each other of facts without giving evidence in open court.[10] The constraints of discomfort were primarily intended to encourage unanimity; for, although traces are found until 1346 of the earlier view that the judges were to umpire any disagreements,[11] the vast majority of verdicts in the rolls were the unqualified verdicts of twelve. A leading case of 1367 put the matter beyond doubt; rejecting earlier precedents, the court held a majority verdict to be void.[12]

Maitland thought the judges had adopted the unanimity requirement as 'the line of least resistance';[13] it saved them from having to make awkward decisions. But the consequence ran deeper than they knew: the trial of the facts had become distinct from the application of the law. This distinction was to separate the common law system from all the European legal systems which were based on an 'inquisition' by the judge. It was to become a constitutional principle sacred to generations of Englishmen that men should be judged by their peers, and that judges should not meddle with questions of fact. But perhaps the most far-reaching effect was that it resulted in the elaboration of the substantive law. The decision as to what were material questions of fact for the jury necessitated a decision as to what the law was. However, such questions of law were not raised after the facts had been discovered by trial, but in the course of deciding what the jury was to be asked to try. This is where we must return to the history of pleading.

9. E.g. *Earl of Arundel's Case* (1500) 94 SS *113*; *Mucklowe's Case* (1576) Plowd at 519. In 1587 four jurors were imprisoned for merely being in possession of raisins and plums: HLS MS 16, f.253v, pl.85.
10. *Anon* (1557) Dyer's circuit reports, Inner Temple MS Petyt 511/13, f.36; *Graves v Short* (1598) Cro Eliz 616.
11. E.g. Fitz Abr *Verdit*, pl.40 (1329); YB Mich 20 Edw III (Rolls ser) ii, 555, pl.110 (1346). Both were eyre cases.
12. YB Mich 41 Edw III, 31, pl.36; Lib Ass 41 Edw III, pl.11.
13. Pollock & Maitland, vol. II, p. 627.

Medieval Pleading and Legal Development

Pleading began when the defendant appeared at the bar of the court and the plaintiff stated his complaint. In the royal courts the complaint was made in French in a *counte* (*narratio* in Latin), meaning a tale or story. Its main object was to amplify the matter outlined in the writ, and to reveal a full cause of action. Before the middle of the thirteenth century a new profession of countors or narrators had emerged,[14] whose business was to compose counts and pronounce them before the judges in the proper set forms of the king's courts. Numerous written collections of precedents of *narrationes* were produced in the thirteenth and fourteenth centuries.

In earliest times, pleading began and ended with the count. The defendant had merely to deny ('defend') everything in the count, and then the proof was awarded. Alternatively he could take 'exception' to the count for insufficiency, or variance from the writ, or for want of capacity to sue. Neither the general defence nor the exception raised points of law, so long as the count was in a known form. The rise of the jury changed the order of things completely. The countors no longer went away when they had recited their counts, but stayed to help formulate the question for the jury. This was called producing the 'issue', which was the question to be tried. The general denial remained the defendant's normal course; it produced the 'general issue', which put in question the truth of every material allegation in the count. But a more precise issue could be produced if the parties agreed to stake everything on a specific point. This was 'pleading' properly so called. Bracton referred to such a move as a jeopardy (*jocus partitus*), a chess term meaning a set problem; and in the earliest year-books it is called a 'peremptory exception', because it bound the party whatever the outcome.[15] The compilers of the year-books became greatly interested in the problems of pleading, which had diverted attention from the count and become the main preoccupation of the countors. Bracton's chess metaphor was well chosen. The twelfth-century *Dialogue of the Exchequer* had described litigation as a game of hazard; but it had become a game of skill, played out by the serjeants at the bar of the Common Pleas.

REACHING THE ISSUE

The issue (*exitus*) was the end and object of pleading, and the way out

14. See further pp. 135–136, post.
15. The procedural exception was called a 'dilatory exception' (later a dilatory plea), because it merely delayed proceedings.

into the country where the answer would be found. A case only reached this stage when the parties had fixed on a point which would decide it one way or the other; and medieval logic taught that this occurred as soon as some affirmative proposition was met by a direct negative. The logic was beautifully simple. The plaintiff narrated his facts. The defendant then had to deny them, or some of them, or admit them and introduce new facts. There was no other logical possibility. These three options were given technical names. The denial of all the facts was a general traverse, or a plea of the general issue. The denial of one material fact was a special traverse. The admission of all the facts, with the addition of new facts to explain them away, was a confession and avoidance. The first two resulted in an issue capable of trial; the third called for a reply, because nothing was disputed. In replying to an avoidance, the plaintiff had the same three logical choices, save that a general denial was only available in certain situations. The pleadings continued in this way until a fact was denied.[16]

An example will illustrate the various possibilities. Suppose the plaintiff brings an action of trespass for beating his servant so that he lost his services. The defendant may tender the general issue by pleading 'not guilty', which puts on trial every allegation in the count. Or he may traverse a single point, for instance by denying that the person allegedly beaten was the plaintiff's servant. Or he may admit that he beat the plaintiff's servant, and allege new facts: for instance, that he was a sheriff arresting the servant by *capias*. Only in this third case is there no issue, because nothing is yet in dispute. In that case the plaintiff must answer the new facts. He may reply generally, so that every new allegation in the plea may be disputed at the trial: for instance, by shewing that the defendant was not acting as a sheriff but was brawling. Or he may traverse a single point, perhaps by denying that the defendant was sheriff when the beating occurred. Or he may confess and avoid: for instance, by admitting that the sheriff had a *capias* to arrest the servant, but asserting that he had used excessive violence. And so on, until an affirmative is negatived. All assertions which are not denied have to be treated as if they are true, because their truth cannot come into question if the parties do not make an issue of them. A fortiori, the court has no judicial knowledge of anything which is not pleaded, nor can such a thing be put to the jury.

16. The names of the stages in pleading were: count *or* declaration (plaintiff), plea *or* bar (defendant), replication (plaintiff), rejoinder (defendant), surrejoinder (plaintiff), rebutter (defendant), surrebutter (plaintiff). It was rare for pleadings to reach this stage, because a party was not allowed to 'depart' from his previous pleading by changing his line of argument.

The pleadings, therefore, define conclusively what is in dispute.

ORAL AND 'TENTATIVE' PLEADING

When the science of pleading was at its zenith, pleadings were exchanged orally by the serjeants at the bar. After the clerk had enrolled them on the parchment record, turning the words into Latin, they became binding and unamendable. But there was no record until the end of term, and until then the oral pleas were flexible, tentative and hypothetical. The possibility of discussing tentative pleas, with a view to withdrawal, enabled questions of law to be raised in court. Suppose in our example of battery that the plaintiff wishes to question the amount of force which a sheriff may use in making an arrest. Is it for the sheriff to say that he used no more force than was necessary or reasonable, or is it for the plaintiff to confess the arrest and avoid by alleging excessive violence, and if so what words should he use? In deciding such questions, the serjeants and the court were primarily thinking ahead to the trial and the practicalities of proof; but they would inevitably have to make assumptions of law. Suppose, again, that the plaintiff wishes to assert that the *capias* was illegally obtained; in deciding whether he may do so, someone must decide whether in law sheriffs are excused even if they execute invalid process, or whether they must verify their authority at their peril. These are sophisticated questions of a kind which could never have been contemplated in the days of ordeals. They came to be asked because they were beyond the knowledge of common jurors, who were summoned to speak to the facts, not to make law.

Instead of pleading, a party had the option of admitting all the facts alleged by the opponent and asserting that the law did not compel him to answer because, even if they were true, they did not entitle the party to succeed. This procedure was called a 'demurrer', and it raised an issue of law for the court alone to decide. Demurrers were sometimes entered of record; but in medieval times the judges were very reluctant to decide them, and the usual effect of a formal demurrer was to confirm and perpetuate the uncertainty which had occasioned it. What happened more often in practice was that demurrers were made tentatively, thus enabling full discussion before the serjeants committed their words to the record. If opinion seemed against the demurrer, the serjeant withdrew it and pleaded something; if it seemed in favour, the other serjeant withdrew the disputed plea and pleaded something else. As a consequence, most of the law made by this means was made informally, off the record, and in a way which could not bind anybody. The law was developed, not in decisions upon the known facts of actual cases, but in discussion of supposed facts which could be tried later.[17] The judges did not, in consequence, render reasoned judgments as they did in later times; their role was more that of umpire and adviser. The judgment which the court did give at the end of the case followed automatically and made no law; it was usually entered up by the clerks in chambers. The law reporters were not interested in such judgments, nor even in trials. They wanted to know what happened to tentative pleas which were tried out before the assembled legal experts in Westminster Hall. In those rambling, inconclusive, technical debates about hypothetical situations we can detect the common law being fashioned.

MEDIEVAL JUDICIAL LAW MAKING

It would be misleading to assume that legal development was the chief concern of the lawyers who took part in it. Serjeants were retained to win cases, not to advance jurisprudence. Judges were as embarrassed by new questions of law as they were by questions of fact, and did what they could to avoid making decisions if there was the least division of opinion. How far it was appropriate to delve into the facts of cases in order to make fine distinctions was not predetermined; and on the whole the judges preferred, in the interests of clarity and certainty, not to do it. It was better, said the judges, to suffer a mischief in an individual case than the inconvenience which would follow from admitting exceptions to general rules.[18] Special pleading was therefore discouraged, and wherever possible parties were driven to plead the general issue. The jury would be expected to do substantial justice. Exceptions were made only when it was clear that the 'lay folk' ran the risk of serious error through ignorance of the law, in cases where the merits were more technical than factual. Exceptions were not made on the ground that it would be useful to know the law. In time even special pleading found its own common forms, and attempts to raise new questions by special pleading were warmly contested. The longest survival of the old attitude is in the criminal trial, where to this day special pleading is forbidden. The prisoner always took the general issue, leaving everything to the jury, and as a consequence criminal law could not be refined through tentative pleading.[19]

It was all very well to cast the burden of decision on to the jury, but

17. For a modern analogy, see *Donoghue v Stevenson* [1932] AC 562. No one will ever know, and it does not matter, whether there really was a snail in the ginger-beer bottle.
18. 94 SS *38*. See also the quotation on pp. 270–271, *post.*
19. See pp. 424–426, *post.*

suppose the jurors themselves demanded to know the law? They had every moral right to do so, since they were liable to serious penalties if they gave a false verdict. 'We are not men of law,' bemoaned a jury in 1314 who had been asked to find whether land granted by an abbot to a layman was 'free alms' or lay fee.[20] They could request informal directions; and directions became the principal vehicle for the development of criminal law. But they could also ask to give in a 'special verdict'; that is, to state the facts in detail and 'pray the discretion of the court' as to the result. In the early days special verdicts were widely used, and a statute of 1285 made it a right of the jurors in the assize of *novel disseisin* to refuse a general verdict 'so that they do show the truth of the deed and pray aid of the justices'.[21] But here again the justices found themselves embarrassed. If juries were given complete freedom to throw questions back at the court, confusion and uncertainty would have reigned. During the fourteenth century the judges let themselves out of this difficulty by putting an end to special verdicts except in the assize, as warranted by the statute, and in analogous cases where counts were devoid of detail.[22] The transition may have been achieved by making special verdicts tentative, so that after discussion they could be entered generally one way or the other; but any such discussion would have occurred at *nisi prius*, where the law reporters did not attend.

The law-making machinery which resulted from the introduction of jury trial was thus, to our eyes, slow and faltering. Yet in the actions where juries were not used, pleading remained at its primeval stage and the law stood still. Thus, in the action of debt on a contract, defendants invariably pleaded the general issue *nil debet* and usually waged their law; for centuries this procedure prevented questions about the law of contract from being asked. The medieval law of debt was a law of procedure and little more, because it was a survival of the ancient pattern of lawsuit.

The System Transformed

In the sixteenth century profound changes occurred in the common law system, and especially in the techniques of judicial law making. One result of those changes was that pleading became, as now, the

---

20. YB Trin 7 Edw II (39 SS) 161, pl.1.
21. Statute of Westminster II 1285, c.30.
22. Arnold in 18 AJLH 270–274; Baker in 94 SS *158*. See also Rot Parl, vol. II, p. 203, s.22.

beginning of the lawyer's task rather than the end. This result is usually linked with the introduction of written pleadings during the fifteenth and sixteenth centuries. Written pleas saved trouble where common forms were used, and aided the memory. But the exchange of written pleadings did not preclude discussion in court, because the paper plea was no more binding than the oral plea. The real change came when paper pleas could no longer be debated in court with the possibility of amendment, so that tentative pleading went out of use. This occurred during the sixteenth century, and one cause may have been the Statute of Jeofails 1540.[23] The act had been passed to prevent objections being taken to trivial errors of form in pleading, by providing that formal exceptions could only be taken on demurrer. The party disposed to quibble about form had to admit all the facts against him, and stake everything on the technicality; and it was thought this would seldom be risked. But the measure backfired, because it led to an avalanche of formal demurrers, and the courts decided that it would defeat the policy of the legislature and would prejudice any decision they might have to make if they gave opinions on pleading before demurrer. Elizabethan judges were still asked to allow tentative debates, but usually refused. By Charles I's time the year-book type of discussion was a thing of the past.[24] Had this happened in isolation, the result would have been to stifle the principal means of developing the law. In fact the result was the opposite. The change was symptomatic of a new judicial confidence, a willingness to make authoritative decisions, and a corresponding desire in the legal profession and its clientele to have the law clearly stated upon known facts or formal demurrers. As the law ceased to be discussed before trial in relation to hypothetical facts, means were found whereby it could be discussed in relation to known facts: facts either admitted by demurrer or found by general or special verdict. The replacement of tentative by binding demurrers was only part of the story; there arose in addition ways of raising questions of law *after* trial.

MOTIONS IN BANC

The procedure whereby questions could be raised after the trial, by motions 'in banc' to the court at Westminster,[25] seems in medieval times to have been limited to badly joined issues or formal defects in the trial. In the sixteenth century it was extended to enable substantive questions of law to be argued after the facts in issue had been

23. Stat 32 Hen VIII, c.30.
24. *Anon* (1641) March NC 156, pl.224. See also 94 SS *156*.
25. For the mechanics of the procedure, see further pp. 119–120, post.

determined by a jury. There were three elementary forms of motion in banc: the motion in arrest of judgment, the motion for judgment *non obstante veredicto*, and the motion for a new trial.

The motion in arrest of judgment was the commonest. It was made by the defendant after a verdict for the plaintiff on the ground that, even though the facts alleged by the plaintiff had been found true, they disclosed no cause of action on which the plaintiff could succeed. This kind of motion would have been of no use in connection with the old actions of debt or trespass *vi et armis*, because the facts were stated in the count in the most general terms, and unless the plaintiff experimented with some fanciful novelty there was nothing to argue about. Two developments brought the motion in arrest into its own. One was the rise of actions on the case, in which the 'special case' on which everything depended was infinitely variable and bursting with legal questions. In medieval times a new action on the case could be attacked either by a plea in abatement of the writ or a demurrer to the count; but by the time of Henry VIII the more convenient procedure was to take the objection by motion in arrest of judgment, so that the defendant could have a trial first. Much of the modern common law arose from such arguments, and it should be remembered that actions on the case eventually replaced those *praecipe* actions in which tentative pleading had failed to make much impact. The second development was the revival of the special verdict. When the policy had been to refuse special verdicts, lawyers had striven to achieve the same effect by means of a 'demurrer to the evidence'; in this procedure the parties agreed on the detailed facts and had them entered on record, so that the jury could be discharged without giving a verdict, and the court had to decide the answer.[26] By the middle of the sixteenth century, however, the courts relented and began to allow special verdicts to be given in special actions, such as actions on the case.[27] This let in a consideration of more detailed problems than appeared on the pleadings; and again the procedure was the motion in banc. Later still, in the eighteenth and nineteenth centuries, a similar result was achieved by the parties agreeing to state a 'special case' for the opinion of the court in banc; in this event a general verdict was taken for the plaintiff, with leave to set it aside if the court in banc so decided.

The motion for judgment *non obstante veredicto* was made by the plaintiff after a verdict for the defendant. Its scope was far more restricted, because the only situation where the plaintiff was entitled

26. See 94 SS *111–112, 158*.
27. *Burgh v Warnford* (1553) Dalison Rep, Brit Lib MS Harley 5141, f.12; *Dowman v Vavasor* (1586) 9 Co Rep 7 at 11–14.

to judgment notwithstanding a verdict against him was where the defendant had confessed a good cause of action without pleading a sufficient avoidance.

The motion for a new trial was the latest and most extensive of the procedures for raising questions of law. It was first used where the trial was a nullity for some technical reason. In the seventeenth and eighteenth centuries it became a means of quashing verdicts given against the evidence, or against the proper legal construction put upon the evidence, or after a misdirection by the trial judge. A distinction was then drawn. Where the defect in the trial was on the face of the record, so that the verdict was null *ab initio*, the previous proceedings were disregarded and a *venire de novo* issued to summon a good jury. Where the defect arose off the record, the verdict was 'quashed' or set aside by the court in banc, and a 'new trial' ordered. The facts which were not of record were communicated to the court in banc by the trial judge. The practice whereby the judge at *nisi prius* kept a note of the evidence began, for this reason, around 1700. Lord Mansfield perfected the method, particularly as a means of refining commercial law; and he would state 'very particularly and minutely, from his own notes taken down at the trial, (which he read to the audience verbatim,) the exact state of the facts as they came out upon the evidence'.[28] Like the priests who had tinkered with ordeals in which they had lost faith, the judges had begun to impose a rational control on jury trial. This procedure went further than the others, by throwing *all* the evidence before the court; and, since it was the judge's account of the facts which mattered, it prepared the way for the end of the civil jury and of the common law system.

Decline of the Common Law System

By the seventeenth century the science of pleading had begun to degenerate from its primitive simplicity 'and to become a piece of nicety and curiosity'.[29] Hale CJ attributed the decline to the introduction of paper pleadings: 'anciently pleading was at the bar, and then it did appear plainly what was stood upon; and if the party did demur, he knew what he did. But pleading is now got all into paper and since that, of late, men make it but a snare and trap and piece of skill.'[30] The reports amply bear him out. In the year-book period difficulties were

28. *Sanderson v Rowles* (1767) 4 Burr 2064 at 2067. For Mansfield's notebooks, see E. Heward (1976) 93 LQR 438.
29. M. Hale *History of the Common Law* (1971 edn), p. 111.
30. *Anon* (1672) Treby Rep, MS in Middle Temple, 717.

eradicated before issue joined, and cases were rarely lost on points of mere form. As was suggested above, the ironic result of the Statute of Jeofails 1540 may have been to increase the use of binding demurrers and to accelerate the end of tentative pleading. No doubt many lawyers found it impossible to distinguish form and substance. There is a safety in forms and precedents which readily commends itself to any professional man who has to advise clients. The judges who were responsible for the state of affairs lamented by Hale doubtless con- ceived it their duty to maintain the forms of the law. Coke CJ, writing in 1628, observed that in his day 'more jangling and questions grow upon the manner of pleading, and exceptions to form, than upon the matter itself, and infinite causes [are] lost or delayed for want of good pleading'. But the lesson he drew was not that there should be a return to informality, rather that lawyers should be more precise. If form were neglected, he wrote elsewhere of writs, 'ignorance, the mother of error and barbarousness, will follow, and in the end all will be involved in confusion and subversion of the ancient law of the land'.[31]

The inflexibility of special pleading after the sixteenth century was one of the chief reasons for the decline which we must now trace.

LATIN AND COURT-HAND

When the plea rolls first started it was unthinkable that they should be in any language but Latin, the language of all Christendom, a language of certainty and elegance. The physical construction was designed to last: a clear, formal hand written on good parchment. Many of the earliest rolls have survived in almost pristine condition. Both the language and the set hand, however, became immutable requirements of the common law. Proceedings in English could be reversed for error. And in 1588 a sheriff was fined for returning a writ in ordinary writing.[32] The judges had good reasons. Court-hand can be read when very worn, whereas plain writing 'would be so worn in a dozen years that no man can read it'. And the translation of facts and ideas into a dead language encouraged economy of words and preci- sion of thought. But such things alienated the lay public from the lawyers, and they were carried too far.

The preciseness of Latin meant that the omission of a single down- stroke or contraction sign, or an error of Latin accidence, were fatal mistakes in a writ. Even the learned author of the new *Natura Brevium* once brought a writ which turned out to contain a grammatical

31. Co Inst, vol. I, p. 303; *Blackamore's Case* (1610) 8 Co Rep 156 at 159.
32. Goulds 111.

error.[33] The slightest slip could affect the sense. In 1533 a convicted murderer was saved by a single letter in the indictment.[34] The rendering of post-classical terms into Latin was an endless source of trouble. English words could be used in conjunction with an *anglice* or *vocatus*. The former was used to clarify an equivalent word: for instance, *tres argentei pixides pro necotiano anglice* 'tobacco boxes'. The latter was used if there was no exact equivalent: for instance, *duo pocula vocata* 'tea pots'. In cases of real difficulty both were combined: *quatuor pocula more Japanie picta duplicatis marginatis anglice vocata* 'Japanned double tipped mugs'.[35] The clerk's worst puzzles were eased by the publication in 1685 of a useful manual of 'words Latinised which you cannot find any Latin for in any Dictionary', such as football (*pilae pedalis lusus*), cork-screw (*cochlea suberea*, which suggests a screw made of cork) or spatterdashes (*lutosae caligae amphibularos ex panno vulgari factae*).[36] A dead language imposed real practical difficulties on a living profession.

Eventually, in 1731, parliament abrogated the use of Latin and court-hand.[37] The remedy hurt as much as the disease. Pleaders thought it unsafe to depart from the grammatical constructions of the past, and so English pleadings read like schoolboy translations. The Latin names of writs had to be restored, because writs of 'he lurks' or 'wherefore he impeded' sounded ridiculous. The literacy of attorneys declined, and so many lawyers were cut off from real understanding of precedents upon which they remained dependent. One pleader lamented that the law had become so uncertain as a result of the change that 'if our laws, pure and unsullied in themselves, receive many more changes, our properties will be as precarious in the hands of the most skilful lawyer as our lives are in the hands of the physician'.[38]

DOUBLE PLEADING

It was an axiom of the common law that a special plea could only be taken on a single point, so that one issue resulted.[39] Numerous expla-

---

33. *Fitzherbert v Welles* (1532) Spelman Rep (93 SS) 15.
34. *R v Rogers and Walker* (1533) Spelman Rep (93 SS) 52. The word *quidam* instead of *quidem* made a substantial difference.
35. Examples from *A Treatise on Trover* (1721), pp. 398–399. For an objection to arabic numerals, see *Hawkins v Mills* (1674) 2 Lev 102.
36. G. Meriton *Nomenclatura Clericalis* (1685).
37. Stat 4 Geo II, c.26.
38. J. Mallory *Modern Entries* (1735), vol. II, p. 367.
39. The rule only applied to each cause of action. In trespass to three cows, the defendant could plead a different plea as to each cow; but he could not plead that he had distrained the three cows and also that he had bought them.

nations have been offered. In the quaint language of 1667 it was alleged to be 'pur avoider le stuffing del rolls ove multiplicity de matter'.[40] Another view was that it kept the jurors' task within their frail comprehension. Another was that it deterred liars. None is wholly convincing. The parties paid for the parchment. The jurors were often asked to decide the general issue, and were then obliged to try to understand every facet of the case. And double defences could be mutually consistent: the buyer of a horse might honestly say that he was an infant, that the debt was statute barred, and that he had given something in satisfaction. The true reason why the common law set its face against double pleading is that it was the only logically certain way of bringing the parties to issue. If the defendant could plead two pleas, and the plaintiff make two replies to each plea, the pleadings might multiply in geometric progression. The single-plea rule alone prevented this nightmarish possibility. Even so, it would have been possible to attain the object without causing hardship by giving the court a discretion to allow double pleading in proper cases. This course was adopted in 1705, when parliament enabled defendants to plead several distinct pleas to the same cause of action with leave of the court.[41] The statute was widely used, and leave seems rarely to have been refused. It was even possible to plead generally and specially in the same action, or plead two mutually inconsistent pleas. But the statute did not extend to replications, and it did not allow a party both to plead and to demur. Neither did it, in strictness, permit double pleas; it permitted several pleas, and doubleness in one of several pleas remained demurrable.

GENERAL AND SPECIAL PLEADING

Pleading originated as a means of controlling juries by narrowing their terms of reference and excluding problems of law from their consideration. The new procedures, however, and especially motions for new trials, enabled juries to be controlled after they had pronounced and enabled verdicts to be set aside on legal grounds. Special pleading then became less necessary, and there was a resurgence of the general issue. The courts encouraged this by relaxing earlier rules of evidence which restricted the evidence admissible under the general issue. Thus, in trespass, a defendant could plead not guilty and show in evidence what amounted to a confession and avoidance. And in ejectment, which had replaced the old real actions, the defendant

40. *Churche v Brownewick* (1667) 1 Sid 334.
41. Stat 4 & 5 Annae, c.16.

was actually obliged to plead the general issue;[42] so that questions of
title, long enmeshed in the intricacies of archaic rules of pleading,
became a matter of evidence to the jury. Parliament recognised the
trend, and in over a hundred statutes between 1600 and 1750 made
provision for pleading the general issue in statutory actions. During
the interregnum a measure of law reform was introduced to enable the
general issue in all cases. The eighteenth-century books of precedents
show a preoccupation with declarations in actions on the case and
contain very few special pleas. As the general issue returned to favour,
the reasons for pleading specially changed. A special plea might alter
the order of speeches at the trial; it might narrow the issue, and
therefore restrict the evidence which could be given; or it might
simply be used to confuse and delay. The expression 'special pleading' then passed into the layman's vocabulary as a synonym for the
deployment of technicalities to perplex an adversary. Some lawyers,
notably Mr Serjeant Runnington, argued that the ends of justice
would best be served by abolishing special pleas altogether.

Against this trend there was a reaction, headed by Mr Serjeant
Stephen, at the beginning of the nineteenth century. Stephen considered the principles of pleading to be the finest achievement of the
human intellect, a thesis which he demonstrated by writing the first
reasoned treatise on them. The general issue failed to define the
dispute before trial, and consequently added to expense by compelling parties to prepare for all eventualities; and it failed to separate
questions of fact and law, so that points of law arose at *nisi prius* where
there were no library facilities. Stephen wished the general issue to be
abolished. And so the serjeants joined issue between themselves as to
the purpose and utility of the science they had created five centuries
earlier.

In 1830 the vexed question was referred to the Committee on
Courts of Common Law. Stephen was a member, and carried persuasion to his fellows. They admitted that special pleading still exhibited
too many bad qualities, but thought the advantages were of superior
weight.[43] Parliament thereupon empowered the judges to make rules
of court so as to implement the spirit of the report, and they promulgated soon afterwards the New Pleading Rules of Hilary Term 1834.

The 'Hilary Rules', which were said to have been the brainchild of
Stephen's judicial ally Parke B, drastically restricted the availability
of the general issue. For instance, not guilty in trespass was limited to
a denial of the breach of duty; justifications (such as self-defence) and

42. See p. 225, post.
43. *Parliamentary Papers 1830*, vol. XI, p. 45.

titles had to be specially pleaded. There was a forced revival of special pleading. But the consequences were less salutary than Stephen had envisaged. One problem was that defendants, prevented from pleading generally, took to traversing specially every single allegation in the declaration.[44] But the greatest defect was that it revived all the ancient learning in the state in which it had been abandoned, without modification of its purely formal technicalities. It proved to be a Baroque revival. Pleaders scuttled back to the black-letter books, and legal history for a while became a vocational subject. But it was imperfectly grasped history. Special demurrers flourished; practising counsel were more concerned to win cases than to perfect Stephen's science in all its intellectual purity. The judges must bear some of the blame for this unfortunate turn of events. Their attitude was summed up by the fictional Mr Baron Surrebutter, who, having failed to explain the system to an uncomprehending litigant, loftily suppressed his complaints by saying, 'I do not conceive that laws ought to be adapted to suit the tastes and capacities of the ignorant'.[45] They were not, however, behaving irresponsibly. They had inherited a tradition that lawsuits were to be treated like a sporting contest; a party who deserved to win on merit but failed to observe the rules of the game could not in fairness be declared the winner.

END OF THE COMMON LAW SYSTEM

The experiment with special pleading went so badly wrong that within twenty years parliament began, with judicial help, to rebuild the system from first principles. The Common Law Procedure Act of 1852, and the Trinity Rules of 1853, retained much the same choice between the general issue and special pleading as before; but special traverses were abolished, and pleadings were to omit all immaterial statements, fictions and legal or formal phrases. No demurrers or motions in arrest of judgment were to be allowed for lack of form in pleadings. It even became possible for parties by mutual consent to proceed to trial without pleadings at all, either by stating a question of fact in the form of an 'issue' or by stating a 'special case' with a question of law; this procedure is said to have been dormant until Mathew J made it a standard practice in the Commercial Court.[46] The Judicature Act 1875, and the new rules of court appended in the schedule, carried the reforms further. The plaintiff was to begin with a

44. *Cooling v Great Northern Rly Co* (1850) 15 QB 486 per Lord Campbell CJ.
45. G. Hayes *Crogate's Case: A Dialogue in the Shades on Special Pleading Reform* (1854), reprinted in Holdsworth HEL, vol. IX, pp. 417–431. This witty lampoon, written by a serjeant, is still good reading.
46. E. Parry *My Own Way* (1932), pp. 80–81, referring to the late 1890s.

'statement of claim' stating briefly the facts on which he relied and what relief he claimed.[47] The defendant was then to make a brief statement of his defence, provided that he did not merely deny generally the facts in the statement of claim. Beyond the defence, the parties could either plead new facts (by way of confession and avoidance) or join issue on the whole or part of the previous pleading. Each pleading was to contain, in numbered paragraphs, 'as concisely as may be a statement of the material facts on which the party pleading relies, but not the evidence by which they are to be proved'.[48] Prolixity was to be punished with costs. These provisions effectively stifled the general issue and reduced special pleading to its most basic premises. The demurrer was swept away in 1883, and parties were then enabled instead to raise points of law by pleading or to apply to have a pleading struck out as disclosing no reasonable cause of action or answer.[49] The resulting system is that still in use, with a few modifications made during the present century. Pleading is still conducted with care, and parties may be held to their pleadings if amendment would cause injustice to their opponents. But it is now the substance of the pleading, never its form, which governs the outcome; and there has been a tendency to permit once more the general traverse.[50]

Even more drastic in its effects than the abolition of the old system of pleading has been the disappearance of the civil jury. The possibility of trying facts by judge alone was introduced by the Common Law Procedure Act 1854. There were at that date already many courts in which juries were not used—particularly courts of equity and the new county courts—and in the court in banc, on motions for new trials, it was the trial judge's account of the facts which really mattered. The experience suggested that judges were more likely to understand the factual issues than laymen and were as competent to assess evidence. The 1854 act enabled parties, by consent, to leave issues of fact to the court; and this was so often done that by the end of the century only half the civil trials in the High Court were by jury. The 1854 act said that the 'verdict' of the judge was to have the same effect as the verdict of a jury; and the rules made under it show that the verdict was to be entered on the record in the same way. Yet, if the judges had taken to

---

47. Common law declarations did not include a 'claim'; the relief was fixed according to the form of action. The statement of claim was an amalgamation of legal and equitable procedures.
48. Supreme Court of Judicature Act 1875, 38 & 39 Vict, c.77, Sch. I, Ord. XIX, r. 4. The rule, slightly reworded, is now RSC Ord. XVIII, r. 7.
49. RSC 1883, Ord. XXV.
50. *Supreme Court Practice 1976*, vol. I, p. 299.

finding general verdicts without directing themselves, it would have been difficult to raise questions of law in banc. Some judges were bewildered by the dual role imposed on them,[51] and for some years it was possible to speak of a judge 'misdirecting himself'. In the course of the twentieth century, however, the alternative of jury trial has largely disappeared. The very existence of the option made it seem that the decision to ask for a jury was prima facie unworthy: it suggested the hope of confusion in a weak case, or the expectation of exorbitant damages in a case involving distressing details or high feelings. Wartime conditions led to temporary prohibitions of civil jury service, and from this further blow the civil jury never recovered. Since 1933 parties have only been allowed juries with leave of the court, except in cases of libel and a few other matters; and in recent years the courts have indicated their unwillingness to give leave.[52]

As jury trial became exceptional, and then virtually extinct, so trial by judge alone became a process different in nature and result. Judges have not adopted the practice of giving general verdicts, nor even, as in some American states, of making separate 'findings of fact'. The notion of a verdict has completely disappeared. Instead, the judges give discursive 'judgments' in which findings of fact are intermingled with legal comment. What is now called the judgment combines in one exercise a trial judge's note on the evidence, a 'direction' in law, and a special verdict, often adding for good measure the arguments of counsel. In a sense the trial judge is stating a case, for potential use on appeal, but he is now doing more than was allowed under common law procedure. The substitution of one man for twelve, and the surreptitious disappearance of the concept of a verdict, have left the judge free to publish his ruminations on the evidence in a way which the common law in its wisdom forbade to juries. The effects of this change have gone far beyond procedure. We have seen how the emergence of the jury, by forcing a separation of fact and law, led to the refinement of substantive principles of law. The disappearance of the procedure which separated fact and law has put the development of the common law into reverse. So long as questions of law arose upon pleadings intended to define the issue for the jury, or upon directions to the jury by the judge, they could remain relatively clear and simple. Now that fact and law are no longer decided separately, it is never certain to what extent judgments turn on the facts and to

51. J. A. Foote, *Pie-Powder* (1911), pp. 84–85, tells an amusing story of a judge who was unsure whether he should find as he himself thought or as he thought a common jury would have found.
52. *Ward v James* [1966] 1 QB 273, [1965] 1 All ER 563; *Williams v Beesly* [1973] 3 All ER 144, [1973] 1 WLR 1295.

what extent the judge's comments on factual minutiae are intended to create legal distinctions. Moreover, the tendency to minimise the importance of pleadings means that cases may change direction during the trial, and yet again in the course of an appeal, so that issues are not 'formulated with the precision necessary to elucidate . . . the principles of law which may be applicable'.[53] Coke and Mallory were right in their predictions of a slide into uncertainty, but perhaps for the wrong reasons. The flight from formality and from the common law has brought a retreat from clear principles into a confusion of particular instances. Equity, in the old sense,[54] has begun to replace and not merely to supplement the law.

Further reading

Pollock & Maitland, vol. II, pp. 574–674

Milsom HFCL, pp. 26–40, 61–73; 'Law and Fact in Legal Development' (1967) 17 *Univ Toronto Law Jo* 1–19

R. Sutton, *Personal Actions at Common Law* (1929), pp. 72–204

M. S. Arnold, 'Law and Fact in the Medieval Jury Trial: Out of Sight, Out of Mind' (1974) 18 AJLH 267–280

THE JURY

J. P. Dawson, *A History of Lay Judges* (1960), pp. 118–129

R. V. Turner, 'The Origins of the Medieval English Jury' (1968) 7 *Jo British Studies* ii, 1–10

R. C. Van Caenegem, *The Birth of the English Common Law* (1973), pp. 62–84

J. H. Baker, 'Trial of the Issue' (1978) 94 SS *103–116*

PLEADING

H. J. Stephen, *A Treatise on the Principles of Pleading* (1826)

Holdsworth HEL, vol. III, pp. 627–656

J. H. Baker, 'Joinder of Issue: the Mechanics of Pleading' (1978) 94 SS *92–103*; 'Pleading and Litigation as Sources of Law', ibid. *142–163*

REFORMS

Holdsworth HEL, vol. IX, pp. 262–335

53. *Banbury v Bank of Montreal* [1918] AC 626 at 709 per Lord Parker.
54. See pp. 89–90, post. It will be noted that the equity of the medieval Chancery was administered by a judge sitting without a jury, and therefore rested on the absence of a formal separation between fact-finding and adjudication.

6. The Court of Chancery and Equity

The courts and procedures described in the preceding chapters embodied the regular 'course of the common law'. Although the courts altered their jurisdictions, and the procedures were distorted and evaded in different periods, the essential premises and outward forms of the common law system went almost unchanged until the nineteenth century. It came to be thought an Englishman's birthright to be subject to this system rather than to any other, and a steady stream of medieval statutes from Magna Carta onwards guaranteed that no free man should be deprived of life, liberty or property save by 'due process of law'.[1] These statutes were intended as legal restraints on the power of the Crown to erect new courts and jurisdictions, on the very power which had introduced the common law and its due process as an extraordinary alternative to regular local justice. They were more than abstract theory. In 1368 the justices at Chelmsford held void a commission to seize a man and his goods without due process.[2] In 1406, Gascoigne CJ said that 'the king has committed all his judicial powers to divers courts',[3] and in the same year the King's Bench declared unconstitutional the courts of the University of Oxford which by royal charter proceeded according to the Civil law of Rome.[4] The notion that the king had exhausted his judicative powers by creating the common law courts was pressed to its limit by Coke CJ when in 1608 he told James I that he had no authority to participate in the judicial decisions of his own courts.[5]

The statutes of due process were provoked by a series of experiments with the judicial system; if litigation had become a game of skill, it was not right to change the rules at random. Yet, despite their lofty phrases, they represented a departure from constitutional

1. Magna Carta 1215, cl. 29; Stat 25 Edw III (sess.v), c.4; 28 Edw III, c.3; 42 Edw III, c.3, 4; 11 Ric II, c.10; 4 Hen IV, c.23; 15 Hen VI, c.4.
2. Lib Ass 42 Edw III, pl.5. See also Co Inst, vol. IV, p. 163.
3. *Chedder v Savage* (1406) YB Mich 8 Hen IV, 13, pl.13.
4. *Peddington v Ottworth* (1406) 88 SS 166. The university courts were subsequently confirmed by statute, and abolished in 1977.
5. *Case of Prohibitions del Roy* (1608) 12 Co Rep 63.

orthodoxy. The king could hardly have lost his sovereignty by exercising it. He was sworn 'to do equal and right justice and discretion in mercy and truth',[6] and so if the regular procedures proved defective it was his duty to furnish a remedy. The king therefore retained an overriding residuary power to administer justice outside the regular system; but the important limitation imposed on that power by the due-process legislation was that it could be invoked only where the common law was deficient. By the fourteenth century numerous petitions (or 'bills') were being presented to the king, asking for his grace to be shown in respect of some complaint. The usual royal answer was 'let him sue at common law'; but in the exceptional cases where the king took some other action we can see the beginning of the newer jurisdictions which came to be associated with the king's council.

Already in the fourteenth century the petitioning of the king by bill was so common that such business had to be referred to sessions of the council or parliament; and in this way the council directly continued the role of the Anglo-Saxon *witan* and the Norman *Curia Regis*. By the end of the century only matters of highest importance were retained in the great council, where, if the bills were assented to, they became acts of parliament. Private suits were more often delegated to individual councillors such as the chancellor, admiral or marshal; and petitioners took to addressing these officers directly. Each officer came to possess a separate court;[7] but the most important, because it ultimately developed a jurisprudence of its own, was that of the chancellor.

The Chancery

The Chancery (*cancellaria*) began as the royal secretariat, and took its name from the latticed screen or chancel behind which the clerks worked. In origin it was no more a court of law than the Exchequer, but was a department of state descended from the Anglo-Saxon *scriptorium* where royal charters and writs were drawn and sealed. The head of department, the chancellor (*cancellarius*), had the custody of the great seal of England, which was used to authenticate the documents prepared by the Chancery. Royal grants of property, dignity or office, treaties, charters and commissions all had to 'pass the seal' in Chancery. The original writs of the common law emanated from the

6. Coronation oath of Edward II, *Statutes of the Realm*, vol. I, p. 168.
7. For the other conciliar courts, see pp. 101–109, post.

same department, and through them the chancellor was associated with the ordinary administration of justice.

The office of chancellor was founded on the keeping of the great seal, which was the most important mark of authority in the realm. The silver seal matrix, bearing the sovereign's effigy, was later carried before the chancellor in an embroidered purse and set before him in court. The authority was necessarily enjoyed by any keeper of the seal for the time being. 'Keepers of the seal' were originally appointed temporarily, between chancellors, but in later times the office of lord keeper of the great seal was sometimes granted permanently. When the seal was placed in the keeping of several persons, these were known as commissioners of the great seal, and they too had the same powers as a lord chancellor. Since 1708 there has been no great seal of England, and no chancellor of England; but the Chancery, and the court of the lord high chancellor of Great Britain, remained purely English institutions.[8]

The chancellor had a large staff of clerks, who were reckoned of his own household and were therefore distinct from other branches of the *Curia Regis*. The first grade of clerks were the twelve *clerici ad robas*, so called because they received liveries of robes; they were known by Tudor times as the masters of the Chancery, were usually doctors of law, and deputised for the chancellor in administrative and judicial affairs. The foremost of the masters was the master of the rolls, who kept the records (including the patent and close rolls) and appointed the lesser clerks. The second grade of clerks were known in medieval times as 'bougiers' and were also twelve in number. The chief officers in this grade were the clerks of the Crown in Chancery, and next were the clerks of the Petty Bag, who controlled the common law business of the Chancery (such as inquisitions post mortem). The third grade comprised the twenty-four cursitors (or clerks *de cursu*) who wrote out the standard-form writs 'of course'. The development of the chancellor's equitable jurisdiction led to the growth of new offices, particularly the department of the 'six clerks', who were originally deputies to the master of the rolls; so much did their work expand that eventually the six clerks had their own deputies, the sixty clerks.

The chancellor has always been primarily an officer of state and a minister of the Crown. Most medieval chancellors were also bishops, or even archbishops. Some chancellors, notably Cardinal Wolsey (1515–29) and Lord Clarendon (1658–67), were prime ministers in all but name. Appointments to the office, which still takes precedence over the newer rank of prime minister, are made on political grounds.

8. Act of Union 1706, 6 Annae, c.8, art. 24; *R. v Hare and Mann* (1719) 1 Stra 146.

Yet the majority of chancellors have been lawyers[9] and until 1876 spent most of their time sitting in court. The anomaly that a politician should hold the highest judicial office in the land was compounded by the undefined nature of the chancellor's jurisdiction. The chancellor received no patent or commission defining his office, which he held at the king's pleasure, and took no part in the ordinary administration of justice as an assize judge. His powers derived from his custody of the great seal and from his pre-eminent position in the king's council.

THE LATIN SIDE

The first signs of judicial activity in the Chancery, as in the Exchequer, began in connection with the specialised work of the department. Questions relating to royal grants went there. The Chancery also controlled inquisitions relating to the Crown's property rights. For instance, on the death of a tenant in chief a writ of *diem clausit extremum* issued from the Chancery commanding a local official to hold an inquisition post mortem to discover exactly what lands he held, and of whom, and on what day he died, and who and how old was his heir; this information would enable the seizure of whatever was due to the king as feudal lord. Such inquisitions were frequently 'traversed' by interested parties, thus raising legal questions for the Chancery. The chancellor in addition had a full common law jurisdiction in personal actions involving his clerks, servants and officials, to the exclusion of the other courts. All such proceedings were described as being 'on the Latin side' of the Chancery, because the records were kept, as in the other central courts, in Latin.

The Chancery also received petitions seeking redress against the Crown; the king could not be sued by his own writ in the other courts. The determination of 'petitions of right' was obviously a function of the king's residuary duty to do justice to his subjects rather than of the regular common law. To that extent it foreshadowed the growth of bill procedure which brought the Court of Chancery into prominence. But the connection between the Latin and 'English' sides was minimal. The latter development made the court in effect an extraordinary court for common pleas, a court which was not tied to the forms or language of the common law and was arguably not even a court of record.

THE ENGLISH SIDE

The chancellor's 'English' jurisdiction, so called because pleadings

9. This is even true of the medieval chancellors, who were mostly graduates in Civil or Canon law.

were in the vernacular tongue,[10] grew not from the departmental work of the Chancery but from the jurisdiction of the king's council to deal with bills of complaint. In the fourteenth century bills addressed to the king in council came to be passed to the chancellor, and before 1400 most petitioners had begun to address their complaints directly to him. The Chancery may have been thought an appropriate place to discuss legal remedies because of its supervision of the original writ system. No one would be sent out of the Chancery without a remedy: *nullus recedat a curia cancellariae sine remedio.*[11] In the twelfth and thirteenth centuries the chancellor's response to a petition might have been the allowance of a new form of original writ. Once the categories of writ were closed, the only general remedy was to refer the bill to parliament with a view to legislation. But the chancellor could instead treat the matter ad hoc, and grant a specific remedy in the form of a decree which bound only the parties to the suit. Decrees were at first made in the name of the king in council, and then by 'the court', sometimes reciting the presence of the judges and serjeants and councillors as advisers; by 1473 at the latest the chancellor was issuing decrees in his own name. In making such decrees, medieval councillors or chancellors did not regard themselves as administering a system of law different from the common law of England. They were making sure that justice was done in cases where shortcomings in the regular procedure, or human failings, rendered its attainment by due process unlikely. They came not to destroy the law, but to fulfil it.

We have seen why it was difficult to conceive of the common law apart from the procedures through which it operated. In the King's Bench and Common Pleas it was circumscribed by the writ system. Cumbersome mesne process made it depend on the good will of sheriffs. It was constrained by the forms of pleading, by the rules of evidence, and by the uncertainties of jury trial. The possibilities of mechanical failure were legion. And the strength of the substantive law could also work injustice, because the judges preferred to suffer mischiefs to individuals than to make exceptions to clear rules; hard cases make bad law.[12] The stock example was that of the debtor who did not ensure that his sealed bond was cancelled when he paid up. The law regarded the bond as incontrovertible evidence of the debt, and so payment was no defence. Here the debtor suffered the obvious hardship of being driven to pay a second time; but the mischief was a

10. Some of the earliest were in French. The court used Latin for its endorsements on pleadings; but the decree books, which begin in 1544, were in English.
11. YB Hil 4 Hen VII, 5, pl.8 per Moreton C.
12. See p. 70, ante.

result of his own foolishness, and the law did not bend to assist fools. Likewise, if a man made an oral contract where the law required written evidence, he would find himself without remedy. Similarly, if a man granted land to others on trust to carry out his wishes, he would find that at law the grantees were absolute owners who could not be compelled to obey him. It was not that the common law held that a debt was due twice, or that a promise or trust could be broken; such propositions would have been as absurd then as now. It was a matter of observing strict rules of evidence, rules which might exclude the merits of the case from consideration but which could not be relaxed without destroying certainty and condoning carelessness. For a creditor, promisor or trustee to take unfair advantage of those strict rules was without question wrong; but it was a matter for their consciences rather than for the common law.

The chancellor was free from the procedural formalities and customs of the regular courts. No original writ was necessary, and so all actions were commenced by informal bill of complaint, usually in English. Process in most actions was begun by subpoena,[13] a simple summons to appear in Chancery or else forfeit a penalty. Pleading was relatively informal, there was no jury, and evidence could be taken by deposition or interrogation, even from the parties themselves. The Chancery was always open; it was not tied to the terms and return-days, though for convenience it observed them as far as possible. It could sit anywhere, even in the chancellor's private house; and causes could be tried out of court by commission of *dedimus potestatem* to country gentlemen. These technical advantages enabled the chancellor to provide swift and inexpensive justice for the poor and oppressed. Sheriffs and juries could be bypassed where unfair pressure was feared. The chancellor's eyes were not covered by the evidential blinkers of due process, and he could concern himself with the exceptional case. He could enforce the dictates of conscience, and protect the foolish. He could order bonds and other writings to be cancelled where they could only serve unjust ends. He could order parol contracts to be performed, and fiduciary obligations carried out. In short, he could coerce parties to do whatever conscience required. And yet, by exercising this jurisdiction he was not causing any of the 'inconvenience' which the law eschewed; in Chancery each case turned on its own facts, and the chancellor did not interfere with

---

13. After the subpoena came attachment, and then a 'commission of rebellion' by which local commissioners were ordered to arrest the defendant and bring him to the Chancery. In the 16th century there developed the further process of sequestration, by which property could be seized.

the general rules observed in other courts. The decrees operated *in personam*; they were binding on the parties in the cause, but were not judgments of record binding anyone else.

The chancellor's jurisdiction in conscience became firmly established during the fifteenth century. At the beginning of the century the majority of petitions complained of weakness or poverty, or the abuse of power by an opponent; and there was no limit on the subject-matter of disputes. During the chancellorship (1432–50) of John Stafford, Bishop of Bath and Wells, the total number of petitions increased sixfold and the court became the fourth major court of Westminster Hall. But, as the court grew independent of the council, its expanding jurisdiction became in practice almost confined to real property. Most of its work by the second half of the century arose from the practice of granting land 'to uses' (in trust).[14] Of its contract jurisdiction, the most important part was ordering the completion of conveyances. The tort jurisdiction was given up. The reasons for this we have already seen. The initial success of the Chancery had spurred the King's Bench into extensive reforms in the law of contract and tort, by means of actions on the case, and into adopting bill procedure, by means of the bill of Middlesex and *latitat*.[15] On the other hand, the kind of unusual violence or abuse of power which the regular system was powerless to redress needed attention at the highest level; complaints of this nature were therefore retained in council and became the foundation of the Star Chamber jurisdiction.[16] The council also found new ways of dealing with poor men's causes.[17] The Chancery then ceased in reality to be an extraordinary court. Although it retained its extraordinary ways, and would develop its own legal principles, it had become a court of constant resort for claimants to property.

Law and Equity

By Tudor times it was a trite saying that the Chancery was not a court of law but a court of conscience. Developments in the system of pleading and discussing cases in banc had by then generated the modern conception of law as a body of rules applicable to given sets of facts.[18] The chancellor, by way of contrast, was not concerned with

14. See pp. 212–213, post.
15. See pp. 37–40, ante.
16. See pp. 102–103, post.
17. See p. 104, post.
18. See p. 72–74, ante.

rules but with individual cases. He combined the role of judge and jury, and in delving as deeply as conscience required into the particular circumstances before him he did not distinguish fact and law. Inevitably the chancellor's justice was seen as something superior to the less flexible justice of the two benches. Indeed, if proceedings in other courts were in themselves unconscionable, the chancellor would issue injunctions to stop them. This transcendant justice acquired the name 'equity'.

Equity was a classical notion, defined by Aristotle as 'a correction of law where it is defective owing to its universality'. The idea was well known to medieval scholars. Glanvill mentions it as an ingredient in the common law,[19] and throughout the year-book period it was applied to the interpretation of statutes.[20] But it was a particularly apt term for the function of the chancellor. As early as 1468, a temporary keeper of the great seal was charged to determine all matters in Chancery 'according to equity and conscience'.[21] Generations later, Lord Ellesmere C explained that the reason why there was a Chancery was 'that men's actions are so diverse and infinite that it is impossible to make any general law which may aptly meet with every particular and not fail in some circumstances. The office of the chancellor is to correct men's consciences for frauds, breaches of trust, wrongs and oppressions of what nature soever they be, and to soften and mollify the extremity of the law.'[22]

The shift from 'conscience' to 'equity' was more than a change of vocabulary. It is not certain how medieval chancellors reached their decisions, but 'conscience' has a subjective ring to it; guided no doubt by their training in theology and Canon law, they were driven back onto their own consciences. The clerical chancellors were exercising the temporal counterpart of the confessional. In the early sixteenth century we hear grumbles amongst the lawyers about such an arbitrary function, and the dissatisfaction came to a head under Cardinal Wolsey (Chancellor from 1515 to 1529), who had no academic training at all. Wolsey delighted in putting down lawyers, had an arrogant confidence in his own untutored common sense, and in his desire to please plaintiffs too often left a sense of injustice. The chancellor's jurisdiction had visibly become another system of secular justice, sharing all the failings of human institutions; and the decisions of an unlearned chancellor, unacquainted with the reasoning of the com-

19. Glanvill, prologue, ii, 7; vii, 1.
20. See p. 181, post.
21. *Rymer's Foedera* (G. Holmes & R. Sanderson edn), vol. XI, p. 579.
22. *Earl of Oxford's Case* (1615) 1 Rep Ch 1 at 6.

mon law, easily offended at least the lawyers' sense of fairness. A strong reaction to the arbitrariness of the Chancery appeared in a treatise written by an anonymous 'serjeant-at-law' shortly after Wolsey's death. The serjeant 'marvelled' that the chancellor should presume to interfere by subpoena with the king's law, which was the inheritance of the subject. Conscience was a variable standard, for 'divers men, divers consciences'; and it offended the rule of law. The serjeant went so far as to assert that the chancellor's jurisdiction was founded on ignorance of the merits of the common law, and that it was contrary both to reason and the law of God.[23]

The rift was partly closed by Wolsey's successor, Sir Thomas More (1529–33), the first chancellor since the fourteenth century to have been trained in the inns of court. More had earlier written that to allow even a good judge to follow his own whim would defeat the principle that justice must be seen to be done, and would leave people in a condition of slavery.[24] He nevertheless thought the common law was too 'rigorous', and he not only exercised the equitable jurisdiction but continued the practice of inhibiting common law actions by injunction. When the judges complained, he invited them to dinner and told them that it belonged to their own discretion 'to mitigate and reform the rigour of the law'; if they would do so, he promised he would issue no more injunctions. The judges declined the offer, because, as More later told his biographer, 'they may by the verdict of the jury cast off all quarrels from themselves upon them, which they account their chief defence'.[25] The judges had no wish to become involved in decisions of fact, and therefore could not tackle questions of conscience. In truth the judges did introduce some equity into the law by means of actions on the case; but their flat rejection of More's proposal destined equity to develop in England as a system separated from the common law. Until More's time it could still be argued that equity or conscience operated in all courts, albeit to an extent which varied with the degree to which individual circumstances could be revealed to the court. As late as 1550 it was said by the King's Bench that 'conscience is *aequum et bonum*, which is the basis of every law'.[26] But thereafter equity would increasingly be regarded as the peculiar prerogative of the Court of Chancery. As a consequence, equity itself

---

23. *Replication of a Serjaunte at the Lawe* [c.1530] in F. Hargrave (Ed) *Law Tracts* (1787), pp. 321–331.
24. From *Responsio ad Lutherum*, as translated in 94 SS *81*. Cf. Audley's reading on uses (1526), p. 216, post.
25. W. Roper *The Lyfe of Sir Thomas Moore* (E. V. Hitchcock edn, 1935), pp. 44–45.
26. Bro Abr *Estates*, pl.78. Cf. speech to Anderson CJCP (1582) Moore KB 116 at 117 per Bromley C ('*aequum et bonum*, which are the life of the law').

became a kind of law, in the sense of a body of rational principles, and the original rationale of the chancellor's bill jurisdiction was forgotten.

CHANCERY AND THE COMMON LAW COURTS

Before the distinction between law and equity hardened in this way, the Court of Chancery and the law courts enjoyed a harmonious partnership. The judges of the two benches frequently attended in Chancery to give legal advice, and seem to have had no difficulty distinguishing the jurisdiction in conscience from the regular common law. In a case of 1452, Fortescue CJ countered a legal argument with the words, 'We are to argue conscience here, not the law.'[27]

The harmony gave way to discord under Wolsey, who did not spare even the greatest judges his contempt for things legal. In 1546 there was a minor explosion during the chancellorship of Sir Thomas Wriothesley, when some common lawyers petitioned the council complaining of attempts to introduce Civil law into the Chancery. The petitioners claimed that the whole profession was jeopardised, and Wriothesley was soon afterwards deposed for abuses 'to the great prejudice and utter decay of the common laws'.[28] The appointment of legally trained chancellors ended further fears of that nature, but there was an explosion of a different kind in 1616.

The trouble in 1616 was largely caused by a clash of strong personalities. Lord Ellesmere, the Chancellor (1596–1617), was an able common lawyer by training; but as he grew older his political and personal prejudices gained the better of him, and he repeated Wolsey's error of antagonising the judges. He encouraged suits in Chancery after judgment had been given at common law, and a backlog of thousands of cases piled up. Any criticism of himself he represented as an attack on the monarchy as established by God. The appointment of a doctor of Civil law, Sir Julius Caesar, as Master of the Rolls in 1614 was perhaps the final straw. In 1613 Sir Edward Coke had been made Chief Justice of the King's Bench, and he joined battle with Ellesmere over the Chancery's claim to reopen cases after judgment at law. Coke had the law on his side; the procedure was an irregular appeal, an illegal challenge to judgments notionally given before the king himself.[29] He began to release, by habeas corpus, prisoners committed by Ellesmere for contempt; and he encouraged such prisoners to prosecute their opponents for the crime of impeaching the judgments of the king's courts. Unfortunately for Coke, his

27. Mich 31 Hen VI, Fitz Abr *Subpena*, pl.23.
28. *Acts of the Privy Council*, vol. II, p. 48.
29. See further pp. 116–117, post.

hints were taken up by the unworthiest of litigants; and, after a misguided attempt by a crank to indict various officials including Ellesmere, the dispute was referred to James I in 1616. Coke was by then in political disfavour, and Ellesmere combined with Bacon and Buckingham to engineer his downfall. Coke was dismissed from office in 1616.[30] The weakness of Coke's position at that moment enabled Ellesmere and Bacon to persuade the king to issue a royal decree confirming the chancellor's jurisdiction to entertain suits after judgment at law. In 1617 Ellesmere died, and Bacon on succeeding him took pains to restore good relations with the profession and the judges. Once the dust had settled, the 1616 decree would be seen as illegal;[31] but never again did the relations with the other courts become so strained that the division of functions led to any hostility.

The lawyer chancellors from Bacon onwards concentrated on refining equity as a body of principles, and the jurisdictional hardships which remained resulted from the procedural inconvenience of having to seek equitable and legal remedies in separate courts. At best the inconvenience could be expensive, at worst disastrous. The problem was not tackled until the 1850s, and not resolved until 1875.

EQUITY ACCORDING TO RULE

The essence of equity as a corrective to the rigour of laws was that it should not be tied to rules. If, on the other hand, no principles whatever were observed, parties would not be treated equally; and equality was a requisite of equity. As Selden quipped, if the measure of equity was the chancellor's own conscience, one might as well make the standard measure of one foot the chancellor's foot.[32] The conundrum was an old one. St German, the anonymous serjeant, and Sir Thomas More, all agreed that subjective equity had no place in a legal system. The chancellor, argued St German, must order his conscience after the common law. He could not attempt to enforce the finest dictates of conscience, for at some point litigation had to be final. The Chancery did not upset a false verdict in an attaint, or a common recovery, or wager of law tainted by perjury. Many of the rules applied to uses had no moral content; the trustee was bound in conscience to follow them merely because they were positive law. A case of 1522 showed that a trustee was not to follow his own conscience, but was to obey the beneficiary; his conscience, like the chancellor's, was ordered by law.[33] Moreover, the acts of a supreme

30. See pp. 144–145, post.
31. *R v Standish* (1670) *Legal History Studies 1972*, p. 4.
32. *Table Talk of John Selden* (F. Pollock edn, 1927), p. 43.
33. *Gresley v Saunders* (1522) Spelman Rep (93 SS) 22–23.

legislature could not be upset by recourse to conscience; statutes might be construed equitably, but they could not be disregarded because they were unconscionable or because a party was unaware of their effect. In all these cases the only 'court of conscience' was the party's own soul.

Another factor which compelled chancellors to regulate their supreme power was the sheer success of the equity jurisdiction in terms of the number of petitioners attracted. Faced with so many thousands of petitions, they were obliged to develop routine attitudes to commonly recurring cases. There had always been a procedural *cursus cancellariae*, a common 'course of the court'; by Elizabeth I's time the *cursus* was coming to embrace substantive doctrine as well.[34] By the time of Lord Ellesmere lawyers were beginning to take notes of what the chancellors said in court, and Bacon C in 1617 appointed an official reporter to sit at his feet.[35] After 1660 Chancery cases were regularly reported. The announcement of general reasons, with a view to their being reported, completed the reduction of equity to known principles. By 1676 a chancellor could repudiate the idea that equity had any dependence on his own inner conscience: 'the conscience by which I am to proceed is merely *civilis et politica*, and tied to certain measures'.[36]

Thus equity hardened into law. Trusts and mortgages were governed by rules as clear as any rules of common law. In matters of contract and tort, the Chancery normally followed the law. There were no equitable torts, nor would contracts be amended to make them less harsh: 'the Chancery mends no man's bargain'.[37] It could be said in 1675, without a hint of paradox, that a contract without consideration was binding in conscience but not in equity.[38] Precedents were as binding in equity as at law, and now even the Chancery would sooner suffer a hardship than a departure from known rules.[39] It is true that equity has remained more flexible than the common law, because it can take greater account of individual circumstances; for instance, remedies can be lost by delay, by the intervention of third-party interests, or by a lack of complete probity on the part of

34. *Duchess of Suffolk v Herenden* (1560) 93 LQR 36.
35. 26 SS xxii; *Legal History Studies 1972*, p. 17. Some dicta by Lord Ellesmere C (1596–1617), survive in manuscript; and there are unpublished reports from the 1630s and 1650s.
36. *Cook v Fountain* (1676) 3 Swan 585 at 600 per Lord Nottingham C.
37. *Maynard v Moseley* (1667) 3 Swan 655. The only major exception was the relief given against penalties: p. 271, post.
38. *Honywood v Bennett* (1675) Nottingham Rep (73 SS) 214.
39. *Galton v Hancock* (1743) 2 Atk 427 at 439 per Lord Hardwicke C. Cf. Bl Comm, vol. III, p. 440.

the plaintiff. The first book on equity was arranged around fourteen general principles of the very broadest nature, such as 'Equality is Equity' and 'Equity prevents Mischief'.[40] But the preoccupation of the court with matters of property, the high intellectual capacity of the chancellors and the leaders of the Chancery Bar, and the superior quality of the reports taken in the eighteenth century, all combined to render equity as certain and as scientific as law. The process may even have gone too far. *Rigor aequitatis* set in,[41] and equity almost lost the ability to discover new doctrines. 'Nothing would inflict on me greater pain in quitting this place,' said Lord Eldon C, in 1818, 'than the recollection that I had done anything to justify the reproach that the equity of this Court varies like the Chancellor's foot.'[42]

Practical Defects of the Chancery

It is the height of irony that the court which originated to provide an escape from the defects of common law procedure should in its later history have developed procedural defects worse by far than those of the law. For two centuries before Dickens wrote *Bleak House*, the word 'Chancery' had been synonymous with expense, delay and despair. That the court survived at all owes something to the vested interests of its officials and still more to the fact that expense and delay do not extinguish hope. Those landed families, if any there were, who escaped the throes of Chancery litigation were fortunate indeed.

The root of much trouble was the principle that the chancellor was the sole judge. Had he been a full-time judge the strain would have been enormous; but the situation was worse, because for much of his time he was engaged on affairs of state or the business of the House of Lords. Necessarily the business of his court was widely delegated. Some of it was transacted before the master of the rolls; yet, as there was but one court, he could only sit when the chancellor did not—often in the evening—and his decisions were subject to review by the chancellor. Enquiries into facts were delegated to the masters, who reported back to the court. Some matters were sent to a form of arbitration, by reference to lay commissioners in the country, who were 'to hear and end according to equity and good conscience'. Even these devices made little effect on the ever increasing lists of unheard and part-heard causes. Chancellors were unwilling to give equitable

40. R. Francis *Maxims of Equity* (1727).
41. Allen *Law in the Making*, p. 417.
42. *Gee v Pritchard* (1818) 2 Swan 402 at 414.

relief until all the facts were ascertained, especially since their decisions were virtually final; and yet they never had the benefit of conducting a trial from beginning to end. If some fact were wanting, the only course was to adjourn; and perhaps when the cause was next moved there would be more time wasted in reconstructing arguments, not to mention the possibility of new insights and doubts to cloud the issue. Throughout the seventeenth and eighteenth centuries the estimates of causes depending reached figures like 20,000, and some of those causes were still undetermined after thirty years.

The second main cause of the trouble was the dependency of the Chancery officials on the fee system. Most of the hundreds of clerks were remunerated by fees paid for individual tasks. Many of the fees seem extortionate in retrospect, and the standards of morality in that respect were too flexible. Two distinguished chancellors (Bacon and Macclesfield) were dismissed for accepting 'presents', but their subordinates made gifts almost respectable. Gold or silver could open paths through the Chancery morass, and by long usage many 'presents' became fees which could be demanded as of right with an untroubled conscience. The masterships were worth so much in fees that in the early eighteenth century they could be sold for £5,000. Since every step in litigation attracted fees, there was no incentive to expedition. One typical innovation was to lengthen masters' reports by reciting the whole of the previous proceedings verbatim in a 'whereas' clause before starting on the substance of the report. The masters were not accountable for funds in court, and when the South Sea Bubble burst in 1725 it was found that over £10,000 was missing; it had been borrowed for investment by some of the masters. The six clerks received £2,000 a year for two months' work filing documents and signing copies. Litigants were obliged to order, and pay for, copies they did not want and which were sometimes never made. The sixty clerks were paid by the page for drawing documents; and so they developed such large handwriting, and used such wide margins, that it was said a skilful clerk could spread six ordinary pages into forty. Attempts to reform these abuses met with hostility and almost complete failure. Offices were property, and reform was resisted as being tantamount to arbitrary confiscation.

A few good words should be said of Chancery procedure, most of which ultimately prevailed over 'due process'. The present High Court writ is modelled on the subpoena rather than the original writ of the common law. Interlocutory proceedings before masters, the use of affidavits and interrogatories, trial by judge alone, the examination of parties as witnesses, not to mention most forms of relief other than damages, all derive from Chancery procedure and were unknown at common law. By the eighteenth century, however, most of the advantages had been lost by abuse. Chancery pleadings had become verbose and complex, and the use of minutely drafted interrogatories served only to hinder proceedings. The documentation produced by most Chancery suits was elephantine. By Lord Eldon's time the office work seemed to be grinding to a halt. Lord Eldon was Lord Chancellor from 1801 to 1827 and has borne much of the blame for the state of affairs over which he presided. He was so renowned for procrastination that his court was said to be a court of 'oyer sans terminer'. He had by no means created the mess, but unfortunately his very high judicial standards were incompatible with the load of work thrust upon him. When, in 1824, he was appointed to head a commission of enquiry into the delays, things had reached their lowest ebb. Even a simple matter could take five years to determine, and vast funds—£39 million—mouldered in court, out of human dominion, the remains of undecided cases and wrecked fortunes. Appalling instances were mentioned to the commission. The case of *Morgan v Lord Clarendon*, commenced in 1808, was still in its interlocutory stages; sixteen years had been spent on routine work, and no counsel had been briefed, yet the costs had already reached £3,719. Eldon was too resigned to the situation to perceive any obvious remedy; his report found little fault with the system, and attributed most of the delays to the carelessness or obstinacy of the parties.

Reform and Abolition

Perhaps the most drastic of the nineteenth-century reforms of the judicial system, and certainly the most urgent, were those which attacked these practical evils in Chancery.

The problem of judicial manpower was tackled by appointing a vice-chancellor in 1813 and two more in 1842, and by increasing the jurisdiction of the master of the rolls. After 1833 the master of the rolls was empowered to sit concurrently with the chancellor in a separate court. Still the chancellor had the final say, until in 1851 a Court of Appeal in Chancery was established, comprising in addition to the existing Chancery judges some additional 'justices of appeal in Chancery'.

The deeper problems were tackled by the gradual abolition of most of the offices in the court. The six clerks went in 1842, the masters in 1852; care was taken to buy out vested interests from public funds, so that no individual was harmed. These officers gone, business in chambers could be streamlined; after 1852 it was conducted, according to new rules, before the master of the rolls or the vice-chancellors and their 'chief clerks'.[43]

These measures prepared the way for still more sweeping reforms. Under the Common Law Procedure Act 1854 the Chancery was empowered to decide questions of law, to try issues of fact by jury, and to award damages; courts of law were empowered to compel discovery, to grant injunctions, and to a limited extent to allow equitable defences to be pleaded. The work of the various courts being now assimilated to a great extent, the division of jurisdictions itself came into question. Could law and equity at last be fused together? The feat was proposed by the Judicature Commission which reported in 1869, and was attained within six years. But was fusion to be regarded as procedural or substantive? And, if there was to be no distinction between law and equity, should the resulting system be regarded as equity or law?

Procedural fusion was the main object of the Judicature Acts of 1873 and 1875. All the judges of the Supreme Court were empowered to administer law and equity, and both the Chancery and the common law courts were abolished. The establishment of a Chancery Division of the High Court merely reflected the convenience of specialisation, not the nature of the remedies available. But the promoters of the legislation also envisaged fusion at a deeper level. The only direct enactment was in s.25(11): 'Generally in all matters not hereinbefore particularly mentioned in which there is any conflict or variance between the rules of equity and the rules of common law with reference to the same matter, the rules of equity shall prevail.' The precise meaning of this proved elusive. Some lawyers at first thought the distinction between law and equity had been obliquely abolished, and that there was, for instance, no longer any distinction between legal and equitable estates in land. Sir George Jessel MR, the first president of the Court of Appeal, was inclined to incorporate equitable doctrines into the common law, and once suggested that damages could be given for innocent misrepresentation prior to a contract. His successor, Lord Esher MR, is said to have complained openly that Jessel 'had been sent to dragoon the Court of Appeal into substituting equity for Common Law, but that he (Esher) and his Common Law colleagues would not have it'.[44] By 1897, when Lord

---

43. The title 'master of the Supreme Court' was substituted for 'chief clerk' in 1896. Analogous officers in other divisions had the same title.
44. A. Underhill *Change and Decay* (1938), p. 87.

Esher retired, it was plain that the effect of s.25(11) had been minimal. Trusts still remained. No new remedies had been created. Indeed, as Maitland pointed out, the section had been based on a false premise. Law and equity were never in 'conflict or variance', because equity was not a self-sufficient system; at every point equity presupposed the existence of common law.

Attempts have been made in more recent years, particularly by Lord Denning MR, to banish the distinction between law and equity. To the extent that they have succeeded, equity has taken on a new meaning. If, for reasons of history, equity had become the law peculiar to the Court of Chancery, nevertheless in broad theory equity was an approach to justice which gave more weight than did the law to particular circumstances. The abolition of the historical, procedural distinction, gave new emphasis to the broad view of equity. The survival of a distinct Chancery Bar, still domiciled in Lincoln's Inn, where Lord Eldon's court used to sit, has ensured the continuance of the specialist traditions of the Court of Chancery in property matters. Chancery judges and practitioners are the least likely to administer equity in the broader sense, because the type of work they do demands as much certainty as clear rules can provide. The Queen's Bench judges, on the other hand, in dealing with agreements and accidents, are more given to the equitable approach. Paradoxically, as equity has hardened into law, so law has been dissolving into something like abstract justice, with a consequent loss of clarity and certainty.[45] At any rate, the Chancery Division is not a court of conscience; and 'it is the common lawyers who now do equity'.[46]

Further reading

Holdsworth HEL, vol. I, pp. 395–476; vol. V, pp. 215–338; vol. IX, pp. 335–408; vol. XII, pp. 178–330, 583–605

Milsom HFCL, pp. 74–87

Radcliffe & Cross, pp. 114–156, 270–277, 306–310

W. P. Baildon, *Select Cases in Chancery 1364–1471* (10 SS, 1896)

A. D. Hargreaves, 'Equity and the Latin Side of the Chancery' (1952) 68 LQR 481–499

J. P. Dawson, *A History of Lay Judges* (1960), pp. 145–172

D. E. C. Yale, *Lord Nottingham's 'Manual of Chancery Practice' and 'Prolegomena of Chancery and Equity'* (1965), esp. pp. 1–80; *Lord Nottingham's Chancery Cases* (73 SS, 1954; 79 SS, 1962)

W. J. Jones, *The Elizabethan Court of Chancery* (1967)

45. This is partly a result of procedural changes: pp. 79–82, ante.
46. *Hill v C. A. Parsons Ltd* [1971] 3 All ER 1345 at 1359 per Lord Denning MR.

M. E. Avery, 'History of the Equitable Jurisdiction of the
Chancery before 1460' (1969) 42 BIHR 129–144; 'An Evaluation
of the Effectiveness of the Court of Chancery under the
Lancastrian Kings' (1970) 86 LQR 84–97

W. H. Bryson, *The Equity Side of the Exchequer* (1975)

THEORY OF EQUITY IN CHANCERY

W. H. D. Winder, 'Precedent in Equity' (1941) 57 LQR 245–279

C. K. Allen, *Law in the Making* (7th edn, 1964), pp. 383–425

J. L. Barton, *St German's Doctor and Student* (91 SS, 1974), pp. xxix–li

D. E. C. Yale, 'St German's Little Treatise concerning Writs of
Subpoena' (1975) 10 IJ 324–333

J. H. Baker (1978), 94 SS *37–43, 74–83*

CLASH OF 1616

J. P. Dawson, 'Coke and Ellesmere disinterred: the Attack on the
Chancery in 1616' (1941) 36 *Illinois Law Rev* 127–152

J. H. Baker, 'The Common Lawyers and the Chancery: 1616'
(1969) 4 IJ 368–392; *Legal History Studies 1972*, pp. 3–4

G. W. Thomas, 'James I, Equity and Lord Keeper John Williams'
(1976) 91 EHR 506–528

L. A. Knafla, *Law and Politics in Jacobean England* (1977),
pp. 155–181

7. The Conciliar Courts

We have now seen how the common law courts were derived from the early king's council or *Curia Regis*, and how at a later stage the Court of Chancery separated from the council as an extraordinary jurisdiction to be invoked where the ordinary procedures failed. Still there remained a residuary royal prerogative of justice. Petitions which were not thought appropriate for the chancellor alone to deal with were retained in the king's council, to be dealt with at its judicial sessions, or were delegated to other, more appropriate officials. In the fourteenth century, when the chancellor's decrees were made in the name of the council, there was no clear distinction of jurisdictions; and it could be argued that the English jurisdiction of the Court of Chancery was not truly distinct from the council's jurisdiction until the second half of the fifteenth century. In the case of the other conciliar courts, distinctions did not clearly emerge until the sixteenth century. Until about 1540 the council was one body with one series of records; but its work was divided as convenience dictated, often by means of informal expedients. It was both the strength and the ultimate downfall of conciliar jurisdiction that it depended on close connection with the king's chief ministers. The original justification for its existence was that extraordinary action by the king and his magnates offered the only escape from the kind of undue influence which could corrupt sheriffs and juries. But the absolute power needed to check abuses was itself open to constitutional objection. In 1510 a wave of reaction to Henry VII's avaricious ministers Empson and Dudley very nearly carried away conciliar jurisdictions; a bill for abolition was rejected only at the new king's personal insistence. In 1511 two plaintiffs recovered damages against opponents who had sued them before Empson, contrary to the statutes of due process; and there was a flood of less successful actions in respect of conciliar jurisdiction in various forms. By the end of the century the vehicle of attack had become the prohibition, which brought about further clashes in the seventeenth century. In 1641, after an unfortunate decade in which the Star Chamber became too closely involved in politics, conciliar jurisdiction in the old sense was swept away for ever.[1]

THE COURT OF STAR CHAMBER

The best known of the conciliar courts was the Court of Star Chamber. It used to be thought that the court was established by the so-called Star Chamber Act of 1487,[2] but this statute in fact set up a special tribunal to deal with particular problems of law and order; its jurisdiction seems later to have been absorbed into that of the Star Chamber. The starred chamber (*camera stellata*), so called from the gilded stars on the ceiling, was a room built within the palace of Westminster in 1347 and thereafter used for judicial sessions of the king's council.[3] For over a century the 'council in the Star Chamber' was nothing other than the council meeting in a particular place. During the chancellorship of Thomas Wolsey (1515–29) its jurisdiction increased and it became a regular court; but it was not until 1540 that the Court of Star Chamber and the Privy Council became so separate that they had their own officials and records, and even thereafter the membership of the two bodies was almost identical. The Privy Council was a more secret institution, concerning itself with government policy and administration; its only jurisdiction from the seventeenth century was of an appellate nature.[4]

At the beginning of the sixteenth century the council in the Star Chamber exercised a predominantly civil jurisdiction. Like the Chancery it was concerned mainly with real property, but petitioners usually complained of riot, unlawful assembly, forcible entry or oppression, and it was this element of disorder which gave the council its theoretical interest in such business. Many of the allegations were probably fictitious, and the council in reality was being asked to decide title: a task it could not in theory undertake because of the statutes of due process.[5] The Star Chamber was not concerned with conscience as such, and did not develop an equitable jurisdiction on the civil side; it was a court of common law in all but procedure, and always had judges in attendance. It even took upon itself in the seventeenth century to award damages, a remedy denied to courts of

1. 94 SS *70–74*; Stat 16 Car I, c.10.
2. Stat 3 Hen VII, c.1. The Star Chamber itself did not rely on the statute: *Chambers' Case* (1629) Cro Car 168; Co Inst, vol. IV, p. 62. The marginal title *pro camera stellata* seems to have been an interpolation.
3. A meeting in 1366 for legal business is mentioned in *Calendar of Close Rolls 1364–68*, p. 237.
4. See pp. 121–122, post.
5. Stat 25 Edw III (sess. v), c.4, prohibited the council from meddling with freeholds.

equity. Since it had no law of its own, its abolition in 1641 left no gap in civil jurisprudence.

By Stuart times the court was more often associated with criminal matters, an aspect of its jurisdiction which in 1500 had been almost negligible. Prosecutions were brought upon information by the attorney-general, and defendants were tried summarily without jury. This gave the Crown a distinct advantage in prosecutions of an unpopular character, and the court was used to suppress sedition and other political offences. Constitutional principle, however, excluded felonies from its purview; a man could only be tried for his life by a jury of his peers. The law of misdemeanours, on the other hand, was developed and refined by the Star Chamber. The court is best remembered for its imaginative punishments, such as the slitting of noses and severing of ears; but the memory is conditioned chiefly by the last ten years of its life, and its true achievement must be sought in the progress of substantive law. Criminal libel, forgery, perjury, subornation of perjury, conspiracy, and attempts to commit crimes, were largely the creation of the Star Chamber. The inventive nature of this jurisdiction might be termed criminal equity; but in this instance the 'equity' was an integral part of the common law, and the offences cultivated in the Star Chamber could also be prosecuted on indictment in the country. The abolition of the court did not, there-fore, destroy its creative work on the criminal side, but merely chan-nelled it into the regular course of prosecutions elsewhere. Political misdemeanours could still be prosecuted by information, but in the King's Bench. And the King's Bench claimed to have inherited the equitable function of developing the criminal law to meet particular new circumstances.[6] It is now commonly believed that this equitable jurisdiction has been abandoned in the interests of certainty.[7] Pun-ishments for misdemeanour remained unfixed at common law, so that whipping and the pillory remained permissible substitutes for pecuniary fines; but Coke urged that novelties were not desirable in penal matters, and the Bill of Rights of 1689 prohibited 'cruel and unusual punishment'.[8]

THE COURT OF REQUESTS

The early Tudor council found itself as over-pressed as the Chancery,

6. E.g. *R v Edgerley* (1641) March NR 135 at 137 (damaging highway with large vehicles); *R v Sidley* (1663) 1 Sid 168 (indecent exposure). For informations, see pp. 418–419, post.

7. Bl Comm, vol. I, p. 92; *Shaw v Director of Public Prosecutions* [1962] AC 220 at 268, 273; *Knuller Ltd v Director of Public Prosecutions* [1973] AC 435 at 471, 473.

8. Co Inst, vol. IV, p. 66 (where he says the Star Chamber cannot order the 'obtrunca-tion' of members other than ears); Stat 1 Will & Mar (sess. ii), c.2.

and relied similarly on delegation and reference. Indeed, conciliar proceedings often had the appearance of a compulsory arbitration process, in which parties were hauled before single councillors or committees of councillors; the adjudication was given force by being embodied in a conciliar decree. Lesser tribunals of this kind were busy under Henry VII, but fell under the odium attaching to Empson and Dudley and were curtailed in the first years of Henry VIII. Wolsey revived experiments with 'under courts', to relieve himself of minor judicial work when he grew weary of it; but they were not a lasting success.

The most enduring of the sub-conciliar tribunals was the Court of Requests. As a distinct department of the council, it may be traced to the promotion in 1483 as a 'clerk of the council of the requests' of an official who had been dealing with the 'bills, requests and supplica- tions of poor persons'.[9] It kept separate records, the earliest entry being a case of 1493. Under the early Tudors it was the special responsibility of the king's almoner and dean of the chapel royal, which indicates its charitable nature; during the sixteenth century it came to be regarded as the court of the lord president of the privy seal, and its usual meeting place was the White Hall. It enjoyed the surge in popularity of all the extraordinary jurisdictions in the Tudor period, and from the 1540s the business was dispatched by the appointment of masters of requests.

The Requests had in theory taken over that aspect of early Chan- cery jurisdiction which gave relief on grounds of poverty, and it did emulate Chancery practice to the extent of becoming a court of equity. But it had even less constitutional foundation than the Chan- cery, and was frequently complained of as an encroachment on the common law. Its opponents were not indifferent to poverty; paupers suing in the Common Pleas were assigned a clerk and a serjeant to help them gratis. Moreover, the allegation of poverty in Requests became a fiction, and the expansion of jurisdiction occurred because men of substance were taking advantage of the simple procedures. Towards the end of the sixteenth century the common law judges began sending prohibitions to the Requests; and in 1598, despite a learned historical essay in defence of the court by Sir Julius Caesar, then a master of requests, the Common Pleas delivered the astound- ing pronouncement that the court simply did not exist and that its proceedings were *coram non judice*.[10] The hostility was relaxed in the

---

9. *Calendar of Patent Rolls 1476–85*, p. 413.
10. *Stepneth v Lloyd* (1598) Kiralfy SB, p. 301, 12 SS xxxix, Cro Eliz 647. The *ratio decidendi* was narrower than Coke (Co Inst, vol. IV, p. 97) stated it to be.

seventeenth century, and the Requests came to be acknowledged as a court of record separate from the council; prohibitions were sent only if the court meddled with the common law. Its new status enabled it to survive briefly the abolition of prerogative tribunals in 1641;[11] but, though never abolished, it was stifled during the Civil War when the privy seal was withdrawn. Since it had developed no distinct equity of its own, nothing substantial was lost. The provision of small-claims courts was more sensibly tackled at a local level, since litigation at Westminster was inevitably more costly. The gap was filled first by urban courts of requests, and eventually by the modern county courts.[12]

REGIONAL CONCILIAR AND EQUITY COURTS

In addition to the council which followed the king, there were for a time two regional councils which exercised similar jurisdiction to the Star Chamber and Chancery in certain parts of the country. The Council in the North Parts[13] originated as the Duke of Gloucester's council in the time of Edward IV, but went into abeyance for some years before it was revived as the Duke of Richmond's council in 1525. The Council in the Principality and Marches of Wales began as the Prince of Wales's council in the time of Henry VII, and was confirmed by statute in 1542.[14] Each council met under a lord president and, by devolution from central government, transacted both judicial and administrative business. For a short time after 1537 there was also a Council in the West Parts, but it proved so unpopular that it was suspended.

The common law courts kept a suspicious eye on these prerogative tribunals to ensure that they did not act *ultra vires* by meddling with common law. The surveillance, by means of prohibition, became hostile under Coke CJ, who even denied the jurisdiction of a court of equity to grant specific performance of contracts, on the ground that a defaulting party had the right to pay damages if he chose.[15] The lords president complained of Coke CJ's attempt to control them, but the Privy Council ruled that both councils 'should be within the survey of

11. Records ceased in 1642. But the power to imprison was upheld by the King's Bench in *ex parte Howsden* (1645) HLS MS 113, p. 229. Masters of requests were appointed at the Restoration, but they exercised no jurisdiction.
12. See pp. 26–27, ante. The model for the urban courts was the London 'Court of Conscience', erected in 1518.
13. These comprised Yorkshire and all the English counties beyond.
14. Stat 34 & 35 Hen VIII, c.26. Until 1604 it exercised jurisdiction in England, but in that year it was held that Herefordshire, Worcestershire, Shropshire and Gloucestershire were outside its bounds: Co Inst, vol. IV, p. 242.
15. *Bromage v Genning* (1616) 1 Rolle Rep 368. The decision was later reversed.

Westminster Hall'. The Lord Treasurer said there was no reason why Yorkshire should be less free than, say, Cornwall; and yet there was the most miserable slavery when the law was vague or uncertain, and men's fortunes decided by discretion.[16] The councils functioned until the Civil War, when they went into disuse. Only the Council in Wales was resurrected in 1660, by reason of its statutory foundation; but its second life was short, and in 1689 parliament dissolved it as being 'contrary to the Great Charter, the known laws of the land, and the birthright of the subject, and the means to introduce an arbitrary power and government'.[17]

Equity jurisdiction was also exercised in the palatinates, but these were not conciliar courts.[18]

The Courts of the Admiral and Marshal

The courts of common law could not properly entertain causes of action arising outside the realm, because of the rule that the issue had to be tried by a jury from the place where it was 'laid'; and a jury could not be summoned from outside an English county. Ordinary justice ended where the power of the sheriff ended. This gap in the system of justice was closed by the king in council. The council needed no juries, and the speed of its process made it easier to deal with foreigners or seamen. By the middle of the fourteenth century the council had allowed its extraterritorial jurisdiction to be exercised in all but the most difficult cases by the two sister courts of the admiral and of the constable and marshal. Some such causes were still heard in the fifteenth-century Chancery or in the council itself;[19] but the two specialised tribunals became courts of regular resort, following Civil law procedure, and under the influence of the doctors of law they enjoyed a history quite apart from that of the other conciliar courts. The sharing of jurisdiction was not in practice as straightforward as the theory of venue dictated, because even in medieval times overseas actions were occasionally tried at common law by means of a fictitious

16. *Case of the Lords President of Wales and York* (c. 1608) 12 Co Rep 50 per Lord Salisbury T.

17. Stat 1 Will & Mar (sess. i), c.27, s.2. Cf. Wales Act 1978 (c.52).

18. There were four equity courts: the Chancery of Durham, the Duchy Chamber of Lancaster (presided over by the chancellor of the duchy), the Chancery of the County Palatine of Lancaster (presided over by the vice-chancellor), and the Exchequer of Chester (presided over by the chamberlain). The last was abolished in 1830; the Duchy Chamber was not abolished, but has not sat since 1835; the remaining two flourished until 1971 (Courts Act 1971, c.23, s.41).

19. The best-known instance is the *Carrier's Case* (1473), p. 433, post.

supposition that the foreign place was in England. If the plaintiff said that Harfleur was in Kent, or that Hamburg or Ireland were in London, and the defendant joined issue on the substance of the matter, then the jury would be summoned from Kent or London without question. The common law therefore acquired concurrent jurisdiction in some cases, and in others it even claimed an exclusive jurisdiction which it defended by prohibition.

THE HIGH COURT OF CHIVALRY

The Court of the Lord High Constable and Earl Marshal of England appeared in the 1340s or 1350s as a court having jurisdiction over military matters such as prisoners of war, ransom and disputed coats of arms. Its attempts to assert a common pleas jurisdiction were restrained by statutes of Richard II, after which it was confined to 'deeds of arms and war' and appeals of treason or felony committed overseas. Because of these serious limitations, and because for political reasons the high office of constable was suppressed in the sixteenth century, the court disappeared. Elizabeth I was once asked by a suitor to appoint a constable ad hoc so that he could bring an appeal, but she refused to do so.[20] The court rarely sat again,[21] but it has understandably been confused with the court of the earl marshal alone. This *Curia Marescalli*, or High Court of Chivalry, was revived by James I as a court of honour, which not only tried the right to distinctions of honour and coat armour but also redressed affronts to honour such as slander. The slander jurisdiction was denied in 1703,[22] and the present jurisdiction is probably confined to disputes over armorial bearings, which are decided according to the law of arms. The court, which has sat only once since 1737, is the last English court to use the procedure of the Civil law.[23]

THE HIGH COURT OF ADMIRALTY

The Court of the Lord High Admiral of England appeared at the same period as its terrestrial counterpart, to deal with matters arising on the high seas. It was not restricted to causes connected with naval warfare, and was much resorted to by foreign merchants. Like its sister court, it encroached in its early days upon the common law and had to be restrained by statutes of Richard II from hearing matters

20. The refusal was doubtless a favour to Francis Drake, the accused: [1972A] CLJ 84.
21. A notorious exception was *Lord Rea v Ramsey* (1631) 3 St Tr 483, in which battle was waged.
22. *Chambers v Jennings* (1703) 7 Mod Rep 125.
23. *Manchester Corporation v Manchester Palace of Varieties Ltd* [1955] P 133, [1955] 1 All ER 387.

arising within the realm, whether or not they concerned the sea. The court was presided over by a judge of the Admiralty, usually a doctor of law, and proceeded according to the Civil law, under which process could issue against ships and goods as well as persons. The law applied was based on the *jus gentium*, or universal law of the sea, which was derived from the ancient Rhodian sea law and the 'customs of Oleron'.

The Admiralty was watched by the common law courts with the jealousy and suspicion which they bestowed upon all jurisdictions tainted with Romanism. In the fifteenth century actions were allowed in the two benches against adversaries who sued in Admiralty contrary to statute,[24] and during the sixteenth century a torrent of prohibitions rained on those who chose the Civil law. In 1536 the criminal jurisdiction was by statute turned over to the common law, so that pirates and other marine criminals could be tried by jury under special commissions of oyer and terminer. By 1600 the admiral's jurisdiction was at a low ebb. According to the Elizabethan judges, he could not try causes arising on land beyond the seas, but only causes arising on the sea; and the sea for this purpose ended at low water-mark, except when the tide was in.[25] This extremely restrictive view excluded charterparties and foreign maritime contracts, which the common law had taken over by means of fictions. The admiral was left to deal with seamen's wages, which were earned at sea, collision and salvage, and prize.[26] The Civilians, of course, took a wider view of their jurisdiction, and retaliated with their own fiction: that contracts were made *super altum mare*. In 1633 the Council directed a settlement, under which the Admiralty was to be allowed actions for freight and actions to enforce charterparties relating to overseas voyages and maritime contracts made on foreign soil.[27] This settlement did not last, however, and by the end of the century the common law had succeeded in depressing the Court of Admiralty to a worse condition than it had enjoyed in Tudor times.

The court revived somewhat during the Napoleonic wars, when the prize jurisdiction benefited from British naval successes. A number of statutes after 1840 extended the jurisdiction to all maritime matters except charterparties, and the value of the specialised tribunal was recognised when in 1875 it was incorporated into the Probate, Divorce and Admiralty Division of the High Court. The president of

24. 94 SS *73*.
25. *Constable's Case* (1601) 5 Co Rep 106.
26. Prize, from *prendre*, is the right to a share in the proceeds of enemy ships and cargoes seized at sea.
27. *Memorandum* (1633) Cro Car 216.

that Division used to sit with the silver oar of the Admiralty before him when trying maritime cases. Coke's final victory came in 1970, when the Division was abolished and admiralty business transferred to the Queen's Bench Division.[28]

Further reading

Holdsworth HEL, vol. I, pp. 477–580

C. G. Bayne and W. H. Dunham, *Select Cases in the Council of Henry VII* (75 SS, 1956)

G. R. Elton, 'Conciliar Courts' in *The Tudor Constitution* (1960), pp. 158–213

C. M. Gray, 'The Boundaries of the Equitable Function' (1976) 20 AJLH 192–226

J. A. Guy, 'Wolsey, the Council and the Council Courts' (1976) 91 EHR 481–505

J. H. Baker, 'The Conciliar Courts' (1978) 94 SS *70–74*

STAR CHAMBER

I. S. Leadam, *Select Cases before the King's Council in the Star Chamber* (16 SS, 1902)

T. G. Barnes, 'Star Chamber and the Sophistication of the Criminal Law' [1977] *Criminal Law Rev* 316–326; 'Star Chamber Litigants and their Counsel' in *Legal Records and the Historian* (1978), pp. 7–28

J. A. Guy, *The Cardinal's Court: the Impact of Thomas Wolsey in Star Chamber* (1977)

REQUESTS

I. S. Leadam, *Select Cases in the Court of Requests* (12 SS, 1898)

L. M. Hill (Ed), *The Ancient State Authoritie and Proceedings of the Court of Requests by Sir Julius Caesar* (1975)

ADMIRAL AND MARSHAL

G. D. Squibb, *The High Court of Chivalry* (1959)

F. Wiswall, *The Development of Admiralty Jurisdiction and Practice since 1800* (1971)

T. J. Runyan, 'The Rolls of Oleron and the Admiralty Court in 14th Century England' (1975) 19 AJLH 95–111

D. E. C. Yale, 'A View of the Admiral Jurisdiction: Sir Matthew Hale and the Civilians' in *Legal History Studies 1972*, pp. 87–109

28. Administration of Justice Act 1970 (c.31).

8. The Ecclesiastical Courts

At much the same time as the common law of England was being fashioned by the centralisation of English justice, the universal law of the Church was developing as a parallel or even rival system of jurisprudence through the centralisation of ecclesiastical authority at Rome. By the twelfth century there was a mass of rules and pronouncements circulating in collections of 'canons', many of which were purely theological in content, such as creeds and doctrinal statements. Canon law became a scientific system, distinct from theology and ecclesiastical history, as a result of the work of the Bolognese monk Gratian. Gratian's *Decretum* (c. 1140) set out to systematise the canons in accordance with a hierarchical scheme of authority with the pope at the earthly summit; whatever the pope decreed was to be obeyed, however intolerable or wrong: if the pope erred, the punishment would be his, and the obedient would be released. The study of this new Canon law became all the rage in medieval European universities, a system of courts developed to cope with the litigation to which it gave rise, and numerous questions found their way to the popes for decision. The popes' answers to such questions, contained in letters called 'decretals', provided additional material for study. By the fourteenth century there was a substantial body of legislation (the *Corpus Juris Canonici*) comprising Gratian's collection, the Decretals of Gregory IX (1234), the Sext (1298), and the Clementine Decretals (1305–14); to which were later added the *Extravagantes* of John XXII (1316–34) and the *Extravagantes Communes* (c. 1300–1480).[1]

Before the rise of royal justice in England, bishops wielded their spiritual authority without the aid of a distinct system of courts, and ecclesiastical matters were dealt with in the old local assemblies.

---

1. The *extravagantes* were unofficial collections, and there was no standard text until they were printed at the beginning of the 16th century. The Roman Church made substantial alterations to the *Corpus Juris Canonici* at the Council of Trent, and abandoned it altogether in 1918. Ironically, the medieval *Corpus Juris Canonici* still has a residual authority in England, where post-Reformation changes in Roman Canon law are inapplicable.

William I in 1072 or thereabouts granted that episcopal pleas should no longer be held in the hundreds, and from this act of separation grew the consistory courts in which Church law was administered by bishops' chancellors. Beneath the bishops were the archdeacons and their courts; their main concern was ecclesiastical discipline and the correction of moral offences, and appeal lay to the 'audience court' of the bishop. From bishops appeal lay to the archbishop of either province: in the north to the Chancery Court of York, in the south to the Court of Arches.[2] From the provincial court, appeal lay to the pope: either to papal delegates, or to the Papal Curia in Rome. At all levels the law was administered by clergy learned in Canon law, and so the jurisprudence of these courts developed quite separately from the king's common law. This inevitably led to conflict.

CANON LAW AND COMMON LAW

The Canon law of the Western Church was taken to apply to all Christians in all places, but its enforcement in the temporal world depended on the co-operation of temporal authority, and therefore varied from one country to another. No English king, nor royal judge, would have dreamed of disputing the spiritual authority of the Canon law of Rome. The popes, on the other hand, sometimes laid claim to temporal as well as spiritual authority; and there was considerable room for argument as to what matters were spiritual and what temporal. The conflicts of jurisdiction were not disputes between an embattled church and a hostile royal power, but disputes over the boundaries between two systems of law which were admitted to operate on the same people within the same geographical area.

The first clash arose in the 1160s over the immunity of clerks from secular criminal jurisdiction. After stormy scenes, the council at Clarendon in 1164 agreed to a compromise. Clerks were to be arraigned before the temporal court; if they proved their clergy, they were to be handed over for trial to the bishop; if convicted, they were to be degraded from their orders and returned to the lay court for punishment as laymen. This sensible settlement fell foul of a personal dispute between Henry II and Thomas Becket, the archbishop of Canterbury, who argued that the procedure resulted in double punishment. That the Church should have sought privilege for murderers now seems shameful, but Becket's assassination earned him a martyr's crown and the Church succeeded in making him the most popular English saint. The clergy won their privilege, and the lay

2. So called because it used to sit in the church of St Mary-le-Bow, which is built over arches.

judges restored equality by extending it to laymen.[3] Becket's victory was, in any case, limited in scope. Popes who wanted temporal power had to descend to human politics; and, on a more practical plane, bishops needed temporal co-operation to enforce their own judicial authority by imprisonment. For the rest of the middle ages, therefore, the conflicts were fought, not between the king and the pope, but between private litigants in particular cases. A party could seek to prevent litigation in a church court by seeking a royal writ of prohibition. His opponent might retaliate by setting in motion the process of excommunication. But these weapons were wielded by subjects, not by Church and State; and the keenest purchasers of prohibitions, it seems, were the clergy themselves.

The issue of writs of prohibition as a matter of course, on a bare application being made, was much complained of by the bishops in the thirteenth century. The constitutional wrangle was won by Edward I, who nevertheless conceded a procedure (called 'consultation')' by which the prohibition could be withdrawn if an adversary satisfied the king's judges that the cause was spiritual. The decision as to what matters were spiritual was therefore reserved to the king and his judges. By the writ *Circumspecte agatis* (1285), and the *Articuli cleri* (1315), the boundary was sketched out. The Church courts had an unquestioned jurisdiction over marriage and bastardy,[4] succession to personal property,[5] and punishment of mortal sin, such as fornication and adultery. The appointment of clergy to benefices was for the bishop; but the right to present a clerk to the bishop for appointment was a temporal right (an 'advowson') which was justiciable in the royal court; questions as to tithes, the principal income of benefices, were subject to a complex division of authority. Contracts were for the temporal law; but 'breach of faith' could be corrected by penance in the spiritual courts.[6] Two torts were allowed to the Church courts: laying violent hands on a clerk, which was also a breach of the king's peace, and defamation, which was not actionable at common law until the sixteenth century.[7] In each case the remedy was penance, not civil compensation; but in practice a civil remedy was achieved by allowing commutation on terms.

This settlement gave the Church a pervasive jurisdiction over the lives of most ordinary people: over family matters and wills, sexual offences, defamation and breach of faith. The king's courts, on the

3. See pp. 422–424, post.
4. See pp. 391–395, 400–401, 401–404, post.
5. See pp. 321–322, post.
6. R. H. Helmholz, 91 LQR 406.
7. See pp. 364–367, post.

other hand, retained a complete control over temporal property, which included advowsons and most of the land owned by the Church; and they enjoyed the extensive patronage of bishops, religious houses and other ecclesiastical bodies when pursuing their not inconsiderable temporal rights.

Effect of the Reformation

By the end of the fifteenth century the uneasy peace between the two jurisdictions was breaking down. Huse CJ had declared in 1485 that the king was answerable directly to God and was superior to the pope within the realm. The King's Bench had begun to receive a stream of actions against parties who had sued in ecclesiastical courts concerning matters which overlapped the jurisdictional boundary. Pamphleteers complained of avarice and extortion by officials, of uncertainties and delays, and of the unfairness of trial by judge alone. They argued that the king's law permitted the ecclesiastical jurisdiction only on trust, and that if the trust was abused the liberty was forfeited. In 1529 the most powerful prelate in England was brought down by the common law. Thomas Wolsey, Lord Chancellor, Archbishop of York, Cardinal of St Cecilia trans Tiberim and papal legate *a latere* was condemned by the King's Bench for improperly using his legatine authority. The precedent enabled the king's advisers to bring the rest of the clergy to heel, and prepared the way for the legal revolution brought about by the Reformation parliament. A greater issue than jurisdictional boundaries had arisen;[8] but the manner of its resolution was a culmination of earlier developments.

From January 1534 the Church in England was severed from Rome, and no appeals could be taken to the pope. Some common lawyers advocated abolition of ecclesiastical courts, but that would have required fusion of Canon and common law. Some kind of fusion was seriously contemplated. A law commission was appointed to prepare a code of 'the king's ecclesiastical laws of the Church of England', and those canons which they did not approve were to be abrogated. Meanwhile the old Canon law was to continue in force, except where it was contrary to the common or statute law or the king's prerogative. The report of the commission was either forgotten or deliberately shelved, and so the transitional provision slipped into permanence.

Henry VIII suppressed the study of Canon law at Oxford and

8. See pp. 404–406, post.

Cambridge, so that the judges and advocates thereafter were all doctors of Civil law. The long survival of the wider jurisdiction of the Church may be attributed to the existence of this small but persistent Civilian profession.[9] But the chief practical effects of the Reformation were the introduction of two new courts to replace the pope. The Court of High Commission exercised the pope's supreme personal jurisdiction, particularly in criminal matters; it was a spiritual Star Chamber, much hated for its proceeding by oath *ex officio*, by which a man could be driven to condemn himself. It was allowed to die with the Laudian Church in the 1640s. More regular in its proceedings was the Court of Delegates, which was established to hear such appeals as would formerly have been assigned to papal delegates; the delegates, a combination of temporal judges and Civilians, were appointed by the Chancery. Apart from these changes at the top, the system of ecclesiastical courts was unaffected. The minor criminal jurisdiction of archdeacons went on at least until the eighteenth century, when it passed de facto to the justices of the peace. The jurisdiction over marriage, divorce and probate lasted until 1857. After 1857 the jurisdiction has been confined to Church matters, such as faculties to alter or sell consecrated property and disciplinary proceedings against clergy.

Further reading

Holdsworth HEL, vol. I, pp. 580–632

Vaisey Commission, *Canon Law in the Church of England* (1947)

B. Woodcock, *Medieval Ecclesiastical Courts in the Diocese of Canterbury* (1952)

R. C. Mortimer, *Western Canon Law* (1953)

J. W. Gray, 'Canon Law in England: some Reflections on the Stubbs v Maitland Controversy' (1966) 3 *Studies in Church Hist* 48–68

W. R. Jones, 'Relations of the two Jurisdictions' (1970) 7 *Studies in Medieval and Renaissance Hist* 77–210

C. Donahue, 'Roman Canon Law in the Medieval English Church' (1974) 72 *Michigan Law Rev* 647–716

REFORMATION AND AFTER

R. G. Usher, *The Rise and Fall of the High Commission* (1913)

A. H. Manchester, 'Reform of the Ecclesiastical Courts' (1966) 10 AJLH 51–75

R. A. Marchant, *The Church under the Law 1560–1640* (1969)

9. See p. 147, post.

G. I. O. Duncan, *The High Court of Delegates* (1971)
G. R. Elton, *Reform and Renewal* (1973), pp. 129–139
D. Logan, 'The Henrician Canons' (1974) 47 BIHR 99–103
J. H. Baker, 'Spiritual Jurisdiction' (1978) 94 SS *64–70*

9. Judicial Review of Decisions

The present judicial system recognises that judges and juries make mistakes by providing for redress by way of appeal to a 'higher' court than that appealed from. People have come to regard the 'right to appeal' as an essential requirement of natural justice, and as long ago as 1723 it was said to be 'the glory and happiness of our excellent constitution, that to prevent any injustice no man is concluded by the first judgment; but that if he apprehends himself to be aggrieved he has another court to which he can resort for relief'.[1] Nevertheless, the machinery of appeals was not built into the common law system from the outset, and the ways in which the central courts have subjected other superior and inferior courts and institutions to judicial review have been many and varied.

It is easy to understand why the earliest legal systems had no appeal process. There was no possibility of human error in a judgment supported by divine intervention and therefore beyond questioning. Human judgment did not play a significant part in the resolution of disputes until the development of the jury as a fact-finding tribunal; but even the establishment of juries, and the consequent separation of findings of fact from rulings on law, did not result in the introduction of appeals. The common law courts were the courts of the king, and there was no justification for allowing appeals from the king to anyone else. The only conceivable outside forum was the Church; but parliament was sufficiently troubled by the prospect of papal intervention in temporal litigation to legislate in the fourteenth century against 'appeals' from the king's courts to any others. Neither was there any obvious sense in allowing the judgments of the king's judges to be reopened before different royal judges. The decision of a court such as the Common Pleas or King's Bench was a decision of the whole bench, not of the trial judge; and provided such a court kept within its bounds it would have produced unnecessary uncertainty to permit another court to say that its judgments were wrong. It is accepted that trial judges cannot give the same detailed attention to legal arguments as can the more sedentary central bodies,

1. *R v Cambridge University, ex parte Bentley* (1723) 1 Stra 557 at 565 per Pratt CJ.

and one of the advantages which would nowadays be claimed for an appeal is that it enables greater legal concentration to be brought on a problem once the facts have been ascertained. The trial judge is now regarded as a 'court of first instance', and so the further consideration by three or more judges after trial must be by way of appeal. At common law, however, the trial judge was not a court; and the verdict was always returned to the full court of three or four judges so that they could give judgment. The kind of attention now given on appeal could therefore be given, under the old system, before judgment was entered. It follows that when judgment was entered it could fairly be treated as final and conclusive. Indeed, the finality of a judgment once entered accounts for the reluctance of the courts to enter judgments when any division of opinion occurred on the bench.[2] In case of doubt, proceedings would be adjourned as often as was necessary to enable the doubts to be fully explored and for the judges to deliver 'arguments' (tentative judgments), which could be reviewed on successive occasions until a consensus of judicial opinion was found. Delays which might now seem intolerable were sincerely defended on this ground, as essential to the deliberative process. The present system has sacrificed some of this circumspection to speed, but insures against error by providing for an appeal.

Corruption and misconduct by jurors were undeniable obstacles to justice, but procedures were available to deal with them. An action called 'attaint' could be brought against jurors for giving a false verdict, and if it was successful the verdict would be upset. Attaint did not permit a review of decisions of fact by way of appeal, to determine their substantial correctness, nor of directions in law by the judge. The only question was whether the jury had found correctly on the evidence before it, and that was the only evidence which could be laid before the attaint jury.[3] By Tudor times the attaint was virtually obsolete, because such severe punishment was due to defeated juries that attaint juries would seldom find for plaintiffs. Misconduct by juries was more easily raised by motion;[4] or, in serious cases, by complaint to the Star Chamber. The motion for a new trial, as we shall see, was to contribute to the modern notion of an appeal. Indeed, it had more in common with an appeal than had proceedings in error. Error bears superficially the closest resemblance to an appeal; but it made nothing other than the record of the court available to scrutiny, and was closer to what is now termed 'judicial review'.

2. See p. 70, ante.
3. *Rolfe v Hampden* (1542) Dyer 53; *R v Ingersall* (1593) Cro Eliz 309 at 310.
4. See p. 74, ante.

Proceedings in Error

The basis of all proceedings in error was the record, or plea roll, containing the formal minute of all the stages in the action down to judgment. The record was invested with such a sacred finality that it was accepted as conclusive evidence of whatever it contained. A writ of error ordered judges to send the record of the proceedings in a named action to a superior court for inspection. The court of error could only concern itself with errors on the face of the record, or with new facts (such as the death of a party) which were not inconsistent with the facts in the record but had to be proved by the plaintiff in error. If the plaintiff after removal of the record assigned errors worth argument, the other party was called in to defend the proceedings. Judgment was either to affirm or reverse the judgment of the lower court. The concept of error on the face of the record gave only limited scope for raising points of law. If the first proceedings were in common form, and correctly entered, there could be no challenge on the grounds that judge or jury had erred in law, because no error appeared on the record. Before the sixteenth century most writs of error were brought on technical, procedural grounds. The rise of actions on the case and special verdicts, in the sixteenth century, placed more detail on the record and enabled points of substance—such as the sufficiency of the consideration for a promise—to be raised by writ of error. Error thereafter played a part in legal development.

COURTS OF ERROR

Every common law court was subject to the surveillance of some other tribunal to ensure that it did not commit patent errors or exceed its jurisdiction. From courts not of record, such as local and feudal courts, there was an analogous procedure by which those courts could be ordered to make up an ad hoc record of a case for review by the Common Pleas. From local courts of record, such as borough courts and palatinates, and from the Common Pleas itself, error lay to the King's Bench. From the King's Bench and the Court of Exchequer, both deemed to be held *coram rege*, error lay to the king in parliament. The parliamentary jurisdiction, which was left to the House of Lords alone, was never very effective. In 1347 the Commons prayed that judgments in the Exchequer might be reviewed in the King's Bench, and the king replied that they should be referred to a commission consisting of the chancellor, treasurer and two justices. Ten years later a statutory tribunal, known as the Exchequer Chamber, was established to hear error from the Exchequer; but this was petitioned against in 1378, and was never a very satisfactory tribunal. In the case of the King's Bench the remedy was delayed until 1585, when another statutory court—also called the Exchequer Chamber—was set up because of the difficulties of securing a hearing in parliament. This court consisted of the justices of the Common Pleas and barons of the Exchequer, and was active after about 1590.[5]

The use of error to question points of substantive law led to some undesirable uncertainty when the major courts found themselves in disagreement over matters within their shared jurisdiction. In 1602 a law student noted with dismay that if the King's Bench overturned a unanimous Common Pleas by three votes to one, three judges prevailed over five. Nine years later, Coke CJ complained that one third of the judiciary could defeat the majority if the Exchequer Chamber reversed the five King's Bench judges by four to three.[6] That problem has never been solved, and such oddities still occur in a hierarchic system.

Two major reforms preceded abolition. In 1830 the error jurisdiction of the King's Bench and of the two courts of Exchequer Chamber was transferred to a new Court of Exchequer Chamber, comprising the judges of all three superior courts; error from any one court was heard by the judges of the others. In 1852 the writ of error was abolished, and proceedings in error became a 'step in the cause' rather than a separate action. Finally, in 1875, jurisdiction in error was itself abolished.[7] It had been rendered otiose by the introduction of appeals.

Development of the Appeal

The assize and *nisi prius* system enabled jury verdicts to be taken by single circuit judges, and in the absence of any defect in the proceedings judgment would normally be entered as a matter of course the following term. But the full court which met in banc at Westminster could refuse to enter judgment if cause were shown why it should not do so. If the verdict had been given for the plaintiff, the defendant's counsel could either move in arrest of judgment or move for a new

---

5. Rot Parl, vol. II, p. 168; Stat 31 Edw III (sess. i), c.12; 27 Eliz I, c.8.
6. *The Diary of John Manningham* (R. P. Sorlien edn, 1976), p. 149; *Maine v Peacher* (1611) MS in Middle Temple, f.124v. Cf. *Fossett v Carter* (1623) Palm 329, Cro Jac 662, 663, where the 1585 Act is construed to require a majority of at least six.
7. Stat 11 Geo IV & 1 Will IV, c.70; Common Law Procedure Act 1852, 15 & 16 Vict, c.76, s.148; Judicature Act 1873, 36 & 37 Vict, c.66, Sch. I, Ord. 58.

trial.[8] If a prima facie case were made upon motion, the court made a 'rule *nisi*': that is, a rule to stay judgment, or to set aside a verdict and direct a new trial, unless cause were shewn to the contrary. The plaintiff's counsel then had an opportunity to shew cause against the rule, and if he was successful the rule was discharged; if he failed, the rule was made absolute. On a motion for a new trial, the trial judge made a report on the evidence from his notebook, and it was therefore possible to raise questions of law which were not on the record and which were beyond the purview of a writ of error. A similar procedure, which developed in the eighteenth century, was the reservation of a point of law for the court in banc. A verdict was taken for the plaintiff, subject to the opinion of the court upon a written point of law, and the defendant then moved the court in banc to set aside the verdict and enter a nonsuit. By means of these procedures, the court in banc enjoyed wide powers after the sixteenth century to consider questions of law arising from facts appearing at the trial. But it exercised the powers before judgment and not in the capacity of a superior court. Once the court had given judgment, the only redress was of the limited kind provided by a writ of error.

RESERVATION OF POINTS BY JUDGES

A circuit judge often reserved difficult cases for further discussion with his brethren at Westminster. The practice was common by the sixteenth century, when such discussions took place at Serjeants' Inn or in the Exchequer Chamber. The meetings were informal assemblies of all the assize judges, or of the 'twelve judges' of the superior courts, and not a court of record. Nevertheless, the opinion of all the judges would be followed both in the instant case and in the future. By the eighteenth century the reservation of points in civil cases had been formalised in the 'verdict or nonsuit' procedure just outlined. In criminal cases, the older practice continued, a case being stated in writing by the trial judge; judgment was usually stayed pending the decision of the twelve judges, but in case of doubt after conviction a pardon was recommended.[9] In 1848 the informal court was regularised by statute as the Court for Crown Cases Reserved, which then began to keep records. The defendant in a criminal case did not acquire a right to appeal until that court was replaced by the Court of Criminal Appeal in 1907.

The reference of difficulties to all the judges was not a liberty confined to trial judges. It was not uncommon for the judges of one

8. See pp. 73–74, ante.
9. See pp. 425–426, post.

bench to send a judge across Westminster Hall to state a case to the judges of the other. The year-books of the fifteenth century mention meetings of the judges in the Exchequer Chamber,[10] or occasionally in a church or hall, to debate matters of legal or public importance in an informal way. We need hardly doubt that similar discussions occurred over dinner in the Serjeants' Inns; reports of Serjeants' Inn opinions first occur in the 1520s and 1530s, and become more common later in the century. At first the Serjeants' Inn meetings were merely professional discussions by members of the particular inn; but during the sixteenth century it became common for all the judges of England to be convoked there, as an alternative to the Exchequer Chamber at Westminster, to argue a difficult case. The pronouncements of these assemblies, though not in themselves judgments, were keenly reported and were followed by the individual courts.

REVIEW IN CHANCERY

Error lay from the Latin side of the Chancery to the king in parliament. But error was not appropriate to the English side, because there was no record. At first the only way of reviewing a decision in equity was by reopening the matter before the chancellor himself, or his successor, or by obtaining a commission of review. After a great deal of argument in the seventeenth century, it was finally decided by the House of Lords in 1675 that it could review decisions on the English side.[11] The importance of the notion of a 'review' in such cases was that the absence of a record enabled all the facts to be taken into consideration; and the absence of juries rendered the new trial unnecessary, so that the court of review conducted a rehearing on the merits, an appeal. In 1851 a Court of Appeal in Chancery was erected for hearing Chancery appeals, and the notion of a full-time appeal judge was introduced.[12]

THE PRIVY COUNCIL

After the abolition of the Star Chamber in 1641, the only jurisdiction exercised by the council in suits of an adversary nature[13] was appellate. It was a royal prerogative to entertain applications for redress in respect of the foreign jurisdictions of the Crown, and this was virtually

10. An important example is *Doige's Case*, p. 278, post.
11. *Shirley v Fagg, Privilege of Parliament Case* (1675) 6 State Tr 1121.
12. The 'justice of appeal in Chancery'. Under the Judicature Acts the office was extended into that of lord justice of appeal.
13. The Privy Council also had, and still has, an authority to advise the Crown on hypothetical questions of law and on constitutional matters. The precedence of king's counsel before serjeants was settled by it: p. 143, post.

the last judicial prerogative to be retained by the king in council and not delegated to a regular court. The jurisdiction of the council over the Channel Islands had been established since at least 1495, and in the seventeenth and eighteenth centuries it was extended to all the plantations and colonies. Appeals of this kind were usually referred to a committee on which legal and colonial expertise was represented. In 1832 and 1833 the appeals committee was placed on a statutory footing. It became the Judicial Committee of the Privy Council, with a fixed judicial membership and a definite and slightly extended jurisdiction. In addition to the foreign appeals, it was also to be the final court of appeal for ecclesiastical causes in place of the Court of Delegates, and for admiralty cases, including vice-admiralty appeals from the colonies.[14] Since the appeals committee had proceeded informally, it was settled practice by 1832 to allow appeals on the substantial merits of the case. Moreover, the Civil law notion of an appeal, as applied to ecclesiastical and admiralty causes, seems to have been closer to equitable review than to common law error. The Privy Council, then, furnished a model for a court of appeal; but it was limited to matters outside the common law system.

THE COURT OF APPEAL AND HOUSE OF LORDS

The appeal, having become fully established in respect of courts of equity, courts of Civil law, and colonial courts, made its debut in the common law system in 1854. The legislature in that year provided for an 'appeal' to a court of error from the court in banc against a decision to award or refuse a new trial or nonsuit. Parliament expressly referred to the court of error as a 'Court of Appeal' for this purpose. When the Exchequer Chamber, and proceedings in error, were abolished in 1873, it was this Court of Appeal which passed into the new scheme of things. The system envisaged in 1873 was that motions 'in banc' would be made to the Divisional Court of the appropriate division of the High Court; and from thence an appeal would lie, as it had between 1854 and 1873, to the Court of Appeal. The Court of Appeal thereupon abandoned the older function of being a court of error, and merged with the Court of Appeal in Chancery, acquiring full-time lords justices of appeal.

The jurisdiction of the House of Lords as the highest court of error would have disappeared under the 1873 system; but before the latter came into operation the role of the House of Lords was reconsidered. In 1876 the House was given a statutory appellate jurisdiction superior but akin to that of the Court of Appeal, and yet another

14. Stat 2 & 3 Will IV, c.92; 3 & 4 Will IV, c.41.

judicial rank was introduced, that of lord of appeal in ordinary.[15] This afterthought indirectly stifled the motion in banc, which would have been a third tier in the appellate hierarchy. To avoid triple appeals the Court of Appeal, rather than the Divisional Court, became the direct successor to the old court in banc and motions in banc were replaced by appeals after judgment. Ironically, the court established in 1873 kept the name *Supreme* Court of Judicature. The judicial House of Lords which in truth occupies the supreme position is no longer the same as the upper chamber of parliament, but is a court composed of professionally qualified judges sitting independently of the parliamentary sittings of the House.

The Prerogative Writs

The notion of an appeal, by way of rehearing on the merits, was extended by these means to enable the judgments of courts of law to be reviewed in the same way as the decrees of courts of equity. The extension removed the need for proceedings in error. But the notion of judicial review represented by error, though restricted to formal errors, could be applied to a broader range of decisions. The notion was that the king's courts could keep all lesser jurisdictions within the bounds which the law gave them, and could provide the subject with a remedy if tribunals or officials exceeded their legal authority or made orders which were patently contrary to law. The writ of error achieved this object where judgment had been given by a court of record; but there was a group of other writs which facilitated the control of inferior jurisdictions, and these were developed to extend judicial review both to all courts not of record and to judicial or quasi-judicial functions exercised by bodies which could not otherwise be regarded as courts at all. The function of controlling authority was regarded as a royal prerogative, and until the sixteenth century was primarily the responsibility of the council. From about 1600, there was a tendency to transfer this surveillance to the King's Bench, for which Coke CJ claimed the jurisdiction to correct 'errors and misdemeanours extrajudicial, tending to the breach of the peace, or oppression of the subjects . . . or any other manner of misgovernment'.[16] Thus began one of the most important and distinctive developments of the common law. The principle known as the 'rule of law' treats all exercise of authority as subject to the control of the regular courts of law and furnishes the subject with a remedy when

15. Appellate Jurisdiction Act 1876, 39 & 40 Vict, c.59.
16. 11 Co Rep 98; Co Inst, vol. IV, p. 71.

any official, however mighty, exceeds the power which the law gives him. No power is outside the law; and any lawful power over the lives, liberty or property of others, even if not conferred on a court, must be exercised in accordance with certain minimum standards of justice. The means by which this principle was put into practice was the adaptation of certain judicial writs which had been designed for purely routine procedural functions. In their extended role, these writs ceased to be obtainable as of course, and the court in granting them had 'a great latitude and discretion . . . not bound by such strict rules as in cases of private rights'.[17] The jurisdiction was, in other words, equitable. As a branch of common law, however, it was more conveniently attributed to the royal prerogative than to 'equity' by that name; and since at least the time of Charles I habeas corpus has been referred to as a 'prerogative writ'. The name was not altogether apt, because in their early stages these writs were mainly used to challenge prerogative acts by councillors and conciliar courts. Lord Ellesmere C objected strongly on this ground to Coke CJ's usurpation of the conciliar supervisory function: 'in giving excess of authority to the King's Bench he doth as much as insinuate that this court is all sufficient in itself to manage the state . . . as if the King's Bench had a superintendency over the government itself'.[18] Subsequent events have made this a greater dispute between law and equity than that which Coke lost in 1616; for in this context Coke's common law brand of equity prevailed, and it has in the long term proved as fruitful as the equitable creations of the Chancery.

PROHIBITION

The oldest member of the 'prerogative' class of writs was the writ of prohibition, which was developed in the thirteenth century as a means of restraining ecclesiastical courts from meddling in temporal affairs.[19] During the sixteenth and seventeenth centuries it was firmly established that the writ would lie to all other jurisdictions whatsoever: to the courts in the palatinates, to provincial conciliar courts, to courts of Civil law (such as the Court of Admiralty, Court of Chivalry and university courts) and to all inferior jurisdictions. By this means the boundaries of jurisdictions, and the interpretation of the charters or statutes on which they rested, fell exclusively to the common law judges. Coke CJ claimed jurisdiction to send prohibition

---

17. *Lord Montague v Dudman* (1751) 2 Ves 396 per Lord Hardwicke C, ruling that the Chancery could not restrain mandamus by injunction.
18. 'Observations on Coke's Reports', printed in L. A. Knafla *Law and Politics in Jacobean England* (1977), pp. 307–308 (spelling modernised above).
19. See p. 112, ante.

even to the Chancery, but this was never settled; it will be recalled that the dispute between Coke and Ellesmere had to be resolved by James I in person.[20] But Coke CJ and his fellow judges did prohibit the High Commission and Court of Delegates, which were prerogative courts. Prohibition has not developed as dramatically as the other prerogative writs, because after 1641 the Crown has not attempted to erect new types of court without parliamentary sanction, and the restraint of non-judicial powers may be achieved by means of other writs. It was, nevertheless, fully settled in the nineteenth century that prohibition would if necessary lie to statutory bodies and central government departments.

QUO WARRANTO

Whereas prohibition enabled a private party to stop a specific action against him, a general challenge to the existence of a jurisdiction or franchise could be made by means of a writ ordering the sheriff to summon the claimant to show by what authority (*quo warranto*) he exercised it. Extensive use was made of this procedure by Edward I in what was intended to be a comprehensive survey of inferior jurisdictions; the investigation proved too ambitious, but one lasting outcome was a statute which fixed at 1189 the time from which prescriptive claims had to be made.[21] The statute also provided that, to save costs, writs of *quo warranto* should be returned before justices in eyre. This had the unintended consequence that *quo warranto* disappeared with the eyre system itself. There was a revival under Henry VIII, and three or four eyres were commissioned for the purpose.[22] At the same time a less cumbrous procedure was devised, in the form of an information in the King's Bench by the attorney-general. This 'information in the nature of a *quo warranto*' thereafter completely supplanted the procedure by writ. The Tudor revival has been interpreted as part of a government campaign to suppress private authority, but it now seems that most of the informations were brought on the relation of private suitors; and by the seventeenth century it was a recognised procedure for subjects to promote such informations in the name of the master of the Crown Office. The last major political use of *quo warranto* occurred when Charles II sought to remodel municipal corporations by forcing new charters upon them. The City of London fought this reform to the bitter end, and was called upon by information to show 'by what warrant' it claimed its privileges; in 1683 the King's Bench delivered the shattering judgment against the city that

20. See p. 93, ante.
21. Statute of Quo Warranto 1290.
22. For one held at Lynn in 1522, see Spelman Rep (93 SS) 199.

its liberty of being a body politic be seized into the king's hands.[23] The following year, by an equally dramatic use of the analogous procedure of *scire facias*, the charter of the province of Massachusetts was rescinded for encroachment on the royal prerogative in founding Harvard College. After this period, the steady suppression of private and irregular jurisdictions by act of parliament reduced the need for *quo warranto*; but its scope was at the same time extended to cover all usurpations of public functions of importance, though not judicial.[24] The information in *quo warranto* was abolished in 1938, but the same remedy may still be given by injunction.

HABEAS CORPUS

The writ of habeas corpus has become the principal safeguard of personal liberty. It is not a little ironic, therefore, that its original purpose was not to release people from prison but to secure their presence in custody. The words habeas corpus occur in the common judicial writ of *capias ad respondendum*, and in the *habeas corpora juratorum* which issued to compel the attendance of jurors in the Common Pleas. The first use of the writ to curtail imprisonment occurred in cases of privilege; an officer of a central court, or a litigant there, could be released from imprisonment in another court by a writ of privilege in habeas corpus form. The Court of Chancery was the first to develop a procedure for reviewing the cause of imprisonment in an inferior tribunal; in this case the species of writ was called *corpus cum causa*, and it became a common remedy against the misuse of borough jurisdiction in the fourteenth and fifteenth centuries.

The King's Bench developed the *habeas corpus ad subjiciendum* in the sixteenth century, chiefly to protect subjects against unconstitutional imprisonment by privy councillors and officers of state. It was held by the judges in 1540 that, although the king had the same powers of imprisonment as his justices, the cause of imprisonment could be reviewed; the subject was protected against illegal imprisonment by Magna Carta.[25] At about the same time it was held that a committal by order of a privy councillor was not a good cause; and the decision was frequently followed. The decision was as frequently disregarded by some statesmen, and in 1592 the judges petitioned the lord chancellor and lord treasurer against interference with the law.[26] The judges persevered. They extended the remedy to unlawful committals

23. *R v City of London* (1682) 8 State Tr 1039.
24. *Darley v Reginam* (1846) 12 Cl & Fin 520, reviewing earlier cases.
25. *Serjeant Browne's Case* (1540) Spelman Rep (93 SS) 184.
26. 94 SS 74 (a case of privilege); *R v Steward of Marshalsea, ex parte Howell* (1587) 1 Leon 71; *Hellyard's Case, R v Warden of Fleet, ex parte Hellyard* (1587) 2 Leon 175; Articles of 1592, 1 And 298; Holdsworth HEL, vol. V, p. 495.

by inferior courts, and in the time of Coke CJ to superior courts such as the High Commission; Coke even released prisoners who had been committed by the lord chancellor.[27] Coke's successor, Mountague CJ, tried to dispel the feeling that the writ was being used to counter prerogative power by explaining that it was itself 'a prerogative writ, which concerns the king's justice to be administered to his subjects; for the king ought to have an account why any of his subjects are imprisoned'.[28] After fierce wrangles in Charles I's time, the general principle triumphed. Habeas corpus would lie in respect of any imprisonment, even by order of the king or council, and would secure the prisoner's release unless good cause were shown.[29]

The prerogative writ of habeas corpus thus replaced earlier civil remedies[30] as the most effective means of challenging a deprivation of liberty. The Habeas Corpus Act of 1679[31] improved the procedure in criminal cases, so that the writ could be obtained in vacation; prisoners had to be produced within three days, and any prisoner not tried within two terms was to be given bail. But the remedy was not confined to persons on criminal charges, for the writ could be addressed to anyone believed to be keeping a subject in confinement, ordering him to 'have the body' in court with the cause of detention 'to undergo and receive' what the court should adjudge. By issuing habeas corpus the King's Bench was able to affirm and protect a wide range of fundamental personal liberties: for instance, by denying the power of parliament to imprison people beyond the period of one session, of courts to coerce jurors by imprisonment, or of husbands to detain their wives in order to exact their conjugal rights.[32] It enabled persons committed to madhouses to secure a proper medical review of their condition.[33] Perhaps most important of all, it enabled the court to declare that English law does not recognise slavery.[34] In the twentieth century its chief use has been to question orders of extradition and deportation, since the writ is available to all persons except enemy aliens who are present within the jurisdiction. Even in its

---

27. See 4 IJ 374–378.
28. *Bourn's Case, R v Lord Warden of Cinque Ports, ex parte Bourn* (1619) Cro Jac 543.
29. *Five Knights' Case, R v Warden of Fleet, ex parte Darnel* (1627) 3 State Tr 1; Petition of Right 1628, 3 Car I, c.1, s.5.
30. The writs *de homine replegiando, de odio et atia*, and mainprise, enabled release in certain cases. Most disputes about imprisonment before 1600 were tried in actions of false imprisonment after the event; but the only remedy was damages.
31. Stat 31 Car II, c.2.
32. *Streater's Case* (1653) 5 State Tr 365; *R v Sheriffs of London, ex parte Bushell* (1670) Vaugh 135, 1 Freem 1; *Lister's Case, R v Lister, ex parte Rawlinson* (1721) 8 Mod Rep 22, 1 Stra 478; *R v Jackson* [1891] 1 QB 671.
33. *R v Turlington, ex parte D'Vebre* (1761) 2 Burr 1115.
34. *R v Knowles, ex parte Sommersett* (1772) 20 State Tr 1.

widest application, however, it does not enable an appeal on the merits of a decision to imprison. Its function is to question the lawfulness, not the inherent correctness, of an imprisonment. But the courts are extending their powers of review by acknowledging that the lawfulness of imprisonment may depend upon the manner in which a discretion is exercised.[35]

MANDAMUS

A good many writs, including the writ of error, contained the word *mandamus* ('we command you'), but the species distinguished by that word was developed at the beginning of the seventeenth century as a means of controlling borough and city authorities. It is likely that, as with habeas corpus, the original application of the writ was in cases of privilege; but from about 1615 the King's Bench asserted a general jurisdiction to order a local authority to do something or else show cause why it did not.[36] At first mandamus was used as a writ of restitution to protect public offices, such as alderman or constable, recorder or churchwarden; it secured a review of local elections to such offices, which were often corruptly mishandled, and helped establish democracy as a principle of common law. Until the last century, the underlying purpose of mandamus was the protection of an office or status which could not be recovered by an assize;[37] and this purpose was extended in the eighteenth century to include ecclesiastical benefices such as prebends, and university degrees.[38] In 1763 mandamus was awarded to restore a presbyterian minister, and Lord Mansfield CJ observed that it was a prerogative writ which 'ought to be used upon all occasions where the law has established no specific remedy'.[39] It would not, however, protect a private employment, for there the remedy was to sue for breach of contract; and it could not be used to establish rights of fellowship or membership of colleges or inns of court, because these are domestic bodies under the control of their 'visitors'. Reforms in local government in the nineteenth century put an end to the older use of mandamus, which has now been turned to the wider use of compelling public authorities or officials to carry out their statutory duties, including the proper exercise of discretionary powers.[40]

35. E.g. *R v Governor of Brixton Prison, ex parte Schtraks* [1964] AC 556.
36. *Bagge's Case, R v Mayor of Plymouth, ex parte Bagge* (1615) 11 Co Rep 93, 1 Rolle Rep 224.
37. As to this, see p. 352, post.
38. *R v Cambridge University, ex parte Bentley* (1723) 1 Stra 557.
39. *R v Barker, ex parte Mends* (1763) 3 Burr 1265 at 1267.
40. *Padfield v Minister of Agriculture, Fisheries and Food* [1968] AC 997, [1968] 1 All ER 694; *Secretary of State for Education v Tameside Metropolitan Borough Council* [1977] AC 1014.

CERTIORARI

The writ of certiorari was originally a means of informing a superior court about the proceedings of another court of record.[41] For instance, it might be necessary during proceedings in error in the King's Bench to inspect the original writ, and in that case a certiorari went to the keeper of the writs for the Common Pleas commanding him to search his files and certify what he could find to the King's Bench. A different form of the writ was used to remove records into the King's Bench so that proceedings could be taken over by the superior court. Until the seventeenth century this procedure was reserved for indictments, which could be brought into the King's Bench from any other court and either tried there, or quashed, or sent for trial in the country. This gave the King's Bench before 1500 a limited power to review criminal jurisdiction; but review was limited to the wording of the indictment, and most judgments to quash were made on purely techn:cal grounds.[42]

In the reign of Charles I the procedure was extended to administrative orders by justices of the peace, first to remove recognisances to enforce orders, and then to remove the orders themselves for scrutiny. By the end of the seventeenth century the King's Bench had a flourishing jurisdiction as a court of review for both summary convictions and quarter sessions orders relating to such matters as the settlement of the poor and licensing. The review was not by way of appeal, but by way of jurisdictional control. The essential features of the jurisdiction were settled by Holt CJ: certiorari would lie to any body created by statute which acted judicially, even if it was not a court of common law; statutes creating powers outside the common law were to be strictly construed; and before conviction or confiscation a man was to be summoned so that he had an opportunity to present his case.[43] Certiorari could not, however, be used to question purely 'ministerial' decisions.

In the nineteenth century the situations which had occasioned the remedy changed. Local administration was taken from the justices of the peace and transferred to councils and boards which could not readily be characterised as judicial. Summary convictions after 1848 were entered in a form which rendered review of the old kind difficult, and doubts in law were thereafter raised instead by case stated to the Queen's Bench. In the present century the growth of the welfare state

---

41. The opening words were '*Quia . . . certiorari volumus*' (because we wish to ascertain).
42. See 94 SS *301–302*. Sometimes the King's Bench seized on technical flaws when there were formally undisclosed grounds for freeing a prisoner on the merits.
43. For these propositions, see *Groenvelt v Burwell* (1700) 1 Ld Raym 454; *R v Chandler* (1702) 1 Ld Raym 581; *R v Dyer* (1703) 6 Mod Rep 41, Holt 157.

has resulted in more and more powers being conferred upon administrative bodies, with no right of appeal to the courts. There are now
over fifty categories of administrative tribunal in England. One of the
most hopeful developments in the common law over the last century,
and more particularly during the last quarter century, has been the
subjection of these new forms of administration to certiorari and to
the other prerogative remedies which had been developed to meet
analogous problems in earlier ages. The courts have achieved this by
relaxing the notion of a 'record', so that they may correct 'errors in
law' in the decisions of any public body which interferes with the
rights or obligations of subjects in a quasi-judicial manner.[44]

DECLARATIONS AND APPLICATIONS

A modern remedy which goes further than the prerogative writs is the
action for a declaration. This was an equitable procedure, of which an
ancient prototype was the petition of right against the Crown; but
until 1883 it could only be granted where some specific relief was also
claimed. Since 1883 the action for a declaration has become a remedy
in its own right, regularly given by the High Court. Although the
declaration when given is not directly enforceable, it would be unlawful to act against it; and it may be combined with an injunction or
damages. It has proved useful in filling gaps between the prerogative
remedies, because it is subject to few technical restrictions; it can be
used, for instance, against the Crown, or a professional body, and
may even be used to question subordinate legislation. In 1978, by the
simple expedient of introducing new rules of court (Ord. LIII), a new
and still more flexible procedure (the 'application for judicial review')
became available to the subject.

Administrative Law

The growth of the prerogative remedies affords an excellent illustration of the way in which the common law can adapt to new circumstances in protecting the individual. The forms of 'oppression and
misgovernment' which Coke CJ sought to control sprang chiefly from
bodies established under the royal prerogative to administer policy or
'equity' outside the safe framework of the common law. Once the
Crown had been painfully brought under the law, it was parliament
which began to indulge in its own democratic form of despotism.
Countless statutory bodies have been created over the last 150 years,

44. See *R v Northumberland Compensation Appeal Tribunal, ex parte Shaw* [1952] 1 KB 338,
    [1952] 1 All ER 122.

many of them with sweeping powers to restrict freedom and redistribute private property and money, others empowered to allocate funds raised from subjects by taxation or other forms of confiscation. The power to take away a man's home or his livelihood is a far greater power than that of fining him £5, and it would be a travesty if it were not regarded as 'judicial' merely because it was not conferred on a 'court' in the traditional sense. The new powers have been entrusted to non-judicial bodies for the very reason that government departments wish to control the membership of those bodies and the policy which they administer in a way which would not be allowed if they belonged to a court. Many of the powers conferred on boards and tribunals and ministers are therefore expressed in absolute terms; the decision is to be final, it is not to be questioned in any court, or it is to be as valid as if embodied in legislation. Even language as plain as this has not stifled judicial review. Similar language had been used by parliament in the eighteenth century in extending the justices' powers; but the courts held that parliament could not have intended that decisions were to be regarded as properly made, and therefore incontrovertible, unless they were made in strict accordance with the legislation and with the principles of natural justice.[45] In the earlier part of the twentieth century, however, the courts felt unable to take a similar stand against the alarmingly absolute discretionary power conferred by modern legislation on administrative bodies.[46] The rule of law had been buried. In place of law there was policy, which was not administered by judges but under the control of civil servants and their masters.

The tide has turned since the last war to such an extent that 'administrative law' is becoming one of the most fruitful and beneficial areas of judicial activity. Parliament, though responsible for the spread of tribunals, has itself contributed to the new spirit. Since 1947 the Crown has been liable to actions in contract and tort. And in 1958 measures were taken to subject tribunals to the rule of law; chairmen were to be appointed by the lord chancellor, and were to give reasons for their decisions, so that certiorari would lie to correct an error, and in some cases an appeal to the High Court was provided.[47] The judges have returned to the attack on language which purports to confer absolute power,[48] and they have blurred the distinction between

45. *R v Moreley* (1760) 2 Burr 1040.
46. See the pessimistic survey by Lord Hewart CJ, in *The New Despotism* (1929).
47. Crown Proceedings Act 1947, 10 & 11 Geo VI, c.44; Tribunals and Inquiries Act 1958, 6 & 7 Eliz II, c.66.
48. E.g. *Anisminic Ltd v Foreign Compensation Commission* [1969] AC 147, [1969] 1 All ER 208 (provision that determination 'shall not be called in question in any court of law' did not oust jurisdiction to decide whether determination *intra vires*).

administrative and judicial bodies. From the old decisions on summary convictions and churchwardens, and the like, have emerged
certain broad principles of 'natural justice' to which all decision-
making bodies are in some degree subject. The judges have so far
stopped short of reviewing administrative decisions on the merits,
where a decision is procedurally in order and properly informed. But
an influential judge has argued that even this barrier must be crossed
unless there is to be 'a world of rights and obligations not amenable to
the control of the ordinary courts'.[49]

Further reading

Holdsworth HEL, vol. I, pp. 213–218, 222–231, 242–246, 368–377,
516–525, 641–645

Radcliffe & Cross, pp. 204–228

Milsom HFCL, pp. 46–50

M. Hemmant, *Select Cases in the Exchequer Chamber* (51 SS, 1933; 64
SS, 1945)

R. Stevens, 'The Final Appeal: Reform of the House of Lords and
Privy Council 1867–76' (1964) 80 LQR 343–369

J. H. Baker, 'The Correction of Errors' in *Crime in England
1550–1800* (J. S. Cockburn, Ed, 1977), pp. 45–48; 'The Stay and
Reversal of Judgments' (1978) 94 SS *116–123*

PROHIBITION

G. B. Flahiff, 'The Writ of Prohibition to Court Christian in the
13th Century' (1944–45) 6 *Medieval Studies* 261–313; 7 *Medieval
Studies* 229–290

R. H. Helmholz, 'Writs of Prohibition and Ecclesiastical Sanctions
in the English Courts Christian' (1975) 30 *Minnesota Law Rev*
1011–1033

QUO WARRANTO

D. W. Sutherland, *Quo Warranto Proceedings during the Reign of
Edward I* (1963)

J. Levin, *The Charter Controversy in the City of London 1660–88* (1969)

PREROGATIVE REMEDIES

Holdsworth HEL, vol. IX, pp. 104–125

S. A. de Smith, 'The Prerogative Writs' (1951) 11 CLJ 40–56

L. L. Jaffe and E. G. Henderson, 'Judicial Review and the Rule of
Law: Historical Origins' (1956) 72 LQR 345–364

E. G. Henderson, *Foundations of English Administrative Law* (1963)

---

49. L. Scarman *English Law—The New Dimension* (1974), pp. 48–50.

10. The Legal Profession

It is a moot point whether, in the first instance, lawyers create legal science or legal science creates lawyers. In England, at any rate, the emergence of the common law as a body of rational principles coincided roughly with the development of a common law profession. Once a system of law has come into being, the course of its future development is in the hands of those who practise it; of the judges who declare what it is, of the advocates who present cases in court, of the counsellors who advise clients as to its effect, of its writers and teachers, and of all who make it their study. The common law of England was developed chiefly by an elite body of advocates and judges who belonged to the order of serjeants-at-law; a body which, in nearly seven centuries of history, numbered less than one thousand men, one quarter of the size of the present practising bar. Beneath the serjeants was a much larger profession centred on the inns of court and chancery. The growth of this peculiarly English professional structure, wholly independent of the university law faculties (where only Roman law was taught), helped preserve the distinctive character of English law and secure its isolation from the influence of Continental jurisprudence. The strength and unity of the profession explains how the reasoning of a small group of men in Westminster Hall grew into one of the world's two greatest systems of law.

ORIGINS OF A PROFESSIONAL BENCH AND BAR

We have seen how the common law grew from the work of the Norman and Angevin *justiciarii*, the members of the *Curia Regis* who toured the country on eyre or remained in the central bench. The first learned *justiciarii* were clergy: it was natural that they should be appointed from the only literate profession. But they made the administration of royal justice into a distinct profession. They devoted their working lives to the system they were helping to establish, and they handed on the traditions of the king's justice to their successors. Already by 1200 there was a habit of appointing to the bench clergy who had served as clerks to the judges of the previous generation, and who had thereby gained expertise in the common law. The professional character of the bench was soon followed by the emergence of a professional bar, and by the fourteenth century it had become the rule that judges could only be appointed from among the senior professional advocates. As a result, England possessed from an early date a bench and bar united by their membership of a common profession. This new profession was independent both of the Church and of the universities, and before 1300 it was producing judges who were not in Holy Orders and whose background was solely in the practice of the law of the land.

The non-clerical legal profession appeared in the course of the thirteenth century. The clergy were not allowed by Canon law to practise in lay courts, except on behalf of the Church or the poor, but it is possible that they did so until a lay profession came into being. The lack of biographical details has so far placed beyond reach the story of how the change took place. But the reasons may be guessed. Litigation in central courts, often far from home, required supervision by men who followed the king's court wherever it might be. Moreover, the growing technicality of the proceedings in the central courts, and the use of the French tongue at the bar, soon made expert assistance indispensable. Even before the change occurred, there was a clearly defined distinction between the person who stood beside and spoke for another subject to correction (the *advocatus* or *prolocutor*) and the person who stood in another's shoes and acted on his behalf so as to bind him (the *attornatus* or *procurator*). There has never been any question of the English legal profession dividing into two; the division of function preceded the appearance of a profession, though the precise allocation of functions has shifted over the centuries.

We cannot speak of a legal 'profession' being established until such time as we can see men following the law for a living, and being subjected to some form of discipline in so doing. The first element may have been present as early as 1200–10, when the names of certain pleaders, attorneys and essoiners[1] are found to recur in the records of the *Curia Regis*; but these habitual practitioners did not act to the exclusion of others, nor were their functions mutually exclusive. The element of professional regulation was probably added later in the thirteenth century. In 1275 a statute enacted that professional lawyers found guilty of deceit should be punished;[2] and in 1280 the City of London made regulations concerning the admission of prac-

1. An essoiner (*excusator*) was employed to make excuses for non-appearance. In the 14th century the function was absorbed into that of the attorney.
2. Statute of Westminster I, c.29.

titioners in the mayor's court, for the administration of an oath to those newly admitted, and for keeping separate the functions of pleader, attorney and essoiner. It is certain that some closely analogous regulation was made for the Common Bench at about the same period, for as soon as there are any records of such matters in the fourteenth century it is found that the pleaders in the Bench were selected by the judges there, made to take an oath, and were then expected to remain aloof from lesser practitioners. A study of the names of pleaders in the records and year-books of Edward I's reign establishes that already by 1300 a small group of advocates took most of the business. At the same time, the attorneys in the royal courts, whose function was to represent clients in the clerical or formal aspects of litigation, managing suits in the absence of the parties, also became a distinct profession. The attorneys came to be selected by the judges, and sworn; as officers of the court they were subject to disciplinary control by the bench. The separation of pleaders and attorneys was a separation of intellectual, court-room lawyers from ministerial, office lawyers, a distinction which was to be copied much later by barristers and solicitors.

THE SERJEANTS-AT-LAW

Soon after 1215, when the Common Bench was established as the principal common law court, a new class of professional advocates began to practise there. Matthew Paris referred to them in 1230 as 'the prolocutors of the Bench, whom we vulgarly call *narratores*'.[3] Their job, as indicated by their name, was to recite the count or *narratio* of the plaintiff, and to engage in any argument which arose. By the end of the century the identity of these narrators is well known from the year-books and records; they were the select group from whom the judges were always chosen, and whose words at the bar were noted down by the reporters for future learning.

During the fourteenth century this select group of narrators in the Common Bench was organised into a fraternity or guild known as the order of serjeants-at-law. Admission to this guild took place every few years, so that (after 1339 at the latest) serjeants were 'called' in batches of about six to eight. By the time of Richard II the admission had been turned into a degree ceremony or 'creation', and the degree of serjeant-at-law (*serviens ad legem*) became a rank which could compete even with knighthood. The degree was conferred by the judges of the Common Pleas, after the issue of a writ of subpoena to the graduand ordering him to make ready to take the degree. The

3. *Chronica Majora*, iii, 619 (Rolls ser). For the 'count', see p. 67, ante.

interposition of a royal writ, which apparently began in 1383, seems to have been necessary to combat a reluctance on the part of some lawyers to undergo the expense of graduation or to confine their working lives to one court. New serjeants took an oath to serve the king's people, gave a sumptuous feast which the king sometimes attended, distributed gold rings with mottoes, and were invested with their distinctive robes and white linen coifs. The coif, originally a head covering tied under the chin, was the badge of the serjeants until the end of the last century; but by then it had diminished into a circular patch on the crown of the wig. The central point of the creation ceremonies was the introduction of the new serjeant at the bar of the Common Pleas, when he was led up by two older serjeants and heard to make his count for the first time; anyone allowed by the judges to perform this function was ipso facto a serjeant, and all the other ceremonial was ancillary to this simple process of admission at the bar.

The serjeants enjoyed their greatest fortunes in the year-book period, when the bulk of all civil litigation took place in the Common Pleas. Fortescue said in the fifteenth century that the serjeants were the richest advocates in the whole world. The decline of the serjeants followed the decline of the court to which they belonged. Although they had audience in the King's Bench and other courts, they shared it, to their cost, with the apprentices-at-law. Furthermore, when written pleadings replaced oral pleading at the bar, and a lawsuit effectively began with the trial at *nisi prius*,[4] the importance of the serjeants as pleaders was lessened. Serjeants retained their monopoly of motions in banc, and of signing special pleas, in Common Pleas cases; but for all other business they had to compete with the lower branches of the profession. The growth of the junior bar also caused the loss of the serjeants' exclusive right to seats on the bench, because from the sixteenth century it became common to appoint judges from outside the order of the coif after a formal creation as serjeant for qualifying purposes. The first documented instance of this occurred in 1519, when John Ernle, the Attorney-General, was made Chief Justice of the Common Pleas; and the precedent was followed in 1545 when Sir Richard Lyster, Chief Baron of the Exchequer but not a serjeant, was made Chief Justice of the King's Bench. The practice became ever more common, so that many eminent judges—including Coke, Mansfield and Blackstone—never practised as serjeants in the Common Pleas. The exclusive character of the order was lost in the seventeenth century when coifs were sold for bribes, and by 1700

4. See pp. 71–74, ante.

there were ten times as many serjeants as there had been in 1500, but with less for them to do. Even the superiority of the serjeants over the rest of the bar gave way in the seventeenth century to the new rank of king's counsel.[5] The attractions of the coif waned when it was found to pin men beneath their juniors who took silk.

The end of the serjeants was finally settled in 1846 when, by a statute passed hurriedly in the long vacation, the Common Pleas was opened to the whole bar.[6] The order was never abolished, but the last non-judicial serjeants were created in 1868. The Judicature Act of 1875 removed the necessity for judges to have taken the coif, and after 1875 no more serjeants were created. The serjeants sold their Inn in 1877, and the last serjeant (Lord Lindley) died in 1921.[7] It is said that the queen could still nominate serjeants-at-law, though it is unclear how they would be created; they would have few privileges save their precedence before junior barristers and their colourful robes.

APPRENTICES AT LAW

The emergence of a non-clerical literate profession in the thirteenth century necessitated an educational system independent of the Church in which future serjeants and judges could be trained. Before 1300 there appeared a body of secular law students or 'apprentices of the Bench', who attended and sat in a gallery in Westminster Hall to listen and take notes. There is no evidence that the apprentices were articled to anyone; but their name (from *appendre*, to learn) clearly indicates their occupation. Not all apprentices became serjeants; some did not want the promotion, but most would never be chosen. The older apprentices of the law who did not take the coif therefore became a junior branch of the profession, and there was plenty for them to do. They practised as attorneys, as counsel in chambers or in Westminster Hall, and as advocates in the King's Bench, Chancery and lesser courts and on circuit. As these functions became increasingly important, in Tudor times, the process of control by the judges—which had produced the order of serjeants two or three centuries earlier—repeated itself. By this time, however, the judges

5. See pp. 142–143, post.
6. Stat 9 & 10 Vict, c.54. For an unlawful attempt by Lord Brougham to do this by warrant, see *The Serjeants' Case* (1840) 6 Bing NC 235; J. Manning *Serviens ad Legem* (1840).
7. Serjeant Sullivan (d. 1959), often called 'the last serjeant', was not a member of the English order, but was the last king's serjeant in Ireland. The rank of queen's serjeant survives even now in the County Palatine of Lancaster; but it has no connection with the order of the coif.

could exercise their discretion by reference to an established standard, the status of the individual in the inns of court. By 1600, if not long before, the title 'apprentice' had been narrowed to denote a double reader in one of the inns.

THE LEGAL INNS

The western suburbs of London were filled, by the fourteenth century, with the town houses or *hospicia* (inns) of the statesmen, civil servants and lawyers whose work brought them to London when parliament and the courts were in session. Of these, only the legal *hospicia*, and the inn or palace of the archbishop of Canterbury at Lambeth, have retained their original character and identity. The judges and serjeants usually had houses to themselves before Tudor times, but the apprentices and clerks found it convenient to live in shared accommodation, sometimes in part of the inn of a magnate who did not need it, occasionally in the household of a judge or senior official. The inns were never 'founded', like the colleges at Oxford and Cambridge, as part of a coherent scheme; they evolved through expediency. About twenty inns are known to have been used by apprentices-at-law, most of them in the parishes of St Andrew, Holborn, and St Clement Dane's. Of these, four major inns came to predominate. Known by Tudor times as the inns of court,[8] the four principal inns had attained a superior position by at least 1388.

The Temple was the *hospicium* or London residence of the knights Templar until their dissolution, and the Inner Temple hall stands on the site of the refectory of the military order. It was let out to lawyers in the fourteenth century, and before 1388 the legal tenants had formed the two societies of the Inner Temple and Middle Temple. Gray's Inn was the town house of the Lords Grey of Wilton before it was let to apprentices-at-law in the fourteenth century. The origin of Lincoln's Inn, which is not mentioned in records before the fifteenth century, is still obscure. Ancient tradition supposes it to have been the inn of Henry de Lacy (d. 1311), Earl of Lincoln, whose arms adorned the Tudor gatehouse. The earliest records of the societies formed in these inns are the Black Books of Lincoln's Inn, which commence in 1422 and show that there was by that time a settled social and educational routine. By that date, too, the judges and serjeants were almost invariably drawn from the membership of the four inns of court.

The other inns were of lesser status, and by the middle of the

8. The earliest use of the phrase, in pleadings, shows that it meant the inns of the men of court: *hospicia hominum curiae legis temporalis.*

fifteenth century were used chiefly by the attorneys and clerks who could not gain admission to the major inns, and by younger students who came to learn the rudiments of the writ system. The number fluctuated, but settled by 1500 at nine,[9] which were known compendiously as the 'inns of chancery'. At about that time they came under the control of the inns of court, the latter sending barristers to lecture and in some cases acting as landlords to the satellite societies. After the educational functions ceased in the seventeenth century, the inns of chancery continued to provide accommodation and social facilities for attorneys until they were sold and the societies wound up in Victorian times. Only one of the medieval buildings survives, the hall of Barnard's Inn, Holborn; but Staple Inn, lovingly rebuilt after war damage, still evokes the atmosphere of these forgotten little colleges of law.

After his elementary grounding in an inn of chancery, the student who aspired to the bar would seek admission to one of the inns of court as a member of 'clerk's commons'. He would spend seven years or so in the capacity of an 'inner barrister', attending the courts, performing exercises such as moots, attending lectures ('readings'), and keeping commons with his fellows. After this training he might expect to be called to the bar as an 'utter barrister'. The description 'barrister' is not found before the middle of the fifteenth century, when it seems to indicate the status of the member at moots; the inner barristers, or young students, sat inside the bar of the inn, and the utter barristers sat outside it. At first the rank had no significance in the courts, since it denoted only a domestic status. The highest ranks in the inns of court were those of bencher and reader, which also originated in the learning exercises. Twice a year, in the Lent and summer vacations, a barrister was elected to deliver a reading, or course of lectures, upon a selected statute. After performing this task he became a senior member of the inn and took part in its management and discipline. Benchers took their name from their function of sitting on the bench at moots. By Tudor times they had become more or less the same body as the readers, although some promising young men were elected to the bench of an inn before they had read. The system of readings never provided a coherent course of legal instruction, and readings were never given on the common law except to the extent that it was relevant to the exposition of a statute; but it initiated the student in the intricacies of legal analysis and debate, teaching him skills which he could himself practise in moots. After 1642 civil war and the

9. Barnard's Inn, Clement's Inn, Clifford's Inn, Davies (later Thavies) Inn, Furnival's Inn, Lyon's Inn, New Inn, Staple Inn and Strand Inn.

interregnum brought the educational life of the inns to an end, and attempts at revival in 1660 were unsuccessful. Law students were thereafter left to fend for themselves.

The New Profession

Since the important litigation of medieval times was concentrated in the Common Pleas, the serjeants and attorneys did all the important contentious work of the nation. The attorneys of the Common Pleas were officers of the court who carried on the formal side of litigation for their clients by issuing process and authorising entries on the plea rolls. Argument in open court was the exclusive province of the order of the coif. But these old branches of the profession had no monopoly of the new legal work which in the fifteenth and sixteenth centuries flooded into the King's Bench and Chancery and conciliar courts, nor of the conduct of trials at *nisi prius*. In the absence of contrary regulation, this work could be done by anyone who held himself out as able to do it. The occasional glimpses which the year-books provide of proceedings outside the Common Pleas show that the senior apprentices were as busy there as the serjeants were in their own court. It had become possible to earn a living by the law without becoming a serjeant or an attorney, and the other 'men of court' had become a third branch of the profession.

In the sixteenth century attempts were made, both by the judges and by the Privy Council, to impose some control on this new branch. Rights of audience had probably de facto belonged solely to readers and barristers of the inns of court; and so, when regulations were required, it was natural to insist upon a certain standing in an inn of court before appearance at the bar. In this way the private degree of utter barrister became a public degree, a sine qua non for practice at the bar; and to reflect this change the degree became better known as that of barrister-at-law. Contemporaneous with this process of definition was the development of yet another new class of lawyers, called 'solicitors'. Solicitors are mentioned in the fifteenth century, and appear to have been men of affairs, estate agents and general legal advisers; they could in some cases act themselves, and in others would instruct attorneys or counsel as appropriate. At first they were not rigidly separated from barristers, and would certainly have been members of the inns of court or chancery. Not only could a Common Pleas attorney be a 'solicitor' when pursuing causes in other courts, but even a barrister could act as a solicitor. Indeed, once the degree of barrister-at-law became a qualification for practice there was a wide-spread feeling that solicitors who were neither barristers nor attorneys were unqualified and could not intervene in litigation without committing the tort of maintenance. The common law judges, and particularly the Star Chamber, waged a fierce campaign between 1580 and 1630 to stamp out these 'mere' solicitors altogether; but they proved indestructible. The attack on solicitors proceeded on the basis that soliciting causes was one of the functions of young barristers, and that the work should not be taken over by under-qualified lawyers. The barristers, however, seem to have had more than enough to do appearing in court and giving opinions and settling pleadings; they did not press their case to be solicitors as well, and by the middle of the seventeenth century solicitors had become a recognised fourth branch of the profession. Barristers ceased to prepare their own briefs, leaving the preliminary meetings with clients in both contentious and non-contentious matters to the solicitors, and in consequence becoming specialists to whom cases were referred by the latter.

The new callings of barrister and solicitor thus came in a sense to mirror the older callings of serjeant and attorney, of *advocatus* and *procurator*. The barristers were particularly aware that their specialist role was superior to that of purely ministerial practitioners and clerks, and steps were taken to emphasise their superiority by excluding attorneys and solicitors from membership of the inns of court, an exclusion which for the last two centuries has been almost absolute. The bar projected an image of itself as an honourable calling for gentlemen, which, in accordance with classical notions of a liberal profession, was to be followed from a sense of duty rather than for gain. Out of this sentiment came the rule that barristers cannot sue for their fees, which are regarded as *honoraria* in the Civil law sense, that barristers should not court the company of solicitors, and that barristers should not undertake the routine work of soliciting causes or attending directly to the everyday affairs of clients. The elevation of the barrister suited the solicitor very well, because it gave him a great deal of exclusive business. By the eighteenth century the solicitor had become acceptable, and even respectable. In 1729 attorneys and solicitors, often the same persons, were subjected to closer professional regulation to exclude undesirables; and at about the same time they formed a 'Society of Gentlemen Practisers in the Courts of Law and Equity'. Through the efforts of this society, and its descendant the Law Society (incorporated in 1826), in supervising its members, the profession of solicitor[10] became in the nineteenth century as

10. The much older office of attorney disappeared in 1875.

respectable as that of barrister. The social differences between the two classes have largely withered away, and the professional differences are now differences in function more than in education or ability.

KING'S (OR QUEEN'S) COUNSEL

The only *degrees* in the common law are those of serjeant-at-law, conferred by the judges upon the nomination of the Crown, and of barrister-at-law, conferred by the inns of court. There have been, however, numerous particular *offices* which members of the bar might fill; an office being a paid public employment rather than a status. The highest offices were judicial, as were some of the lowest—such as recorderships of boroughs, and stewardships of leets and manors. Of offices appropriate to practising advocates the most rewarding were those relating to the litigation of the Crown. The king retained counsel and attorneys in each court: the king's serjeants in the Common Pleas, the king's attorneys there and in the King's Bench, and the king's serjeants and attorneys in the palatinates and in Ireland. In the fifteenth century the single office of king's attorney-general combined the older separate offices in the two benches, and in 1461 the first king's solicitor-general was appointed. The king's serjeants were usually between two and four in number and by virtue of their rank and office preceded the rest of the English bar. But in 1623 the attorney-general and solicitor-general were by warrant given precedence over all but the two senior king's serjeants, known thereafter as the king's prime and second serjeants; and by another warrant in 1813 they were given their present pre-eminence over the whole bar. The standing of the two senior law offices increased steadily after the fifteenth century, when they were already a stepping-stone to judicial office. In Tudor times two serjeants gave up the coif to become law officers, technically a loss of status, because it was more influential and lucrative. A seventeenth-century attorney-general might earn over £4,000 a year, while in the eighteenth century several earned over £10,000 a year.

The attorney-general, solicitor-general and king's serjeants were the king's counsel in ordinary. The first king's counsel 'extraordinary' to be granted that office by patent was Francis Bacon. He had been 'called within the bar' in 1597 as Queen Elizabeth I's 'learned counsel extraordinary, without patent or fee'; and in 1603 James I granted him the office of king's counsel, with place, precedence and preaudience. Further king's counsel were appointed by James I and Charles I. It is doubtful whether the office was really needed; but this was an age for bestowing titles, as a favour or at a suitable price, and the right of preaudience was valuable. In theory the king's counsel were law officers who, in return for a small salary, held permanent retainers which prevented them from appearing against the Crown; until 1920 it was necessary for king's counsel to obtain a licence to appear in a criminal case for the defence. In practice, it was the precedence which made the silk gown[11] beneficial. The institution of king's counsel extraordinary, which resulted from an attempt to placate a greedy Bacon, proved to be the principal death blow against the order of serjeants. It was unsettled until 1670 whether serjeants took precedence of the new officers, but in that year King Charles II in the Privy Council personally delivered the damaging decision that they did not. Thereafter the most junior king's counsel preceded the oldest serjeant, not being a king's serjeant, and the prospect of continuous demotion deterred the most able lawyers from applying for the coif. A serjeant could, of course, take silk and become a king's serjeant; but this would carry him in a leap over the heads of many of his seniors, and in all but a few cases would have been unacceptable and professionally dangerous. By the nineteenth century nearly all barristers with high aspirations chose a silk gown in preference to the scarlet habit of the serjeants; and this tendency contributed greatly to the decay and eventual extinction of the order of the coif.

The Judiciary

The highest responsibility of the bar has been the exercise of public offices of judicature. By 1400 it had become the invariable practice to grant judgeships in the two benches, and commissions of assize, only to serjeants-at-law. The chief baron of the Exchequer was as often as not a serjeant, but it was not until the last decade of the sixteenth century that the coif became an invariable qualification for all the barons except the junior ('cursitor') baron.[12] These judges received their salaries and robes from the Crown, but made up much of their income from court fees. Permanent judgeships, unlike recorderships and other inferior offices, prevented the holders from continuing in private practice at the bar; but in medieval times judges were allowed to give private advice, and habitually acted as private arbitrators, in

11. The proper dress of all king's counsel was a gown with black lace and tufts; but since the eighteenth century they have worn black silk gowns. Junior barristers wear stuff mourning gowns.
12. See p. 46, ante. The custom began too late to be regarded as binding, and parliament always distinguished the 'barons of the degree of the coif' when conferring judicial functions.

which capacity they took fees and alimentary gifts from the public. Thus, the judiciary were removed from the profession of the bar only by office, and in the two Serjeants' Inns[13] the judges kept common table with their brethren of the coif. If a judge lost his office he could return to practice as a serjeant, and this was not an infrequent occurrence in the troubled years of the seventeenth century.

The independence of the judiciary is now rightly regarded as one of the pillars of the constitution, but it was built on an unsure foundation. The judges were servants of the king, appointed and paid by the king, and in theory removable at the pleasure of the king. On paper they were no more secure than a minister such as the attorney-general, who held office on similar terms. And in reality kings often expected subservience from their judges in matters affecting the Crown. But the professional training of the judiciary, and the notion of a constitutional monarchy as expounded by Fortescue CJ in the fifteenth century,[14] transformed the personal loyalty which judges owed the king into a more objective form of loyalty to an impersonal Crown and to the king's common law. The independent stance of particular chief justices may have paved the way for the general principle. The famous story that Gascoigne CJ committed Prince Henry (later Henry V) for contempt, whether true or not, was a popular story in the sixteenth century. In 1485 the king desired the judges to give preliminary opinions in a treason case, and Huse CJ successfully resisted, saying that 'it would come before the King's Bench judicially, and then they would do what by right they ought to do'.[15] Under Henry VIII, however, there were occasions when the judges seem to have conformed their opinions to the king's wishes.[16] Before Stuart times there were very few removals from office, which may be more consistent with judicial subservience than with independence. Probably the Crown did not often apply extreme political pressure; but when it did so the reaction depended on the quality of the men in office and the extent of their agreement with royal policy.

In the seventeenth century the judiciary came into head-on collision with the Crown on several occasions. The sorry story began in 1616, when the judges were brought before the council to say whether they would stay a suit if the king so ordered. All the judges submitted except Coke CJ, who answered (doubtless remembering the example of Huse CJ) that 'when that case should be, he would do that should

13. One was in Fleet Street, the other in Chancery Lane. In 1730 the former was given up and the two societies merged.
14. J. Fortescue *De Laudibus Legum Anglie* (S. B. Chrimes edn, 1942).
15. *R v Stafford* (1485) YB Trin 1 Hen VII 26, pl.1.
16. E.g. *Lord Dacre's Case* (1535), pp. 216–217, post.

be fit for a judge to do'.[17] A few months later Coke was dismissed by a writ giving no reasons, notwithstanding his reputation as the greatest lawyer of the time. During the next twenty-five years James I and Charles I removed a number of judges who refused to behave as the government wished, and judicial office became less secure than it had ever been. The judges who survived in office were often associated with the government, and in a few decades the awesome judiciary which the people had revered at the turn of the century came to be regarded, rightly or wrongly, as an instrument of prerogative rule. The decision of a majority of judges in favour of the imposition of ship-money in 1638 brought their reputation to its lowest ebb, and in 1641 several of the ship-money judges were impeached.

Contemporaries saw the solution to be the granting of life tenure to judges. The appropriate words of limitation in a patent granting office for life were *quamdiu se bene gesserit* (so long as he should behave well). Bryan CJ had (perhaps uniquely) had such a patent in 1472,[18] and since about that period barons of the Exchequer had been given tenure, a practice not broken until 1631. In 1642 Charles I was persuaded to appoint judges during good behaviour, and the practice was followed under Charles II by Lord Clarendon; but from 1668 there was a quiet return to grants during pleasure. Even judges who had been appointed for life were insecure, for in 1672 such a judge was suspended from sitting; he established his right to remain technically a judge, but took no further part in decisions.[19] Charles II also began the practice of forced retirement. Two judges, Hale CJ (in 1676), and Twisden J (in 1678), had been allowed to retire with a pension on grounds of old age and ill health; but the same procedure was used in 1678 to remove Rainsford CJ, to make way for a dissolute court favourite (Scroggs CJ), and in 1679 to remove several judges for political reasons. These scandals were exceeded by James II, who removed twelve judges in four years, mostly for refusing to recognise his claim to dispense with statutes. The lesson was learned. William III appointed all his judges during good behaviour, and after 1700 tenure during good behaviour was guaranteed by statute.[20] Even

17. *Acts of the Privy Council 1615–1616* (1925), p. 607.
18. His predecessor, Danby CJ, had apparently been dismissed; but history does not tell why.
19. *Re Justice Archer* (1672) T Raym 217; Lincoln's Inn, MS Misc. 500, f.206v. His name was still used in final concords, and he is said to have received his share of court fees. The cause of his dismissal is unknown.
20. Act of Settlement, 12 & 13 Will III, c.2. Some modifications have recently been made, in that judges appointed during good behaviour must retire at 75 and may be removed for permanent infirmity: Judicial Pensions Act 1959, 8 & 9 Eliz II, c.9, s.2; Administration of Justice Act 1973 (c.15), s.12.

tenure during good behaviour ended with the demise of the Crown. Upon the king's death all judicial proceedings ceased, and all judicial authority returned to the new king; one of the first acts of a king was to deliver the great seal to a chancellor, who could use it to seal patents appointing judges. On the death of a sovereign, therefore, judges and other officials could be effectively dismissed by not renewing their patents. Queen Anne discontinued some judges in this way in 1702. After 1707, however, patents were continued for six months after the demise of the Crown; and since 1760 continuity in office has been secured by statute.

Once judges achieved security of tenure, the principal form of political influence was in the appointment of new judges. There is no constitutional machinery for reviewing appointments. Until 1946, when Lord Goddard was appointed, it had been a very frequent practice[21] for four centuries to offer chief justiceships when vacant to government law officers. Politics sometimes played a part in the appointment of puisne justices as well, even as late as the turn of this century, when Lord Halsbury C made some nominations which were widely condemned for showing party bias. It has to be said, nevertheless, that most of the judges appointed in this manner after the seventeenth century conducted themselves with complete propriety in office; the tradition of independence from government interference was strong enough to prevail over party loyalty. Lord Ellenborough CJ was (in 1806) the last of many chief justices to serve in the Cabinet; and thereafter the judges have remained aloof from government politics.

It may seem strange that the tenure secured for judges of the superior courts is not given to other judges. The reason is partly historical. Until 1972 justices of assize were appointed by commission, and until 1973 justices of the peace were appointed in the same way. Commissions were made ad hoc from time to time, and there was no guarantee that a judge would be continued from one commission to the next. Circuit judges are now appointed by royal warrant, justices of the peace by an instrument signed by the lord chancellor; but these instruments confer no greater security of tenure than if there had been a commission. The majority of judges are, therefore, to this day removable at the behest of the lord chancellor, who is an active member of the government. So far the high traditions of their office have restrained lords chancellor from abusing the power, despite growing political pressure to interfere with judicial independence.

21. With two exceptions (Lord Tenterden CJKB and Erle CJCP) all 19th century chief justices were either law officers on appointment or judges who had previously served as law officers. Tenterden had been Treasury counsel.

The Civilian Advocates

The practitioners and judges in the English courts of Civil and Canon law were until 1857 wholly separate from the common law profession just described. Corresponding to the serjeants were the advocates, and corresponding to the attorneys were the proctors. The proctors were bred up in the routine of those courts, and sometimes had a bachelor's degree. The advocates were doctors of law from the universities of Oxford and Cambridge who had been admitted to practise by the Dean of Arches upon receipt of a mandate from the archbishop of Canterbury.[22] After the reign of Henry VIII, the doctors were mostly doctors of Civil law (D.C.L. at Oxford, LL.D. at Cambridge), because Canon law studies were discontinued at the Reformation. They practised not only in the ecclesiastical courts, but also in the Admiralty and the Court of Chivalry. From them were appointed the judges in those courts, and the king's advocate, who acted as law officer there. Many, though not all, of the advocates belonged to a society called Doctors' Commons, where they kept a common table and a precious library of foreign law books. This society was formed by the 'doctors of the Arches' in the fifteenth century, for reasons of social convenience, and in 1768 was incorporated by charter as the 'College of Doctors of Law exercent in the Ecclesiastical and Admiralty Courts'. The doctors' ancient traditions and scarlet robes resembled in many respects those of the serjeants, and their end came in a similar way. Upon the establishment of secular divorce and probate courts in 1857 the doctors were deprived of their monopoly of audience in those important spheres, and as a profession they lost heart. The library of Doctors' Commons was sold in 1861, the buildings in 1865. No new advocates were admitted. The last member of the profession, Dr T. H. Tristram, died in 1912.

Legal Education

If the common law sometimes appeared to be an orderless science, it was chiefly because it lacked a comprehensive system of education. No one ever had to attempt to teach or learn the law as a coherent whole, and for many the sole objective was to obtain a grounding in practice. The universities taught Civil and Canon law to the exclusion of the law of the land, perhaps because they disdained any sciences

22. There were also a few doctors who practised exclusively in the northern province, presumably by licence from the archbishop of York.

which were not expressed in Latin. The vast majority of law graduates before the middle of the nineteenth century took Holy Orders and became country parsons; a few chose administrative positions in the Church, or became advocates in Doctors' Commons. The common lawyers with equal insularity rejected any special knowledge of the Civil law. The inns of court provided learning exercises which produced skilful and quick-witted advocates; but they did not aim to give a complete course of instruction in law, and in any case the exercises disappeared in the seventeenth century. The principal method of legal education was, therefore, self-help. The student would try to obtain a seat in a lawyer's office where he could study the routine of pleading and conveyancing at first hand; and during term he would attend the courts, with notebook in hand, to learn legal method. His law would be gathered from such books as he could afford to buy or borrow. If he began practice too soon the chances were that he would never learn much law; but if he put it off too long he might confuse himself beyond salvation.

By a curious twist of history the universities were destined to succeed where the inns of court eventually failed. England was perhaps the last European country to admit the profession of the municipal law into its academic curriculum,[23] a process which began when Dr William Blackstone began to lecture on English law at Oxford in 1753. In 1758 the Oxford lectures were endowed by the foundation of the Vinerian Chair, and within the next fifty years similar chairs were founded at Trinity College, Dublin, and at Cambridge. Blackstone's success proved, ironically, an obstacle to further advances. His lectures were not aimed at professional law students, but at country gentlemen and clergymen; yet his exposition of the law was the first successful presentation since Bracton of the whole of the law in an elementary but rational method. The publication of the lectures in 1765 as the *Commentaries on the Laws of England* provided law students with a primer and rendered further lectures for the time being unnecessary. None of Blackstone's immediate successors, nor the early Downing professors at Cambridge, had large audiences. We do not know whether they deserved better. We do know that at times lectures in English law ceased altogether.

A new impetus for legal education came from the efforts of Andrew Amos, a practising barrister who accepted the first Chair of English Law in the new University of London in 1828. He gave evening classes and lectures in Gower Street for bar students and articled clerks who had spent the day in an office, and his avowed intention

23. F. Sullivan *Principles of Feudal Law* (1772), p. 10.

was to combine practical observation with academic discussion. His classes were a notable success, and in 1839 the University awarded the first academic degrees in the common law. Again, however, it was chiefly a one-man success; and before long legal education returned to the doldrums. There were insufficient endowments to attract professors of distinction, and students preferred to learn their law in the rival professional law schools which sprang up at that time. It is a sad reflection on the law faculties that most of the distinguished lawyers between about 1850 and 1950 were either not university graduates at all or had read subjects other than law. The state of legal education was constantly debated. In 1846, and again in 1971, it was recommended that universities should teach the elements of legal science and that professional law schools should teach the practice. The profession responded first, by establishing the Council of Legal Education in 1852 to serve the inns of court;[24] but lectures were voluntary and were soon virtually superseded by crammers, and examinations for the bar were not compulsory until 1872. In 1850 Oxford introduced a B.A. course in law and history, and in 1858 Cambridge established a law tripos. Towards the end of the nineteenth century the university law faculties revived under such brilliant names as Maitland, Dicey, Anson and Pollock, and in the twentieth century the study of law at university has become a normal—and now very nearly compulsory—preliminary to the vocational training which has also been made compulsory for both branches.[25]

Further reading

Holdsworth HEL, vol. II, pp. 311–318, 484–512; vol. VI,
     pp. 431–499; vol. XII, pp. 4–101
H. Cohen, *History of the English Bar and Attornatus to 1450* (1929)
E. W. Ives, 'Promotion in the Legal Profession of Yorkist and early
     Tudor England' (1959) 75 LQR 348; 'The Common Lawyers in
     pre-Reformation England' (1960) 18 TRHS (5th ser.) 145–173
M. Birks, *Gentlemen of the Law* (1960)
J. P. Dawson, *The Oracles of the Law* (1968), pp. 1–50
G. O. Sayles, 'The Serjeants at Law' (1971) 88 SS xxviii–xli
J. H. Baker, 'Counsellors and Barristers: an historical Study'
     [1969] CLJ 205–229; 'Solicitors and the Law of Maintenance'

24. Before that date, the Law Society had introduced lectures and examinations for articled clerks, and the inns had experimented with lectures.
25. Articles for solicitors had been compulsory since the 17th century. But pupillage for practising barristers was not made compulsory until 1958. Compulsory attendance .at learning exercises, after they lapsed in 1642, was not reintroduced until around 1970.

[1973] CLJ 56–80; *Creations of Serjeants at Law 1339–1875*
(forthcoming)

R. C. Palmer, 'The Origins of the Legal Profession in England'
(1976) 11 IJ 147–169

INNS OF COURT

S. E. Thorne, *Readings and Moots in the Inns of Court* (71 SS, 1952);
'The early History of the Inns of Court' (1959) 50 *Graya* 79–96

R. F. Roxburgh, *Black Books of Lincoln's Inn* (1968), vol. V,
pp. 448–476; 'Lawyers in the New Temple' (1972) 88 LQR
414–430; 'Lincoln's Inns of the 14th Century' (1978) 94 LQR
363–382

A. W. B. Simpson, 'The early Constitution of the Inns of Court'
[1970] CLJ 241–256; 'The early Constitution of Gray's Inn'
[1975] CLJ 131–150

W. R. Prest, *The Inns of Court 1590–1640* (1972)

R. E. Megarry, *Inns Ancient and Modern* (1972)

J. H. Baker, 'The Inns of Court in 1388' (1976) 92 LQR 184–187;
'The Original Constitution of Gray's Inn' (1977) 81 *Graya* 15–19;
'The Education of Lawyers' (1978) 94 SS *125–137*

CIVILIAN ADVOCATES

B. P. Levack, *The Civil Lawyers in England 1603–41* (1973)

G. D. Squibb, *Doctors' Commons* (1977)

JUDICIARY

A. F. Havighurst, 'The Judiciary and Politics in the Reign of
Charles II' (1950) 66 LQR 62–78, 229–252; 'James II and the
Twelve Men in Scarlet' (1953) 69 LQR 522–546

D. A. Rubini, 'The Precarious Independence of the Judiciary
1688–1701' (1967) 83 LQR 343–345

W. J. Jones, *Politics and the Bench: the Judges and the Origins of the
English Civil War* (1971)

J. H. Baker, 'Independence of the Judiciary' (1978) 94 SS *137–142*

LEGAL EDUCATION

H. G. Hanbury, *The Vinerian Chair and Legal Education* (1958)

J. H. Baker, 'University College and Legal Education 1826–1976'
[1977] *Current Legal Problems* 1–13

11. Legal Literature

The literature produced by a profession is usually the clearest guide to the state of its intellectual sophistication. It is, of course, possible for courts and administrative systems to function without books; but it is not possible for a body of law to develop very far without the interposition of writing. The ways in which law came to be written about were as various as the reasons for writing about the law. Once the opinions of the court, and of the serjeants, were recognised as providing good evidence of the law and of accepted practice, it was sensible for someone to note them down for future reference. When the inns of court organised readings and debates in which accepted doctrine was tried and tested in the presence of judges and benchers, it was again sensible for those present to keep notes. Forms and procedures called for formularies, first of writs and then of pleadings; and formularies attracted notes of explanation and commentaries by which the beginner could understand as well as learn the forms. Medieval lawyers must have spent countless hours writing out their own libraries. Even a century after the introduction of the printing press, the copying of legal texts by hand remained a feature of legal self-education. As books became the repositories of legal learning, so lawyers of all classes became hungry for books. By 1500 the inns of court all had libraries, and a century later there were over a hundred law books in print. After 1600 the publication of law books grew with such rapidity that by 1800 the printed literature of English law extended to over 1,500 separate titles.

Reports of Cases

The official record kept by the clerks of each court preserved precedents of the particular forms of pleading, and of judgments given upon them. As early as the 1220s and 1230s lawyers were extracting interesting cases from the plea rolls as illustrations of the law. The rolls remained the most authoritative source of precedents, and until at least the end of the seventeenth century it was common for counsel to 'vouch the record' when citing a previous case. But the record contained only the formal phrases, so many of which were common form, and omitted the legal discussion which took place at the bar. The arguments of the judges and serjeants, the tentative pleading which obliquely revealed the principles of the common law,[1] took place off the record, and only the formalised results of their deliberations went down on parchment. Yet, for the development of abstract legal principles, these forensic exchanges could often be of greater importance than the record. This explains why long attendance in Westminster Hall was an indispensable part of a common lawyer's education. The natural store for such learning was the human mind. Royal judges of the thirteenth century and before must have relied almost entirely on memory and experience, prompted by the rolls. But memory is frail and unsafe, and if continuity was to be preserved from one generation to another, and if legal discussions in the Bench were to reach a wider audience than those who happened to hear them at the time, then some additional kind of record was required. The first idea was to add new material into a schematic exposition of the law; but this, at a time when the law was changing rapidly, was too unwieldy and untidy a method to succeed.[2] What lawyers required was a report of the oral proceedings in court.

THE YEAR-BOOKS

After some early experiments at presenting forensic debates in an abstract way, written out in the form of a brief treatise or as teaching exercises, there appeared in the 1280s the first specifically dated reports of arguments (in French) attributed to named judges and serjeants in the Common Pleas or in eyre. By the 1300s these reports had become an established chronological series with a wide circulation. Their authorship is unknown, and so they have been given the generic name 'year-books'.[3] The first year-books were obviously the creature of the new legal profession, but opinion is divided as to whether they were produced primarily by or for young students, or serjeants, or court officials. From about 1550 to 1900 tradition firmly attributed the year-books to official reporters, conjecturally identified

1. See pp. 69–70, ante.
2. See pp. 161–162, post.
3. They were later cited by year and folio. Contemporaries called them *livres de termes* (term books), because the basic unit was the law term rather than the whole year. Printing enabled citation by years, when the foliation was standardised. Year-books may still be cited by term, since the cases within each term are separately numbered.

by some as the prothonotaries of the Common Pleas. This thesis was exploded by Maitland, who pointed out that there were no records of the appointment or payment of official reporters, that no year-books were preserved with the records and office books of the courts, and that the style of the earliest books was informal and sometimes even boisterous when compared with the stereotyped Latin formality of the plea rolls. The purpose of the year-books cannot have been to supplement the rolls, because they frequently omit details (such as the names of parties) which would be needed to identify the cases in the record. The purpose must rather have been, in the broadest sense, academic; to circulate and preserve for future learning, both by students and by their practising elders, the possible moves in the recondite games of legal chess played by the pleaders in open court.

The anonymity of the year-books is not without significance. It could be taken to indicate that they were not individual compilations at all, but resulted from the communal interchange of notes in the inns of court and chancery. But it could also indicate that the original value of the reports lay not so much in their historical authenticity as precedents, in which respect they are often worthless, as in the ideas and doctrines which they contained. It mattered little who wrote them, because any sense they made was self-evident, and any nonsense could be freely corrected by the owner of the manuscript.

THE LATER YEAR-BOOKS

The mystery and anonymity surrounding the year-books of Edward II is almost as deep two centuries later with respect to those of Henry VII and Henry VIII. One remarkable feature is that from before 1350 until about 1450 there seems to be only one basic text. The continuity of such a text from year to year implies some form of organisation, with either a single line of reporters or a definite editorial body; but no evidence as to the form of that organisation has survived. In the 1450s, and again in 1465,[4] there were clearly at least two reporters producing different texts of the same cases; and from the 1480s the number of reporters increased. Whatever system there had been must have broken down. By this period, too, we can begin to identify some of the reporters. The first[5] of whom mention is found

---

4. For this year there are two reports in print, the vulgate year 5 Edward IV and the much longer text called the *Long Quinto*. The second texts of the 1450s are not in print.
5. A possible earlier candidate is Robert Aspere, admitted to Lincoln's Inn in 1442, who in the 1440s had a year-book with cases as recent as 20 Henry VI: *English Legal Manuscripts*, vol. II, p. 49.

was Roger Townshend, admitted to Lincoln's Inn in 1454, created serjeant in 1478, and a justice of the Common Pleas from 1485 to 1493. His reports extended from the 1450s to the 1480s, which proves that at that time reporting was not the exclusive province of any particular class of person, but rather the life-long occupation of individuals. A similar pattern is found in the work of another early reporter, John Caryll, whose reports extended from his student days in the Inner Temple in the 1480s through his time as a prothonotary of the Common Pleas and throughout his career as a serjeant from 1510 to 1523. Other reports of the 1480s and 1490s were evidently the work of a member of Gray's Inn. It would be an attractive speculation to suppose that there was by then one recognised reporter in each inn; but there are reasons for doubting whether this was true in the fifteenth century, and it certainly does not hold true in the sixteenth.

In early Tudor times the character of the reports began slowly to change. This was not the result of any breakdown in organisation, but simply the consequence of the transformation of the legal system in the renaissance period. There was actually an increase in the amount of law reporting, and many of the new reports were of cases in the King's Bench, where the most interesting reforms were initiated. With the demise of oral pleading, the reports concentrated more and more on motions in banc raising questions of law after trial; and this direct discussion of substantive law has a distinctly more modern appearance than the inconclusive tentative pleading of the classical year-books. Yet, despite these differences, there was no break in continuity between the year-books and their successors. The year-books did not end at any fixed date. What has usually been taken as their end is the result of two concurrent factors: the advent of printing, and the identification of reports by the name of the author.

THE ADVENT OF PRINTING

Within ten years of the introduction of printing into England in the 1470s, the London printers had found a market in the legal profession. The first printed law book was Littleton's *Tenures* (1481), but in Henry VII's reign a number of year-books were printed and offered for sale at a few pence a year. By 1558 the canon of printed year-books was complete; they were reprinted numerous times, still as single years, by the Elizabethan law printer Richard Tottell, and between 1590 and 1610 other printers collected them into ten thick volumes. The first attempt to print the whole at once was not until 1679–80, when what was destined also to be the last edition was produced in tall folio.[6] The effect of printing the year-books was that in time the manuscripts were ousted from practitioners' libraries. The printed version, with all its many defects, had the advantage of appearing to be a complete set of reports of accepted authenticity and having a standard method of citation.

Unfortunately for the historian, the magic of the printed word has tended to obscure the original state of the texts. A number of interesting year-books, including the entire reign of Richard II, were for no good reason altogether omitted. In the later reigns a wide variety of texts, no longer recoverable because of the destruction of the manuscripts, was confused into a deceptively uniform series. Our suspicion is aroused only when we find judges speaking after they were dead, and similar chronological solecisms; moreover further investigation shows that what appear to be different cases, or successive arguments in the same case, are sometimes reports of the same argument by different hands. The last printed year-book of all, ending with Michaelmas term 27 Henry VIII (1535), has been taken to represent some definitive line between old and new; an ominous event, as Maitland thought, which marked the decline of the common law at the zenith of Henrician despotism. In fact law reporting was by then busier than before; it was simply the printing press which fell behind with its programme. The only surviving manuscript of the year-books of 1535 continues into the 1540s without change of style. The reports of the mid-Tudor period are in general indistinguishable from the 'last' year-books save in the bibliographical particular that no one published them as year-books.

THE NAMED REPORTS

In the sixteenth century came a personalisation of law reports, occasioned probably by the proliferation of texts and the need to distinguish different series. Some of the earliest known reporters of the century, such as Sir John Spelman (d. 1546) and Sir James Dyer (d. 1582), produced reports no different in character from the year-books; and, like Townshend and Caryll before them, both reported continuously from their student days through their careers as serjeants and judges. *Dyer* was printed posthumously in 1585. *Spelman* did not reach the press until 1977. There are others which have still to be printed.

6. The reprint of 1679–80 has been wrongly associated with the name of Mr Serjeant Maynard (d. 1690), who had just promoted the first publication of the year-books of Edward II in 1678. The 'Maynard' edition has been the standard text ever since, though it is arguably the least accurate.

Only a minority of the named reports were printed, and those usually long after they were written. The profession was accustomed to using manuscript reports, which could be obtained in mass-produced copies from law stationers down to the Civil War; and even in the eighteenth century it was not uncommon for manuscripts to be cited in court. Some of the reporters, for instance William Dalison (d. 1559), William Bendlowes (d. 1584), Sir Edmund Anderson (d. 1605) and Sir Francis Moore (d. 1616), were well known long before their work was printed, and numerous manuscript copies of their work survive to this day. Much of the printing was carried out in the middle of the seventeenth century, to a low standard. Some notes of appallingly poor quality were printed, while the better manuscripts were for reasons of length or unavailability passed by. Unscrupulous publishers placed on title-pages the names of distinguished lawyers of the past, even if the texts were in reality as anonymous as the year-books. The *English Reports*[7] before 1660 present considerable textual problems. At least half of them are wrongly attributed. *Keilwey*, named after an owner, is really a part of Caryll's year books bound up with Inner Temple moots (probably by Caryll) and fourteenth-century *quo warranto* cases. Parts of *Dalison, New Benloes, Owen, Noy, Popham* and *Winch* are demonstrably spurious in their attribution because they contain cases decided after the alleged reporters' deaths; on page 125 of *Winch* we even find a note of Winch's own death. A glance at the reports called *Dalison, Old Benloes* and *Anderson* will reveal a substantial quantity of common material, albeit in a different sequence in each collection: it was a common practice to collect together cases from borrowed manuscripts without acknowledgment. One case occurs three times, in identical words, in Leonard's collections alone.[8]

Of the pre-1660 reports, three series stand out as being of excellent quality. All were seen through the press by their authors, a feature which alone marks them out as unusual. The first, which made the greatest departure from the year-book style, were the *Commentaries* of Edmund Plowden (d. 1585). Plowden reported cases from the 1550s to the 1570s, and took great pains to check details with the counsel and judges and to procure a transcript of the record. He selected for publication only those cases in which questions of law were raised for solemn argument on demurrer or special verdict, and edited them carefully with references and comment added. Plowden's conception

---

7. This name was given to the reprint of 1900–32, in which the principal reports before 1865 were reprinted in 178 volumes.
8. *Anon* (1566) 3 Leon 13, 4 Leon 167, 224. For its identity, see note 4 on p. 353, post. Even the publisher did not pretend that these reports were *by* Leonard.

of a law report as a reasoned exposition of the law, with learned gloss, was taken up by Sir Edward Coke (d. 1634). Coke edited eleven volumes of reports between 1600 and 1616, and left further reports in manuscript from which two posthumous parts were printed in 1658 and 1659. He added rather more of his own comment than Plowden had done, often working into one report his own notes of earlier cases, and often failing to distinguish (as Plowden had done, by using italics) his own views from those he was reporting. Coke's intentions were not dishonest; like Plowden he still held the medieval view that the correctness of the doctrine reported was more important than the historical precision of the report, and his reports were conceived as instructional law books built around actual cases. Coke's volumes have the distinction of being cited simply as *The Reports*, and they have been perhaps the most influential series of named reports. The third series worthy of mention was that of Edward Bulstrode (d. 1659), a Welsh judge, who in the last three years of his life published three copious volumes of King's Bench reports taken under James I and Charles I. These reports were not so distinguished as those of Plowden or Coke, but they continued the tradition of careful and detailed reporting into a period better known for books which should never have been printed. Bulstrode's were also the first reports to be published by their author in English.[9]

The reports of the period 1650–1750 were mostly of an inferior nature, consisting of short notes and scattered arguments. For long periods there are no printed reports of what was happening in the Common Pleas. This period did, nevertheless, witness the beginning of continuous if irregular reporting in the Chancery and Exchequer. Lord Mansfield's distinguished tenure of the office of Lord Chief Justice of England (1756–88) made its impact on the law partly by attracting reporters of high calibre, of whom the best was Sir James Burrow (d. 1782). The haphazard state of law reporting was eventually remedied by the reintroduction of periodical series: a publishing venture which, once the profession accepted the high price of the volumes, ensured a steady succession of accurate reports. No longer did publishers have to assemble reports of dubious accuracy from the jottings of the dead. The first regular series to be brought out almost contemporaneously with the cases reported were Durnford and East's *Term Reports* (King's Bench, 1785–1800), *Henry Blackstone* (Common Pleas, 1788–96) and *Vesey Junior* (Chancery, 1789–1817). Thereafter a

---

9. Before 1650 all reports were in French. A statute of 1650 required law books to be printed in English. After 1660 some further reports were printed in French, but by 1700 English was invariably used.

succession of professional law reporters maintained these and parallel series until 1865, when the Council of Law Reporting was set up to produce the *Law Reports*.

Abridgments

By the middle of the fifteenth century the body of year-books was so large that lawyers were finding it necessary to compile commonplace books or abridgments to help them find material when they needed it. In commonplaces, points which were encountered in casual reading were entered up, ideally under pre-ordained titles, for future reference. The abridgment was more systematic and comprehensive. A blank volume would be divided up into alphabetical titles—say, from *abatement* to *withernam*—and the compiler would work through year-books, inserting under the appropriate headings a precis or abridged text of each major proposition of law. The existence of these volumes indicates that year-books were being treated as sources of law.

Three abridgments of year-books were printed. The first was published in Rouen in about 1490 and has no title-page; it is called *Statham*, because tradition attributes it to Nicholas Statham (d. 1472), a baron of the Exchequer. In the sixteenth century came the larger and more widely used 'grand' abridgments of Fitzherbert and Brooke. Sir Anthony Fitzherbert (d. 1538) was a learned Common Pleas judge who owned a large collection of old legal manuscripts, including 'Bracton's Notebook' and many year-books now lost. His *Graunde Abridgement*, first published without title in 1514–16 when he was still a serjeant, was the prime example of this type of book and had a considerable effect on techniques of research and citation. It contained 13,845 entries. The *Graunde Abridgement* of Sir Robert Brooke (d. 1558), printed posthumously in 1573, was in some ways an improvement on Fitzherbert. It contained more items (over 20,000), including cases reported by Brooke himself, but the abridging was more drastic. These two great abridgments relieved the less industrious lawyers from having to make their own, and made it unnecessary for law students to read all the year-books through.

In the seventeenth century efforts were made to abridge the post-medieval reports. Epitomes of Plowden, Dyer and Coke were published in little pocket volumes; and three larger abridgments were produced. William Sheppard's *Epitome* (1656), later enlarged into a *Grand Abridgment* (1675), may have resulted from an attempt at codification; but it was a muddle, superficially analysed and inaccurate.

Of higher quality were William Hughes' *Grand Abridgement of the Law* (1660–63) and Henry Rolle's *Abridgment des Plusieurs Cases* (1668). The latter, published posthumously, had a stormy reception. Its publication was delayed by a lawsuit over copyright, and when it appeared it was castigated as a mere student's commonplace book. Vaughan CJ said he wished it had never been printed, since it contained so many conflicting opinions that it made the law ridiculous.[10] Yet, although the contents did little credit to a distinguished judge,[11] Rolle set the pattern for the future by using subdivisions which enabled the law to be analysed more minutely. Rolle's entries were incorporated in the later abridgments of Comyns and Viner.

Abridgments still more compendious were printed in the eighteenth century. Comyns' *Digest*, not printed until the 1760s, was the work of Sir John Comyns (d. 1740), Chief Baron of the Exchequer, and in its original state was the last English law book written in French. Matthew Bacon's *New Abridgment* (1763–66) shared with Comyns a high reputation well into the nineteenth century, and both passed through several editions. But the greatest of all the abridgments was the monumental *General Abridgment of Law and Equity* produced in twenty-three volumes between 1741 and 1753 by Charles Viner. It contained nearly all the substantive points to be found in the earlier abridgments and later reports, in carefully subdivided titles, with marginal annotations and cross-references. It is the eighteenth-century counterpart to Halsbury's *Laws of England* and the *English and Empire Digest*, and remains the first recourse for lawyers searching into pre-1800 law.

Although the abridgments were not of the same intellectual order as reports or textbooks, they provided a bridge between the two by systematising the confused mass of ideas in the reports and bringing together for comparison the authorities on particular areas of the law.

Formularies

During the first half of the thirteenth century were produced the first compilations of forms of writs. A collection of writs was called a 'register'. Whether there was ever one authoritative Chancery register is not known, but some of the early surviving manuscripts were owned by Chancery clerks and it seems probable that each master

10. *Legal History Studies 1972*, p. 7. For the suit, see Carter 89.
11. Rolle (d. 1656) was Chief Justice of the Upper Bench from 1648. After the Restoration he was usually known as Serjeant Rolle, having taken the coif in 1640.

made his own collection, basing himself on earlier versions which came to hand. All registers contained copies of original writs, in Latin; but they differed in scope and arrangement. Their size increased enormously in the thirteenth and fourteenth centuries, but they reached their final form when the older writs ceased development. The classical register was that printed from a fifteenth-century exemplar as *Registrum Omnium Brevium* in 1531. The register contained only a few early specimens of actions on the case, and no attempts were made to update it when those actions transformed the common law in the sixteenth century. That role fell to another type of formulary.

The other type appeared within a generation or two of the first registers, and was for the use of countors. The books of *narrationes* contained specimen counts, in law French, with occasional interspersed instructions for their use. They reached the peak of their development in the fourteenth century, when the manuscripts called *novae narrationes* (or 'new counts') gave a wide selection of counts and also of defences. The books went out of use, except for elementary educational purposes in the inns of court, when attention shifted to tentative special pleading.

The full art of tentative pleading could only be learned by observation, and study of the year-books, since it was a dynamic process and could not be captured in set formulae. However, once particular forms of special plea became established, there was a need for accessible precedents; and the rolls themselves were not readily accessible. The need was primarily that of the clerks who had to make the entries on the rolls, and it was the prothonotaries of the Common Pleas who first compiled 'books of entries' in the late fifteenth century. Since these were for assistance in drawing written pleadings, they were in Latin, not French. The replacement of the *narrationes* by the books of entries is itself clear evidence of a shift of emphasis from oral to written pleading.[12] By the sixteenth century there was a public demand for books of entries, to assist attorneys and counsel in drawing pleas themselves. The first to be printed was the *Intrationum excellentissimus liber* (1510), the authorship of which is unknown. The best were compiled by judges: William Rastell's *Colleccion of Entrees* (1566), based on at least three earlier collections, and Sir Edward Coke's *New Booke of Entries* (1614). Rastell and Coke both included a good selection of actions on the case, and in later books of entries these came to predominate. The later books of precedents of actions on the case effectively combined the functions of both registers and *narrationes*,

12. See pp. 71–72, ante.

and for this reason they continued to be produced from ever more modern precedents until the eighteenth century. The genre survives in Bullen and Leake's *Precedents of Pleading* (1st edn, 1860; 12th edn, 1975). The old books of entries are the least used of all early law books; but they are replete with learning which, though difficult to extract, the legal historian ignores at his cost.

Treatises

Treatises are not accorded the same authority in English jurisprudence as decisions of the courts, and for this reason we have placed them after law reports and books of entries. Yet it cannot be doubted that the greatest treatises have contributed materially to the development of the law as a coherent body of reasoned principles. A remarkable feature of the history of English legal literature, however, is the paucity of works deserving to be called literature. With a handful of notable exceptions, law books until recent times were devised not as original contributions to jurisprudence but as ancillary aids to practice or keys to source material.

'GLANVILL' AND 'BRACTON'

The story begins with the two early treatises *De Legibus et Consuetudinibus Angliae* ('of the laws and customs of England'). The first, attributed since the thirteenth century to the justiciar Ranulf de Glanvill but probably by another royal official, was written in about 1187 and is chiefly a compilation of writs with dilemmatic commentary in Latin. We have already noted its significance in the emergence of the common law.[13] The second, much larger treatise bears in some versions the name of Henry de Bracton (d. 1268). Maitland thought it was written in the 1250s, using plea rolls of the previous generation, which had first been collected into a notebook. Recent scholarship suggests that it was written in the 1220s and 1230s, using current plea rolls, and then brought up to date by Bracton, who added cases decided while he was a judge *coram rege* in the 1240s and 1250s, before it was variously treated by a succession of later editors. It gives a detailed and comprehensive account of the early common law, again based heavily on the writ system, but with much speculative substantive law as worked out by the compiler with help from decided cases and from Roman law. The number of surviving copies shows that it

13. See pp. 12–13, ante.

circulated very widely in the thirteenth and fourteenth centuries; but it failed to have a deep and lasting influence because it was written too soon. The compiler was able to survey the whole of English law with confidence only because it had not yet become clogged with sophisticated detail; special pleading had barely begun, and there were still no inns of court. There are signs in the treatise itself of reversals of opinion, and of successive attempts at updating. The work of the nascent legal profession soon left it completely behind. For background reading, the student of Edward I's time preferred smaller French introductions; while, for full initiation, the year-books and practice manuals were found more serviceable than a massive Latin treatise by a clerical judge of the old order. The obsolescence of Bracton left the common law without systematic exposition for five hundred years.

THE FOURTEENTH CENTURY

The principal contribution of the fourteenth century to legal literature was the year-books, but two little tracts on particular subjects pointed the way towards the textbook of later times. The *Old Tenures* presented a child's eye-view of the feudal land law, and the *Old Natura Brevium* gave a simple explanation of the original writs. Both are often bound together, and we know they were student primers in the fourteenth and fifteenth centuries. No one knows who wrote them.

THE FIFTEENTH CENTURY

More detailed exposition of particular branches of the law became the task of the readers in the inns of court, and many readings were taken down in writing by those present and circulated in later years. No full texts have survived before the time of Henry VI, though some fragments of fourteenth-century discussions of statute law have come to light. Readings were delivered on the legislation of the thirteenth century, and in treating of statutes such as *De Donis* readers were able to give ingenious and minute accounts of the intricacies of land law. The principles of property law and criminal law were repeatedly discussed and refined during these exercises, while points of pleading and procedure were discussed at moots. The written copies of readings might well be regarded as treatises, although none of the medieval readings were printed and they had a diminishing influence as sources of law in later centuries. Certainly the readings, written and unwritten, influenced the style and content of the treatises which eventually displaced them.

The only legal textbook of the fifteenth century[14] belongs to the same genre as the readings in court, but is cast in a more elementary form and was probably an attempt to replace the *Old Tenures*. The *New Tenures* was the work of Sir Thomas Littleton (d. 1481), a celebrated Common Pleas judge under Edward IV. He claimed to have written it for his son, Richard (d. 1518), who later became a bencher of the Inner Temple. Perhaps Richard turned it to profit in a way his father had not intended; but it is possible that manuscripts were in circulation before the author's death, and the private purpose may have been expressed out of professional modesty. From the date of its first publication in print in 1481 it was seized upon by the whole profession as a faithful guide to the common law of real property. Littleton wrote as the common law system was being overlaid by the complications of uses;[15] and this, helped by the easy fluency of his style, was to give his every word an authority enjoyed by no other writer before or since. In 1550 *Littleton* had been reprinted more often than the English translation of the Bible, and by 1600 it was 'not now the name of a lawyer, but of the law itself'.[16] With Coke's commentary it was basic reading for all law students until the mid-nineteenth century.

THE SIXTEENTH CENTURY

No writer in the sixteenth century applied Littleton's technique with the same brilliance to other branches of the law, but there was nevertheless a turn for the better in the production of good law books. The *Natura Brevium* was rewritten by Sir Anthony Fitzherbert, whose *New Natura Brevium* (1534) took account of recent developments and contained references to his *Graunde Abridgement*. Sir William Staunford (d. 1558), another Common Pleas judge, used the latter in compiling his two books on Crown law: *Les Plees del Coron* (1557) on the criminal law, and *An Exposicion of the Kinges Prerogative* (1548, but printed in 1567). In these works we see already a departure from Littleton. No longer, it seems, could a judge write on his own authority from well-known first principles. He must instead digest authorities. Style and clarity were, almost unwittingly, sacrificed to a profusion of citations. Staunford expressed the hope that other learned men would digest the whole of the common law, following the titles of Fitzherbert but with sufficient subdivision to lay bare the principles, so as 'to help

14. The writings of Fortescue are here excepted as being mainly on constitutional and philosophical topics. His *De Laudibus Legum Anglie* (c. 1470) discusses some features of English law by way of comparison with French law.
15. See pp. 212–219, 238–241, post.
16. W. Fulbecke *Direction or Preparative* (1600), f.27v.

the students of their long journey'.[17] Even to the best legal minds, therefore, digesting authorities seemed more worthwhile than expounding principles. That was the chief fault of the abridgments.

If settled law fared badly, the developing law fared worse. It is only in an advanced state of legal scholarship that nascent ideas find their way into print, and this accounts for the absence of any books about the evolving law of contract and tort or the actions on the case. Christopher St German's *Doctor and Student* (1528–31)[18] was for that reason alone a remarkable enterprise. Cast in the form of a dialogue between a doctor of divinity and a student of the common law about the relationship between law and conscience, a debate relevant at that time both to the controversy over the chancellor's jurisdiction[19] and to the extent of the spiritual jurisdiction of the ecclesiastical courts on the eve of the Reformation, it was not intended as a law book so much as a lawyer's view of moral philosophy written mainly for lay consumption. But it became very popular for its legal content, and the number of editions shows that it was second only to Littleton as a standard textbook until the eighteenth century.

THE SEVENTEENTH CENTURY

The increased printing activity of the seventeenth century brought a torrent of new law books, many of them badly written and of little value. The one noteworthy feature of these miscellaneous tracts is the range of subjects which they covered, including for the first time contract and tort. The best of the works touching on these newer topics was Sir Henry Finch's *Nomotechnia* (1613), a bold and enlightened essay at methodising the common law by dialectical techniques learned at Cambridge. Finch's analysis and definitions influenced later writers, though his book, written in law French, did not become a standard textbook and was not reprinted.[20] Attempts to expound the personal actions, for instance by William Sheppard in *Marrow of the Law* (1651), *Action upon the Case for Slander* (1662) and *Actions upon the Case for Deeds* (1663), were vastly inferior jumbles of cases and were barely an improvement on the abridgments. The two greatest legal writers of the century, as in the two preceding centuries, were judges.

17. *Exposicion of the Kinges Prerogative* (1567), preface.
18. Part I is said to have been printed in 1523, but no impression survives. The first known edition of Part I is dated 1528. Part II came out in 1530, but additions were made in 1531.
19. See pp. 90–91, ante.
20. Finch's *Law or a Discourse thereof* (1627), published posthumously in English, was more successful; but it was based on an earlier and less finished version of Finch's work.

When Sir Edward Coke was dismissed from office in 1616, and thereby effectively prevented from continuing his *Reports*, he channelled his literary energy into writing his *Institutes of the Laws of England*. Already 64 years of age, and with a heavy parliamentary career still ahead of him, Coke did not live to finish the complete project; but the four parts which he left are a lasting monument to his industry. The first part, published in 1628 and the only part Coke saw in print, was a *Commentary on Littleton*. Coke shovelled out his enormous learning in vast disorderly heaps,[21] piled around Littleton's *Tenures* to form a phrase by phrase gloss on the text. He delighted in wandering off at tangents, and in doing so covered many aspects of the common law which Littleton never hinted at. Coke seems to have been oblivious to the disorder, but the reader can easily forgive him. He wrote like a helpful old wizard, anxious to pass on all his secrets before he died, but not quite sure where to begin or end. The comment on the first section of *Littleton* provides a typical foretaste. The text is a definition of 'fee simple'; but the commentary wanders through such disparate topics as etymology, alien status, misnomer in grants, interest rates and usury, the precedence of earth over the other elements, the correct Latin words for ponds, marshes, rushes, willows, elders, and boileries of salt, the Domesday Book, the eight parts of a deed, the styles and titles of the kings of England, the ownership of the isle of Man, and the legal status of monsters and hermaphrodites. With all its faults, *Coke on Littleton* was the principal textbook on property law until the last century; and the nineteenth edition, encrusted with notes by Hale, Nottingham, Hargrave and Butler, is still much valued. The remaining three institutes consisted of a commentary on the older statutes, a treatise on the criminal law, and an account of the courts. The manuscripts were suppressed by the government for fear of any politically dangerous matter they might contain, but were printed in the 1640s.

Far superior to Coke, and indeed to all previous legal writers, was Sir Matthew Hale (d. 1676). Regarded, like Coke, as an oracle in his own time, Hale has had a more lasting influence and his views on criminal law are not infrequently cited in the courts to this day. His are the first English law books to possess a coherence and style with which the modern reader can feel at ease. Yet Hale's influence was delayed, because of his rather singular attitude to publication. Whereas he was quite prepared to unwrap his theological and scientific speculations to the public gaze, he consistently refused to publish what he had written on the subject he knew best, and even

21. F. W. Maitland *Collected Papers* (1911), vol. II, p. 484.

forbade publication by his descendants. The legal works were therefore posthumous publications, from his *History of the Common Law*
(1713) and the influential *History of the Pleas of the Crown* (1736) to the
more recent *Prerogatives of the King* (1976). Hale made considerable use
of history, but he was not truly a historian. The old rolls and year-
books which he used were a guide to the present, when properly
understood. His principal distinction was that he was able to organise
and present this arcane material in thoughtful and analytical treatises
marked by the clarity of their literary style.

THE EIGHTEENTH CENTURY

The slight character of the generality of law books continued in the
eighteenth century, the first half of which was more distinguished by
abridgments than by textbooks. The most prolific theoretical writer
was Sir Jeffrey Gilbert (d. 1726), who wrote elementary accounts of
most branches of the law, few of which were published in his lifetime.
His treatises served a useful purpose for a century or so, but hardly
stand comparison with Hale.

The magnum opus of the eighteenth century was Sir William
Blackstone's *Commentaries on the Laws of England* (1765), which were
based on the lectures he gave as Vinerian Professor at Oxford.[22] As
with Littleton and St German, the success of Blackstone is attributable partly to the discipline of trying to explain the law to educated
laymen. This Blackstone achieved in his lectures with such effect that
before long lecture-notes were being passed round, and it was the
circulation of corrupt copies which finally induced him to commit the
lectures to the press. Blackstone has been accused of complacence
about the state of the law, and of superficiality in his interpretation of
history; but no amount of criticism can destroy the fact that the
Commentaries were the first comprehensive survey of English law since
Bracton, and perhaps the most stylish and readable contribution ever
made to English legal literature. Just as Littleton had embalmed the
logic of medieval land law on the eve of its eclipse, so Blackstone
conveyed to a wide readership on both sides of the Atlantic ocean the
essential beauty and logic of a system of law and constitutional theory
about to be submerged by a wave of massive reform. Blackstone was
both a final survey of the old common law and the first textbook of a
new legal era.

THE NINETEENTH CENTURY

After Blackstone, the old 'black letter' type of law book was dead, but

22. See p. 148, ante.

the profession proved perfectly capable of rising to the high standards
he had set. Two distinct schools of writer may be identified in the
nineteenth century. The first was associated with a slightly reactionary burst of traditional common law scholarship in the face of the
drastic reforms, and it produced some of the greatest practical works
of reference of modern times. Examples which have stood the test of
time, although they have been rewritten by successive editors, are
Woodfall's *Landlord and Tenant* (1st edn, 1802; 27th edn, 1968), Archbold's *Pleading, Evidence and Practice in Criminal Cases* (1st edn, 1822;
39th edn, 1976), Chitty on *Contracts* (1st edn, 1826; 24th edn, 1977),
Byles on *Bills of Exchange* (1st edn, 1829; 23rd edn, 1972) and Williams
on *Executors and Administrators* (1st edn, 1832; 15th edn, 1970). The
second school resulted from the revival of academic law schools in the
later Victorian period, which switched the limelight from the special
pleaders and conveyancers to the universities, where our classic
textbooks—for instance, those of Pollock,[23] Anson[24] and Maitland[25]—were, like *Blackstone*, being born in the lecture rooms.[26]

Further reading

P. H. Winfield, *Chief Sources of English Legal History* (1925)
W. S. Holdsworth, *Some Makers of English Law* (1938)
T. F. T. Plucknett, *Early English Legal Literature* (1958)
J. H. Baker, 'The Dark Age of English Legal History' in *Legal
History Studies 1972*, pp. 1–27

YEAR-BOOKS

W. C. Bolland, *The Year Books* (1921); *Manual of Year Book Studies*
(1925)
F. W. Maitland, 'Of the Year Books in General' (1903) 17 SS ix–xx
G. J. Turner, *Year Book 4 Edward II* (1911) 26 SS ix–lxiv
A. W. B. Simpson, 'The Circulation of Yearbooks in the 15th
Century' (1957) 73 LQR 492–505; 'The Source and Function of
the later Year Books' (1971) 87 LQR 94–118
E. W. Ives, 'The Purpose and Making of the later Year Books'
(1972) 89 LQR 64–86
J. H. Baker, 'The last Year Books' (1978) 94 SS *164–170*

23. *Contract* (1876); *Partnership* (1877); *Jurisprudence* (1882); *Land Laws* (1883); *Torts*
(1887); etc.
24. *Contract* (1879); *Law and Custom of the Constitution* (1886).
25. *History of English Law before the time of Edward I* (1895); *Constitutional History of England*
(1887, first printed 1908); *Equity* (1888, first printed 1909).
26. This wave of scholarship affected the contemporary American law schools, particularly Harvard, which boasted the presence of Ames, Thayer, Holmes, Langdell and
Wigmore.

NAMED REPORTERS

J. W. Wallace, *The Reporters Arranged and Characterized* (4th edn, 1882)

T. F. T. Plucknett, 'The Genesis of Coke's Reports' (1942) 27 *Cornell Law Qly* 190–213

L. W. Abbott, *Law Reporting in England 1485–1585* (1973)

J. H. Baker, 'Coke's Note-Books and the Sources of his Reports' [1972A] CLJ 59–86; *The Reports of Sir John Spelman* (93 SS, 1977); *170–178;* 'Sir Thomas Robinson (1618–83), Chief Prothonotary of the Common Pleas' (1978) 10 *Bodleian Library Record* 29–40

ABRIDGMENTS AND FORMULARIES

J. D. Cowley, *A Bibliography of Abridgments* (1932)

E. Shanks and S. F. C. Milsom, *Novae Narrationes* (80 SS, 1963)

E. de Haas and G. D. G. Hall, *Early Registers of Writs* (87 SS, 1970)

PARTICULAR TREATISES

G. D. G. Hall (Ed), *Glanvill* (1965)

H. G. Richardson, *Bracton: the Problem of his Text* (1965)

S. E. Thorne (Ed), *Bracton De Legibus et Consuetudinibus Anglie* (1968–   ), esp. introduction to vol. III (1977)

C. M. Gray, *Hale's History of the Common Law* (1971)

G. Jones (Ed), *The Sovereignty of the Law: Selections from Blackstone's Commentaries* (1973)

T. F. T. Plucknett and J. L. Barton (Eds), *St German's Doctor and Student* (91 SS, 1974)

D. E. C. Yale, *Hale's Prerogatives of the King* (92 SS, 1976); *Hale as a Legal Historian* (SS Lecture, 1976)

P. Brand, 'Hengham Magna' (1976) 11 IJ 147–169

W. R. Prest, 'The Dialectical Origins of Finch's *Law*' [1977] CLJ 326–352

12. Law Making

Common lawyers liked to think of their law as an unchanging body of common sense and reasoning which was part of the heritage of the English people. If man's reason does not change, the law cannot change; it is only the application of old ideas to new social circumstances which creates the appearance of change. Judges are not appointed to change the law; 'their office is *jus dicere*, and not *jus dare*'.[1] Judicial decisions, therefore, do not make law but merely declare what it is; and the progress of legal history is a slow revelation and refinement of doctrines essentially immutable. Change when it comes must be imposed from without, by the legislature. And legislative changes, almost by definition, are at odds with natural reason. Sir Edward Coke wrote that it was 'a maxim of policy, and a trial by experience' that the alteration of any fundamental point of the common law was most dangerous, 'for that which hath been refined and perfected by all the wisest men in former succession of ages, and proved and approved by continual experience to be good and profitable for the common wealth, cannot without great hazard and danger be altered or changed'.[2] Sir John Davies, in the same vein, wrote that 'the customary law of England . . . doth far excel our written laws, namely our statutes or acts of parliament; which is manifest in this, that when our parliament have altered or changed any fundamental points of the common law, those alterations have been found by experience to be so inconvenient for the common wealth as that the common law hath in effect been restored again'.[3] Sir Matthew Hale, looking back over the preceding centuries, was not convinced that there had been any fundamental changes in the law, because 'the mutations hath not been so much in the law as in the subject matter of it'.[4]

1. F. Bacon *The Essayes* (1625), p. 316.
2. *Le Quart Part des Reportes* (1604), sig. B2ᵛ. Cf. Co Inst, vol. I, p. 379: 'Commonly a new invention doth offend against many rules and reasons of the common law, and the ancient judges and sages of the law have ever . . . suppressed innovation and novelties in the beginning.'
3. *Le Primer Report des Cases en Ireland* (1615), preface.
4. H. Rolle *Abridgement des Plusieurs Cases* (1668), preface.

This view of the common law and its relation to legislation is a reflection of lawyers' attitudes rather than of historical fact. The notion that the principles of the common law are somehow in existence before anyone has discovered what they are is a convenient figure of speech but not a statement of reality. At no time has the common law stood still. If it had not changed it would have no history. Changes in the law have sometimes come about through barely perceptible modifications and clarifications from case to case; at other times they have occurred swiftly and deliberately, through bold judicial decisions or reforming legislation. But never has the law been exempt from the ceaseless alteration to which all human creations are subject. Even the distinction between judicial and legislative change has not always been as fundamental as modern theory supposes. It is one of degree. The courts do make new law, but they do so within the framework of common law reasoning, whereas a sovereign legislature may legislate irrationally or unreasonably. Yet parliament has not always acted in a despotic manner. Few legislative acts before the last century could be regarded as radical departures from the common law tradition, and some lawyers genuinely regarded the acts of the medieval high court of parliament as the decisions of a supreme court of law.

In considering the techniques of law making, it is convenient to have in mind the famous thesis put forward by Sir Henry Maine. Referring to early societies in general, Maine advanced a 'general proposition of some value' regarding the agencies by which law can be brought into harmony with the current mores of a changing society: 'These instrumentalities seem to me to be three in number, Legal Fictions, Equity and Legislation . . . Their historical order is that in which I have placed them. I know of no instance in which the order of their appearance has been changed or inverted.'[5] The thesis implied a natural progress from making changes while pretending not to (fictions), through making exceptions in particular cases (equity), to direct change by virtue of authority or power. Nevertheless, in so far as it imposed an historical sequence on the harmonising influences, it is difficult to square with the English experience. To be fair to Maine, he used the terms 'fiction' and 'equity' in a broad sense rather than in the technical sense familiar to English lawyers. But, in focusing on English law, we shall be less liable to confusion if we separate fictions in the technical sense from the development of case law and if we separate the equity of the Court of Chancery from the equity which pervades the common law.

5. *Ancient Law* (1861), pp. 24–25.

CASE LAW AND PRECEDENT

There was probably never a time when the common law was not in some sense 'case law'. Glanvill, it is true, based his account of English law on the writs and only once referred to a specific case; but it is not unlikely that many of the writs were granted in particular cases after argument in council. By the time of the treatise called 'Bracton' (c. 1220–50), the influence of judicial decisions is apparent on the face of the text. The author of the preface expressly stated that he had written in order to prevent the newer generation of judges from unwittingly leaving the right course settled by their wise predecessors. The law made by those predecessors was preserved in their enrolled decisions. By the 1280s the very words of the judges and pleaders were being taken down in the year-books, and by the fourteenth century we find these books being cited as evidence of law and practice. When a judge of Edward II's time remarked, 'one may safely put that in his book for law',[6] he may have been addressing the reporter himself. As we read the year-books, we find the judges openly admitting that their decisions will be taken as precedents in future ages, and we find it maintained that a clear line of precedents should be followed even if the reason was not immediately apparent, for otherwise the 'young apprentices' would lose faith in their books of 'terms'.[7]

On the face of it, the present notion that cases are a source of law might seem to have been always the first principle of English jurisprudence. In truth, the differences from the current notion of precedent were greater in the year-book period than the similarities. The strict meaning of 'precedent' was a judgment entered on the roll; but the formal entry of the judgment gave no reasons, and in the majority of cases no law was made on the record.[8] Where a novel point was raised by demurrer, the medieval judges were notoriously reluctant to enter judgment at all if there was any disagreement between themselves; and so the plea rolls contain mostly common-form entries, with the occasional interesting question raised by the appearance of a new form. To the extent that new forms of pleading raised questions of law, they hardly ever settled them in a definitive way. If the parties went to issue without demurring in law, the record did not reveal whether the court had given the pleading its approval, or whether a serjeant had not chosen to stake his case on a doubtful point, or whether no one had thought the point worth arguing. The development of legal principles, in so far as it occurred in court, therefore

---

6. *Midhope v Prior of Kirkham* (1313) 36 SS 178 per Stanton J.
7. *Wyndham v Felbrigge* (1454) YB Mich 33 Hen VI, 38, pl.17, at f.41 per Prysot CJ.
8. See pp. 70–71, ante.

belonged to the oral part of the legal process which attracted the reporters. Yet we have already noticed that in this period much of the debate was tentative, extempore and inconclusive.[9] Case law could not, as a consequence, be based on judicial decisions.

The law which emerged in the course of argument was not law laid down by the court so much as law which was accepted learning within the profession: 'common erudition', as it is called in the old books. The judges were the chief repositories of this common learning, but what they said as a body was law mainly because it conformed to the reasoning of the little intellectual world of Westminster Hall. A common opinion of all the judges and serjeants in the Exchequer Chamber was the highest authority there could be. But if the judges could not agree on the law, the point under discussion could hardly be common learning and no majority judicial decision could make it so; judgment was accordingly withheld. This explains the seeming paradox that counsel's decision to withdraw points from argument, by reframing his plea, sometimes indicated the state of the law more clearly than the pressing of doubtful points on the court by demurrer. It also explains why there could have been no suggestion that a court was bound by a previous decision. To this extent it was true that judges did not make law. Their decisions were not sources of law, but simply evidence as to what the law was. Legal learning and reasoning transcended single instances, because the law must be free from error even if judges are not.

Increased emphasis on the judicial decision came in early Tudor times, and the change was connected with the new ways of raising questions of law. Those new procedures were, indeed, developed because lawyers and their clients consciously wanted more definitive rulings from the bench. As more law came to be settled upon demurrer or special verdict or motion after trial, the courts began to look at old precedents in a new way and to belittle the authority of those in which no considered decision was reached. The publication of abridgments, coupled with the printing of the year-books, facilitated the use of specific citations in argument. Fitzherbert, in his *New Natura Brevium* (1534), was the first writer to make a practice of discussing earlier cases critically.[10] At the same time, the courts took to a more methodical evaluation of precedents; cases could now be dismissed as out of date, or as aberrations, or as mere exchanges of opinion. The formal, deliberate judicial decision was thus becoming a source of

9. See pp. 69–70, ante.
10. See also p. 163, ante. No cases are cited in Littleton's *Tenures*, except in some later interpolations.

law, to be distinguished from the opinion or obiter dictum. By the time of Plowden, the distinction was fully recognised; earlier reports had mostly been based on 'the sudden speech of the judges upon motion of cases of the serjeants and counsellors at the bar: but all the cases here be matter in law tried upon demurrers, or be special verdicts containing matters in law, of which the judges had copies, studied them, and in most of them argued, and after great deliberation have given judgment. And so (as I think) there is most firmness and surety of law in this report.'[11]

Notwithstanding this fundamental change of attitude, the doctrine of the binding force of precedent did not appear for another three centuries or more. Vaughan CJ explained that, since judges sometimes made mistakes, precedents might be wrong. And, although error in a particular case could only be corrected by a court of error, because of the principle of *res judicata*,[12] judges were not bound to repeat the error in similar cases. If a judge considered a previous decision to be wrong, then, being sworn to do justice according to law, he ought not in conscience to follow it: 'for that were to wrong every man having a like cause, because another was wronged before'.[13] The desire for certainty was the chief restraining factor; but it could not be assured by rigidity. A strict adherence to precedent can actually increase uncertainty because it encourages over-subtle distinctions between cases essentially alike.[14]

It is sometimes suggested that the tide turned in the early nineteenth century, and that the principle of *stare decisis* was then elevated into inflexible dogma by conservative judges such as Lord Kenyon CJ and Parke B (later Lord Wensleydale). The *locus classicus* of the new thinking is said to be an opinion of Parke J (as he then was), in 1833, that rules derived from precedents were applied for the sake of uniformity and consistency even when they were 'not as convenient and reasonable as we ourselves could have devised'.[15] But the learned judge only said that precedents were to be followed 'when they are not plainly unreasonable and inconvenient'. Pollock CB later recalled that 'even Parke, Lord Wensleydale (the greatest legal pedant that I believe ever existed), did not always follow even the House of Lords; he did not over-rule . . . but he did not act upon cases which were nonsense'.[16] There was nothing new in Parke J's sentiment that

11. *Les Comentaries* (1571), prologue.
12. The principle that parties are estopped from denying the correctness of a final judgment. Without it there would be no end to a lawsuit.
13. *Bole v Horton* (1673) Vaugh 360, 383.
14. See *Darley v Reginam* (1846) 12 Cl & Fin 520 at 544 per Lord Brougham.
15. *Mirehouse v Rennell* (1833) 1 Cl & Fin 527 at 546.
16. Lord Hanworth *Lord Chief Baron Pollock* (1929), p. 198 (citing a letter of 1868).

accepted principles ought to outweigh judicial idiosyncrasies; it had often been said in the year-books. The truth is that, from the earliest period, there have been on the bench both 'timid souls' and 'bold spirits';[17] and that to seek uniformity of practice at different periods is to seek what never existed. It has also been the case that judges have treated rules of property law—including in due course the principles of equity relating to property—as standing in greater need of certainty than matters of contract and tort. Coke CJ, who spoke constantly of the need for certainty in the land law and strove to banish all the new-found conceits which had crept in since the Statute of Uses, promoted with equal vigour new developments in the law of contract and in the prerogative remedies of the subject against administrative bodies. Lord Mansfield CJ, perhaps the boldest of judicial spirits, often acted on the principle that 'as the usages of society alter, the law must adapt itself to the various situations of mankind'.[18] But in property matters he recognised the need for fixed rules; so much so that 'if an erroneous or hasty determination has got into practice, there is more benefit derived from adhering to it, than if it were to be overturned'.[19] In 1834 a learned barrister published a large collection of interesting but conflicting judicial pronouncements on the subject of precedent. He concluded that a court could be bound by a previous decision, but only if it was 'wholly unimpeachable' or if the objection to it was insufficient to shake its authority.[20] The judicial approach to precedent, far from being inflexible, could only be summarised by drawing a vicious circle.

The duty of repeating errors is a modern innovation, and one which many have come to regret. It may have resulted from the improved quality of law reports following the introduction of shorthand, which made the *ipsissima verba* of the judges available as an authentic text and made bold distinguishing more difficult. But it was more likely a result of the reformation and strengthening of the hierarchy of appellate courts in the last century. It is obviously a sensible discipline to require lower courts to abide by the rules settled by their superiors. But the hierarchical logic did not require courts to be bound by their own decisions, or by those of courts of comparable authority. That step was taken by the House of Lords in 1898, and by the Court of Appeal not until 1944. The theory would presumably require the

---

17. See *Candler v Crane, Christmas & Co* [1951] 2 KB 164 at 174, 178 per Denning LJ.
18. *Johnson v Spiller* (1784) 3 Doug 371 at 373. The remark prompted Lord Kenyon CJ to reply, 'I confess I do not think that the Courts ought to change the law so as to adapt it to the fashions of the times': *Ellah v Leigh* (1794) 5 Term Rep 679 at 682.
19. *Hodgson v Ambrose* (1780) 1 Doug 337 at 341.
20. J. Ram *Treatise on Legal Judgment* (1834).

Court of Appeal to follow without question decisions of the Exchequer Chamber, although that uncomfortable proposition has not yet been squarely faced.[21] The House of Lords in 1966 freed itself from the self-imposed fetter,[22] leaving only the Court of Appeal (Civil Division) and in some situations the divisional courts subject to such restraint. There has been some controversy in recent years as to whether the Court of Appeal should not revert to its earlier practice; but since 1969 there has been a procedure for by-passing that court where the House of Lords is to be invited to overturn a decision binding on the trial judge.[23]

After 1972 all English courts have been bound by statute to follow decisions of the European Court of Justice in matters of community law; but that court does not regard itself as bound by its own decisions, and an English court which has doubts may reopen a point by making a reference.[24] This radical innovation marks the beginning of a future chapter of legal history.

FICTIONS

Maine used the term 'Legal Fiction' in its widest sense, 'to signify any assumption which conceals, or affects to conceal, the fact that a rule of law has undergone alteration, its letter remaining unchanged, its operation being modified'.[25] An example of such a fiction is the extension of benefit of clergy to enable courts to avoid imposing the death penalty, first by treating anyone who could read as a 'clerk' and then by allowing clergy to persons who could not read or who were disqualified from being clergymen.[26] The more usual sense of the term is that of the Roman *fictio*, a false averment of fact which could not be traversed and so could not be shown to be false. We have seen how several English courts in the fifteenth and sixteenth centuries enlarged their jurisdictions by allowing fictitious allegations.[27] Fictions were also used to extend substantive remedies, the most familiar examples being the false allegation of deceit in *assumpsit*,[28] the false

---

21. Hints have been dropped, in *Drive Yourself Hire Co (London) Ltd v Strutt* [1954] 1 QB 250 at 272, 274; *Beswick v Beswick* [1966] Ch 538 at 552 per Lord Denning MR; *Tiverton Estates Ltd v Wearwell Ltd* [1975] Ch 146, [1974] 1 All ER 209.
22. *Practice Note* [1966] 3 All ER 77.
23. Administration of Justice Act 1969 (c.58), ss.12–16. The wording of s.12(3) recognises, perhaps for the first time in a statute, that a decision may be 'binding'.
24. European Communities Act 1972 (c.68), s.3(1); *Bulmer Ltd v Bollinger SA* [1974] Ch 401 at 419–420 per Lord Denning MR.
25. *Ancient Law* (1861), p. 26.
26. See pp. 422–423, post.
27. See pp. 38–40 (bill of Middlesex and *latitat*), 45 (*quominus*), 102, 104 (conciliar courts), 108 (admiralty), ante.
28. See p. 279, post.

allegation of a loss and finding in trover,[29] the false allegation of a lease and ouster in ejectment,[30] and the collusive common recovery.[31] In all these cases the pretence was of a fact which, if true, would have led to the desired result under established rules of law. If the untrue fact was not substantially material to the cause of action, but merely went to jurisdiction or to some procedural requirement of the forms of action, then no harm was done by pretending it to be true. No one was deceived by fictions, and there was nothing fraudulent about them. They were only allowed where their operation was fair and the effect desirable in the eyes of the court: *in fictione juris semper est aequitas*.[32] Nevertheless, once they had done their work of bringing about a change in the operation of the law, their continued repetition as common form added unnecessary mystery if not absurdity to the law. Eighteenth-century writers urged procedural reforms which would render them unnecessary, and one of the achievements of the nineteenth century was indeed to end fictions in the classical sense of the term. It is no longer permissible to make a false assertion in pleading, whatever the purpose. But fictions in the wider sense are by no means defunct, and are frequently combined with legislation in the form of conclusive presumptions, 'deeming' provisions and terms implied into contracts by law.

EQUITY AND LEGAL CHANGE

The equity of the Court of Chancery, like the fictions of the common law courts, proceeded from the premise that the course of the common law was notionally immutable. The just remedy was provided in Chancery, not by changing the law, but by avoiding its effect in the special circumstances of particular cases. So long as chancellors thought of themselves as providing ad hoc remedies in individual cases, there was no question of their jurisdiction bringing about legal change or making law. When, however, equity was regularised and reduced to known principles and rules, the overall content of English law could be said to have been thereby changed. The use and the trust, the equity of redemption, the doctrine of relief against forfeitures and penalties, and the equitable remedies of discovery, injunction and specific performance, were permanent additions to the substantive law which survived the abolition of the court.

The trust is an example of a legal institution which was later taken

29. See pp. 332–333, post.
30. See pp. 254–255, post.
31. See pp. 235–236, post.
32. Co Inst, vol. I, p. 150.

over and modified by legislation. It had begun as a mere trusting of someone, a situation where there was no legal protection; but it became a regular species of property and, under the legislation of 1925, became the sole means of creating future interests in land. There were other ways in which equity protected convenient arrangements which were originally outside the notice of the law but eventually came to be recognised legal institutions. The medieval landowner was enabled to leave his land by will, by conveying to third parties with instructions to carry out his last wishes; such an arrangement was protected by equity, whereas a legal power to devise land directly by will was not introduced till 1540.[33] Married women were given the capacity to own property by means of the 'separate use', centuries before they were given legal capacity in 1882.[34] New kinds of property, such as copyright and trademarks, were recognised in equity before parliament took them over.[35] And, in the last century, equity was moving towards the recognition of joint-stock companies with limited liability before the statutory foundations of modern company law were laid in 1844 and 1856.[36] Since the Judicature Acts there has been little sign of creative activity in the equitable jurisdiction of the Supreme Court, and it has been supposed that equity is 'past the age of childbearing'.[37] The principal equitable offspring of the twentieth century, the deserted wife's interest in the matrimonial home, was judicially exterminated; yet it did, even so, lead to a change in the law, because it was resurrected in statutory form.[38]

Legislation

Maine regarded legislation as operating in a completely different way from fictions and equity, because it changes law directly as an exercise of authority, whereas the other two techniques of modification rest on the assumption that the law does not change. Although it is doubtless correct to regard all forms of royal legislation as an exercise of

33. See pp. 217–218, post.
34. See pp. 396–397, post.
35. See pp. 380–381, 385–386, post.
36. C. A. Cooke *Corporation, Trust and Company* (1950), pp. 86–88. For a short history of company law, see L. C. B. Gower *Principles of Modern Company Law* (1969), pp. 22–64.
37. Harman J said in 1951 that 'Equity is not to be presumed to be of an age past childbearing': R. E. Megarry *A Second Miscellany at Law* (1973), p. 293. But the tag has passed into circulation in the reverse sense.
38. *National Provincial Bank Ltd v Ainsworth* [1965] AC 1175; Matrimonial Homes Act 1967 (c.75).

sovereign power, it may nevertheless be going too far to suppose that the earliest legislation was primarily intended to alter the course of the law. The Anglo-Saxon codes, as we have seen, were more concerned with clarification and unification than with innovation. The Normans and Angevins were fond of legislation, which they produced in various forms: the Assize of Northampton, the Constitutions of Clarendon, the Great Charter, the Provisions of Oxford, and so on. These enactments, however, and many more which have been lost, were not changing the common law; they were making it. And it is not to be assumed that contemporaries thought of this method of law making as different in character from the function of the judges. What in later times were seen as two distinct features of the constitution—the king as head of the legislative assembly in parliament, and the king as head of the judicial system—had their origins in a less sophisticated notion of kingship in which legislation and adjudication were not distinguishable. If the judges could reserve cases of difficulty for the king to decide in person or in council, so the king and council could give general directions to the judges for the future. It is likely that the writ system was first developed in this way, and possible that rules of law were treated in similar fashion.

The parliamentary form of modern legislation is rarely encountered before the end of the thirteenth century, and the consent of the House of Commons was probably not regarded as indispensable until after 1400.[39] The present bill procedure was not settled until early Tudor times. It is therefore anachronistic to regard medieval legislation as an authoritative text in quite the modern sense. The text was written law, certainly, but it was not a text which had been pored over word for word in both houses, with debates upon verbal amendments. In the case of some early statutes, the drafting was done by the clerks and judges after assent had been given. A statute represented the terms of a decision upon a complaint or petition; a decision of the highest authority in the land, but not different in kind from decisions by inferior branches of the *Curia Regis*. This accounts both for the freedom with which statutes were interpreted and for the otherwise inexplicable lack of early definitive texts. Until 1299 there was no official procedure for enrolling parliamentary statutes; from that year an official, but still incomplete, roll was kept in the Chancery. A parallel record, the rolls of parliament (which began in 1290), contained only part of the legislation together with other acts of parlia-

---

39. It was established in the principle that amendments contrary to the terms of Commons' bills had to be resubmitted to the Commons: Rot Parl, vol. IV, p. 22, no. 10 (1414); *Pilkington's Case* (1455) YB Pas 33 Hen VI, 17, pl.8.

ment, including decisions in litigation. In the absence of official records, the public and their lawyers relied on private collections of statutes, many examples of which survive from monastic or legal libraries. These manuscripts varied from each other and were never wholly complete; indeed, there was no definitive guide as to what should be included, and the occasional statute may have escaped notice altogether.[40] They sometimes contained writs and ordinances, and even passages from Glanvill, masquerading as statutes. By professional usage some of these spurious texts became 'statutes' for practical purposes, although properly they were regarded as evidence of the common law rather than of legislation.[41] These private statute-books formed the basis of the series of printed statutes which began to appear in 1481 and were frequently re-edited in later generations as the 'statutes at large'. Not until 1822 was an official edition of the old statutes (down to 1713) published; but even the impressive volumes of *Statutes of the Realm* were acknowledged to be incomplete and to contain apocrypha. In the case of medieval legislation, it may be said that tradition was of greater practical force than sovereign authority.

In Tudor times the character of parliamentary legislation underwent a significant change. The reason was partly procedural, for developments in bill procedure towards the end of the fifteenth century meant that legislation was 'no longer the government's vague reply to vaguely worded complaints, but rather the deliberate adoption of specific proposals embodied in specific texts'.[42] And it was partly political. The Tudors exalted parliament, and expected somewhat in return. The king in parliament became prodigiously industrious. Under Henry VIII, some 677 statutes were passed, occupying almost as much space as all the preceding legislation from Magna Carta onwards, and many of the statutes were of immense political significance. The achievements of the Reformation Parliament in spiritual matters established the legislative supremacy of parliament against its only remaining rival, the once universal Church. And in the temporal sphere parliament ventured to the limits of legal possibility: entailing the Crown, fictional livery of seisin,[43] new treasons of

---

40. E.g. the Royal Marriages Act 1428, which was discovered in 1977: R. A. Griffiths, 93 LQR 248; G. O. Sayles, 94 LQR 188.

41. *Re Sir John Skrene, decd.* (1475) YB Mich 15 Edw IV, 13, pl.17 per Littleton J (who also points out that Magna Carta 1215 was not a parliamentary statute); *Swaffer v Mulcahy* [1934] 1 KB 608. Some of these texts may represent legislation, but of a pre-parliamentary kind.

42. T. F. T. Plucknett, 60 LQR at 248.

43. For the Statute of Uses 1535, see p. 217, post.

appalling width, even boiling in oil. Attempts were made to control the environment and the economy by legislation. The changes wrought by parliament in the Tudor period were no more significant than those effected by the courts, but they were definitely seen as changes, the work of humanist legislators confident in their ability to improve things by the right use of power. With this new concept of legislation came a new reverence for the written text. Legislative texts were now drawn with such skill by Crown lawyers, in advance of parliament, and explained in such extensive and explicit preambles, that the judges were manifestly being discouraged from the creative exegesis they had bestowed on medieval statutes.

ACTS OF PARLIAMENT AS 'JUDGMENTS'

The changes in the character of legislation were disguised by constitutional theory. Parliament continued to be regarded as a 'high court', distinguished from other courts chiefly in that its acts were not reversible for error and were therefore not tied to the course of the common law. Sir Henry Finch wrote of parliament as having 'absolute power in all cases, as in making laws, adjudicating upon matters in law, trying capital cases, and reversing errors in the King's Bench; and especially is this the proper court where there is some common mischief which the ordinary course of the law has no means to remedy. And all things that they do are like judgments.'[44] The judgments were not *inter partes*, but they bound everyone, on the medieval principle that since all the estates of the realm were represented in parliament every person was 'privy' to its acts. By Finch's time, however, there were obvious procedural differences between the bill procedure and the judicial procedure. Sir Matthew Hale perceived and demonstrated the ambiguity of the phrase 'high court of parliament', which at different periods had borne different senses. Most of the judicial work had long been appropriated to the House of Lords; for, 'although in truth the king and both houses of parliament make the entire supreme court of this kingdom; yet very often, in parliamentary records of writs, *curia nostra in parliamento*, and *curia parliamenti*, is applicable to the lords' house'. Hale therefore distinguished the legislative or 'deliberative' function of parliament from the contentious or 'judicative'. The former looked to the future, the latter to things already done. Even so, Hale treated the functions as being of like nature. The House of Lords, he argued, could not be the supreme court of final appeal because, if it were, 'then is the legislative power virtually and consequentially there also'. The test was whether the

44. *Nomotechnia* (1613), ff.21v–22 (translated).

House could give judgment against an act of parliament. Hale said that it could not, and therefore it was not supreme. The argument now seems rather academic; but it shows us that, as late as the seventeenth century, lawyers saw no fundamental difference between judicial and parliamentary law making. For Hale, the supreme power of making laws and the supreme power of deciding cases had to reside in the same body.[45] *Jus dicere* was *jus dare*.

STATUTE LAW AND THE COURTS

English lawyers never doubted the authority of parliament to make new laws and to bind all courts, excepting only future parliaments. Sir John Fortescue said in 1453 that 'this high court of parliament . . . is so high and so mighty in its nature, that it may make law, and that that is law it may make no law'.[46] Nearly two centuries later, Sir Edward Coke wrote that the power and jurisdiction of parliament in making statutes 'is so transcendant and absolute as it cannot be confined either for causes or persons within any bounds'.[47] Nevertheless, in the application and interpretation of the legislative acts of this supreme court, the judges formerly enjoyed the like freedom as they had in applying and interpreting the common law of their own courts. The judges as assistants to the Lords often helped to prepare legislation, and were well acquainted with the policy behind it. In applying the spirit of the law, the medieval judges paid scant respect to the letter. This freedom was rationalised in terms of the Aristotelian concept of equity as a corrective of general laws.[48] 'It is not the words of the law but the internal sense of it that makes the law . . . and it often happens that when you know the letter you know not the sense, for sometimes the sense is more confined and contracted than the letter, and sometimes it is more large and extensive'.[49] Equity, which would 'enlarge or diminish' the letter of the law, was in this sense to be applied in all the courts and not solely in the Chancery. The test which Plowden proposed for finding the equitable construction of a statute was remarkably like the officious bystander test so familiar to modern students of contract: 'Suppose that the lawmaker is present, and that you have asked him the question you want to know touching the equity; then you must give yourself such an answer as you imagine he would have done if he had been present.'[50]

45. *The Jurisdiction of the Lords House, or Parliament* (F. Hargrave edn, 1796), esp. pp. 17, 85, 205–207; *The Prerogatives of the King* (D. E. C. Yale edn, 1976), p. 181.
46. *Re Thomas Thorp, speaker-elect* (1453) Rot Parl, vol. V, p. 239.
47. Co Inst, vol. IV, p. 36.
48. See p. 90, ante.
49. Plowden's note to *Eyston v Studde* (1574) Plowd 459 at 465.
50. Ibid., 467.

Some judges may have taken the equitable approach so far as to believe that an unreasonable statute could be totally disregarded. Theoretical justifications for such a belief would have been hard to formulate, and few attempts were made. One interesting fifteenth-century suggestion was that the clerk of parliament might be presumed to have erred in recording what no parliament could be taken to have intended.[51] The boldest statement, which has been the foundation of the practice of 'judicial review' of legislation in America, was that of Coke in reporting a case of 1610: 'it appears in our books that in many cases the common law will control acts of parliament and sometimes adjudge them to be utterly void; for when an act of parliament is against common right and reason, or repugnant, or impossible to be performed, the common law will control it and adjudge such act to be void'. There is no doubt that this was Coke's considered opinion at the time, and the passage has been found written out twice in his own hand.[52] There is some doubt, however, as to whether it reflected the views of his brethren. Lord Ellesmere C reacted sharply, saying it was more fitting 'that acts of parliament should be corrected by the same pen that drew them than to be dashed in pieces by the opinion of a few judges'.[53] In his speech to Coke's successor as Chief Justice, Ellesmere inveighed against the view that judges 'have power to judge statutes and acts of parliament to be void if they conceive them to be against common right and reason', which was for the king and parliament to judge.[54] The context of Coke's remark was a statute which appeared to infringe a principle of 'natural justice'. Hobart CJ shared Coke's view that 'even an act of parliament, made against natural equity, as to make a man judge in his own cause, is void in itself, for *jura natura sunt immutabilia*'.[55] It seems from Coke's *Fourth Institute*, however, that on further consideration Coke relented. As to natural justice, he recounted a story that Henry VIII had asked his judges whether an attainder in parliament could be called in question if the person attainted had not been given an opportunity to defend himself; they had replied that they hoped parliament would never do it, but if it did the act could not be questioned. Coke then listed some oppressive

51. Reading cited in 94 SS *44*, n.10. No court, however, could question the record of parliament for error.
52. *Dr Bonham's Case* (1610) 8 Co Rep 114, 118; Cambridge Univ Lib MS Ii. 5. 21(2), f.93v; Yale Law Sch Lib MS G.R. 24/1, f.157v.
53. 'Observations on Coke's Reports', printed in L. A. Knafla *Law and Politics in Jacobean England* (1977), p. 307.
54. *Speech to Sir Henry Mountague* (1616) Moore KB 826, 828. He added, however, 'I speak not of impossibilities or direct repugnancies.'
55. *Day v Savadge* (1614) Hob 85 at 87.

statutes, and the lesson he drew was moral rather than legal; they were 'a good caveat to parliaments to leave all causes to be measured by the golden and straight metwand of the law, and not to the incertain and crooked cord of discretion'.[56] Little more was heard of judicial review in England, and Coke's earlier doctrine was whittled down into a presumption to be applied only where a statute was ambiguous. The moral proposition alone has remained. Parliament cannot make bad good, nor can it make possible the impossible. But it can make bad law, and it can prescribe a punishment for those who fail to do the impossible.

Blackstone said that to permit judicial review of unreasonable legislation 'were to set the judicial power above that of the legislature, which would be subversive of all government'.[57] Now this principle has in turn been carried too far, so as almost to eliminate the equitable approach to interpretation. When Denning LJ tried in one case to find the intention of parliament and give effect to it by filling in gaps in the wording, Lord Simonds rebuked him for 'a naked usurpation of the legislative function under the thin disguise of interpretation'.[58] The only survival of the doctrine of the equity of a statute is the 'mischief rule', another of Coke's formulations, which permits ambiguous legislation to be interpreted in such a way that it will be effective to suppress the mischief which it was designed to eliminate.[59]

Law Reform Movements

The many reforms effected by judicial decision and statute before the eighteenth century were sometimes sweeping, but rarely if ever radical. They presupposed and followed established reasoning and known concepts. The resulting edifice was likened by Blackstone to a gothic cathedral, an amalgam of different styles of architecture, full of venerable monuments alongside modern embellishments, always in need of repair but nonetheless a pleasing structure, its utility and unity unimpaired by the vicissitudes of time and the changing fashions of the outside world. The legal profession in general would have relished the metaphor. Lawyers well know the danger and uncertainty which attend drastic changes in the law. Coke, who effected many moderate reforms himself as a judge, saw the dangers and wrote repeated warnings. Hale, a notable law reformer, thought that much

56. Co Inst, vol. IV, pp. 37, 41.
57. Bl Comm, vol. I, p. 90.
58. *Magor and St Mellons RDC v Newport Borough Council* [1952] AC 189 at 191.
59. *Heydon's Case* (1584) 3 Co Rep 7.

of the 'itching' for change among the people at the time of the interregnum was caused by ignorance, fear, and envy of the lawyers; it was as necessary to avoid 'error in the excess, the over-busy and hasty and violent attempt in mutation of laws' as it was to avoid 'error in the defect, a wilful and over-strict adhering in every particular to the continuance of the laws in the state we find them'.[60] The sword of justice must be kept free from rust, but it cannot be brandished at random without doing untold harm. Professional conservatism is, however, a virtue easily misunderstood by the lay public. In a world of *latitats* and demurrers and rebutters, when lawyers wrote notes in French and kept records in Latin, and when every lawsuit followed a labyrinthine path strewn with parchment and ink and fictions and fees, laymen could be forgiven for thinking that the whole structure had been designed to increase the income of lawyers. At two periods of history popular dissatisfaction with the state of the law reached such a peak that parliament initiated extensive programmes of reform. Both movements were concerned mainly to improve the procedure and institutions of the law rather than its substantive doctrines. In more recent times, planned law reform has spread to every branch of the law and has become a permanent and unsettling feature of the legal system.

THE CIVIL WAR AND INTERREGNUM

The period from 1640 to 1660 is usually characterised as an age of revolutionary reform. In 1640 there had not been a parliament since 1629 and dissatisfaction with the common law had reached a climax following the *Case of Ship-money* (1638). The Long Parliament wasted no time in starting; away went the Star Chamber and High Commission and conciliar courts in 1641, to be followed in a few years by all the ecclesiastical courts. Then there was the Norman yoke to be cast off, by the abolition of military tenures and the Court of Wards in 1645, and of the use of Latin and law-French in 1650. In 1649 the monarchy itself was displaced. What was to be done next? If kings could be done away with, no other legal institution could be beyond question, and in the years that followed there was protracted discussion of law reform. Hundreds of pamphlets circulated, more than at any previous period, as a result of the withdrawal of press licensing. The revolutionary voices were the loudest, and they did not spare law or lawyers. The Levellers wanted to abolish the whole of the common law, including its courts and practitioners, and replace it by a

---

60. *Considerations touching the Amendment of Lawes* in F. Hargrave (Ed) *Law Tracts* (1787) vol. I, pp. 249, 253.

pocket-book code in plain man's English. Their law would be administered by laymen who conformed to party standards. This was not to be, save at the level of county magistrates.[61] The questioning spirit did, however, enter more moderate hearts and it was the reforming lawyers who achieved the most in practice. The weightiest proposals were those produced by Sir Matthew Hale's law commission of 1652, which contained a few radicals but was dominated by lawyers who laboured to keep discussion on a technical plane. The commission looked into the simplification of mesne process, the abolition of fictions, the reform or abolition of special pleading, the introduction of county courts for small claims, the abolition of imprisonment for debt, and the introduction of civil marriage and of land registration. In all these areas they anticipated the reforms of the nineteenth century by nearly two centuries. Many of the suggestions were acted upon. Some steps were even taken to reform the Chancery, the thorniest problem for reformers then and later.

The reforms were mostly reversed in 1660, saving that the conciliar courts and feudal revenue were not resurrected. As for the rest, including the use of Latin in records, and fictions,[62] the interregnum legislation was treated as void. The disinclination to sever the good from the bad was an understandable reaction to the repressive illiberality of the bad legislation. Military dictatorships are not renowned for their jurisprudence, and the unlearned members of parliament had not known when to stop. Their High Court of Justice was worse than the Star Chamber had ever been, because it could inflict the death penalty without the safeguards of indictment or jury trial; it was the most fearsome political tribunal ever suffered in England. The Blasphemy Act of 1648 had made it a capital offence to deny the Trinity, or the authority of the scriptures, or that the bodies of men rose again after death, or that there would be a last judgment. Two years later, fornication (on a second conviction) and adultery were made capital offences. Actors and popular musicians were to be punished as rogues and whipped. The licentiousness of Charles II's court was an overreaction against this state of affairs; but it is small wonder that the legislative reaction was blind. Reform was not killed stone dead. Many of the ideas continued to be discussed later in the seventeenth century. But 1660 marked the end of a powerful, and to many rather frightening, law-reform movement. England would be

61. Revised guides to the law of justices, for the use of the party men now placed on the benches, were produced at government instigation by William Sheppard.
62. For an unsuccessful attempt to abolish the fictitious bill of Middlesex in 1661, see p. 42, ante.

free of law commissions for centuries to come. Men of Hale's quality were better employed on the bench than as committee men trying to reconcile absurd opinions and thrash out irrational compromises.

THE NINETEENTH CENTURY

The second wave of systematic reform hit the English legal system in the second quarter of the nineteenth century, and we have already noticed many of its effects. The changed intellectual climate which brought it about has often been associated with the name of Jeremy Bentham (1748–1832), an eccentric genius who wished to reduce jurisprudence to the principles of a natural science. Bentham had attended Blackstone's lectures at Oxford in 1763 and had been called to the bar, but he disliked Blackstone's attitude in apologising for the status quo with such eloquence, and he regarded the common law with contempt. He set himself the life-long task of constructing a rational legal system from first principles. To this end he evolved a method called 'deontology', the logic of the will, the science not of what is but of what ought to be. The basic premise to which this method was to be applied was the principle of utility which Bentham had distilled from the works of Beccaria and Priestley. The end of all law should be the greatest good of the greatest number, the optimum balance between pain and pleasure. Bentham proceeded to try the 'whole province of jurisprudence' by this test of expediency, setting pleasures against pains and reconciling conflicting human interests in minutest detail by applying his 'felicific calculus'.

The peculiar originality of Bentham's ideas, and the oddity of his language, held little attraction for contemporary lawyers. Preoccupied as he was with the elaboration of his abstract jurisprudence, he would not cultivate the ability to compromise which was necessary if specific reforms were to be carried through parliament. The one scheme with which Bentham did persevere on a practical level—the Panopticon, a new kind of prison based on the beehive—met with failure and financial loss. Bentham himself despaired of seeing his legislative science put into practice, and contented himself with writing for future generations. His death came, with ironic symbolism, on the eve of the 1832 Reform Act. Yet, if Bentham's writings were esoteric, his personal influence on the leading reformers of the next generation cannot be doubted. He provided the practical men with the theoretical justifications for what they were trying to do. To Lord Brougham (1788–1868), 'the age of law reform and the age of Bentham are one and the same thing'.[63]

63. *Lord Brougham's Speeches* (1838), vol. II, p. 287.

It was Brougham who took the lead in setting the parliamentary reforms in motion. Brought up in Scotland, arrogant and impetuous of character, Henry Brougham had sufficient contempt for the English common law and its practitioners to be capable of pressing forward drastic measures regardless of professional feeling. His ideas, though not as extravagantly radical as Bentham's, must have seemed anathema to men steeped in the ancient lore and practice of Lincoln's Inn and Westminster Hall. Brougham began his campaign as a young advocate, in the pages of the *Edinburgh Review*, and continued it in Bentham's *Westminster Review*. On coming to England, and being elected as a Whig member of parliament, he represented himself as the broom which could sweep the cobwebs from Westminster Hall. He announced his programme from the floor of the House of Commons on 7 February 1828 in a celebrated speech which lasted six hours. The notable spiders who had spent their lives spinning the threads of the old system in the dusty purlieus of the law immediately voiced their terror at the thought of impending doom. Brougham swept on, becoming Lord Chancellor in 1830, and after a mass of preliminary investigations and reports by parliamentary committees most of his proposals were put through in the following decades.

Dicey discerned two consecutive trends in the reforms of the nineteenth century. The first, which he assigned to the period 1825–70, he labelled 'Benthamism, or Individualism'. The reforms of this period were characterised as promoting individual liberties, or improving the means of protecting the rights of the individual. This was followed by a 'period of Collectivism' stretching from about 1865 until Dicey's time and beyond. The principal objects of collectivist legislation were groups of people rather than isolated individuals, and the interests of groups were promoted to the detriment of individual freedom. To some extent this reflected a shift of emphasis from the middle to the inferior classes; there was, for instance, the rise of trade unionism and its legalisation, the improvement of factory conditions and the protection of workmen against loss from industrial injuries by compulsory insurance. The latter period is also marked by paternalistic legislation which, at the expense of individual liberty to do what one liked with one's own resources, imposed minimum standards for the good of the community and paid for improvements out of compulsory taxation. This last trend greatly increased the range of government activity and power and led to what in the twentieth century is called the Welfare State. The new style of governance demands an awesome volume of legislation and delegated legislation. It has encouraged modern governments to encroach further and further on individual liberty in promoting ideological programmes of social reform. Political programmes such as these can hardly be termed law reform movements, since the results are by their nature insecure and relatively impermanent. But one direct consequence of constant sweeping change has been its neutralising effect on the judiciary. The old values embodied in the common law have been so shaken that the judges no longer have confident views as to what is right and wrong. Rather than embroil themselves in politics, the judges shelter behind the doctrine of sovereignty of parliament and adhere to the letter of the law. Even the task of improving the common law and ironing out inconsistencies has, by the establishment of the Law Commission in 1965, effectively been withdrawn from the judges and from the adversary system of exploring problems. Law reform has itself been institutionalised. Some have heralded this as progress. But when judges conceive their only role to be the discovery of facts and the interpretation of words, while the legislators are interested only in political warfare, then justice is a precarious commodity.

CODIFICATION

Roman law began, and ended, with a code. However little English law owed to Roman ideas, the example of the Romans always lurked in the background and inspired would-be codifiers of the common law in every century since at least the fifteenth. The idea behind 'codification'[64] is that legal principles should be laid down authoritatively in written form, so as to dispel the doubts and uncertainties which attend law derived from cases or from juristic literature. In its most extreme form, the compilation of a code may involve rewriting the whole law; at its least drastic, it is a matter of editing the existing sources of the law under legislative authority. Many have been the visions of a code of English law, but little has been the practical achievement.

Two or three university men in Henry VIII's reign advocated the reduction of English law into a Latin code after the Roman example, but the only attempt at a draft chapter was not calculated to inspire confidence in the idea. Staunford, a learned judge, put forward the more attainable proposition of a digest of the common law, following the titles of Fitzherbert's *Abridgement*, but with the material so ordered that the governing principles were made apparent.[65] Francis Bacon spent over twenty years working out a scheme for reshaping the law. In the parliament of 1593 he introduced his plan for reducing the

64. The word was introduced into the English language by Bentham.
65. See pp. 163–164, ante.

volume of statutes, which were 'so many in number, that neither the common people can practise them nor the lawyer sufficiently understand them'. Four years later, that task was committed to all the lawyer members of the House of Commons. Nothing seems to have been achieved. In 1607, James I invited parliament to scrape the rust off the laws, so that they 'might be cleared and made known to the subjects', a suggestion which he elaborated (probably at Bacon's behest) in 1609. The idea was to reconcile conflicting decisions, discard obsolete material, and prepare an authoritative restatement of the law. Bacon himself expounded this plan in his *Proposition touching the Amendment of the Law* (1616), and called for digests of the common and statute laws, with law commissioners to revise them and keep them up to date. The prospect was daunting, and Bacon's hopes were not fulfilled. His own attempt to formulate the elements of the common law was as lacking in order and analysis as Coke's *Institutes*. Coke himself was against the project, because he thought abridgments confused those who used them. If Coke and Bacon could not produce a code, who could?

Bacon's 'great law reform project' was very much a lawyer's project. He did not wish to abolish the common law and put all its principles into statutory form, because like most of his contemporaries he regarded written law as technically inferior: 'there are more doubts that arise upon our statutes, which are a text law, than upon the common law, which is no text law'.[66] He wished merely to arrange and prune the sources of the law in order to simplify research. Later projects tended to be more far-reaching. Hale, the most restrained of the campaigners, wanted to see a *Corpus Juris Communis* in the Roman manner; he alone could have written such a code, but we have seen how reluctant he was to put his learning in print. Less informed writers wanted a little booklet which could be carried in the pocket and read aloud in church on Sundays; none of them seems to have prepared a draft. Bentham, as might be expected, went further than anyone. His code was to be derived from the principle of maximum felicity, and was to take no account whatsoever of the previous common law; he thought he could as easily produce a code for Russia as for England. This was an age of codification, and Bentham lived to see the French *Code Napoléon* (1804) adopted or imitated by many European countries. But he did not live to see even a draft English code, and his notions of codification have received no serious support since his death.

Some experiments in more modest types of codification were carried

66. *Life and Letters of Bacon* (J. Spedding edn, 1872), vol. VI, p. 67.

out in the nineteenth century. Much of the common law was codified between 1830 and the 1860s for use in India, and with such success that the matter was reopened in England. In 1853, Lord Cranworth C proposed a consolidation of statute law which he hoped would form a Code Victoria. The proposal foundered in a profusion of different ideas as to what it was meant to achieve. The principal outcome was the Criminal Law Consolidation Acts of 1861, and there also began the long series of Statute Law Revision Acts. Lord Westbury C raised the matter of codification in parliament in 1863, and his plea resulted in the establishment of a royal commission under the chairmanship of Lord Cranworth in 1866 'to enquire into the expediency of a Digest of Law'.[67] The commission recommended the preparation of digests of particular branches of the law, and jurists were invited to submit specimen drafts. At first it looked as though no one would be so bold or immodest as to take up the challenge, and in 1875 one writer said the scheme was universally considered worse than useless.[68] But in 1876 Sir James Fitzjames Stephen published his *Digest of the Law of Evidence*, and the following year his *Digest of the Criminal Law*. Interest in the latter led to the appointment of another royal commission, which in 1879 actually produced a Criminal Code; but the enactment of this code was defeated after opposition from Cockburn CJ. Meanwhile Professor Pollock had published a *Digest of the Law of Partnership* (1877), and Judge Chalmers, acknowledging the example set by Stephen and Pollock, put out a *Digest of the Law of Bills of Exchange* (1878). The last-named was the first to make the statute book, as the Bills of Exchange Act 1882, followed by Pollock's work as the Partnership Act 1890. Chalmers also drew up a digest of the law of sale, which became the Sale of Goods Act 1893. These digests were more in the tradition of Justinian, Staunford and Bacon than of Bentham. Their object was to restate in clear language the case law of the time, and the texts were supported by reference to the decisions on which they were based. Chalmers believed this was the only way to start: 'I am sure,' he wrote in 1883, 'that further codifying measures can be got through Parliament if those in charge of them will not attempt too much. Let a codifying bill, in the first instance, simply reproduce the existing law, however defective. If the defects are patent and glaring, it will be easy enough to get them amended.'[69] Pollock took an even more conservative view of the function of a code:

67. See T. E. Holland 'Codification' (1867) 27 *Edinburgh Rev* 347–376; *Plan for the Formal Amendment of the Law of England* (1867).
68. R. K. Wilson *History of Modern English Law* (1875), pp. 184–185.
69. *Digest of the Law of Bills of Exchange* (1964 edn), p. xlii.

'Codes are not meant to dispense lawyers from being learned, but for the ease of the lay people and the greater usefulness of the law. The right kind of consolidating legislation is that which makes the law more accessible without altering its principles or methods.'[70] There is little reason, however, why clear expositions of this nature should not remain in textbook form. Textbooks may guide without relying on force. Textbooks have indeed proliferated, whereas proposals for codification in recent times have usually been coupled with law reform. Since 1965 the Law Commission has had a standing charge to review the law with a view to its development, reform and possible codification.[71] Few regard the latter prospect with any pleasure, since 'to reduce unwritten law to statute is to discard one of the great blessings we have for ages enjoyed in rules capable of flexible application'.[72]

Further reading

Holdsworth HEL, vol. II, pp. 299–311, 406–484; vols. IV and XI, passim; vol. XII, pp. 146–162

Plucknett CHCL, pp. 315–350

J. W. Gough, *Fundamental Law in English Constitutional History* (1955)

C. K. Allen, *Law in the Making* (7th edn, 1964)

D. E. C. Yale, 'Hobbes and Hale on Law, Legislation and the Sovereign' [1972B] CLJ 121–156

COMMON LAW

T. E. Lewis, 'The History of Judicial Precedent' (1930–32) 46 LQR 207–224, 341–360; 47 LQR 411–427; 48 LQR 230–247

J. U. Lewis, 'Coke's Theory of Artificial Reason' (1968) 84 LQR 330–342

J. P. Dawson, *The Oracles of the Law* (1968), pp. 50–99

J. H. Baker, 'Pleading and Litigation as Sources of Law' (1978) 94 SS *142–163*

LEGISLATION

T. F. T. Plucknett, *Statutes and their Interpretation in the first Half of the 14th Century* (1922); 'Dr Bonham's Case and Judicial Review' (1926) 40 HLR 30–70; 'Ellesmere on Statutes' (1944) 60 LQR 242–249

H. G. Richardson and G. O. Sayles, 'The Early Statutes' (1934) 50 LQR 201–223, 540–571; *Law and Legislation from Aethelberht to Magna Carta* (1966)

70. *Digest of the Law of Partnership* (1915 edn), p. viii.
71. Law Commissions Act 1965 (c.22).
72. *Parliamentary Papers 1854*, vol. LIII, p. 391, per Talfourd J.

S. E. Thorne, 'The Equity of a Statute and Heydon's Case' (1936) 31 *Illinois Law Rev* 202–217; 'Dr Bonham's Case' (1938) 54 LQR 543–552

G. Barraclough, 'Law and Legislation in Medieval England' (1940) 56 LQR 75–92

C. M. Gray, 'Bonham's Case Revisited' (1972) 116 *Proc American Philosophical Soc* 35–58

M. S. Arnold, 'Statutes as Judgments: the Natural Law Theory of Parliamentary Activity in Medieval England' (1977) 126 *Univ Pennsylvania Law Rev* 329–343

17TH-CENTURY LAW REFORM

M. Cotterell, 'Interregnum Law Reform: the Hale Commission of 1652' (1968) 83 EHR 689–704

D. Veall, *The Popular Movement for Law Reform 1640–60* (1970)

B. Shapiro, 'Law Reform in 17th Century England' (1975) 19 AJLH 280–312

19TH-CENTURY LAW REFORM

A. V. Dicey, *Law and Public Opinion in England during the 19th Century* (1905)

C. H. S. Fifoot, *English Law and its Background* (1932), pp. 145–274; *Judge and Jurist in the Reign of Victoria* (1959)

G. Keeton and G. Schwarzenberger (Eds), *Jeremy Bentham and the Law* (1948)

J. H. Burns (Gen Ed), *The Collected Works of Jeremy Bentham* (1968–   )

A. H. Manchester, 'Simplifying the Sources of the Law: an Essay in Law Reform' (1973) 2 *Anglo-American Law Rev* 395–413, 527–550

Part two
13. Real Property: Feudal Tenure

The most fundamental distinction in the English law of property was between real property and personal property. Land is a place to live for man and beast, a source of food and of all other commodities, including (if one has enough to let) money. It outlives its inhabitants, and therefore provides a suitably firm base for institutions of government and wealth. Control of land could not, indeed, be readily divorced from power and jurisdiction, from 'lordship'. Land therefore became the subject of feudal tenure, which will be explained presently. Schemes of provision for the interests of members of landed families led in due course to an elaborate doctrine of estates and rules of inheritance. Personal property, on the other hand, was not subject to tenure, inheritance or the system of estates.

The characteristics which for convenience we have attributed to 'land' belonged more strictly to 'real property'. Some interests in land, such as leases for years, were not subject to tenure or to the rules of inheritance and were classed as chattels. On the other hand, some interests not directly concerned with land, such as an advowson (the right to present a clerk to an ecclesiastical benefice) or a franchise, were real property. There is not much logic in the way various rights were classified as realty and others as personalty, and there must have been a time when there was no distinction. Possession, the fact of control, was of the same nature in all cases and could be protected with force. Right, or ownership divorced from possession, was a legal rather than a factual concept, and may at first have been closer to our ideas of contract than of property. Right to land would usually be a claim against a grantor, who under the feudal arrangement would be the lord, and so a claim to land would be to recognise the contract between lord and man. This kind of right became enforceable *in rem*, binding the land itself, and then tenure moved from the realms of contract to those of status or property.[1] Other rights which, for various reasons, escaped this process and remained closer to contract—for instance, leases for years, debts, and the right to goods

1. See pp. 200–201, post.

bought—followed a different course and became 'personal property' because the remedy lay *in personam*. The division occurred before lawyers perceived it, and before the technical terms 'realty' and 'personalty' were introduced to explain it. By the time it achieved legal recognition, it was a distinction built into the forms of action, to be observed and accepted as axiomatic, without need for explanation. When leases for years were given protection *in rem*, in the Tudor period, they were not reclassified as realty; it was too late for such a fundamental alteration.[2]

Since there is no principle of logic to guide us, the only way we can understand the separate nature of the law of real property is by tracing the development of the rules governing the ownership of land. The starting point, however, is not ownership; it is tenure.

Tenure

The notion of tenure, though it no longer affects the ownership of land, has been the foundation of the law of real property for nine centuries. Tenure is the name given to the relationship whereby a tenant 'holds' land of a lord. *Holding*, as opposed to *owning*, must be explained in terms of the 'feudal system' which was the economic basis of society at the time of the Norman conquest. The expression 'feudal system' is an anachronism, an historiographical image which conveniently describes certain common features of medieval life which had no contemporary name given to them; and it is particularly important to remember that the 'system' which the common law fossilised never existed as contemporary ideology. The neat, logical scheme described by Littleton in the fifteenth century was an attempt to impose order on tenures for fifteenth-century purposes, purposes far removed from those for which tenures had first arisen. Tenure was not in origin a legal concept at all, but a social fact, a state of affairs beyond precise definition.

Much has been written about the origins of feudalism in the dark ages. The controversy as to whether it was a Germanic or a late Roman institution need not concern us here. We know that feudal institutions of a kind existed in Anglo-Saxon England. But it was the conquest of England by a Norman king in 1066, and the ensuing occupation and settlement by a French elite, which led to the regularisation and centralisation of those institutions. Under Norman rule

2. They were, however, called 'chattels real': see pp. 251–252, post. The law of chattels personal is dealt with in chap. XVIII.

all the land in England was held by the tenant in possession from someone else, either from the Crown as lord paramount or from a 'mesne' (middle) lord. There was no allodial land.[3] The simplified explanation is as follows. William I, having acquired the whole realm by lawful conquest, sent his warriors into different parts to preserve order, giving them rights over the people living there and duties to govern them, to exact military service and raise provisions and taxes when called upon. These chief lords themselves then parcelled out their dominions in like manner, in consideration for such services and provisions as they needed. The transaction whereby the grantee held property as tenant of the grantor in return for services has been called 'subinfeudation'. The process of subinfeudation created chains of tenures from the king to the men who actually possessed the land. As a matter of social history, it is unlikely that the occupation of land at the bottom end of the chains was much disturbed by the conquest. The peasantry after 1066, the unnamed country folk of the Domesday survey (1086), kept their humble allotments and went about their daily chores much as they had done in King Edward's day. Their immediate lords were often the same Englishmen as had been their lords before 1066. The Norman feudal structure was erected above them, and self-evidently it therefore had no direct bearing on land ownership as now understood. The relationship between lord and tenant was in a sense contractual, though it can hardly be likened to that of vendor and purchaser. The person who wished to occupy land within the lord's fee had to make a personal arrangement with him. The tenant obliged himself to perform services, and he forfeited his interest if he committed a fundamental breach by failing in this service or by being unfaithful. The lord in return protected the tenant in his holding, ruled over him, and held court for him and for all his other tenants. But tenure was more than a contract. It was a life-long status, comparable in some respects with marriage, which also began by contract. The special relationship was sealed by the ceremony of homage, when the tenant knelt and placed his hands between those of his lord and swore to become his man in life and limb and earthly honour against all men except the king.[4]

A typical Norman baron would have held numerous parcels of 'land' from the king or from other barons. Some of these would have been retained for his own personal use: his 'desmesne lands'. Others

3. *Allodium* is land which is not held of any feudal superior.
4. The similarity with the marriage ceremony was recognised by the rule that a woman could not use these words on doing homage, but said 'I do unto you homage'.

would have been subinfeudated, in consideration of services, either by himself or an ancestor to tenants; and in respect of these the baron would not enjoy the land but a 'seignory' which comprised the services and other profits which were due to him as lord. The same pattern applied to lesser landowners, the proportion of a man's subinfeudated wealth depending on the magnitude of his real estate. Only the poorest landowners needed all their land for themselves; they were always tenants, never lords. Most of these lowest tenants, or tenants 'paravail', held of manors. The manor had been an economic and social unit before the conquest, comprising a vill or hamlet of perhaps a hundred or two hundred inhabitants, centred upon the mansion house or hall of a lord. In feudal legal theory the manor became a nucleus of tenants holding of the same lord and having a court to which all the tenants of the manor owed suit. This court controlled the agrarian activities of the manor, and often many other aspects of village life—from personal conduct to the manufacture of flour, bread and ale. Each manor was therefore a little feudal state, with its own customs and legislation administered through its own supreme court. Not until the common law took to overseeing these courts did the lord and his court become something less than a feudal sovereign whose decree was as good as law.

TYPES OF TENURE

The nature of the lord's moral obligations to his tenants was universal. But the tenant's obligations, or 'services', were almost infinitely variable. At the upper level of the feudal order there were three main kinds of tenure: military, civil and spiritual. The principal military tenure was *knight service*, whereby the tenant was obliged in time of war to provide one soldier in combat order for every knight's fee which he held of his lord. Other forms of military tenure were *castlegard* (garrison duty) and *cornage* (border patrol). In theory, military feudalism provided the king with a reserve army. Civilian services were also provided for by feudal grants. Tenants who held immediately of the Crown (tenants in chief) and who were bound to perform personal services for the king were said to hold by the tenure of *grand serjeanty*; of which there were as many forms as there were services to be done. Then there were the services which required the tenant to provide things, such as horses, arrows or armour for military uses, or wine, wax, fish and such like provisions for the king's household or army. Such services, when due from tenants in chief, were called *petty serjeanty*. Spiritual tenure arose when the pious made grants to ecclesiastical bodies to hold by the regular celebration of *divine service*, or the general duty of saying prayers for the soul of the donor (*frankalmoign*).

Tenures were less easy to subdivide at the lower levels. The duties of the average manorial tenant were usually menial. If his services were unfixed, so that the lord might in theory (but subject to the custom of the manor) demand all manner of work, the tenure was 'unfree' and was called *villeinage*. If the services were fixed, such as helping the lord with sowing or reaping at fixed times, the tenure was usually called *socage*. This originally denoted plough-service, but by Littleton's time was a generic term for all free services owed to mesne lords other than military or spiritual services.

Under a hypothetically perfect and complete feudal economy the type of tenure denoted not merely the services due but also the status and way of life of the tenant. The king at the top of the feudal pyramid had the greatest bargaining power, while the peasant at the bottom had none. Everyone had his place in the feudal hierarchy; tenure, rank and economic position were interdependent. Knight service and serjeanty denoted high rank; villeinage was the state of the peasant. Life was not, however, as neat as this in reality. A man might hold different fees for different kinds of service, or he might hold the same fee for a mixture of services. It was quite possible for a tenant to hold part of his lands by knight service and another part by socage; or he might hold one fee by knight service and an annual rent, in which case the tenure was military but with an element of socage added. Nor did tenure by knight service make the tenant a knight, any more than tenure in villeinage made him a villein.[5] In later legal theory a knight could hold land in villeinage, and a villein by knight service.

Moreover, the system of services itself proved impracticable within a century or two after the Norman conquest. The notional perfect feudal relationship was a bond lasting for life; it was personal to the tenant, inalienable and uninheritable. Yet in reality inheritance and free alienability were grafted onto the feudal system at an early stage,[6] and as a result the system of services lost its economic and social effectiveness. The military system was imperfect in its conception and it is unlikely that an English army was ever raised solely by feudal levy. Service was normally limited to forty days in the year, and there was no provision for training. Methods of warfare changed, and cavalry lost pride of place to archery; but tenure in chivalry, as its name indicates, was confined to cavalry. And then, when knight's fees descended or were sold to women, children, old men, or monasteries,

5. Villein status (*villeinage de sank*) was an hereditary personal disability.
6. See pp. 200–201, 208–209, post.

personal service became impossible. The division of estates by inheritance or subinfeudation created fractions of knight's fees, and no
tenant could be expected to find a fraction of a knight. The only
answer to these problems was to collect money from the tenants and
use it to pay mercenaries. This was effected with respect to most
knight's fees within the century after 1066. The knight service was
converted into *scutage*, a payment based on the number of knights to
be provided. When the king went to war, the rate of scutage was
proclaimed and levied proportionately on the tenants of knight's fees.
Probably these payments did not exempt tenants in chief from personal service, but if they were not inclined to the sword they could buy
licences to stay at home. By the fourteenth century, scutage itself had
become practically obsolete and money for wars was raised by other
forms of taxation.

Similar commutations were made of other forms of service.
Hereditary servants are not necessarily the best, because there is no
guarantee that their personal qualities are inheritable, and the sure
expectation of an employment removes the impetus for training and
self improvement. Again, the practical solution was to hire deputies,
or to commute the services to a money rent which the lord could spend
on servants of his own choosing. By the fourteenth century most
services had been commuted into quit-rents. Once fixed in sums of
money, the commutation payments constantly lost their value
through inflation, until in many cases they were hardly worth collecting. By the fifteenth century the feudal services, once the basis of the
feudal economy, had almost ceased to have any economic
significance. Nevertheless, as we shall see,[7] the importance of tenure
continued.

Feudalism and Land Ownership

If the question were posed, whether under the feudal system the
owner of the land was the lord or the tenant, one could not give a
direct answer. Feudal tenure was the antithesis of ownership as we
know it. Possession, to be sure, belonged to the tenant; but the tenant
enjoyed few of the privileges of an owner. He could not do what he
liked with the land. He could not sell it. He could not pass it on to
others by will, and there was no guaranteed succession in his family
after his death. His only protection against dispossession by the lord
was the feudal obligation of the lord to protect those within his

7. See pp. 204–219, post.

homage. The tenant's interest therefore stopped at possession, which is a fact and not a legal right. The fact of being in possession as a feudal tenant was called 'seisin'; and the means of acquiring seisin was by being received to do homage to the lord. For similar reasons, the interest of the lord could not accurately be called ownership. It may be that some lords had power enough over their tenants to seize profits and produce, or even to dispossess, when they felt like it. But, in so far as feudal theory was practised in feudal courts, lords owed a duty to recognise and protect the possessions of tenants from whom they had received homage. When the feudal bond was dissolved by death of the tenant, the lord might seem to be in a position akin to ownership: he could keep the land in his own hands, or select a new tenant if he wished. Yet, even in respect of such land, he was himself a tenant of someone else. Under such a simple system, the only problem which might seem to turn on ownership rather than possession occurred if a lord inadvertently or dishonestly received homage from two men in respect of the same land. But, here again, the solution rested on the fact of possession. The unlucky claimant had a grievance, and was perhaps entitled to be compensated by the lord with land of equal value, but there was no question of upsetting seisin by reference to some more abstract notion of title. In this feudal world, then, we should think always of seisin and never of ownership. The tenant was seised of the land, and the lord was seised of the tenant's services, but neither of them 'owned' in any sense which can be intelligibly divorced from that of seisin.

If the pristine feudal system had ever exhibited this simple character, it had certainly lost it by 1166. Two unfeudal forces had combined to strengthen, and in strengthening to transform, the interest of the tenant. The first of these forces was custom. As soon as records of manorial courts begin, we see that lords were not in reality autonomous despots; or, if they were, they took pains to pretend not to be. The management of the manorial land was controlled in open court by decisions purporting to follow the 'custom of the manor'. These customs tied the lord's hands very considerably, and most lords probably submitted to the restraint. The customs which made the most impact were those which tied the lord's hands on the death of a tenant. In most places there were customs of inheritance: that is, designated members of the deceased tenant's family had the expectation of succeeding him, and the lord was supposed to accept the heir into his homage on the same terms as his ancestor. But custom alone could not make inheritance a legal right. Until the heir did homage he was not seised; if he were passed by, and someone else did homage

and took seisin, his expectation was effectively frustrated by events.
An heir might be passed over for a number of reasons; for instance, if
he was not around to make claim, or if he was thought personally
unfit, or if there was some dispute as to which relative should be
the heir. Some manorial courts took the trouble to formulate
qualifications of their customs to meet such exigencies. But whether
the custom was modified, reformed, reversed, or utterly disregarded,
could make no legal difference within the world of the feudal court.
The decisions of the lord and his court were as much legislative as
judicial. Inheritance might be a widespread social fact, a custom to
guide the court, and a strong expectation based on precedent; yet
seisin was still the only interest which ultimately meant anything, and
that could only result from a compact between living people. Only the
lord could make a tenant.

The second unfeudal force was the common law. At an early date
the king, both as the ultimate feudal superior and as the fountain of all
justice within the realm, took upon himself the surveillance of feudal
jurisdictions. The king would, upon complaint, order a lord to do
right to one who claimed to hold of him. But what was 'right'? The
twelfth-century writ of right, addressed (unlike the later original
writs) to the lord himself, ordered him to do 'full right' to a claimant
who had been 'deforced' by another. Already we see a substantial, if
unconscious, change of thinking. For the first time, someone who is
out of seisin can claim to oust someone who is in seisin; and he does so
on the basis of some right. In the writ *praecipe in capite*,[8] used where the
claimant sought to be put in seisin as a tenant in chief of the king, the
claim becomes worded as a 'right and inheritance'. This right which
the king would protect was therefore hereditary; and from other
sources we learn that inheritance was to be traced from whomever
could be shown to have been seised first. The thinking behind these
new remedies was doubtless unsophisticated and straightforward.
Inheritance was a well known and reasonable custom which could
only be given full effect if lords, against their own economic interests,
treated it as binding; where, therefore, land was customarily inheritable, lords would be constrained by the king to honour the custom.
The result of the policy was, however, far more profound. A *right* to
seisin could only be protected at the expense of the person who
actually had seisin, and, less directly, at the expense of the lord who
had given it to him. Where once the fact of seisin had been all that
mattered, the tenant in seisin now had but a precarious interest. A
tenant who had been duly awarded seisin by the manorial court, and

8. For the forms of these writs, see pp. 438–439, post.

had done homage, was now liable to be dislodged as a result of historical enquiries into events which might have occurred before he or his lord were born, perhaps even before the writ of right had been invented. The choice of an heir by the lord's court was no longer an administrative act; it was a judgment subject to review if it broke the rules. At this point, we may say the law has begun to recognise ownership; for the 'right' to seisin was an abstract legal concept which transcended, and could be invoked to displace, actual seisin. In the non-feudal language of Roman law, seisin was the bare fact of possession, as against the legal right or *dominium* of the owner.

It is difficult to guess how far back local memory could have stretched in the twelfth and thirteenth centuries, but the reliable tracing of ancestral seisin beyond human memory must have been virtually impossible. The mode of trial in the writs of right was therefore battle, which conveniently excused humans from undertaking impossible enquiries. The violence and irrationality of battle, however, must have seemed a high price to pay for the new remedy; a man with a strong arm or the money to pay good champions could too easily abuse the system and dispossess the weak. So Henry II introduced for defendants the option of the grand assize, a form of jury. Further concessions to human reason had to be made to allow for possibilities not envisaged when the writs of right were introduced, such as a transaction between the parties' ancestors. The claim in the writ of right treated the defendant's presence on the land almost as an irrelevance; how he came to be there did not matter, unless his ancestor were seised first. But if the only permissible claim of right had been the hereditary claim from the dawn of memory, there would have been no way of acquiring title save by inheritance. The logic of the action could not accommodate alienation, and if this did not trouble the God of battles it might well perplex the men of the grand assize.

THE PETTY ASSIZES

An alternative and more direct way of controlling feudal lords was invented in the 1160s. Whereas the writ of right was designed to settle the right for all eternity through the solemnities of judicial combat, the 'petty assizes' of Henry II were intended to afford a speedy enquiry by neighbours into more readily ascertainable questions of fact. The assizes did not go into the right, but protected the status quo against wrong. If a man died seised of an hereditary fee, and the lord despotically refused to admit his heir, the heir could bring an assize of *mort d'ancestor* against the lord or against the tenant who had been put in his stead; and if the assize found that the ancestor had been seised on the day he died, then the heir was entitled to be put in seisin. The assize of *mort d'ancestor* was responsible for compelling lords to recognise inheritance; but the assize procedure was not confined to cases of disinheritance. If a tenant in seisin were disseised, that is, forcibly ousted, he could if he acted promptly bring the assize of *novel disseisin*. Here again the usual defendant was the lord; and the function of the assize was to enforce the lord's feudal duty towards those he had received as tenants. The assizes, like the writs of right, could be seen as protecting a kind of ownership, albeit of a lesser kind usually (but rather misleadingly) characterised as 'possessory'. No longer could lords, even in theory, give and take seisin as they chose. If the right lay elsewhere than with the person seised, it could be raised in a writ of right; but it could not be vindicated privately and without judgment.

WRITS OF ENTRY

The assizes as first conceived were concerned with recent events: the death of an ancestor in seisin, or a 'novel' (recent) disseisin. A claim which went beyond such matters of current news had to be raised by a *praecipe* writ. In the thirteenth century a wide range of special *praecipe* writs developed, which in their wording followed the writs of right by reciting an hereditary claim of right but went on to specify some flaw in the means by which the defendant had come by the land. Thus, if the defendant had entered by reason of a grant made by the plaintiff's ancestor, the plaintiff could anticipate his defence by showing in his writ that the grant was invalid, and thereby forcing the defendant to take issue on that point. The additional clause asserted that the defendant 'had no entry' in the land except by some specified means; and so these writs were called writs of entry. There were almost as many types as there were defects in title;[9] for example, the writs of entry *dum non fuit compos mentis* and *dum non fuit infra aetatem* (where a grant had been made by an insane or infant ancestor), *cui in vita* (where a husband had granted away his wife's lands, and after his death she sought to recover them), and *sur disseisin* (where there had been a disseisin too remote to be remedied by the assize). The writs of entry represented a more sophisticated notion of title than the primeval writ of right, because they recognised that title could pass by alienation.[10] They went further into the past than the assize, and were therefore concerned more with right than with upsetting the status quo; and yet by confining enquiry to specific historical

9. For specimen writ of entry, see p. 439, post.
10. See pp. 208–209, post.

facts they enabled the irrationality of battle to be avoided. Their attraction for plaintiffs resided chiefly in that. In narrowing their claim of right to discoverable facts, plaintiffs not only ousted battle but also gained direct access to the king's courts. The ultimate or 'mere' right which could be discovered only by combat or grand assize became a mystery into which litigants grew less and less inclined to delve, and so the writs of entry and petty assizes between them gradually pushed the writs of right into disuse.

LATER DISTORTIONS OF THE REAL ACTIONS

Of all the means of protecting tenants' interests, the assize was in practice the most useful and its history after 1200 is one of continuous and even strained expansion. The subject matter was extended beyond land to include such things as rents and offices. The 'novelty' required of the disseisin was relaxed, because the limitation period was defined as running from a fixed date which was not moved forward. The notion of disseisin was extended to include wrongful feoffments, such as a feoffment by a minor; and this enabled the assize to do some of the work of writs of entry. And then the idea of seisin was broadened from actual possession to include an attempt to gain possession by someone entitled to enter. This was an extraordinary turn; for now, if *A* had a right to enter on land of which *B* was seised, and *B* prevented his entry, this was a disseisin of *A* by *B* and *A* could bring the assize. The assize had by then ceased to try factual questions of dispossession, and was being used to try rights of entry. Not that everyone with a right to land had a right of entry. Originally a person who was disseised was allowed but a few days to re-enter with force, after which he was obliged to seek his remedy at law. In the fourteenth century, however, many of the restrictions on rights of entry were removed, particularly by the doctrine of 'continual claim', which enabled them to be preserved for a long time provided there was notionally a continuous claiming and being kept out. As a result of these changes, the assize became a 'droitural' action—that is, it tried right rather than recent possession—and by 1400 the writs of right and entry had largely been driven out of use.

From about 1400 the assize itself began to decline, and was replaced by a miscellany of personal actions: replevin, detinue of title deeds, trespass *quare clausum fregit*, actions on the statutes of forcible entry, and (in Tudor times) ejectment. The feudal dimension had completely gone. In 1413 it was argued that the use of trespass to try title was an innovation which ought to be stifled; but Thirning CJ, admitting the change of practice, defended the innovation on the grounds that trespass could be tried in banc, whereas the assize was subject to 'great maintenance in the country'.[11] Another reason for the eclipse of the assize was the complexity of the rules of pleading and procedure which had grown up around its transformation from one use to another. Trespass, in contrast, enabled a straightforward question of title to be put to a jury. Although it was a personal action which lay only for damages, it was not beyond the ingenuity of the common lawyers to escape even that difficulty. The change, when it came in the sixteenth century,[12] enabled the law of title to land to be reconstructed, free from the shackles of medieval rules of pleading rooted in feudalism.

The Incidents of Tenure

We have noted that during the middle ages feudal services lost all economic importance. By 1300, at the latest, the feudal system of economy was dead, perhaps without anyone knowing it. Yet, ironically, tenure was as important as ever; and it was now that lawyers began to classify tenures according to their incidental consequences for the lord. The reason is that the casual side-effects of tenure had become more valuable than the services, and the accidental collection of rights to which lords were entitled made it worth the while of lords to preserve their seignories. Long before Littleton wrote his celebrated treatise on tenures,[13] men had usually worked for money; and the attractions of being a feudal lord were neither the services nor the jurisdiction, but the windfalls which might be expected from time to time as incidents of the tenurial relationship. Had feudal lords resisted the control of the common law, then those incidental benefits would have been whatever they could exact from tenants. A necessary result of subjecting feudalism to the control of the king's courts was that seignorial powers were restricted and defined. The incidents of tenure as defined in the law books thus represented what the lord had left under the common law: the vestiges of a notional suzerainty which had been cut down to a standard of reasonableness.

1. *Aids*

The omnipotent lord might exact aids from his tenants to assist him in meeting any extraordinary financial difficulties. Such a power of

11. YB Hil 14 Hen IV, 35, pl.52, at f.36. 'Maintenance' was the use of improper pressure on sheriffs and jurors.
12. See pp. 254–255, post.
13. See p. 163, ante.

random confiscation, though it was tolerated in relation to villeins until Tudor times, was inconsistent with personal freedom. As to free men, it was therefore curtailed. By Magna Carta aids were limited to three cases: where the lord needed money to ransom himself from captivity, or to knight his eldest son, or to endow his eldest daughter on marriage. Such aids were to be reasonable, and in 1275 the two latter were fixed at twenty shillings per knight's fee. The king was not to levy aids without the consent of the great council of the realm; but taxation by king in parliament could reach all subjects and it was destined to outlive feudal taxation, becoming the principal source of national revenue after the abolition of knight service in 1660.

2. Fines on alienation

Because tenure was a personal relationship, alienation of the land by substitution, that is, by replacing one tenant with another, required in theory the consent of the lord. When the theory prevailed in practice, as it did (at least after 1256) in respect of the king's tenants in chief, the lord could charge money for his consent: the fine for licence to alienate. The fine was not payable on subinfeudation, which did not disturb the relationship between lord and tenant. Fines for alienation were abolished when alienation by subinfeudation was ended in 1290.[14] But the statute of 1290 did not bind the Crown, and fines from tenants in chief continued to add to the royal revenues until the seventeenth century.

3. Relief and primer seisin

On the death of a tenant, the land went back or reverted to the lord. If the tenant's interest had been merely for life, the lord was free to choose a new tenant. But if the tenant's interest had been inheritable, the lord was supposed to admit the heir as the new tenant. Before inheritance was protected by the common law, lords might seize the land and take the profits for themselves until the heir bought back the land by paying 'relief'; unscrupulous lords might even frustrate the inheritance by demanding excessive relief. When the law began to protect inheritance, the lord might still claim to take the deceased tenant's land into his hands until the new tenant did homage; this 'primer seisin' entitled the lord to the profits during the feudal limbo, and was also a security to ensure that the tenant paid relief. The common law necessarily regulated such claims, which if abused would obstruct the heir's legal rights. In the twelfth century, lords were prohibited from demanding unreasonable reliefs, and by Magna Carta reliefs were fixed at five pounds for a knight's fee or one year's

14. *Quia emptores terrarum*: pp. 208–209, post.

profits for land held in socage. Primer seisin was abolished in 1267, except as to tenants in chief; in the latter case, it survived as a valuable royal prerogative until the seventeenth century.

4. *Escheat*

If the tenant died without leaving an heir, the land necessarily fell to the lord by way of escheat.[15] Likewise, if the tenant was convicted of felony, his land fell to the lord. The latter kind of escheat was later called 'forfeiture'. Forfeiture, in the original sense, occurred when a tenant committed treason; in which case his land went to the Crown, and the rights of mesne lords were extinguished.

5. *Customary dues*

In many places there were customary obligations to be performed on the death of either the lord or the tenant, and the common law allowed these if they were reasonable. The most widespread was the custom of heriot, which entitled the lord to seize the best beast or chattel of a deceased tenant.

6. *Wardship and marriage*

A different problem to that of escheat arose if the heir was under age, and so unable to perform his feudal obligations. The heir was then subject to wardship. The guardian was supposed to look after the land for the ward and see to his education until he came of age. Here there arose a substantial difference between military tenure and socage. The guardian in socage, usually a near relative of the infant heir, exercised a genuine guardianship and (after 1267) could be made to account to the heir when he came of age at 14. But if the tenure was military, the guardian was the feudal lord and there was no accountability; lords unashamedly helped themselves to the profits of the land until the ward was 21. Indeed, before Magna Carta, lords had even been able to waste the ward's land by taking natural resources such as timber. Guardianship in chivalry was probably a Norman institution. Apologists argued that the lord was the appropriate guardian because grasping relatives could not be trusted with the life of an heir, and that lords ought to keep the profits of the land to defray the expenses of an education in feats of arms. In truth there was no logical defence for a usage which turned a burden or trusteeship into a regular income.

Guardians received into ward not only the heir's land but also the heir's body. No doubt this also originated as a form of protection for the ward, but in practice it was exploited for profit. The guardian was entitled to select a suitable marriage for the ward, and because large

15. From *eschier*, to fall.

sums of money or exchanges of property were involved in arranging suitable matches for young heirs and heiresses this right could be highly valuable. The marriage could not be forced on unwilling children, because it was a rule of law that consent was essential to true matrimony. But if a ward declined a suitable marriage when it was offered, he or she had to compensate the lord to the value of the marriage. And if a ward married without the lord's consent, he or she incurred the penalty (after 1236) of remaining in ward until the lord had received double the value of the marriage. The only legal concession made to the infant was the provision that guardians should not disparage their wards by offering marriages with unsuitable persons.

THE VALUE OF INCIDENTS

Those incidents which, like the services, were fixed in monetary terms suffered the same economic fate as the services. But those which were tied to the value of the land, or gave a right to take the profits of the land, survived inflation. The most profitable incidents for lords, and the most onerous to tenants, were those which attached on a descent to an heir; and these death duties hit the hardest at tenants by knight service. Being casual windfalls they did not provide a regular source of income except for great lords who had many tenants. But, until means were found of avoiding descents, the incidents attached whenever a tenant in fee died, and that was an event he could not avoid. The greatest profits of all came to the Crown, which was ultimate lord of all land in the realm and also had special prerogative rights which mesne lords did not possess. On the death of a tenant in chief, the king's escheator seized all his lands into the king's hands until an inquisition post mortem had been held to ascertain the king's rights. In addition to the ordinary rights of a lord, the king had primer seisin (a year's profits), and priority as to wardship over all other lords of whom lands had been held. The value of the feudal revenue to the Crown, and the special machinery used for its collection, explain why the feudal system of tenures was preserved long after its purpose, in terms of services, had become obsolete. All the most important legislation concerning real property, from 1215 to 1540, was directed principally at the preservation of the incidents of tenure from devaluation or avoidance.

MORTMAIN

An early means of avoiding incidents was to alienate the land to a monastic house in order to hold it of the house. The tenant would arrange to acquit the monks in respect of the services to the chief lord, but by interposing a corporation between himself and the lord the tenant avoided all the incidents vis-à-vis the chief lord which would otherwise have fallen due on his death. A corporation was immortal and had no heirs. An alienation to a corporation was a grant to a dead hand, 'in mortmain'. As a means of cheating the lord, mortmain was prohibited by Magna Carta. If land was given to a religious house in order to resume it again to hold of the same house, it was forfeited. But even a genuine charitable gift to a monastery had the same effect on the lord's incidents. In 1279, therefore, a more sweeping measure was introduced, forbidding all alienations in mortmain whatever the purpose.[16] The Crown could grant licences of exemption from this prohibition, but would only do so after a proper composition had been made for the loss of incidents. The last vestiges of the mortmain legislation remained in the law until 1960.

QUIA EMPTORES TERRARUM 1290

The system of paying for services with land had become virtually obsolete by 1290, and the continuation of subinfeudation as a means of alienating land was a source of complaint because of its effect on the valuable incidents of tenure. If property were sold to raise money, the vendor could either put the purchaser in his place (substitution) or make the purchaser his tenant (subinfeudation). The latter was preferable even if the services were nominal, because it did not require the lord's approval, and because the vendor retained a seignory which might yield occasional profits, whilst the purchaser lost nothing that he would gain by substitution. Indeed, the purchaser himself benefited from subinfeudation if the services were made nominal, such as a peppercorn or a rose at midsummer, because he took free of any older obligations higher in the feudal pyramid. The only loser was the vendor's lord. If his tenant died possessed of the land and leaving an infant heir, the lord had wardship of the land. But if the tenant had in his lifetime subinfeudated for a peppercorn rent, the lord had wardship of the rent alone and was entitled merely to a few peppercorns. Furthermore, the likelihood of the land escheating was reduced if there were more tenants in the chain. Alienation by substitution could damage the lord in a different way: for instance, if a very old tenant substituted a young man so that the chances of a death were reduced. Once lords lost control of alienation, however, the greater evil was seen as subinfeudation.

The statute *Quia emptores* is proof of the importance of the incidents

16. *Magna Carta* 1217, cl.43; Stat *De viris religiosis* 1279, Statutes of the Realm, vol. I, p. 51.

of tenure in 1290. In order to save them, the statute enacted that alienation was thenceforward to be by substitution, which was to be allowed without fine. Curiously enough, the statute did not expressly prohibit subinfeudation; but such a prohibition was soon read into it. As a consequence, no tenures in fee simple[17] have been created since 1290, and as mesne tenures have lapsed over the years most of the land in England has come to be held in chief of the Crown. Another consequence of the statute was the increasing use made of the husbandry lease for years, which had many of the advantages of subinfeudation without being caught by the feudal rules.[18] The statute is still of importance, because it keeps the feudal system in abeyance; and an attempt to repeal it in 1967 was defeated for that reason.

EVASION AND PRESERVATION OF INCIDENTS

An equally important consequence for the land law of the economic value of the incidents of tenure followed from the constant attempts of lawyers to arrange their clients' property interests in such a way that they attracted the least amount of incidental taxation. The incidents which most needed avoidance were reliefs, wardships and primer seisin, all of which arose when a tenant died and the fee descended to his heir. These were not merely death duties, but inheritance duties. And, whereas death could not be escaped, inheritance could. The essence of most feudal tax dodges was therefore to ensure that the land did not descend to an heir. Provision against descent had to be made during the tenant's lifetime, because at common law land could not be disposed of by will. We have already noticed an early device for achieving the object by grants in mortmain; but that way had been stopped. Another obvious method was for the tenant to transfer the land to his heir apparent before he died; few fathers thought it wise to do so. Another method, which generally had no legal success, was to create a succession of life interests so that the tenant and his heir and his heir's heir, and so on, each had separate life estates under the original grant and took nothing by descent.[19] Another method was to make a collusive grant to friends, who were trusted to convey the land back to the heir when he attained his majority; this was forbidden in 1267. Each form of evasion was countered at an early date by legislation or by judicial decision. But all the evasions were superseded by

17. The statute did not extend to estates less than fee simple, and so it was thought that tenants of particular estates (such as tenants for life) held of the reversioner or remainderman who had the fee simple. The meaning of these terms will be discussed in the next chapter.
18. See pp. 252–253, post.
19. See pp. 236–237, post.

the institution of the 'use', which enabled the real owner of the land to hide behind a legal façade.

Feudalism and Uses

The modern system of estates in land[20] is founded on the division between legal and equitable interests. This division is not readily comprehensible until the historical reasons for its existence are known; and the initial reasons had little or nothing to do with the later notion of concurrent interests in the same property. The 'equitable interest' originated not as an estate in land, but as a factual situation requiring recognition in conscience if not in law. The situation existed whenever the feudal tenant was personally obliged, either by contract or by the requirements of good faith, to allow another person to have the beneficial enjoyment of land vested in himself. Such an arrangement did not at first have a technical name. The nominal owner was obliged in conscience to observe the trust reposed in him, and in Latin he was said to hold the property *ad commodum* (to the advantage) or *ad opus* (to the use or benefit) of the beneficiary.

That this did not originate as a technical concept may be seen by comparing the language used in analogous situations. Bailiffs and guardians had a trust reposed in them to look after property for the benefit of another. In their cases the property was not vested in them, and yet they were said to keep (*custodire*) the property *ad opus* of the ward or owner. Thus, a statute of 1275 spoke of a guardian as holding to the use of his ward. The word *commodum* is also the Latin for 'easement', a right enjoyed over another person's land, such as a right of way.[21] No doubt the case where the tenant had no beneficial interest in his own property was difficult to describe except by analogy with these more familiar situations. But the law could only admit one 'right', and that belonged to the feudal tenant. The holding *ad opus* therefore of necessity involved a separation of legal title from true ownership.

ORIGINAL PURPOSES OF HOLDING AD OPUS
The earliest instances of holdings *ad opus*, in the twelfth century, were of a temporary nature. Thus, if a tenant wished to alienate his land, the proper feudal procedure was to surrender his interest to his lord on trust to admit the new tenant; this remained the mode of conveying

20. See next chapter.
21. See p. 355, post.

copyhold estates until 1925. Between surrender and admittance the lord kept the land *ad opus* of the transferee. Another example is provided by the case where a man wished to transfer property into the name of himself and his wife, or to settle property on himself and others; he could not grant the land directly to himself, and so he would grant it to friends on trust to reconvey it in the required manner. An extension of this enabled a man to avoid the rule prohibiting wills of land; he would grant the land to the group of friends on trust to regrant it after his death to such beneficiary as he should name. This in effect enabled land to be devised, and since the title did not pass by descent the feudal incidents were avoided.

It was soon realised that arrangements of this kind could be even more advantageous if they were permanent. Grants to the Franciscans afford an early instance. The Order of St Francis, forbidden to own land, was permitted to enjoy the use of property vested in another; and so a person wishing to benefit the order would grant land to a group of feoffees[22] to hold to the use of the friars. On the same principle, the statutes of mortmain could be avoided. Pending the issue of a licence, while the fine was being raised, the grantor or his nominee might hold the land to the use of the corporation. Yet, if this arrangement was effective, where was the point in purchasing the licence? A further mortmain statute was passed in 1391 to stop this means of evasion, but by that date the holding to uses was becoming a recognised institution.

Secular persons could also employ the arrangement to their advantage. It was noted above that a landowner could make a grant so as to take a regrant to himself and others, or to others after his death. If he made it a *condition* of the feoffment that the feoffees should make the regrant, the condition was enforced by the law with unbending exactitude; on failure of the condition, the land automatically returned to the feoffor or his heirs. If the condition was to convey the land after death to someone other than the heir, this means of enforcement was useless. But if the feoffor made the feoffment merely *on trust* to regrant, without imposing a condition, the feoffees held the title solely to the feoffor's use. Whatever he directed, they were expected to obey. This was very convenient to the feoffor. He remained the absolute owner in effect, because he possessed the land for his own benefit and took the profits, and he could sell the fee whenever he wished by directing the feoffees to convey to his purchaser. But he could in addition defer the selection of his successors to the point of his own death, if he so

22. A feoffee is a person to whom a fee simple is granted. The grant in fee is called a feoffment.

wished, and thus achieved the power of disposing of his property by will or of conveying *inter vivos* as he pleased. It was this function of the holding *ad opus*, the permanent arrangement which gave the beneficial owner the power to devise without impairing his other powers, which principally assured its establishment as a common institution. It also ensured that the device had to be a mere trust, because the effect of a will was to disinherit the only person capable of enforcing a condition.

THE 'USE' AS AN INTEREST IN LAND

Each of the arrangements just described began as a temporary expedient which was found to have advantageous effects if extended into a permanent state of affairs. The permanent institution which resulted was called a 'use', the law French word for *opus*, and the beneficiary was called *cestuy que use*.[23] The common law did not recognise any interest at all in the *cestuy que use*; he had 'no more to do with the land than the greatest stranger in the world',[24] and if he remained in possession of the land he was accounted a tenant at sufferance of the feoffees. It was said in 1464 that the feoffees could sue the *cestuy que use* for trespass if he cut trees,[25] and the dictum was often approved as a statement of abstract theory in later cases. Yet the feoffees, being charged with a trust, were not supposed to obstruct the *cestuy que use* or appropriate the land for their own advantage. By choosing a group of feoffees, usually lawyers, the feoffor ensured against individual unscrupulousness. But if any difficulties arose, the feoffees were obvious candidates for Chancery supervision, because they had obligations imposed on them by conscience which were not enforceable in the common law courts. By the accession of Henry VI at the latest,[26] uses were a major part of the chancellor's jurisdiction.

The principles established by the courts in the fifteenth century turned the interest of the *cestuy que use* into a new kind of ownership, which was later called the equitable estate. If the feoffees died, the trust passed to the heir of the last survivor; this was settled between 1450 and 1483. If the feoffees alienated the land, the trust passed to the purchaser, unless he bought for value without notice of the trust, in which case his conscience was free; this was settled before 1465. By

23. Probably short for *cestuy a que use le feoffment fuit fait* (he to whose use the feoffment was made). The word 'use' in this sense has no connection with the verb 'to use', but was derived from *opus* via the old French *oeps*.
24. *Anon* (1502) Keil 42, pl.7 per Frowyk Sjt.
25. YB Pas 4 Edw IV, 8, pl.9 per Moyle J.
26. In 1502, Vavasour J dated the Chancery intervention to Edward III's time: Keil 42. See also Plucknett CHCL, p. 578. Barton put it in Richard II's reign, and Bean in Henry IV's. See Rot Parl, vol. III, p. 511 (1402). By 1425 uses formed about two thirds of the chancellor's work.

the sixteenth century a use could also be raised by implication. If the owner of land bargained and sold it to another, then before the conveyance an implied use was raised in favour of the purchaser, which the chancellor would protect by specific performance. And if the owner enfeoffed another without any consideration being given or any express use declared, the feoffee held the land to the use of the feoffor and was bound to observe his instructions. The recognition of this 'resulting use', possibly as early as 1465, confirms how usual it had become in the fifteenth century for feoffments to be made on secret or undisclosed trusts, or to perform the feoffor's will. Where there was a use, the legal owner had nothing but the bare title, a right to expenses, and a possibility of taking a beneficial interest if the *cestuy que use* died intestate without heirs. The interest of the *cestuy que use* was even recognised by the common law courts as the result of a statute of 1484 which enabled him to make feoffments.[27] It became regular practice for pleaders to trace the *jus usus* in common law pleadings, and the rules relating to this right were discussed and settled by the common law judges. The use was by this process assimilated to legal property concepts; it descended to heirs on an intestacy, it could be bought and sold, and it could be settled on a succession of bene-ficiaries. Nevertheless, despite the legal fiction to which the statute gave rise, and the tendency to receive the use into the law, the new kind of ownership which the *cestuy que use* enjoyed was inherently foreign to the common law because it conflicted with the feudal system.

EVASION OF FEUDAL PRINCIPLES

By 1500 it could be asserted that the greater part of the land in England was held in use.[28] The main reason for this state of affairs was that it provided an escape from the automatic certainty of the legal rules of succession; by last will the landowner could provide for younger sons, daughters, bastards, remote relations or charities, could vary the provision given by law to his widow, and could charge the payment of his debts on real property. These objects could be achieved either by directing the feoffees to convey property directly to the devisees, or by directing them to retain the property and apply the income as directed, or by directing them to sell the land and apply the proceeds as directed. Whichever course was taken, it was the use and not the land which passed on death.

The social changes made possible by uses were accompanied by

27. Stat 1 Ric III, c.1. The object was to protect purchasers who took feoffments from possessors who appeared to all the world to be owners: p. 214, post.
28. YB Mich 15 Hen VII, 13, pl.1 per Frowyk Sjt.

two main evils. First, because most of the land in the country was vested in nominees who had no visible connection with the land, it could be difficult for third parties to discover the identity of the true owner. This difficulty was eased by the statute of 1484, which was passed to protect the purchaser who took a feoffment from the person seen to be in receipt of the profits. Added to this difficulty was that the use, unlike the land itself, could be transferred informally without livery of seisin. Conveyancing was made less sure by the danger of the hidden use, and fraud was encouraged because debtors and defendants could, by alienating to obscure uses, prevent their land being taken in execution. This difficulty was tackled in a similar way, by allowing actions to be brought against the 'pernor of the profits'; uses might be secret, but pernancy was an external manifestation of which notice could be taken.

Second, and this was the cause of all the trouble which came in Tudor times, the employment of uses deprived lords, and most of all the Crown, of their feudal revenues. It is unlikely that this was the prime motive behind uses, but it was their inevitable result and doubled their attraction. The devise of land in itself displaced inheritance and, therefore, the incidents which attached to inheritance; and even if the *cestuy que use* died intestate there was no descent of land to which incidents could attach. So long as the number of feoffees was kept up there would never be a descent at all, for if one feoffee died the others absorbed his share by the *jus accrescendi*. There was an 'unassailable mortmain'.[29] It was unassailable because the lord continued to have living tenants to whom the feudal rules applied; and in that situation, if he suffered economic loss, it was *damnum absque injuria*. Once this became common knowledge, it was foolish for any man to leave land vested in his own name. By vesting it in others he paradoxically became a more absolute owner than the common law allowed, because he was released from all the incidents of feudalism and also from the inflexible rules of inheritance. As a result of the use, the feudal system was by 1500 virtually a dead letter in England. Littleton's account of it might well have seemed an obituary.

TUDOR LEGISLATION AND FISCAL FEUDALISM

Between Edward I and Henry VII little was done to preserve the financial profits of feudalism against the encroachments of uses. Weak efforts were made in the fifteenth century by royal advisers to amplify the scope of the legislation passed three centuries previously, and to control feoffments to uses by tenants in chief; but no king before

29. Milsom HFCL, p. 180.

the Tudors felt strong enough to plug the gaps which had been made in these early provisions by means of the use. Henry VII and Henry VIII were determined to revive at least some of the feudal revenues which had belonged to their predecessors, and which they needed to defray the expense of government and of supporting themselves in royal state. They could see no reason to tolerate an institution, not even recognised by the common law, which enabled so much tax avoidance to be perpetrated. Ad hoc parliamentary taxation did not have as much to commend it as a regular feudal revenue which could be collected simply by enforcing the old law of the land.

Henry VII did not tackle the main problem, the will of land, but by statutes of 1489 and 1504 the heir of an intestate *cestuy que use* was subjected to the same incidents as if his ancestor had died seised.[30] These statutes contained the important new idea that for tax purposes the beneficiary might be treated as if he were the legal owner, whether or not there had been fraud or collusion. They ended a glaring anomaly, but were not designed to and in fact did not greatly enrich the Crown. Their chief practical effect was simply to remind men to make wills. It was Henry VIII who, for revenue purposes, raised feudalism from the grave. Historians have given to this artificial revival the name 'fiscal feudalism'.

In 1529, Henry VIII and his advisers made an agreement with some of the peers whereby feudal incidents would be restored, but only to the extent of one third of the amount due at common law. As mesne lords were also to have one third of their revenues restored, this seemed a fair compromise. But, when the proposal was laid before parliament in 1532, the Commons rejected it outright. They knew that taxation could only be imposed with their consent; and uses were an established legal institution which they were keen to preserve, not least because they acquired thereby the power to devise land. Henry threatened them that if they would not accept the one-third principle he would set in motion the full rigour of the dormant feudal law. They declined this offer, and the king kept his word.

The king's counsel were able to take advantage of a growing body of hostile opinion on uses. There were two lines of attack. The judges of the Common Pleas, in applying the statute of 1484, were coming to the view that uses were governed by the common law. If that were taken to its logical conclusion, wills of uses would be void, because wills of land were void. The other school of thought was that uses were inherently dishonest and that chancellors in enforcing them were

30. Stat 4 Hen VII, c.17; 19 Hen VII, c.15. The former dealt with the wardship of tenants in chivalry, the latter with relief and heriot from tenants in socage.

countenancing large-scale fraud. Perhaps uses were not to be regarded as binding in conscience after all. The anonymous serjeant who replied to *Doctor and Student*[31] proclaimed uses to be an 'untrue and crafty invention' to deprive the king and his subjects of their feudal incidents. 'What a falseness,' he wrote, 'to speak and do one thing, and think another clean contrary to the same'. Thomas Audley, as reader of the Inner Temple in 1526, complained of landowners who had 'connived of evil purpose to destroy the good laws of the realm', which laid down certain rules of inheritance, but 'now by reason of these trusts and confidences are turned into a law called "conscience" which is always uncertain and depends for the greater part on the whim of the judge in conscience; by reason whereof no man is certain of knowing his title to any land . . .'[32] No one present would have missed the dig at Wolsey. What they could not have known was that seven years later Audley would himself become that 'judge in conscience'. No doubt his promotion was helped by the lecture. Certainly the king expected Audley to put his preaching into practice; and so he did. With the assistance of the king's secretary Thomas Cromwell, appointed to sit beside him as Master of the Rolls in 1534, he assembled the judges to discuss a test case adjourned from the common law side of the Chancery. The question was whether a will made by a tenant in chief, Lord Dacre, which would have deprived the king of primer seisin and wardship, was valid. The judges, having been coerced or coaxed by King Henry himself into apparent unanimity, declared that it was against the nature of land to be devisable by will, and that a will of the use of land which deprived the king of his feudal incidents was ipso facto collusive and invalid.[33] The decision accomplished what parliament had refused to do, and within a few months the Commons were persuaded to assent to a new measure concerning uses. The reason why the Commons gave way in 1535 was not merely that their theoretical position had been undermined. If wills were invalid in 1535, it followed that wills had always been invalid, and doubts could be cast upon a great many titles throughout the country.[34] One clause in the 1535 bill provided that wills of persons dying before May 1536 should be accounted as

31. See p. 91, ante; Hargrave *Law Tracts*, vol. I, p. 329; 94 SS 199.
32. 94 SS *198*.
33. *Re Lord Dacre of the South, decd.* (1535) Spelman Rep (93 SS) 228; Bean *Decline of English Feudalism*, pp. 275–283. The true division of judicial opinion at the outset seems to have been 5 against 5.
34. Serjeant Mountague, arguing the case for the Dacre family, said 'it would be a great mischief to change the law now, for so many inheritances in the realm depend today on uses that there would be great confusion if this were done': YB Pas 27 Hen VIII, 10, pl.22 (translated).

effectual as they had been until recent decisions had brought their validity in doubt. This in effect reversed the decision in *Lord Dacre's Case* as to the past. Almost certainly this was the inducement which persuaded the Commons to accept the sweeping legislative change which was to govern in future.

The Statute of Uses carried the royal policies to the extreme of abolishing the power to devise for the future. This it did by the statutory fiction called 'executing the use'. Wills had only been valid where the legal title was vested in feoffees to uses. The abolition of uses would nevertheless have been absurd, because its effect would have been that nearly all the land in England would have become beneficially vested in the lawyers who happened to be acting as feoffees. The legal title had instead to be taken from the feoffees and given to the *cestuy que use*. The statute therefore provided that where *A* was seised of property to the 'use, confidence or trust' of *B*, then *B* was thereafter to be deemed to be seised of the property 'to all intents, purposes and constructions in the law, of and in such like estates as [he] had or shall have in use'.[35] In other words, whenever *A* was enfeoffed to the use of *B*, the statute effected a second, notional or fictional livery of seisin from *A* to *B*. *B*, the *cestuy que use*, was to be statutory owner of the legal estate, and the feoffees (*A*) merely a channel through which the seisin passed in an instant of time to *B*. A similar fictional passing of seisin occurred if *A* covenanted to stand seised to the use of *B*, or bargained and sold the land to *B* (in which case there was an implied use).[36] The purpose and effect of executing the use was that the beneficial owner of the land would die seised, so that his last will was ineffective and the feudal incidents attached on the descent to his heir.

Financially, the statute was a tremendous success. But it aroused much popular opposition. It not only restored feudal incidents, but it imposed compulsory primogeniture on a society which had accustomed itself to greater flexibility; and it did so for socage tenants as well as for tenants by knight service. For this reason, it has been called 'a piece of short-sighted political vindictiveness'[37] in which Henry VIII pushed his hand just too far. Lawyers immediately set about finding loop-holes, and landowners set about demanding the repeal of the statute. Within four years, after the Pilgrimage of Grace had brought to light the strength of feeling, the king restored to the

35. Stat 27 Hen VIII, c.10.
36. Even more strangely, if *A* conveyed land to *B* without consideration and without saying 'to the use of *B*', nothing passed, because the resulting use in favour of *A* was executed and the seisin which *A* delivered to *B* immediately rebounded on *A*.
37. E. W. Ives, 82 EHR at 695.

landowner the power to devise land. The Statute of Wills 1540 conferred for the first time the legal power to dispose of freeholds by will.[38] The preamble referred to the king's 'grace, goodness and liberality' towards his loving subjects; but it was a major political retreat. The king reduced his fiscal demands to the one-third principle of 1529; tenants in chief who held their lands by knight service were allowed to devise no more two thirds of those lands, so that the Crown would enjoy wardship and the other incidents in respect of the remaining one third which devolved on the heir by descent.

Even after this compromise of 1540, the royal revenue from fiscal feudalism was vast. In 1540 the Court of Wards was established, under the presidency of the master of the king's wards, an office created by Henry VII. Its purpose was to supervise the collection of the feudal revenues of the Crown and to settle incidental questions of law. It enjoyed a thriving jurisdiction for one century. Yet the policy of fiscal feudalism came under constant criticism. It was suggested that if the Crown helped itself to the property of wards it ought to discharge its educational duties towards them. One master of the wards in the time of Elizabeth I went so far as to prepare plans for a new university for this purpose, but nothing came of them. It was also urged, under Elizabeth I and James I, that Crown and people alike would benefit if the irregular burdens imposed by fiscal feudalism were replaced by annual composition payments or other more rational forms of taxation. This was not finally achieved until the end of Charles I's reign. Resolutions of the Long Parliament in 1645 were confirmed by a statute of 1656, and this statute was one of the few to be continued at the Restoration. The Military Tenures Abolition Act 1660 abolished tenure by knight service, and all its incidents, and abolished the onerous incidents of grand serjeanty.[39] From that date the feudal system has been little more than abstract theory in this country. Public revenue was thereafter raised by other forms of taxation which spread the burden more widely: excise duty, house tax (measured by the number of hearths or windows), purchase tax, income tax, death duty, and so on. Mesne lords have had no reason to preserve their claims to seignories, except where manors have been preserved as units. Since there has been no new subinfeudation since *Quia emptores*, most landowners today hold their lands in chief of the Crown by free and common socage,[40] the only incident of which is the duty of fealty.

38. Stat 32 Hen VIII, c.1.
39. Stat 12 Car II, c.24.
40. Where the details of tenure were unknown, the common law presumption was, in favour of the Crown, that the land was held in chief by knight service: 94 SS *195*, n.1. The presumption now is of a tenancy in chief by socage.

The abolition of knight service and casual feudal revenue did away with most, if not quite all, of the rules of law which were built on feudal foundations. But the Statutes of Uses and Wills wrought changes in jurisprudence which would never have occurred if Henry VIII's wishes had been met by the parliament of 1532. The side effects of the brief conflict of 1532–40 ultimately proved more enduring than the resuscitation of feudal revenue, and enabled the emergence of new conveyancing devices. The effects will be discussed in the next chapter.

Further reading

Pollock & Maitland, vol. I, pp. 229–406; vol. II, pp. 1–6, 29–106, 228–239

Holdsworth HEL, vol. III, pp. 29–87

Plucknett CHCL, pp. 506–520, 531–545, 575–587

Simpson IHLL, pp. 1–43, 163–186

Milsom HFCL, pp. 88–136, 169–192

T. F. T. Plucknett, *The Legislation of Edward I* (1949)

J. L. Barton, 'The Medieval Use' (1965) 81 LQR 562–577

E. W. Ives, 'The Genesis of the Statute of Uses' (1967) 82 EHR 673–697

J. M. W. Bean, *The Decline of English Feudalism 1215–1540* (1968)

S. F. C. Milsom, 'The Real Actions', introduction to Pollock & Maitland (1968 edn), pp. xxvii–xlix; *The Legal Framework of English Feudalism* (1977)

D. W. Sutherland, *The Assize of Novel Disseisin* (1973)

S. D. White, 'English Feudalism and its Origins' (1975) 19 AJLH 138–155

P. A. Brand, 'The Control of Mortmain Alienation in England 1200–1300' in *Legal Records and the Historian* (1978), pp. 29–40

J. H. Baker, 'Uses and Wills' (1978) 94 SS *192–203*

Table A. Classification of property

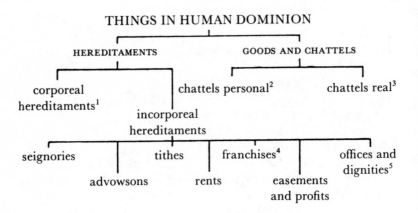

THINGS IN HUMAN DOMINION

HEREDITAMENTS   GOODS AND CHATTELS

corporeal   chattels personal[2]   chattels real[3]
hereditaments[1]
                  incorporeal
                  hereditaments

seignories   tithes   franchises[4]   offices and
                                                                dignities[5]
          advowsons   rents   easements
                                            and profits

1. Land, including minerals, vegetation, buildings, fixtures, wild animals, heirlooms, title deeds.
2. Of two kinds: (i) choses in possession, (ii) choses in action.
3. Including terms of years, tenancies at will, wardships severed from seignories.
4. Including regal or palatine privileges, private liberties and jurisdictions, markets and fairs, tolls, forestry rights, and rights to take royal revenues or profits, such as treasure trove, wreck, swans.
5. Including peerages and baronetcies, names and armorial bearings.

Table B. Classification of tenures

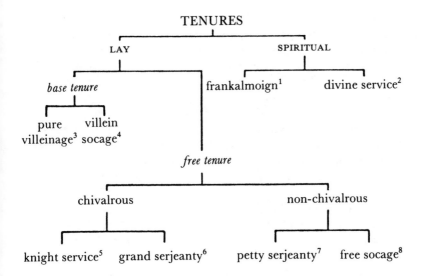

TENURES

LAY   SPIRITUAL

base tenure   frankalmoign[1]   divine service[2]

pure villeinage[3]   villein socage[4]

free tenure

chivalrous   non-chivalrous

knight service[5]   grand serjeanty[6]   petty serjeanty[7]   free socage[8]

1. Uncertain religious services such as saying mass for the soul of the donor.
2. Certain religious service, such as saying mass on certain days, or finding a chantry chaplain, or distributing alms.
3. Uncertain villein services, e.g., copyhold, tenancy by the virge.
4. Certain services, e.g., tenure in ancient demesne.
5. Military service, including castle-gard and escuage.
6. Certain non-military service to the king's person.
7. Service of rendering something to the king. According to some definitions it must have a military use.
8. Of two kinds: (i) common socage, the only form of tenure apart from frankalmoign and grand serjeanty remaining after 1925; (ii) customary socage, e.g., gavelkind, burgage.

14. Real Property: Estates and Settlements

The subject matter of feudal tenure was the 'fee' (*feodum*) which, as we have seen, in theory belonged neither to the lord nor the tenant. The lord was seised of the fee 'in service', and the tenant was seised of the fee 'in demesne' (*in dominico suo*). In a notional feudal world, the interests of lord and tenant lasted for life: the tenant became tenant when he took the oath of homage and ceased to be tenant when either he or his lord died. But we have seen that the common law before 1200 recognised a more extensive interest in the tenant, which was both inheritable and alienable. The common law recognised the life interest also, but it so favoured the position of the free tenant that the 'fee' for common law purposes was an alienable inheritance. Where there was a tenancy for life, the inheritable fee remained in the lord. If we may treat the tenant in possession as 'owner', there was in such a case a temporal division of ownership; the tenant owned the land for his lifetime, and then the lord, as owner of the inheritance, became tenant in demesne. The notion that ownership of land can be divided up on a time scale into present and future interests, and into interests of varying duration, was expressed in terms of the tenant's 'estate', a word derived from the Latin *status*. 'An estate in the land is a time in the land, or land for a time.'[1]

The tenancy for life and the inheritable fee were the basic units of the scheme of estates. Other kinds of interest could be created by act of the parties, since freedom to alienate included freedom to alienate on terms. In the course of time some of the interests created by act of the parties evolved into legal estates, while others were refused admission to the common law scheme.

The establishment of inheritance as a right[2] did not, in itself, necessitate a differentiation of estates in land. A grant to *A* and his heirs, even when it was enforced by law, might have been construed as creating an infinite succession of life tenancies. The idea that the fee was not a succession of interests but a single estate, owned in its

1. *Walsingham's Case* (1573) 2 Plowd 547, 555.
2. See pp. 200–201, ante.

entirety by the tenant in fee, arose when the tenant in fee was permitted to alienate to another person in fee in such a way as to disinherit his own heirs. It is therefore appropriate to consider first the legal effects of alienation.

Alienation

Alienation is the transfer of the ownership of land from one owner to another. There was no reason inherent in feudalism why a tenant should be accorded the privilege of free alienation, because if the feudal tie were a truly personal one the lord had as much right as the tenant to decide who should enter his fee. The tenant could no more impose a substitute on his lord than a servant could sell his job without the employer's consent. Yet the demands of a land-based economy would not have been satisfied by an absolute ban on the disposition of land. In fact the possibility of alienation was never denied, and in a feudal context it could take either of two forms: substitution or subinfeudation. In the former case the grantor left the fee altogether, and the grantee became the lord's immediate tenant in his place. In the latter case the grantor remained the tenant of his lord, and the grantee held the land of him; this was the most usual type of alienation before 1290. It was seen in the last chapter how subinfeudation prejudiced lords paramount; but substitution could also prejudice the lord, since his tenant would be changed. The lord lost no theoretical entitlement, either to services or incidents, by substitution; but so long as the tenant's identity was a matter of feudal significance it made sense to require the lord's assent to either form of alienation. By Bracton's time the feudal reality had so faded away that the tenant's individual identity was legally immaterial. And after 1290 alienation of the fee was always by substitution, without the lord's permission.[3]

EFFECTS OF ALIENATING THE INHERITABLE FEE

The right to alienate freely could be reconciled with the right of inheritance, but not without conceptual difficulty. If a grant to a tenant and his heirs had been held to confer life interests on each tenant in succession, no tenant in possession would have been able to alienate for a period exceeding his own life. Had that been so, the first grantor of the fee would have had the power to tie the land to the grantee's family until the end of time. Freedom of alienation would

3. See pp. 208–209, ante.

have stultified itself, because one grant of land to a person and his heirs would have precluded any further grant of the same land to another person and his heirs. No human disposition could be allowed such eternal force. Freedom of alienation could not include the freedom to prevent future alienation. Glanvill (c. 1190) tried to resolve the conflict by distinguishing a man's acquisitions from his patrimony. What he had himself purchased he could alienate without restriction; but what he had inherited he could only alienate in exceptional circumstances.[4] But Glanvill's approach would have done no more than delay the same unacceptable consequences; a single descent was effective to render the land inalienable. Within a generation Glanvill's restriction had been abandoned. If land were granted to *A* and his heirs, *A* received an inheritable fee which he could alienate in its entirety to *B* and *B*'s heirs.

The new doctrine may have originated from the protective force of warranties, which were guarantees of title made by grantors. *A*'s obligation to warrant the title of *B* and *B*'s heirs descended to *A*'s own heirs, who were thereby barred from claiming back the fee for themselves. Bracton, however, treated it as a substantive principle that the words 'and his heirs' in a grant gave no interest to individual heirs but merely defined as inheritable the character of the interest granted. This became the common law. An heir took his land by right of succession and not by a direct grant to himself; in legal language, he took 'by descent' and not 'by purchase'. The heir had no right unless his ancestor died seised; in that event his right was absolute and neither a will nor the power of the lord could disinherit him. But if the ancestor alienated in fee during his lifetime, the heir had nothing to inherit and no legal standing. The reason given was that the identity of the heir could not be known until the ancestor's death. Heirs were made by God not man: *solus Deus facit haeredem*. No ascertained individual was therefore cut off by an alienation *inter vivos*; an heir apparent or presumptive had an expectation of inheriting, but not a vested estate.

The tenant who was granted land 'to himself and his heirs for ever' thus had something quite different from a life estate. His estate was of infinite duration and during his lifetime he could alienate it for ever. If he died seised, the estate did not determine but descended to his heir. His estate was called a 'pure fee' or 'fee simple' and it was the totality of ownership out of which all lesser estates were carved. Unlike lesser estates it was as perpetual and indestructible as the land itself, neither the subject of creation nor of determination by parties. The fee simple

4. Glanvill, vii, 1.

was a right to land for ever. It had always to be vested in someone, and if it was in no subject it would be in the Crown. All that men could do with it was to pass it from one to another or carve it up.

EFFECTS OF ALIENATING THE TENANCY FOR LIFE

The life estate could not be subject to the same rules as the fee simple. Being finite, it was tied to the life span of the original grantee notwithstanding alienation. Once the lord lost the power to control his tenant's alienations and select his tenants it would have been an injustice to him if, say, an aged tenant for life could alienate the remaining portion of his estate to a young man for the rest of the young man's life. A series of such alienations might have kept the land from ever returning to the lord, who had only parted with it for one life. It was therefore held that, although the life tenant was free to alienate the whole of his interest, that interest necessarily determined on the death of the person for whose life the land was originally given.

The estate which arose by the purchase of a life estate from another person was called an estate *pur auter vie*. The tenant *pur auter vie* had a freehold which lasted until some other person (*cestuy que vie*) died. A problem insoluble by logic arose if the tenant *pur auter vie* died before *cestuy que vie*; the estate could not pass to his heirs because it was not a fee, and yet it could not be disposed of by will or by administration because it was a freehold and not a chattel. The estate was conceded, in default of any logical rule, to the first occupant. A grantor of a life estate could specify in advance who such successors were to be, as by saying 'to *A* and his heirs for the life of *B*'; in that case, if *A* predeceased *B*, *A*'s heirs would have the estate, not by descent but as 'special occupants'. The chaotic situation where there was no special occupant was altered by the Statute of Frauds 1677, which conferred on tenants *pur auter vie* the power to devise their estate by will, and provided for the estate of an intestate tenant *pur auter vie* to be distributed by his personal representatives in the same way as a lease for years.[5]

The standard case of tenancy *pur auter vie* is where a life estate is assigned or granted by the original life tenant to another. But another form occurred in the lease for lives, where the estate was made to last *pur auter vies* from its inception and was not derived out of an ordinary life estate. Such leases were widely used as an alternative to leases for years where it was desired to create an uninheritable freehold; and colleges and ecclesiastical corporations often leased property for lives by virtue of statutory powers to make short leases. Renewal was

5. Stat 29 Car II, c.3, s.12.

effected by the addition or substitution of a new life. In 1925 the commercial lease for lives was finally converted into a chattel interest by the provision that a lease for lives reserving a rent to the lessor should be treated as a lease for ninety years.[6]

Succession: The Canons of Descent

The landed aristocracy and gentry depended for their continuity on patrimony, on the devolution of land from one generation to the next. The rules governing succession determined where the wealth of the family would go, and the inadequacy of the rules in providing for all who needed support caused landowners to experiment with their own arrangements for the purpose. Before we examine the history of settlements, we must first outline these legal rules.

When inheritance operated solely by virtue of custom, it was the custom which determined who would be heir, and there were variations from place to place. When the common law intervened by writs of right and the assize of *mort d'ancestor* to give the heir a legal right, it had to define the heir. Customs as to who should inherit were now elevated into rules as to who did inherit. A grantor had no say in these rules; he could choose whether to use the words 'and his heirs' in the grant, but he could not choose who those heirs would be.

The principal canons of descent were as follows:

1. *The parentelic scheme*

Proximity of kinship for the purposes of inheritance was measured according to a 'parentelic' calculus. The *parentela* of a deceased person comprised all living persons who traced their blood from him: that is to say, his issue. The search for the heir went successively through the *parentelae*, beginning with that of the deceased himself, then that of his father, and so on. Each degree had to be exhausted before the next could be considered. The result was that lineal descendants of the deceased were preferred to his collateral relatives. Only if there were no children, grandchildren, or other issue, did the law look to brothers, cousins or other collaterals for the heir. And collaterals on the father's side were preferred to those on the mother's side, however remote.[7] Moreover, if the land had descended from the father, the

6. Law of Property Act 1925, 15 & 16 Geo V, c.20, s.149(6).
7. *Clere v Brooke* (1573) 2 Plowd 442. In the 13th century alternation from one side to another in each degree had been favoured. Even in the 18th century it was unsettled whether the preference for the 'male line ascending' applied to different parentelic degrees; whether, for instance, the brother of the paternal grandmother was preferred (as Hale thought) to the brother of the paternal grandfather's mother (as Blackstone thought): Bl Comm, vol. II, pp. 238–240.

mother's side was totally excluded and in the absence of heirs on the father's side the land would escheat. Similarly, if land descended through the mother, the father's side of the family was excluded by the same *jus recadentiae*; and the search for the mother's heir went through her male line ascending according to the same principles.

A second aspect of the parentelic scheme was that a deceased person was 'represented' by his own issue, however remote. Thus if A has an elder son B and a younger son C, and B dies before A leaving a son B_1, and then A dies; A's heir is B_1 and not C, because B_1 represents his father. This rule was not clear in the time of Glanvill or Bracton and was only established after bitter struggles between grandchildren and their grasping uncles; King John was such an uncle, and his accession to the throne delayed the acceptance of the principle until the end of the thirteenth century.

2. *Males preferred to females of same degree*

When most people believed without question that male superiority was ordained by God, and that men were more reasonable and capable of managing affairs than women,[8] it was natural that men should be preferred as heirs. Thus a brother would always be heir in preference to his sisters, even if they were born before him. But the common law did not exclude female heirs. Women were allowed to inherit if there were no males of the same degree. Thus, if a deceased tenant left no sons, his daughters would be preferred before his brother because they were lineal descendants within his own *parentela*.

3. *Primogeniture and coparcenary*

Coparcenary, the equal partition of land among all the sons or daughters, seems to have been the usual custom of succession before the Norman conquest. Military feudalism introduced the principle of primogeniture, the preference of the first-born to the exclusion of all others.

Before the common law rule was clearly settled, the younger sons were considered to share with their eldest brother 'in parage'. This meant that the eldest only was tenant *quoad* the lord, but his brothers held their shares of him by a strange form of tenure in which there were no services or incidents and the tenant was somehow a peer of his lord. By Glanvill's time (c. 1190) knight's fees had ceased to be partible in this way and all went to the firstborn, but land held in socage was partible if it had been so of old. Since every new tenure was subject to primogeniture, the common law began to prevail as local customs died out. Partibility was once common in Norfolk, but it

8. See Plowd 305, 444–445.

survived to a noticeable extent only in Wales (until 1536) and in Kent (until 1926). Primogeniture never applied to women, however, and if a female heir had sisters they all inherited equally as coparceners. Originally the women coheirs held of the eldest in parage, but parage died out before the fourteenth century because lords had more to gain by way of incidents if all the coheirs were treated as his own immediate tenants.

4. *Exclusion of collaterals of half-blood*

When an heir was sought among issue it mattered not whether the issue had been born of one marriage or another, because all the issue were the blood descendants of the deceased. A son by a second marriage would be preferred to a daughter by the first. Half-sisters could be coparceners as heirs to their father. But if a tenant died seised without issue, having a half-brother, the brother could not inherit because he was only related by the half blood. The reason for this rule was the subject of much speculation and controversy until the rule itself was abolished in 1833.[9]

Succession: Dynasty and Family

These rules of inheritance lasted, with few alterations, until 1926, when inheritance as a principle of succession was virtually abolished. Their endurance may be attributed less to their intrinsic value than to the freedom with which, in later times, they were modified. The common law ensured that unless land was disposed of or settled *inter vivos*, it would benefit a family only in a lineal, dynastic sense. Spouses, younger sons, daughters having brothers, and illegitimate children, were unprovided for because they could not inherit. The dynasty, on other hand, was totally unprotected against disherison. Inheritance operated only when the owner for the time being died seised of the land, and there was nothing to prevent an owner selling his patrimony for cash whenever he pleased.

The owner of land could attempt to circumvent either deficiency in the law of succession by making express provision for the future. He could withdraw parcels of land from the patrimony to make gifts to members of his immediate family, especially upon marriage; or he might settle the entire patrimony in such a way as to restrict the dispositive powers of his successors. In deciding whether, and to what extent, to give effect to such arrangements, the law had to resolve the

9. Inheritance Act 1833, 3 & 4 Will IV, c.106. If the elder brother had predeceased the
   father, then the half brother inherited at common law, as heir to the *father*.

conflict between the interests of the living family group and the dynastic instinct to preserve the unity of the patrimony in the male line; between the social and economic desirability of ensuring that land remained freely alienable and the paternalistic concern to restrain the rash prodigality of youthful heirs. In short, the law had to hold a balance between the dead, the living, and the unborn.

DOWER

The wife was not a descendant of her husband, and so she was outside the scope of inheritance. Husband and wife were accounted one person in law,[10] and grants from one to the other were generally void, with one important exception. A gift from husband to wife on the day they were married, at the church door, could take effect on the husband's death if he predeceased his wife. This was 'dower', and under the supervision of the Church the endowment of wives at the church door became a regular feature of the Christian marriage service. The dower lands were nominated before the marriage, and after the husband had given his wife a ring, saying 'with this ring I thee wed', he gave her tokens symbolising dower with the words 'with this dower I thee endow'. This symbolic livery gave the wife the right to an estate for life in the lands so nominated, if she survived her husband. An increasingly common arrangement in medieval times was for the husband to endow his wife generally of all his lands, without nominating any particular property. She was then entitled to claim a reasonable part of all lands owned in fee by the husband during the marriage, including land acquired or disposed of during the marriage. The law fixed her reasonable share as one third, and gave her a writ of right of dower to recover it.

The general endowment grew so common by the fourteenth century that dower ceased to depend on agreement and became a common law right. If the husband made no specific assignment of property, the widow was automatically entitled to one third, although nothing had been said at the church door. She was even entitled to her third if she rejected an offer of specific dower. This kind of dower, arising by operation of law, was called dower *ad communem legem* (at common law). By the mid-fifteenth century specified dower was exceptional.

Dower was an estate for life arising by operation of law. But estates arising by operation of law have usually proved inconvenient, for men prefer to make their own arrangements. Equity never recognised dower, and so the practice of vesting land in feoffees to uses almost put

10. See pp. 395–400, post.

an end to it. It became usual instead to provide in a marriage settlement—and sometimes in a post-nuptial settlement—for lands to be settled on the husband and wife jointly for the life of the survivor, so that a widow would have the lands during her widowhood in lieu of dower. Such a provision was called a 'jointure'. The Statute of Uses 1535, by executing uses, would have revived dower generally; so it was provided that jointresses were to elect to take their common law dower or their jointures, but not both. By the Dower Act 1833 husbands were empowered to bar dower by will or by alienation *inter vivos*,[11] and in 1925 dower was abolished in respect of persons dying after that date.

CURTESY

Dower was a one-way arrangement. A wife could not endow her husband. But often a man would marry an heiress and enjoy her lands during the marriage. If on her death the lands went immediately to her heir, the husband might be left in an unfortunate position. The common law prevented such a situation from occurring by allowing the husband to continue his seisin of his wife's inheritances until his own death. The widower in this case was called tenant *per legem Angliae*, or tenant 'by the curtesy of England'. Apparently English law was more courteous, or bounteous, to the widower than were other laws in that the life estate it gave him was not determined by remarriage. A mysterious prerequisite to tenancy by the curtesy was that a child of the marriage, capable of inheriting, should have been born.

Maitland endeavoured to explain the origin of curtesy in connection with guardianship. If the father was to be guardian of the wife's children he ought to be allowed her lands for his support. If this had ever been true, it was forgotten as a reason at a very early date. Another possibility is that curtesy originated in connection with the marriage-gift and the concomitant concept of joint ownership. If land were granted to a husband and wife and their lineal heirs, their interest became a fee only if such heirs were born alive, and if it became a fee in this way the survivor of the spouses continued to own the fee by the *jus accrescendi*. This would explain some of the features of curtesy, but not the extension of the rule to fees simple and fees vested in the wife alone before marriage, in which case the husband had only a life interest by the curtesy. Perhaps English law was 'courteous' in applying the marriage-gift rules to all estates of inheritance.

Curtesy was abolished with respect to the fee simple in 1925, but it survives as a doctrine of equity[12] in relation to entailed interests.

11. Stat 3 & 4 Will IV, c.105.
12. Equity allowed curtesy, but not dower.

THE MARRIAGE-GIFT

The assignment of *dos* at the time of marriage was recognised by the universal Church and was practised throughout Europe and beyond. But to the Civil lawyer *dos* did not mean dower; it meant dowry, a gift to the husband or wife or both of them by their parents or other relatives. In England this was called the 'marriage-gift' or *maritagium*. Gifts of this nature were very commonly made, either to establish a cadet branch of the family or to assist a daughter who was not an heiress to make a good match. Since the purpose of such gifts was to provide for the couple and their progeny, the couple were not usually given an absolute or pure fee, but an inheritance limited to their issue. This was a curtailed fee or fee tail (*feodum talliatum*). The typical form was 'to *H* and *W* and the heirs of their bodies begotten' or 'to *H* and *W* and to the heirs of *H* begotten on *W*'. The words of inheritance, as used to create a fee simple, were thus cut down by the addition of 'words of procreation'. Sometimes the gift would be in frank-marriage (*in liberum maritagium*), in which case the donees held of the donor free of all feudal services for three generations.

The marriage-gift or fee tail was not perpetual, because it would terminate when there were no longer any heirs of the body as prescribed by the form of the gift. Hence, if the couple or their issue died without issue, the land did not go to collateral heirs but 'reverted'[13] to the donor. The intentions of donors, however, could easily be defeated by alienation. According to the lawyers of the early thirteenth century, if a man gave away an inheritable fee there was no way he could restrain the donee from alienating it. A condition against alienation—that is, a provision that on an attempt to alienate the estate should cease—was, and still is, void for repugnancy. The words of procreation were therefore construed simply as a condition precedent to the existence of the fee. Until issue was born capable of inheriting, the donees had only a life interest, but on the birth of issue the fee became fully alienable. This was felt to be a mischief. For one thing, family arrangements of this nature were intended to benefit the issue alone, yet the law allowed the benefit to be carried away from the issue by alienation. For another, if the spouses had issue and then one spouse died leaving no issue capable of inheriting, the survivor had the fee absolutely and could alienate it so as to deprive the donor of his possibility of reverter. In 1258 the barons complained of the inability of the law to control these abuses, and the remedy was enacted in 1285 in the important first chapter of the second Statute of Westminster, 'of conditional gifts' (*De donis conditionalibus*).

13. For reversions, see pp. 232–233, post.

THE STATUTE DE DONIS 1285

The statute of 1285 protected the benevolent intentions of donors from frustration, in the most liberal terms. It ordained that in future when land was given to a man and wife and the heirs of their bodies, or to one person and the heirs of his body, or in frank-marriage, the will of the donor manifestly expressed in the terms of the gift (*in forma doni*) was to be observed. The issue, and the donor, were given writs of 'formedon' (from *forma doni*) to protect their statutory interests by allowing them to enforce the terms of the gift. The statute was widely construed, to enable donors to restrict categories of heirs in ways not possible at common law. Thus, a gift could be made to *A* and the heirs *male* of his body, whereas a gift to *A* and his heirs male, without words of procreation, at common law passed a fee simple, which could descend to females.

The statute produced the odd legal result that two fees could exist simultaneously in the same land; an unfeudal notion, comprehensible only in the sense that the fee had become an estate or time in the land which could vest either in possession or in the future. The fee tail created by the statute was different from the pre-1286 curtailed fee in that it was not freely alienable.[14] It was a particular estate which might come to an end; therefore, when a fee tail was given, the fee simple continued in the donor. This fee simple would not fall into possession unless the donee's issue failed, which might never happen, but it was logically necessary that it should be vested in someone, to fill the residue of eternity which would be left if and when the fee tail ended. In this respect the statute was partly responsible for the doctrine of future estates.

Reversions and Remainders

By 1300 the common law recognised the tripartite classification of estates in possession, in remainder, and in reversion. This classification is not based on the duration of the estate but on the time of its enjoyment.

The reversion is the most natural future estate. If a tenant in fee granted a life estate or a fee tail to another, something stayed behind in himself; for when the grantee's interest (the 'particular estate') ended, the land would come back (*revertere*) to him. If the particular estate had been created by subinfeudation, the reversion was the same thing as an escheat. But the reversion proper had little to do

14. It later became so: pp. 235–236, post.

with tenure; it was an absolute fee simple, an estate of infinite duration, as freely alienable as the fee simple in possession, but with the
right to possession postponed until the particular estate ended. Thus,
to say that a reversion is a 'future estate' is true only of the right to
possession; the estate was 'vested in reversion' from the moment when
the particular estate was created. Therefore, if the tenant in possession tried to alienate the fee so as to bar the reversion, the reversioner
could forthwith bring a writ of entry.[15]

If a grantor limited successive interests by the same grant, for
instance 'to *A* for life and then to *B*', the future interest of *B* was not a
reversion because it was to stay away (*remanere*) from the grantor. It
was therefore called a remainder. The remainder could be an estate of
shorter duration than a fee simple, in which case the grantor would
still have a reversion in fee simple. But if the remainder was in fee
simple, there could not be a reversion. For the same reason, successive
remainders could be carved out of the same fee simple; for instance,
'to *A* for life remainder to *B* for life remainder to *C* for life' and so on, or
'to *X* for life remainder to *Y* in tail remainder to *Z* in fee simple'.
Examples of this kind might be multiplied; provided all the remaindermen were ascertained persons, the only restriction was that a
remainder could not follow a fee simple.[16]

The law had greater difficulty in accommodating the remainder
than the reversion. The reversion may have grown up in connection
with the escheat, and it is common sense that a man who gives away a
slice of his cake keeps the cake. But a remainderman took by a form of
succession unknown to the law; he had no prior seisin, he was no one's
heir, and it was not clear what remedy he had to recover his interest.
Bracton regarded him as a quasi-heir, to whom the land 'descended',
in a loose sense, according to the *forma doni*. Perhaps the implication
was that the remainderman should use a fictitious action of formedon
in the descender. In fact the writ of formedon in the reverter seems
occasionally to have been used for the purpose, until in 1279 the
Chancery invented a new writ of formedon in the remainder.[17] In this
action the remainderman relied on the seisin of both the grantor and
the first grantee, and it came to be thought that the seisin passed to
him *via* the first grantee. But this theory availed nothing if the
remainder were 'contingent' and not vested. A contingent remainder

---

15. Statute of Westminster II 1285, c.24. The remedy where the prior estate ended in
    due course was the writ of entry called formedon in the reverter.
16. See further pp. 236–238, post.
17. *Ferlington v Brewosa* (1279–81) 10 IJ 322. Here the remainder followed a 'reversion'
    for life to the grantor after an entail. The jurors found that no seisin had passed to
    the donee in tail, and so judgment was given for the defendant.

was a remainder limited to take effect upon the happening of an uncertain event, which might not happen before the determination of the particular estate or at all, or limited to a person not ascertained at the time of the grant.[18] The common example in the year-book period was the remainder to the heir of a living person; for example, 'to *A* for life remainder to the heir of *B*'. If this contingent remainder were in fee, the location of the fee during *A*'s life was elusive. Either it stayed in the grantor until the remainderman was ascertained and the remainder vested; or it stayed until the particular estate determined and the remainder vested in possession; or it just went into thin air (*in nubibus*) until it vested. On any of these views, the remainder could only be valid if it vested before the particular estate ended; otherwise there would be an abeyance of seisin and no feudal tenant, which was a legal impossibility. The validity of contingent remainders remained a moot point in the fifteenth century, and does not seem to have been settled until the mid-sixteenth century.[19] Its subsequent importance grew out of the attempts of conveyancers to make perpetual settlements.

Settlements[20]

We have considered the ways in which a landowner could provide for living members of his family who were outside the scope of heirship. The second motivation for landowners to vary the automatic rules of law was the dynastic instinct, the desire to control the devolution of land after death and to restrain descendants from disposing of the patrimony for their own personal benefit. This instinct was especially strong as regards marriage-gifts, and we have seen how the statute *De donis* was passed in 1285 to protect these and similar gifts according to the donors' intentions.

THE FEE TAIL AND ITS DURABILITY

Did *De donis*, however, permit the tying up of land to descendants without limit of time? Were the issue in tail to have successive life

18. Gray defined a remainder as contingent when 'in order for it to come into possession, the fulfilment of some condition precedent other than the determination of the preceding freehold estate is necessary': *Rule against Perpetuities*, p. 89. A reversion could never be contingent because by definition it belonged to an ascertained person and fell into possession when the particular estate ended.

19. *Colthirst v Bejushin* (1550) Plowd 21. See also *Melton's Case* (1535), cit. Plowd 34v per Fitzherbert J.

20. A settlement was a disposition whereby several estates in succession were created by the same grant.

interests for ever? The statute was silent as to the period for which the *forma doni* was to be inviolable. Some opinion immediately after the statute was that it was only intended to postpone the fee for one generation. Bereford CJ in the early fourteenth century thought the intention was that the fee should be inalienable for three generations. Before 1400, however, the better opinion was that, in the absence of any restriction in the wording of the statute, the fee tail was inalienable for ever. Each successive heir in tail, until the end of the line, could bring formedon to thwart any attempt to discontinue the tail.

This construction gave the fee tail almost opposite characteristics from the common law fee simple. It was a rigid, unalterable, inalienable perpetuity: a 'juridical monster'.[21] No one could 'own' entailed land beyond his own lifetime. Unless some escape could be found, vast quantities of land would be tied up indefinitely. But the pressures in favour of free alienation necessarily prevailed, and ways were soon found of 'barring' the entail by converting it into a fee simple.

The earliest means of barring the entail was the warranty: an obligation to guarantee the title of the grantee, which bound the issue of the warrantor. Remaindermen and reversioners could only be barred by devices of great complexity and uncertainty, and it could not be said that the fee tail was freely alienable until the last quarter of the fifteenth century. By about 1475 a more effective means had been found, by combining the warranty with a collusive real action called a 'common recovery'. In its simplest form, the alienee brought a real action against the alienor, the tenant in tail, on an imaginary title; the tenant called upon or 'vouched' a third party to warrant his title; the vouchee defaulted; and judgment was given for the alienee to recover the land. But for the voucher, the recovery could have been avoided ('falsified') by the issue in tail bringing actions of formedon. But the effect of the voucher was that the recoveror took an indefeasible title by the judgment, and the issue in tail were compensated by judgment against the defaulting vouchee for lands of equal value. The trick which was established by 1475 was for a humble, landless official of the court to lend his name (for a fee of 4d) as the 'common vouchee'. The common vouchee would deliberately make default, and the issue would then be cut off with a worthless right to execute judgment against the lands of the landless defaulter.[22] This legal trick could hardly be faulted, since in theory the issue were not injured, and by 1500 the common recovery had made the fee tail freely convertible

21. Milsom HFCL, p. 146.
22. For the origin of the common recovery, see 94 SS *204–205*. For details of the methods of barring, see Simpson IHLL, pp. 118–129.

into a fee simple. St German raised the question whether it was consistent with conscience to allow the defeat of entails by fictions; but the Student concluded that the device was too common to question, and that the policy of *De donis* in 'magnifying the blood' was not to be favoured.[23] The recovery was especially effective since it barred the remaindermen and reversioner as well as the issue in tail.[24]

No sooner had the common recovery been established than conveyancers began to experiment with conditions to prevent barring. It was impossible to restrain the alienation of a fee simple by condition, but it could be argued that a condition restraining the barring of an entail accorded with the policy of the legislature. Sixteenth-century settlements commonly limited successive entails to each of the settlor's sons in remainder, with a perpetuity clause providing that if any tenant in tail attempted to alienate in fee his interest should determine as if he were dead and pass to the next remainderman. Such clauses were thought acceptable until Elizabeth I's time,[25] but were later held to be invalid as contravening the policy of the law that, notwithstanding *De donis*, an entail was inherently barrable.[26] The judges had contrived, first by fiction and then by judicial law making, to circumvent the unforeseen consequences of an unfortunately loose act of parliament. Thereafter it could be said that the most practical difference between the fee tail and the fee simple was the mode of conveyance.[27]

LEGAL REMAINDERS

Behind these developments may be detected the recurrent theme that the owner of land in fee, be it fee simple or fee tail, is the absolute owner and must have the power to alienate the land for a period exceeding his own life. The way to avoid such alienations, if it could be done at all, was not to impose a restraint on the fee, but to postpone the fee in such a way that the tenant in possession for the time being had only a life interest. If the fee could be kept always in remainder, no tenant in possession would be able to alienate more than a life estate unless he had the concurrence of the remainderman in fee.

The remainder could not be used, however, simply to split up a fee between a person and his own heirs so that the heirs took by way of

---

23. *Doctor and Student* (91 SS) 159.
24. *Capel's Case* (1581) 1 Co Rep 61. They too were left with a nominal right to compensation from the common vouchee.
25. See, e.g., *Scholastica's Case, Newis v Larke* (1571) 2 Plowd 403.
26. *Germin v Ascot* (1595) Moore KB 364; *Hethersall v Mildmay, Mildmay's Case* (1605) 6 Co Rep 40; *Mary Portington's Case, Portington v Rogers* (1613) 10 Co Rep 35.
27. D. Barrington *Observations on the Statutes* (4th edn, 1775), p. 132.

remainder and not by descent from their ancestor. Thus, if land were granted 'to *A* for life, remainder to *A*'s heirs', this gave the fee simple at once to *A*; it would otherwise be a fraud on the lord as causing a loss of incidents.[28] In such a case, *A* could alienate as owner in fee, because his heirs had no estate by purchase; while, if *A* died seised, there would be a descent to his heir and the feudal incidents would attach. For the same reason, a grant 'to *B* in tail, remainder to *B*'s heirs in fee simple' gave *B* a fee simple forthwith. To have held otherwise would have enabled the creation of a fee simple which could not be alienated by lineal heirs.

The ability to create a perpetual succession of remainders would have depended on the extent to which the law permitted contingent remainders. While medieval lawyers may have admitted the validity of a remainder to the heir of a living person, other forms of contingent remainder were uncommon and did not achieve full recognition until 1550. It was then declared that 'anyone who is the lawful owner of any land may give it to what person, in what manner, and in what time he pleases, so long as his gift is not contrary to law or repugnant'.[29] But, as we have seen, it was necessary that the remainder should vest at the latest by the time the particular estate came to an end. Moreover, until vesting the remainder had no legal existence; it did not belong to anyone, and was not property. Therefore, as a corollary to the principle that the remainder had to vest before the determination of the particular estate, the remainder could be destroyed by the bringing to an end of the particular estate before it vested. Thus, if land were granted to *A* for life, remainder to the heirs of *B*, and *A* made a grant in fee to *C* during *B*'s lifetime, the remainder was destroyed because by the time *B*'s heir was ascertained there was no precedent estate left to support it.[30] The common law, therefore, brooked no substantial risk of perpetuities once the entail became barrable. The usual settlement before 1536 was in the form of successive entails to named sons, who took not as heirs but as named living persons with vested remainders. A remainder after an entail might, of course, come into possession at a remote time; but there was no perpetuity because it could be barred by common recovery. The conveyancer could only give secure interests to living persons, because remainders to unborn persons were by definition contingent and as such liable to destruction.

The Statutes of Uses and Wills shook this common law system to

28. *Provost of Beverley's Case* (1366) YB Hil 40 Edw III, 9, pl.18.
29. *Colthirst v Bejushin* (1550) Plowd 21 at 34, 35 per Mountague CJ.
30. See 1 Co Rep 135v–136 (1595). The year-book opinions conflicted: Plucknett CHCL, pp. 562–564.

the foundations, by raising new possibilities which for a century and a half threw the law into turmoil.

Before 1535 there had been little occasion to create permanent settlements in use. The 'use in tail' had been discussed, and had given lawyers nightmares. *De donis* did not expressly apply to equitable interests; but if it could be taken to extend to uses, then it was impossible to bar the tail by common recovery.[31] If the status of remainders in use had been discussed, there would have been no reason to subject them to the nascent legal principles governing the time of vesting: so long as the feoffees' estate conformed to the rules, the seisin would never be in abeyance, and the feoffees would be obliged in conscience to hold the land to the use of the remainder. The problem here began with the Statute of Uses. The statutory magic of 1535, whereby the interest of *cestuy que use* was transubstantiated into a legal estate, gave rise to two bewildering conundrums.

The first conundrum was whether the Statute of Uses operated on future interests at all, and if so how. Let us suppose a grant 'to *A* to the use of *B* for life remainder to *C*'. The statute executed the use for *B*'s life by giving seisin to *B*. But what happened on *B*'s death? *B* had not been seised to the use of *C*, and yet the statute only operated where one was seised to the use of another. If the remainder was to be executed by the statute, it had to be supposed that *A* was somehow still seised to *C*'s use upon *B*'s death. The theoretical obstacle to this was that the statute had already taken *A*'s seisin and given it to *B*. There was nothing in the statute to say that *B*'s seisin could go back to *A*, because *B* had never been seised to the use of *A*. Legal ingenuity solved the puzzle by supposing that, when the use was executed in *B*, a spark of title (which Dyer called the *scintilla juris*) remained in *A* in order to ignite the remainder on *B*'s death. *C*'s interest was called an 'executory interest'; it was due to be executed, or turned into a legal estate, upon some contingency, but until it was executed it was a mere expectancy. Similar, if not worse, problems arose under the Statute of Wills 1540, because there might not be feoffees in whom the spark could be kept alight. The courts dealt boldly with such nice problems, and by the end of Elizabeth I's reign it was quite clear that future interests in use were 'executory' and subject to the statutory magic.

The second conundrum followed from the solution to the first. Executory interests became legal interests when executed, but did

31. See 94 SS *207–208.*

this make them subject to the legal rules about remainders? Strict logic at first denied the possibility. There had been no restriction on future interests in uses before 1536, and whatever had been effective in equity was now by statute turned into law. The Statute of Uses decreed that the *cestuy que use* should be deemed to be seised 'in such like estate as he had in use'; while the Statute of Wills gave full liberty to a freeholder to devise the legal estate 'at his free will and pleasure'. As late as 1575 it was said that 'uses are not directed by the rules of the common law, but by the will of the owner of the lands; for the use is in his hands as clay is in the hands of the potter, which he in whose hands it is may put into what form he pleaseth'.[32] Within a few years the courts were regretting the consequences of this logic, and were slowly but surely abandoning it. If these statutes really had been intended to make the legal rules obsolete, conveyancers could achieve whatever they wished by adding the magic words 'to the use of' in their settlements. Seisin, which for centuries had only passed with clods of earth or solemn ceremonies on the land, could now change hands in private chambers; and it could be made to skip and jump as never it could before, or even put into cold storage to await future contingencies. The spectre of perpetuities haunted the courts once again. In the sixteenth century, the search for the unbreakable settlement, following the success of the common recovery in breaking entails, led conveyancers to experiment with this new-found magic and to introduce (in Coke's words) 'upstart and wild provisoes and limitations such as the common law never knew'.

The first indication that executory interests should be governed by the legal rules came in *Shelley's Case* (1581), in which Coke made his legal reputation by persuading the King's Bench that a grant 'to the use of *X* for life, remainder after 24 years to the heirs male of the body of *X* in tail male' gave *X* a fee tail.[33] There was no discussion of perpetuities, but what had in medieval times been a feudal rule was now turned into a rule of construction applicable to uses, that 'where an ancestor by any gift or conveyance takes an estate of freehold, and in the same gift or conveyance an estate is limited to his heirs "the heirs" are words of limitation of the estate and not words of purchase'. Soon after this the courts considered some attempts to create perpetual successions of life interests by way of executory devise. The intention was that every generation the eldest son should take by

32. *Brent's Case*, *Brent v Gilbert* (1575) 2 Leon 14 at 16 per Manwood J.
33. *Woulfe d. Shelley v Shelley* (1581) 1 Co Rep 88, Dyer 373. The question arose because *X*'s heir male by descent, his great-grandson, was *en ventre sa mère* at *X*'s death; a remainder, if it were so, would therefore have vested in *X*'s second son, who was the nearest male heir living at *X*'s death.

remainder and not as heir. The courts refused to allow such schemes, and in their refusal applied the spirit of the legal remainder rules. Although it was possible to devise a remainder to an eldest son, or an 'heir' (in the singular), if the intention was that he should not take by inheritance, this could not be done in indefinite succession because all the contingent remainders had to vest before the determination of the first particular estate.[34] The courts also held that the executory interest, like the contingent remainder, was destructible; if the supporting estate of the feoffees was destroyed before the interest was executed, the *scintilla juris* was snuffed out and with it the power of executing the interest.[35]

Had the matter rested there, a good deal of confusion might have been saved. Coke foresaw this, and was firmly of opinion that uses should follow 'the rules of the common law, which are certain and well known to the professors of the law, and should not be made so extravagant that no one will know any rule to decide the questions that will arise upon them.'[36] But the matter did not rest there. Conveyances had been drawn in the belief that there was greater freedom, and there was a diversity of legal opinion as to how strictly the rules should be applied. In the confusion, various exceptions to the general principle were conceded. The judges allowed shifting uses: that is, where a fee was to pass from one to another upon a contingency. They allowed springing uses: that is, where the freehold was to commence after a term of years. Both kinds of interest were forbidden by the common law remainder rules.[37] Then, in 1620, they reached the stunning conclusion that executory interests of this kind were indestructible precisely because they did not depend upon a prior estate of freehold. The case arose from a devise 'to *A* in fee simple, with remainder to *B* in fee simple if *A* should die without heirs of the body during *B*'s life'. This could not be a legal remainder, because it followed a fee simple; and its effect if allowed would have been to create something like an entail. *A*, thinking that he *was* tenant in tail, suffered a recovery to his own use in fee simple. But the recovery was held ineffective to destroy *B*'s interest. The devise had therefore created a fee simple which in reality was an unbarrable

---

34. See *Perrott's Case, A.-G. v Perrott* (1594) Moore KB 368, in which cases from the 1580s were cited.
35. *Chudleigh's Case, Dillon v Freine* (1595) 1 Co Rep 113, 1 And 309, Poph 70; *Archer's Case, Baldwin v Smith* (1597) 1 Co Rep 66.
36. 6 Co Rep 34.
37. In 1597 a bill 'to take away future uses creating perpetuities' was introduced to ban springing and shifting uses, but it failed. Its wording shows that they were clearly established by that date. See 35 LQR 258.

entail during *A*'s life. Dodderidge J dissented vigorously on traditional grounds: 'Common recoveries are the anchor-hold and assur-
ance which subjects have for their inheritance, and it would be
dangerous to give liberty to anyone to invent such an estate as cannot
be cut down by some means . . . and although it is a praiseworthy
thing for someone who has risen from little or nothing, or has an estate
descended from his ancestors, to desire the continuance thereof in his
name and family so long as he leaves this to the providence of God;
yet, when a man endeavours to make it so firm and stable that neither
the law of the realm nor the providence of God may alter it, then it is
an unlawful thing . . . And if such perpetuities were allowed it would
in a short while take away all commerce and contract from the realm,
for no one would be able to buy or sell my land for any cause, be it
never so important.' The other judges replied that there was no
perpetuity here, for two reasons: first, that the contingency might
never happen, and second, that the fee was not inalienable because *A*
and *B* could together suffer a recovery.[38] They also had in mind a
common clause in a devise, whereby the devisee was directed to make
payments to the executors or to younger brothers, and for default of
payment the land should go to them; it was thought vital that this
form of security, although it depended on a shifting fee, should be
protected.[39]

The failure of the judges to produce a coherent system from the
confusion was perhaps the worst legacy of the sixteenth-century legal
revolution. Even in the mid-seventeenth century the average landowner must have found the land law, as Oliver Cromwell did, an
ungodly jumble. From about that time, however, the practical
difficulties were eased by the introduction of standard patterns of
strict settlement which were known to achieve what they intended.[40]
And the juristic confusion over the validity of executory interests was
ended by the definite, if unsatisfactory, rule in *Purefoy v Rogers*.[41] If a
contingent limitation could not be a common law remainder at the
outset, it was presumed to be a valid executory interest under the
Statutes of Uses or Wills. But if it could by possibility take effect at
law, the legal rules applied, and if the remainder did not vest in time it
failed. Other difficulties were solved by the survival of the unexecuted
equitable interest in the form of the trust.

---

38. *Pells v Brown* (1620) Palm 131, Cro Jac 590, 2 Rolle Rep 196, 217, HLS MS 2073,
 ff.22v, 24v. The quotation is assembled from Palmer and the MS.
39. See *Purslowe v Parker* (1600) Rolle Abr, vol. II, p. 793, to the same effect.
40. See pp. 245–247, post. Tradition attributed them to Sir Orlando Bridgman.
41. (1671) 2 Wms Saund 380. The facts of this case are extraordinarily complicated,
 and the 'rule' is usually quoted out of context.

TRUSTS

Although the Statute of Uses executed uses by turning them into legal estates, it did not abolish conscience or eradicate equitable interests in land. In situations not covered by the words of the statute, the chancellor's jurisdiction to enforce the use or trust continued as before. There were several such situations. First, if *A* made a lease for years to *B* to the use of *C*, the use was not executed because *B* was not technically 'seised' to the use of *C*. The same was true where copyholds were granted in use, because the copyholder had no seisin in law. Second, the 'active use' was not executed. If the feoffee had duties to perform, such as the collection and distribution of profits, the payment of debts, the management of an estate, or the execution of a conveyance, it would have been futile to execute the use because the duties of the trustee would have been thereby destroyed. These were called active or special trusts,[42] as opposed to the passive or general use which alone was contemplated by the statute. Third, a use in favour of a purpose rather than a person was not caught by the statute. The feoffees had to retain seisin in order to perform the trust; a purpose could not be fictionally executed. Thus charitable uses in support of educational institutions or the relief of poverty, and so forth, were protected and enforced by the Chancery. The fourth situation was the double use, were land was held by *X* to the use of *X* to the use of *Y*, or by *X* to the use of *Y* to the use of *Z*.

Where there was such a use upon a use, the statute only executed the first use and the second use was void at law because it was repugnant to the first.[43] If, however, the first *cestuy que use* was not intended to hold the land beneficially, it would have been unconscionable not to enforce the second use in Chancery. There is evidence that the chancellor enforced second uses, in proper cases, from at least 1560. The earliest reported case concerned a duchess who had sold land to a lawyer, ostensibly to his own use, but in truth subject to a secret understanding that the lawyer would hold the land to the use of the duchess. This arrangement, which had been rendered necessary by the flight of the duchess to Poland for religious reasons under the Marian persecution, was enforced by Sir Nicholas Bacon LK after Elizabeth I's accession. The reporter noted that the equity of the Chancery differed from the common law in allowing a secret trust to

42. 'Trust' originally meant the same as 'use', but came to be used for equitable estates which were not executed by the Statute of Uses: see Style 40 per Twisden.
43. *Jane Tyrrel's Case* (1557) 2 Dyer 155 (express on implied use); *Anon* (1557) 1 And 37 (implied on express use); *Anon* (1563) Moore KB 45 per Browne J (express on express use).

be set up contrary to an express use.[44] By the time of James I, deliberately created trusts were commonplace.[45]

By enforcing the second use the Chancery was not infringing the letter or the spirit of the Statute of Uses, but was properly exercising its jurisdiction in conscience. This application of the jurisdiction followed from the legal decision not to execute the second use, for the intervention of equity would have been otiose if the second use had been caught by the statute. Until the repeal of the Statute of Uses in 1926, it was common form to create trusts by a conveyance 'to *A* and his heirs unto and to the use of *A* and his heirs in trust nevertheless for *B*'. This vested the legal estate in *A* as trustee for *B*; the interposition of the first use was necessary to prevent the execution of the second use. Once again the courts had allowed policy to triumph over unintended legislative hindrances; and so 'a statute made upon great consideration, introduced in a solemn and pompous manner . . . had no other effect than to add at most three words to a conveyance.'[46]

The reasons for the creation of trusts in the sixteenth and seventeenth centuries were quite different from those which, much earlier, had brought about the use. They had nothing to do with wills, which were now valid at law. There was no intention of evading feudal revenues; if there had been, it is unthinkable that chancellors before 1645 would have connived at the evasion of fiscal legislation by recognising trusts. There were good non-feudal reasons for wishing to separate the legal from the beneficial ownership of land. The purpose might be merely temporary, for instance where the trustee was to make a conveyance at the direction of the feoffor. Or the purpose might be more permanent, as for instance to look after the land and its revenues during the minority of a beneficiary.

Perhaps the chief reasons for creating trusts were the advantages gained in settlements. For instance, they could be used to protect the estate from unthrifty sons: if land were granted 'to *X* for life, remainder to trustees for the life of *X*'s eldest son, remainder to the eldest son's heirs', the interposition of trustees prevented the eldest son from becoming the owner of any legal estate.[47] The interposition of trustees

44. *Duchess of Suffolk v Herenden* (1560) 93 LQR 36. For the background, see also 2 Dyer 176.
45. Henry Sherfield's reading (1624) 93 LQR 37, 38. See also *Sir Moyle Finch's Case* (1600) Co Inst, vol. IV, pp. 85 at 86; *Sambach v Dalston* (1635) Tothill 188, Nelson 30, 74 LQR 550.
46. *Hopkins v Hopkins* (1738) 1 Atk 581 at 591 per Lord Hardwicke C. His lordship's historical sense on this occasion was as questionable as his arithmetic. The real object of the statute had been spent since the abolition of military tenures in 1645.
47. *Corbet's Case* (1600) Brit Lib MS Lansdowne 1074, f.312. It was some time, however, before it was settled that the trustees' estate was indestructible.

had the added advantage of preserving contingent remainders and barring dower. From the seventeenth century a familiar mode of settlement was 'to *X* for life, remainder (after the determination of *X*'s estate for any reason in his lifetime) to trustees for the life of *X* in trust to preserve the contingent remainders expectant upon his decease from being destroyed, remainder to *X*'s eldest son'. A very similar device was perfected by Fearne in the eighteenth century in order to bar a widow from her dower by splitting the fee into a life estate and a remainder and interposing trustees to prevent the estates from merging; for instance, 'to *H* for life (with unlimited power of disposition), remainder (after the determination of *H*'s estate for any reason in his lifetime) to trustees for the life of *H* upon trust for *H* and to the express intent that *H*'s wife may not be entitled to dower, remainder to *H* and his heirs for ever'. Another useful device, which appeared in the sixteenth century, was the trust for a married woman's 'sole and separate use', which enabled her to own property independently of her husband during the marriage.[48]

THE DOCTRINE OF PERPETUITIES

There was no logical reason why trusts should be subject to the legal rules which prevented perpetuities, because their rationale did not extend to equitable interests. Trusts were also theoretically exempt from the confusion over executory interests, and should have continued in the supposedly uninhibited state which uses had been in prior to 1535. But obviously the policy of forbidding unbreakable settlements was applicable in equity as much as in law. As early as 1624, a reader of Lincoln's Inn, unconsciously echoing Audley's strictures on uses in 1526, attacked trusts as introducing yet more uncertainty into the land law and went so far as to urge their total extirpation.[49] Hostility was still felt in mid-century,[50] but the trust was by then firmly rooted. In the Restoration period, chancellors such as Lord Nottingham set about to formulate the law of trusts, which by then were treated as equitable estates governed by known rules. One of the chief principles settled in Lord Nottingham's time was the perpetuity doctrine, which, though formulated in relation to trusts, was based on legal decisions and offered such an acceptable compromise that it was generally accepted in all the courts thereafter. The doctrine was commendable for its simplicity. Instead of testing settlements by a mass of abstract and arbitrary principles relating to

48. See pp. 396–397, post.
49. 93 LQR 37 at 38 per Sherfield, Lect.
50. See *R v Holland* (1647) Style 20 at 40.

the character of the contingency, such as the rule against uncommon possibilities and the rule against double possibilities, Lord Nottingham proposed that the validity of a contingent interest be tested by the remoteness of its time of vesting. If it would necessarily vest within the lifetime of a person or persons in being at the date of the settlement, it was valid.[51] Though often called the 'rule against perpetuities', the decision was seen by contemporaries as introducing a degree of relaxation in favour of complex contingencies which were not remote in time. Lord Guilford, who succeeded to the great seal in 1682, thought the principle too liberal: 'A perpetuity is a thing odious in law, and . . . is not to be countenanced in equity. If in equity you should come nearer a perpetuity than the rules of the common law would admit, all men being desirous to continue their estates in their families would settle their estates by way of trust; which might indeed make well for the jurisdiction of the court, but would be destructive to the commonwealth.'[52] He reversed the decision, but Lord Nottingham was upheld by a unanimous House of Lords. The decision approved a particular perpetuity period (a life in being), but it did not set the limits of remoteness. Eighteenth-century decisions added twenty-one years plus the gestation period. It had always been acceptable to settle land on A for life, remainder to the heirs of B in fee tail. This postponed the fee during A's life, and also for practical purposes during the minority of the remainderman in tail, because an infant could not suffer a common recovery. In the extreme case that on A's death B had just died leaving an infant *en ventre sa mère*, the fee would have been postponed for a further twenty-one years and nine months beyond the life of A. That was the maximum the law would allow, but it came to be regarded as a period 'in gross' which did not have to be related to a settlement of the kind just mentioned. The maximum permissible period for postponing the fee, both at law and in equity, was therefore a life in being plus a term of twenty-one years, whether or not the life was that of a beneficiary, and whether or not the twenty-one-year period related to the infancy of a beneficiary.[53]

THE STRICT SETTLEMENT

The form of settlement which was perfected in the seventeenth century, and remained in use for three hundred years, was essentially the common law arrangement which gave only a life estate to the owner of

---

51. *Howard v Duke of Norfolk, Duke of Norfolk's Case* (1680–83) 3 Cas in Ch 1 at 2, 2 Swanst 454.
52. S.C., 1 Vern 163, 164.
53. *Cadell v Palmer* (1833) 1 Cl & Fin 372.

the land for the time being and limited remainders in tail to each of his children in order of seniority. This was combined with the appointment of trustees to raise various sums of money for the maintenance of other members of the family and to preserve contingent remainders.

The settlement was set out in a conveyance to the trustees of the settlement 'to the uses hereinafter declared'; the uses in favour of the life tenant and his issue were turned into legal estates by the Statute of Uses, while the uses in favour of the trustees (being uses upon uses) subsisted in equity. The typical uses, where no son had yet been born to the settlor, were:

1) To the settlor for life, subject to a rent-charge to provide the settlor's wife with pin-money (an annuity for her personal use) during her husband's lifetime. In the case of a marriage settlement, the first use would be to the settlor in fee simple until the solemnisation of the marriage and subject thereto to the husband for life.

2) Remainder to the trustees during the life of the life tenant, to preserve the contingent remainders from destruction in the event of a premature determination of the life estate.

3) Remainder to the trustees for a long term of years (say, 500 years from the death of the life tenant), to raise a jointure for the life tenant's widow and portions (lump sums of money by way of advancement) for his younger sons.

4) Subject thereto, remainders to each of the sons of the life tenant severally and successively in order of seniority, in tail male; followed by remainders to each of the same sons successively in tail general. The first remainder in tail vested on the death of the life tenant, but it was subject to the portions term; usually the remainderman in tail paid off the jointure and portions, if necessary borrowing the money on mortgage, so that he could take possession free of the trustees' term of years.

5) Also subject to the portions term, successive remainders to the daughters of the life tenant severally in tail; *or* (more usually) remainder to the daughters as tenants in common in tail, with cross remainders. The effect of cross remainders was that on the death of one daughter her share remained to the others as tenants in common, so that the land would descend only to the issue of the last surviving sister.

6) Remainder or reversion in fee simple: usually to the settlor and his heirs for ever.

This type of settlement was intended to last only for one generation. It was binding on the life tenant and his eldest son until the latter came of age, because a minor could not suffer a recovery. If the eldest son came of age while his father was living, he would be persuaded to co-operate in a 'resettlement', achieved by means of a common recovery to bar the entails of the former settlement. Under the new settlement the son's interest would be reduced to a life estate in remainder, with the usual remainders in tail to his own sons and daughters. He would be encouraged to assent to this by the grant of an immediate income charged on the land during his father's lifetime, by the advancement of his female issue in the order of succession (because they would now precede his brothers and sisters and their issue), and if he was already married by the provision of pin-money and a jointure for his wife. If the eldest son came of age after his father's death, he would himself make a resettlement upon marriage for similar reasons. The idea was that there should be a resettlement each generation, making appropriate adjustments for changes in the family, so that no tenant in possession would normally have more than a life estate or be in a position to dispose of the fee. The general employment of the strict settlement and resettlement by the landed classes shackled much of the land in England to the same families until Victorian times and beyond.

The economic undesirability of keeping so much land out of circulation was keenly felt in the nineteenth century. It was not simply that the land could not be sold out of the family and that the *nouveaux riches* could not acquire real property. The 'owner', the tenant for life, could not without special powers exercise the normal functions of leasing, mining and felling timber which belonged to an absolute owner. In this way the strict settlement might inhibit the proper exploitation of the landed wealth. The requisite powers could be conferred on the tenant for life by each individual settlement, according to the foresight of the settlor and his counsel; in many cases unforeseen situations compelled landowners to seek private acts of parliament as the only escape. In Victorian times the most commonly needed powers were by public general statutes conferred on all tenants for life of settled land.[54]

The final stage in the history of the settlement realised the economic fact that, local sentiment apart, a settlement of land was a settlement of wealth which need not be tied to specific pieces of land. Settled land could be made freely alienable without destroying settlements in economic terms. So the tenant for life was given the ultimate power of an owner, the power to sell the land in fee simple.

54. Settled Estates Act 1856, 19 & 20 Vict, c.120; Settled Estates Act 1877, 40 & 41 Vict, c.18; supplemented by the Settled Land Act 1882, 45 & 46 Vict, c.38.

On his doing so, the settlement was not destroyed but attached itself to the proceeds of sale.[55] The power of sale may be given to trustees rather than the tenant for life, and if the trustees are obliged to exercise this power the arrangement is a 'trust for sale'. In practice the trust for sale has become a less cumbersome way of conferring wealth on a succession of beneficiaries than the traditional strict settlement, which is generally used only for large country mansions and estates which are intended to remain in the same family as long as circumstances permit. Settlements of this latter kind have in the present century suffered severely from the crippling effect of increased death duties on successive life interests. Between 1900 and 1970 the rate of death duties increased about a hundred-fold, and many settled estates were eaten away by taxation deliberately aimed at destroying hereditary wealth and preventing the establishment of landed families in the dynastic sense. As in medieval times, the conveyancer has sought ways of avoiding the incidence of taxation; and as Chancery counsel have exercised their ingenuity in parrying fiscal onslaughts, so the law of property has become still more complex. The old law, enshrined in *Littleton* and *Coke*, has declined with the landed gentry whose fortunes it governed for so long.

Further reading

Pollock & Maitland, vol. II, pp. 1–28

Holdsworth HEL, vol. III, pp. 101–197; vol. VII, pp. 78–238

Plucknett CHCL, pp. 521–530, 546–623

Simpson IHLL, pp. 44–96, 112–129, 195–224

Milsom HFCL, pp. 140–168, 196–210; 'Formedon before De Donis' (1956) 72 LQR 391–397

P. Bordwell, 'The Common Law Scheme of Estates Revisited' (1933) 18 *Iowa Law Rev* 425–444; 'The Conversion of the Use into a Legal Interest' (1935) 21 *Iowa Law Rev* 1–49; 'Alienability and Perpetuities' (1937–40) 22 ILR 437–460, 23 ILR 1–23, 24 ILR 1–66, 635–659, 25 ILR 1–32, 707–736

J. C. Gray, *The Rule against Perpetuities* (4th edn, 1942), pp. 126–190

D. E. C. Yale, [on the perpetuity rule] (1954) 73 SS lxxiii–xci; 'Equitable Estates in the 17th Century' [1957] CLJ 72–86

J. L. Barton, 'The Statute of Uses and the Trust of Freeholds' (1966) 82 LQR 215–225

P. A. Brand, 'Formedon in the Remainder before De Donis' (1975) 10 IJ 318–323

55. Settled Land Acts 1882 (ante), 1890, 53 & 54 Vict, c.69, and 1925, 15 Geo V, c.18.

G. L. Haskins, 'Extending the Grasp of the Dead Hand:
  Reflections on the Origins of the Rule against Perpetuities'
  (1977) 126 *Univ Pennsylvania Law Rev* 19–46
J. H. Baker, 'The Use upon a Use in Equity 1558–1625' (1977) 93
  LQR 33–38; 'Family Settlements' (1978) 94 SS *204–209*

Table C. Classification of estates

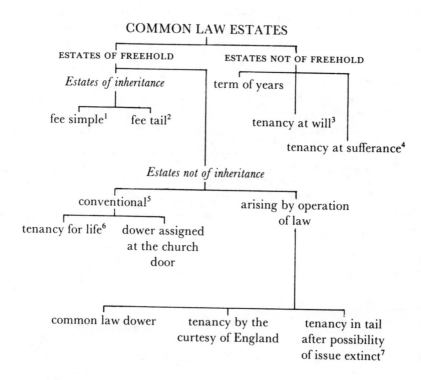

1. Absolute, conditional or qualified.
2. General or special (e.g., limited to male heirs).
3. Including the copyhold tenancy, which was at the will of the lord of the manor.
4. Including the interest of the *cestuy que use* in possession.
5. I.e., arising by act of the parties.
6. A tenancy *pur autre vie* might be an estate *quasi* of inheritance by special occupancy:
   e.g., to *A* and his heirs for the life of *B*.
7. A fee having some attributes of the life estate, because it cannot descend.

Table D. Modes of conveying real property

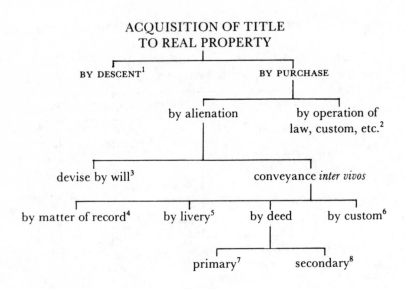

ACQUISITION OF TITLE
TO REAL PROPERTY

BY DESCENT[1]   BY PURCHASE

by alienation   by operation of law, custom, etc.[2]

devise by will[3]   conveyance *inter vivos*

by matter of record[4]   by livery[5]   by deed   by custom[6]

primary[7]   secondary[8]

1. Three modes: (i) at common law, (ii) in tail, under the Statute *De Donis* 1285, (iii) customary, e.g., gavelkind.
2. E.g., by escheat, forfeiture, limitation, general occupancy.
3. Either by borough custom (as in London) or by statute.
4. E.g., Act of Parliament, letters patent under the great seal, deed enrolled, final concord, bargain and sale enrolled.
5. Only appropriate to corporeal hereditaments; the livery of seisin was usually accompanied by a charter to evidence the estate granted.
6. E.g., surrender and admittance in court customary.
7. Creating an estate, e.g., feoffments, gifts, grants, demises.
8. Dealing with a pre-existing estate, e.g., releases, quitclaims, confirmations, surrenders, assignments, disentailing devices.

15. Interests in Land less than Freehold

Not all interests in land were subject to the developments described in the last two chapters. Two important kinds of interest grew up outside the common law scheme of real property. For quite different reasons, the lessee for years and the copyholder were not regarded as freehold tenants; but, as their social and economic positions changed, their interests were assimilated to that of the freeholder by the development of the action of ejectment.

The Term of Years

A 'term of years', or lease for years, is the right to the occupation of land for a fixed period of time, usually but not necessarily a number of years. The term was not a freehold interest and was therefore exempt from the feudal rules about seisin, inheritance and future interests. It may be surprising that an estate in land for nine hundred and ninety-nine years is a chattel whereas an estate which lasts only for one man's lifetime is a freehold. The distinction obviously does not represent the quantity of an estate, in respect of its duration; it is a distinction of quality which lost its rational basis many centuries ago.

The quality of the lessee's interest as a chattel is usually accounted for by showing that it was not protected by the writ of right or the assize of *novel disseisin*. If the lessee had no real action for his protection, his property was not real but personal. Bracton's explanation for the denial of the real actions to the lessee was that the possession of land for a certain period could not be called a 'free' tenement (*liberum tenementum*), and the real actions lay only for a free tenement or freehold. Both explanations are somewhat circular. The true reason for the lessee's exclusion must be sought in the feudal context. The freeholder who made a lease for years did not part with his seisin or his fee. The lessee was regarded as a usufructuary rather than an absolute owner, and had only the possession of the land without any 'right'. If he were ejected, that was a disseisin not of himself but of his lessor.

Maitland criticised Bracton for finding an analogy with the Civil law usufruct, and said that 'English law for six centuries and more will rue this youthful flirtation with Romanism'.[1] But it seems that Bracton was simply borrowing Roman vocabulary to explain an existing English state of affairs. The lessee in fact had no feudal existence, and so in law he could not be seised of a free tenement.

The question why the lessee had no place in the feudal framework cannot be answered by the application of abstract logic. The answer is to be found in the original purpose and function of the term of years. The unit of feudal ownership was the holding for life, and the hereditary fee was by its nature the property of a family. The tenant in fee took an oath of homage for life and not for a limited number of years. The real actions were developed to protect feudal and family interests of this nature. But the letting for years did not, in its original form, confer any family interest. It was a temporary commercial or financial interest, commonly granted to secure a loan of money. A landowner who needed cash could hand over the possession or profits of his land to a money-lender for the period of the loan, so that the profits would slowly pay off the debt. This was the living gage, as opposed to the dead gage or mortgage in which the land was a passive security. In Glanvill's time (c. 1190) the mortgage was tainted with usury, and was tolerated only with misgivings; but the lease was free from moral or legal difficulty. The intention behind the gage was that the fee should belong to the borrower throughout, but that the use or profits of the land should be surrendered to another until the loan was repaid. The arrangement was a matter of contract, not subinfeudation, and the legal remedy of the lessee against his lessor was accordingly the writ of covenant rather than a real action. The lessee's possession was protected against grantees of the lessor by the writ *quare ejecit infra terminum*. Against the rest of the world his only remedy was in damages for trespass *de ejectione firmae* (ejectment); the freehold was for the lessor alone to protect.

The tenant for years owned a capital interest which by 1300 enjoyed the name 'chattel'. It could be bought and sold, but not entailed or settled, and on the death of the lessee it passed to his legatees or next-of-kin together with his movables.

CHANGE IN NATURE OF TERM OF YEARS

Most leases at the present day involve letting the beneficial enjoyment of land at a rent. The lessee is regarded as the owner of the land for many purposes, and the lessor as the owner of a reversion which

1. Pollock & Maitland, vol. II, p. 115.

entitles him during the term to the rent. Here is a parallel with the sort of arrangement achieved before 1290 with freehold interests. The landowner before 1290 could subinfeudate to a tenant in fee, at a rent, and this was called 'fee farm' from the Latin word for rent (*firma*). The purpose of the fee farm was usually to produce a regular periodic income for the feudal lord. But the rent-payer or farmer (*firmarius*), though he might have paid a premium, was not a money-lender; he wanted possession of the land for his own use and that is what he was paying for. He could not afford to buy the fee outright, so he bought it for a rent and became a tenant farmer.

When the statute *Quia emptores* ended subinfeudation in 1290,[2] it incidentally deprived landowners of this method of securing an income. They could still alienate their property in fee farm by substitution, so that the rent was a charge on the land rather than a feudal service, but would then have to part with their property permanently and their manors would be broken up. A similar effect to subinfeudation could, however, be achieved by leasing the land for years to a rent-paying tenant or *firmarius*; and within a century of *Quia emptores* the husbandry lease to farm (*dismissio ad firmam*) became very common.

By the fifteenth century the typical lessee for years was a farmer in the modern sense, a husbandman with insufficient capital to buy estates in fee but able to pay rent out of the fruits of his labour. The lease for years had come to do the work of feudalism; the lessor came to be called the 'landlord', and it was said that the lessee owed him fealty.[3] The farmer needed legal protection as much as the freehold tenant, and the fact that the subject of his ownership was only a chattel was an historical accident which ought not to stand in the way of a remedy. The action of ejectment, being a form of trespass, properly lay only for damages. A precedent has been found as early as 1389 in which a lessee recovered his term in an action of ejectment,[4] but another century passed before the lessee's right to recovery *in rem* was established beyond dispute. The objection to such a remedy was that a trespassory action, such as ejectment, was concerned only with wrongs already done and not with continuing rights. The judges may have overcome their doubts in the fifteenth century because the Chancery had begun to offer relief to the lessee; at any rate the law was settled by a decision of 1500.[5] The form of judgment in the action of ejectment was that the plaintiff recover his term and also the

2. See p. 208, ante. For the implications in this context, see Milsom HFCL, p. 100.
3. Littleton *Tenures*, s.143.
4. Plucknett CHCL. p. 373, n.5.
5. *Gernes v Smyth* (1500) 94 SS *181* n.7. The decision was upheld in 1525 and 1530: ibid. n.8.

damages occasioned by the trespass. The giving of possession could be enforced by the judicial writ *habere facias possessionem*. By these means ejectment became, in effect, a real action. The common law managed to digest the incongruity of a chattel interest having the character of realty, and named it the 'chattel real'.

USE OF EJECTMENT TO TRY FREEHOLD TITLE

The action of ejectment, as a result of this bold development, gave the leaseholder a remedy superior in practice to anything available to the freeholder. It enabled him to recover possession by a form of action free of the technicalities of the writs of entry and the possessory assizes, and in which trial was by jury. Naturally, freeholders envied the new real action, and by about 1570–80 they had, through a simple expedient, assumed the use of it as their own standard remedy. Indeed, its use became so prevalent that Lord Ellesmere complained of 'a great decay of the true knowledge and learning of the law in real actions'; it had 'almost utterly overthrown all actions real that be possessory, as assizes of novel disseisin and writs of entry'.[6]

The freeholder would lease the land in question to a friend for the purpose of bringing the action, and would contrive to put him in possession so that he would be ejected by the defendant. The nominal lessee would then bring ejectment against the defendant, and issue would be joined on the title to the freehold; in other words, the question to be tried would be which of the two real disputants had the better title. Judgment for the plaintiff lessee would in effect entitle the freeholder to possession, for the lessee would surrender the lease once its object had been attained. This action was so much more convenient than the older real actions that the judges encouraged its use, and refused to allow defendants to evade the issue of title by disputing the details of the lessee's entry and physical ejectment. As a result, the whole process was by the later seventeenth century the subject of a remarkable series of fictions.

In its perfected form, the action of ejectment was brought by a wholly imaginary lessee, usually called John Doe, against an equally imaginary person, sometimes called Richard Roe, William Styles or Shamtitle, who was supposed to be the lessee of the person in possession and to have ejected John Doe. These fictitious creatures were puppets of the real claimant, who could pull the strings without incurring the trouble, and the possible danger, of making a physical entry, granting an actual lease, and waiting for the lessee to be personally ejected by the real defendant. The puppet defendant was

6. 'Memorialls for Judicature' in L. A. Knafla *Law and Politics in Jacobean England* (1977), p. 276. Mr Knafla's note on this passage was evidently appended in error.

made to inform the real defendant that an action had been commenced against him, asking him to intervene to defend his title. The court, of course, allowed the real defendant to intervene, but only on condition that he signed the 'consent rule'. This rule obliged the defendant to accept the fictions and to enter a plea of not guilty. As a result, questions of title were raised in evidence to the jury on the general issue, and the more slippery technicalities associated with pleading title were eliminated.

Ejectment replaced the old real actions in all the cases where it would lie, but it was not quite universal. The fictions enabled the plaintiff to take a short cut only where he could have gone the long way. Since a valid lease could only be granted by a person entitled to enter the freehold, the fictitious apparatus could not be set up if the real plaintiff had no right of entry; the courts would not admit the pretence of a situation which was incapable of existence as a fact. The action was not available if the plaintiff's right of entry had been 'tolled' (taken away by law) through failure to exercise it in time; for instance, after a descent from the disseisor to his heir, or after the expiration of the twenty-one year limitation period ordained in 1623.[7] Furthermore, ejectment would not lie for those types of property which in their nature could not be entered upon and leased; such as advowsons, rights of way, and unassigned dower.

For two and a half centuries then, the usual action to recover real property involved two fictitious parties. Even the title of an ejectment action—*Doe d. Smith v Roe*[8]—concealed the truth. In 1833 ejectment was raised to the status of being the only permissible real action, except for the writ of right of dower and the action of *quare impedit* for advowsons. John Doe and Richard Roe were retired in 1852 when fictions were abolished.[9] The present action to recover possession of land is the direct successor of ejectment, and the rules about proof of title are, with statutory alterations, those developed in actions of ejectment rather than in the old real actions.

LEASES AND SETTLEMENTS

The usual husbandry lease was not for a long period; twenty-one years would have been normal. The ninety-nine year building lease was the longest beneficial term created in the ordinary course of events. Longer leases may in medieval times have been regarded as unsafe because they were precarious; if the lessor died leaving an

7. Statute of Limitations 1623, 21 Jac I, c.16.
8. I.e. Doe (nominal plaintiff) on the demise of Smith (real plaintiff) against Roe (casual ejector).
9. Real Property Limitation Act 1833, 3 & 4 Will IV, c.27; Common Law Procedure Act 1852, 15 & 16 Vict, c.76.

infant heir, the guardian's rights in the land took priority over the lease.[10] The social and economic transformation of the lease rendered this state of the law unacceptable and so, after considerable vacillation in Henry VIII's reign, it was settled by the mid-sixteenth century that the lessee should be preferred to the guardian.[11] This was pure judicial legislation, but it was no more shocking than allowing the lessee a real action. An unforeseen consequence of this change of view was that it opened the way to very long leases. In the sixteenth century leases for as long as a thousand years were made, perhaps in some cases with the intention of avoiding feudal incidents.[12] The new status of the lessee gave the conveyancer much to think about in the sixteenth century. The lease was now a protected estate with many of the attributes, but none of the burdens, of feudal tenure. If long leases could be used in creating settlements, there might be a way of avoiding the rules about contingent remainders and executory interests; while the splitting of ownership between a lessee and a reversioner, neither of whom could convey the freehold in possession, brought perpetuities within reach.

The first obstacle in the way of using leases in settlements was that estates could not be created in chattels. It was, however, possible to settle the use of chattels, and such uses were not executed by the Statute of Uses.[13] The widest possibilities were those opened up by the Statute of Wills 1540, which empowered a testator to dispose of his real and personal property 'at his will and pleasure'. Soon after the statute it was held that a testator could devise a term of years to X, and if X should die during the term then to Y.[14] Y's interest could not technically be a remainder, since there could be no remainder in a chattel; it was a quasi-remainder or 'possibility of remainder'. If and when the time came, the whole term passed from X to Y. The exact nature of an executory devise of a term was much in doubt in the later sixteenth century. The better opinion in the 1550s was that the first devisee took the whole term and could therefore bar the executory devise,[15] but it was later settled that the second devisee had more than a mere possibility and that his interest could not be destroyed by the first devisee.[16] Each devisee took the whole term, but subject to the rights of the other.

10. See Arnold [1976] CLJ at 326.   11. For the controversy, see 94 SS *182*.
12. See *Risden v Tuffin* (1597) Tothill 122; *Anon* (1599) Cary 9.
13. *Mayntell's Case* (a. 1553) cit. in Brit Lib MS Harley 1691, f.91v. See also p. 242, ante; and p. 324, post.
14. *Anon* (1551) Brit Lib MS Hargrave 4, f.116v; *Anon* (1553) Brit Lib MS Harley 5141, f.6v.
15. *Anon* (1541) Bro NC 49; *Anon* (1552) 1 Dyer 74.
16. *Welcden v Elkington* (1578) 2 Plowd 516. See also *Lampet's Case, Lampet v Starkey* (1612) 10 Co Rep 46.

Since the executory devise was indestructible and inalienable, and the carving up of leases was not subject to the rules about the abeyance or postponement or shifting of the freehold, these developments might have opened the way to effective perpetuities. Yet a perpetuity for a thousand years would have been as mischievous as a perpetual fee, and an entailed lease would have contravened the policy of the law in that it could not have been barred by common recovery. The judges recognised these problems and refused to allow a term to be entailed,[17] or to be devised in a way which would infringe the legal rules designed to prevent remote possibilities and perpetuities.[18] In the seventeenth century, executory devises for years seem (from the law reports) to have been much used in creating future interests, and the decisions concerning leases played an important part later in the century in the formulation of the perpetuity doctrine by Lord Nottingham.[19]

LEASES AND CONVEYANCING: LEASE AND RELEASE

Another appendix to the history of leases for years is the story of the replacement of livery of seisin as the only mode of conveying a freehold estate in possession. The Statute of Uses introduced a second mode of legal conveyance by effecting a constructive transfer of seisin when a use was executed; thus, a bargain and sale of land by A to B raised a use in favour of B which the statute executed. A contract would therefore have been simultaneously completed, by a fictional livery of seisin; but it was enacted that, to have this effect, the sale was to be enrolled in the plea rolls of one of the courts at Westminster.[20] After 1535, therefore, the freehold in possession could be conveyed either by livery of seisin or by bargain and sale enrolled. Both were public and formal, and the secret and informal modes of transferring the use before 1536 were not allowed to pass legal title. There was, however, a chink in the legislation which was discovered within a century. The Statute of Uses executed a contract to grant a lease, because the lessor on making the contract stood seised to the use of the lessee. The Statute of Enrolments did not, however, provide for the compulsory enrolment of such a contract. Therefore if A contracted to make a lease to B, and then granted ('released') the reversion to B by deed, the freehold would have passed from A to B in two stages without any livery or enrolment being necessary.[21] This was probably

17. *Peacock's Case* (1576) cit. 10 Co Rep 87; *Lovies's Case* (1613) 10 Co Rep 78.
18. *Child v Baylie* (1623) Cro Jac 459, Palm 48, 333, 2 Rolle Rep 129.
19. See p. 245, ante. Lord Nottingham expressly overruled *Child v Baylie*.
20. Statute of Enrolments 1535, 27 Hen VIII, c.16.
21. The device was recognised in *Lutwich v Mitton* (1620) Cro Jac 604.

discovered in genuine cases, but in the seventeenth century a nominal lease followed by a release became a usual mode of conveyance. The device was traditionally attributed to Sir Francis Moore (d. 1616), a serjeant-at-law. In making a settlement, a settlor would enter into a bargain and sale to trustees for a short term at a nominal premium and then execute a deed releasing the reversion to the trustees upon the trusts of the settlement. In the course of time, the release became the only deed actually made, and the recital of the bargain and sale in this deed would estop the parties from denying its existence. This fiction by estoppel was given the force of law in 1841, but four years later practice was simplified by a statute which enabled corporeal hereditaments to be transferred by grant.[22]

Tenancy at Will

Sometimes the occupier of land has a beneficial interest and yet has no recognisable estate, because he does not hold the land for any defined period. Examples are where a lessee for years 'holds over' at the end of his term, with the lessor's consent, or where *cestuy que use* enjoys the possession of land belonging in law to feoffees. In the sixteenth century these were classified as tenants 'at sufferance' because, although they were not trespassers, they had no legal rights in the land at all.[23] Then there were cases where a person was directly and purposely given an interest in land to last as long as the grantor liked. This was called 'tenancy at will'. Such a tenancy would arise if a lease were made without a fixed term being defined; the lessee could be given notice to quit at any time, but the law gave him a reasonable time to leave and also any crops he had sown during the tenancy (his *emblements*). In the sixteenth and seventeenth centuries the courts inclined to the view that a periodic tenancy, a tenancy from year to year at the pleasure of the parties, was a lease for one year or two, depending on the words used, followed by a tenancy at will.[24] Later the courts tended to construe demises for uncertain terms as successive yearly leases.[25] Thus the precarious position of the tenant at will was avoided wherever possible by finding that an estate of certain duration was intended.

22. Conveyance by Release Act 1841, 4 & 5 Vict, c.21; Real Property Act 1845; 8 & 9 Vict, c.106. A few forms of property still 'lie in livery' and not in grant: e.g. ecclesiastical benefices and fellowships in some colleges (which require induction), and degrees in some universities.
23. Cf. licences, pp. 261–262, post.
24. The leading case is *Burgh v Potkyn* (1522) Spelman Rep (93 SS) 136; 94 SS *183–184*.
25. *Right d. Flower v Darby* (1786) 1 Term Rep 159; Bl Comm, vol. II, p. 147.

The most important kind of tenant at will in medieval times, and the principal example given by Bracton and Littleton, was the unfree tenant who held at the will of his lord. The interest of the villein underwent a radical transformation in Tudor times into an estate as sure as any freehold or leasehold: the copyhold tenancy.

Copyhold

Much of the land in medieval England, especially that comprised within manors, was held by unfree tenure. The distinguishing mark of villeinage, for lawyers, was that the services were uncertain; the tenant had to do what his lord demanded, and had no rights in the property beyond those which the lord acknowledged in his own manorial court. In practice the tenant's position might be secure, and his lord's demands reasonable. In many manors there were customs allowing the tenant's heir to succeed on paying relief, as in the case of freehold land. In so far as it was governed by custom, the lord's rule was not arbitrary; but it did not fall under the control of the common law in the twelfth century when the 'right' of the freeholder achieved recognition in the royal courts.[26] The ancient real actions were devised at a time when villein tenure and villein status were not clearly distinguished, and when the Crown would only interfere with the feudal establishment at the behest of a free man. So the legal analysis of tenure in villeinage in Littleton's time was that the lord was the freehold tenant, seised in fee and protected by the real actions, and the tenant was merely his tenant at will.[27]

The tenant in villeinage had no seisin and he could not transfer his interest without the lord's consent. The only way in which his interest could be alienated was by surrender to the lord on trust to admit the alienee; the alienee was admitted at a session of the manorial court and the fact entered on the court rolls. Hence the tenant by the custom of the manor was called 'tenant by copy of court roll', the roll being the only evidence of his title. For the same reason, this kind of holding was named 'copyhold'. The copyhold tenant could not sue or be sued in the common law courts in respect of his holding, but all actions concerning copyholds were brought in the lord's court by plaint. Such was the medieval law.

Social and economic change, the supposed effect of the Black Death

26. See pp. 200–202, ante.
27. Littleton *Tenures*, s.77.

on peasant labour, the commutation of unfree services for fixed payments, and the ownership of copyholds by freemen, all combined to make villeinage an anachronism by the fifteenth century. Even if the tenant had no protection against his lord, there was no good reason why he should not be protected against the rest of the world. And in truth there was no good reason why he should not be protected against his lord. The decline of feudal reality had made the freehold tenant the legal landowner vis-à-vis his lord, and reason demanded that the same should happen to the copyholder.

LEGAL RECOGNITION OF THE COPYHOLDER

The common law hardened too early for the copyholder to be accommodated directly; he was only a tenant at will. It was clearly unconscionable, however, for a lord to flout the established custom of his manor, and if he failed to do right to his copyhold tenant the Chancery, by the fifteenth century, would compel him to do so.[28] Perhaps spurred on by the Chancery, some common law judges of the late fifteenth century began to contemplate actions of trespass by the copyholder against the lord to protect his tenancy; but such a right of action was never established.[29] The common law solved the difficulty in the 1570s or 1580s, by allowing the copyholder's lessee to bring ejectment and by recognising the copyhold title in such an action.[30] By this means copyholds were at last protected by what was in practice a real action. In strict theory, estates in copyhold land were not subject to the common law rules, but to the customs of each particular manor; but the tendency in the sixteenth and seventeenth centuries was to assimilate copyholds as far as possible to freeholds, and the common law was presumed to apply unless the contrary could be proved. In spite of this liberal approach, many of the peculiar rules remained embedded in the law and the distinction between freehold and copyhold, necessitating for the latter the ancient form of conveyance by surrender and admittance, remained a vital distinction until 1926.

---

28. Fitz Abr *Subpena*, pl.21.
29. It was established that the tenant could plead the custom of the manor against the lord, in trespass brought *by* the lord: *Tropnell v Kyllyk* (1505) Keil 76. But it did not follow that the tenant could sue his lord on the custom, and this remained uncertain until ejectment made the question obsolete: see 94 SS *184–187*.
30. *Melwich v Luter* (1588) 4 Co Rep 26, is a clear example.

Licences

A licence to go upon or use land, being merely an authority to do what would otherwise be a tort, does not possess the characteristics of a property right. It is inalienable: if I license *A* to visit my house for dinner, he cannot substitute *B*. It is not enforceable *in rem*: a countermand is effective, though it may be a breach of contract, and the licensee who ignores it becomes a trespasser.[31] A fortiori, a licence cannot be invoked against a purchaser from, or lessee of, the licensor.

Nevertheless, just as the use and the lease for years turned from being mere personal arrangements into property rights, so licences appear to be undergoing a similar transformation. Even in the year-books there were said to be limits to the power of countermand. A licence could not be revoked if it amounted to a lease for years, or if it was coupled with a grant of an easement or profit. And if the licence were to take a profit, the licensee could assign it, or could at least exercise it through agents.[32] The medieval explanation was that things of pleasure were purely personal and could be revoked without loss, whereas things of profit were more highly regarded by the law. In later times, however, the explanation advanced was that, whereas a bare authority was inherently revocable, a grant of property was not. The critical distinction was between a bare licence and a grant.[33] A grant of an easement or profit required a deed; a lease did not, but it required an intention to confer the right of exclusive occupation for a fixed period. With this distinction the common law rested; despite contrary rumblings from time to time, the law could not confer the attributes of real property upon a bare licence. As with uses, the change in character was wrought by equity. By the nineteenth century it was settled that equity would restrain the revocation of a licence if the licensee had been allowed to improve land on the understanding that it would not be revoked, or if the licensee had given consideration for a 'contractual licence'. It has been maintained in the twentieth century that, as a result of the Judicature Acts, the equitable doctrine prevails over the law to the extent that a contractual licensee may exercise a countermanded licence without becoming a trespasser. But the most remarkable development has occurred

---

31. YB Mich 39 Hen VI, 7, pl.12. The later cases are reviewed in *Wood v Leadbitter* (1845) 13 M & W 838.
32. *Duchess of Norfolk v Wiseman* (1497) YB Trin 12 Hen VII, 25, pl.5; Hil 13 Hen VII, 13, pl.2. Cf. Mich 18 Edw IV, 14, pl.12.
33. Spelman Rep (93 SS) 161 per Broke Sjt. (c. 1520); *Webb v Paternoster* (1619) 2 Rolle 143, 152, Poph 151, Palm 171, Gcdb 282, Noy 98. See also *Bringloe v Morrice* (1676) 1 Mod Rep 210 (licence to ride horse not assignable, but otherwise where horse leased).

within the last quarter of a century, when some judges have held that an irrevocable licence to occupy land raises an 'equity' which binds purchasers with notice.[34] The precise characteristics of this new species of property are still a matter of controversy; but it does seem that an interest is being elevated from the realms of contract into those of status, in order to protect the interests of those who have bargained for the use or occupation of real property without becoming tenants. The historical parallel with the recognition of the use and of the lease for years is obvious and striking.

Further reading

Pollock & Maitland, vol. II, pp. 106–124

Holdsworth HEL, vol. III, pp. 198–217

Simpson IHLL, pp. 135–162, 206–210, 225–237

Milsom HFCL, pp. 127–139

C. M. Gray, *Copyhold, Equity and the Common Law* (1963)

P. Bordwell, 'Ejectment takes Over' (1970) 55 *Iowa Law Rev* 1089–1147

W. M. McGovern, 'The Historical Conception of a Lease for Years' (1976) 23 *UCLA Law Rev* 501–528

M. S. Arnold, 'The Term of Years' in [1976] CLJ at 323–330

J. H. Baker, 'Agrarian Changes and Security of Tenure' (1978) 94 SS *180–187*

---

34. *Errington v Errington and Woods* [1952] 1 KB 290, [1952] 1 All ER 149; *National Provincial Bank Ltd v Ainsworth* [1965] AC 1175, [1965] 2 All ER 472. For the trespass proposition, see *Winter Garden Theatre (London) Ltd v Millennium Productions Ltd* [1948] AC 173, [1947] 2 All ER 331.

16. Contract

From the law of real property we now turn to the law of obligations, which comprises the law of contract (and of quasi-contract) and the law of torts. In general, the law of torts governs infringements of interests protected by the law independently of private agreement, whereas the law of contract governs those expectations of good faith which arise out of particular transactions between individual persons. The latter type of obligation may be analysed in terms either of the *right* to performance of the contract, or of the *wrong* of breaking the contract and thereby causing loss. The modern common law knows only the latter aspect; it awards damages to compensate for breach of contract, but cannot compel specific performance of a contract in the future. This is somewhat remarkable when one learns that the earliest form of action concerning contractual obligations was designed to compel performance. Moreover, the story begins, rather than ends, with an apparently comprehensive contractual remedy. But the history of the English law of contract has not been an unbroken evolution of principle. It has been caught up in evidential problems, in jurisdictional shifts, and in the process by which trespass actions were extended to remedy the deficiencies of the *praecipe* writs.

Before embarking on the subject, it is necessary to understand the terminology of the medieval common lawyers. The word 'contract' possessed a more confined meaning in the year-book period than it now has. It denoted a transaction, such as a sale or loan, which transferred property or generated a debt; to borrow the language of the Civil law, it meant a *real* rather than a *consensual* contract. The modern sense of 'contract', as a legally binding agreement, was provided by the word 'covenant' (*conventio*). 'Covenant' later came to have a restricted technical meaning because of the limiting evidential requirements in the action of covenant, and it then became necessary to find a word to replace it. 'Contract' was not, because of its special connotations, immediately appropriate. Pleaders had invented the law-Latin verbs *agreare* and *barganizare*, but the word which ultimately prevailed as the substitute for covenant was 'undertaking' or *assumptio*. We shall see in this chapter how this was brought about by the evolution of forms of action designed to remedy wrongdoing by those who took upon themselves to do things. By about 1600 the action of *assumpsit* had expanded to take over the work of the older actions based on covenants and contracts, and thereafter the word 'contract' was increasingly used in a looser sense as a description of the subject-matter of *assumpsit*. 'Contract' then came to have two shades of meaning. Serjeant Sheppard explained in 1651 that 'a contract, taken largely, is an agreement between two or more concerning something to be done, whereby both parties are bound to each other, or one is bound to the other. But more strictly it is taken for an agreement between two or more for the buying and selling of some personal goods whereby property is altered.'[1] It will be noted that even this distinction no longer incorporated precisely the old notion of contract as a transaction *re*. By the middle of the seventeenth century, 'contract', however defined, denoted agreement; and it is in the sense of a legally binding agreement that it has passed into current use.

The legal problem is not merely one of terminology or classification, but of deciding what agreements or promises or undertakings are to be enforced, and what remedies are available to enforce them. In the ancient communal assemblies, and in the medieval town courts, where mercantile litigation was mostly conducted, the answer to this problem was hidden behind the more practical question of proof. Everyone knew that contracts ought to be performed; but there was no more law than that.[2] In the royal courts—that is, at common law—the answer was governed by the writ system.

The Action of Covenant

Before 1200 there was a royal writ in the form *praecipe* by which the sheriff was to order the defendant to keep the covenant he made with the plaintiff (*praecipe* A *quod teneat* B *conventionem inter eos factam*).[3] This writ was usually brought to enforce covenants concerning land, such as leases, but its wording comprehended all sorts of covenant. According to the Statute of Wales 1284, there were as many writs of covenant as there were kinds of agreement. At that date, therefore, there existed a form of action applicable to all consensual contracts. But history did not stop in the thirteenth century, and time left the action of covenant behind.

---

1. *Faithful Councellor* (1651), p. 93.
2. See pp. 63, 71, ante.
3. For the form in full, see p. 440, post.

A covenant relating to land was usually in a charter, sealed and witnessed. But many private agreements, not concerning land, raised evidential problems which the royal courts were not prepared to tackle. The common law of Glanvill's day was not much concerned with agreements;[4] and oral agreements were best left to the local courts, where proof by compurgation was used. Nevertheless, covenant could in the early days be brought in the royal courts without written evidence, provided the plaintiff had 'suit' (transaction witnesses),[5] and in such cases the proof was by wager of law.[6] The royal courts simply followed the practice of local courts. Then, some time between 1290 and 1320, the royal judges made the momentous decision that the methods of proof which were acceptable at the local level were inadequate to support covenants in suits before themselves. The only proof they would admit was a deed, a written document under seal. In the London eyre of 1321 an action of covenant was brought against a carrier who had covenanted to carry a load of hay from Waltham to London. In spite of counsel's plea that one could not put every little covenant into writing, the action failed for want of a deed. Herle J said: 'We will not undo the law for a cartload of hay. Covenant is nothing but an agreement (*assent*) between parties in words, but the words can only be proved by specialty.'[7] After this, we hear no more of plaintiffs bringing actions of covenant without deeds.

An inevitable result of this decision was that the word 'covenant' itself came to be equated with an agreement under seal. It was all very well to say that all agreements were enforceable, provided the plaintiff could produce a deed in evidence; the truth was that informal agreements were no longer actionable in the king's courts, and that a person who made a covenant without a deed did so at his peril. The development of a law of consensual contracts had for the moment been stifled by the formal requirement of a seal.

Contemporaries would not have viewed the new common law rule as a drastic denial of justice. True, one could not put every little covenant into writing; but then one should not be able to bother the royal courts with every little unwritten covenant. The restriction applied only in the king's central courts. The local courts in the time of Edward II were quite competent to deal with informal agreements,

---

4. Glanvill, x, 18.
5. E.g. *Berkshire Eyre 1248* (90 SS), 119.
6. E.g. *Berkshire Eyre 1248* (90 SS) 189, 192. In one case the defendant waged law on the existence of the covenant, in the other on its performance. See also Pollock & Maitland, vol. II, p. 220n.
7. *Case of the Waltham Carrier* (1321) London eyre 1321 (86 SS) 287 (quotation from combined texts). 'Specialty' means deed, or sealed writing.

while royal justice remained available to those with the wisdom and foresight to invest their agreements with the solemnity of parchment and wax. Thus there was no change in the law itself, but only a demarcation of jurisdictions. In fact people did use deeds for their most important transactions, but because they found the conditioned bond the most effective formula their enforcement was through the writ of debt and not covenant.[8] Moreover, it was not long before breaches of informal agreements could be remedied by means of the writ of trespass on the case.[9] The action of covenant therefore went into decline. Even to the extent that it survived, it suffered from what narrow interpretation turned into a conceptual restriction. The Chancery clerks never enlarged the ancient formula *praecipe quod teneat conventionem*,[10] which was appropriate to compel performance but not to compensate for imperfect or tardy performance. Suppose, for instance, that a man covenanted to build a house to certain specifications, but in building it made the joints so badly that the house collapsed. The writ of covenant was inapt. Or suppose that he finished building it long after he was supposed to, so that the other party was put to inconvenience and expense. It would have been futile to order him to keep his covenant in this case. Or suppose a tailor promised well and sufficiently to cut cloth and make it into a suit, and he cut the cloth so carelessly that the suit would not fit the customer. Here the tailor had disabled himself from performing the covenant because the cloth was ruined. Or suppose a man sold goods which turned out to be defective. Here was not even a covenant which he could be ordered to keep. In all these cases there was no remedy by writ of covenant even if there was a deed. Covenant was designed, as it seemed from its wording, to remedy nonfeasance (not doing) but not misfeasance (doing badly).

The Action of Debt

At least as old as the writ of covenant was the writ of debt, by which the defendant was to be ordered to render or yield up a sum of money, or a quantity of fungibles,[11] which he owed to and unjustly withheld

8. See p. 269, post.
9. See p. 273 et seq, post.
10. This is an example of the unintended consequences of freezing a particular form. In the 12th century there were precedents for a writ *quare non tenet conventionem*. Even in the form which prevailed, it was impossible (certainly after 1345) to obtain any remedy other than damages.
11. Goods defined by weight or measure and generic character, but not identified in particular. They are interchangeable, so that a loan of fungibles is repaid in kind. The term *res fungibilia* is Roman; there was no technical term in English law.

from the plaintiff: *praecipe* A *quod reddat* B £x *quas ei debet et injuste detinet*. There was no theoretical overlap with covenant because, contrary to the present approach, the medieval lawyers saw debt as a different type of obligation from agreement. A debt could arise out of a transaction such as sale or loan without any express covenant being made; only later lawyers would have to import into the transaction an implied promise to pay. The *praecipe quod reddat* formula suggests an analogy with actions to recover property. Debt was indeed the twin sister of the action of detinue, which lay for personal property detained. The distinction between them came to be that while detinue was based on property, on an owning, debt was based on duty, on an owing.[12] Thus, if *A* owed *B* a quarter of barley, this was a debt because *B* could not assert property in any identified barley. But if *A* detained a specific sack of barley which belonged to *B*, then *B*'s remedy was detinue. Again, if *X* lent *Y* £10, this was a debt because the actual coins became *Y*'s property and his duty was to render the sum of £10 in whatever lawful coin he chose. But if *X* delivered to *Y* a bag of coins to the value of £10 to look after for him, the property in the coins remained in *X* and they could be recovered *in specie* by the action of detinue. Covenant would lie only if *Y* promised to pay *X* £10, but this was not necessarily a debt because a promise to pay was not in itself a 'contract'. When twentieth-century lawyers say that a debt is a breach of a promise to pay money, this is a refined distortion brought about by the action of *assumpsit*; the action of debt still looks very like an action to enforce the contract, notwithstanding that the legal mind regards it as an action for damages for failing to pay as agreed.[13] The writ of debt, however, was not at all concerned with the enforcement of promises or agreements; that was the province of covenant. It lay to enforce the obligation or duty of payment which arose out of a contract *re*.

The existence of a debt, as of a covenant, might depend on private transactions and thus present difficulties of proof. But the royal courts did not insist on a deed as the only means of proving a debt. Certainly a deed was an acceptable, and superior, mode of proof; and debt would not lie on a mere promise to pay money, without a deed, for this was a naked pact and *ex nudo pacto non oritur actio*. But they also allowed an action to recover a debt arising out of an informal transaction, and in such a case continued to allow proof by wager of law. The reason for the divergence in this respect from covenant was that an oral covenant

12. See p. 325, post.
13. See 2 Burr 1086 per Lord Mansfield CJ. As regards the burden of proof of payment, it may still be incorrect to regard a debt as a breach of contract: see *Young v Queensland Trustees Ltd* (1956) 99 CLR 560.

consisted but in fleeting words, and no action was allowed in the royal courts for mere breath. A sale, a loan, a hiring, on the other hand, were all acts done; the act could in theory be proved, since it had lasting effects, and the act itself generated the duty to pay regardless of any words spoken.[14] The deed likewise was an act done (*factum*), in that the specialty was sealed and delivered before witnesses as an 'act and deed'. The distinction between words and deeds ran deep in English law.[15]

DEBT ON A CONTRACT

If he had no deed, the creditor had to show in his count some *causa debendi*, a transaction or 'contract' which gave rise to the owing. Glanvill and Bracton may have theorised about *causa* in a Roman law sense, but in the year-books it is explained in terms of *quid pro quo*. A plaintiff could maintain an action of debt if he had conferred some valuable recompense, or *quid pro quo*, upon the defendant in return for the duty; the furnishing of *quid pro quo* executed the contract on his side and created the relationship of debtor and creditor between them. The borrower of money had *quid pro quo* in the use of the money, the buyer in the goods bought, the hirer in the use of the thing hired, the employer or client in the services rendered, and so on. Debt did not lie on a wholly executory contract because a mere promise to perform an act was not *quid pro quo*. Thus, if a carpenter were retained to build a house for £10, there was a covenant which bound him if he had executed a deed; but not until he built the house was there *quid pro quo* to enable him to bring debt for his £10.

Like covenant, the action of debt on a contract was hindered by the problems of proof. And because the judges did not insist on formal evidence under seal, they had to cope with the difficulty of secret transactions. Even if the contract itself was open and well-known to neighbours, the defendant might set up a secret payment in discharge of the debt. The judges therefore denied jury trial, and permitted the defendant to wage his law. The peculiarities of this method of proof when used at Westminster have already been pointed out,[16] and as a result of them creditors may have been deterred from trying to enforce simple debts in the central courts. Indeed, it became very unwise to give substantial credit without the security of a deed.

The availability of wager of law also hindered the development of a concept of contract. If defendants always pleaded the general issue,

14. *Anon* (1338) YB Trin 12 Edw III (Rolls ser) 587 per Sharshulle J.
15. See pp. 364–365, post.
16. See p. 65, ante.

there was no way in which detailed questions could arise. *Quid pro quo* was no more than an explanation of the common features in the common debt counts. Discussion of *quid pro quo* only arose when a new kind of count was tried out: the leading cases concerned contracts to pay money on marriage, so that the *quid pro quo* was both 'spiritual' and moving from a third party.[17] When such discussion occurred, there was manifestly no uniformity of views on the subject. Some judges thought *quid pro quo* could be extended to the case where the plaintiff conferred a benefit on a third party or performed an act of charity at the defendant's request. Others thought that *quid pro quo* was not always essential anyway, and that a perfect contract could sometimes be made without it. Others held to the orthodoxy as stated above. The law of contract might in time have developed in the context of debt something like the present notion of consideration or even of mutual promises. But it did not have the time or the opportunity to do so, because debt on a contract went slowly out of use.

DEBT ON AN OBLIGATION

More important in practice was the action of debt founded on an 'obligation' under seal. This was a very common action until the eighteenth century, and its popularity derived from the widespread use of the conditioned bond.

A bond, or obligation, was a sealed document containing an acknowledgment that a sum of money was due. When it was desired to draw up an important written agreement, a common practice was for both or one of the parties to make a bond to pay a sum of money to the other unless a certain condition was performed; the condition, endorsed on the bond, set out the terms of the agreement or referred to more detailed terms in an indenture. The bond, usually in Latin, was in the form: 'Know all men etc. that I, *AB*, have bound myself to *CD* in £x to be paid at Michaelmas next following.' The condition, usually in English, might read: 'The condition of this obligation is that if *AB* shall build a house etc. [*or*, perform the covenants in an indenture dated etc.] then this obligation shall become void, or else it shall stand in full strength.' The principal advantages which this device had over a straightforward covenant were that damages could be obtained, as a debt, for mere non-performance of the condition; and the damages could be fixed in advance by the parties. And the promisor could be

17. *Anon* (1458) Fifoot HSCL, 249. In a similar case, *Elys v Hobard* (1480) CP 40/871, m. 136; YB Hil 19 Edw IV, 10, pl. 18, there was a demurrer to a plea that the *causa actionis* was spiritual; but no decision was reached.

made liable for misfeasance, which was outside the scope of covenant. Even an agreement to pay money could be strengthened by making a bond to pay a larger amount in default of payment on the day. So popular were conditioned bonds that actions of debt on an obligation were the commonest single class of actions in the Common Pleas rolls before the eighteenth century. Since the action of debt was brought to enforce the penal obligation and not the substantive agreement itself, many of the problems of the later law of contract never came into the open; they were hidden on the other side of the bond.

The action could cause hardship to a defendant because the truth of the relationship between the parties was of subsidiary importance to the obligation under seal. A deed was of such a 'high nature' that few defences were allowed against it. The only defence generally open to the defendant was to show that the deed was for some reason invalid. The plea that the writing was not his deed (*non est factum suum*) enabled the defendant to show that a document was not a deed at all, or that it was a forgery, or that he had been tricked into executing because he was illiterate and the contents had been misread to him. The deed could be invalidated for duress, incapacity (such as infancy) and 'suspicion', where the deed appeared to have been tampered with after execution. It was also open to the defendant to show that the deed had been executed upon condition, and that the condition had been performed or discharged. Here parol evidence was admitted of the condition and its discharge, because the writing did not indicate on its face whether it was absolute or conditional. All these defences focused on the validity of the deed. If, however, the defendant acknowledged the deed to be his, he could not without evidence under seal plead such defences as payment of the debt acknowledged by the obligation.[18] Hence an 'obligor' might be forced to pay twice on the same obligation; the law said it was his own folly not to have had it destroyed or to have obtained an acquittance under seal. Even if the debtor paid, and the bond was returned, the obligee could snatch back the bond by force and sue upon it; there was no way in the world that a valid deed could be overturned by oral evidence.[19] 'It is better to suffer a mischief to one man than an inconvenience to many, which would subvert the law; for if matter in writing could be so easily

18. It was otherwise in covenant, where the deed evidenced the agreement but not its breach. An obligation evidenced a state of indebtedness, and was in effect a grant of the debt rather than an agreement or contract. Equity gave relief in such a case: p. 88, ante. The plea was not allowed at law until 1705: Stat 4 & 5 Annae, c.3.

19. *Donne v Cornwalle* (1486) YB Hil 1 Hen VII, 14, pl. 2. The remedy was for the obligor to sue in trespass for taking the bond, and he would recover back the payment in damages.

defeated and avoided by mere breath (*nude vent*), a matter in writing would be of no greater authority than a matter of fact.'[20]

Debt on an obligation remained in use until the nineteenth century, for it was the only form of action which could be used to enforce a debt evidenced by a deed. It preserved the distinction between formal and parol contracts, which is still part of the law. But the use of bonds to secure an extortionate advantage over a contracting party was seriously curtailed when the chancellor began to give equitable relief against 'penal' bonds. In the sixteenth century it was established that it was inequitable for the obligee to recover a sum which exceeded his actual loss arising from the breach of condition, and obligors could obtain relief in Chancery against penalties which they had incurred at law.[21]

Gaps in the Medieval Law

Compared with the local and ecclesiastical courts, the medieval royal courts played a limited part in the field of contract. The action of debt was subject to wager of law; and, however well this may have worked in the country, it seemed an artificial obstacle at Westminster. Wager of law was restrictive not merely because of the hired oath-helpers and obvious dangers of misuse. One could not wage another's law, and so if a debtor died his simple debts[22] died with him; his executors could not wage law for him, and in the absence of any method of trial they could not be sued at all. Debt had other limitations. It could only be brought for a sum of money fixed at the time of the contract. If a house were built, but no price fixed beforehand, nothing could be recovered for work and materials even if a sum were subsequently agreed. Neither could debt be brought on a sale of goods which had no existence at the time of the sale; for instance, the sale of a crop not yet grown, or of all the butter to be produced in a year from a herd of cows. The doctrine of *quid pro quo* probably prevented a contract being made by mutual promises. Thus, if *A* promised *B* £10 in return for *B* doing something, then if this amounted to a contract for services *B* could bring debt for the £10 when he had done the act. But if *A* promised *B* £10 in return for *B* promising to do something, the contract was wholly executory and *B* had no action for the £10.

A contractual claim other than for money or personal property would only succeed if the plaintiff could show a deed. And even if he

20. *Waberley v Cockerell* (1542) Dyer 51. In Plowd 82 (1553) words are described as nothing but *le verberation del ayer*.
21. See E. G. Henderson, 18 AJLH 298 (1974).
22. Executors could be sued in debt on an obligation.

had a deed, unless it was a conditioned bond, his only remedy was for nonfeasance. The carpenter who did not build was liable in covenant, if he had covenanted by deed; but the carpenter who built badly was not amenable to this action. The vendor of land was liable in covenant for failing to convey; but if he conveyed to someone other than the plaintiff, covenant was inappropriate because he could no longer be ordered to keep his covenant. The practical answer to all these problems was to make conditioned bonds, and many people did so. But this was not a wholly adequate remedy. Even if laymen were conscious of the magic of parchment and wax, they often trusted the words of others without further security. They saw no reason why a man's word should not have been as good as his bond.

RELIEF IN CHANCERY

If, as is suggested, the medieval solution to these problems was found in the local courts of the boroughs and cities, and in the ecclesiastical courts, nevertheless the royal courts could not continue indefinitely to wash their hands of informal contracts on the supposition that litigants could find relief elsewhere. As the local courts decayed, and the ecclesiastical courts were effectively prohibited from meddling with contract, so practical justice in all but minor matters became coterminous with the law of Westminster Hall. And, if the common law remained inflexible, the Chancery was an obvious source of relief. It could give better remedies than the common law courts, and could give remedies where the regular courts gave none. The creditor who had lost his deed might yet enforce his debt, while the debtor who had paid would be relieved from paying again. Sometimes petitioners sought relief simply on the ground that if they sued in the Common Pleas they would be barred by wager of law. Claims were entertained in Chancery for a just reward for services where no certain sum had been fixed, and for specific performance of parol contracts, even of wholly executory contracts. By 1500 the chancellor had assumed a general jurisdiction in matters of contract, and it was said that 'a man shall have remedy in the Chancery for covenants made without specialty if the party have sufficient witnesses to prove the covenants'.[23]

The intervention of the Chancery was no slight factor in influencing the common law judges to recognise new or better remedies than those obtainable through the *praecipe* writs. Equity, in the widest sense of the word, was not the sole prerogative of chancellors. The Chancery, moreover, suffered from a limitation in that it could not award

23. *Diversite de courtz et lour jurisdictions* ('1523'), sig. Avi. This was first printed in 1526, but may have been written before 1500.

damages; and so a contract which circumstances had placed beyond performance could no more be upheld in Chancery than it could by a writ of covenant. For the purpose of competition, the nearest common law equivalent of the Chancery subpoena was the writ of trespass, complaining of a wrong done. Yet, whereas the chancellor could in each case act upon free-ranging principles of conscience and equity, the common lawyers in turning to a different form of action were compelled to dress up contractual causes of action as trespasses. The earliest cases involved no real distortion; but by 1600, as we shall see, the whole law of contract had been temporarily subsumed under the law of tort.

Trespass and Covenant

A trespass (*transgressio*) or wrong is fundamentally different from the right to performance of a contract. If a medieval plaintiff brought a writ of trespass for not performing a covenant, he would be met by the argument 'this sounds in covenant' and the action would fail because he had used the wrong writ. Trespass could not compel a man to keep his promise where he had done nothing towards it, but required the defendant to come and explain why he had done something wrong. The mere fact that a plaintiff had no deed to evidence the covenant gave him no greater right to bring trespass for its non-performance than if he had a deed and could sue in covenant.

In some cases, however, a breach of covenant which caused damage could properly be classed as a wrong. If a surgeon covenanted to cure a person and then attempted an operation which made him worse than before, this could be regarded either as the non-performance of the covenant or as a physical wrong having a close resemblance to battery. It was not battery, because the patient had consented to surgery and so the conduct could not be said to be *vi et armis*.[24] Neither was it a simple breach of covenant, because the complaint was not merely that the plaintiff had not been cured, but that he had been made worse. Once actions of trespass were admitted in the central courts without the words *vi et armis*, there was no difficulty in allowing actions in which the plaintiff's special case was an undertaking which had been badly discharged so as to cause damage. Such cases were already known in London and the local courts; the change was therefore not a change in the substantive law but an enlargement of royal jurisdiction and a partial retreat from the earlier exclusion of informal covenants from the purview of royal

24. *The Surgeon's Case* (1329) Kiralfy SB, p. 184.

justice. By the fifteenth century the phrase used in writs on the case was that the defendant 'took upon himself' (*assumpsit super se*) to do something, and then did it badly to the damage of the plaintiff.

The first known case in the superior courts where liability was imposed on a person who had undertaken[25] to do something and done it badly is the famous *Humber Ferry Case* of 1348.[26] The plaintiff complained by bill of trespass in the King's Bench that the defendant, a ferryman, had received his mare to carry across the River Humber and had so overloaded the ferry that the mare perished. Counsel for the defendant argued that the action should have been covenant. His reasons are not reported, but it is obvious that if he had succeeded the plaintiff would have been without a remedy. Covenant did not lie in the King's Bench, and it is unlikely in any case that the consignor had a deed. But the argument failed. The judge said that overloading the ferry, whereby the mare perished, was a trespass. The report again omits the reasoning, but the decision was sensible enough; there was a wrongful act which was not governed by the covenant, and which would have been wrong even if there had been no covenant. It would have been useless to order the ferryman to keep his covenant, because the mare was dead; and the damages in covenant ought presumably to have been for the not ferrying rather than for the loss of the beast. So the only apt remedy was trespass.

The second reported case was an action on the case against a veterinary surgeon who had killed a horse by his negligence. The word used for the undertaking was *manucepit* (he took in hand), a word familiar to pleaders in London. This time it was argued, perhaps rather desperately, that the action should have been either covenant or trespass *vi et armis*. Serjeant Belknap frankly submitted in reply, 'We cannot bring covenant without a deed . . . so it is more reasonable to maintain this special writ according to the case than to abate it, for we can have no other writ.' The writ was upheld.[27] A few years later, in a similar action against a surgeon for negligently maiming the hand he had undertaken[28] to cure, the plaintiff failed because he had omitted to name the place where the undertaking was made. The decision indicates that the undertaking was the basis of the action. Cavendish CJ significantly called it an action of 'covenant' and said

25. The report says *emprist*, which is French for *assumpsit*; but the record says *recepit ad salvo cariandum*.
26. *Bukton v Tounesende* (1348) Kiralfy SB, p. 187; Kiralfy AC, p. 222. Kiralfy's text is more correct than the others in print.
27. *Waldon v Marshall* (1369) Fifoot HSCL, p. 81.
28. The year-book says *emprist*, but the record says *manucepit sanare*. A similar case, but with *assumpsisset*, is *Birchester v Leech* (1390) 88 SS 63.

that it could be maintained without a deed, 'since a man cannot always have a clerk to make a specialty for him for every little thing'.[29]

Numerous cases of a similar nature followed. These were cases of trespass, and it is no distortion of language to describe them as claims in tort. But everyone knew that they were beginning to encroach on covenant, and the possibility that a breach of covenant might be treated as a trespass had been established. The law which could not be undone for a cartload of hay could at least be circumvented.

ASSUMPSIT AND NONFEASANCE

The development so far was as much a part of the history of tortious negligence[30] as of the law of contract. The cases all involved positive wrongdoing. But there is all the difference in legal theory between doing something wrong (misfeasance) and wrongly not doing something (nonfeasance). The difference is easy to understand in terms of duty. Misfeasance is wrong if there is a negative duty to refrain from doing harm, whereas nonfeasance is only wrong if there is a positive duty to act. The law is commonly associated with the proscription of misconduct, with commands of the form 'Thou shalt not. . . .' But it does not normally order 'Thou shalt . . .' unless there is a contract to do something. It is trite learning that if one sees a man drowning there is no legal duty to attempt to rescue him; but there is a clear legal duty not to push him under the water or actively prevent his rescue.

This was the conceptual obstacle to allowing the action of *assumpsit*, as the new action was called, for the mere failure to perform a covenant. In the misfeasance cases, the 'undertaking' had not necessarily been promissory; it was the taking on of a task. The notion of an undertaking to do something in the future reflected a subtle difference of meaning which alert lawyers had already foreseen in the fourteenth century. Undertaking in this sense was the same as promising or covenanting; and since in a case of nonfeasance the duty to perform arose solely from the covenant, the action 'sounded in covenant' rather than in trespass. Not doing could not naturally be called trespass.[31] A benevolent promise to build a house, followed by inaction, was not more obviously a legal wrong than a malevolent promise to knock a house down, followed by inaction; and the latter was no tort, because a man was not liable for his intentions without an act done.[32] The argument about nonfeasance often sounded unreal,

29. *Stratton v Swanlond* (1375) Kiralfy, SB, p. 185; Fifoot HSCL, p. 82.
30. See pp. 337–338, post.
31. For a modern instance, see *Fagan v Metropolitan Police Commissioner* [1969] 1 QB 439.
32. YB Trin 17 Edw IV, 3, pl. 2 per Wode. The assumption in the old cases is that words were not acts.

especially as both the misfeasance and the nonfeasance cases concerned a harmful default following an undertaking. Lawyers are retained, however, to present arguments which have a chance of success; and so whenever an action on the case was brought for breaking a covenant it was a standard objection that it was nonfeasance and therefore did not sound in trespass. As late as 1493, when a carrier was sued for the loss of a cargo of corn through his default in looking after a ship, it was argued that this neglect was only nonfeasance; but the court held it to be *un graund mysfezance*.[33]

The year-book discussions, fragmentary as they are, suggest that the argument against nonfeasance sounding in trespass prevailed until about 1500. The plea rolls, on the other hand, contain many undetermined actions based on nonfeasance dating back to the four-teenth century. It is not certain how many of these cases came before the court judicially; but obviously the clerks of the court were happy to issue mesne process upon writs alleging nonfeasance. The distinc-tion between misfeasance and nonfeasance, as a last-ditch argument in court, doubtless broke down because it was difficult to apply. If the doctor gave the patient inert medicine, or treated the wrong limb, was this misfeasance or nonfeasance? What is more, the distinction led to seemingly anomalous results. A good many instances of nonfeasance could be regarded as tortious if some damage resulted other than the mere cost of paying someone else to perform the covenant. Thus, if a carpenter undertook to build a house and then did nothing about it, that was pure nonfeasance and sounded only in covenant.[34] But if he started the work and then left the roof unfinished, so that the rest of the house was spoiled by the weather, this might be called trespass; at any rate, it might if the customer owned the wood. Medieval crafts-men did not usually provide materials, and so a bad job was an injury to the client's property falling short of trespass *vi et armis*. On the same principle, if the carpenter undertook to repair the roof of an existing house and did nothing at all, so that the timbers rotted or collapsed, this nonfeasance could reasonably be called trespass. The carpenter had caused the damage, and the only difference between these cases and the misfeasance cases was that the damage was consequential and indirect. Any remaining distinction between non-feasance causing physical loss and nonfeasance causing economic or financial loss would not have been very substantial. For instance, if

33. *Anon* (1493) Caryll Rep, Brit Lib MS Harley 1691, f. 76v.
34. *Watton v Brinth* (1400) Fifoot HSCL, p. 340; *Anon* (1409) ibid. In the MSS of the latter report, the action is called 'a writ of covenant' and in two the marginal catchword is 'covenant on his case'.

the carpenter had totally failed to build or repair a mill, his inactivity might ruin the miller's livelihood. Was not this as plain a tort as where the mill was physically damaged? Or suppose a man had promised to sow crops, and defaulted, so that the profits of the land were lost for the season. The landowner had entrusted the task to one man until it was too late to employ another to do the same task: was not this damage going beyond a mere failure to act? In a case of 1425 problems of this kind were fully discussed, and they were treated not as arbitrary questions of misfeasance or nonfeasance but as questions of causation: whether the defendant's conduct had damaged the plaintiff. Martin J remarked in the course of the discussions that if this approach were adopted 'a man could have an action of trespass for every broken covenant in the world'.[35] This is almost what happened.

The full recognition of *assumpsit* for nonfeasance may have been facilitated by other factors. However irrational the distinction between misfeasance and nonfeasance might become in practice, and however galling the competition from the Chancery, there was still the objection to using trespass in place of covenant. If, besides the nonfeasance, there was some other source of liability, then the cause of action was not merely covenant and the difficulty vanished.

1. *Status*

We have seen how the feudal system turned contractual services into a status which became a property right. Despite the collapse of feudalism as a means of securing services, the status approach to a limited extent survived. Under the Ordinance and Statute of Labourers (1349–51), workmen were compelled to remain with their employers and their contracts were enforceable by criminal sanctions. A refusal to work as agreed was a punishable 'departure from service'. It was also held that the employer could sue on the legislation; such an action in effect sought damages for breach of the covenant to serve, and yet in form it was trespass for the wrong of infringing the public duty to serve.[36] In the early carpenter cases it was suggested that a carpenter fell within the ambit of the legislation. Probably he did not; an engagement to build a house was not a permanent employment. But it is easy to see how the independent contractor may have been thought within the equity of the legislation, and how by analogy a failure to build could be classed as a trespass. Many callings were, in

---

35. *Watkins' Case* (1425) Fifoot HSCL 341.
36. See, e.g., *Thelnetham v Penne* (1378) 88 SS 7, where the question was expressly raised whether the claim was in covenant or trespass. Hankford J in 1410 said it sounded in covenant: YB Mich 11 Hen IV, 24, pl. 46.

any case, controlled by the common law or custom independently of contract; an innkeeper, for instance, was liable under the 'custom of the realm' for his failure to look after a guest's goods or for refusing to accommodate a traveller. Again, liability for nonfeasance was imposed by public law. And similar duties could be imposed on professional men. In 1455 *assumpsit* was brought against a clerk of the juries who failed to make an entry in his roll as promised; the argument that this was nonfeasance does not seem to have occurred to anyone.[37] Another kind of status was that of the bailee or custodian of property; it was held in 1487 that a shepherd having the custody of sheep was liable in *assumpsit* for failing to look after them, so that they were killed.[38]

2. Deceit

A second idea transferred from the local merchant courts was the action on a warranty of goods sold.[39] This was also connected with a criminal jurisdiction, under which the precursors of the inspectors of weights and measures invigilated the standards of wares offered for sale. The false purveyor of food was carted ignominiously around the town so that everyone would be put on their guard when dealing with him in the future. In the royal courts the remedy was the action on the case for deceit, for tricking someone into a purchase he would not otherwise have made.

The action for deceiving someone offered the means of extending *assumpsit* beyond the cases of physical damage. Among the earliest examples were actions against lawyers for 'ambidextry', the offence of taking fees from both sides, or for disclosing counsel to adversaries. Again the cause of action was a public offence.[40] In *Somerton's Case* in 1433,[41] a counsellor who had been retained to purchase a manor fraudulently and collusively revealed his counsel to a third person and conveyed the manor to him. The judges thought an action would lie because of the deceit. Although the essence of the complaint was the failure to obtain the manor, which was nonfeasance, there was also positive malpractice (or malfeasance) in revealing secrets to another. Nine years later, in *Doige's Case*,[42] a similar action was brought

37. *Holt v Chevercourt* (1455) CP 40/778, m. 432; sub nom. *Ceveront's Case* YB Mich 34 Hen VI, 4, pl. 12 (where the main objection is that the omission was not the sole cause of the plaintiff's losing the first action).
38. *Anon* (1487) Fifoot HSCL, p. 86. As to the bailee's liability for negligence, see pp. 329–330, 338 post.
39. See pp. 293–294, post.
40. Statute of Westminster I 1275, c. 29.
41. *Somerton v Colles* (1433) Fifoot HSCL, p. 343.
42. *Shipton v Dog* (1440–42) Fifoot HSCL, p. 347, Kiralfy AC, p. 227, Kiralfy SB, p. 192, 51 SS 97. Cf. *Anon* (1441) Simpson *History of Contract*, p. 626. The decision was followed by the Common Pleas in *Cook v Iwyns* (1475) CP 40/856, m. 334.

against a vendor who had prevented herself from performing the agreement by enfeoffing a third person of the land which she had promised to convey to the plaintiff. The defendant felt sufficiently sure of her ground to demur to the declaration, on the ground that the action should have been covenant, and the point was debated by all the judges in the Exchequer Chamber. The plaintiff eventually succeeded, because the defendant had deceitfully disabled herself from performance. Covenant would have been a futile remedy in such circumstances, because the writ would have commanded her to do what she had already rendered impossible; and for the same reason there could have been no relief in Chancery by way of specific performance. By the sixteenth century it was usual to allege deceit in all *assumpsit* actions, even where there was no deceit in fact; the allegation itself was thought by some to dispose of the technical objections about nonfeasance.[43]

'PURE NONFEASANCE' AND CONSIDERATION

The final abandonment of the older objections to *assumpsit* for nonfeasance is usually traced to a dictum of Fyneux CJ in Gray's Inn in 1499. He said that a man who had paid for land could bring *assumpsit* against the vendor for not delivering seisin; and likewise that a man could sue a carpenter for failing to build a house.[44] Fyneux was something of an innovator, and in his thirty years as Chief Justice did much to restore the fortunes of the King's Bench by developing new remedies. But his view was soon shared by the judges of the Common Pleas, and there is no reported case in which it was ever again questioned. All the early statements of the doctrine, however, stress the prepayment: according to Frowyk CJ, in 1505, 'if I covenant with a carpenter to build a house, and pay him £20 to build the house by a certain day, and he does not build the house by the day, now I shall have a good action on my case because of the payment of my money; and yet it sounds only in covenant, and without payment of money in this case there is no remedy'.[45]

The argument that not performing a promise was not actionable in trespass was never completely vanquished. It was side-stepped, by the recognition of factors which lifted the case above the level of pure nonfeasance. There might be fraud, there might be misfeasance, or

43. It is doubtful, however, whether deceit, having opened up an exception, continued to play a central role in the story: see 94 SS *274–275*.

44. Fitz Abr *Accion sur le Case*, pl. 45. The passage is dated Trin 14 Hen VII (1499), and marked 'In greis Inne'; but it was later inserted in the printed year-books for 1505 (whence the text in Fifoot HSCL, p. 353).

45. *Orwell v Mortoft* (1505) as reported at Keil 78, pl. 25 per Frowyk CJ.

there might be injurious reliance on a promise, for instance by payment in advance or by entrusting a particular job to someone. All these things were causes of action. There was no single concept of *assumpsit* before 1550, but a miscellany of very diverse formulae.

In his judgment of 1505, quoted above, Frowyk CJ did not explain why he regarded the prepayment as the 'cause' of action. It seems probable from other early-sixteenth century sources that, besides the need to avoid the technical problem over covenant and nonfeasance, two substantive principles of liability were merging. One was the notion that bargains ought to be reciprocal. If a man built a house for £10, or conveyed land for £10, he could bring debt for the £10. Why then, if the other party paid £10 for a house or for land, could he not have an action if the recipient defaulted? *Quid pro quo* should produce mutual obligations, and the only reason it did not was that debt lay only for money or fungibles. The second principle was that if a man made a promise on which the promisee relied to his detriment the promisor ought to make good the loss. The notion was not so much that the promise should be enforced, for the promise in itself was not binding, but that the damage incurred in reliance on the word of another should be restored. This squared very comfortably with the reasoning which had prevailed against the nonfeasance doctrine: *assumpsit* did not lie to enforce the covenant, which was not enforceable without specialty, but redressed the injury suffered by acting or reposing in the belief that it would be kept. But it was also a principle of moral philosophy, very similar to the modern doctrine of promissory estoppel. It could be said that a broken promise to build a house was not in itself legally wrong, because the promisee was in no worse position than if it had never been made. If, however, the promisee was put in a worse position by relying on the promise—for instance, by loss of the advance payment, or by reason of consequential loss flowing from a failure to repair, or by lack of a home after the date for completion—then an action on the case lay.

These two principles may well have become confused in lawyers' minds before any effort was made to isolate them. The first writers who attempted to generalise about contractual liability turned to Roman law for words to explain what was happening in the common law. St German's discussion of the subject relies on an acquaintance with the canonist notion of *causa*. Morally one was bound by all one's promises, but in law one was bound only by those made seriously and with good cause.[46] In 1565 it was explained that 'because words are

46. *Doctor and Student* (91 SS) 228–233; discussed at lv–lix.

oftentimes spoken by men unadvisedly and without deliberation, the law has provided that a contract by words shall not bind without consideration'.[47] By that date, but not for very long before, 'consideration' was becoming a legal doctrine. *Assumpsit* would lie only upon a promise given for sufficient consideration. Some have seen the doctrine as an English adaptation of *causa*; but there was no deep familiarity with Roman learning in the English legal profession, and the common law seems rather to have produced its own theory of contractual liability. The English consideration was as much *causa actionis* as *causa promissionis*. It was the reason or cause why the defendant's promise should bind him. 'If I promise to build you a house by a day, and do not, this is only *nudum pactum* for which you will not have an action . . . [but] if I give certain money to one to make a house by a day, and he does not make it by the day, there this is a consideration why I should have an action on my case for the nonfeasance.'[48] About the middle of the sixteenth century pleaders began to explain how the promise or *assumpsit* had been made in an *in consideratione* clause, which set out the prepayment or *quid pro quo* or act done in reliance on the promise. Thus the miscellaneous elements which had been introduced to make nonfeasance tortious came to be associated in the pleadings with the word consideration. The plaintiff alleged that in consideration of something done by him for the defendant the defendant promised to do something else, and that the defendant deceitfully failed to keep his promise. By Elizabethan times the consideration for the promise was regarded as the gist of the action, so that it was possible to arrest judgment if the pleadings disclosed no sufficient consideration. The substantive law of contract was then argued out in the new context of consideration; some things would be 'good' consideration for a promise, and others would not. Consideration had to be of some value, though the courts would not investigate its adequacy: 'a penny or a jug of beer is as much obliging in a promise as £100'.[49] So long as the parties made their agreement in a binding form, they were treated as being the best judges of their own bargains. But it was necessary that the consideration should be present or future; something already done could not 'move' the promise, and therefore a promise to pay for something past was gratuitous. Before 1600 *assumpsit* could be defined in modern terms as 'a mutual agreement between the parties for a thing to be performed by the defendant in consideration of some benefit which must

47. *Sharington v Strotton* (1565) 1 Plowd 300, 308.
48. Passage in Yorke's reports (c. 1530) 94 SS *296–297*.
49. W. Sheppard *Grand Abridgment* (1675), vol. I, p. 64. Cf. Hetley 4.

depart from, or of some labour or prejudice which must be sustained by, the plaintiff'.[50]

Assumpsit and Debt

The failure to pay money owed is a particular species of nonfeasance which sounded only in debt. Perhaps it is not a serious abuse of everyday language to classify a debt as a wrong. The thirteenth-century treatise *Fet Asaver* treated debt *a tort detenue* as a form of trespass, and the variant texts of the Lord's Prayer use the words 'debt' and 'trespass' interchangeably.[51] Yet the lawyer sees a clear difference between a wrong, which is a spent act requiring redress, and a duty such as a debt, which is continuous and requires enforcement. 'Debt commences by contract and agreement between the parties, and the ground of action is *duty*; trespass commences by wrong (*tort*), without the assent of the parties, and the demand is to have a wrong punished.'[52]

The reasons for wishing to extend *assumpsit* to money claims were not the same as those for extending it to breaches of covenant. There was already a remedy in the royal courts, unlimited by the requirement of a deed. Simple debts could be recovered at common law, and the action of debt lived on as covenant faded into relative unimportance. But the disadvantages of debt have already been noticed: wager of law, the narrowness of *quid pro quo*, the need for a sum certain, and the lack of a remedy against executors. The King's Bench was more eager to furnish litigants with an alternative than was the Common Pleas, which had the exclusive cognisance of writs of debt and had a conservative outlook. It began the extension of *assumpsit* in this direction in the reign of Henry VIII.

The action on the case would not lie for a mere debt any more than it would lie for a mere breach of covenant; but once it had been established that it could lie for not performing a promise to *do* something, it was at least arguable that it could lie for not performing a promise to *pay* something. It must be remembered that a promise to pay was not the same thing as a 'contract', in the medieval sense of a real transaction, an exchange of grants. If *A* sold *B* a horse for £10,

---

50. *Slade's Case* (1598), from text in [1971] CLJ at 55 per Tanfield. Cf. *Manwood v Burston* (1587) 2 Leon 203.
51. Matthew, vi, 12, 14; Luke, xi, 4 (*debita, peccata, delicta*). Cf. Woodbine *Four 13th Century Law Tracts* (1910), p. 112.
52. *Warden of the Fleet's Case* (1428) YB Mich 7 Hen VI, 6, pl. 9 per Vampage (freely translated and abridged).

then *B* owed *A* the £10 by virtue of the sale alone. Modern lawyers would find in such a sale a promise to pay, but very often it would only be a tacit or implied promise. In the sixteenth century, however, it was legitimate and proper to say that an undertaking to pay money was different from a contract. If, therefore, an *assumpsit* or promise to pay was made at the time of the contract, or afterwards, and the promise was supported by consideration, and was broken so that loss ensued, this could provide the basis for an action on the case. The action would not be brought to enforce the contract, but to remedy the deceitful breach of the undertaking.

The earliest King's Bench actions so far discovered date from the 1510s. The form of pleading was that the parties had entered into some transaction, which was set out, that the defendant undertook to pay the resulting debt, and that the defendant not regarding his promise but scheming to defraud the plaintiff had failed to pay, as a result of which the plaintiff had suffered loss by being unable to pay his own debts, or by losing the profits of further bargains he could have made with the money. Many of the earliest actions were to enforce payments which could not be recovered in debt: actions by or against sureties, actions by or against executors, cases where the sum was not fixed in advance, and so on. Whether case would lie in a situation where debt would also lie became a vexed question in the 1520s. It was settled by a judgment of the King's Bench in 1532. The plaintiff had paid the defendant for a quarter of malt and now brought *assumpsit* for non-delivery. The defendant argued that the proper action was debt. But the court held, with one dissentient, that the plaintiff could elect in such a case to bring either debt or *assumpsit*. According to Spelman J, 'the action of debt is founded on the *debet et detinet*, whereas this action is founded on another wrong, that is, on the breaking of the promise'.[53] The decision was a natural extension of the views of Fyneux CJ in 1499, and of Frowyk CJ in 1505; but it opened up a far more fruitful line of business for the King's Bench. By the 1540s *assumpsit* for money was becoming the principal form of action on the case; and the King's Bench, now able to entertain suits upon charterparties, insurance contracts, partnerships, and bills of exchange, was rapidly becoming a commercial court.

As with the other forms of *assumpsit* for nonfeasance, it became

---

53. *Pykeryng v Thurgoode* (1532) Spelman Rep (93 SS), 4, 5; 94 SS 247. The question had been inconclusively raised in two earlier unreported cases: *Cremour v Sygeon* (1521–25) and *Haymond v Lenthorp* (1528–31): 94 SS *283*. The decision was confirmed in two actions against sureties who had promised to pay debts: *Squyer v Barkeley* (1533) Spelman Rep 7; *Holygrave v Knyghtysbrygge* (or *Jordan's Case*) (1535), ibid., Fifoot HSCL, p. 353.

necessary to show some 'cause' or consideration for the promise to pay. Various usages had developed by Elizabethan times, though it is difficult to assess how far the allegations were fictions introduced for the sake of preserving a trespassory formula which did not quite fit the facts. If the jury found for the defendant, the law would hardly ever be discussed; while, if the jury found for the plaintiff on the general issue *non assumpsit*, it was impossible to go behind the verdict into the details. The facts could not, of course, be disputed on a demurrer. Therefore the plea rolls tell us only the forms which were acceptable, not the true facts of cases.

One way of framing the action was to allege a pre-existing debt and a promise to pay it in consideration of a forbearance to sue for the debt for a certain time. By Elizabeth I's time pleaders were alleging nominal forbearances of a day or so in order to put their case into this form; the Common Pleas refused to accept such a consideration as genuine, but the King's Bench was satisfied.

A second device was appropriate where tradesmen or merchants had accounted with each other or with customers and an agreed total debt was acknowledged. It was possible to bring *assumpsit* in consideration that the parties had accounted together (*insimul computassent*) and that the sum was found owing.[54]

Third, the plaintiff could rely simply on a promise to pay a pre-existing debt. Without more, this was open to the objection that it sounded in debt; the consideration was past, and in any case the performance of an existing duty was not good consideration because there was already a remedy by writ of debt. These objections would be avoided by saying that the contract was entered into at the request of the defendant, and by alleging a consideration and a loss over and above the debt. Thus, it might be shown that the plaintiff paid a nominal sum of a few pence in return for the promise, or that the plaintiff suffered special loss as a result of not having his money on time. Very common was the familiar allegation of deceit, by means of which the non-payment was presented as a fraudulent scheme to cheat the plaintiff of his money. Here again, the Common Pleas judges would reject these considerations unless they were genuine. It was not really fraudulent to fail in the payment of a debt if the sole reason for non-payment was lack of money. But the King's Bench generally allowed the action in all cases where an action of debt would lie, to the extent even of implying promises to pay into all contracts. Coke summed up the attitude of the King's Bench in 1587 by saying that 'conscience has encroached this action upon the common law, for

54. See p. 306, post.

by the common law one could not have action on the case if he could have some other action, but now this old law is altered and it is now taken for a rule that upon such matter whereon he could have a bill and *subpoena* in the Chancery he may now have an action on the case *sur assumpsit* at common law'.[55]

The King's Bench approach came under fire from the Common Pleas during the sixteenth century. A host of objections was raised. First, it was said that the flagrant attempt to introduce an alternative remedy to debt was depriving debtors of their birthright to wage their law.[56] Second, it was wrong to allow actions of *assumpsit* unless an express *assumpsit* could be proved. Third, the damages for breach of a promise to pay a debt should represent only the consequential loss and not the debt itself. Fourth, a general form of pleading had developed in which the details of the contract were not set out; the plaintiff merely said that the defendant, being indebted to him, promised to pay the debt (*indebitatus assumpsit solvere*). This *indebitatus assumpsit* formula, it was argued, took defendants by surprise because they had no idea of the case they were to answer until they heard the witnesses. Moreover, the vague words might include debts arising from obligations under seal, and it was not proper for those to be tried by jury. Fifth, the King's Bench was allowing *assumpsit* against executors to enforce the debts of the deceased, and this was not possible by writ of debt.[57]

SLADE'S CASE (1602)

These differences of opinion generated much uncertainty. Probably the judges of the two benches had given conflicting directions to juries on circuit; and, since a King's Bench case might come before a Common Pleas judge at *nisi prius*, there was little predictability. In the last decade of the sixteenth century, a number of King's Bench decisions were reversed by the statutory Exchequer Chamber, composed of the Common Pleas judges and barons of the Exchequer.

At the end of the century, in an effort to end the discord, the problems were considered by all the judges of England in *Slade's Case*.[58] Slade had bargained and sold a field of corn to Morley, who, according to the pleadings, assumed and then and there promised to pay £16 for it. Slade brought *assumpsit* for the non-payment, Morley

55. *Anon* (1587) HLS MS 116, f. 401v.
56. This objection was first raised in *Anon* (1543) Gell Rep 94 SS *298* per Shelley J.
57. This was the earliest objection: *Anon* (1535) YB Trin 27 Hen VIII, 23, pl. 21 per Fitzherbert J, who said that the King's Bench decision of *Cleymond v Vincent* (1520) should be taken out of the year-books because it was not law.
58. *Slade v Morley* (1597–1602) 4 Co Rep 92; [1971] CLJ 51–67.

denied the promise, and the jury found specially that the sale had taken place but that there was 'no promise or undertaking other than the said bargain'. This special verdict was no doubt procured in order to compel the court in banc to face the controversial issue whether case would lie on a contract, in the strict sense of that word, in the absence of an express promise to pay the debt which the contract generated. The King's Bench had no doubts about this, but if they gave judgment they would certainly be reversed by the Exchequer Chamber and the battle would be lost: So Popham CJ referred the question before giving judgment to all the judges of England, thereby giving the King's Bench judges a voice as well. The point was argued by the best lawyers of the day, including Coke and Bacon, over a period of five years. No real agreement was reached, and the King's Bench decided in the end to act upon a bare show of hands.[59] The Common Pleas were outvoted, and the plaintiff succeeded. No detailed reasons were reported, as was usual with leading decisions in the Exchequer Chamber, but it seems that two main questions were answered. First, it was settled by precedents that actions on the case could sometimes be brought where an older action also lay, and so the duplication of remedies was not of itself an objection to the newer action. Second, every executory contract 'imported' in itself an *assumpsit* to pay what was due under it; the man in the street could not be expected to use the precise words 'I assume' or 'I undertake' when making bargains, but the law would treat the bargain as including an undertaking.

Slade's Case therefore established the right to recover debts by the action of *assumpsit*, and thereby practically put an end to wager of law. Although it had been argued that the damages in *assumpsit* should not automatically equal or include the debt, Coke asserted that the whole of the debt could be recovered by way of damages, and the point does not seem to have been pressed again. As a necessary corollary, a judgment in *assumpsit* would bar an action in debt for the same sum, and vice versa. Thus, a plaintiff who had brought debt and had been met by wager of law could not start again in *assumpsit* for the same sum. Consequently, the action of debt on a contract went almost out of use. The judges expressly left open the question whether *assumpsit* for money would lie against executors. In 1611 it was resolved by all the judges that it would.[60] The only reason why debt did not lie

59. See the recollections of Walmsley J, in 1604: 21 AJLH 340. The procedure was irregular inasmuch as the tradition of such meetings had been, in the case of deadlock, to withhold judgment. Cf. the comments of Hale CJ, p. 289, post.

60. *Legate v Pinchon* (1612) 9 Co Rep 86, Fifoot HSCL, p. 374.

against executors was that they could not wage the law of the testator; but that argument was irrelevant in *assumpsit*, since trial was by jury. Although the general rule for torts was that *actio personalis moritur cum persona*, the action of *assumpsit* was by 1611 sufficiently contractual in nature to constitute an exception to the rule.

A Unified Law of Contract

Slade's Case marked the final stage of the unification of the law of contract through the action of *assumpsit*. There was now one law of parol contracts. Deeds apart, the subject-matter of the old actions of debt and covenant had been fused. Of course there were protests. Vaughan CJ objected to the confusion of debt and covenant, and ventured to deny the authority of *Slade's Case*.[61] Nevertheless, 1602 may be regarded as the date whence the modern law of contract traces its life as a single entity.

It must not be thought, however, that all actions of *assumpsit* were the same in form. The historical differences lingered in the pleadings until the procedural reforms of the last century. *Assumpsit* for misfeasance continued to be brought as an action in tort without the need for consideration in the contractual sense;[62] and to this day a negligent surgeon may be sued in tort or in contract at the plaintiff's election. *Assumpsit* for breach of covenant, for not performing an act as promised, varied from case to case and has therefore been labelled 'special *assumpsit*'. *Assumpsit* to recover a debt separated out into several standard forms represented by the 'common counts'.

THE COMMON INDEBITATUS COUNTS

The objections to the general form of declaration in *indebitatus assumpsit* did not arise in *Slade's Case* itself, because the transaction of sale was there set out in detail and the undertaking was imported into that transaction by the court. Yet it was decided soon afterwards, by the Exchequer Chamber, that a general statement of indebtedness followed by a promise to pay was insufficient.[63] The next step was to inject the spirit of *Slade's Case* into the more desirable *indebitatus* action. Pleaders managed to avoid the objection to generality by stating the nature of the contract by which the debt arose. Thus, the seller of goods counted that the purchaser was indebted to him 'for goods sold

---

61. *Edgcomb v Dee* (1670) Vaugh 89, 101; *Anon* (1673) 1 Mod Rep 163.
62. See p. 330, post.
63. *Woodford v Deacon* (1608) Cro Jac 206. For other cases, see 21 AJLH 341 n. 20.

at his request', and being so indebted he, in consideration thereof, promised to pay. This formula was thought just sufficient to put the defendant on due notice as to the substance of the claim, but gave the plaintiff the advantage of not having to set out any specific details. By the mid-seventeenth century this revised *indebitatus* formula had probably replaced the *Slade's Case* type of formula. During that century the standardisation of pleading according to the new practice resulted in the common counts, which were used until 1852. The main varieties were the counts for goods sold and delivered, or bargained and sold, for work done, for money lent, for money spent to the plaintiff's use, for money had and received to the plaintiff's use, and for money due upon an account stated.

The subsequent promise on which these actions were founded was fictitious, in that there was no need to prove it; and the consideration seems to have been almost equally fictitious, since it was an existing duty incurred in the past.[64] No one was in any doubt that the courts had allowed the forms of law to be twisted so that the transactions represented by the common counts could be enforced without resort to an action of debt. That had been the object of the majority in *Slade's Case*. But the means were different from those approved in *Slade's Case*, and the effects of the fiction were to be more far-reaching, because they enabled the use of the action to enforce non-contractual obligations to pay, obligations which had never been actionable in debt or in any other form of action.[65] To the development of 'quasi contract' we shall return in the next chapter.

PAROL CONTRACTS AND PERJURY

A direct consequence of *Slade's Case* was the complete replacement of wager of law by jury trial for the trial of simple debt actions. Coke had made this a positive argument in favour of Slade, 'for now experience proves that men's consciences grow so large that the respect of their private advantage rather induces men (and chiefly those who have declining estates) to perjury'. Unfortunately, the jury, with the limitations of the seventeenth-century law of evidence, was not wholly suited to the new task. Wager of law, for all its defects, had protected the innocent defendant from fraudulent claims by unscrupulous tradesmen in cases where there was no evidence of contract or payment to go before a jury. After 1602 there was little protection against such claims except the good discretion of the jury. The parties them-

64. See *Hodge v Vavisour* (1612) 1 Rolle Rep 413, 3 Bulst 222.
65. Holt CJ tried unsuccessfully to restrain the fiction to the rationale of *Slade's Case*: p. 309, post.

selves, and interested persons, were excluded from the witness box at common law on the assumption that their testimony would be biased and therefore worthless. If the professional perjurer changed his occupation from oath-helper to hired witness, the jurors might have no evidence to salve their own consciences but perjured evidence, and the loss caused by such perjury now fell on defendants rather than plaintiffs. During the course of the seventeenth century the harm done by perjury in *assumpsit* cases was keenly felt. Hale CJ remarked in 1672 that perjury was so rife that two men could not safely talk together without a promise being sprung on them. All the fears of the Common Pleas judges had been realised, and Coke had it all to answer for: 'for the common law was a wise law, that men should wage their law in debt on a contract, and if they proved their reputation with twelve hands should be discharged, that so things might be reduced to writing. And *Slade's Case*, which was hardly brought in (for it was by a capitulation and agreement among the judges) has done more hurt than ever it did or will do good.'[66]

It was too late to undo *Slade's Case*, except by legislation, and so it was to a legislative solution that Restoration lawyers looked. Hale's solution would have been to reintroduce wager of law, or to require some 'signal ceremony' or writing to bind the parties. The reintroduction of wager of law was not actively pursued, but the requirement of writing for certain types of contract seemed to provide a convenient solution. It was almost as if the history of covenant was repeating itself; save that the revival of compulsory writing was only partial, and that an unsealed writing was considered adequate for evidential purposes. The first draft of the Statute of Frauds, believed to have been written by Sir Heneage Finch (later Lord Nottingham) in 1674, adopted a simple solution. Its main object was to provide that transactions concerning land should be in writing, but it also provided that in actions upon parol contracts whereof there was no written memorandum no damages were to be recovered beyond a stated amount.[67] This policy of restricting the damages recoverable for breach of oral contracts was copied from earlier Continental legislation, which had in 1667 been re-enacted by Louis XIV of France.[68] Finch's preliminary bill was not concerned with debts and the problem left by *Slade's Case*, but with the wider problem of perjury in the proof of oral contracts. The bill was drastically altered, by Sir Francis North and others, before it became law. In place of the limited

---

66. *Anon* (1672) Treby Rep (MS in Middle Temple) 747; *Legal History Studies 1972*, p. 5.
67. Holdsworth HEL, vol. VI, Appendix I.
68. See E. Rabel, 63 LQR 174.

damages principle, the new proposal was to make certain classes of oral contract completely unenforceable. The contracts to which this proposal was to apply were: (1) a promise by an executor to answer for damages out of his own estate, (2) a promise to answer for the debt, default or miscarriage of another (a guarantee), (3) an agreement in consideration of marriage, (4) a contract for the sale of land or any interest therein, and (5) an agreement which is not to be performed within one year. No action was to be brought upon such contracts unless there was a memorandum in writing signed by the party to be charged. It was also provided that no contract for the sale of goods for more than £10 should be good unless the buyer accepted part of the goods and actually received them, or gave something in earnest to bind the payment or in part payment, or there was writing. All this was enacted in the Statute of Frauds 1677.[69] The subsequent history of the statute has not been entirely happy. Strict enforcement of its terms could easily have protected more frauds than it was designed to prevent. Courts of law and equity therefore took every opportunity to limit its scope by construing it in such a way as to promote the policy of inhibiting frauds;[70] but this policy only added to the obscurity of some of the provisions. The provision as to sale of goods was an attempt to change the trading habits of the nation; yet, two hundred years after the statute, it had made little difference to the habits of buyers and sellers and had become a dead letter, repudiated in practice by mercantile men.[71] It was, nevertheless, incorporated in the Sale of Goods Act 1893 and survived until 1954.[72] The requirement as to contracts for the sale of land has been accepted as wholly desirable, and was incorporated in the legislation of 1925.[73] It remains, however, subject to the important equitable gloss which permits an action to be brought—not on the contract, but on something like an equitable estoppel—where an oral contract has been partly performed.

Elaboration of Contract Law

Even as late as 1800, the content of the law of parol contracts was slight by comparison with the position in 1900. There were old cases

69. Stat 29 Car II, c. 3, ss. 4, 17.
70. See *Simon v Metivier* (1766) 1 Wm Bl 599.
71. See J. F. Stephen, (1884) 1 LQR at 24.
72. Sale of Goods Act 1893, 56 & 57 Vict, c.71, s.4; Law Reform (Enforcement of Contracts) Act 1954, 2 & 3 Eliz II, c.34.
73. Law of Property Act 1925, 15 Geo V, c.20, s.40.

on consideration, and a great deal on pleading; material enough for a handbook on *nisi prius* practice, but not for a scientific textbook. Nothing was yet heard of offer and acceptance, of mistake, or of principles of remoteness of damage. Misrepresentation belonged to the law of tort, and the principles of illegality and discharge were only just emerging in a quasi-contractual context.[74] The reason for the absence of detailed rules was that in most *assumpsit* cases the defendant pleaded *non assumpsit* and the merits were left to the jury. What was a contract, and what was not, were questions of fact. The change seems to have occurred within a fairly short space, and was probably a response to pressure from commercial men for the formulation of clear rules of commercial law. Those rules began to be formulated by Lord Mansfield CJ, in the third quarter of the eighteenth century. In 1787 a judge recalled that, 'Within these thirty years . . . the commercial law of this country has taken a very different turn . . . Before that period we find that in courts of law all the evidence in mercantile cases was thrown together; they were left generally to a jury, and they produced no established principle. From that time we all know the great study has been to find some certain general principles, which shall be known to all mankind . . . Most of us have heard these principles stated, reasoned upon, enlarged, and explained, till we have been lost in admiration at the strength and stretch of the human understanding.'[75] The technique used by Lord Mansfield has already been described.[76] The intellectual sources were the writings current throughout Europe of natural lawyers such as Grotius, Pufendorf, Heineccius and Vattel, and the standard international textbooks on the law merchant. Bench and bar became imbued with a new European spirit.

ATTEMPTS TO RATIONALISE CONSIDERATION

The notion of consideration had grown into a legal doctrine in a haphazard way, but it could be seen as performing a single function: that of providing the vital element which caused parol promises to be legally binding. Little effort was made to identify or express the underlying principle until the eighteenth century, and lawyers managed with the lists of cases on one side or the other which were found in the abridgments. In an early treatise on the law of contracts, Sir Jeffrey Gilbert (1674–1726) explained that English law had adopted the middle course between holding men to a rigid fidelity in all their

74. See p. 310, post.
75. *Lickbarrow v Mason* (1787) 2 Term Rep 63 at 73 per Buller J.
76. See pp. 74, 120, ante.

promises, and only enforcing pacts supported by *quid pro quo* or recompense. If the party used the formality of a writing under seal then his contract was taken to be binding without more ado, for it would be 'down right madness to trifle with the solemnity of law and pretend after the sealing that there was nothing seriously designed'. Where, however, the contract was merely by parol it needed consideration to clothe it with binding force; 'otherwise a man might be drawn into an obligation without any real intention by random words and ludicrous expressions, and from thence there would be a manifest inlet to perjury because nothing were more easy than to turn the kindness of expressions into the obligation of a real promise'.[77]

Lord Mansfield sought to carry this approach further in the case of *Pillans v Van Mierop*,[78] where he refused to accept the proposition that a parol written contract without consideration was *nudum pactum*, at any rate in a commercial case. Mercantile men expected written contracts to bind. 'I take it,' he said, 'that the ancient notion about the want of consideration was for the sake of evidence only; for when it is reduced into writing, as in covenants, specialties, bonds, and so on, there was no objection to the want of consideration.' This was not a sound historical argument, but a deliberate rejection of the magic of the seal. Wilmot J, concurring, said that the theory of consideration had been 'melting down into common sense of late times'. He thought that the purpose of consideration, both in the common law and the Civil law, was to guard against rash undertakings made without due reflection. Writing supplied that purpose as well as parchment and wax.[79]

When Lord Mansfield reiterated his point of view in 1778, however, it was reversed on error. Counsel argued in the House of Lords that sealing was no more than a ceremony, and that a parol writing should displace the need for consideration in the same way as a deed had always done. Skynner CB, delivered the unanimous opinion of the judges to be that, whatever the Civil law meant by the maxim *ex nudo pacto non oritur actio*, the common law clearly meant that an action could only be founded on a parol promise if it were supported by consideration. There was no difference in English law between written and oral contracts, only between deeds and parol contracts. The House of Lords gave judgment accordingly,[80] and the decision has been treated as law ever since. As most contracts which give rise to

77. *Of Contracts* (c. 1720) Brit Lib MS Hargrave 265, ff. 75–77.
78. *Pillans and Rose v Van Mierop and Hopkins* (1765) 3 Burr 1664.
79. See a learned refutation of this view in J. Fonblanque *Treatise on Equity* (1793), vol. I, p. 326–337.
80. *Rann v Hughes* (1778) 4 Bro Parl Cas 27, 7 Term Rep 350n.

litigation are in writing, the decision practically ensured the survival into modern times of the doctrine of consideration.

THE NINETEENTH CENTURY

In the first half of the nineteenth century the courts were given the opportunity to formulate the classical law of contract, as counsel increasingly took advantage of the procedures for raising detailed questions of law in banc. The courts took the opportunity, and, following Lord Mansfield's example, sought guidance outside the black-letter texts of the common law. The most influential sources were the *Traité d'Obligations* (1761) by the French jurist R. Pothier (1699–1772), which was published in English in 1806, and the university textbook *Principles of Moral and Political Philosophy* (1785) by William Paley (1743–1805), Archdeacon of Carlisle. Both works included discussions of elementary contractual principles so long absent from the common law. In them we find the seeds of the English law of offer and acceptance and mistake, and much else which we now tend to regard as the eternal customs of England.[81] It is, ironically, only with Britain's entry into the European Economic Community that Pothier's authority has been emphatically rejected.[82]

Contractual Terms

The origins of the law relating to the 'terms' of a contract are to be found in the law of warranties. A warranty or guarantee was a statement about the quality or quantity of goods sold, made by the seller at the time of sale. It was not a promise to do something *in futuro*, but an assertion of present fact. If, therefore, the warranty was false, the wrong was not a breach of promise but a deceit.

Suppose, for example, that *A* undertook to deliver to *B* ten yards of blue cloth, and he sent ten yards of red cloth. *B* could sue *A* in *assumpsit* for failing to carry out his promise. But if *A* sold *B* a specific bale of cloth and said that it contained ten yards, whereas it only contained five, there was a perfect sale of the cloth and the wrong was that *B* had been tricked into buying it. In such a case *B* had an action on the case for deceit against *A*, in that *A* had sold the cloth by warranting it to be

---

81. E.g. *Hadley v Baxendale* (1854) 8 Exch 341 (damages); *Offord v Davies* (1862) 12 CBNS 748 (formation of contract); *Taylor v Caldwell* (1863) 3 B & S 826 (frustration); *Smith v Hughes* (1871) LR 6 QB 597; *Phillips v Brooks* [1919] 2 KB 243 (mistake).
82. *Lewis v Averay* [1972] 1 QB 198 at 206E per Lord Denning MR.

of a certain length when it was not.[83] This form of action in tort appeared in the royal courts in the fourteenth century, and was in the same class as the action for playing with false dice and for other forms of trickery. It lay only if the plaintiff had been deceived by relying on the warranty, and was not available if the untruth of the statement was obvious to the senses of the buyer. Thus, if *A* in the last example warranted the cloth to be blue, when it was red, *B* could not allege a deceit unless he was blind, because it was a matter he should have discovered for himself by inspection. Neither would the action lie in respect of statements relating to the future; for instance, a 'warranty' by *A* that the cloth would last so long, or that seeds would grow, or that a horse could be ridden so many miles in a day. Such things were either outside human control, and therefore inherently unpredictable, or they were promises which sounded in covenant; they were not statements about the present condition of the goods when sold, and so they could not deceive.

It is clear from these examples that the action of deceit on a warranty lay for the tort of deceit, and not for the breach of any contractual undertaking. If there was no warranty, there was generally no remedy if the goods turned out to be of poor quality. Since the seller had not deceived the buyer, the rule was 'let the buyer take care' (*caveat emptor*).[84] Nevertheless, the line between tort and contract was here very thin. A promise that cloth would last so long was not unlike a warranty that the cloth was of a certain quality. A promise that a horse would work hard was almost a warranty that it was a strong horse. Such promises were not actionable unless they were given in return for some consideration; but the sale itself might be treated as consideration for this purpose. It is not wholly surprising that eventually a breach of warranty came always to be regarded as a breach of contract.

WARRANTIES AS PROMISES

In the seventeenth and eighteenth centuries, pleaders began to treat a warranty on a sale as a promise or contract that the facts stated were true. The motive for so doing was to enable the joinder of actions. Thus, an action on the warranty if framed in *assumpsit* could be joined with an action to recover back the price for a total failure of consideration. As late as 1778 it was argued that a promise could only relate to

---

83. E.g. *Langham v Spencer* (1414) 88 SS 222; *Anon* (1471) Fifoot HSCL, p. 349. The action also lay in respect of a hiring, e.g., of a defective horse.

84. Co Inst, vol. I, p. 102. See *Chandelor v Lopus* (1603) Cro Jac 4, 8 HLR 282. And for a precursor of that case see *Audrey v Boby* (1415) 88 SS 230.

the future, and not to past or present facts; but by this date the boundaries between contract and warranty had broken down, and the Court of King's Bench upheld the established practice of suing in *assumpsit* for breach of warranty. As Grose J remarked eleven years later, 'All the cases of deceit for misinformation may be turned into actions of *assumpsit*.'[85]

The chief consequence of the new practice was that the tort of deceit grew more distinct from contract, and was held to rest upon fraudulent misrepresentation.[86] The word 'warranty', on the other hand, lost its strict meaning and was applied both to representations of fact (affirmative warranties) and to promises (promissory warranties). The bifurcation of remedies for deceit created an unfortunate gap, in that no action for damages would lie on a misrepresentation unless it was made fraudulently or became a term of the contract.[87] Another consequence was that contracts ceased to be regarded as single obligations, and were analysed as bundles of stipulations, of varying degrees of importance, called the 'terms' of the contract. Some terms were so fundamental to the contract that if they were broken the other party could repudiate his own obligations; these were conditional promises, because their fulfilment was a condition of the other party's liability. Warranties which did not amount to conditions entitled the party to sue for damages.

IMPLIED TERMS

In the old action of deceit, it had been established that a seller was liable to an action for *knowingly* selling something unsaleable even if there was no express warranty. If the seller's liability was to survive the rearrangement of remedies, the law would have to imply an *assumpsit* as to merchantability, and this is what happened in the early nineteenth century. While *caveat emptor* remained the general rule,[88] it was decided in 1815 that it had no application where the buyer was given no opportunity to inspect the goods. In all such cases the seller was to be taken as contracting that the goods were of merchantable quality.[89] Best CJ explained in 1829 that the doctrine *caveat emptor* had been convenient in relation to horses; 'no prudence can guard against latent defects in a horse', and so in the absence of fraudulent concealment no more is implied on the sale of a horse than that the creature

---

85. *Stuart v Wilkins* (1778) 1 Doug 18, 20; *Pasley v Freeman* (1789) 3 Term Rep 51, 54.
86. *Pasley v Freeman* (1789) 3 Term Rep 51; *Derry v Peek* (1889) 14 App Cas 337.
87. *Heilbut, Symons & Co v Buckleton* [1913] AC 30. The gap was filled by the Misrepresentation Act 1967 (c.7), s.2(1).
88. *Barr v Gibson* (1838) 3 M & W 390; *Burnby v Bollett* (1847) 16 M & W 644.
89. *Gardiner v. Gray* (1815) 4 Camp 144; *Laing v Fidgeon* (1815) 6 Taunt 108.

sold is a horse. A manufacturer of goods, however, bore more responsibility for the condition of articles which he had brought into being; and so he was taken to contract not only that his goods were merchantable but also, if he knew the purpose for which they were intended, that they were fit for that purpose.[90]

As a corollary to these principles, the buyer was usually entitled to reject goods tendered to him if they were unmerchantable or unfit for the purpose for which they were supplied. It was a 'condition precedent' to the buyer's obligation to accept and pay for the goods that they should be of the quality contracted for, and the sale had no force unless the condition was fulfilled. When the law relating to the sale of goods was codified in 1893, the draftsman, Judge Chalmers, framed the implied terms as to merchantibility and fitness for purpose as 'conditions'.[91] Under the Sale of Goods Act, as at common law, the implication of terms could always be excluded by express language. In the twentieth century, parliament has taken to imposing unexcludable 'implied terms' in order to confer minimum standards upon persons entering into certain classes of contract. Of course, such terms are fictitious. The object is to protect classes of persons who are thought incapable for economic reasons of protecting themselves when making contracts. Protection was extended first to leasehold tenants, then to employees, and now to consumers. The result is that the law of contract is diminishing in importance as regards the ordinary non-commercial man; all the important transactions he is likely to make are governed not by the common law of contract but by the statutory law of landlord and tenant, labour law, or consumer law.

STANDARD-FORM CONTRACTS

The growth of large-scale manufacturing, trading and public utility companies after the Industrial Revolution brought changes in contract-making practices. It is convenient and time-saving for a company to make the same form of contract with each of its customers. The terms are contained in a standard document, upon which the company has had legal and business advice; there is no room for negotiation. Since most of the written contracts made by the ordinary person are in standard forms, the freedom of contract which the law assures everyone has become abstract theory. The law did not easily adapt to this state of affairs, because the man who submits to a standard form is under no legal duress and must be taken to have

90. *Jones v Bright* (1829) 5 Bing 533.
91. Sale of Goods Act 1893, 56 & 57 Vict, c.71, ss.11–14; p. 190, ante.

assented to the terms as a free bargain. Every party is equal, be he a pauper or an international corporation.

The aspect of standard-form contracts which has provoked the most discussion has been the exclusion or limitation clause. Such clauses, inserted into printed contracts to cut down or negative the liability of the party who dictates the terms, seem to have been introduced by carriers; and they came to prominence with the expansion of the railways in the last century. By 1850 the railway companies were using a clause which exempted them from 'responsibility for any damage, however caused'. The courts were sympathetic to these clauses, because the invention of the railway had conferred new benefits on the public, and so the proprietors who exploited the invention were entitled to protect themselves against the unprecedented risks inherent in rail transport.[92] The clauses were not, of course, welcomed by the public, who soon came to regard rail travel as a natural right. When the Railway and Canal Traffic Bill was passing through parliament in 1854, the subject of exclusion clauses was fully debated in the House of Lords, and strong criticisms of the law were advanced by Lords Lyndhurst and Brougham. The latter, in characteristically strong language, said that the railway exemption clauses ought in justice to be void for duress since the passengers had no freedom of choice; either they agreed to the terms or they could not use the railways. A clause was therefore added to the bill to provide that railway companies were to be liable for negligence notwithstanding any condition limiting or excluding their liability, unless the clause was held to be just and reasonable.[93] This reform attempted to introduce a convenient balance between the functions of the legislature and those of the judiciary. The courts were to enforce reasonable contracts to the letter, but had a power to review exclusion and limitation clauses if freedom of contract was missing in reality. But the principle of reasonableness proved difficult to apply in practice, and was not adopted in subsequent legislation. As exclusion clauses spread into all kinds of contracts, the courts themselves endeavoured to reduce their effects. They were always construed *contra proferentem* and given the narrowest effect consistent with the words used. In the absence of clear language, a clause would not protect a party who acted outside the terms of the contract, and if the contract as a whole manifested an intention by one party to be bound a clause purporting

---

92. See *Carr v Lancashire and Yorkshire Rly Co* (1852) 7 Ex 707; *Peek v North Staffordshire Rly Co* (1863) 10 HLC 473 at 556 per Cockburn CJ.
93. *Parliamentary Debates* (HC), cxxxiii (3rd ser.); Railway and Canal Traffic Act 1854, 17 & 18 Vict, c.31, s.7.

to exempt him from liability would be rejected as repugnant. From these general principles of construction, some of the common law judges of the 1950s, notably Lords Devlin and Denning, attempted to extract a rule of law that a party who committed a 'fundamental breach' of contract could in no circumstances retreat behind the protection of an exclusion clause. In 1966, however, the House of Lords decided that there was no such rule of law. The courts should lean against construing a clause to cover a serious breach if there was any looseness in the language, but there was no principle of construction which could compel them to deny contractual force to an unambiguous clause.[94] Attempts by the Court of Appeal to distinguish the decision of 1966 have led to considerable confusion, and the good objections to standard-form contracts were lost sight of in a farrago of illogical and artificial distinctions. Meanwhile the Law Commission suggested the introduction of different rules depending on the bargaining power of the parties; for instance, by drawing a distinction between consumer contracts and business contracts. The reforms have now begun, and in some respects they represent a complete departure from the traditions of the common law of contract. It may now be possible in some circumstances to enforce a 'reasonable expectation' which exists contrary to the express terms of a contract.[95]

Further Reading

Pollock & Maitland, vol. II, pp. 184–228

Holdsworth HEL, vol. III, pp. 412–454

Fifoot HSCL, pp. 217–443

Milsom HFCL, pp. 211–227, 271–315

W. T. Barbour, *History of Contract in early English Equity* (1914)

W. Friedmann, *Law and Social Change* (1951), pp. 34–72

A. W. B. Simpson, 'The Place of Slade's Case in the History of Contract' (1958) 74 LQR 381–396; 'Innovation in 19th Century Contract Law' (1975) 91 LQR 247–278; *History of the Common Law of Contract: the Rise of Assumpsit* (1975)

H. K. Lücke, 'Slade's Case and the Origin of the Common Counts' (1965–66) 81 LQR 422–445, 539–561; 82 LQR 81–96

W. M. McGovern, 'Contract in Medieval England' (1968) 54 *Iowa Law Rev* 19–62; (1969) 13 AJLH 173–201; 'The Enforcement of Oral Contracts prior to Assumpsit' (1970) 65 *Northwestern Univ Law Rev* 576–614; 'The Enforcement of Informal Contracts in the later Middle Ages' (1971) 59 *California Law Rev* 1145–1193

---

94. *Suisse Atlantique Société D'Armement Maritime SA v N.V. Rotterdamsche Kolen Centrale* [1967] AC 361, [1966] 2 All ER 61.

95. Unfair Contract Terms Act 1977 (c. 50), s.3(2)b.

J. L. Barton, 'The early History of Consideration' (1969) 85 LQR 372–391

J. H. Baker, 'New Light on Slade's Case' [1971] CLJ 51–67, 213–236; 'The Establishment of Assumpsit for Nonfeasance' (1978) 94 SS *255–298*

G. Gilmore, *The Death of Contract* (1974)

M. Horwitz, 'The Historical Foundations of Modern Contract Law' (1974) 87 HLR 917–956

R. H. Helmholz, 'Assumpsit and Fidei Laesio' (1975) 91 LQR 406–432

S. J. Stoljar, *History of Contract at Common Law* (1975)

M. S. Arnold, 'Fourteenth Century Promises' [1976] CLJ 321–334

17. Quasi-Contract

There are various situations in which, independently of any contract giving rise to a debt, a person may be obliged in justice or in good faith to pay over money to another. The interest of the beneficiary is closer to property than to a contractual right; but the beneficiary has no legal title to the 'money', because no specific coins are his.[1] Such an obligation to pay money to a beneficiary therefore had much in common with the fiduciary obligation of a feoffee to uses of land; the legal ownership was in one person, the beneficial ownership in another. Yet the obligation was enforced by the common law without recourse to equity in the Chancery sense. The ultimate development cf this common law use or trust of money, before the abolition of the forms of action, was achieved by a fictitious extension of *indebitatus assumpsit*. Since the essence of the fiduciary obligation was that it was not contractual, the fiction was no slight one; now not only the tortious dressing but the promise itself had to become a figment of the legal imagination. For this procedural reason, it became customary to treat what was accordingly labelled 'quasi-contract' as an appendix to the law of contract, consisting of 'contracts implied by law'. As a reflection of historical accident this was understandable. But in substance there is no affinity between quasi-contract and contract. As we trace the history of this rather amorphous category of money claims, we must ever keep that in mind. The growth of quasi-contractual obligations is perhaps the most striking example of the way in which the common law could be developed, whatever the formal procedural restraints and however devious the subterfuges needed to evade them, in order to achieve equity.

The Action of Account

The foundation of many of the later developments lay in the medieval action of account. An accounting between two parties, either before auditors or by mutual reckoning, was itself a cause of action in debt;

1. If, however, *A* handed specific coins in a sealed bag to *B* to deliver the bag to *C*, *C* did own the coins and could bring detinue.

and by 1400 debt *sur insimul computaverunt* (later called 'account stated') would lie to recover the sum agreed to be outstanding.[2] The action of account was not concerned with the obligation to pay this sum, which sounded in debt, but with the antecedent obligation to enter into an account in order to discover what if anything was owing. The writ, which is coeval with debt and covenant, was in the *praecipe* form: command the defendant that he render a reasonable account (*praecipe quod reddat rationabile compotum*). If the court decided that he should account, the defendant was committed to prison and auditors were assigned to hear the account. The imprisonment at one time could be continued until the account was settled, but it was no part of the judgment that any sum should be paid, and in later times it was necessary to bring an action of debt if the defendant declined to pay what was found due.

At first the duty to account rested upon a status akin to what we now call agency. The early actions were brought against bailiffs (estate managers) and guardians in socage.[3] In the fourteenth century it was extended to commercial relationships, first by treating various kinds of agent as constructive bailiffs, and then by admitting a count against one who had received money in an accountable way (*ad compotum reddendum*). The recognition of the count against a receiver opened up the possibility that account would lie even where there was no prior relationship of agency between the parties; for instance, where *A* paid money to *B* for the benefit of *C*. At the beginning of the fourteenth century, *C* was not allowed to bring account against *B* unless *B* commonly acted as his receiver; but by the end of the century this restriction had disappeared.[4] Here, therefore, *B* was obliged to pay over money to *C* even though he was not in any contractual relationship with him. Moreover, in the example given, it was possible for *A* to bring account against *B* if *B* failed to pay *C*; *B* had no more contracted to pay *A* than to pay *C* but he was accountable. It was by this means possible for a party to a failed transaction to recover back a deposit, and thus to obtain rescission for failure of consideration.[5] Much later, in the 1590s, it was decided that account would lie where *A* paid *B* by mistake; *B* was not in that case a debtor, but he could be said to have received the money to the use of *A* since *A* had not parted with the beneficial ownership.[6] The action was never

2. See S. F. C. Milsom, 82 LQR 534.
3. For the latter, see p. 206, ante.
4. YB Hil 11 Edw II (61 SS) 264, pl. 41; *Hastynges v Beverley* (1379) YB Pas 2 Ric II (Ames Foundation), 121, pl. 4.
5. *Anon* (1367) Fifoot HSCL, p. 285.
6. *Framson v Delamere* (1595) Cro Eliz 458; *Hewer v Bartholomew* (1598) Cro Eliz 614.

extended, however, to tortfeasors. If a disseisor of land took profits, or a bailee sold the bailor's goods and appropriated the purchase money, there could not be said to be a receiving to the use of the disseissee or bailor because the wrongdoer had received and converted the money to his own use; the remedy was therefore the assize or trespass.[7]

These developments split the cause of action in account into two. Account against a bailiff, guardian, or other agent, was intended primarily to secure an inquiry into a series of transactions over a period; some of the individual transactions might themselves have been contracts between the parties, others might not; there might be set-offs and allowances: all the individual items merged in the finding of the auditors, who were supposed to follow equity rather than law. The other kind of account lay against the receiver of some specific sum of money which could not be recovered in debt, where there was no dispute as to the calculation of a balance and no question of allowing expenses or adjusting mutual claims. It is this latter type which may be termed quasi-contractual. But the development from this point was not continuous. By the sixteenth century it was becoming apparent that the action of account was not the most convenient method of achieving either of the objects.

DECLINE OF ACCOUNT

In the middle of the fourteenth century account was the most frequently used personal action, more common even than debt. A century later it was far less common, and was beginning a gradual decline into oblivion. The reason usually given is that the defendant could wage his law. Too much should not be made of this. Wager of law was not permitted where the defendant received money from a third party to the use of the plaintiff,[8] and most actions of account were of this kind. By 1600 wager of law had also been denied to the bailiff.[9] There must have been other procedural disadvantages. One, no doubt, was the archaic process of imprisonment and of hearing before auditors who had no powers to compel discovery and (according to some writers) could not take evidence from the parties. In an embarrassing case of the 1520s, a defendant was incarcerated for five years without an account being taken.[10] Parties faced with a cumbersome procedure might just as well submit voluntarily to an accounting; and this explains why debt *sur insimul computaverunt* became more common as

7. For the assize, see p. 201, ante. For the action for conversion, see pp. 332–334, post.
8. *Huntley v Fraunsham* (1559) Dyer 183, Coke's *Entries*, f. 47v.
9. *Shyfield v Barnfield* (1600) Cro Eliz 790.
10. *Earl of Northumberland v Wedell* (1523–27), Spelman Rep (93 SS) 9; YB Mich 18 Hen VIII, 2, pl. 13.

account declined. A voluntary accounting of this kind barred an action of account. In the quasi-contractual kind of case, on the other hand, it is difficult to see what possible function the auditors could have had. The count alleged the receipt of a specific sum by the hands of a named person, and the defendant could plead before the judges that the sum was received for a specific purpose which had been fulfilled and not *ad compotum reddendum*.[11] The judgment 'that the defendant do account' ended the dispute, and yet it brought about only the appointment of auditors, not payment. Here there must have been a great temptation to bring debt instead, and the courts did what they could to permit it. It was said that debt would lie if *A* paid *B* money for a purpose which was not carried out.[12] Accordingly, in a leading case of 1536, it was held that where a grocer had paid money to be invested in prunes, and the payee died before buying any prunes, debt could be brought against his administrator. Wherever money was paid on trust, and the trust was not observed, the payer could elect to bring account or debt.[13] Soon afterwards it was settled that where *A* paid money to *B* to pay to *C*, *C* could bring debt against *B* if the money was not paid.[14] These decisions virtually put an end to the quasi-contractual use of account. The action continued to be used for its older purpose, where debt was precluded because of the uncertainty as to the total amount due, into the seventeenth century; but from the middle of that century the common law jurisdiction collapsed as the Chancery offered a more efficient procedure for taking accounts.

Actions on the Case

The substitution of debt for account was not to be a lasting solution to the problems of quasi-contract. Debt, as we saw in the previous chapter, had too many shortcomings of its own. Therefore, just as debt on a contract was replaced by *assumpsit*, so debt in lieu of account was replaced by various actions on the case.

11. YB Mich 19 Hen VI, 5, pl. 10 per Newton CJ. E.g. *Clerk v More* (1452) YB Trin 30 Hen VI, 5, pl. 4 (received the money to obtain a patent, not to trade with and account); *Earl of Worcester v Bodringan* (1469) CP 40/830, m. 403 (received the money to pay over to the master of two ships for victualling purposes, not to trade with and account).
12. *Orwell v Mortoft* (1505) Fifoot HSCL, p. 352 per Frowyk CJ.; *Bretton v Barnet* (1599) Owen 86.
13. *Core v May* (1536) Spelman Rep (93 SS) 132; 94 SS 327; Dyer 20. There was a deed, and so the objection that personal representatives could not wage law did not arise.
14. Bro Abr *Dette*, pl. 129 (citing 15th-century cases); *Shaw v Norwood* (1600) Moore KB 667. The proposition is expressly denied in Spelman Rep 132.

The first possibility which occurred to lawyers was to treat the failure to account for money as a conversion. In a case of 1530, a plaintiff (x) showed that he had bought pieces of camlet from y, that at his request the defendant (z) had received them from y to resell at a higher price and pay x the proceeds, and that z undertook to do this but instead converted the proceeds to his own use. X recovered in damages somewhat more than the price paid to y, presumably the higher sum he expected from the resale.[15] The difficulty with the conversion approach, however, was that money was not specific property, and so the accountant who appropriated money was not converting property belonging to the plaintiff.[16] In 1600 the Exchequer Chamber put a temporary stop to the idea of using trover and conversion for money claims. The King's Bench had given judgment against a factor alleged to have converted the proceeds of corn sold on behalf of the plaintiff; but the judgment was reversed, primarily on the technical ground that the plaintiff, by alleging (albeit fictitiously) a loss of the money, admitted that he no longer owned any specific coins which could be converted.[17] The better ground, on the real facts revealed by the special verdict, was that the actual coins received for the corn belonged to the factor, whose obligation was to account for the sum received.

According to the Exchequer Chamber in the factor's case, the proper remedy was account. But there remained the alternative of *assumpsit*. The objections to a trover count could not apply to an *assumpsit* count. The plaintiff in the 1530 case had alleged an undertaking. As *assumpsit* became a distinct action on the case, it became necessary to show consideration, but the King's Bench was not too particular in this regard. The question arose in 1591, in an action against one who had been paid money to pay over to the plaintiff, which he had undertaken to do. The defendant argued that the proper action was account, and that *assumpsit* did not lie because there was no consideration; but the court held that an action on the case was proper to recover the damages which were not recoverable in account, and that there was sufficient consideration in the defendant's having the money temporarily in his hands.[18] We shall see that in such

---

15. *Miller v Dymok* (1530) KB 27/1077, m. 72A; 93 SS *250* n. 4.
16. See *Orwell v Mortoft* (1505) Fifoot HSCL, p. 351, Kiralfy SB, p. 151 per Kingsmill J.
17. *Holiday v Hicks* (1598–1600) Cro Eliz 638, 661, 746. The *ratio decidendi* was overruled in *Kinaston v Moor* (1627) Cro Car 89, but no more is heard of trover against accountants. In *Orton v Butler* (1822) 5 B & Ald 652, an attempt to bring trover for money had and received to the plaintiff's use was rejected with scorn.
18. *Glanvill v Spurlinge* (1591) HLS MS 16, f.315v. Cf. the identical arguments for using *assumpsit* instead of debt: pp. 283–285, ante.

situations a further development would enable the receiver to be sued on a fictitious undertaking. The action on a genuine *assumpsit* remained of use only in situations where there was a contractual relationship between the parties, a true agency. But this was precisely the kind of case where auditors were needed to go over the items of account; and Hale CJ is known to have rejected the use of such actions because of the inconvenience of unravelling accounts before juries. By 1689, nevertheless, it was established that *assumpsit* could always be used as an alternative to account against an agent, because by acting as an agent a receiver of money was understood to promise an account.[19] It was around this time, however, that the Chancery remedy effectively removed the need for such a remedy at law.

IMPLIED AND FICTITIOUS UNDERTAKINGS TO PAY

Slade's Case decided, amongst other things, that a promise to pay could be implied in any contractual debt. Such an implication was not a fiction, but a recognition that the obligation to pay such a debt was tantamount to an undertaking to pay it, even though the words 'I promise to pay' were omitted. The promise was too obvious to be expressed. This may have set lawyers wondering whether similar implied promises could not be read into contracts which were not debts and into debts which were not contracts. One could safely allege an *assumpsit* in pleading if the trial judge could be relied upon to tell the jury that in certain situations they could imply or presume an undertaking from the circumstances. Since the proceedings at *nisi prius* were not reported, it is very difficult for the historian to trace the steps by which the law came to permit the *assumpsit* to be raised, first by genuine implication and then by pure fiction. But there are two common cases in which the process seems to occur at around the time of *Slade's Case*, and it is likely that these paved the way for further extensions later in the century.

The first was the *quantum meruit* count. If a person ordered goods or services without fixing the sum to be paid for them, he could be sued upon an *assumpsit* to pay what the goods were worth (*quantum valebant*) or what the performer of the services deserved (*quantum meruit*). Of course, there may in some cases have been an express promise to pay whatever was deserved; but this seems inherently unlikely. When we see a *quantum meruit* count it is a fair guess that the undertaking was to be implied from the circumstances. This was openly stated to be so in 1609, and in 1632 the judges decided that whenever 'I bid one do work

19. *Wilkins v Wilkins* (1689) Comb 149, Carth 89, 1 Salk 9.

for me, and do not promise anything, the law makes it'.[20] Here we are well on the way from implication to fiction. There is doubless an understanding that the work is to be paid for, but the promise to pay a reasonable sum is inferred as a matter of law.

The second case was the *insimul computassent* count. This was the direct successor to debt *sur insimul computaverunt*, but for some reason the *indebitatus assumpsit* formula was not used. The form was to recite that the parties had accounted together and that the defendant had been found in debt in a specific sum, and then to allege that in consideration thereof the defendant undertook to pay the sum. Actions of this type were in use by the mid-sixteenth century, but in Elizabethan times they met the stumbling block of consideration. The King's Bench held in 1587 that a deferment of payment for a short while was sufficient consideration for the promise to pay the outstanding sum, and in 1605 it went further and held that the debt itself was sufficient consideration.[21] By the latter date, at least, both the promise and the consideration had clearly become legal fictions; being found in arrear upon an account raised an undertaking in law to pay the debt. This action ensured the survival into modern law of the concept of an 'account stated' as a cause of action sui generis, independent of contract. The modern importance of this concept grew from the use of *insimul computassent* in Georgian times to recover money due under contracts rendered unenforceable by the Statute of Limitations or the Statute of Frauds. It was established for this purpose that an acknowledgment of the existence of a debt arising from a single transaction is a cause of action separate from the contract, because it is tantamount to an accounting together and the law implies a subsequent promise to discharge it.[22]

Indebitatus Assumpsit

The action of *indebitatus assumpsit* as it developed in the seventeenth century always rested on a fictitious promise, because whenever one person was indebted to another the law implied a promise, in consideration of the indebtedness, to pay off the debt. Where the debt arose from a contract, the fiction merely reproduced the truth. Whereas in *Slade's Case* the promise to pay was implied in the contract itself, in

20. *Warbrook v Griffin* (1609) 2 Brownl 254, Yelv 66; *The Six Carpenters' Case* (1610) 8 Co Rep 146; *Anon* (1632) Sheppard's *Marrow*, p. 125.
21. *Whorwood v Gybbons* (1587) Goulds 48; *Egles v Vale* (1605) Cro Jac 69, Yelv 70. For earlier precedents, see 94 SS *61, 282.*
22. E.g. *Knowles v Michel* (1811) 13 East 249. For the survival, see *Camillo Tank SS Co Ltd v Alexandria Engineering Works* (1921) 38 TLR 134.

indebitatus assumpsit the alleged promise was subsequent to the contract and therefore wholly imaginary, but in either case the result was the same. The fictitious subsequent promise, however, soon let in an extension of *indebitatus* beyond the realms of contract: first to indebtedness arising by custom or operation of law, and then to the kind of equitable indebtedness arising from the receipt of money which belonged beneficially to someone else.

NON-CONTRACTUAL DEBTS

Debt would lie in a number of situations where the duty to pay arose from custom or law, but in theory *assumpsit* could only perform this task if there was a promise to pay. If the law implied a promise in such a case, it was pure fiction. There are cases beginning in 1588 which raise a suspicion of fiction,[23] but the first clear decision that the law would raise such a promise occurred in a case of 1677. An action was brought to recover a customary imposition (called 'scavage') owed by the defendant, and the jury found a special verdict that although there was a customary duty there was no express promise to pay it. The court held that the plaintiff should recover. The indebtedness itself was sufficient to ground an action of *indebitatus assumpsit*, and the allegation of a promise given for consideration was in such cases mere form.[24] This rapidly became accepted doctrine, and *assumpsit* was used to recover a wide range of customary dues. In *Shuttleworth v Garnett* (1688)[25] it was allowed even in respect of a manorial fine arising from tenure; the objection that *assumpsit* would not lie for a right of inheritance was brushed aside with the response that when a particular fine fell due it was like a 'flower fallen', or severed crops, and was to be treated as personalty.

Assumpsit was never allowed to take over the work of debt on an obligation or debt on a record, because it was not thought convenient to allow the general issue where there was a deed or record; but in the eighteenth century the fiction of *indebitatus assumpsit* was extended to enable the enforcement of judgments given by foreign courts.[26]

MONEY HAD AND RECEIVED

The doctrine that *indebitatus assumpsit* lay wherever debt lay enabled the action on the case to be used in place of those forms of debt which

23. *Lord North's Case* (1588) 2 Leon 179 (fine *pro licentia concordandi*); *Ayton v Van Somer* (1665) Brown's *Vade Mecum*, p. 50 (fees as Black Rod); *City of London v Gould* (1667) 2 Keb 295 (custom called water-bailage).
24. *City of London v Goree* (1677) 2 Lev 174, 1 Vent 298, 1 Freem 433, 3 Keb 677.
25. 3 Mod Rep 240, 3 Lev 261, 1 Show KB 35, Comb 151, Carth 90, Fifoot HSCL, p. 381.
26. *Bowles v Bradshaw* (1748) and *Crawford v Whittal* (1773) 1 Doug KB 4.

had themselves supplanted account. By 1616 the form of the remedy was established as the count in *indebitatus assumpsit* for money 'had and received to the use of the plaintiff'. It was no objection to such an action that account lay on the facts, and it was not necessary to specify from whom the money had been received.[27] It could be brought in all the quasi-contractual situations where account had lain: for instance, where *A* paid money to *B* to pay to *C*, or where *C* paid *B* by mistake or under a void contract. In these cases *B*, being indebted to *C* for money had and received by him to *C*'s use, was fictitiously presumed to have promised in consideration of that indebtedness to pay *C*.

But *indebitatus assumpsit* did not stop there. The count merely supposed a receipt of money to the use of someone else, and if this was construed broadly it could include situations not covered by account. The first and main extension seems to have come about more by accident than design, in a trio of cases in the 1670s concerning the profits of disputed offices. The first arose from a dispute over the office of Clerk of the Papers of the King's Bench; it was resolved to try the title by bringing *indebitatus assumpsit* in respect of £10 in fees received by the officer in possession, which the claimant regarded as having been received to his use; the arguments were confined to the question of title, not the form of action. In the second case, the Court of Exchequer allowed a similar action, despite the objection that a usurpation of office was a tort for which the proper remedy was an assize or an action on the case for disturbance.[28] The only reason given was that account lay for the profits of an office, and that *indebitatus* would lie wherever account lay. This reasoning seems false, because account would not lie against a disseisor who received income to his own use. In the third case, the court agreed 'that it might be hard perhaps to maintain it if this were a new case, and the first of this nature; but they said two or three actions of this kind had been held before'.[29] However thin the reasons behind it, the extension opened up still more possibilities: could *assumpsit* now be brought whenever money was taken or detained tortiously, or whenever the profits of property were tortiously intercepted?

SCOPE OF THE MONEY COUNTS

Sir John Holt, Chief Justice of the King's Bench from 1689 to 1710,

27. *Beckingham and Lambert v Vaughan* (1616) 1 Rolle Rep 391, Moore KB 854. Cf. *Gilbert v Ruddeard* (1607) 3 Dyer 272n (special count, but *assumpsit* implied).
28. See p. 359, post.
29. *Woodward v Aston* (1672) 2 Mod Rep 95, 1 Vent 296, 1 Freem KB 429; *Arris v Stukeley* (1677) 2 Mod Rep 260; *Howard v Wood* (1678–80) 2 Lev 245, 2 Show KB 21, T Jones 126, 1 Freem 473, Fifoot HSCL, p. 380.

answered these questions with an emphatic 'no'. He was strongly critical of the two extensions just mentioned, because they involved an undesirable distortion of the forms of action which could bear hard on defendants. He dissented from the decision in *Shuttleworth v Garnett*, saying that it was not axiomatic that *indebitatus assumpsit* was coextensive with debt: 'where wager of law doth not lie, there an *indebitatus* don't lie, and it is mischievous to extend it further than *Slade's Case*; for an *indebitatus assumpsit* is laid generally, and the defendant can't tell how to make his defence'.[30] He also thought the office cases were wrongly decided. Again and again he attacked the fictitious use of *indebitatus* and promised to stop its spread: 'it shall go as far as it has gone, but not a step further'.[31] There was no reason to allow this action to be brought in place of debt where jury trial was available, or in place of special *assumpsit* or actions in tort. Had Holt CJ not called a halt, there is no telling where the action might have gone; certainly it bid fair to overtake, at one time or another, most of the other forms of action.

1. *Real property*

The office cases established that *indebitatus* could be used to try the title to freehold offices, even though an assize was available for the purpose. If this was so, why should not the remedy be used for land? The logical conclusion had been reluctantly conceded before 1700, when it was admitted that *assumpsit* would lie against someone who had received rent without title from tenants who had attorned to him.[32] How far *assumpsit* jostled with ejectment in reality is not known, but an obvious attraction would have been that it could be brought against personal representatives and persons against whom ejectment would not lie. The orthodox view in the later eighteenth century turned against allowing *assumpsit* to be brought for accepting rent where adverse title was claimed. In such a case the proper remedy was ejectment, which was brought against the tenant; or, if ejectment was unavailable, *assumpsit* against the tenant for the 'use and occupation', supposing him to be in occupation with the licence of the plaintiff and owing him rent. If the tenant was made to pay rent a second time, in an *assumpsit* for the use and occupation, it was then for

30. Comb 151. The one case which Holt CJ seems to have accepted as a fait accompli was the overpayment by mistake: Comb 341, 2 Ld Raym 1217.
31. *Hussey v Fiddell* (1698) 12 Mod Rep 324.
32. It was said in *Arris v Stukeley* and *Hussey v Fiddell*, ante, that such actions had already been allowed, the first having been brought by Serjeant Rolle in the 1640s. An example is *Hasser v Wallis* (1708) 1 Salk 28.

him to sue the ousted landlord for money had and received.[33] The office cases were distinguished on the ground that fees paid to a de facto officer discharged the payer, so that the *de jure* officer had to sue the usurper; whereas payment of rent to a disseisor was no discharge as against the disseisee.

An attempt was once made to use *indebitatus* instead of replevin, where the plaintiff had paid the defendant to release his cattle from distress even though he intended at the time to challenge the defendant's right to distrain. Again convenience triumphed over logic. The court said that it would be prejudicial to the defendant to allow title to be put in issue in such a devious way.[34]

2. Contract

In the count for money had and received, there was no need to set out the circumstances in which the money was received. This gave the plaintiff a considerable advantage when compared with special *assumpsit*, in which all material details had to be shown. Attempts were therefore made to use the former instead of the latter. Holt CJ opposed this where there had merely been a breach of contract. In a case where the plaintiff paid money to the defendant to perform a service, which he failed to perform, he exclaimed: 'Away with your *indebitatus*, 'tis but a bargain'.[35] Neither would he allow *indebitatus* for the purpose of recovering back money where a party had been led into a contract by a false warranty.[36] He accepted, however, that the money count was appropriate where money was paid under a void contract or where there was a failure of consideration.[37] By the beginning of the nineteenth century the distinction here was coming to be regarded as one of substance: a contract could not be rescinded for mere breach of warranty, but only for a breach going to the root of the contract followed by prompt rescission, or for frustration, or where the contract was void *ab initio*. The principles governing the discharge of contracts, conditions and warranties, and illegality, were for this reason mostly worked out in actions for money had and received and not in actions for breach of contract.

3. Tort

The office cases represented a major departure from the old law of

33. *Birch v Wright* (1786) 1 Term Rep 386; *Cunningham v Lawrents* (1788) Bacon Abr, vol. I, p. 344 (7th edn); *Newsome v Graham* (1829) 1 B & C 234. For the contrary view, see 1 Freem 479n.
34. *Lindon v Hooper* (1776) 1 Cowp 414.
35. *Anon* (1695) Comb 341.
36. *Anon* (1698) Comb 447.
37. *Martin v Sitwell* (1690) 1 Show 156, Fifoot HSCL, p. 383; *Holmes v Hall* (1704) 6 Mod Rep 161.

account in that they allowed *indebitatus assumpsit* to be brought for money appropriated by tort. In such a case the plaintiff was said to 'waive the tort', but in so doing he was not acting from charitable motives. By suing on a contract, albeit a fictitious one, the plaintiff gained advantages in pleading, a more favourable limitation period, and the possibility of suing executors. For these reasons, waiving the tort became a common practice in the eighteenth century and was indulged by the courts. Even Holt CJ grudgingly accepted that if personal property was converted by a tortious sale, the person wronged could waive the tort by affirming the sale and bringing *indebitatus* for the proceeds.[38] This was the most frequent case of waiver, and it was extended to the conversion of negotiable bank notes (which were treated as money) and in one case to the disappearance of a masquerade ticket for which value could be presumed to have been given.[39] But there was no count for goods received, and if goods were converted without being exchanged for money then the proper remedy was trover. It was possible to waive other torts, such as trespass or deceit, where money was obtained by force or dishonesty. But the concept was not appropriate to torts such as assault or slander, where no money changed hands. Legal ingenuity did nevertheless stretch the notion further in the early nineteenth century, through the fictitious use of other *indebitatus* counts. Thus, where *B* tortiously lured away *A*'s apprentice, *A* could waive the tort and recover the profits of his labour in a count for work done.[40] Here the fiction was to suppose that *B* had requested *A* to supply the services of his apprentice. And in the case where *B* obtained *A*'s goods by fraud, and converted them without selling them, *A* might be allowed to waive the tort and sue for *quantum valebant* in an action for goods sold and delivered to *B*.[41] Here the contract of sale was fictitious. On the same principle, it was later held that where a trespasser travelled on a railway with intent to avoid paying the fare, he could be sued on a fictitious 'implied promise' to pay.[42] By this stage, the quasi-contractual claim gave more than a procedural advantage, because the sum claimed was greater then the sum recoverable in trespass.

MONEY LAID OUT

There was one other of the common counts which did not rest on

38. *Lamine v Dorrell* (1705) 2 Ld Raym 1216, Fifoot HSCL, p. 384.
39. *Longchamp v Kenny* (1779) 1 Doug KB 137.
40. *Lightly v Clouston* (1808) 1 Taunt 112. For the tort of enticing a servant, see pp. 381–382, post.
41. *Hill v Perrott* (1810) 3 Taunt 274; *Russell v Bell* (1842) 10 M & W 340.
42. *London & Brighton Railway Co v Watson* (1879) 4 CPD 118.

contract. Where the plaintiff paid or 'laid out' money to the defendant's use, he could bring *indebitatus assumpsit* to obtain reimbursement. Already by 1624 it was accepted that the promise to reimburse might be 'implicative' or fictitious.[43] It was not necessary to allege specifically how the money came to the defendant's use; yet, since English law does not allow one person to foist good works upon another without his consent, reimbursement could only be obtained if the payment was authorised by the defendant. It was therefore necessary to allege that the money was laid out 'at the special instance and request' of the defendant. In certain cases, however, the law implied a request as well as a promise to repay, and by means of this double fiction created another form of quasi-contractual obligation. This did not occur until the late eighteenth century, and then only in two clear cases.

The first case established the doctrine of contribution between co-sureties and joint contractors. If several persons stood surety for a debt, or broke a joint contract, and an action was sued to execution against one of them, that one could sue the others for a contribution. The principle of contribution was first established in equity, but the common law came to accommodate it by supposing that the money recovered in the first action had been laid out by the one at the request of the others.[44] The element of legal compulsion overcame any objection that a person could not spend another's money without authority. But the common law stopped short of giving the same remedy to joint tortfeasors, a remedy which was introduced by statute in 1935.[45]

The second case was where the plaintiff's property was distrained for the defendant's debt, so that the plaintiff had to pay off the debt to redeem his property. Here again, because of the legal compulsion, the law implied a request to pay off the debt and a promise to indemnify.[46] The principle was later extended to other cases where the plaintiff conferred a benefit on the defendant under compulsion and without acting officiously.

A General Principle

In the eighteenth and nineteenth centuries, the count for money had and received became one of the most extensively used actions in the

43. *Anon* (1626) Sheppard's *Marrow*, p. 124.
44. *Cowell v Edwards* (1800) 2 Bos & P 270.
45. *Merryweather v Nixan* (1799) 8 Term Rep 186; Law Reform (Married Women and Tortfeasors) Act 1935, 25 & 26 Geo V, c.30, s.6.
46. *Exall v Partridge* (1799) 8 Term Rep 308.

law. The reasons for its popularity, as was suggested above, were partly procedural; and the object of keeping the defendant in the dark as to the true cause of action, as Holt CJ had recognised, was not a very worthy one. But the action was also a flexible means of plugging gaps which had appeared in the other actions, and Blackstone described it as 'a very extensive and beneficial remedy, applicable to almost every case where a person has received money which *ex aequo et bono* he ought to refund'.[47] Having escaped the buffets dealt it by Holt CJ, at the beginning of the century, the remedy was carefully culti-vated by Lord Mansfield CJ, in the second half. Lord Mansfield favoured 'a liberal extension of the action for money had and received; because the charge and defence in this kind of action are both gov-erned by the true equity and conscience of the case'.[48] To compensate for the generality of the plaintiff's count, the defendant could raise at the trial every legal and equitable defence or allowance open to him without having pleaded it, because the only issue for the jury was whether *ex aequo et bono* the money ought to be deemed to belong to the plaintiff. By establishing that the basis of this common law action *quasi ex contractu* was an obligation to refund money arising from 'the ties of natural justice' and equity,[49] Lord Mansfield began to free the underlying principles from procedural technicalities. At the end of the following century, jurists at Harvard took up Lord Mansfield's approach and began to analyse what they identified as an equitable principle that a man should not unjustly enrich himself at the expense of another.[50] The principle was not peculiar to the English action of *indebitatus assumpsit*, but was also found in the *condictiones* of Roman law and the concept of *enrichissement illégitime* in French law.

Meanwhile, the principle had been virtually forgotten in England. *Indebitatus assumpsit* and legal fictions were abolished in 1852, but the fictitious promise seemed to be immortal. Lawyers still spoke of implied promises and waiving the tort, but as they lost familiarity with the forms in which those ideas had been clothed it was easy for misconceptions to flourish. For instance, it was held in 1904 that money paid under a contract could not be recovered back on frustra-tion, because the contract had been in force when the money was paid and frustration only discharged future obligations. When the House of Lords unanimously overruled this decision in 1943, Viscount Simon said the Court of Appeal had overlooked the distinction

47. Bl Comm, vol. III, p. 163, paraphrasing Lord Mansfield in *Moses v Macferlan*, post.
48. *Longchamp v Kenny* (1779) 1 Doug KB 137 at 138.
49. *Moses v Macferlan* (1760) 2 Burr 1005 at 1010; Fifoot HSCL, pp. 387, 389.
50. See J. B. Ames, 2 HLR 66 (1888); W. A. Keener *The Law of Quasi-Contracts* (1893).

between *indebitatus assumpsit* for money had and received and express *assumpsit*. The action to recover money on a failure of consideration was of the former kind, and was not brought on the contract but on the equitable obligation to restore the money. Lord Wright attributed that obligation to the principle of unjust enrichment, which was neither contract nor tort but a third category sometimes called quasi-contract which rested on an equitable foundation. Lord Mansfield's view was thus reinstated as English law.[51] Since that time, English writers have attempted to identify the applications of this principle without undue reference to the forms of action, and have found parallel examples in the equity of the Chancery and in the salvage law of the Admiralty. American lawyers had already suggested the wider heading 'restitution' for the whole class of obligations of this nature, but it was only in the last twenty years that restitution began to be firmly established in England as a discrete body of principles wholly independent of contract and no longer confined to the 'quasi-contract' of the old money counts.[52]

Further reading

Holdsworth HEL, vol. III, pp. 425–428; vol. VIII, pp. 88–98; vol. XII, pp. 542–549

Fifoot HSCL, pp. 268–288

J. B. Ames, 'Implied Assumpsit' (1888) 2 HLR 53 at 63–69

T. A. Street, *Foundations of Legal Liability* (1906), vol. II, pp. 199–241

C. D. Hening, 'History of the Beneficiary's Action in Assumpsit' (1909) *Essays AALH*, vol. III, pp. 339–367

E. O. Belsheim, 'The Old Action of Account' (1932) 45 HLR 466–500

R. M. Jackson, *The History of Quasi-Contract in English Law* (1936)

S. J. Stoljar, 'The Doctrine of Failure of Consideration' (1959) 75 LQR 53–76; *The Law of Quasi-Contract* (1964); 'The Transformations of Account' (1964) 80 LQR 203–224; *A History of Contract at Common Law* (1975), pp. 105–117, 181–187

A. W. B. Simpson, *A History of the Common Law of Contract* (1975), pp. 489–505

51. *Chandler v Webster* [1904] 1 KB 493; *Fibrosa Spolka Akcyjna v Fairbairn Lawson Combe Barbour Ltd* [1943] AC 32, [1942] 2 All, ER 122.
52. The turning point was the publication of R. Goff & G. H. Jones *The Law of Restitution* (1966).

18. Property in Chattels Personal

The common law relating to movable property was totally separate and distinct from the law of real property. The reason is not that movables were formerly of minimal importance: 'Not even in the feudal age,' jested Maitland, 'did men eat or drink land.'[1] There was, nevertheless, a marked difference between the economic value of land, which produced a permanent livelihood or income, and ordinary chattels, such as sacks of grain or cattle, which were consumable. Until the Industrial Revolution land was the chief form of wealth, and litigation about landed property was one of the principal concerns of the royal courts. Every piece of land was geographically a parcel of the realm, the subject of tenure, immovable, indestructible and recoverable by real action. Chattels, in contrast, could be passed around by hand, damaged, consumed, lost. The live chattel was mortal, provisions were perishable, and a great many commodities such as grain and meat were fungibles with no individual characteristics. To such things the notions of seisin and feudal tenure were quite inappropriate, and for many of them the processes of litigation in the royal courts were too solemn and dilatory. Most disputes about chattels were still heard in the local courts in early medieval times, when the common law already had a complex law of real actions. Moreover, the elusive 'law of personal property' was so submerged in the law of tort and contract as to be almost denied an independent existence. Without a Littleton to analyse it, the rational structure of the law of personal property has to be constructed from less coherent sources than those available for the law of real property. Yet there was a law of personal property, which could be conceived of as distinct from the forms of action. The owner had a right to seize his property extrajudicially; and questions of ownership could come in issue in less direct ways than in actions for direct interference or denial. What is more, it appears that the abstract principles were often discussed in the inns of court. The rules of law were, however, for the most part expounded in the actions of detinue and, later, conversion.

1. Pollock & Maitland, vol. II, p. 149.

CHATTELS PERSONAL DEFINED

For the purposes of this chapter, 'chattels personal' means all corporeal or tangible property which is not real property. The nature of this distinction has already been touched upon.[2] The words 'goods' and 'chattels' are used indiscriminately to denote tangible personal property. 'Goods' (*bona*) is a general word which to Civil lawyers indicated all kinds of property, movable or immovable. In the common law the word had much the same meaning as 'chattels' (*catalla*), a law French word having the same root as 'capital'. The English equivalent 'cattle' after about 1500 was usually confined to livestock, but the legal word included all goods which were not in the nature of freehold[3] and also intangible personal property such as terms of years.[4]

The fact that some movables might be part of the realty sometimes made the line between land and chattels nebulous. Movables such as title-deeds, door-keys, heirlooms and uncollected loose minerals and windfalls were all part of the realty for the purposes of succession. They went to the heir rather than the executors. They also passed on a grant of the realty. Here there could be fine distinctions. Domesticated animals were personal property, but unreclaimed wild animals were accounted part of the land on which they lived. Ploughshares were personal property, but the mill-stone of a mill was regarded as part of the realty even if it was away being mended. On the other hand, things affixed to the realty might nevertheless be regarded as chattels for the purposes of succession; for instance, certain classes of fixture placed by a tenant. The purpose and degree of annexation have always been guides; thus, in 1647 a meeting of all the judges was convened to establish that, whereas a heap of dung was a chattel, dung spread on the ground was part of the realty.[5] Yet, to say that something was part of the realty for the purposes of the law of succession or construing grants was not to say that a real action lay for the thing independently of the land. There was no writ of right for muck or loose stones, but recovery of the land in a writ of right carried such things with it. The same things when reduced into possession became chattels, could be recovered by the action of detinue and were the subject of larceny.

2. See pp. 193–194, ante. Of course, it is the thing owned rather than the property in it which is 'tangible'.
3. *Termes de la Ley*, s.v. catal.
4. For the term of years, see pp. 251–258, ante.
5. *Yearworth v Pierce* (1647) Aleyn 31; sub nom. *Carver v Pierce* Sty 66 at 73.

HOW PERSONAL PROPERTY ARISES

Under the feudal system all the land in England must belong to someone, for if no tenant can be found the land must be part of the demesne of the Crown. But it is not necessary to suppose that anyone owns the atmosphere, the rain, the birds of the air, the water running in streams and rivers, and other movables in their natural state. Such things, according to Bracton and his Roman sources, are outside our patrimony (*extra patrimonium nostrum*) and common to all mankind. Ownership of them arises, in the first place, by 'occupation'; for whoever first reduces a wild thing into his possession is its owner. A man owns the air in his lungs, rain water in a butt, birds in a cage, or fish on his dinner plate. The precise distinction between the limited property of the freeholder in unreclaimed wild animals or things on his land, and the interest of the occupant or captor, caused long disputes. It was held that birds flying in the air belonged to no one, birds nesting in trees (and their eggs) belonged to the owner of the trees, and birds in a cage were chattels personal. Likewise, fish in a river belonged to no one, fish in a pond belonged to the owner of the pond, and fish in a net or in a fishmonger's pipe or trunk were chattels personal. The worst problem arose when a bird or beast was reduced into possession by a poacher on another man's soil; eventually, after centuries of disagreement, the law gave such things to the tenant of the land.[6]

The common law prohibited the occupation of certain classes of natural resources by private subjects because they belonged to the Crown by virtue of the royal prerogative: namely, gold and silver ore,[7] swans,[8] venison in a royal forest, and great fish such as whales, sturgeons, porpoises and dolphins. These natural 'flowers of the Crown' could be acquired by subjects only through royal grant or prescription.

Another way in which property arises is by the creation or manufacture of a new thing. A young bird or beast born in captivity belongs to the owner of the mother.[9] Wool and milk belong to the owner of the animal from which they are taken. When a new thing is made by human industry (*specificatio*) it generally belongs to the maker; but a problem arises if he uses materials belonging to another person. In the time of Edward IV it was held that the property vested in the maker if

6. See *Blades v Higgs* (1862) 12 CBNS 501.
7. *Case of Mines, A-G v Earl of Northumberland* (1567) 1 Plowd 313.
8. *Case of Swans, R v Yong* (1592) 7 Co Rep 15.
9. *Case of Cygnets, Male v Hole* (1472) CP 40/842, m.303; YB Pas 12 Edw IV, 4, pl.10. Where animals are leased, however, the young belong to the lessee: *Wood v Ash* (1586) Godb 112.

the new thing was so different from the materials from which it was made that the materials could no longer be demanded in an action of detinue as being in existence.[10] But the fact that property could not be demanded in detinue did not necessarily mean that it could not be recovered at all, for instance by seizure. If goods were taken wrongfully and made into something new, the owner of the materials was entitled to seize the new article without bringing any legal action. Accordingly, the property was only changed by specification in three cases. First, if the materials were no longer identifiable, because there would then be nothing specific to seize; for instance, if corn were made into bread, or barley into ale, or silver were melted down and cast in a new form,[11] at any rate if this was done by a tradesman who had other corn, barley or silver from various sources. The second case was where the only remedy available to the owner was detinue, because that action presupposed the continued existence of a thing belonging to the plaintiff. And the third case was where the thing was made to accede to the realty, in which case there was no right of seizure or action of detinue; for instance, if wood was built into a house or seeds sown in the ground.

An overlapping problem occurred where property belonging to two persons was combined. Obviously, if a tailor added his own thread to A's gown, the property in the gown remained in A. This was originally explained on the *de minimis* principle: the lesser acceded to the greater. But it apparently became a general principle that where B mixed his own property with A's—as, by adding his sheep to A's flock, or mixing his hay with A's—the property passed to A.[12]

A different problem arose where things became chattels personal by severance from the realty. Fruit and crops, for instance, became pure personalty when gathered or harvested. If a tenant had an estate of uncertain duration, such as a life estate, which ended before he could take the produce, a fair division was made: crops which were the product of human industry (*emblements*)[13] belonged to the tenant who had sown them or his executors, while natural fruits and produce belonged to the reversioner. It was a moot point whether a disseisor was entitled to emblements sown before the disseised tenant re-entered.[14]

10. See pp. 328, 331, post.
11. *Hoode's Case* (1490) 94 SS *212–213*. See also *Anon* (1560) Moore KB 19, pl.67 (trees made into boards may be retaken); *Anon* (1596) Sheppard's *Abridgment*, vol. I, pp. 273, 543.
12. *Anon* (1591) Yale Law Sch MS G.R. 29.7, p. 444; *Smoote v Futball* (1593) Cambridge Univ Lib MS Dd. 10. 51, f. 7v; same case (1594) Poph 33, pl.2.
13. From the law French *embler* (to sow).
14. *Pope v See* (1534) Spelman Rep (93 SS) 215.

Modes of Transfer

A person may acquire a chattel either by occupation or by transfer from another person. There have been three principal modes of transferring property in chattels.[15]

DELIVERY

The common law has always refused to recognise a gift of chattels unless accompanied by a delivery of possession to the donee. The Civil law regarded transfer by *traditio* as taking effect by the law of nature, and the reason behind it is simple. If property depended on occupation it could be transferred by changing the occupant, just as property in land followed seisin.[16] Delivery did not itself pass the property, because it might simply separate the property from the physical custody; but property passed upon delivery if there was an intention to give or sell it to the recipient.

SALE

Sale, as an institution, is as old as English history: so much may be assumed from the discovery of ancient coins. But it does not follow that a sale passed any property from the seller to the buyer before the latter took delivery. In the early common law, sale was one of the transactions which would generate a debt; but it would only do so if the goods were delivered. Conversely, there is no indication before the fifteenth century that an executory contract of sale gave the buyer any action for undelivered goods. Yet, if the buyer had paid for the goods, justice demanded a reciprocal remedy. When it was given, buyers felt it necessary to allege a constructive delivery to themselves at the instant of sale, followed by a deposit of the goods with the seller. This was not a very untruthful fiction: probably the buyer did handle the goods at the time of sale and then hand them back. But it was stressed because of the dominant notion that property was derived from occupation. The plaintiff in detinue had to trace the goods from his own hands into those of the defendant. The possibility that an abstract property or 'title' could pass independently of the physical transfer may have presented itself because of the close affinity between the action of detinue and the action of debt. If the seller contracted to deliver an unspecific quarter of barley, and received *quid pro quo*, the buyer could bring debt. It would have seemed irrational if

---

15. There are others, e.g., by deed. Upon the death of a pawnor before redemption, the property passed to the pawnee.
16. See p. 199, ante.

the buyer lost his remedy where the quarter of barley was in specific sacks; and, since the same writ (omitting the word *debet*) would apply to his case, there was no point in maintaining the distinction. If this be correct, however, the claim to goods in either case was not based on property at all but on a contract to deliver them.

The distinction between contract and property was of no importance so long as there was a specific remedy. But it was axiomatic that a sale could not pass more than the seller had: *nemo dat quod non habet*. Sale by a non-owner could pass no property. Yet at some point it is desirable that the claim of the original owner should give way to the demands of commerce, and to the expectations of *bona fide* purchasers of goods in the open market. The law therefore protected honest sales which took place openly in a market or fair, to the extent that the purchaser thereby acquired a good title even against previous owners who had lost their goods; only if the goods had been stolen could the sale be upset, and then only if the thief had been successfully appealed of felony or, after 1529, convicted on indictment. To have the effect of divesting the original owner, the sale had to be in 'market overt', that is, openly in a market established by royal grant or prescription. A sale in a secret place in or out of the market did not bind the first owner, since the rationale of the doctrine was that the owner could enquire after lost goods in the market, and if his goods were displayed for sale and he did not see them it was his oversight. It was not reasonable for the owner to have to search outside the market, or to enquire after goods sold privately.[17] For the same reason, a sale in a shop did not have the same effect as a sale in a market because the true owner could only enter the shop with the shopkeeper's consent. But the City of London enjoyed, and still enjoys, a custom that every shop within the city is a market for the purpose of the rule.[18] By 1600 other cities were claiming similar privileges, but the custom was not extended because of the hardship to owners. Another way of dealing with the problem of sales by non-owners was to require registration of title to certain kinds of goods. An attempt to introduce compulsory registration of title on the sale of horses[19] was ultimately unsuccessful, and in four centuries few changes have been made in the law of sale in market overt. The principle of protecting those who deal in good faith with non-owners in the open market has received some statutory extension.[20]

17. *Sir Gervase Clifton's Case* (1600) Brit Lib MS Add. 25203, ff.63v, 279.
18. *Case of Market Overt, Palmer v Wolley* (1596) 5 Co Rep 83.
19. Sale of Horses Act 1555, 2 & 3 Ph & Mar, c.7. (Repealed in 1968.)
20. Beginning with the, 4 Geo IV, c.83.

SUCCESSION ON DEATH

Before the Norman conquest, English customs of succession seem to have been designed to provide for the whole family of the deceased by dividing his estate into aliquot parts, usually halves or thirds. Under the influence of Christianity, the deceased was also given a 'part', to dispose of by testament or to be disposed of on his behalf for the good of his soul. The other parts went to the widow and children equally. This system survived Norman feudalism in the case of movable property, and remains in Scotland at the present day. The early common law provided a writ, analogous to detinue, called *de rationabili parte bonorum*, for the widow and children to recover their 'reasonable parts'. In the twelfth and thirteenth centuries, however, the spiritual and lay courts came into jurisdictional conflict, and the dispute was compromised so that the inheritance of land became the sole concern of the royal courts while the administration of the goods of a deceased person fell solely to the Church courts.

The Church encouraged men to make wills, even to the extent of disposing of all their movables, no doubt because testators were likely to be less partial than executors and administrators in distributing the estate. As a result the fixed parts of the widow and children could be claimed only if the deceased died wholly or partly intestate, or if local custom preserved the older principle, or if the Church restricted testation. Before 1600, the Province of Canterbury (excepting Wales and London) came to permit complete freedom of testation, whereas the Province of York adhered to the old parts scheme until 1692. Freedom of testation was not universal in England until 1724, when it was extended to the City of London.

The administration of intestates' goods also fell to the Church authorities, and in 1357 it was enacted that bishops were to commit their responsibility in this connection to persons called administrators, who were empowered to sue and be sued in the same way as executors. In the course of time, partly through inefficiency and partly through interference from the common law courts, the Church courts lost effective control over administrators, who usually kept the property for themselves after paying debts. A statute was therefore passed in 1670[21] laying down a statutory scheme of distribution which administrators were obliged to observe. The thirds rule was retained, but the dead man's part abolished. The rules for distribution have been changed many times by statute, though the rules are of necessity árbitrary. One of the most important later reforms was the reintroduction of automatic provision for close members of the deceased's

21. Statute of Distributions 1670, 22 & 23 Car II, c.10.

family who had been cut out by will. The extension of free testation had led to the harsh result that widows and children could be completely cut off by their husband or father if he made a will in favour of someone else. It was over two centuries before the remedy was found.[22]

Termination of Property in Chattels

Since chattels do not necessarily have an owner, property in them may in some circumstances come to an end.

RETURN TO NATURAL STATE

Animals which are wild by nature (*ferae naturae*) belong to humans only so long as they are in human control. If they are set free, or escape, and have no inclination to return to their captor, then property in them ceases and they become *res nullius*. The same principle applies to water poured into a river; or to combustion, whereby chattels are converted into fumes which diffuse in the atmosphere.

DEODAND

A strange and irrational principle of the common law was that which required the forfeiture of objects which occasioned, or were the instruments of, a man's death. The rule may have originated in barbaric notions of retribution, but by the thirteenth century chattels seized as 'deodands' were appropriated to charitable purposes by the king's almoner. At its most equitable, the deodand system provided a primitive form of insurance for the dependants of the deceased, if the almoner was disposed to assist them; at its worst, it could inflict undeserved hardship on the innocent owner of offending objects for the profit of the Crown or of private franchise owners. The most valuable types of deodand commonly found were horses and carriages involved in fatal accidents. The doctrine was not finally abrogated until 1846, after its application to railway engines brought its irrational nature to public notice.

ABANDONMENT AND LOSS

The common law has never clearly decided whether a person can divest himself of personal property by waiver or abandonment, though the best authorities deny the possibility.[23] The question is

22. Inheritance (Family Provision) Act 1938, 1 & 2 Geo VI, c.45.
23. E.g. St German *Doctor and Student* (91 SS), p. 292. As to waiver by a thief in flight ('waif'), see *Foxley v Annesley* (1601) 5 Co Rep 109, Cro Eliz 693.

rarely of importance, because the first finder of a derelict may be regarded as a donee acquiring by constructive delivery, while before it is taken up the first owner is at liberty to retake it. A mere accidental loss, without intention to derelinquish, certainly cannot alter property; even a waiver of all enjoyment of the property, for instance by burying it in a grave, does not divest the owner of his title.[24]

The finder of lost goods acquired a property against all the world except the loser, because the law would not, in an action between two parties, try to discover the absolute title, but only the relative rights of the parties. The finder who appropriated lost goods was not considered a thief until the notion of larceny by finding evolved in the early nineteenth century.[25]

Certain categories of lost property belong to the Crown by the royal prerogative, and these can only be taken by private persons if they have the royal perquisite by franchise. Thus, treasure trove—that is, gold or silver artefacts, coin or bullion hidden by a person unknown but not abandoned—belongs to the Crown unless and until the true owner makes good his claim; and it may be seized into the queen's hands by a coroner. Wreck of sea belonged to the Crown unless the owner claimed the goods within a year and a day.[26] The rhetorical Elizabethan explanation for this was that it compensated the king for his expensive naval obligations. Estrays, which are lost cattle or valuable domestic beasts, belong to the Crown if proclamations are made in public places and the owner does not claim them within a year and a day.

Interests in Chattels

Movable wealth could not be settled on a succession of owners, because the common law did not allow future estates to be created in chattels. A gift of a chattel for an hour was a gift for ever. But a lesser interest could be conferred by the contract of hire, as on a lease of sheep or furniture. The effect of such a transaction was explained by later lawyers as a separation of ownership from possession; but it is unclear how far this dichotomy was known in the early common law. To some extent ownership and possession coincided in the medieval concept of 'property' (*proprietas*), a word used only in connection with personal property. Property arose, as we have seen, from occupation

24. *Haynes' Case* (1613) 12 Co Rep 113.
25. See p. 434, post.
26. *Constable v Gamble* (1601) 5 Co Rep 106.

and was transferred by delivery. There was no such thing as *dominium*, absolute ownership or right. The most a person out of possession could claim was a better right to possession than the possessor. Property therefore described the relationship between two parties rather than a status against the world at large. Thus, if *A* lent his horse to *B* for a week, *A* remained its owner as against *B*. But if *B* lost it, or lent it to *C*, *B* was regarded as the owner for the purposes of recovering the horse by legal action.

The relationship between property and mere possession was seen most clearly where there was some dealing between two parties. There is a natural distinction between handing over a thing with the intention that all the property should pass to the recipient (gift or sale), and handing over the thing with the intention that the recipient should only have the temporary use or profits of the thing (loan or hire) or hold it as a pledge or as a mere deposit. These latter transactions were all forms of 'bailment', the technical name for a transaction whereby a thing is delivered (*baillé*) on the basis that the bailor shall retain his property. Situations can readily be envisaged where a similar separation of property and physical possession might occur without a bailment; for instance, where goods are stolen, or lost and then found by a stranger. Even in these cases, the terms 'property' and 'possession' relate only to the relationship between two people; the relationship being that the proprietor has a better right to possession than the possessor. A refinement was made shortly before 1500, when it was decided that, for the purposes of the law of theft, the custody of a chattel could be entrusted to another without loss of possession: as in the case of a household servant or personal attendant having the control of his master's goods.[27]

In the fifteenth and sixteenth centuries a further distinction was drawn, between the property in and the 'use and occupation' of a chattel. Whereas the property could not be settled, it was possible for the use of a chattel to be limited to a succession of persons, and such a settlement would bind the executors; but no one could prevent the possessor for the time being from destroying the chattel and with it the future expectations under the settlement. The analogy with the use of land is obvious. But this was common law.[28]

27. See p. 433, post.
28. This was the interpretation later put on the inconclusive leading case of *Glover and Brown v Forden* (1459) CP 40/794, m.291; YB Trin 37 Hen VI, 30, pl.11; Dyer 359 (devise of a grail). Cf. p. 256, ante, for the settlement of the use of a chattel real in equity.

Detinue

The remedy ordained in the register of writs for the enforcement of the right to possession, where it became separated from the actual possession, was the action which came to be called 'detinue'. The writ, which shares a common ancestry with the writ of debt, commanded the sheriff to order the defendant to yield up to the plaintiff the chattels which he unjustly detained from him: *praecipe* X *quod reddat* Y *catalla quae injuste detinet*. The clearest case of a possessor who would be subjected to the action as a matter of course was that of the bailee.

DETINUE ON A BAILMENT

The bailee's duty to return the chattel at the end of the period of bailment was contractual—in the medieval rather than the modern sense[29]—and not different in kind from the duty to pay a debt. Lawyers only found it necessary to distinguish a debt from a withholding (*detentio*, detinue) of goods in so far as the difference between owing and owning carried certain consequences. The owner claimed *in specie*, the debtee *in genere*. If a debtor lost his money, he continued to owe the sum lent because he could not identify any specific coins as representing the debt; the debt, as opposed to the coins lent, could not be lost or stolen. But if a borrowed horse died or ran away, without fault in the bailee, the bailee might with reason claim to be discharged; he was no longer detaining the bailor's property.

In the thirteenth and fourteenth centuries the common law seems to have allowed a special plea of accidental loss or destruction in the action of detinue, but in the majority of cases the law was obscured behind the general plea 'he does not detain' (*non detinet*). In the fifteenth century a stricter theory came into vogue, that the bailee was only excused if the loss were caused by act of God or the king's enemies. The reason was that the bailee had a right of action, save in those cases, against the wrongdoer; and since it would have been unjust to allow him to keep the damages to himself he ought in turn to be liable to his bailor. It was then suggested that theft ought to be an excuse if the identity of the thief were unknown, or if the thief had been hanged and his property forfeited, because the bailee's right of action in such cases would be useless. But the better opinion was that these circumstances did not excuse, because there remained a remedy in law if not in fact. The bailee could only excuse himself in detinue by pleading theft or loss if the bailment had been on terms which excused

29. See p. 263, ante.

him in such cases; for instance, if the terms were to keep the goods with the same care as he would bestow on his own.[30]

The bailee's liability thus became so stringent that further encouragement was given to the general issue and wager of law. In all cases of theft or loss, even where the bailee had been careless, the plea of *non detinet* was truthful if disingenuous. Indeed, the bailee who drank or gave away wine committed to his safe keeping could truthfully, though at great danger to his soul, plead that he no longer detained it. It is far from clear whether the common law courts had sufficient control over the consciences of bailees to prevent them waging their law in such cases. Justice might suggest the development of a doctrine of constructive detaining in these circumstances, but there was no procedure whereby the question could be raised as a question of substantive law; it could only be a matter of exhortation to a man about to swear an oath. On any view, detinue would not lie against a bailee who had returned the goods, but in a damaged condition. In such cases, where damage was irrecoverable in detinue, or where a bailee had wrongfully put himself beyond the reach of detinue, the remedy would have to be sought in trespass.

DETINUE AGAINST A STRANGER

When the plaintiff in detinue showed a bailment to the defendant, it was plain that he had a better right than his own bailee—unless, of course, the defendant had had the property earlier. But suppose the defendant was a mere stranger, a finder or a thief. What sort of claim did the plaintiff make? It could not be based on some transaction between the parties. Nevertheless, the wording of the writ of detinue was perfectly apt to cover the case. A plaintiff was therefore allowed to bring detinue if in his count he could trace the chattel from his own possession and show how it came into the hands of the defendant (*devenit ad manus defendentis*). The point of telling the tale in full was to establish the relative right of the parties, and also to establish the identity of the thing in question. Thus the *devenit ad manus* tale performed a similar function to the bailment set out in the first type of detinue, and there was no need to introduce a novel concept of ownership as the basis of the action. The plaintiff did not have to assert any abstract right reposed in himself; instead he told a story which showed that the defendant had come into possession without gaining any property which would stand against his own. Nevertheless, the two forms of detinue could be seen as conceptually distinct causes of

30. See *Southcote v Bennet* (1601) 4 Co Rep 83, Cro Eliz 815, Fifoot HSCL, p. 169.

action accidentally united by the wording of a writ which happened to cover them both.

Every step traced in the *devenit ad manus* count was arguably material to the plaintiff's case and could be challenged by the defendant. This feature made it a very unsafe mode of pleading, particularly because the plaintiff was often not in a position to know precisely what had happened to the goods between leaving his possession and coming into the hands of the defendant. It might also raise difficult questions of law which the courts preferred to avoid. For both reasons, pleaders were eager to abandon the *devenit ad manus* count and to find a less vulnerable general count.

DETINUE SUR TROVER

The solution was found in the second half of the fifteenth century. The plaintiff simply alleged that he had accidentally lost the chattel, and that the defendant found it and unjustly detained it. No property could pass to the defendant by finding, and it was not too dishonest to speak of a loss even where the plaintiff suspected a more devious history. The courts would not allow the defendant to traverse the loss and finding (*trover*) unless he could plead specially that he had acquired the property by a recognised means.[31] The count on a *trover* therefore became the usual form of count in detinue against anyone who was not a bailee, and was in many cases fictitious. The fiction could not obstruct the proper working of the action because the question of property would be raised either by a special plea or, more usually, by the general issue.

The liability in detinue *sur trover* was less strict than in detinue on a bailment, because there was no contract to impose a strict obligation on the defendant. Accidental loss of the chattel by the defendant would be a genuine defence, because the only obligation which could be imposed on a finder arose from his being in possession; as soon as he lost possession, from whatever cause, the nexus between plaintiff and defendant dissolved away.[32]

SHORTCOMINGS OF DETINUE

We have seen that the history of contract involved first the supplementation and then the replacement of the *praecipe* actions of debt and covenant by actions on the case. The history of the law of personal

---

31. *Carles v Malpas* (1455) CP 40/778, m.482; YB Trin 33 Hen VI, 26, pl.12; Fifoot HSCL, p. 42. Carles set out the details but ended with a *trover*; issue was joined on the title but there was a nonsuit.
32. *Anon* (1536) Fifoot HSCL, p. 34, n.51.

property was likewise a story of the supplementing and replacing of detinue by actions on the case. The reasons are closely analogous in both stories. First, a *praecipe* action was barred by performance, even by an imperfect performance, and so in detinue damages were only awarded if the goods were not restored at all. The bailee who returned goods in a damaged state, or who starved a horse to death, or rode it further than agreed, was not liable in detinue. The plaintiff in detinue could not count of a bailment or loss of the thing demanded if the thing was no longer the same thing as it was when he had bailed or lost it: as where it had been made part of something else by accession or confusion, or had been fashioned into something new by specification. A fortiori, he could not allege a detaining of a thing which no longer existed at all: 'If you bail to me a tun of wine, and perchance I drink it up with other good companions, you cannot have detinue for it because it is not in being.'[33] Detinue did not lie against anyone who had dealt wrongfully with another person's property, but only against the person who happened to be in possession at the time the action was brought. The defendant might therefore be innocent, or at any rate less culpable than the intermediary; or he might have acquired a good title in market overt, in which case detinue was barred. Finally, the availability of the general issue, and the proof of the issue by wager of law, meant that the substantive law of personal property was stunted and suppressed by the process of oath-taking, and the plaintiff in danger of being defeated by perjury.

Trespass to Chattels

The solution, as in the law of contract, was found in the law of wrongs. From an early date, actions of trespass for taking away goods (*de bonis asportatis*), or for destroying or damaging goods, had been available to plaintiffs who sought monetary compensation; but at first these writs could be brought in the central courts only if the interference with the chattels could be described as *vi et armis*. The bailee who took away goods bailed to him could not be said to commit a trespass with force and arms, because he had been given possession by the bailor and had appropriated it without force. Neither could a finder, unless he damaged the thing found, or knew the identity of the owner at the time of the 'finding' and kept it nevertheless. In the fourteenth century, wrongs such as these may have been remedied in trespass by the

33. YB Hil 20 Hen VI, 16, pl.2 per Brown.

expedient of bringing a *vi et armis* writ and hoping that the defendant would not be allowed to plead the bailment or finding as a technical defence. This was an unsatisfactory fiction, because it gave the plaintiff the advantages belonging to suits for forcible wrongs when the wrong was not forcible; and for this reason the courts may not have favoured it. The problem was solved when, in the mid-fourteenth century, it was decided that writs of trespass might be brought in the royal courts with a special case instead of the force and arms.

The 'case' on which a plaintiff might rely in complaining of a wrong to chattels might incorporate any number of tortious concepts, such as deceit, negligence, breach of an undertaking, or conversion. Later history was to separate these as distinct actions, according to the element which predominated as the gist of the action. The process of separation did not occur until the sixteenth century; when it did take place, the rules of law concerning personal property were distributed between the law of contract and what came to be called the torts of conversion and negligence.

UNDERTAKINGS TO KEEP OR CARRY SAFELY

The commonest of the earlier actions on the case against bailees were of the kind typified by the *Humber Ferry Case* (1348).[34] The plaintiff counted that he had delivered the goods to the defendant to look after, or carry safely (*tradidisset ad salvo et secure custodiendum,* or *cariandum*), and that the defendant so neglected them that they perished or sustained damage. Sometimes the pleadings alleged an undertaking (*assumpsit*) to carry, but this was not necessary. Little turned on the use of the word *assumpsit* in this context, where it clearly retained the older sense of an assumption of physical custody and risk and did not import an express promise. Sometimes words such as *recepit* (received) were used instead. Very probably the undertaking was something which could be read into any bailment in the absence of a contrary explanation. In modern language, the action was based on tort rather than contract.

When in the sixteenth century the action of *assumpsit* became nearly always an action for breach of contract, confusion arose as to the nature of actions against bailees. At the beginning of the century, the courts clearly laid down that the undertaking was not the gist of the action and could not be traversed.[35] But when the doctrine of consideration evolved in the time of Elizabeth I some thought a bailee

---

34. See p. 274, ante.
35. *Bourgchier v Cheseman* (1504–08) 94 SS *249–250*; *Rycroft v Gamme* (1523) Spelman Rep (93 SS) 3; *Warton v Ashepole* (1524) ibid. 4.

could not be sued in case unless consideration had been given for his undertaking. In order to avoid this objection, some plaintiffs relied on the delivery of the goods as being itself a consideration; but this was plainly bad because the defendant derived no benefit from the mere custody, and the promise to give up the goods on demand was *nudum pactum* because it was no more than he was bound to do by law.[36] A deposit of goods was different from a loan of goods or money, for in these cases the use of the goods or money is a benefit to the defendant and therefore good consideration for an undertaking to return or repay.

The unnecessary intrusion of the principles of contract into the matter forced lawyers to distinguish bailees for reward from gratuitous bailees. The former were liable in contract, and were therefore strictly liable unless the contract was to take no more than reasonable care. The latter were liable for negligence; and in such an action, even if the word *assumpsit* was used, there was no need to show consideration.[37]

The true position of the gratuitous bailee was explained in *Coggs v Bernard* in 1703.[38] The defendant had undertaken gratuitously to move hogsheads of brandy from one cellar to another, and in doing so he put them down so negligently that they were staved and many gallons of brandy were spilled. It was objected that no consideration had been shown for the undertaking, and therefore *assumpsit* would not lie. The Court of King's Bench, after a full debate, dismissed this argument. First, the negligence was itself actionable since it was a deceit to the plaintiff, who had trusted the defendant to be careful. Second, the word *assumpsit* did not in this context denote a future promise, but 'an actual entry upon the thing, and taking the trust upon himself'. Holt CJ took the opportunity in his judgment to restate the law of bailment in Roman terms, on the authority of Bracton, as an escape from the effects of formalism. The result of his labour, as he himself foresaw, was a little unsettling, in that it led some lawyers to suppose that bailment was a transaction sui generis, not dependent on the general rules of either contract or tort.

NEGLIGENCE, CONVERSION AND DETINUE

The above form of the action on the case against a bailee lay for negligent keeping, but there were cases where liability could be founded on a different kind of wrong. If the bailee of a deed tore off the

---

36. *Riches v Bridges* (1602) Cro Eliz 883, Yelv 4; *Pickas v Guile* (1608) Yelv 128.
37. *Powtuary v Walton* (1598) Rolle Abr, vol. I, p. 10.
38. 2 Ld Raym 909, Fifoot HSCL, p. 173.

seal to make it invalid, or the bailee of a horse rode it so hard that it died, or the bailee of a gown cut it into pieces, the complaint was not of carelessness but of deliberate damage, and the special case was adjusted accordingly. It was in actions of this nature that allegations of 'conversion' first made their appearance. The bailee of coins who spent them, or the bailee of goods who sold them and spent the proceeds, was liable not because he had 'so negligently kept the goods that they were lost' but because he had wrongly taken them and 'scheming to defraud the plaintiff converted them to his own use'. In 1500 this was just one of several ways of framing a complaint against someone who had undertaken to look after goods; but in the next fifty years it grew into a general remedy which replaced detinue, as the action on the case for conversion.

The actions against bailees for damaging goods entrusted to their care filled gaps in the old action of detinue, but did not overlap with it. Their justification, indeed, was that they lay for damage which could not be recovered in detinue. There were compelling reasons for extending the remedy to acts of conversion, and in the earliest cases there was likewise no overlap with detinue. If a bailee destroyed the thing bailed by converting it to his own use, as by drinking wine, he was liable in case precisely because detinue did not lie. But the possibility of overlap was soon discerned, both by plaintiffs who wished to avert wager of law, and by defendants who sought to upset actions on the case by arguing that detinue should have been brought instead. In 1472 a sub-bailee of gold cloth and rich embroideries cut some of them up, and was sued by the executor of the bailor both in detinue *sur trover* and in an action on the case for damaging the cloth; both actions stood undecided for three years, but the nature of the difficulty may be gathered from the sources. The plaintiff apparently argued that by cutting up the material and making it into clothes the defendant had altered the property by specification; therefore, since detinue was barred, an action on the case was proper.[39] Then, in 1478, case was brought against a sub-bailee of silver cups who had broken them up and made them into silver vessels of different shape and converted them to his own use. Again it was argued that detinue was unavailable, and the case of gold cloth was cited. Choke J accepted the plaintiff's argument. Bryan CJ, however, held that detinue was the appropriate action and that it was improper

---

39. *Rilston v Holbek* (1472) CP 40/844, m.332 (case), 335d (detinue); YB Mich 12 Edw IV, 11, pl.2, and f.14, pl.14; Kiralfy AC, p. 220. The year-book reports only the pleading difficulties in detinue; the argument as to case appears from the citation by Choke J, in the next case.

to use case in order to oust wager of law.[40] The defendant was liable if the facts alleged were true; but the outcome was left by law to his conscience. The reports are then silent until the beginning of the sixteenth century, but by then the action on the case against a bailee for conversion was as firmly established as *assumpsit*, at any rate in the King's Bench. The conversion, often aggravated by an allegation of deceit, was treated as a tort distinct from the detaining of the goods.

Trover and Conversion

Although the earliest actions for conversion were brought against bailees, the principle of the action was equally applicable to strangers and finders: indeed more so, because such persons could not be sued in detinue unless they still possessed the goods at the time the action was brought. In 1510 an action was brought in the Common Pleas by a man whose silver had been stolen against another who had bought it, melted it down and converted it to his own use. And in 1519 a plaintiff brought conversion in the King's Bench against a person into whose hands his goods had come. The *devenit ad manus* form of count, clearly reminiscent of detinue, resulted in six years of discussion; and we may guess that the reason was one of the same difficulties which had led to the disuse of the analogous count in detinue.[41] The consequence was that history repeated itself, or rather that lawyers followed the lesson they had learned in detinue. Conversion would be brought on a *trover*. In 1531 the classical *trover* declaration was approved in the King's Bench, in a case where the plaintiff alleged that he had lost a purse, which had come to the defendant by finding, and that the defendant had refused to deliver it up and, scheming to defraud the plaintiff, had taken out the contents, sold them, and converted the proceeds.[42] By the 1540s the *trover* was non-traversable, and doubtless usually fictitious. The action soon became common form in the King's Bench, and later in the century it was even allowed against bailees. The fiction went so far that in 1600 it was decided that a defendant who had taken goods with force and arms could be sued as a 'finder':[43] an instance of case replacing trespass *vi et armis*.

40. *Calwodelegh v John* (1478) CP 40/868, m.428; YB Hil 18 Edw IV, 23, pl.5; Fifoot HSCL, p. 113. The record shows that issue was joined on the bailor's title; no judgment is entered.
41. *Astley v Fereby* (1510) 94 SS *251* (and cf. Fifoot HSCL, p. 114); *Audelet v Latton* (No. 1, 1519) and (No. 2, 1520–26) ibid. *252*.
42. *Wysse v Andrewe* (1531) 94 SS *252*.
43. *Bishop and Jurdain v Viscountess Montague* (1601) Cro Eliz 824, Fifoot HSCL, p. 114.

The first reported case in which this form of action was discussed came before the Common Pleas in 1555. Dyer argued that the plaintiff should have brought detinue, but most of the judges approved the action because the finder was only liable in detinue so long as he retained possession of the goods found.[44] This argument finally vanquished any remaining scruples as to the use of case instead of detinue, and of course gave further encouragement to the fictitious use of the *trover* formula. Arguments founded on the rule against double remedies were thereafter confined to the cases where *trover* was used against bailees. Bailees were liable to detinue. But a fiction which was good for strangers had to be good for bailees as well; if the *trover* was not issuable, there was no way in which the fact of the bailment could be disclosed. By Elizabethan times, the only cases where the bailor would count on a bailment when suing his bailee were cases of damage falling short of conversion: a finder was not liable for negligence, and could not be said to have converted to his own use merely because he failed to preserve what he had found.[45]

The final triumph of the action for conversion came when it was allowed to overlap completely with detinue. The development was exactly paralleled, both in point of time and in the judicial attitudes involved, by *Slade's Case* in the law of debt.[46] The bare withholding of property was a nonfeasance closely analogous to the withholding of a sum owed. But, as with *assumpsit* for money, the controversy could not be ended so long as defendants pleaded the general issue and juries found general verdicts; for the record, with its formal allegations of fraudulent conversion, was unimpeachable. If King's Bench judges directed juries that a mere detention, or refusal to deliver, was evidence of a conversion, there was no ground for interfering with the subsequent verdict and judgment. The Exchequer Chamber did, nevertheless, reverse several King's Bench judgments in the 1590s; and at length, shortly before *Slade's Case*, the question was raised in a test case by means of a special verdict. The jury found that the defendant had simply refused to restore goods to the plaintiff, and asked the opinion of the court whether this was conversion. After long debates, using much the same arguments as in *Slade's Case* about overlapping special and general actions, the majority view seems to have been that the plaintiff could choose to bring case if he wished.[47] No clear decision was announced in the test case, but the law was

44. *Lord Mounteagle v Countess of Worcester* (1555) Dyer 121.
45. *Mulgrave v Ogden* (1591) Cro Eliz 219, 1 Leon 224, Owen 141.
46. See pp. 285–286, ante.
47. *Eason v Newman* (1596) Cro Eliz 495, Goulds 152.

clearly stated in 1614.[48] The court then said that a refusal to deliver
was equivocal, because it might be justified in cases where it did not
amount to an assertion of adverse title; for instance, if the goods were
held as a pledge or lien, or if the holder simply wished to verify the
claimant's identity. But in the absence of such a justification, a refusal
to deliver goods to the owner on demand was itself a conversion, and
therefore it was proper for the jury to find for the plaintiff even though
there was no evidence of misfeasance.

The result of this last development was that the tortious origins of
the action for conversion went into the background, and the action
became a proprietary action used in place of detinue. The gist of the
action was no longer the wrongdoing, but the denial of title. There
had been a debate in 1590 as to whether conversion would lie against
a bona fide purchaser for value who had resold the goods.[49] It was
thereafter settled that a voluntary dealing in good faith with the goods
of another could constitute conversion;[50] and it could then be said
'trover is merely a substitute of the old action of detinue . . . [it] is not
now an action *ex maleficio*, though it is so in form; but it is founded on
property'.[51] The title which the action protected was relative, as in
detinue; and so a finder could himself bring *trover*.[52] But the change of
character left its scars in the strange rule of English law that the
proprietary remedy for chattels lies not merely against the person who
has the chattels when the action is commenced, but against any
intermediate possessor who may be said to have converted them
(however innocently) by dealing with them as if he were owner. And
the 'proprietary' action, being in form a purely personal action, did
not enable specific recovery of the chattel claimed.[53]

REVIVAL AND ABOLITION OF DETINUE

The abolition of wager of law in 1833 and the reform of the common
law processes had the effect of reviving detinue as a viable remedy.
From then until 1978 the common law suffered two distinct causes of
action for personal property to exist side by side. The precise historical differences were not revived as well, and detinue was regarded in
modern times, save by purists, as a tort. Yet the choice of action

48. *Isack v Clarke* (1614) 1 Rolle Rep 126, 2 Bulst 306, Fifoot HSCL, p. 117.
49. *Vandrink v Archer* (1590) 1 Leon 221; sub nom. *Galliard v Archer* ibid. 189. Cf. *Fines v Spencer* (1571) Dyer 306.
50. *Hartop v Hoare* (1743) 2 Stra 1187, 1 Wils 8; *Cooper v Chitty* (1756), 1 Burr 20. See also *Hollins v Fowler* (1875) LR 7 HL 757.
51. *Hambly v Trott* (1776) 1 Cowp 371 at 374 per Lord Mansfield CJ.
52. *Armory v Delamirie* (1722) 1 Stra 505.
53. This had been attempted, perhaps by mistake, in *Knight v Browne* (1588) Cro Eliz 116, but the judgment was reversed.

remained of practical importance, for a reason which was little more than an historical accident. Since the action of detinue lay to recover the goods or their value, the value was assessed at the date of the action, whereas in conversion the damages were based on the value of the goods at the moment of conversion. The plaintiff therefore elected to base his claim on a detinue or a conversion according to whether the goods had appreciated or depreciated in value since the date of conversion.[54]

On 1 June 1978 detinue was 'abolished'. The precise meaning of this terse enactment is unclear. The writ of detinue had been abolished long before. The fact of detinue cannot be abolished, because people will continue to detain goods. The legal consequences of detaining (as opposed to converting) goods may be abolished, but parliament seems to have gone to much trouble to prevent that happening. The court retains the discretion to order the return of the goods, or their value, or the payment of damages.[55]

Further reading

Holdsworth HEL, vol. III, pp. 401–544

Fifoot HSCL, pp. 24–43, 102–125

Milsom HFCL, pp. 227–235, 321–332

J. B. Ames, 'History of Trover' (1897) 11 HLR 277–289, 374–386

P. Bordwell, 'Property in Chattels' (1916) 29 HLR 374–394, 501–520, 731–751

A. W. B. Simpson, 'Introduction of the Action on the Case for Conversion' (1959) 75 LQR 364–380

S. F. C. Milsom, 'Sale of Goods in the 15th Century' (1961) 77 LQR 257–284

J. M. Kaye, 'Res addiratae and Recovery of Stolen Goods' (1970) 86 LQR 379–403

J. H. Baker, 'Property in Chattels' (1978) 94 SS *209–220*; 'Conversion' ibid. *248–257*

54. *Rosenthal v Alderton & Sons Ltd* [1946] 1 KB 374, [1946] 1 All ER 583.
55. Torts (Interference with Goods) Act 1977 (c.32), s.2(1): 'Detinue is abolished'. S.I. 1978 No. 627.

19. Negligence

THE CONCEPT OF TORT

The law of torts, or civil wrongs, is extensive and its boundaries are indistinct. An understanding of the process by which a number of miscellaneous causes of action came to be classified as 'torts' will depend partly on semantics. The nearest medieval equivalent of the modern technical word 'tort' was trespass, while the old law-French word *tort* denoted any kind of legal injury (*injuria* in Latin).[1] In the preceding chapters we traced the development of trespass in the areas of contract and property law, and noticed that in the early sixteenth century there was nothing incongruous in describing a breach of contract as a tort or trespass. But when the action of *assumpsit* became a truly contractual remedy, based on a promise in return for consideration, it became necessary for various reasons to distinguish breaches of promise from those other kinds of trespass which reflected a wider notion of wrong. One reason for the distinction, which was being drawn soon after 1600, was that actions for breach of contract could be brought against personal representatives, whereas actions for personal wrongs could not.[2] Another reason was that the rules concerning joint and several liability were different in contract and tort.[3] The appearance of the new terminology is perhaps seen most clearly in the rule that claims in contract and tort could not be joined in one action. Thus, when an action was brought in 1665 against the hirer of a horse for misusing the animal and for not paying the hire, counsel argued that the joinder of the two causes of action was erroneous because one action sounded in tort and the other 'in breach of promise only'.[4] In another case the same year, counsel treated tort and contract as mutually exclusive: 'tort can never be done where there is a special agreement, unless there be duty by statute or common law incumbent'. This is near the modern understanding of the word,

1. Even in contractual *praecipe* actions the defence was in the words *defendit vim et injuriam* (denies the force and tort).
2. *Fossett v Carter* (1623) Palmer 329 at 330 per Jones J.
3. *Boson v Sandford* (1689) 1 Show KB 101.
4. *Golding v Goteer* (1665) 1 Keb 847.

although Twisden J in the same case considered that tort connoted malice, fraud or negligence and did not include *trover*.[5] Already by 1663 indexes were classifying 'tort' in the modern sense, as a sub-heading under 'actions on the case'.[6]

As different kinds of action on the case acquired separate identifiable characteristics in the sixteenth and seventeenth centuries, further subdivisions of the law of torts were possible; subdivisions which survived the abolition of the writ system itself. During the last century or so, however, the law of torts has been undergoing a gradual reclassification as a result of the rapid expansion of the new tort of negligence.[7] Liability for negligence alone was rarely imposed before the eighteenth century, and even at the beginning of the twentieth century Sir John Salmond denied the existence of a separate tort of negligence. Not that there is anything modern about the concept of negligence; but for most of its history it occupied an ancillary position as the fault element in other torts.

Negligence is not merely the name of the most recent tort to have emerged; it is a new way of approaching tortious liability, and it has become the principal concept around which the modern law of tort is arranged. But the story of negligence must begin in the days when it was a factor in other torts; and in this capacity it made its debut in writs which alleged a non-forcible wrong.

UNDERTAKINGS AND NEGLIGENCE

The word *negligenter* (negligently), as an adverb designed to indicate wrongful conduct, first appeared in writs of trespass as the antithesis of force and arms. If damage was done in the course of performing carelessly a task undertaken with the plaintiff's consent, it could not be described as having been done *vi et armis*. If, on the other hand, the wrong was forcible, the complaint was not of mere negligence and so there was no need to mention it in a special case. Negligence and force were thus mutually exclusive.

In all the early cases where negligence was part of the special case in the writ, there was a pre-existing relationship between the parties which precluded an allegation of force against the peace. The relationship arose from some undertaking which brought the defendant into contact with the plaintiff or the plaintiff's property; and, since the plaintiff had consented to this physical contact, the careless defendant

5. *Matthews v Hopping* (1665) 1 Keb 870. But in 1 Sid 244 it is said that conversion *is* founded on tort.
6. E.g., *An Exact Table to the Three Parts of Reports of Mr William Leonard* (1663), sig. Rr1v. See also G. Townesend *Tables* (1667), p. 27.
7. See further pp. 348–349, post.

who caused harm was liable not for *doing* the act but for doing it *carelessly*.

Some of the leading cases have already been examined in reviewing the history of contract and bailment.[8] Actions on the case for negligence were brought against bailees, carriers, surgeons, workmen and tradesmen. They all had a common form: the defendant was alleged to have undertaken to perform some specific task, and to have done it so carelessly that some specified harm resulted. The undertaking was only to do the work, not to use skill or care; so to that extent the obligation to use care was imposed by law rather than by contract. A bailee's undertaking to keep goods 'safely' may actually have fixed him with strict liability. The nature of the negligence relied on in these *assumpsit* actions never clearly emerged in the cases, because the defendant normally pleaded the general issue and the question of negligence was then a question of fact for the jury alone to decide.[9] Whatever it was, it found expression always in negative adverbs, such as *negligenter, improvide, inartificialiter, indebite,* and so forth. But the adverb always governed a verb of positive action. The best generalisation we can make is that a person who embarked upon a service which brought him into contact with the person or property of another was liable if he performed the service with want of care or skill and damage resulted.

The same form of pleading continued in use after the word *assumpsit* became associated almost exclusively with contractual undertakings. But where there was negligence there was no need to show consideration for the undertaking, because (as we should say) the action was founded on tort rather than contract.[10] Nevertheless, the confusion resulting from the use of the word *assumpsit* has caused contract and tort to overlap down to the present day, inasmuch as surgeons, carriers, bailees and others who cause damage by performing negligently an undertaking which they were paid to perform diligently may be sued either in tort or in contract at the plaintiff's election.

NEGLIGENCE IN THE ABSENCE OF UNDERTAKINGS

Actions on the case were brought in the fourteenth century against innkeepers for the loss of goods belonging to their guests by their 'default'. The relationship between innkeeper and traveller with respect to luggage was not sufficiently close to be treated as bailment,

8. See pp. 273–275, 329–330, ante.
9. An exception, which raised a number of potentially interesting questions and shows that such questions were by no means overlooked, is *Terry v White* (1528) 94 SS *226–227*.
10. See p. 330, ante.

especially since common innkeepers were bound by law to accept all travellers who wished to stay and for whom there was room. The plaintiff in such an action therefore relied on a 'custom of the realm' that all keepers of common inns were bound to accommodate travellers, and to look after their goods so that no harm came to them through their default. The gist of the action was the innkeeper's default in custody, but precisely because there was no liability for negligence without a pre-existing duty of care it was thought necessary to show a custom of the realm which imposed the duty.

By 1400 the custom of the realm approach had been extended to cover liability for fire. Again, it would seem, the necessity for laying such a custom arose from the absence of a pre-existing relationship between the parties. The only relationship was that of being a neighbour. The alleged custom of the realm was therefore stated to be that everyone was bound to keep his fire safe and sound so that it did not injure his neighbour. The operative clause, that the defendant nevertheless kept his fire so negligently that the plaintiff's property was damaged, was borrowed from the action against bailees; but as the complaint was of a default in the custody, not of the plaintiff's goods, but of a dangerous force set in motion by the defendant, it was necessary to allege a customary duty of care and control.[11]

The liability for allowing fire to spread is not dissimilar from that imposed on the owners or keepers of dangerous animals which escaped from their custody and did damage. The *scienter* action,[12] which had appeared by 1367, imposed strict liability; the fault lay in the keeping with knowledge of the danger. But that liability was imposed independently of an undertaking or custom of the realm, and this may account for the unresolved but otherwise absurd doubt whether it was not a form of trespass *vi et armis*.

The modern lawyer may see in the so-called customs of the realm the antecedents of the 'duty of care';[13] but there was in fact no continuity between the old doctrine and the new, and the custom of the realm was abandoned as a source of legal development for the simple reason that such a custom could not be other than the common law itself. The legal position until the later seventeenth century, therefore, was that liability for negligence was generally imposed only for default in undertakings, and for breaches of duty by innkeepers or

---

11. *Beaulieu v Finglam* (1401) Fifoot HSCL, pp. 166–167.
12. So called from the assertion that the defendant 'knowingly retained' (*scienter retinuit*) the dangerous animal.
13. See pp. 346–348, post. The connection was later made in *Ansell v Waterhouse* (1817) 6 M & S 385 per Lord Ellenborough CJ.

persons who lit fires. No thought was given to liability for negligence as such, and an Elizabethan judge could state without undue conservatism, 'Here there is nothing alleged except negligence, and I have never known an action to lie for negligence save where one is retained to do something for someone and does it negligently; and the reason why it lies in that case is because he had undertaken to do it.'[14] An obvious explanation for such a restriction would be that the common law could not impose a duty of care on a person who had not undertaken it of his own volition. But the real reason why such a state of affairs was for so long tolerated was the wide scope of trespass *vi et armis*.

TRESPASS VI ET ARMIS AND NEGLIGENCE

If negligent conduct caused direct physical harm, the appropriate remedy, in the absence of an undertaking, was an action of trespass alleging force and arms. Such an action was not based on doing something negligently which would have been lawful if done carefully, but on doing something which there was no right to do at all. The short-sighted archer who shot a passer-by unawares, or the careless driver who ran him down, were just as guilty of battery as if they had injured him deliberately. Negligence in the sense of inadvertence was irrelevant.

A wide range of accidents qualified as battery, but the range was obscured by the sameness of the writs and counts. Whatever the real facts, defendants always 'assaulted, beat and wounded' the plaintiff 'with force and arms, to wit with swords and staves'. In the general writ there were no further particulars, and no mention of negligence. The degree of fault of the defendant would only become relevant if he tried to make it so by excusing himself on grounds of accident. Yet, if he did so, he would not usually plead the accident specially, but would plead the general issue 'not guilty' and explain the circumstances in evidence to the jury. As a result, the law relating to accident was suppressed for centuries; what happened before the jury was not entered on the record and raised no legal questions for the court in banc. If the short-sighted archer were sued in battery, he might satisfy the jury that the accident was not his fault, and they would then find him not guilty; but the details of his defence would nowhere be set down in writing. It is therefore an unreal question whether the *law* recognised a defence of accident; the question was treated as being purely of fact. The question only presented itself on the face of the

14. *Bradshaw v Nicholson* (1601) Inner Temple MS Barrington 6, f.127v per Walmsley J.

record in one or two exceptional cases where, through mistaken policy by the pleader, accident was raised by a special plea. The plea was regularly rejected, but the cases did not thereby establish that accident was no defence: merely that it could not be pleaded in the manner which had been attempted.

In the *Case of Thorns*[15] a man was sued for trespassing on his neighbour's land to collect thorns which had fallen there in the process of clipping. He pleaded, as to the trespass by the thorns, that they had fallen against his will (*ipso invito*); but Choke J held this plea bad because the will was only relevant in felony. It was agreed that if the thorns had been blown by the wind that would not have been the defendant's act, but the act of the wind. Gravity is a more continuous natural phenomenon than wind, and its effects were reasonably predictable even before Newton. A defence that the force of gravity had been overlooked was not a defence consistent with having taken due care. The plea was bad in substance, and so the question of form did not arise.

The problem occurred again in cases arising out of shooting accidents. In *Weaver v Ward*[16] the defendant, who had shot the plaintiff during military exercises, pleaded that the wounding was accidental and against his will. The court held the plea bad, but said that if he had shown that the plaintiff ran against his gun as he was firing it, or had shown that the accident was 'inevitable' and not his fault, then he might have been excused. Then, in 1682, a defendant adopted this advice and pleaded that as he was firing his pistol the plaintiff accidentally walked across the line of fire and was shot, against the will of the defendant. But even this was held to be a bad plea, 'for in trespass the defendant shall not be excused without unavoidable necessity, which is not shewn here'.[17] Even if the facts alleged in the plea were true, the defendant might yet have been negligent.

These decisions led subsequent generations to suppose that liability in trespass *vi et armis* had been strict, and excusable only by 'inevitable accident'.[18] When examined carefully, the decisions were by no means as sweeping as random dicta suggested. None of the

---

15. *Hull v Orynge* (1466) CP 40/815, m.340; YB Mich 6 Edw IV, 7, pl.18; Kiralfy SB, p. 128; Fifoot HSCL, p. 195. There is an inconclusive discussion of the same point in *Jankyn's Case* (1378) YB Mich 2 Ric II (Ames Foundation), 69, pl.7.

16. (1616) Moore KB 864, Hob 134, Fifoot HSCL, p. 198, Kiralfy SB, p. 132 (record). The action was eventually settled: HLS MS 112, p. 319. A similar plea was entered, with no objection, in *Ustwayt v Alyngton* (1534) 94 SS *223–224.* See also *Middleton v Bridelyngton* (1388) YB Hil 12 Ric II (Ames Foundation), 125, pl.16 (child justified battery as arising from play *sine voluntate et absque malicia*).

17. *Dickenson v Watson* (1682) T Jones 205, Fifoot HSCL, p. 200.

18. See *Wakeman v Robinson* (1823) 1 Bing 213; *Hall v Fearnley* (1842) 3 QB 919.

pleas had put the defendant's fault in issue. It did not follow because the damage was accidental (*per infortuniam*) or against the will of the defendant (*ipso invito*) that the defendant had been without fault. The judges therefore wished to know whether the defendant could have taken steps to avoid the accident; in other words, whether it was 'inevitable'—not in the sense of being predestined, but in that there was no reasonable opportunity of prevention. A man who had done wrong could not offer as a defence that he had not wished it to happen. If he had some justification for acting as he did, he could plead by way of confession and avoidance. If he had not done the act at all, if his own act had not caused the accident, or if he had done all he could to prevent it, then his proper course was to plead the general issue and tell his story to the jury.[19]

Thus, although negligence played no formal part in the action of trespass *vi et armis*, it seems likely that a man was only considered guilty of such a trespass if he had at least been negligent in causing direct, forcible harm. It was not clearly laid down that the standard of liability was exactly the same as in actions on the case until the tort of negligence was established and the forms of action abolished;[20] but there is no reason to suppose it was ever different, since in either action it was for the jury to decide. The writ of trespass *vi et armis* had been an archaic survival, in that unlike most of the other actions which continued in use its wording almost totally suppressed the real facts. But this formal, procedural distinction between trespass and case was engraved on the heart of the pleader, and it was not until 1959 that a plaintiff complaining of a direct trespass was held obliged to allege negligence as part of his own case.[21]

The Tort of Negligence

We now know that the distinction between trespass and case was the result of the jurisdictional accident that the royal courts entertained complaints of forcible wrongs before letting in the rest[22]. There ought, therefore, to have been no substantive gaps between the two. Any wrong which was not forcible ought to have been remediable in case. Harmful carelessness was on the face of it legally wrong, and there was probably no absolute rule to the effect that there could be no duty to take care without an undertaking; it was just that between battery

---

19. *Gibbons v Pepper* (1695) 4 Mod Rep 404, 1 Ld Raym 38, Fifoot HSCL, p. 200.
20. *Stanley v Powell* [1891] 1 QB 86.
21. *Fowler v Lanning* [1959] 1 QB 426, [1959] 1 All ER 290.
22. See pp. 56–59, ante.

and *assumpsit* most accidents were provided for. When exceptional cases arose, new actions on the case could be devised. We have already noticed the fourteenth-century device of customs of the realm; but there was no peculiar magic in the two customs, and new duties could be recognised at common law without the use of that label. In 1473 we find an action for putting a pile of firewood near the highway, knowing the danger of its falling, where it did fall on the plaintiff; issue was joined on the negligence.[23] In 1520 we find a mill-keeper sued for breach of his duty *ratione officii* to control a mill-sluice so that flooding did not occur.[24] In 1530 a person into whose hands the plaintiff's goods had come was successfully sued for negligent keeping, there being no *assumpsit* or conversion;[25] similar actions were also brought against bailees. And in 1582 an action was brought for damage caused by a spark from a gun, which was a fire accident not covered by the custom of the realm.[26] These cases are few and far between, not because the law had difficulty in recognising the existence of a duty, but because the situations not covered by trespass *vi et armis* or *assumpsit* were few and far between. Problems only arose, as elsewhere in the law, when attempts were made to use case instead of an existing remedy. In this sphere the conflict was between case and trespass *vi et armis*.

The first signs of a tort of negligence, in the more pervasive sense which included forcible wrongs, are found in a long series of running down cases beginning in the seventeenth century. If a man negligently drove his horse and cart or ship into another man or his property, that was a trespass with force. But there could be many disadvantages in bringing trespass. For one thing, the accident might be shown to be the fault of the horse, or of the unpredictable forces of nature, or perhaps partly of the plaintiff himself, and so the jury would be persuaded to find the defendant not guilty of the trespass. Also, for similar reasons, the jury might reduce the damages if the battery turned out to have been unintentional.[27] Moreover, the plaintiff often wished to sue the driver's master, and vicarious liability could only be imposed by an action on the case. And then there was the serious practical danger that recovery of nominal damages in

---

23. *Loughton v Calys* (1473) CP 40/847, m.382.
24. *Fynamore v Clyfford* (1520), and two similar cases of 1508 and 1529, 94 SS *229*.
25. *Watson v Wodward* (1530) KB 27/1077, m.30. Cf. *Mulgrave v Ogden* (1591), p. 333, ante.
26. *Anon* (1582) Cro Eliz 10. An earlier precedent, without judgment, is *Clerk v Terrell* (1507) 94 SS *229*.
27. *Angell v Shatterton* (1663) 1 Sid 108 (negligent discharge of gun); *Burford v Dadwell* (1669) ibid. 433 (running down).

trespass *vi et armis* carried nominal costs.[28] In all these situations the plaintiff did well to waive the force and sue in an action on the case for negligence.

In the seventeenth century there was some doubt how negligence of this kind, where there was no pre-existing relationship between the parties, ought to be set out. One pleader, doubtless mindful of earlier history, actually invented a new custom of the realm, that drivers were bound so to control the horses that no damage befell anyone through their want of care;[29] but this experiment led nowhere. The breakthrough appeared to later generations to have been made in 1676. But it was only a significant step to later eyes. At the time there was no awareness that a new principle of liability was in the making. It was just another new case which did not quite fit into the existing formulae.

Mitchil v Alestree[30] was an action against a master and servant who had broken in horses in Lincoln's Inn Fields, where many people were walking about, including the plaintiff who was kicked and injured. In his first action the plaintiff alleged that the defendant had negligently permitted the horses to injure the plaintiff; but Hale CJ ruled at the trial that there was no evidence of want of care in controlling the untamed horses. The essence of the wrong was in bringing horses to a public place for breaking in, and so a second action was brought alleging that the defendants had acted *improvide, incaute* and without consideration of the danger of breaking in horses in a busy place. The action succeeded, even though there was no undertaking, no custom of the realm, and no force and arms. The arguments show that the judges were conscious only of making a slight enlargement of the *scienter* principle: The negligence was in creating a dangerous situation, rather than in the way the situation was controlled. The new principle was to give some trouble in relation to dogs, which were not normally confined; but as early as 1700 it was contended that the effect was to make a man 'answerable for all mischief proceeding from his neglect or his actions, unless they were of unavoidable necessity'.[31] Subsequent writers regarded *Mitchil v Alestree* as having opened up a new category of actions on the case, and by George II's time a

---

28. Duties on law proceedings Act 1670, 22 & 23 Car II, c.9, Schedule [s.9 in *Statutes of the Realm*, s.136 in *Statutes at Large*]. There was also a difference in the limitation periods: Limitation Act 1623, 21 Jac I, c.16, s.3 (4 years for battery, 6 for case).
29. Cited by Prichard, [1964] CLJ at 236.
30. (1676) 1 Vent 295, 3 Keb 650, 2 Lev 172, Exeter College Oxford MS 108, p. 183 (which alone mentions the first action).
31. *Mason v Keeling* (1700) 1 Ld Raym 606 at 607.

significant chapter headed 'Of injuries arising from negligence or folly' had been built around it.[32]

Towards the close of the eighteenth century, numerous problems raised by running down cases vexed the superior courts. Two reasons have been suggested for the glut of these cases in the last three decades of George III's reign. First, there was a heavy increase in the number of driving accidents, as a result of the greater speed and volume of traffic following the improvement of road surfaces by the turnpike trusts and the technical achievements of Telford and Macadam. Stage coaches, driven as often as not by men undistinguished for their sobriety, competed for the fastest journeys; and during such races they not infrequently overturned, collided with other vehicles, or went out of control. Second, the litigation which resulted from busier roads raised numerous legal difficulties, which were accentuated by the rigid insistence of the courts on the artificial boundary between trespass (direct forcible injury) and case (mediate or consequential injury).[33] The metaphysics of directness, as also the problems surrounding vicarious liability, were a constant trouble to courts and practitioners for over thirty years. The solution was found by Tindal CJ, in 1833, when it was laid down that a plaintiff could waive the force and sue in case whenever the injury complained of was not both direct and wilful.[34]

The effect of this decision was that trespass became more and more associated with wilful injuries. Few lawyers today would classify a running down accident as an assault and battery. And since the essence of the action on the case was negligence, the negligence had to be expressly pleaded and proved. The Industrial Revolution and the development of the railway added to the possibilities of frequent, novel and expensive accidents, and litigation about negligence enjoyed a further boom. By the beginning of Victoria's reign, cases on negligence were sufficiently numerous for writers on the law to put them into a separate compartment. The first collection of cases arranged in this way appeared in Mr Serjeant Petersdorff's *Abridgment* in 1843. A generation or two later, the subject had its own textbook: Thomas Beven's *Principles of the Law of Negligence* (1889).

32. *An Institute of the Law relative to Trials at Nisi Prius* (1768), p. 35. For this work and its date, see p. 347, post.
33. E.g. *Day v Edwards* (1794) 5 Term Rep 648; *Leame v Bray* (1803) 3 East 593, Fifoot HSCL, p. 205. The *locus classicus*, arising from a firework accident, was *Scott v Shepherd* (1773) 2 Wm Bl 892, Fifoot HSCL, p. 202. See also p. 59, ante.
34. *Williams v Holland* (1833) 10 Bing 112, Fifoot HSCL, p. 209.

The Nature of Tortious Negligence

Negligence, or neglect, is simply a failure to exercise care; and the failure to do something is only a legal wrong if the law imposes a duty to do it. Even in factual situations revealing apparently positive misconduct, 'negligence' could be regarded as a wrong of nonfeasance, consisting in not taking care. It all depends on whether the misconduct or the negligence is regarded as the core of the complaint. It is a fine point whether the driver of a .vehicle which runs over a pedestrian is liable for misfeasance in running him down or for nonfeasance in failing to apply the brake or take evasive action. The distinction no longer matters, since the negligence amounts in either way to a breach of the duty to take care; but before the nineteenth century it could affect the choice of writ and the classification of the wrong.

Sir John Comyns (d. 1740), in his *Digest of the Laws of England* (published in 1762), juxtaposed the separate headings 'Action upon the Case for Misfeasance' and 'Action upon the Case for Negligence'. The former category, which covered damage caused by 'misadventure', seems closer to the later tort of negligence than the latter. The latter included the neglect of miscellaneous duties imposed by law: the duties of an office, the duties imposed by customs of the realm, local customs or statutes, and the duties imposed by undertakings. In modern language we would describe Comyns' misfeasance as comprising negligent acts, his negligence as comprising neglectful omissions; and his misfeasance, as is evident from the cases abridged, cut across the categories of trespass and case. The tort of negligence was to fuse both aspects of carelessness, and to focus attention on the breach of a duty to take care, rather than upon the miscellaneous consequences of not taking care.

Leaving aside the choice of writ, the problem for the substantive law was to indicate the cases in which the law imposed a duty of care in the absence of an undertaking or custom. Duties of care could not be imposed on everyone in every situation. The finder of lost goods, for example, was under no duty to take care of them. The casual passer-by is under no duty to rescue a drowning man. At the beginning of the eighteenth century no one, it seems, could see any pattern emerging; the kinds of case were 'almost infinite, daily increasing, and continually receiving new forms'.[35] By the middle of the century, however, a clear answer had been formulated in an influential

35. T. Wood *An Institute of the Laws of England* (1724 edn), p. 542.

treatise, based on a manuscript supposedly written by Lord Bathurst (1714–94) in the 1740s or 1750s, which became a standard practitioners' manual in its subsequent editions by Buller and Onslow. The author suggested for the first time[36] a principle which is now familiar to every law student: 'Every man ought to take reasonable care that he does not injure his neighbour; therefore, wherever a man receives hurt through the default of another, though the same were not wilful, yet if it be occasioned by negligence or folly the law gives him an action to recover damages for the injury so sustained . . . However, it is proper in such cases to prove that the injury was such as would probably follow from the act done.'[37]

The 'neighbour' principle was redefined in the classic speech of Lord Atkin two centuries later in *Donoghue v Stevenson*.[38] As Lord Atkin explained, the law has to define who is a neighbour for this purpose. The general solution to this problem has been developed from Lord Bathurst's concept of the probability of injury; neighbours in the law of tort are 'persons who are so closely and directly affected by my act that I ought reasonably to have them in contemplation as being so affected when I am directing my mind to the acts or omissions which are called in question'.[39] Yet there are situations where a man may lawfully do or omit to do something, even though his act or omission will harm another person. A man may open a shop which ruins the livelihood of a neighbouring shopkeeper by drawing away his trade; but it is no legal wrong.[40] A man may know that his neighbour is starving; yet he is not bound in law to go and feed him. The definition in advance of all the situations in which a duty of care exists independently of agreement is impossible. The recognition of a duty of care is the recognition of a cause of action having no technical name by which it may be identified, and that must ultimately be a matter of policy incapable of precise formulation. But it remains true that mere nonfeasance is not usually actionable in the absence of a pre-existing relationship between the parties: 'when a person has done nothing to put himself in any relationship with another person in distress or with his property mere accidental propinquity does not require him to go

36. The 'neighbour' figure may have been suggested by the form of words used in fire cases. See *Turberville v Stamp* (1697) 12 Mod Rep 152: 'he must at his peril take care that [the fire] does not through his neglect injure his neighbour'.
37. *An Institute of the Law relative to Trials at Nisi Prius* (1768), pp. 35–36. This later acquired the name Buller's *Nisi Prius*. For the date and attribution, see W. Selwyn *Nisi Prius* (1869 edn), preface.
38. [1932] AC 562 at 578. See also *Langridge v Levy* (1837) 2 M & W 519; *Heaven v Pender* (1883) 11 QBD 503.
39. *Donoghue v Stevenson*, last note, at 580 per Lord Atkin.
40. See p. 376, post.

to that person's assistance. There may be a moral duty to do so, but it is not practicable to make it a legal duty'.[41]

THE REASONABLE MAN

Just as there are degrees of carefulness, so there are degrees of want of care. English law occasionally experimented with 'gross negligence', borrowing ideas from Roman law with little understanding, or even with malicious negligence.[42] In the case of fire (until 1707[43]), and of undertakings to keep safely, the duty to take 'care' was strict. But, as a general principle, the judges of the eighteenth and nineteenth centuries settled for Lord Bathurst's standard of *reasonable* care. In 1781 Sir William Jones surveyed the various alternatives, in an attempt to determine the standard of care expected of a bailee. He rejected Bracton's test of the utmost diligence as too strict, and the duty to look after goods 'as one's own' as too subjective. As a solution, he proposed a new 'fixed mode or standard of diligence', that of the 'generality of rational men'.[44] This we take to be the origin of the standard of care of the reasonable man. Doubtless it proved a useful way of putting the idea of negligence across to juries. By 1856 it could be made part of the substantive definition of the new tort: 'Negligence is the omission to do something which a reasonable man would do, or doing something which a reasonable man would not do.'[45]

THE MODERN LAW OF NEGLIGENCE

The recognition of negligence as being a cause of action in itself represented more than the birth of a new tort, because it brought about a reclassification of legal ideas. The basis of the old writ system was the classification of torts according to the kind of *harm* done to the plaintiff. Each form of action developed its own approach to the kind of fault which made the defendant liable for causing that kind of harm, be it force, deceit, malice, negligence, or whatever. The new approach is to classify torts according to the type of *fault* for which the defendant is to be made liable, and only within that framework to

41. *Home Office v Dorset Yacht Co Ltd* [1970] AC 1004 at 1027 per Lord Reid.
42. *Algar's Case* (1591) Brit Lib MS Lansdowne 1067, f.146 ('negligence de male purpose'). This is a variant report of *Mulgrave v Ogden*, p. 333, ante.
43. Act preventing Mischiefs from Fire 1707, 6 Annae, c.31 [c.58 in *Statutes of the Realm*], which took away the action for damage by fire beginning in a house 'accidentally'.
44. *Treatise on the Law of Bailments* (1781), p. 6. This was intended to displace the different standards of care propounded by Holt CJ, in *Coggs v Bernard* (1703) 2 Ld Raym 909. See also *Jones v Bird* (1822) 5 B & Ald 837, 845–846; *Vaughan v Menlove* (1837) 3 Bing NC 468.
45. *Blyth v Birmingham Waterworks Co* (1856) 11 Ex 781 at 784 per Alderson B.

settle the types of harm for which the law will give redress. Theoretically there has been no change in the legal results, but the method of arriving at them is back to front. It is now the defendant's fault, rather than the damage which results from it, which is the primary cause of action. Thus, in place of the old scheme of torts based on the writs, we have torts of negligence, of deceit, and of strict liability. Some writers add torts of intentional wrongdoing; but no general tort of malice has emerged from the debris of the forms of action,[46] and in fact most of the so-called 'intentional torts' would also be torts in the absence of intention.

The expansion of the tort of negligence has produced a more profound result, in that the concept of negligence has grown to encompass the greater part of the law of tort. It has swallowed up many of the older torts, but in doing so it has come to contain within itself a number of diverse concepts masquerading as one. For instance, the doctrines of *res ipsa loquitur* and vicarious liability sometimes enable strict liability to be imposed under the guise of liability for negligence. Also, the degree of care may vary with the risk; a reasonable man takes more care when doing something dangerous than when doing something normally safe. The tendency of these developments, although ironically they coincide with the expansion of 'negligence' as a tort, has been interpreted as favouring the allocation of loss not on proof of moral fault but according to the degree of risk created by the defendant's activities and the extent to which he should be expected to insure against it. The common law has not overtly proceeded far in that direction, and in a paternalistic age it has been advocated that legislation should be introduced to put an end to fault-based liability in certain areas. The result of imposing strict liability on those who engage in hazardous or commercial activities would be that such persons would insure themselves, at the expense of all their customers, against the consequences. A more radical suggestion even than this is to abolish accident litigation altogether, and provide compensation by way of 'social security' from money raised by compulsory national insurance. A recent report has recommended the retention of actions in tort based on negligence or strict liability, but that there should be a shift of emphasis towards social security, which should be recognised as the principal means of compensation for injuries.[47] It is too early to say whether the recommendations will

---

46. See *Bradford Corporation v Pickles* [1895] AC 587; and also pp. 373, 385, 387–389, post.
47. Report of the Royal Commission on Civil Liability and Compensation for Personal Injury [Pearson Report] (1978), Cmnd 7054.

be implemented, but it is difficult to resist Professor Millner's conclusion that the shadow of its decline has fallen upon the concept of negligence in the very moment of its triumph.[48]

Further reading

Fifoot HSCL, pp. 154–213

Potter HIEL, pp. 375–394

Milsom HFCL, pp. 344–352

P. H. Winfield, 'The History of Negligence in the Law of Torts' (1926) 42 LQR 184–201

C. H. S. Fifoot, *Judge and Jurist in the Reign of Victoria* (1959), pp. 31–56

M. J. Prichard, 'Trespass, Case and the Rule in Williams v. Holland' [1964] CLJ 234–253; *Scott v Shepherd (1773) and the Emergence of the Tort of Negligence* (SS Lecture, 1976)

J. H. Baker, 'General Principles of Liability' and 'Fault in Negligence Actions' (1978) 94 *SS 220–230*

48. M. A. Millner *Negligence in Modern Law* (1967), p. 234.

20. Nuisance

If 'trespass' proved a useful word to lawyers because it was capable of describing a wide variety of wrongs, so to a lesser extent did 'nuisance'. They both began life as ordinary English, or rather French, words with no inherent technical significance.[1] Nuisance comprises, for legal purposes, such unlawful conduct as causes annoyance or disturbance rather than direct physical harm. It can be regarded as a species of trespass, but it cannot be a trespass *vi et armis*. When, in the mid-fourteenth century, the central courts began to entertain actions of trespass on the case, nuisance was brought within the broad common law concept of trespass; but it had already had a separate existence, both in the local courts and in a number of special real actions in the royal courts. It is from these latter forms of action that the original legal character of nuisance derived: it was a disturbance of the enjoyment of real property, falling short of a forcible trespass or ouster.

The concept of nuisance grew up with the real actions because the ordinary real actions required supplementation in two types of case. The first was an interference with a servitude over another's land, such as a right of way or pasture. The owner of the right had no seisin of the servient land itself. Instead, therefore, of the writ of right to recover the land he was given an analogous *praecipe* writ to recover the servitude. The writ instructed the sheriff to order the defendant that he permit (*quod permittat*) the plaintiff to have his pasture, or right of way, or whatever. A variant of the writ *quod permittat* lay to permit the plaintiff to abate a nuisance; for instance, to knock down a wall built across his right of way (*quod permittat prosternere murum*), or to restore a diverted watercourse. The second situation was a consequential interference with the land itself. For instance, if a neighbour stopped up a watercourse on his own land so that the adjoining land was flooded, or left his land unfenced so that cattle strayed onto adjoining land, this was neither a disseisin of the land nor a trespass *vi et armis*, but merely

1. The Latin root is *nocumentum*, from which come also the nouns 'annoyance' and 'noise' and the adjectives 'noisome' and 'noxious'.

the indirect result of something done on the wrongdoer's property. In such cases the injured freeholder could obtain a remedy by means of the writ *quod permittat* or something analogous. The writ *de curia claudenda*, for instance, lay to order the defendant to enclose his land 'which is open, to the nuisance of the free tenement' of the plaintiff.

THE ASSIZE OF NUISANCE

There may have been a reference in the legislation which established the assize of novel disseisin (c. 1166) to acts done to the nuisance of a free tenement. At any rate, there was from about that time a species of the assize, later called the assize of nuisance, which lay to abate a nuisance. The party aggrieved by a nuisance had a limited right of self-help analogous to the disseisee's right of re-entry; he could enter the servient tenement and abate the nuisance or exercise his servitude notwithstanding the obstruction. After the limitation period had expired, this right of entry and abatement was turned into a bare right of action, so that a *quod permittat* was necessary. But the de facto enjoyment of the right could be restored, in the same way as the seisin of land could be restored, by an assize. The plaintiff in the assize of nuisance complained that he had been disseised of his right of way, or common of pasture, or whatever, or that the defendant had done some act to the nuisance of his free tenement. Recognitors were then summoned to view the tenement and to recognise whether there had been a disseisin or nuisance as alleged. If they found for the plaintiff, the defendant had to abate the nuisance and pay damages. The assize lay not only for nuisances to land, but also for disturbing the franchise of market and the common of pasture, and by a statute of 1285 it was extended to other profits *a prendre*, tolls, and offices in fee.[2] But the remedy availed only freeholders, and it only lay against freeholders.

Just as the assize of novel disseisin gained popularity at the expense of the writ of right, so the assize of nuisance almost replaced the *quod permittat*. Yet, by the later fifteenth century, it was virtually unheard of. It had gone the way of all the old actions and was being replaced by trespass.

NUISANCE AND TRESPASS

The real actions suffered from a number of limitations in relation to nuisance which were analogous to the limitations in respect of land. There was no remedy for or against a tenant for years. The assize did not lie for nonfeasance, such as a failure to repair a ditch, because one

2. Statute of Westminster II 1285, c.25.

could not be disseised by inaction or by the forces of nature. Neither did it lie, as a rule, for a partial interference with an easement, such as polluting (without stopping up) a watercourse. These were cases of 'nuisance' in a broad sense, but because there was no interference with the realty there was no real action. They were also cases of 'trespass' in a broad sense, but in the absence of force and arms— which could only be alleged where there was a direct invasion of the plaintiff's close—no general writ of trespass was available. A remedy opened up when the royal courts dispensed with the necessity for force and arms and allowed the development of actions on the case.

One of the earliest actions of this nature was brought in 1341 for nonfeasance, where the defendant had failed to repair sea walls so that the plaintiff's land was flooded. The nonfeasance was a legal wrong because it was in breach of a customary duty to repair, and since no other remedy was available the court allowed an action of trespass 'formed on the case'.[3] Similar actions for failing to repair roads, bridges and fences, and for failing to scour ditches and water-courses, abound in the records and year books after this date. Other early actions on the case were brought where for some other reason the assize did not lie; for instance, where the nuisance was perpetrated by someone other than the freeholder, or where the plaintiff was a lessee for years, or where the nuisance was over and done with when the action was brought. In these cases it could be argued that case lay for the 'personal' wrong, as distinct from the proprietary wrong which was redressed by the assize.

The argument that trespass could not be brought in any case where there was already a remedy by real action—the argument which, as we have seen, was raised to prevent trespass for a time from doing the work of debt, detinue and covenant—was also a standard objection to the use of trespass on the case for nuisance. As in the sphere of contract, the impact of this objection remains uncertain, because the plea rolls of the fifteenth and sixteenth centuries contain numerous undetermined actions which appear to defy the theory. By 1566, at least, the Common Pleas was prepared to make a definite stand on the principle that case would not lie for a 'local or real disturbance', as where a right of way was stopped.[4] The familiar story of disagreement with the King's Bench then repeated itself. The King's Bench, which seems always to have entertained such actions without qualms, was

---

3. *Bernardestone v Heighlynge* (1342) YB Pas 16 Edw III (Rolls ser), vol. I, p. 257; Kiralfy AC, pp. 208–210.

4. *Yevance v Holcombe* (1566) 2 Dyer 250, 3 Leon 13, 4 Leon 167, 224, Coke's *Entries*, f.11b. Accord. *Beswick v Cunden* (1596) Cro Eliz 520. For two cases of the 1520s where the matter seems to have resulted in an impasse, see 94 SS *233*n.

equally emphatic that case lay as an alternative to the assize.[5] The justifications advanced by the King's Bench, and the objections raised by the Common Pleas, resemble very closely the arguments between the courts over the expansion of *assumpsit* and *trover*. Formal propriety was maintained by the usual expedient of alleging deceit and special loss. Perhaps the allegation of deceit was once taken seriously, though in what sense is unclear; the common-form suggestion that the defendant who committed a nuisance did so 'craftily scheming to defraud' the plaintiff of the use, enjoyment or profit of his property was obviously fictional in the majority of cases. The allegations of consequential loss stressed the 'personal' aspect of the wrong: even the Common Pleas judges, in the 1566 case, accepted that case was appropriate for 'personal disturbance'. Thus, if a way had been stopped, the plaintiff made out that he had been prevented from carrying on his business and household activities, and from fetching victuals to his house. If a watercourse had been stopped or narrowed, a miller could complain of the loss of profit while his mill was put out of action or slowed down. These injuries were injuries to the person rather than to the realty; yet, inasmuch as they were the natural consequences of 'local or real disturbance', the difference between the courts rested on a flimsy foundation. In the 1590s the Exchequer Chamber began to reverse King's Bench judgments on the grounds that the proper action for nuisance was the assize. The matter came to a head shortly before *Slade's Case*, and was debated by all the judges of England, who decided (with two dissentients only) that the plaintiff should have the right to choose the action on the case if he preferred.[6]

The Nature of Nuisance

When actions on the case supplanted the assize, the concept of nuisance as a personal wrong diverted attention for a time from the proprietary aspect of nuisance. The resolution of disputes about good neighbourliness raised questions of policy which could be approached in terms of the general principle, borrowed from Ulpian, that a man should not use his own property so as to hurt another: *sic utere tuo ut alienum non laedas*. But the application of so vague a principle could be a matter of grave doubt. A man may build on his own land according to the dictates of his own taste. But may he build so as to block his neighbour's light and air, to spy on his private life, or to obstruct his

5. *Aston's Case* (1586) 2 Dyer 250 n.88.
6. *Cantrel v Church* (1601) Cro Eliz 845, Noy 37.

view? When does a bad neighbour become a legal nuisance? One way of solving such problems of policy was to treat the enjoyment of light and air and other 'commodities' as property rights, so that their infringement was ipso facto a tort. But this approach was not comprehensive, because some rights were recognised as attaching to the occupation of property independently of any grant or long usage. It was therefore convenient to divide the interests protected by actions for nuisance into those which had to exist as property rights created by grant or prescription, and those which were the natural incidents of land ownership in general.

ACQUIRED RIGHTS: EASEMENTS

Easements originally included both natural rights and acquired rights over the land of another person which enured to the 'ease', advantage or profit of the property of the person who enjoyed them. None of these terms was technical. The plaintiff commonly alleged a loss of *proficuum, commodum et aisiamentum*, as if all three were synonymous, and the phrase even occurs in a contract case to denote the profit and advantage of a bargain.[7] Next the word 'easement' came to be confined to such rights as could be regarded as distinct property rights in themselves, and not merely as incidents to the ownership or occupation of property. Then easements were separated from profits *a prendre*, which include a right to take something from the servient tenement; for instance, a pasture or fishery. Examples of easements in this narrower sense are rights of way, of light, and of water and air flow. These are not profits, for nothing is taken; nor are they natural rights, for they must be acquired by grant or prescription. The decision as to what could only subsist as an easement rested upon the determination of what might subsist as a natural right. Commons and rights of way were never natural rights. Illumination for a house may once have been regarded as a natural right, acquired by whomsoever built his house first.[8] It was allied with the right to enlarge buildings, which also went by priority: 'one who has an old house may build as high as he pleases, even though he thereby stops up his neighbour's lights; but no one is allowed to erect a new house in a vacant space where there was none before, to the damage of neighbours in their lights'.[9] On this principle, new building near other houses could not

7. 94 SS *234* n.8.
8. *Hales' Case* (c. 1560), p. 357, post; *Anon* (1569) Lincoln's Inn MS Maynard 86, f.91.
9. *Hughes v Keme* (1612) 1 Bulst 115, Yelv 216, Godb 183, Coke's *Entries*, f.20. Quotation from HLS MS 109, f.10v.

be justified even by a city custom.[10] Experience and discussion soon showed this to be unsound policy as well as illogical where neighbours both had houses of similar age; and so the principle which prevailed was that a plaintiff must prescribe for each of his 'ancient lights' by showing uninterrupted user from time immemorial.[11] Similarly, the right to have support for a building, originally considered a natural right, could exist in later law only as an easement.[12]

When an easement was interfered with, an action on the case lay as a matter of course. There was no need to balance the interests of the parties, or to introduce questions of policy, because the matter was one of property. Such an interference is called 'cognate nuisance' to distinguish it from disturbances of the personal enjoyment of the incidents of occupying land.

NATURAL RIGHTS

As the owner of land was protected against forcible invasions of his close by the writs of trespass and forcible entry, so he was protected up to a point against the disturbance of his environment by the action of nuisance. Where noxious matter came onto the plaintiff's land indirectly by reason of the dilapidated state of the defendant's premises, the collapse or putrefaction of something placed near the boundary, the flowing of water, force of wind, or the permeation of damp and mould, this was not a trespass *vi et armis*. If damage resulted, such an injury was remedied by the action on the case.

Several such cases have been found in fourteenth-century plea rolls. Defendants built so near the edge of their land that water dripped onto the plaintiff's house and caused damage; or put filth in a stream and polluted the plaintiff's water supply; or put putrid refuse so near the boundary that the plaintiff's home was infected or rendered uninhabitable. The action on the case for *fedities* became one of the commonest forms of nuisance in times when there were few, if any, public health regulations and the standards of hygiene were low. It was brought against butchers who did not adequately dispose of blood, offal and carrion. It was brought against tanners and glovers whose limekilns emitted poisonous fumes which destroyed pasture and fruit and spoiled drinking-water. It was brought against dyers for corrupting the air and water with their chemicals. It was brought against private householders for keeping leaky or ramshackle latrines

10. Ibid. (custom held good, but rebuilding must be on old site); *Bland v Moseley* (1587) cit. 9 Co Rep at 58; Kiralfy AC, pp. 213, 214 (custom held bad); *Hammond v Alsey* (1592), cit. 1 Bulst 116 (custom to build on old foundation good).
11. *Bury v Pope* (1587) Cro Eliz 118, 1 Leon 168.
12. *Palmer v Fletcher* (1663) 1 Lev 122, 1 Sid 167. The right of support for the land itself remained a natural right.

in inconvenient places. It seems that a nuisance might also be committed by failing to remove noxious matter from the plaintiff's property, where there was a legal duty to do so; for instance, where tithes of milk and butter were set aside and the rector did not collect them until they were mouldy. It was even suggested, in the early days of Elizabeth I, that 'if one who hath a horrible sickness be in my house, and will not depart, an action will lie against him; and yet he taketh not any air from me, but infecteth that which I have'.[13] The remaining on the land was a trespass, but the infection was a nuisance.

In the sixteenth and seventeenth centuries there was increasing speculation about the scope of the action of nuisance, particularly with respect to nuisances affecting the senses. Already by Tudor times the law recognised that nuisances could be occasioned by noise, heat and smell. Nevertheless, every inconvenience could not be the subject of legal redress. The law had to strike a balance between a man's freedom to do as he liked with and upon his own property, and his duty not to injure his neighbour. The first noteworthy debate to be reported concerned the right to light, where a man blocked the side windows of his neighbour's house by erecting a building on his own land. Counsel for the plaintiff said that when light and air were stopped up 'his house remaineth as a dungeon', and referred to the Roman rule that a man may obstruct a view but not light. Counsel for the defendant said that light and air received only through side windows were not necessaries, and that in any case the side windows themselves infringed the defendant's privacy. No judgment is reported;[14] but, as we have seen, in a few years' time light was held not to be a natural right. In another early Elizabethan case, a barrister brought an action on the case against a neighbouring schoolmaster because the 'jabber of boys' disturbed the quiet of his chambers. The action failed, apparently on the ground that it was lawful to set up school anywhere; and the lawyer had to move his study to another side of the house.[15] It was further settled, in 1587, that although an action would lie for obstructing ancient lights, it could not be brought for 'a matter of pleasure only', such as a pleasant view, however ancient the prospect.[16] In the case of smell, liability was probably founded on the danger of infection rather than the distastefulness as

---

13. *Hales' Case* (c. 1560), published as *A Briefe Declaration for what manner of speciall Nusance . . . a man may have his remedy* (1636), per Mounson. The cheese problem was discussed in *Wiseman v Denham* (1623) Palm 341, Ley 69.
14. *Hales' Case* (c. 1560), last note.
15. *Jeffrey's Case* (bef. 1567) HLS MS 2069, f.206v. The plaintiff, John Jeffrey, became a serjeant in 1567 and was later Chief Baron of the Exchequer.
16. *Bland v Moseley* (1587) cit. 9 Co Rep at 58 per Wray CJ.

such; fresh air was a matter of health as well as feeling. In the leading case, the defendant had erected a pig-stye so near the plaintiff's land that unhealthy odours flowed through his hall and made the house uninhabitable. Counsel argued that pigs were necessary as food, and that a man should not have such a delicate nose as to object to them. But it was held that the action lay, for putrefying the air.[17]

In all these cases argument turned in part on the utility or necessity of the defendant's conduct. Someone had to keep pigs, and school-boys, and the trades of butcher, tanner and dyer were well established and necessary to the common wealth, notwithstanding the unpleasant side-effects of their activities. Yet a line had to be drawn somewhere. The problem was fully discussed in 1629, in a case concerning the burning of sea-coal in a brewhouse erected within six feet of the office of a bishop's registrar, so that the fumes damaged the registrar's papers and utensils. The court considered that it was not inherently unlawful to burn sea-coal, 'though it is not as sweet as wood', and that '*si home est cy* tender-nosed *que ne poit endurer* sea-coal *il doit lesser son mease*'. They allowed the action, nevertheless, because the fumes were excessive by reason of their continuous emission and had actually caused damage to property.[18] From this point it became clear that if an activity amounted to a nuisance, it was actionable regardless of its utility; and this is the present law. Noxious processes must be carried out in such places and in such manner that they do not hurt individual landowners; a butcher, said Jones J in the 1629 case, was acceptable in Newgate shambles but not in Cheapside.[19] Whether an activity amounts to a nuisance depends on whether those affected by it ought reasonably to be expected to put up with it; and although the law does not protect oversensitivity, it will provide a remedy against anything insalubrious or offensive which renders the enjoyment of life and property unduly uncomfortable. The standard of reasonableness is, of course, ever shifting. In Victorian times it was held very low, and the law of nuisance proved helpless in controlling some of the very unpleasant industrial processes considered vital to the nation's economy. The most effective weapon against large-scale industrial nuisances in modern times is public-health legislation, such as the statute which abolished London smog overnight.[20]

17. *Aldred v Benton* (1610) 9 Co Rep 57. On 'infectious smells', *R v Rockett* (1607) Exeter College Oxford MS 93, f.62v per Williams J.
18. *Jones v Powell* (1629) Palm 536, Hutton 135, HLS MS 106, ff.190v, 342v, HLS MS 1083, ff.50v–53; Cambridge Univ Lib MS Dd. 12. 48, ff.115v–120.
19. Ibid., from HLS MS 1083. See also *St Helen's Smelting Co v Tipping* (1865) 11 HL Cas 642.
20. Clean Air Act 1968 (c.62).

DISTURBANCES

In the same way as the action on the case came to replace the assize for easements and profits, so also it came to replace the assize for franchises and offices. These latter are not properly within the ambit of nuisance, in the technical sense of the word, but the remedies are so closely analogous that there is no material difference between them. Thus, trespass on the case could be employed to protect the franchise rights attaching to markets or ferries, where competitors set up rival markets or ferries contrary to the franchise. Economic rights other than franchises, such as the manorial right of mill-suit, were similarly protected.[21] An office of profit, granted by letters patent as a freehold interest, was protected after 1285 by the assize. Unlike a mere employment, an office was granted by or through the Crown, to have and to hold for life or in fee, and had to be exercised in a certain place. It was a form of real property not unlike an easement exercised over the place where the office was performed. For example, an officer of a court of law could bring the assize to recover his office, and the proprietary nature of the claim is shown by the allegation of seisin by taking fees in the place where he sat in court. In 1608 an assize was brought by the master of the king's tennis games (*magister ludorum pilarum palmarium regis*), and the judgment was that he recover his seisin in the tennis courts (*in spheristiis*).[22] The assize for an office survived into the seventeenth century, but where there was no complete usurpation of the office, or where the claimant had had no prior seisin, the action on the case was more appropriate. Case for disturbance in an office did not enjoy a long history, however, because a better remedy was found in the quasi-contractual claim for money had and received in respect of the intercepted fees.[23]

The disappearance of alienable and inheritable offices made actions concerning title to offices obsolete. But the action on the case was not confined to the situations covered by the assize, and it lay for disturbing miscellaneous rights which were not otherwise protected; for instance, the right to sit in a particular pew in a church.[24] The development of this innominate class of actions for disturbances reached its furthest point in the important constitutional case of *Ashby v White*, which settled the right of a parliamentary elector to sue a returning officer who wrongfully refused to receive his vote. The pleadings show an affinity to more conventional nuisance and

21. See p. 376, post.
22. *Webbe v Knivet* (1608) 8 Co Rep 45.
23. See p. 308, ante.
24. *Dawney v Dee* (1620) Cro Jac 605, 2 Rolle Rep 139, Palmer 46.

disturbance actions, but the right to vote was not a property right in the strict sense and the majority of the King's Bench judges thought the action would not lie because it was unprecedented. Holt CJ, in an outstanding judgment which was later upheld by the House of Lords, dissented, on the grounds that 'if the plaintiff has a right he must of necessity have the means to vindicate it and a remedy if he is injured in the enjoyment or exercise of it'.[25] *Ubi jus ibi remedium*. The action for disturbance would not, however, avail a plaintiff who could not assert some legal right. Purely economic nuisance, in the absence of a franchise, custom or prescriptive privilege, was not actionable.[26]

Isolated Occurrences

Since the essence of nuisance was an interference with the enjoyment of property, it was usually a continuing wrong. The plaintiff's inconvenience and damage were increased by the duration of the nuisance; and the older real remedies depended on its continuance, because their object was abatement. The real actions would not have lain for a spent nuisance; but in the action on the case it was irrelevant whether the act complained of was past or continuing. The medieval action against the owner of straying cattle, later called 'cattle-trespass', is perhaps best regarded as a species of nuisance in respect of occasional escapes. But there is no reason why it should have been confined to animals: presumably each time rain dripped from the defendant's eaves onto the plaintiff's house there was a nuisance, and each little hurt merged in the whole continuing nuisance.

That a single unrepeated catastrophe might be actionable was confirmed in 1704. The defendant had failed to repair the wall of his 'privy house of office' (latrine), and when the wall collapsed the filth flowed into the plaintiff's cellar and contaminated his beer and coal supply. Holt CJ applied the *alterum non laedere* principle and allowed the action; the law would be the same, he observed, if a large dung heap collapsed onto the plaintiff's land.[27] The principle underlying that decision and also the actions for fire, *scienter* and cattle-trespass was reformulated in a celebrated case of 1866 in terms of a general strict liability for damage caused by the escape of something brought onto adjoining land and which is liable to do mischief if it escapes.[28]

25. (1703) 2 Ld Raym 938, 953.
26. See pp. 376, 387, post.
27. *Tenant v Goldwin* (1704) 2 Ld Raym 1089, 3 Ld Raym 324, 6 Mod Rep 311.
28. *Fletcher v Rylands* (1866) LR 1 Exch 265; affd. sub nom. *Rylands v Fletcher* (1868) LR 3 HL 330 (water in reservoir).

Harmful escapes of this kind have remained a separate category in the law of tort, because they are actionable without proof of negligence; and the principle has been extended far beyond the traditional scope of nuisance to include such 'escapes' as sparks from a railway engine or the collapse of a flag-pole in Hyde Park. Nevertheless, the modern tendency is to impose liability only for fault, and so the judges have expressed their unwillingness to extend the principle beyond escapes.[29]

Common or Public Nuisances

The word 'nuisance' was used in the criminal law to describe the wide class of misdemeanours which were said to be committed 'to the common nuisance of the king's liege subjects'.[30] The scope of common nuisance was far wider than that of private injury to land. There was an area of overlap, because many forms of private nuisance became common when committed in a city or town; for example, by piling rubbish in public places so as to increase the risk of plague, or setting up butcher's stalls in the street and leaving entrails in the gutters, or generating industrial fumes. The health hazards in a city like London were enormous; even in the seventeenth century it was necessary to dissuade visitors to St Paul's from urinating in the doorways and aisles, and such unseemly practices in public places, there being no public lavatories, were complained of as late as the 1750s.[31] The rights of the general public to use the highway and the navigable river were analogous to easements, in that to pollute, obstruct or encroach upon them was an indictable nuisance. But common nuisance also comprehended such diverse wrongs as storing gunpowder in a dangerous place, keeping a dovecote, and being a common scold. Bawdy houses and gambling dens were indictable nuisances, and even inns and alehouses could be illegal if they exceeded reasonable local requirements. In 1671 a rope-dancer in the Strand, whom the judges had espied on their way to Westminster, was convicted of creating a public nuisance; apart from blocking the highway, he had inveigled apprentices from their shops and encouraged idle persons to stand and gape.[32]

---

29. See *Read v J. Lyons & Co Ltd* [1947] AC 156, [1946] 2 All ER 471 (explosion in munitions factory causing injury on premises) esp. at 171 per Lord Macmillan.
30. A nuisance merely to *'divers* of the king's liege subjects' was not indictable: *R v Hayward* (1589) Cro Eliz 148.
31. J. Weever *Funeral Monuments* (1767 edn), p. 163; *An Essay on Decorations and Embellishments for the City of London* (1734).
32. *R v Hall* (1671) 1 Vent 169.

The relevance of these miscellaneous misdemeanours to private law is that no private action in tort could be brought to recover damages for a nuisance which was common to the whole locality. If it were otherwise, a wrongdoer might be subject to hundreds of actions for the same offence. The proper course was for an indictment to be preferred against the offender;[33] or, in later times, a 'relator' action by the attorney-general to secure an injunction. It was nevertheless admitted in the sixteenth century that an action could be brought for any extraordinary damage which an individual suffered over and above that which he suffered in common with everyone else. The point was still uncertain in 1535. In that year a plaintiff complained that the highway had been obstructed with offal, and that he and his visitors had been thereby prevented from reaching his close, which adjoined the highway. Baldwin CJ thought no action would lie, and recommended an indictment for common nuisance. But Fitzherbert J said that if a particular person suffered more hurt or inconvenience than the generality he could maintain an action. He gave the example of a man who fell into a ditch across the highway; he should be allowed to sue the malefactor in respect of this special loss.[34] Fitzherbert J's view prevailed; but the reasoning continued to deny a private action to someone who had suffered no damage greater than that suffered by the rest of the community.[35]

Some conceptual confusion has arisen from calling these private actions 'nuisance'. They have little, if any, affinity with private nuisance and were in fact innominate actions to recover compensation for the special loss. If they belong to any particular genus it is the tort of negligence. The significance of common or public nuisance in the realms of tort is not that it furnishes a distinct cause of action which would not otherwise exist, but that it takes away existing causes of action in order to prevent a multiplicity of lawsuits.

Further reading

Holdsworth HEL, vol. III, pp. 153–157; vol. VII, pp. 318–342

Fifoot HSCL, pp. 3–23, 93–101

Potter HIEL, pp. 417–425

P. H. Winfield, 'Interference with Public Office' (1940) 56 LQR 463–478

F. H. Newark, 'The Boundaries of Nuisance' (1949) 65 LQR 480–490

33. *Note* (1465) YB Pas 5 Edw IV, 2, pl.4 per Heydon, who refers to a 'popular action' by presentment.
34. *Sowthall v Dagger* (1535) Kiralfy AC, p. 211, Fifoot HSCL, p. 98.
35. *Fineux v Hovenden* (1599) Cro Eliz 664; *Iveson v Moore* (1699) 1 Ld Raym 486.

A. K. R. Kiralfy, *The Action on the Case* (1951), pp. 55–72

J. F. Brenner, 'Nuisance Law and the Industrial Revolution'
(1974) 3 *Jo Legal Studies* 403–433

J. Loengard, 'The Assize of Nuisance' [1978] CLJ 144–166

J. H. Baker, 'Nuisance' (1978) 94 SS *232–236*

21. Defamation

Words can be more harmful than deeds, and in some circumstances honour may be more tender than personal safety. Yet the common law has always been more reluctant to award remedies for damage caused by words than for damage caused by deeds. It was centuries before mere words were considered capable of constituting an assault or imprisonment, and only within the last fifteen years that words causing financial loss have been brought within the scope of liability for negligence. The reason usually advanced for the lack of a common law remedy for defamation before 1500 is that it was a spiritual matter more properly within the jurisdiction of the Church courts. These courts heard complaints of defamation and could sentence the guilty party to penance. What was in form a criminal proceeding could be turned virtually into a civil remedy by allowing the penance to be redeemed for a fine payable to the plaintiff. But if the defamation touched any temporal matter, for instance an accusation of felony, the ecclesiastical courts would be restrained by prohibition from proceeding in the matter. There was thus a real gap in the law, not just an exclusive principle of jurisdiction. The most serious kinds of false accusation—those which concerned a man's life—could be remedied neither in the royal courts nor the Church courts. There may at an early date have been adequate remedies in some of the local courts; but it is unlikely that the existence of such remedies, which were soon caught by the forty-shilling limitation on local courts, satisfied popular demand. The absence of a common law remedy for defamation in medieval times is therefore not entirely attributable to jurisdictional boundaries. There was in addition the deep-rooted feeling that mere words were not as serious as sticks and stones and could not give occasion to actions of trespass. It was wrong to tell lies, but the wrong was a form of immorality best punished by the Church. It was wrong to provoke disorder, but that was a matter for the criminal law and the minor local courts. Harsh words hurt feelings, but the only material damage they could cause was an indirect result of their effect on the conduct of third parties.[1] Such evanescent or indirect harm was at fist

1. Compare the 'economic torts', chap XXII, post.

beneath the notice of the courts at Westminster. Defamation, like breach of a parol promise, according to the common law of the fourteenth and fifteenth centuries was *damnum absque injuria*: a damage, but not a tort.

Nevertheless, the exclusion of actions for defamatory words was never absolute. From the beginning of the fourteenth century there had been actions by judges accused of misconduct, a kind of civil action for contempt. Later in the century there appeared an action of trespass for 'lying in wait' and threatening to seize a man as a villein; although ostensibly founded on an ambush, the essence of these increasingly common actions was merely the assertion of a wrongful claim (on which the status could be tried), and in 1483 after long debate it was held that the action lay even if no threats had been made.[2] By that time several actions had also been brought on the 1378 statute of *scandalum magnatum* by peers, bishops and judges who had been defamed. The policy of parliament in 1378 (three years before the peasants' revolt) had been to prevent discord between classes, but the purpose of an action on the statute was clearly to vindicate the magnate's name. There had been isolated attempts at a more general remedy. In 1382 a married man recovered damages for a false statement that he had precontracted marriage with another woman, which he presented as a fraudulent scheme to separate him from his wife and ruin him.[3] Again, in the 1430s, a court official sued in respect of an allegation of misconduct which had led to his suspension while the allegation was investigated.[4] And it may be that, as with the villein cases, wrongs of a defamatory nature were sometimes coloured by allegations of real or pretended violence; only if the defendant pleaded the facts specially would the real cause of action appear on the record.[5]

The judges changed their minds, to permit a general action on the case, in the decade 1508–17. One reason may have been the decline of the ecclesiastical and local courts in the early Tudor period, and another may have been the threat of jurisdictional competition from

2. *Broune v Haukyns* (1476–83) 94 SS *237*, Fifoot HSCL, p. 139. For the other cases in this paragraph, see 94 SS *236–237, 244.*
3. *Roshale v Thorne* (1382) 88 SS 22. Thorne was a notary who had promised the wife to arrange a divorce, and the *falsum instrumentum* on which the action was brought may have been a document in the cause.
4. *T.B. v R.S.* (undated) 94 SS *236*.
5. *Prior of C's Case* (1384) YB 7 Ric II, Lincoln's Inn MS 77, f.208v. The prior brought trespass *sur son case* for an assault (with force and arms) which disturbed him from holding court; the defendant pleaded that he had merely accused the prior of ruling contrary to law. (This was brought to our attention by Dr M. S. Arnold.)

the Star Chamber.[6] It is no mere coincidence that the actions on the case for not paying debts, for converting goods, and for breach of promise, were all sanctioned by the King's Bench in the same period. The very first actions on the case for words are undetermined suits in the plea rolls, and there is no accompanying year-book discussion from which the reasons for the new policy may be discovered. Yet it is noticeable that the actions were all brought for damage suffered as a result of words which were excluded from the spiritual jurisdiction, and it seems probable that the main reason for admitting the new actions by the royal courts was the absence of an alternative remedy.

WORDS ENDANGERING LIFE OR LIBERTY

The first actions on the case for slander are found in the plea rolls of 1508 and concern accusations of theft. Over the next thirty years, over one hundred allegations of theft were made the basis of King's Bench actions, in addition to accusations of murder and other offences, and also villein-claims made without threats or lying in wait. The common factor in these cases is an accusation which endangered the life or liberty of the plaintiff, for instance by arrest and trial, or seizure by the lord; and in some cases an actual imprisonment was mentioned in aggravation. The pleadings usually also contained formal allegations of deceit, and of special damage through the loss of credit with persons who had stopped dealing with the plaintiff as a result of the scandal. An action on the case could be founded on this economic or financial loss without running the risk of objection on the grounds that it was purely spiritual.

WORDS ALLEGING PROFESSIONAL INCOMPETENCE

A second situation where financial loss regularly gave rise to actions on the case for words, in the first half of the sixteenth century, occurred when the words endangered the plaintiff's income from his profession or calling. Here, again, was the kind of damage for which the common law ought to give redress and for which there was no remedy elsewhere. Thus, a lawyer could show that he had lost clients and fees, or a merchant his customers and their trade, as a result of allegations of dishonesty or incompetence. By Elizabethan times all sorts of imputation might be actionable because they touched the plaintiff in his occupation or calling, which would not otherwise have been actionable. Thus it was not in itself actionable to call someone a

6. A slander case had been heard in Star Chamber as early as 1433: 94 SS *236*. See also *Ravensworth's Case* (1339) 76 SS 83, Co Inst, vol. III, p. 174. These were private complaints, but also public or 'criminal' inquiries.

bankrupt; but to call a merchant a bankrupt would obviously threaten his livelihood. Likewise, there was no remedy simply for saying that a man was ignorant or illiterate; but the same words spoken of a barrister would be actionable, because it was necessary to his vocation to be able to read, and no one would engage him if they believed he could not.

'SPIRITUAL' MATTERS

The use of actions on the case to fill the obvious void probably met little resistance. But it was not clear at first whether the new action could also be used as an alternative to the ecclesiastical remedy where the slander was of a kind within the permitted jurisdiction of the Church. The conservative view was that there could be no overlapping, because the king's courts should not meddle with spiritual matters. The Common Pleas accordingly held in 1535 that they would not entertain an action by a man who had been called a heretic, for they had no power to try heresy. The bolder view, held by the ecclesiastical reformers and the King's Bench judges, was that 'spiritual' defamation was actionable provided it caused temporal loss. The King's Bench accordingly gave judgment in 1537 in favour of another man falsely accused of heresy. The King's Bench also allowed actions where an allegation of sexual misbehaviour resulted in a lost marriage, or an allegation of bastardy—which, although a spiritual matter, was not even defamatory—resulted in problems over inheritance. As was later explained, the cause of action was not the accusation itself but the temporal damage which it caused. Proof of temporal damage was therefore essential.[7]

WORDS IMPUTING CERTAIN DISEASES

The frequency with which irate Elizabethans accused each other, usually in anger, of having the pox produced a third category of slander actions, which has enjoyed a separate existence in the text-books down to the present day. It was not actionable to say that someone was ill, unless the illness affected his calling; for instance, to whisper abroad that an attorney was insane, or that a barber was prone to fits of *delirium tremens*. But the imputation of pox, meaning the French pox (syphilis), was obviously a form of abuse, and a particularly harmful allegation because it could easily lead to the ostracism of the person concerned. The courts met the heavy demand for redress

---

7. *Davis v Gardiner* (1593) 4 Co Rep 16, Fifoot HSCL, p. 144. For the earlier cases, see 94 SS *238–242*.

in such cases[8] by giving an action without proof of special loss. The actions were effectively confined to French pox, though it was said that an action lay for imputing leprosy to the plaintiff, because lepers could be ostracised by process of law (the writ *de leproso amovendo* to put them in quarantine).

Attempts to Abate the Flood of Actions

Within half a century of their first appearance, the new actions for words had become part of the everyday business of the common law courts, in particular the King's Bench. An analysis of a King's Bench plea roll of 1566 showed that there were thirty bills or declarations in slander compared with forty-two in *assumpsit* and only two in conversion.[9] At times slander probably outnumbered even *assumpsit*. The judges began to regret the freedom they had given to plaintiffs, especially since juries frequently awarded sums of money quite disproportionate to the harm and to the ability of the wrongdoer to pay. A spirit of repression therefore began to manifest itself.

As early as 1566, Staunford J approved a remark by Dyer that actions on the case for words had become too common because they were brought for 'every trifling thing', and that they properly lay only for an accusation of an offence or an imputation upon a person's 'mystery' or profession.[10] No doubt he should have added 'without proof of special damage', for that would render anything actionable. One reason for the increase in slander actions was that the courts had not allowed issue to be joined on the special damage, which therefore came to be presumed or fictitious. The more restrictive approach, which is still repeated in modern textbooks, was to insist on proof of special damage in all but the established categories mentioned by Staunford J, with the later additions of allegations of pox and libels.

A second line of attack was directed against actions for words spoken in anger or sport. It was held in 1565 that such words were not actionable, and that the plaintiff had to allege malice.[11] This requirement made little sense where the words had caused actual damage, and so it was not developed. The allegation of malice, though it

---

8. The first instance noted in the rolls is *Thumworth v Potte* (1543) KB 27/1127, m.104d.
9. Kiralfy AC, p. 195.
10. *Anon* (1556) Anthony Gell MS Rep, f.32v ('false knave' not actionable).
11. *Anon* (1565) Lincoln's Inn MS Maynard 86, f.34.

became common form, was not normally investigated, and it only became important when certain defences were raised.

The third and most effective attack began in the 1580s when the courts embarked upon a policy of construing ambiguous or doubtful words in the milder sense (*in mitiori sensu*) so that they would not be actionable. Even the King's Bench, normally keen to attract litigation, espoused this policy. They did so because, as Wray CJ lamented in 1585, 'the intemperance and malice of men increase' and were not to be judicially encouraged.[12] The policy was carried to absurd extremes, and ambiguities were exposed where no ordinary person would have felt any doubts. Thus, a mere imputation of 'pox' would be taken to mean small pox, which (for some reason now obscure) was not actionable unless further words were added which made it clear that only French pox was intended; even the expression 'pocky whore', which gave rise to a number of cases, was held not to refer necessarily to the French pox. On the same principle, the courts would construe a statement that a man had stolen apples to mean that he had purloined growing apples, in which case there was no felony. It was not even actionable to say that a physician had killed a patient with his pills; the patient might have suffered an unusual reaction, and so there was not necessarily any medical incompetence alleged, let alone murder.[13] Two cases of 1607 illustrate the absurdities which the *mitior sensus* approach encouraged. In the one, the defendant had said that the plaintiff 'struck his cook on the head with a cleaver, and cleaved his head; the one part lay on the one shoulder, and another part on the other'. The court held that an action would not lie, because the cook might have survived 'and then it is but a trespass'.[14] In the other case the defendant had said that a justice of the peace 'reported that he hath had the use of the Lady Morrison's body at his pleasure'. Lady Morrison's action succeeded, but no less a lawyer than Hobart, Attorney-General, argued that the words should be taken in the best sense: 'to have the use of her body as a tailor, in measuring'.[15]

Such cases continued to exercise the ingenuity of the legal profession until the later seventeenth century, but it is doubtful how far the unrealistic hair-splitting did in fact deter prospective litigants. Plaintiffs in slander are not always primarily interested in damages.

12. *Stanhope v Blith* (1585) 4 Co Rep 15, Fifoot HSCL, p. 142. Coke said (preface to 1604 edn) he had reported this and similar cases to deter men from bringing expensive suits 'for words, which are but wind'.
13. *Poe v Mondford* (1598) Cro Eliz 620.
14. *Holt v Astgrigg* (1607) Cro Jac 184.
15. *Morrison v Cade* (1607) Cro Jac 162, HLS MS 105, f.106v.

Litigation enabled the aggrieved sense of honour or pride to be vindicated by jury verdicts, and allowed the plaintiff to retaliate openly in court, even if the verdict was later upset by the lawyers. The author of a book on slander in 1647 attested that actions for words continued to bring 'as much grist to the mill, if not more, than any one branch of the law whatsoever'.[16]

The Scope of Defamation

The *mitior sensus* rule adds amusement to the older law reports, but it has had little ultimate effect on the law. A reaction against it began in the mid-seventeenth century. Rolle CJ, who collected many of the ridiculous cases in his *Abridgement*, as a judge disliked strained interpretations because they enabled a man to be 'abused by subtlety'. By 1714 the judges had finally put an end to the old approach, on the ground that 'people should not be discouraged that put their trust in the law, for if [men] could not have a remedy at law for such slanders they would be apt to carve it for themselves, which would let in all the ill consequences of private revenge'. Words were therefore to be taken in their 'most natural and obvious' sense.[17] The rule about special damage, on the other hand, had the important effect of putting the emphasis in slander actions on the kind of damage suffered rather than on the kind of words spoken. The remedy was given for the damage caused by the words, not for the words alone. In the absence of special loss, the only remedy for defamatory words was in the spiritual courts, and this was available only if the words charged the party with a 'spiritual offence', such as fornication, heresy or drunkenness. Defamation continued to provide the consistory courts of the seventeenth century with much business, even though they could not award damages; the sentence of penance, performed in a white sheet, gave the plaintiff better satisfaction than money. Nevertheless, there remained a large number of cases in which there was no remedy at all, because the words were not spiritual and did not cause temporal loss.

The law did not at first consider whether the false words disparaged the plaintiff's character, but only whether they resulted in loss. A right-thinking person does not think less of another for being poor or illegitimate or foreign, and yet a person might well suffer loss from being wrongly given such attributes. It is hardly infamous to have a

16. J. March *Actions for Slander* (1647), p. 2.
17. *Hamond v Kingsmill* (1647) Style 22, 23; *Harrison v Thornborough* (1714) Gilb Cas 114 at 117 per Parker CJ (citing Treby), 10 Mod Rep 196, 198.

sweetheart; it might be thought flattering. But if a stranger wrote to a woman calling her his sweetheart, and the letter came to the notice of her fiancé, who as a consequence broke off the engagement to marry, the woman might have been able to sue for damages.[18] If untruths caused harm there was no need to show that they were also defamatory. On the other hand, plainly disparaging words might be irremediable. Until 1891 there was no redress for calling a woman a whore, unless she could prove special loss.[19] And there is still no action for imputing unchastity to a man; and so a parson had no remedy at common law against those who spread a 'very scandalous' rumour that he had slept with all the women between his parish and another.[20]

In the eighteenth century, the courts began to require not only that there should be loss but also that the words which caused it should be capable of bearing a defamatory meaning. The purpose was to withhold frivolous actions from juries, paticularly once the *mitior sensus* method of doing that had been abandoned. The old word slander (*scandalum*) may always have imported the idea of 'infamy, discredit or disgrace',[21] but it was difficult to define a legal concept of defamation which would also include such sinless misfortunes as poverty and illness. The formulation which was adopted in the eighteenth century was that the words should expose the plaintiff to 'hatred, contempt or ridicule'[22] or tend to cause him to be shunned or avoided.[23] This remains the essential characteristic of the tort of defamation, though it is unduly restrictive. Were it not for this narrowing of definition, the action for causing financial loss by careless misstatements about a person's credit might have been developed with less trouble from the action on the case for words.

Since the basis of the action[24] for words was the loss of credit or fame, and not the insult, it was always necessary to show a publication of the words. A man could not lose credit as a result of words

---

18. *Sheppard v Wakeman* (1662) 1 Keb 255, 269, 308, 326, 459, 1 Sid 79. Cf. slander of title, p. 385, post.
19. *Lynch v Knight* (1861) 9 HL Cas 577; Slander of Women Act 1891, 54 & 55 Vic, c.51.
20. *Yates v Lodge* (1681) 3 Lev 18. It would have been otherwise if it had cost him his living.
21. *Smale v Hammon* (1610) 1 Bulst 40 per Williams J. This formulation was criticised in *Holt v Scholefeld* (1796) 6 Term Rep 691 at 694 per Lawrence J.
22. W. Hawkins *Pleas of the Crown* (2nd edn, 1724), vol. I, p. 193, defining *criminal* libel. (This was brought to our attention by Mr J. R. Spencer.)
23. See *Villers v Monsley* (1769) 2 Wils. 403.
24. This was not so of criminal libel, which was punished by the Star Chamber as a 'provocation to a challenge or a breach of the peace': *Sir Baptist Hicks' Case* (1618) Hob 215.

which reached no one's ears but his own. At one time it was said that publication had to be to someone other than a friend of the plaintiff, presumably because a friend could be relied on to discount the scandal; but in the time of Elizabeth I it was established that communication to anyone other than the plaintiff was sufficient, provided that it either resulted in actual special loss or fell within one of the categories where the formal allegation of loss was non-traversable and immaterial. The one essential was that the words should have been understandable in a defamatory sense by the persons to whom they were published.[25] If that sense was not evident from the words themselves, which were invariably set out verbatim in the bill or declaration, it was explained in an *innuendo* clause, a pleading device first developed in the 1540s to explain indefinite pronouns in defamatory speech.[26]

JUSTIFICATION AND PRIVILEGE

In 1535 it was held that a man could sue for defamation even though he was of bad fame already; the essence of actionable slander was not the general reputation of the plaintiff, but the untruth of the particular assertion and the damage it caused.[27] Every man, however wicked, had the right to protection against false statements to his detriment. As a corollary, the defendant in slander could justify his words by pleading that they were true;[28] truth, even when it hurt, was an absolute defence. The courts were careful, even at the height of the *mitior sensus* cult, to prevent the abuse of the defence. The defendant's words might be literally true and yet carry a defamatory meaning; for instance, 'I think X is a thief', or 'I value Y no more than a dog', or 'someone told me that Z stole a sheep'. The defendant was not permitted to justify by proving his thoughts or opinions to be genuine; and, although it was for a while held on high authority that he could justify by identifying the source of his information[29]—a sort of voucher to warranty—the repetition of the rumour came to be considered a new publication to which the defence of truth was not allowed. There had been a school of thought in Henry VIII's reign that truth should not always be a defence, but that accusations of crime should only be made in due course of justice. This was exploded at an early date, except as to criminal libel, to which truth is still no defence.

25. See *Jones v Dawkes* (1597) Rolle Abr, vol. I, p. 74 (Latin); *Price v Jenkings* (1601) Cro Eliz 865 (Welsh).
26. E.g. 'he (meaning [*innuendo*] the plaintiff) is a thief'.
27. *Maunder v Ware* (1535) YB Hil 26 Hen VIII, 9 pl. 1; 94 SS *247* n.5.
28. *Legat v Bull* (1533) Spelman Rep (93 SS) 7.
29. *Earl of Northampton's Case, A.-G. v Gooderick* (1612) 12 Co Rep 132.

When truth became a justification, or absolute defence, the defence of 'privilege' was seen as something different and more qualified. Privilege is an excuse for speaking words believed to be true, though in fact they are false, on occasions when public policy requires openness. What is said in the course of judicial proceedings has always been privileged; the reason being that the public interest requires witnesses and counsel and judges to be unfettered by fear of actions being brought against them. The recognition of this privilege accounts for the origin of the tort of malicious prosecution in the 1540s to provide a remedy in cases where the privilege was abused.[30] By Lord Mansfield's time a similar result could be achieved in a slander action, by allowing the plaintiff to rebut the defence of privilege by proving malice; malice destroyed privilege and rendered the speaker liable to an action.

Libel

Before 1660 the common law drew no distinction between written and spoken defamation, and the distinction was disregarded by Blackstone a century later. 'It matters not how the words (if they be actionable) be published or divulged, whether by writing or by speech; for the action is maintainable in both cases.'[31]

The distinction now made between libel and slander is founded on the principle that where the defamation is in written or permanent form there is no need to prove special damage. We have seen that in the sixteenth century three categories of defamation were actionable without proof of special damage: accusations of criminal offences, unfitness for a calling, and certain infectious diseases. There was never any decision to close this list, though as a general principle 'spiritual defamation' and other harmful words were only remedied on proof of temporal damage. The distinction was not always sharp, because it might depend on whether damage could be presumed; and it was perhaps once orthodox learning that damage could be presumed in cases of 'great and malicious scandal' even if they did not fall within the three common categories.[32] As a result, there was an undeveloped fourth category of words actionable per se by reason of

30. 94 SS *247*. Doubts about the action were settled by *Knight v Jerman* (1589) Cro Eliz 70, 134.
31. W. Sheppard *Epitome* (1656), p. 21.
32. E.g. *Barnabas v Trawnter* (1640) Rolle Abr, vol. I, p. 37 (excommunication). An earlier example is *Morrison v Cade* (1607), p. 369, ante, where Popham CJ said the words were so foul and unclean that £100 damages were scarcely sufficient.

their being particularly malignant or widely disseminated. In the earliest cases in which writing was said to displace the need for special damage, it seems the libel was of a nature which fitted this fourth category.[33] Soon the courts lost sight of the principle, and came to regard writing as itself constituting the fourth category. By 1812, Mansfield CJ pronounced the rule as clear, even though he could not discern the reason behind it.[34] As a consequence, English law now draws a distinction between libel (permanent forms of defamation, even if not in writing) and slander (evanescent forms of defamation, such as speech). The distinction is not very useful, nor very practicable in an age of gramophone records and television; and although scholars have found some pleasure in its intricacies, their discussions betray the want of a rational foundation.

Further reading

Holdsworth HEL, vol. VIII, pp. 333–378

Fifoot HSCL, pp. 126–154

Milsom HFCL, pp. 332–344

R. H. Helmholz, 'Canonical Defamation in Medieval England' (1971) 15 AJLH, pp. 255–268

J. M. Kaye, 'Libel and Slander—Two Torts or One?' (1975) 91 LQR 524–539

J. H. Baker, 'Defamation' (1978) 94 SS *236–248*

J. R. Spencer, 'The Press and the Reform of Criminal Libel' in *Reshaping the Criminal Law* (P. R. Glazebrook, Ed, 1978), 266–286

33. *King v Lake* (1668) Hard 470, Kiralfy SB, p. 154. Cf. *Austin v Culpeper* (1683) Skin 123, 2 Shower KB 313, Fifoot HSCL, p. 146, which could be read in either sense.
34. *Thorley v Lord Kerry* (1812) 4 Taunt 355, Fifoot HSCL, p. 149.

22. Economic Torts

The actions of trespass *vi et armis*, and the actions on the case for negligence, conversion, and nuisance, all lay in respect of some interference with the person or property of the plaintiff. The action for words protected a more subtle kind of interest; we have seen that it did not lie for the insult to the plaintiff, but for the economic and social damage done to the plaintiff through the withdrawal of third parties from relationship with him. The narrowing of that action to defamatory words made it a fairly distinct legal compartment, but in its origin and in its nature it was one of a family of actions which have never earned a comprehensive name.[1] The innominate torts which consist in the infringement of economic or social interests are coming to be known as the 'economic torts'. Their common feature is that they usually involve three or more parties: the plaintiff, the defendant, and the party whose relationship with the plaintiff is interfered with, or unspecified people (such as potential customers) who might but for the interference enter into a relationship with the plaintiff. The indirectness of the harm does not diminish the wrong: one may break bones with sticks and stones, but to ruin a man usually requires the use of influences upon others. Yet the balancing of interests can be uncommonly difficult. It is not unlawful to ruin a man by fair competition, and so the mere fact that the defendant has caused damage to the plaintiff by his activities does not give the latter a cause of action. Unless some legal right is infringed, the loss is *damnum absque injuria*. Moreover, the law is loath to recognise a right to be exempt from economic rivalry, because freedom of trade is more in the public interest than monopoly. Broadly speaking, there are two situations where the law protects economic interests by actions in tort. The first is where the law has given the means of acquiring a monopoly, a right to be exempt from competition. The second is where an existing relationship or state of affairs is interfered with by unlawful means. In both situations innominate actions on the case were devised to enable

---

1. F. A. Shaw dubbed it in 1942 the tort of 'interference', but English writers now use this term in a narrower sense and it has therefore been avoided here.

aggrieved persons to obtain compensation in damages; and in some cases equity assisted by means of injunctions.

Monopolies

It has always been a cardinal principle of the common law that a person does not, by having a de facto monopoly of a particular trade in a particular place, thereby acquire a legal monopoly which will entitle him to prevent others from setting up in competition. The only advantage gained by being first in the field is the goodwill thereby accumulated. This was laid down in 1410 in a celebrated case which the courts have followed ever since. Two masters of an ancient grammar school brought an action in the Common Pleas against another master who had recently set up a rival school in the same town and compelled them to halve their fees in order to compete. It was held that they had no cause of action, because they had no exclusive proprietary right in education and it was lawful for any qualified master to teach children.[2]

It was agreed in the argument of that case that a miller had no action if he lost business through the erection of a new mill. However, it was possible in the case of a mill and certain other trades to acquire a monopoly by prescription; that is, by showing that residents had been compelled to grind their corn only at that mill since time immemorial. Such prescriptive rights were usually manorial customs; but it seems they did not have to be, so long as the plaintiff could claim through an immemorial succession of owners. The best known monopoly of this nature was a market. The lord of a market profited from the tolls taken from those who traded there, and his privilege usually excluded any other sales without toll within a certain precinct. If someone sold goods outside the market but within the precinct, in derogation from the lord's rights, an action on the case lay against him.[3] If someone set up a rival market, an assize of nuisance lay, or later an action on the case. The monopoly of grinding corn, called mill-suit, and that of baking bread, called oven-suit, were protected by the real actions *secta ad molendinum* and *secta ad furnum*. These lay only against the disloyal customers, and were in due course supplemented by actions on the case against the rivals.[4] To what extent

2. *Case of Gloucester School* (1410) YB Hil 11 Hen IV, 47, pl. 21.
3. *Prior of Coventry v Graumpé* (1309) YB Hil 2 Edw II (19 SS) 71, pl. 141; *Prior of Dunstable's Case* (1433) YB Hil 11 Hen VI, 19, pl. 13.
4. *Farmer v Brook* (1590) Cro Eliz 203, 8 Co Rep 126, 1 Leon 142 (bakery); *Hix v Gardiner* (1614) 2 Bulst 195 (mill).

other monopolies could be acquired in this way is largely an academic question, since precedents are few and discussions of principle non-existent; but there must have been a limit, because the schoolmasters of 1410 had not been allowed to assert a prescriptive title.

The other way of acquiring a monopoly was by grant from the Crown. Most markets were created in this way, by medieval charters. So also were the livery companies, which were guilds or trade associations having the privilege of being a corporation. The main object of the earlier company charters was to confer the right to associate and to set up a governing body, but in order to make these privileges more effective it was usually granted that none should follow the trade within the city in question unless he was a member. This was only a partial monopoly, since membership of the guild was not closed, and was intended to impose regulation and discipline upon a particular trade rather than to restrict the trade to specific individuals. In Elizabeth I's time, however, the Crown adopted the recent continental practice of granting monopolies to individuals who introduced new inventions into the realm. Thus began the history of patents for inventions. The first patents were in respect of manufactures, and conferred industrial rather than trading monopolies. Being confined to new manufactures, they did not harm any existing trade and no one could complain of damage. A third type of monopoly which the Crown began to grant with increasing frequency at this period was the exclusive right to conduct a trade in foreign parts. Such a right was conferred upon the incorporation of a merchant trading company by virtue of the royal prerogative to license overseas trade; and again no subject could complain of loss, because without royal licence no subject could trade overseas. Soon the known world had been shared out by charter: the medieval Merchant Venturers took central Europe, the Russia Company (1553) took northern Europe and beyond, the Levant Company (1581) took the mediterranean region, and the East India Company (1600) took Asia; Africa and America were shared out in the seventeenth century, though most of the American charters were for colonising bodies.

THE ATTACK ON MONOPOLIES

The Crown reaped much profit from these sixteenth-century monopolies. Not only could cash be demanded for issuing the patent, but royalties could be extracted from the exploitation of new inventions and explorations. By the end of Elizabeth I's reign there was a large number of monopolies, and the matter was raised as a grievance in the parliaments of 1597 and 1601. The prerogative power of granting monopolies became a grave constitutional issue which was eventually left to the courts to settle. In 1602 an action on the case was brought for infringing a patent granting the plaintiff the sole right to import foreign playing cards. The court declared the patent void, and gave judgment for the defendant. Monopolies were declared to be generally invalid because they operated in restraint of trade and tended to cause increased prices and reduced quality.[5] The decision was not intended to impeach the rights conferred on inventors; playing cards were no novelty, and in any case were not in the public interest. Nor did it strike at companies which existed to regulate rather than to limit trade, although it was established at the same period that a company could not use a power to make bye-laws to confer a monopoly on itself.[6] James I, though professing to dislike monopolies, nevertheless found it difficult to repress the greed of his ministers, and in 1624 it was felt necessary to embody the spirit of the 1602 decision in an act of parliament. All monopolies for the sole buying, selling, making or using of any thing within the realm were declared void, with certain exceptions. The exceptions were: patents for the 'sole working or making of any manner of new manufacture' granted for not more than twenty-one years to 'the first and true inventor', patents concerning printing and certain other trades of public importance, licensing of taverns, and charters to 'corporations, companies or fellowships of any art, trade, occupation or mystery'.[7]

The last proviso gave ministers the means of evasion. After the decision of 1602 a weird new batch of companies had appeared, such as the pinmakers (1605), starchmakers (1607), gold and silver thread makers (1611), brickmakers (1614), tobacco-pipe makers (1619), and so on. Even after the 1623 act, this method of evasion flourished, so that instead of granting a patent to an individual, the individual and his fellow investors were made into a company. Such foundations as the Westminster soapmakers (1631) and the Yarmouth saltmakers (1636) were blatantly private monopolies. The arrangements by which these companies paid duty to the Crown on sales yielded a vast income, and paved the way for the excise duty of post-Restoration times. The era of the monopolistic company ended, however, in the seventeenth century. The merchant companies also came under

---

5. *Case of Monopolies, Darcy v Allen* (1602) 11 Co Rep 84, Moore KB 671, Noy 173. The importation of playing cards was prohibited by Stat 3 Edw IV, c.4, and so the grant to Darcy was a dispensation.
6. *Davenant v Hurdis* (1599) 11 Co Rep 86, Moore KB 576, 591; *Tailors of Ipswich v Sheninge* (1614) 11 Co Rep 53.
7. Statute of Monopolies 1623, 21 Jac I, c.3. The principal provisions remained on the statute book until 1969.

attack. The prerogative power to create monopolies in overseas trade was vindicated in the case of the East India Company in 1683,[8] but it was also decided that the Crown could not grant the right to enforce such a monopoly by forfeiture,[9] and in fact after this period the prerogative was no longer claimed.[10]

LATER PATENT LAW

The main species of monopoly created by grant under present law is the patent for a new invention. The original justification for permitting such a privilege was that it encouraged the importation of foreign innovations into England, and thereby increased trade and employment; it seems few inventions began at home. In the eighteenth century the theoretical foundation shifted, and the judges laid it down that the object of patent law was to secure the revelation of beneficial secrets which could be generally exploited when the inventor's term was up. Increasingly it was not the right to manufacture some material which was granted but the industrial process itself, and this no doubt because of the greater sophistication of industry and an increase in home inventions. The new theory required that the inventor should prepare a specification sufficient to enable the invention to be used by posterity. A line had to be drawn, however, at pure ideas. It was not possible to gain a monopoly in an abstract idea, for scientific truths could not be owned privately; the patent could only be granted in respect of the working process, not the underlying theory.[11] The chief defect of the common law was the extraordinarily cumbersome and expensive procedure involved in obtaining letters patent under the great seal. This was remedied by a statue of 1852, which introduced the present procedure.[12]

COPYRIGHT

Closely analogous to rights in patented inventions are the rights of authors. The first forms of copyright did in fact result from patents conferring the sole rights to print particular classes of book. The prerogative of the Crown to grant this kind of copyright was limited, however, to books on subjects in which the Crown claimed a special

8. *East India Co v Sandys* (1683) 10 State Tr 371.

9. *Horne v Ivy* (1670) 1 Sid 441 (Canary Island Co); *Nightingale v Bridges* (1690) 1 Show KB 135 (Royal African Co).

10. The point was inconclusively reopened in *Merchant Adventurers Co v Rebow* (1689) 3 Mod Rep 126, Comb 53.

11. *Liardet v Johnson* (1778) 18 LQR at 285 per Lord Mansfield CJ; *Boulton and Watt v Bull* (1795) 2 Hy Bl 463. The latter case, concerning Boulton and Watt's improvements to the steam engine, proved so difficult that no decision was reached.

12. Patents for Inventions 1852, 15 & 16 Vict, c.83.

interest, such as the law, service books and bibles. Patentees could enforce their rights in the courts, but since they prevailed over the rights of the owner of the manuscript[13] their monopoly was not akin to copyright as later understood. The first suggestion that the owner of the copy had a common law right to prevent unauthorised publication occurs in an undecided action brought in respect of Bunyan's *Pilgrim's Progress* in 1679.[14] The matter was clarified by a statute of 1709, which gave fourteen years' protection to authors of books or other writings who registered them with the Stationers' Company.[15] Authors could seek an injunction in the Chancery, or an action on the case, for piracy of their work within the term. In the eighteenth century a great controversy arose as to whether literary copyright existed at common law independently of the statute. Lord Mansfield CJ and the majority of the judges held that it did, but in 1774 the House of Lords succumbed to the eloquent opposition of Lord Camden C and ruled that upon publication a book became public property at common law.[16]

The subsequent development of copyright law is a story of piecemeal legislation introduced to clear up specific doubts in the law or to assuage particular pressure groups. The old system had only contemplated copyright in printed books. It was decided in 1758 that the owner of a manuscript could restrain its publication; but doubts were cast on this by the decision of 1774, and the point was settled by statute in 1801.[17] Works of art were given protection more slowly; first by a statute of 1735 in favour of historical mezzotints, which was extended to all prints and maps in 1776, and then by a statute of 1798 covering sculptures of busts or other parts of human beings or animals. It was not until 1861 that copyright was extended to paintings, drawings and photographs.[18] Printed or engraved music was held to be within the 1709 act, but the statute of Anne could hardly be expected to accommodate live performances or gramophone recordings.[19] Oral publication of writings raised similar problems, which were solved first by equity and then by parliament: a person could be

13. *Roper v Streater* (1672) cit. Skin 234 (concerning the publication of Coke's reports).
14. *Ponder v Braddill* (1679), Lilly's *Entries*, vol. I, p. 67.
15. Copyright 1709, 8 Annae, c.19. The Stationers' Company had since the 16th century exercised considerable de facto control over book piracy.
16. *Millar v Taylor* (1769) 4 Burr 2303; *Donaldson v Beckett* (1774) 4 Burr 2408.
17. *Duke of Queensberry v Shebbeare* (1758) 2 Eden 329 (Clarendon's manuscript history of Charles II's reign); Stat 41 Geo III, c.107.
18. Stat 25 & 26 Vict, c.68 (which recites that authors of paintings etc. had no copyright). Cf. *Prince Albert v Strange* (1849) 1 H & Tw 1, 1 Mac & G 25, 2 De G & Sm 652.
19. *J. C. Bach v Longman* (1777) 2 Cowp 623; *Boosey v Whight* [1900] 1 Ch 122.

restrained from publishing notes taken down at a play or lecture,[20] and conversely a person could be restrained from performing a dramatic or musical work published by another.[21] In 1911 the mass of copyright enactments was consolidated, and since then the law has been governed by the Copyright Acts.

Loss of Services

The medieval common law allowed an action of trespass for assaulting or threatening tenants or servants so that they went away or were unable to perform their services for the plaintiff. This type of action belongs conceptually with the economic torts because, although force and arms were alleged, no force was used against the plaintiff; the action lay for the loss occasioned to the plaintiff by the interference with an existing relationship of benefit to him. Since the action lay in respect of the loss of services rather than for the forcible wrong, it was natural that it should have been extended by analogy to situations where the plaintiff was deprived of services by non-forcible conduct. The extensions led to the diverse torts of enticement, criminal conversation and inducing breaches of contract.

SERVANTS AND APPRENTICES
It is possible that the writ of trespass *vi et armis* for taking a servant was used fictitiously for competitive retaining, but by 1400 a direct remedy was available. The Ordinance and Statute of Labourers (1349–51) imposed criminal sanctions on workmen or servants who departed from their employers within the agreed term without reasonable cause, and upon those who retained or harboured deserting servants. It was soon held that a master could bring an action founded on the legislation against both the servant and his new master for damages.[22] By 1530 at the latest there was in addition an action on the case for retaining apprentices or independent contractors, who were outside the statutory remedy; and also for procuring or enticing a servant to depart from service, a wrong which could be committed by an intermediary who did not himself retain the servant.[23] This extension engendered another. If causing a loss of service was actionable, then it ought not to matter whether it occurred

---

20. *Macklin v Richardson* (1770) Amb 694 (play); *Abernethy v Hutchinson* (1825) 1 H & Tw 28 (lecture); Stat 5 & 6 Vict, c.45 (lecture right).
21. *Morris v Kelly* (1820) 1 Jac & W 481; Bulwer Lytton's Act 1836, 3 & 4 Will IV, c.15.
22. See p. 277, ante.
23. 94 SS 253–254.

because of a new retainer or for any other reason. In the sixteenth and seventeenth centuries, therefore, we find actions brought for causing loss to the master by negligently injuring the servant,[24] or even by enticing an apprentice to waste time and money at dice.[25] The master could sue for any wrong to the servant 'whereby he lost his service' (*per quod servitium amisit*). There was also an attempt in 1529 by a master to recover compensation not merely for the loss of an apprentice's service but also the wasted expenditure on the apprentice's education and clothing.[26]

WIVES AND DAUGHTERS

The servant cases were matched by similar actions in respect of wives. In these, however, the real grievance was almost always an act of infidelity or adultery. In the absence of divorce, there could be no exact analogy with the departure of a servant, but the law had no difficulty in treating the marriage relationship as equivalent for this purpose to one of service. Early actions for forcibly taking and abducting a wife with all her possessions almost certainly conceal elopements to which the wife in fact consented. On the principle that the wife's consent to adultery was unlawful and void, coupled with the notion of unity of person, the husband could bring an action jointly with his wife for battery in respect of an illicit sexual act, though it is unclear whether the wife's actual consent was needed to continue such proceedings. In the case of a daughter, where there was no possibility of a joint action, there was a medieval action of trespass for abduction; but it lay only if she were an heir presumptive, to protect the proprietary interest in her marriage.[27] It was later suggested that if an act of debauchery occurred on the property of the father he could bring trespass *quare clausum fregit*, since any implied licence to be on the premises was negatived by such behaviour, and he could recover damages for the debauchery as matter of aggravation.[28] In all these cases, however, the wrong appeared on the record as a forcible trespass to the plaintiff.

The analogy of the action on the case for causing a loss of service gave rise by the early seventeenth century to a more straightforward

---

24. E.g. *Clerk v Terrell* (1507) 94 SS *229* (shooting accident); *Everard v Hopkins* (1614) 2 Bulst 332 (negligent doctor).
25. *Whalley v Richmont* (1602) Cambridge Univ Lib MS Gg.2.5, f.331; Herne's *Pleader*, p. 161.
26. *Southworth v Blake* (1529) 94 SS *254*.
27. *Barham v Dennis* (1600) Cro Eliz 770.
28. *Russell v Corn* (1704) 6 Mod Rep 127, 2 Ld Raym 1032 per Lord Raymond CJ. Cf. *Sippora v Basset* (1664) 1 Sid 225.

remedy for interference with family relationships. The husband alone was permitted to bring an action for beating his wife 'whereby he lost her companionship' (*per quod consortium amisit*).[29] A similar action lay for seducing a maid or daughter *per quod servitium amisit*.[30] These actions were stretched to achieve their real object of providing a redress for injured feelings against adulterers and seducers. Where a wife eloped with a paramour, the old action for taking or abducting a wife was replaced by the action on the case for 'enticement',[31] which bore a strong resemblance to the action for enticing away servants. Another action, called the action for criminal conversation, appeared at about the same time to redress an act of adultery, as amounting in itself to a loss of *consortium*. The action became a necessary preliminary to statutory divorce proceedings,[32] but it would not lie if the spouses were already separated, because there could then be no loss of *consortium*. The action for seducing daughters was also extended, by means of a presumption of services performed for the father: a fiction which protected the rich man whose daughter occasionally made his tea but left without redress 'the poor man whose child was sent unprotected to earn her bread amongst strangers'.[33] In 1857 the action for criminal conversation was replaced by a statutory action for damages, to be brought in the Divorce Court, for adultery. Both that action and the action of enticement were abolished in 1970.[34] Although the principal use made of this class of actions has ended, it remains a tort to deprive a person of services by rendering a relative incapable of continuing to perform them.

INDUCING A BREACH OF CONTRACT

In the action for assaulting a servant *per quod servitium amisit* it was not necessary for the plaintiff to allege a contract between himself and the servant. The fact that the servant was in service when the assault occurred was sufficient to ground the action, which therefore protected a status rather than a contract. In the case of departures from service, however, it was necessary to show that the defendant knew the servant had been retained for a specific term which had not expired; and it may have been this allegation which led to the notion

29. *Cholmley's Case* (1586) cit. Cro Eliz 502 (*per quod negotia infecta remanserunt*); *Guy v Livesey* (1618) ibid. 501 (*per quod consortium amisit*); *Hyde v Scyssor* (1619) ibid. 538 (*per quod solamen et consortium necnon consilium et auxilium in rebus domesticis amisit*).
30. *Notton v Jason* (1653) Style 398.
31. *Winsmore v Greenbank* (1745) Willes 577.
32. See p. 407, post.
33. Serjeant Manning's note to 7 M & G 1044.
34. Law Reform (Miscellaneous Provisions) Act 1970 (c.33), s.5.

that the tort consisted essentially in bringing about a breach of contract between the plaintiff and a third party. As early as 1529 an action was brought against a purchaser of land which the plaintiff had previously contracted to buy from the vendor, on the basis that the purchaser had maliciously procured the vendor to break his contract with the plaintiff.[35] There are few reported discussions of this new basis of liability over the next three centuries, though Blackstone regarded the basis of the action for retaining a servant to be 'the property which the master has by his contract acquired in the labour of his servant'.[36] Recognition of the tort of inducing a breach of contract, a term coined by Blackstone in discussing loss of services, is generally attributed to a decision of the Queen's Bench in 1853. The manager of a theatre had retained Mlle Wagner, the cantatrice to the King of Prussia, to sing there. The defendant offered her more money to sing at Covent Garden instead, and she accepted. In an action for enticing and procuring her to break her engagement with the plaintiff, her counsel argued that the action lay only for servants because it was derived from the Statute of Labourers. Coleridge J thought that since the only cause of damage was a breach of contract, and since the contract was not made with the defendant, the doctrine of privity precluded an action. The court decided, nevertheless, that it was a tort to induce another by persuasion to break a contract with the plaintiff.[37] Later decisions confirmed the law which had been anticipated in 1529, that the tort is not confined to contracts of service.

Unfair or Deceptive Competition

As between buyer and seller, the action of deceit remedied most kinds of deceptive practice.[38] The concept of deceit was wide enough to embrace also those situations where the plaintiff was hurt by reason of a deceit practised on third parties. Here was the strongest analogy with defamation, because there the action on the case lay for false assertions which drew persons from trading with the plaintiff.[39] The earliest cases of injurious falsehood were indeed cast in the form of defamation, by treating the aspersion on the plaintiff's wares or

35. *Palmer v Wryght* (1529) 94 SS *254*.
36. Bl Comm, vol.III, p. 142.
37. *Lumley v Gye* (1853) 2 E & B 216. Cf *Lumley v Wagner* (1852) 1 De G M & G 604 (injunction).
38. See pp. 293–294, ante.
39. See pp. 366–367, ante.

business as being an aspersion on his personal reputation.[40] A false denial of the plaintiff's title to property, whereby he was hindered in selling it, was even called 'slander of title'; and this action was almost as old as the action on the case for defamation.[41] When, around 1700, the tort of defamation crystallised out of the wider action on the case for words,[42] these economic torts were regarded as having a different basis and it became necessary to show actual malice. Both slander of title and unfair disparagement of property or wares were then seen as species of the tort of maliciously making false statements so as to injure another,[43] a tort which Salmond named 'injurious falsehood' and others have called 'malicious falsehood'. Rather surprisingly, parliament has in recent times extended to the tort of malicious falsehood some of the accidental attributes of the tort of defamation.[44]

The second category of deceptive competition arose from the wrongful copying of a trademark or the trade name or get-up of the plaintiff's wares. This could injure the plaintiff both by attracting customers to the defendant in the belief that they were buying the plaintiff's wares and also by driving away customers from the plaintiff as a result of putting around inferior wares purporting to be his. Both types of injury were alleged in the first known case dealing with this problem, a decision of the Common Pleas in 1584 that an action on the case would lie for counterfeiting the cloth and trademark of the plaintiff so that his own cloth was discredited.[45] The reports of this case varied so much that doubts were later entertained as to whether the action had been given to the purchaser of the goods, in which case it was an orthodox case of deceit on a sale, or to the original user of the mark. There was not at first thought to be any property or monopoly in a trademark, any more than in the trader's own surname or in an inn-sign; an action would lie only if some fraudulent use was made of another's mark or sign.[46] From the time of Lord Eldon, however, the user of a trademark was treated as having a species of property akin to

---

40. E.g. *Levet's Case* (1593) Cro Eliz 289 ('thy house is infected with the pox' spoken of an innkeeper); *Fen v Dixe* (1639) W. Jones 444 (gross remarks about plaintiff's beer); *Harman v Delany* (1731) 2 Stra 898 (gunsmith).

41. Some examples from the 1510s are noted in 94 SS *244* n.2. The tort does not seem to have been extended to personal property until the 19th century.

42. See pp. 370–372, ante.

43. The two elements were virtually indistinguishable in *Green v Button* (1835) 2 C M & R 707 (maliciously asserting lien over goods bought by the plaintiff, so that the seller would not deliver).

44. Defamation Act 1952, 15 & 16 Geo VI & 1 Eliz II c. 66, s.3.

45. *Sandford's Case* (1584) reported in MSS; record in Cory's entries, Brit Lib MS Hargrave 123, f.168v; inaccurately cited, Cro Jac 471, Poph 144, Latch 188.

46. *Blanchard v Hill* (1742) 2 Atk 484 (injunction refused); *Sykes v Sykes* (1824) 3 B & C 541 (damages for passing-off).

copyright, or goodwill, and this equitable concept of incorporeal property was embodied in legislation in the 1880s.[47] The rise of mass-production industries in the nineteenth century gave new importance to this branch of the law, and further analysis caused the tort to divide into two categories. Usurping a trademark was an infringement of a proprietary right, whereas passing-off by other means remained actionable only on showing deceit or at least a tendency to deceive. When passing-off was extended to literary property, however, it came close to merging with defamation.[48]

Intimidation

We began the chapter by observing that the common law never allowed an action for drawing away customers by fair competition. It was another matter if the customers were kept away by unlawful conduct, such as defamatory statements or deception, or by threats of unlawful conduct. The first known decision to allow an action for depriving a man of business by menacing potential customers was in 1621. The principle was later applied where shots were fired at natives in the Cameroon to deter them from trading with the plaintiff.[49] On a somewhat similar but broader principle, Holt CJ thought any malicious injury of another in his trade to be actionable. The plaintiff owned a pond with a duck-decoy, and the defendant had fired shots on his own land to scare off the ducks. Now, it is not in itself unlawful for a man to discharge a gun on his own land. The wrong here might have been treated as nuisance by loud noise, but it was put as an unlawful interference with trade: 'the decoy is in the nature of a trade, and there is the same reason that he should be repaired in damages for his decoy as for any other trade. It is true that there may be *damnum absque injuria*. If a man set up the same trade as mine in the same town, this is a damage to me, but it is *sine injuria*, for it is lawful to him to set up the same trade if he please. But this action is brought for disturbing him from exercising his trade.' The Gloucester schoolmasters would have been able to sue, on this principle, if the defendant had kept scholars away by shooting at them.[50]

47. Patents, Designs and Trademarks Act 1883, 46 & 47 Vict, c.57; Merchandise Marks Act 1887, 50 & 51 Vict, c.28.
48. *Archbold v Sweet* (1832) 1 Mood & R 162 (lawyer's reputation injured by publishing inaccurate edition of law book in his name).
49. *Garret v Taylor* (1621) Cro Jac 567, 2 Rolle Rep 162; *Tarleton v M'Gawley* (1793) Peake 270.
50. *Keeble v Hickeringill* (1705) 11 Mod Rep 73, 130, 3 Salk 9, Holt 19, 11 East 574 n.2 (from Holt's MS).

The nature and scope of this tort became a vexed question in the nineteenth century, largely as a result of the introduction of a complicating element, conspiracy. From medieval times until 1843 the action on the case for conspiracy had been brought only for conspiring to indict the plaintiff for an offence of which he was subsequently indicted and acquitted. It is doubtful to what extent the combination of two or more prosecutors was considered essential to the cause of action, the gist of which seems rather to have been maliciously procuring an indictment. In any case, the old action had been largely supplanted in Tudor times by the action for malicious prosecution, in which it was unnecessary to allege a conspiracy. There was, therefore, little precedent in 1843 for the proposition that what might be lawful if done by one person might be a tort if done by confederates. In that year an action was brought by an actor against a duke who had hired two hundred persons to 'hoot, hiss, groan and yell at and against the plaintiff' while on stage, and so to disrupt the performance that his engagement was terminated. The plaintiff succeeded. The court might well have treated this as an application of Holt CJ's general principle, since it is hard to see why such an action could not have been brought against a single person who had contrived to make sufficient noise to achieve the same result. Instead, however, the court treated the conspiracy as the cause of action.[51]

The innovation led some to believe that injurious trade competition, if carried out by a combination, would be actionable as a conspiracy to injure a man in his trade. On this argument, the Gloucester schoolmasters would have succeeded if the new school had been set up by two masters rather than one. This very propostion was urged on the House of Lords in 1892, in a case where a trade association had endeavoured to secure a monopoly by driving out of business other traders who refused to join. The means used were under-cutting at a loss, and withdrawing rebates from customers who dealt with the outsiders. One of those injured by these dealings sued as for a conspiracy to induce customers not to deal with him. There was no intimidation, and no contracts were broken. The House decided that this was lawful competition, because it was not legally wrong to aim at driving a competitor out of business in order to advance one's own business interests. The existence of a combination to effect this end did not make it less lawful.[52] The decision was consistent with earlier law, but it introduced a new complication in treating motive as a relevant factor. If the justification for injurious

51. *Gregory v Duke of Brunswick* (1844) 6 Man & G 205.
52. *Mogul SS Co v Macgregor, Gow & Co* [1892] AC 25.

competition was the advancement of self interest, would it be a tort to injure a trader by identical means if it could not be shown to advance the interests of the competitor? And why should motive be relevant in the law of tort?

This problem soon became of crucial importance in a series of leading cases concerning the liability of trade unions for damage done by strikes or threats to strike. The unions wanted the right to put individuals out of work as a means of securing monopolies of labour. But, unlike the medieval guilds and professional bodies, their object was not to impose educational or ethical standards on members but rather to put themselves on an economic footing with corporate or wealthy employers when negotiating terms of employment. The common law was disposed to favour the working man as against such combinations. If a union dictated to employers whom they might employ and whom not, this had been held an indictable conspiracy under the combination laws. Erle CJ had expressed the common law philosophy by explaining that the right to dispose of one's labour as one wished necessitated a correlative duty (enforceable by action or indictment) to permit others to enjoy the same freedom.[53] If a union deployed all its might to prevent a man exercising his right to work, and thereby to deprive him of the means of existence, the law had to try to protect him. But there could only be a right to work if there was a remedy; and what specific remedy could the law provide? If the union persuaded the employer to dismiss the employee in breach of contract, that would clearly amount to the tort of procuring a breach of contract. But if the union simply persuaded the employer to give the employee due notice, or to refuse a renewal of his contract, the matter was more difficult. It was not easy to distinguish those cases from that of persuading a customer not to deal further with a tradesman; and that was only tortious if the means of persuasion were unlawful. This was where the questions of conspiracy and self-protecting motives became vital. In 1898 the House of Lords held by a majority, contrary to the advice of most of the judges, that no wrong was done where someone threatened to do something he was entitled to do in order to induce someone else to do what he was entitled to do. That it was done with a malicious motive could make no difference. Lord Macnaghten said that 'questions of this sort belong to the province of morals rather than to the province of law'.[54] The decision was taken as a victory for the trade unions against the working man,

---

53. W. Erle *Law relating to Trade Unions* (1869), p. 12.
54. *Allen v Flood* [1898] AC 1. This was the last occasion when the judges were summoned for their opinions.

but the wide conflict of judicial opinion it revealed did little to clarify the law and only three years later the House felt compelled to qualify the decision. A butcher had been injured by a withdrawal of labour intended to penalise him for failing to effect a closed shop. He was allowed an action on grounds of conspiracy and threats.[55] Conspiracy had not been formally alleged in the 1898 case. The 1901 decision was considered by the Court of Appeal to have revived the right to work; if a man prevented another from obtaining or holding employment in his calling, either by threats or improper influence, this was actionable even in the absence of conspiracy.[56] Neither were malice or motive relevant. Although a union might be under a 'duty' by its rules to protect the interests of its members, this was a duty the members had conferred on themselves privately and could not confer a right to injure others contrary to law.[57]

These latter decisions drove the trade unions to seek their ends in parliament as well as in the courts, and at their behest the new Liberal government of 1906 introduced the Trade Disputes Act. This provided that procuring a breach of contract, conspiracy, and interfering with a trade or employment or with 'the right of some other person to dispose of his capital or his labour as he wills' should no longer be actionable if done in furtherance of a trade dispute; and that actions in tort could not be brought against trade unions.[58] Confused law was thus replaced by irrational law. Certain classes of men were given the right to place themselves outside the reach of the ordinary law of the land, whatever it might be, merely by combining to further their own interests or by involving themselves in a dispute with their employers.

A slight but short-lived attempt was made by the courts to curtail misuse of the power to strike by salvaging from the 1892–1906 chaos a tort of intimidation. This tort has its origins in the cases where trade was lost because of threats of violence. If threatening a tort against a third party, to induce him to act against the interests of the plaintiff, constituted intimidation, then so should threatening a breach of contract.[59] This tort is now thought to consist in threatening to commit or procure any unlawful act vis-à-vis a third party in order to intimidate him into acting to the harm of the plaintiff. It is thus distinct from the torts mentioned in the 1906 act. Where damage to a

55. *Quinn v Leathem* [1901] AC 495.
56. *Giblan v National Amalgamated Labourers Union of Great Britain and Ireland* [1903] 2 KB 600.
57. *South Wales Miners Federation v Glamorgan Coal Co* [1905] AC 239.
58. Trade Disputes Act 1906, 6 Edw VII, c.47.
59. *Rookes v Barnard* [1964] AC 1129, [1964] 1 All ER 367. The effect was largely undone by the Trade Union and Labour Relations Act 1974 (c.52), s.13.

trade or employment is done by threats of conduct not unlawful in itself vis-à-vis the third party, then it seems that to be actionable there must be both a conspiracy and the absence of a motive of self-advancement.[60]

Further reading

Holdsworth HEL, vol. IV, pp. 340–354; vol. VI, pp. 360–379; vol. VIII, pp. 392–397, 425–431; vol. XI, pp. 477–501

T. E. Scrutton, *The Laws of Copyright* (1883), pp. 67–116

T. A. Street, *Foundations of Legal Liability* (1906), vol. I, pp. 263–272, 322–325, 342–373, 417–434

E. W. Hulme, 'The early History of the English Patent System' in *Essays AALH*, vol. III, pp. 117–147

F. I. Schechter, *The Historical Foundations of the Law relating to Trademarks* (1925)

C. H. S. Fifoot, *English Law and its Background* (1932), pp. 211–220

D. S. Davies, 'Further Light on the Case of Monopolies' (1932) 48 LQR 394–414; 'The early History of the Patent Specification' (1934) 50 LQR 86–109, 260–274

W. P. M. Kennedy and J. Finkelman, *The Right to Trade: an Essay in the Law of Tort* (1933)

D. O. Wagner, 'Coke and the Rise of Economic Liberalism' (1935) 6 *Economic History Rev* 30–44

H. G. Fox, *Monopolies and Patents* (1947) [with bibliography]

G. H. Jones, 'Per Quod Servitium Amisit' (1958) 74 LQR 39–58

B. Malament, 'The "Economic Liberalism" of Sir Edward Coke' (1967) 76 *Yale Law Jo* 1321–1358

60. *Sorrell v Smith* [1925] AC 712; *Crofter Hand Woven Harris Tweed Co Ltd v Veitch* [1942] AC 435, [1942] 1 All ER 142.

23. Marriage and Divorce

The law of marriage is the most important part of the English law of persons. Marriage is not merely a civil contract, but a relationship which at common law altered the status of a woman for the purposes of the law of actions, obligations and property. Moreover, since the union of man and woman in matrimony has been consecrated by the Christian Church as an 'holy estate', it has been the concern of theologians and canonists as well as secular lawyers. In England, questions of matrimony were regarded as spiritual questions as early as the seventh century, and after the separation of lay and spiritual jurisdictions by William I the subject of matrimony fell exclusively within the province of the Church. Thereafter, when the lawfulness of a marriage came in issue in the lay courts, the question was referred to the bishop to be determined and certified according to the law of the Church. The division of functions persisted until the last century, until when it was true to say that the English law of marriage was part of the Canon law as used in England.[1]

THE LAW OF MARRIAGE

The earliest canonists held marriage to be effected by the physical union of man and woman in carnal copulation. They became one flesh by *commixtio sexuum*. But, since there could be copulation without marriage, a mental element was also necessary. The early view, as stated by Gratian (c. 1140), was therefore that marriage began by agreement but became complete and indissoluble once the agreement was executed in a physical union. This theory led to embarrassing questions about the married status of Mary and Joseph at the time of Christ's conception, and was accordingly superseded by a more sophisticated but infinitely more troublesome doctrine. According to the later Canon law, marriage could be contracted by consent alone, without any physical act or ecclesiastical ceremony, provided the consent was notified in words of the present tense (*per verba de*

---

1. By the 18th century the Church courts recognised Jewish and Quaker marriages also: *Lindo v Belisario* (1796) 1 Hag Con 216.

praesenti). Such a marriage was irregular, in so far as the parties could be compelled for the sake of order and decency to solemnise the marriage publicly at the door of a church and punished for any sinful connection they may have had before so doing. Yet it created an indissoluble bond, before consummation, and would be upheld in preference to a subsequent church marriage with a different spouse. The promise to marry in the future (*sponsalia per verba de futuro*) gave rise to an executory contract of marriage which could be turned into the indissoluble bond of present matrimony by consummation. Before consummation, however, the espousals *per verba de futuro* were but an engagement to marry and could be dissolved by mutual consent.

Thus, in the absence of carnal copulation, the validity of a marriage depended on whether the contract was by words *de praesenti* or *de futuro*. Maitland remarked that this distinction was 'no masterpiece of human wisdom . . . of all people in the world, lovers are the least likely to distinguish precisely between the present and future tenses'.[2] It is hardly surprising that it gave rise to much wrangling and fraud, and that the commonest species of matrimonial suit in the medieval consistory courts was to interpret and enforce marriage contracts. Despite legal pressure, marriages were frequently effected at home or in the open air, using such words as 'I here take you as my wife, for better or worse, to have and to hold until the end of my life, and of this I give you my faith'.[3] The legal effect of such declarations was probably widely misunderstood, and since no set form was necessary difficulties of interpretation frequently arose. What was one to make of 'I will have you as my wife'? Was it a present marriage, or an engagement? There were four schools of thought by the sixteenth century on that phrase alone. Since the courts required two witnesses to prove a marriage, there were additional problems where the *verba de praesenti* were spoken in private, and then a subsequent marriage with another woman took place before witnesses. In such a case, the Church would have to order the man to live in adultery with the second woman; but the better moral opinion was that the man ought to disobey the Church and suffer excommunication on earth, safe in the knowledge that he would be absolved at the last judgment.

If it now seems strange that the Canon law should have given protection to such informal marriages *per verba de praesenti*, it is still more remarkable that an unwilling party could be admonished by the Church to marry, before any carnal connection, simply because of a

2. Pollock & Maitland, vol. II, pp. 368–369.
3. Helmholz *Marriage Litigation* p. 28 (quoting from a case of 1372).

rash promise. It was rather inconsistent to recognise duress as a defence to a forced marriage, and yet to use the force of law to compel someone to marry against his will. But the notion of the 'happy marriage' did not yet exist; it was more important that solemn promises should be kept. This was the law of England until as late as 1753,[4] and it was still doubtful in Blackstone's time whether the impediment of precontract had disappeared. Even after the ecclesiastical forms of specific compulsion had been abolished, an action lay for damages for breach of promise of marriage until 1970.[5]

Concubinage, where there was no marriage contract of either kind, was punishable as a sin. Medieval spiritual courts occasionally gave the parties the option of marrying or forswearing each other's company: the *abjuratio sub poena nubendi* took the form of a compulsory conditional marriage *per verba de praesenti*, that they took each other for man and wife *if* (but only if) they had future sexual relations. This procedure was not consistent with the notion that marriage should be a free act, and it was abandoned in the fifteenth century.

FORMALITY OF MARRIAGE

Both the ecclesiastical and secular authorities were insistent on publicity as a requisite of a completely regular marriage. To prevent clandestine marriages, Archbishop Hubert Walter promulgated a constitution in 1200 requiring banns to be published on three successive occasions before solemnisation of the marriage, and this practice was universally established by the Lateran Council in 1215. The purpose of banns was to call upon the congregation to declare any known impediment to the proposed union, such as consanguinity or precontract. In medieval times it was not unknown for rival lovers to 'make reclamation' at that stage, with the result that the question of contract had to be referred to the consistory court. If no objection were raised, the ceremony took place at the church door. The priest charged the parties themselves to declare any impediment known to them, the parties spoke the words of betrothal and present matrimony, and the husband placed a ring on the wife's finger as a token or *wed*, and delivered to her the tokens (usually coins) representing dower.[6] The ceremony would conclude with a nuptial mass inside the church, and would often be followed by secular festivity. The purpose

4. The sanction was removed by Stat 26 Geo II, c.33, s.13.
5. Law Reform (Miscellaneous Provisions) Act 1970, c.33, s.1. *Assumpsit* for breach of promise began in the 16th century, but was resisted by Vaughan CJ as late as 1673: Cart 236, 1 Freem 98.
6. See p. 229, *ante*.

of the ceremony was not merely to impress on the parties the solemnity of what they were doing, but also to secure the event in the minds of witnesses; registration of marriages was not introduced until the mid-sixteenth century. In essence, however, the church wedding was the same as the meadow wedding. The parties were not married by the priest or by the use of incantations; they married each other.

For most purposes, the common law recognised only the marriage contracted publicly *in facie ecclesiae*. This was simply a rule of evidence, not unlike the rule which excluded covenants unless they were clothed with formality. Whereas the Church was primarily concerned with sin, the temporal judges felt that property rights ought not to depend on clandestine marriages which might be incapable of proof. If, therefore, the validity of a marriage came in issue in a common law case, the bishop would be required to certify not merely whether the marriage was canonically valid but also whether or not it was clandestine.

By Lord Hardwicke's Act 1753, secret marriages were completely abolished for legal purposes; and the publication of banns, or purchase of a licence, the presence of at least two witnesses, and the recording of the marriage in a public register, were made compulsory. Falsification of the register of marriages was made a capital offence.[7] Although this act exempted Quakers and Jews from its operation, because they had for nearly a century been allowed to marry according to their own usages, there was no special provision for Roman Catholics, nonconformists and non-believers. This situation was remedied in 1836 when the alternative of a civil marriage ceremony in a registry office or registered building (such as a nonconformist chapel) was introduced by statute.[8] Both the civil and ecclesiastical forms of marriage have continued in use ever since.[9] These statutory provisions were not applicable to members of the royal family, to marriages with the special licence of the archbishop of Canterbury,[10] or to marriages outside England and Wales. In the case of marriages abroad, the law applicable is the law of the place of celebration, which in some other countries is the common law or the Canon law. In all these cases the courts may have to pronounce on the validity of marriages contracted at common law, without regard to the legislation as to form. In 1843 the House of Lords was called upon to decide the validity of an Irish marriage celebrated without the presence of an

---

7. An Act for the better Preventing of Clandestine Marriages, 26 Geo II, c.33.
8. Marriage Act 1836, 6 & 7 Will IV, c.85.
9. Marriage Act 1949, 12, 13 & 14 Geo VI, c.76.
10. Ecclesiastical Licences Act 1533, 25 Hen VIII, c.21.

ordained clergyman. It was decided at first instance that the presence of a priest was essential, and because the House was evenly divided the decision stood as the law of England.[11] Most scholars are now agreed that the prevailing view was an unconscious distortion of history. The error was confined to the British Isles, because when a marriage is celebrated in a foreign place where the services of a priest are not available it may yet be regarded as valid at common law.[12] In all these cases there must, of course, be *verba de praesenti*; it is one of the most absurd solecisms of the twentieth century to regard concubinage as a 'common law marriage'.

Unity of Person

It was a common saying among canonists and common lawyers alike that in the eyes of the law husband and wife (*baron et feme*) were but one person: *erunt animae duae in carne una*. This one person was the husband, since 'the very being or legal existence of a woman is suspended during the marriage, or at least is incorporated and consolidated into that of the husband'.[13] This was, of course, a legal fiction, and it did not always commend itself to laymen. It was the fiction which prompted Bumble the beadle to utter the immortal words, 'if the law supposes that . . . then the law is a ass'.[14] Like most legal fictions, it was not universally applicable; for instance, the wife was not executed for her husband's crimes or made answerable for his debts. The origin of the doctrine, and its one-sidedness, may be found in the traditional inferiority of women, and the power which social custom vested in the husband over his wife. According to the scriptures, woman was created for man and bound to obey him. The married woman was said to be *femina cooperta* (in law French, *feme covert*), and her husband or *baron* was both her sovereign and her guardian. If she killed him it was not simple murder, but treason. He looked after her and her property during the 'coverture', while she was incapable of owning separate property or of making her own contracts. She could not sue or be sued at common law without her *baron*, and this prevented her from suing him for any wrong done to her. Like feudal wardship, therefore, the guardianship of a wife by her

11. *R v Millis* (1844) 10 Cl & Fin 534. But see *Beamish v Beamish* (1861) 9 HL Cas 274.
12. E.g. *Catterall v Catterall* (1847) 1 Rob Ecc 580.
13. Bl Comm, vol. I, p. 442.
14. C. Dickens *Oliver Twist*, chap. 51.

husband redounded to the guardian's material profit and was not subject to judicial review.

PROPERTY OF MARRIED WOMEN

Any property which the wife had owned as a single woman (*feme sole*) became the husband's on marriage. A wife's personal property vested in the husband absolutely; and, since there could be no estates in chattels, he could if he so pleased dispose of it absolutely. If the husband died first, the widow had no right to claim back any of her personal property disposed of during coverture, but she could have what remained. Likewise upon divorce, the wife could only reclaim such of her goods as had not been disposed of bona fide while the marriage was believed to be valid.[15] If the husband died testate, the widow could only claim whatever legacies had been left her, and her *paraphernalia*: her personal clothes and jewels. The wife's claim to *paraphernalia*, as against a legatee, was limited to necessaries and personal ornaments appropriate to her degree; but ornaments were liable to the husband's debts, 'for it is not fit she should shine in jewels, and the creditors in the mean time to starve'.[16]

The wife's real property vested in the husband only during coverture, although if she died first he was entitled to a tenancy by the curtesy.[17] During the marriage the husband could enfeoff a stranger of the wife's land, but after his death the widow or her heir could recover the land by writ of entry *cui in vita*. If the wife wished to alienate her own land during the marriage she had to obtain her husband's assent, and they would together levy a fine; before the fine was accepted, the judges questioned the wife privately to ensure that she was not acting under coercion; the fine would then bar the wife and her heirs.

The doctrine of unity also affected property conveyed *to* the wife during coverture. Such a grant to her vested the property in the husband alone, at common law. Even if the wife saved a little cash out of her housekeeping allowance, the benefit of her frugality redounded to the husband; the intention was to keep her in necessaries, 'not that she should grow rich and lay up treasure for herself alone'.[18]

By the end of the sixteenth century, many of these rules could be avoided as a result of the equitable doctrine of the separate use. In

15. *Anon* (1534) YB Mich 26 Hen VIII, 7, pl.1; Dyer 13, pl.63; Spelman Rep (93 SS) 216, pl. 5.
16. *Shipton v Tyrrell* (1675) Freem 304, 2 Eq Cas Abr 155, Nottingham Rep (73 SS) 150 per Finch LK.
17. See p. 230, ante.
18. *Shipton v Tyrrell*, ante, per Finch LK. But in equity the husband might agree to the wife saving her own pin-money: *Slanning v Style* (1734) 3 P Wms 334.

equity, husband and wife were separate persons, and it was unconscionable that a husband should appropriate property given to the
wife alone. Property could therefore be settled, either upon marriage
or during a marriage, on trust for the wife's 'sole and separate use'.
The Court of Chancery enforced such trusts by giving the married
woman beneficiary the same independence of ownership, in respect of
the equitable estate, as if she had been single.[19] In the course of time it
was seen that the separate use could be abused, because a weak-willed
wife might be induced to dispose of her equitable estate to her
husband, or to charge it with the payment of his debts, contrary to the
intention of the settlor. Conveyancers—some say Lord Thurlow C
while at the bar[20]—solved this problem in the late eighteenth century
by inventing the 'restraint on anticipation', which was a condition
inserted in a settlement to prevent a wife from alienating or charging
the property during coverture. After 1800 clauses of this nature were
inserted in almost every marriage settlement. By this means, the
wife's absolute property in equity was postponed in her own interest
until widowhood, and she was forbidden to anticipate that estate on
pain of forfeiture.

Equity thus protected the married women of the landed classes, but
it did nothing for the middle and poorer classes whose wealth consisted in personalty, nor for the woman wage-earner. For centuries no
such protection was necessary, because women were rarely in a
position to earn money; cooks, household servants, and secretaries,
were invariably male before the eighteenth century. As the social
position of women began to change, and the opportunities for their
education and respectable employment increased, the archaic rule
which gave a woman's earnings absolutely to her husband became a
source of complaint. In 1856 a number of eminent ladies petitioned
parliament to alter the law, on the basis that modern civilisation had
begun to break down the financial dependence of women upon men.
They begged the legislature to consider the plight of the woman who
'worked from morning to night only to see the produce of her labour
wrested from her and wasted in a gin-palace'.[21] In 1870 their plea was
answered by a modest reform. Instead of making such a radical
change as conferring upon married women the capacity to own
property, the legislature simply extended the equitable concept of the

---

19. See *Herbert v Herbert* (1692) 1 Eq Cas Abr 66. Early cases recognising the separate
   use are *Sanky v Golding* (1579) Cary 87; *Witham v Waterhouse* (1596) Toth 91, HLS MS
   110, f.177v (settled by all the judges).
20. 3 Bro CC 340 n.1 per Lord Eldon C.
21. 'The Property of Married Women' (1856) 10 *Westminster Rev* (NS) 336n.

separate use to wages and earnings.[22] In 1882 the doctrine was further extended to all the property of married women, whether acquired before or after marriage.[23] These statutes effected a fictional settlement whereby the rules of equity, framed for the daughters of the rich, were at last extended to the daughters of the poor.[24] The reform was awkward and confusing; but the married woman was not released from the paternalistic protection of the restraint on anticipation, and given the same legal rights of ownership as a man, until recent times.[25]

CONTRACTS OF MARRIED WOMEN

The wife's inability to contract was the inevitable result of her inability to own separate property. As an agent, or personal representative, she could make valid contracts, because she was dealing with another person's property. For the same reason, she could make contracts in relation to property which she owned by virtue of any local custom which permitted wives to own separate property for trading purposes.[26] Except in these cases, a purported contract by a married woman was merely void, and neither she nor her husband could be sued upon it.

As an agent, however, the wife could sometimes bind her husband to contracts made on his behalf. Thus, it was settled by 1300 that she could bind her husband by buying goods which came to his use or profit. It was clear by 1500 that the husband was bound in such a case only if he had either given his wife prior authority to act for him, or subsequently ratified a contract made for his benefit. He could not be bound by his wife's prodigality or extravagance. If a wife were accustomed to order household goods on credit, an agency might be presumed; but the husband was free to revoke the presumed authority if he chose.

There was no question of the married woman making such contracts as agent for her own separate benefit, and this limitation caused injustice if a wife was neglected or evicted by her husband. Although she could sue for alimony in the ecclesiastical courts, such proceedings cost time and money which she might not have. The courts therefore began, in the seventeenth century, to find in such cases an implied authority to pledge the husband's credit for necessaries for

22. Married Women's Property Act 1870, 33 & 34 Vict, c.93.
23. Married Women's Property Act 1882, 45 & 46 Vict, c.75.
24. Dicey *Law and Public Opinion during the 19th Century*, p. 393.
25. Law Reform (Married Women and Tortfeasors) Act 1935, 25 & 26 Geo V, c.30; Married Women (Restraint upon Anticipation) Act 1949, 13 & 14 Geo VI, c.78.
26. As to the custom of the City of London, see *Beard v Webb* (1800) 2 Bos & P 93.

her own support.[27] Of course, the implication could not be raised if the husband expressly warned traders not to trust the wife, or if the wife were the guilty party. Because of these restrictions, the doctrine was not enormously helpful to wives in distress. Traders gave credit to married women at their peril, and a separated wife might find difficulty in obtaining necessaries without ready cash. If she borrowed money to buy necessaries, the law would not oblige the husband to repay the loan; though equity helped by allowing the lender of money which had actually been spent on necessaries to recover the money from the husband as if he had supplied them himself.[28] In the present century the ability of women to support themselves from their own earnings, and their right to claim maintenance by summary proceedings in magistrates' courts, assisted by legal aid, made the implied authority to pledge credit of little practical value. It had virtually fallen into disuse when it was abolished in 1970.[29]

A married woman who owned separate property in equity was able to make contracts in respect of such property, provided the property was held to her separate use at the date of the contract. But the employment of restraints on anticipation usually prevented the wife from contracting in this way. The contractual capacity of married women was accordingly unaltered by the legislation which increased their rights of ownership, and even after 1882 the married woman's liability in contract attached only to her property and not to her person. The *feme covert* was finally given the same contractual capacity as a *feme sole* in 1935.[30]

TORTS BY AND AGAINST MARRIED WOMEN

Her inability to own property did not render a married woman less capable of committing torts, any more than it exempted her from criminal liability. But it rendered her ircapable of paying compensation, and as a matter of procedure an action for a wife's tort had to be brought against husband and wife jointly. The wrong was not visited on the husband personally, even in a vicarious sense, for if the wife died his liability came to an end; nevertheless he bore the financial brunt. Husbands were not relieved from this consequence of the doctrine of unity of person until 1935.[31] The converse principle

27. *Sir Thomas Gardener's Case* (1615) Rolle Abr, vol. I, p. 351; *Dent v Scott* (1648) Aleyn 61. Cf. *Manby v Scott* (1663) 1 Sid 109, 1 Keb 482, 1 Lev 4, 1 Mod Rep 124, O Bridg 29.
28. *Harris v Lee* (1718) 1 P Wms 482, Prec Ch 502, 2 Eq Cas Abr 135.
29. Matrimonial Proceedings and Property Act 1970 (c.45), s.41.
30. Law Reform (Married Women and Tortfeasors) Act 1935, 25 & 26 Geo V, c.30, s.1.
31. Ibid., s.3.

applied to torts committed against a wife. The husband and wife had
to bring the action jointly, and the damages belonged to the husband.
The husband could, in addition, claim for any loss he had suffered
through the loss of his wife's services or *consortium*.[32] Since 1935, a wife
has been able to sue independently for torts committed against her,
though in general she is still unable to sue her husband.

Bastardy

Bastardy, or illegitimacy, was a condition imposed upon a child as a
punishment for the sin of parents who conceived it by illicit connection. By legal fiction, a child born out of wedlock was no one's child,
filius nullius. This status was visited by the Canon law on children
born of a single woman, of an adulterous union, of a clandestine
marriage which was found to be void, or of a church marriage where
both parties knew of an impediment. The Canon law, however,
treated the children of a bona fide putative marriage as legitimate if
they were born before divorce, and also allowed that a bastard born
out of wedlock was legitimated by the subsequent marriage of his
parents. The Church took notice of illegitimate parentage to the
extent of requiring a putative father to contribute to the support of his
child; but affiliation proceedings in the spiritual courts seem to have
been uncommon in medieval times.

In English law bastardy was not an inferior status or condition.
The bastard had the same legal rights as any other free man, with the
single exception that he could not be heir to his parents nor have any
collateral heir himself. In one case, that of villeinage, this was a
distinct privilege, because the natural child of a villein was accounted
free. The obvious disadvantage was that the bastard could not inherit
real property. It was settled in the twelfth century that bastardy could
be pleaded in bar of a real action, in which case the question was to be
referred to the ecclesiastical authorities. From an early date, however,
there was a conflict between the Canon law and the common law over
the doctrine of legitimation and the effect of divorce. The common law
took the coldly logical view that a bastard could not be legitimated by
subsequent marriage, because this would render inheritance precarious, and that divorce always bastardised the issue. Since inheritance
of land was a question of temporal law, the judges felt their rule
should prevail; yet, on reference to the bishop, his certificate would

32. See p. 383, ante.

preclude them from applying it. The judges therefore proposed in 1236 that bishops should be expressly asked whether the birth was before the marriage. The bishops retaliated by suggesting the introduction of the Canon law doctrine into English law, and received a scornful rebuff from the assembled earls and barons, who 'with one voice answered, that they would not change the laws of England'.[33] After this, the judges decided that in all except the old real actions a party could plead 'special bastardy' (that is, birth out of wedlock), and that such a question was a question of fact capable of trial by jury. On such a question the bishop's certificate of legitimacy was not conclusive, because a person legitimate by the Canon law might yet have been born out of wedlock. As a result of this division of function, coupled with the decline of real actions, questions of bastardy were rarely referred to bishops, and then only when parties wished to bastardise themselves to escape the throes of villeinage.

The common law allowed one exception to its harsh doctrine of bastardy. Where the eldest son was born out of wedlock (the *bastard eigné*) and the next son was born to the same parents after marriage (the *mulier puisné*), and upon the ancestor's death the *bastard eigné* entered as heir and remained in undisturbed possession until his own death, the *bastard eigné* was treated as if he had been legitimate with respect to the inheritance of that land.[34] The reason given was that a person who was legitimate by the Canon law could not be bastardised posthumously, when he no longer had the opportunity to contest the issue.

The doctrine of legitimation by subsequent marriage did not become English law until 1926.[35] Since 1969 an illegitimate child takes on the intestacy of his parents (but not other relatives) as if he were legitimate, and will take under a bequest to 'children' unless a contrary intention appears.[36]

Divorce

The contract of matrimony was the most important contract two persons could make, and yet, unlike all other contracts, there was no way of escaping from it if it proved unsatisfactory. This followed from

---

33. Statute of Merton 1236, c.9. See Maitland (Ed) *Bracton's Note Book*, vol. I, pp. 104–115; Thorne (Ed) *Bracton*, vol. III, pp. xv–xvii.
34. Littleton *Tenures*, ss. 399–401.
35. Legitimacy Act 1926, 16 & 17 Geo V, c.60.
36. Family Law Reform Act 1969 (c.46), ss. 14–15.

the teaching of the medieval canonists, to whom the common law referred all matrimonial questions. In the earliest days of Christian England, divorce by consent was not unknown, and there is evidence that the Church itself sanctioned divorce for adultery and desertion. The medieval canonists, however, adopted that interpretation of the scriptures[37] which held that the bonds of matrimony were indissoluble during the lives of the parties. Marriage was an holy estate, and what God had joined together no man could put asunder. When the Church courts granted a divorce from the bond of matrimony (*a vinculo matrimonii*), they did so on the ground that the putative marriage had been void from its commencement by reason of a 'dirimentary impediment'. They could not break the chains, but they could declare that the chains never existed. Whether a marriage existed or not was a question for the Church and its law; but once a valid marriage was shown to have been contracted *per verba de praesenti*, or by physical union following espousals, only God could end it by extinguishing the life of one spouse. The law of divorce was, therefore, the same as the law of marriage.

NULLITY: DIVORCE A VINCULO

According to the classical Canon law, persons who had undergone the forms of marriage could only be divorced, in the full sense of being free to remarry, if they could establish either a want of capacity to intermarry or a want of consent to the marriage. In those cases the marriage was a nullity from the beginning, and no legal proceedings were needed to make it so.[38] In medieval times divorce was usually a matter of self-help rather than litigation; if a party conceived that he was not lawfully married, he left his 'wife' and, if he was so entitled and so desired, married another. The Church did not interfere. There was, nevertheless, a presumption at common law in favour of the validity of a solemn church marriage: 'even if one marry his mother, this is lawful matrimony before it is defeated'.[39] If, therefore, the question of marriage was likely to come in issue in a property suit in the royal courts, it was advisable to seek a formal divorce in the consistory court.

Consent might be negatived not only by proof of duress, or insanity,[40] or mistake, but also by showing that the parties were of such

---

37. See esp. Mark, x, 2–12; Luke, xvi, 18. Cf. Matthew, v, 31–32; xix, 3–9. See also Deuteronomy, xxiv, 1–2.
38. See *Riddlesden v Wogan* (1601) Cro Eliz 858.
39. YB Trin 9 Hen VI, 34, pl. 3 per Paston J.
40. In *Stile v West* (1605) Rolle Abr, vol. I, p. 340, it was held that idiocy did not avoid consent.

tender age that they were presumed incapable of consenting. The age of consent was fixed at seven, but until the age of puberty either party could avoid the marriage. The age of puberty was, however, fixed arbitrarily by the common law at twelve years in the case of girls and fourteen in the case of boys. The minimum age of consent was raised to sixteen in 1929.[41] In the upper classes, marriages were often arranged while the children were very young, but the practice was rarely contested by those concerned. Even if pressure from guardians or parents verged on duress, the children usually submitted. In any case, voluntary coition and cohabitation after reaching full age purged any inherent defects of this nature. Conversely, parental consent was not under Canon law an essential prerequisite,[42] though as a result of legislation it did have that effect in the period between 1753 and 1823. The Canon law rule which once more prevails does not avoid a marriage for want of such consent once it has been celebrated; if the parents make no objection when the banns are called, or at the solemnisation, they must thereafter for ever hold their peace.

The other impediments to a marriage went to capacity, and were: precontract, consanguinity, affinity, and impotence at the time of marriage. Since Christian marriage has always been monogamous, a church marriage between *A* and *B* could be upset by proving a previous clandestine marriage between *A* and *C* by consent alone; and in this case *B* would be free to remarry. A person could not marry a blood-relation within the prohibited degrees. This prohibition was founded on genetic principles which are incapable of precise formulation, and its scope has varied from time to time. Affinity, which is the relationship created by marriage or carnal connection, was also an impediment within certain degrees. Thus, a man who had fornicated with *X*'s sister was forbidden to marry *X*. Some of the subtleties of the canonists in this regard seem very remote from theology, morality or human feeling, and served merely to facilitate divorces on flimsy grounds, by the discovery of forgotten indiscretions or genealogical obscurities. Moreover, some of the impediments could be dispensed with in return for money paid to the Church. At the time of the Reformation in England the old learning was replaced by a statutory table of the prohibited degrees, derived from scripture.[43] The table was clear, but still rather restrictive; and the removal of some

41. Age of Marriage Act 1929, 19 & 20 Geo V, c.36.
42. For the feudal consequences of this, see p. 207, ante.
43. Marriage Act 1540, 32 Hen VIII, c.38. After 1835 marriages within the prohibited degrees have been absolutely void: Lord Lyndhurst's Act 1835, 5 & 6 Will IV, c.54.

unreasonable impediments based on affinity was left until recent times.[44]

A putative marriage could also be declared void if one of the parties failed to consummate it on account of incurable impotency which existed at the date of the marriage. Failure to consummate did not itself invalidate a marriage contracted by present words: it was the inability to consummate which made the marriage void *ab initio*. Impotency might arise from malformation or from invincible frigidity. Assertions of frigidity raised difficult problems of proof, which in the fourteenth and fifteenth centuries were solved by surprisingly forthright methods of testing.[45] They were obviously open to abuse, especially when it was argued that frigidity could be relative; for, as a witty serjeant quipped in a case of 1599, 'he that is *frigidus quoad unam* and *calidus quoad alteram* is like to prove *callidus nebulo*'.[46]

DIVORCE A MENSA ET THORO

To satisfy the feeling that spouses should be released from conjugal duties where a matrimonial wrong had been committed, the canonists devised the compromise of judicial separation. This they called divorce from board and bed (*a mensa et thoro*) because the parties, though indissolubly united, were licensed to live apart. Such a separation was not a divorce in the modern sense, because the parties were not free to remarry; and it was different from nullity in that the issue of the divorced partners were legitimate. A divorce *a mensa et thoro* could be decreed by the ecclesiastical courts for such misconduct as adultery, cruelty, sodomy, and heresy, or for fear of future injury; and an innocent wife could be awarded alimony for her support after separation. There was an element of discretion or canonical equity in granting this type of divorce, which could be refused if the petitioner had been guilty of 'conduct conducing' to the offence, or had condoned the offence subsequently.

DIVORCE AND THE REFORMATION

One of the immediate causes contributing to the separation of the Anglican Church from Rome in the 1530s was the clash between King Henry VIII and Pope Clement VII over the matter of the king's divorce from his first wife, Queen Katharine of Aragon. The dispute

---

44. Deceased Wife's Sister's Marriage Act 1907, 7 Edw VII, c.47; Deceased Brother's Widow's Marriage Act 1921, 11 & 12 Geo V, c.24; Marriage (Enabling) Act 1960, 8 & 9 Eliz II, c.29.
45. Helmholz *Marriage Litigation*, p. 89.
46. *Berrie's Case* (1599) Brit Lib MS Lansdowne 1074, f.291. (*Callidus nebulo*, crafty rogue.)

made divorce a topic of widespread debate and provoked fresh think-ing on the subject. We may also take the matrimonial history of Henry VIII as an illustration of the intricate workings of the unreformed Canon law.

Henry married Katharine in 1509. As she was the widow of his deceased brother Arthur, Henry had first obtained a papal dispensa-tion from the impediment created by affinity. After eighteen years of married life, and the birth of a daughter, Henry wanted the marriage declared void so that he could marry Anne Boleyn. He persuaded himself that God had denied him a son as a punishment for marrying his brother's widow, and that this was an impediment which could not be dispensed with by the pope because it was derived from divine law and not merely an arbitrary rule of Canon law. This being a theological rather than a legal question, it was referred to Cardinal Wolsey as papal legate. No decision was reached, because it was certain that if the decision went in favour of the king, the queen would appeal successfully to the pope; and in any case the queen had complicated the issue by claiming that her marriage to Prince Arthur had not been consummated and therefore created no impediment at all. The king's advisers instead set about collecting scholastic opin-ions on the proposed divorce, and in 1533 the king felt sufficiently sure of his ground in treating the marriage as void without obtaining a formal divorce. The king's foremost protagonist, Dr Thomas Cranmer, was appointed Archbishop of Canterbury, the king secretly married Anne Boleyn, the archbishop delivered a judicial sentence confirming that the marriage with Katharine was contrary to God's law and void, and parliament abolished appeals to the pope. Those who spoke against these arrangements were guilty of statutory treason.

The king now had his matrimonial affairs virtually within his own control. Three years later Cranmer again exercised his archiepiscopal jurisdiction, this time to declare void the marriage with Anne. No reasons were published, though it was rumoured that a precontract had been established; more likely it was the king's prior misconduct with Mary Boleyn, the queen's sister, which was taken to render the marriage void on grounds of canonical affinity. Anne was beheaded for treason two days later, which would have enabled the king to remarry in any event; the real purpose of the divorce was to bastardise Princess Elizabeth, the child of the marriage. In the course of time Henry also divorced Anne of Cleves, on the grounds of precontract *per verba de praesenti* with Francis of Lorraine, of incapacity, and (rather surprisingly) of duress. There was no need to divorce Queen

Katharine Howard, because she had given the king no daughters to bastardise. In fact there was evidence of a precontract with one Denham, but the king's advisers preferred to suppress this evidence in order to have the queen convicted of treason for committing adultery with Denham.

These proceedings show how the old Canon law was capable of manipulation when pressure was brought to bear. We shall not attempt to assess the sincerity of Henry VIII or Cranmer in making their interpretations of the law, but it is likely that many churchmen genuinely felt the divorce law to be in need of reform. Even in St Thomas More's Utopia—admittedly not a Christian state—divorce was allowed for adultery and cruelty. Henry VIII had not gone so far; he wished to conform, or to be seen as conforming, to the old law. But Cranmer had definite views on reform. He wrote that separation *a mensa et thoro* was a travesty of Christian marriage, which was founded on the cohabitation of man and wife. In his draft code of reformed Canon law for the Church of England, he proposed that full dissolution of marriage should be permitted for good causes. The causes suggested were adultery, cruelty, desertion, and bitter enmity. These proposals were never officially implemented, but for a time there remained a doubt whether the Reformation had somehow in itself altered the nature of divorce *a mensa et thoro*. In the time of Edward VI a precedent was set for a new approach by the Marquess of Northampton. In 1548 he divorced his wife for adultery and then sought to remarry. Cranmer, asked to pronounce on the propriety of a remarriage, procrastinated; and so the marquess remarried without archiepiscopal authority. Eventually the validity of the second marriage was upheld by the Court of Delegates and confirmed by act of parliament. The precedent was first followed and then overruled in Elizabeth I's reign,[47] since when there was no doubt that the old law was unaltered.

DIVORCE BY ACT OF PARLIAMENT

In manipulating the Canonical rules to his own advantage, Henry VIII had been careful to avoid introducing a novel approach to divorce, and such statutes as he passed concerning his marriages were merely confirmations of his interpretation of the universal law of the Church. But his divorces had bastardised two future queens of England: Mary, the daughter of Katharine of Aragon, and Elizabeth, the daughter of Anne Boleyn. Needless to say, each of them upon her

47. *Sir John Stawell's Case* (1572) 29 LQR 86; *Rye v Fuljambe* (1602) Moore KB 683, Noy 100.

accession restored her legitimacy by act of parliament, and in so doing demonstrated more finally than Henry had done the sovereign power of parliament to interfere with the laws of marriage. The statute passed for the Marquess of Northampton provided another example of the sovereignty of parliament in matrimonial affairs. Parliament had begun to do what the Roman Church had considered the exclusive province of God. Even so, legislation at first interfered only with the interpretation and application of the rules to particular cases, not with the rules themselves.

In 1670 the view that the law of God permitted divorce for adultery was given effect by statute, when the Lord Roos' marriage was dissolved and he was enabled to remarry. After this, the promotion of private divorce bills became common. What could not be done in the ecclesiastical courts could now be done in parliament, often with the votes of the bishops. Adultery remained the only ground, and it had first to be proved in the ordinary courts. The husband had to bring an action for criminal conversation to establish the adultery, and then to obtain a divorce *a mensa et thoro* from the ecclesiastical court on the ground of that adultery. Then a petition for dissolution was presented to the House of Lords and voted upon.

In this way divorce for adultery was introduced into English law. There was no alteration in the procedure or jurisdiction of the Church courts, no abrogation of the distinction between separation *a mensa et thoro* and divorce *a vinculo matrimonii*. The parliamentary procedure was long-winded and expensive, and although it was invoked about three hundred times in the eighteenth and nineteenth centuries it was for that reason exclusive to the wealthy and (for reasons based on scripture) exclusive to male petitioners.

REFORM OF THE DIVORCE LAWS

An accident of politics prevented Cranmer's proposal to introduce regular divorce *a vinculo* for adultery and cruelty from becoming law for several centuries. Once the opportunity for reform after the break with Rome was lost, any further hope of change was stifled by the conservatism of the ecclesiastical authorities. But the Church was no longer taking a stand on principle, for the principle could be dispensed with ad hoc by parliament; and its attitude bore hard on those who could not afford to buy release from a broken home life.

Jeremy Bentham (d. 1832) advocated a utilitarian approach to divorce in his *Theory of Legislation*, published posthumously in 1864. He admitted that the natural duration of marriage was life, but viewed the notion of marital imprisonment with horror. The law, knowing full well the misfortunes which sometimes befell the most well-meaning couples, put them in chains which it would never loose. Bentham thought a dissoluble marriage would be a stronger and more loving union, because 'what is now done only to gain affection, would then be practised to preserve it'. He concluded that divorce ought to be allowed in certain cases, at the behest of the innocent party.

The introduction of civil marriage in 1836 removed the ecclesiastical obstacle to remarriage after divorce, but it did not facilitate divorce itself. A strong movement for reform stirred in the early years of Queen Victoria, and according to tradition it was brought to a head by a much publicised observation which Maule J addressed to a prisoner at Warwick assizes in 1845. The prisoner, a pauper whose wife had deserted him, had gone through a form of marriage with another woman and had consequently been convicted of bigamy. In terms of mordant irony, the judge told him that the proper course would have been to obtain a divorce by act of parliament; true, it would have cost him about £500 and the man had not so many pence, but the law was the same for rich and poor alike. The sentence was four months' hard labour, which the judge 'hoped would operate as a warning how people trifled with matrimony'.[48] During the next few years, the Society for Promoting the Amendment of the Law worked out proposals for transferring the divorce jurisdiction of parliament to a special court of law, with cheaper procedure. The proposals were considered in detail by a Royal Commission which reported in 1853. The commission recommended the retention of divorce *a mensa et thoro* (now called judicial separation), but urged the establishment of a divorce court with jurisdiction to grant dissolution in the same circumstances as acts of parliament could be obtained but without the need for previous proceedings in any other court. This recommendation was carried into effect in 1857, when the Court for Divorce and Matrimonial Causes was established and the divorce jurisdiction of the Church courts abolished.[49]

The reform was modest. There were no changes in the grounds for divorce, only in the procedure for obtaining it. The machinery was improved, and the cost reduced, but adultery remained the sole ground for dissolution; and, in the case of a wife petitioner, cruelty or desertion had to be proved as well. The court sat only in London, and its costs were still too high to put divorce within the reach of the lower classes. The abuses of the Victorian divorce court by society families

48. *R v Hall* (otherwise *Rollins*) (1845) *Times* 3 April, p. 8.
49. Matrimonial Causes Act 1857, 20 & 21 Vict, c.85.

became a scandal; formal evidence of adultery was often 'provided' by the respondent, no defence was offered, and unless the prying nose of the queen's proctor smelt collusion the effect was virtually divorce by consent. In 1909 the government was pressed to introduce more effective reforms; but, in the words of Judge Parry, they 'took refuge from their own want of judgment and energy in the constitutional asylum of a Royal Commission'. The grievances were well known, but 'to put the plain fact in the language of the man in the street, the government of that day funked a quarrel with the organised priest-hoods'.[50] The commission, under the chairmanship of Sir Gorrell Barnes, reported that they could find no unanimity among theologians on the subject of divorce and no logical secular reason for confining the grounds to adultery. They recommended as additional grounds, inter alia, cruelty or desertion for three years; and also that wives should possess the same rights as husbands. The Convocations of Canterbury and York immediately declared their hostility to any proposal to facilitate divorce, and the bill which was drawn up to implement the suggestions of the Barnes Commission was defeated in 1914 by the Churches. Another attempt, by Lord Buckmaster in 1923, was also defeated, though it succeeded in giving wives the same grounds for divorce as husbands.[51]

In the twentieth century most churchmen came to reconcile themselves to a divergence between the secular law of marriage and the ideals of Christian doctrine and discipline. In 1935 a committee of churchmen recognised the validity of such a divergence, and soon afterwards the reforms recommended in 1912 were accomplished.[52] The Church of England promptly legislated that divorced persons should not be allowed to remarry with the rites of the Church. The dilemma was ended: the law of divorce and the Canon law of marriage were themselves divorced. After the second world war, further discussion centred on the question whether it was right that divorce should depend upon proof of a matrimonial offence. After a bill had been presented in 1951 to permit divorce after separation by consent for seven years, the matter was referred to yet another Royal Commission, which reported in favour of retaining the matrimonial offence.[53] Lord Walker, in an impressive dissent, argued that divorce should be permitted where a marriage had broken down, and ten years later a

50. E. A. Parry *The Gospel and the Law* (1928), p. 238.
51. Report of the Barnes Commission (1912) Cd 6478; Matrimonial Causes Act 1923, 13 & 14 Geo V, c.19.
52. *The Church and Marriage* (1935); A. P. Herbert's Act 1937, 1 Edw VIII & 1 Geo VI, c.57.
53. Report of the Morton Commission (1955) Cmnd 9678.

commission appointed by the archbishop of Canterbury recommended that 'the doctrine of breakdown of marriage should be comprehensively substituted for the doctrine of the matrimonial offence as the basis of all divorce'. This was brought about in 1969. The new law of divorce still lays stress on the matrimonial offence as the principal manifestation of a breakdown, but it also embraces for the first time the possibility of divorce by consent, after a separation of two years, where a marriage has irretrievably broken down.[54]

Further reading

Pollock & Maitland, vol. II, pp. 364–436

H. Thurston, 'The Canon Law of the Divorce' (1904) 19 EHR 632–645

A. V. Dicey, *Law and Public Opinion in England during the 19th Century* (1905), pp. 369–396

O. R. McGregor, *Divorce in England* (1957)

J. Ridley, *Thomas Cranmer* (1962)

J. Jackson, *The Formation and Annulment of Marriage* (1969), pp. 7–77

G. de C. Parmiter, *The King's Great Matter* (1967)

R. H. Helmholz, *Marriage Litigation in Medieval England* (1975)

H. A. Kelly, *The Matrimonial Trials of Henry VIII* (1976)

BASTARDY

F. E. Farrer, 'The Bastard Eigné' (1917) 33 LQR 135–153

N. Adams, 'Nullius Filius' (1946) 6 *Univ Toronto Law Jo* 361–384

R. H. Helmholz, 'Bastardy Litigation in Medieval England' (1969) 13 AJLH, 360–383

J. L. Barton, 'Nullity of Marriage and Illegitimacy in the England of the Middle Ages' in *Legal History Studies 1972*, pp. 28–49

54. *Parliamentary Debates* (HL) ccl (5th ser.), col. 1547; *Putting Asunder* (1966); *Field of Choice* (Law Comm, 1968); Divorce Reform Act 1969, c.55.

24. Criminal Justice

The criminal law is not at first glance the most rewarding subject for historical study. In operation it has fluctuated from almost ineffectual leniency to brutal severity. In substance it has been slow to develop. It is not only that legal principle so often took second place to punctilious formalities or irrational privileges. There was little for centuries to parallel the reasoning processes which shaped the private law. The absence of pleaders and of special pleading from the criminal courts meant that nearly all criminal cases were tried, as they still are, on the general issue 'not guilty'; and so the only substantive question which could arise on the record was whether the accused was charged with a known offence. So long as the detailed facts which might constitute an offence, or furnish an excuse, were matters purely of evidence, sophisticated definitions of crimes were needless. Reason and jurisprudence, if any there were, remained irretrievably obscured behind the inscrutable and final verdicts of juries. All the usual prerequisites for legal development seem to have been lacking. Yet criminal law has a history. And it is not an uninteresting story, because amongst other things it shows how law can develop from practice and discussion without formal judgments to serve as recorded precedents. Such law is, in the first place, more akin to custom, in the sense that little can be done if the rules are not followed. But it was not local custom. As principles of criminal law became part of the common learning of the legal profession, their misapplication became so insupportable that procedures had to be devised to secure compliance and to resolve doubts. When that occurred, however informal the procedures, the principles became the law of the land.

CRIME AND TORT

The distinction between criminal and civil justice has been so familiar to everyone for so long that it is tempting to regard it as eternal. Not only are there different courts and procedures, but there is a fundamental difference of function. The civil law is designed to provide private redress for wrongs to individuals, whereas the criminal law is concerned with public order and the treatment of offenders against that order. Yet there was a time when the notion of public order was so undeveloped or weak that no such distinction could be made.

In early societies there is no concept of the 'state'. Both compensation and retribution are enforced at the instance of the wronged individual and his kin. Either there will be a feud between one family and another until satisfaction is wrought, or the potential feud will be averted by customary arbitration processes designed to secure the payment of money by way of 'emendation'. The purpose of monetary compensation is overtly retributive, but it is also compensatory; in modern language, it is both a fine and damages at the same time. In so far as feuds and their settlement were governed by rules, there was a law of wrongs. But there was no division of wrongs into crimes and torts. And the main purpose of introducing law into the matter was to protect the wrongdoer against excessive vengeance, rather than to punish him or deter others.

The notion of crime as a species of wrong requiring punishment at the instance of the community or state is based more on procedure than substance. It came to the fore when the responsibility for pursuing the punitive or retributive process shifted from the domestic community of the kin to the wider local community and thence to the king. The transfer of primitive police functions from the kin to the community at large now seems, for want of records, to have been imperceptible; but the acquisition by kings, and their grantees, of valuable and powerful jurisdiction over malefactors marked a new era of procedure in which the kin began to lose all significance, and the fiscal profits of punishment fell into the coffers of powerful individuals or of the Crown by right of jurisdiction.

The rather different notion of crime as a species of wrong requiring punishment or atonement because it is sinful is a more substantive notion which may have played a greater role than procedure alone suggests. Such an approach was fostered by the early Church and its teaching on the need to atone for sin by penance. Even when it was admitted that penance could be compounded for by pecuniary payments, resembling feud-compensation, the penal theory behind it was maintained. Penance was punitive; wrongdoers deserved, and needed, afflictive punishment. The ecclesiastical concept of infamy, exemplified by the form of the sentence of anathema, may have contributed to the idea that 'corruption of the blood' should follow conviction of a serious crime. In English law, the doctrine acquired a feudal dimension, because a felony was treated as a fundamental breach of the contract of homage; the felon forfeited his holding, and the sins of the father were visited on his children[1] by disinheritance until 1870.

Criminal justice in England was born of the union between these two notions when the Crown assumed the power to punish those who broke the 'king's peace', and the blood-feud system went into disuse.

FELONY AND TRESPASS

The firm rule of the Normans and Angevins has already been adverted to as one of the main causes of the common law system of judicature. It also settled that the judgment of transgressors against the king's peace belonged to royal justice. This was necessary to preserve law and order throughout the kingdom, and was incidentally beneficial to the king's purse. The shift of jurisdiction, however, did not in itself alter the fact that the initiative for bringing criminals to justice lay with the victim and his kin. In place of the feud-arbitration processes of communal justice there was a formal action, alleging breach of the king's peace, to be commenced before the king's judges. If the wrong was particularly heinous, it was 'unemendable' and the wrongdoer lost everything he had: his life, his lands, and his personal goods. Wrongs of this nature were called 'felonies', from an old word meaning wicked or treacherous, and the suit against the felon was called an appeal of felony. Lesser wrongs put the offender in the royal mercy and entailed imprisonment to secure a fine to the king, and an award of damages to the victim. The action in this case was the action of trespass *contra pacem regis*.[2] The division of wrongs into felonies and mere trespasses (or misdemeanours) had important consequences until 1967.[3]

The appeal of felony, though much used for several centuries, suffered from a number of defects which must often have deterred victims from the trouble and expense of prosecution. Its principal object was retribution, the invaluable satisfaction to be gained from annihilating an aggressor by legal process. The monetary compensation which had quenched the Anglo-Saxon thirst for revenge was not recoverable at common law in the case of felony, because under the new scheme of things conviction brought forfeiture of all the felon's property: his chattels to the king, his lands to his feudal lord. An appeal could be compromised for money, but it was an offence to do so without the king's licence. The victim who sought financial

1. See Psalms, xxxvii, 28; cix, 13. Cf. Ezekiel, xviii, 20.
2. See pp. 57, 340, ante.
3. Criminal Law Act 1967 (c.58), s.1. This does not explicitly abolish felonies and misdemeanours, but only the distinction between them.

compensation might have done better to settle privately without bringing an appeal, but this too was made an offence against royal justice: that of 'compounding a felony'. At risk of punishment for concealment, the complainant could always disregard the felony and sue in trespass. Trespass did indeed develop rapidly at the expense of the appeal. But the practice, though satisfactory to the individuals concerned, hindered the royal interest in punishing criminals and seizing their goods. The king accordingly developed his own means of discovering and prosecuting criminals, and these 'public' criminal procedures took precedence over any private action of trespass based on the same offence; moreover, conviction at the king's suit barred any subsequent civil suit for damages.[4] Even if the victim were content to pursue his appeal, his chances of success were slight; yet, if he lost, he might himself be punished. The proper mode of trial was not the jury, as in trespass, but battle; and the delays and evasions which accompanied judicial combat made the proceedings cumbersome and ineffectual. It is doubtful whether any appeal after the fourteenth century proceeded to an actual clash of arms; the main object of appellants after this period was to institute prosecutions which would be taken over by the Crown. Intermittent appeals of murder were brought until 1818,[5] but as a means of prosecuting crimes to judgment the appeal had been defunct since medieval times. Criminal justice had been taken over in all its stages by the Crown.

Trial on Indictment

The imperfections of the appeal procedure, and the consequent discouragement to criminal prosecutions, necessitated the introduction in the twelfth and thirteenth centuries of criminal process at the suit of the Crown. If all felonies were not coming to light through the private prosecution of appeals before the king's justices, the king had to take steps to compel the presentment of felonies to his justices by other means. The recording of serious crime as it occurred throughout the country was entrusted to royal officials called coroners, who had to record and investigate every violent or suspicious death by means of an inquest 'upon the view of the body' (*super visum corporis*). The duty of identifying and producing the persons guilty of each crime fell upon the community;[6] and if they failed, to the knowledge of the coroners,

4. These propositions seem to have been taken for granted before the 17th century:
   Higgins v Butcher (1607) Yelv 89; *Markham v Cobb* (1626) HLS MS 106, ff.256v–258v.
5. *Ashford v Thornton* (1818) 1 B & Ald 405, was the last; Stat 59 Geo III, c.46.
6. See p. 23, ante.

then the community as a whole was punished. When the royal justices visited each county in their eyres, or to execute lesser commissions, the representatives of each hundred and township were called upon to report crimes and present suspects for judgment; and their presentments were checked against the coroners' rolls. This system may have been as old as the eyres themselves, and may even have embodied procedures used in the shires before eyres began. It became mandatory under the Assizes of Clarendon (1166) and Northampton (1176).

THE GRAND JURY

The presentment procedure persisted after the disappearance of the eyres, when offences were presented on behalf of the community to the justices of oyer and terminer, or of gaol delivery, or to justices of the peace. The general presenting body at quarter sessions or assizes was called the 'grand jury', which was supposed to represent all the hundreds in the county. The grand jury strained its memory, and also scrutinised informations received in the form of 'bills of indictment',[7] to decide whether there was sufficient evidence to put individuals on trial before the justices. If the grand jurors considered that there was a case to answer, they found the bills 'true' by writing *billa vera* on the back; if not, they endorsed the bill *ignoramus* (we do not know) and proceedings on the bill ended. The finding of a true bill by the grand jury was not a judgment or a finding of guilt, and it required only a majority vote of twelve;[8] it was an accusation upon reasonable suspicion, the effect of which was to initiate proceedings between the king and the accused person to try the issue of guilt. Thus was the criminal prosecution on indictment commenced.

THE TRIAL JURY

The mode of trial on indictment under the Assizes of Clarendon and Northampton was the ordeal of water. When ordeals were abandoned in 1215, the justices were faced with an awkward dilemma. They could hardly discharge all suspected felons on the ground that they could no longer be tried, and they could not simply keep the suspects indefinitely in prison. Neither could the justices take it upon themselves to decide guilt, since the facts were outside their knowledge. The best solution was to ask the men of the country, who were present at the session, to tell the truth of the matter. By the end of the thirteenth century the regularisation of this practice had produced

7. 'Indictment' (from the Latin *indicare*, to point out or accuse) means an accusation.
8. The number of jurors was usually greater than 12, in later times invariably 23.

the 'petty jury' of twelve countrymen, a body identical with the jury used to try civil actions of trespass. It became a matter of course for the sheriff to summon potential jurors before judicial sessions began, and after 1352 at least[9] they had to be different from the members of the grand jury. Trial by jury became the palladium of English liberty. For seven hundred years, the only tribunal capable of deciding the guilt of a man accused upon indictment has been a jury of his peers. But the change to jury trial was an innovation; and, although it happened early enough to be received as common law, it remained in form optional to the accused. Every prisoner who pleaded not guilty was asked how he wished to be tried; to which the correct and only answer was, 'by God and the country' (meaning, by jury). If the prisoner declined to 'put himself on the country', as the law demanded, then he was to be put in a *prison forte et dure*.[10] By a grisly misunderstanding, the *prison* of the statute was inexplicably read as *peine*, and the hard pain or 'penance' involved pressing the accused to death under heavy weights. Some prisoners with little hope of acquittal actually chose this horrible fate in order to die unconvicted, and thus save their dependents from forfeiture of their property. Even when the *peine forte et dure* was abolished—so late as 1772[11]—silence at first led to automatic conviction rather than the imposition of compulsory jury trial.

TRIAL PROCEDURE

Little is known of the courtroom procedure at a trial on indictment before Tudor times, because such things did not attract the attention of reporters or descriptive writers. But the procedure described by sixteenth-century writers had quite probably been in use for a century or even two.

When the justices were seated and the commissions had been read, all the prisoners were brought to the bar of the court, chained together at the ankles, and their names checked with the indictments which the grand jury produced. Those who were to be tried were then arraigned individually by the clerk; their shackles were struck off, and they were asked to plead to the indictments against them. If a prisoner pleaded not guilty, he put himself on the country, and jurors were sworn in from the panel provided by the sheriff. The clerk then called for anyone to give evidence against the prisoner. The witnesses who came

9. Stat 25 Edw III (sess. v), c.3.
10. Statute of Westminster I, 1275, c.12.
11. Stat 12 Geo III, c.20. The last instance of pressing is said to have occurred at Cambridge in 1741. After 1827 a refusal to plead has been treated as equivalent to a plea of not guilty: Stat 7 & 8 Geo IV, c.28.

forward were sworn to tell the truth, and in telling their story might have to dispute with the prisoner.

The blessing of trial by jury certainly benefited the accused in some ways. He was able to challenge up to thirty-five jurors without giving any reason, and more with cause. The twelve who were selected had to be unanimous before they could convict him. If the jury acquitted him, however perversely, the verdict was final and unimpeachable. Yet the accused was, to modern eyes, at a considerable disadvantage compared with the prosecution. His right to call witnesses was doubted, and when it was allowed the witnesses were not sworn.[12] The process for compelling the attendance of witnesses for the prosecution, by taking recognisances, was not available to the defendant. The defendant could not have the assistance of counsel in presenting his case, unless there was a point of law arising on the indictment; since the point of law had to be assigned before counsel was allowed, the unlearned defendant had little chance of professional help. This harsh rule was defended on the grounds that the evidence to convict the prisoner ought to be so clear that it could not be contradicted, and that the judges would take care of that and also ensure that the trial proceeded according to law.[13] Another reason, if not expressly articulated, was the fear that trials would be lengthened if advocates took part. If counsel were allowed, it was pointed out with some alarm in 1602, every prisoner would want it.[14] There was little of the care and deliberation of a modern trial before the last century. The same jurors might have to try several cases, and keep their conclusions in their heads, before giving in their verdicts; and it was commonplace for a number of capital cases to be disposed of in a single sitting. Hearsay evidence was often admitted; indeed, there were few if any rules of evidence before the eighteenth century. The judge's charge was usually short and uninformative, since there was no requirement that the judge should sum up the evidence as he now does. The unseemly hurry of Old Bailey trials in the early nineteenth century was disgraceful; the average length of a trial was a few minutes, and 'full two thirds of the prisoners, on their return from their trials, cannot tell of any thing which has passed in court, nor even, very frequently, whether they have been tried'.[15] It is impossible to estimate how far these conditions led to wrong convictions, but the plight of the uneducated and unbefriended prisoner was a sad one.

12. This was altered by Stat 1 Annae (sess. ii), c.9.
13. Co Inst, vol. III, 137.
14. *R v Boothe* (1602) Brit Lib MS Add. 25203, f.569v.
15. Anon *Old Bailey Experiences* (1833), pp. 59–60. See also *Reminiscences of Sir Henry Hawkins* (1904), vol. I, p. 33.

The most important reforms were put off until the nineteenth century. In 1836 prisoners on trial for felony were at last given the right to 'make full answer and defence thereto by counsel learned in the law'.[16] In 1867 they were given facilities, comparable to those of the prosecution, for calling witnesses to depose evidence before the trial and having such witnesses bound over to attend the trial.[17] And in 1898 prisoners were accorded the dangerous privilege of giving sworn evidence themselves.[18]

Trial of Misdemeanours

All offences which were not treason or felony were classed as trespasses or misdemeanours. These could be, and usually were, tried on indictment in the same way as capital offences. Trial procedure was similar, except that defendants charged with misdemeanours were allowed counsel both to address the jury and to speak in mitigation of sentence. But the safeguards conferred by the indictment procedure in matters of life and death could in some cases be bypassed in respect of lesser offences, either by excluding the grand jury or by excluding both the grand and trial juries.

INFORMATIONS

Criminal informations were accusations made by an individual complainant, or a law officer of the Crown, which initiated proceedings without the intervention of a grand jury. The *ex officio* information by a law officer was the regular procedure in the Star Chamber and was also used for commencing controversial prosecutions in the King's Bench. Informations by private persons were encouraged by legislation imposing penalties for economic offences, and a breed of 'common informers' arose, who made a living by prying for reward. But there was no theoretical limitation on the use of informations, so long as they were not for felony, and from the time of James I the procedure became quite common; the attraction was that they saved the trouble and risk of first persuading a grand jury to approve the prosecution. In 1690 an unsuccessful attempt was made to shake the validity of informations at common law. The grievance was that the procedure

16. Trials for Felony Act 1836, 6 & 7 Will IV, c.114. Counsel had been allowed in treason cases since 1692, and had sometimes been allowed de facto in trials for felony.
17. Criminal Law Amendment Act 1867, 30 & 31 Vict, c.35, s.3. The prosecution had enjoyed these facilities since the 1550s at least.
18. Criminal Evidence Act 1898, 61 & 62 Vict, c.396.

could too easily be abused in bringing unfounded prosecutions, and in 1692 parliament ended that problem by forbidding informations to be filed in the King's Bench without leave of the court and by making the prosecutor liable to costs. Thereafter, prosecutions were commenced by information in the King's Bench only for those 'gross and serious misdemeanours which deserve the most public animadversion', such as riot or sedition.[19] The procedure cut out the grand jury, but not trial by jury.

SUMMARY CONVICTIONS

Trial by jury could in some cases be dispensed with as well. At common law, summary trial (that is, without indictment or jury) was permitted only in respect of offences, such as contempt, committed in the view of the judges sitting in open court. The need for a jury was displaced by the judges' own witness of the facts. The idea was extended in late-medieval statutes which gave justices of the peace the power to punish offences committed in their view out of court, and then in Tudor statutes which gave similar powers in respect of offences which, though not committed in the justices' presence, were discovered by 'examination'. The creation of powers of summary conviction upon examination accelerated in the seventeenth and eighteenth centuries. Such powers were appropriate only for minor offences, but even so they infringed the principle that a man should only be judged by his peers, and they were regarded with deep suspicion by the superior judges. In the seventeenth century the King's Bench took upon itself to review summary convictions by means of certiorari, and would examine the justices' record carefully to ensure not only that they had pursued the relevant statute precisely but also that the accused had been served with a summons and given an opportunity to defend himself.[20] Some thought this an undue interference with local authority, and parliament sometimes expressly excluded judicial review; after 1670 it became common to provide for an appeal to quarter sessions, which kept the matter in the county without denying an opportunity to correct mistakes. Each summary power, however, depended on the wording of the statute which introduced it. Summary jurisdiction was homogenised in 1848.[21]

---

19. *R v Berchet* (1690) 5 Mod Rep 459, 1 Shower KB 106; Stat 4 Will & Mar, c.18; Bl Comm, vol. IV, p. 309.
20. *R v Dyer* (1703) 6 Mod Rep 41, 1 Salk 181. And see p. 129, ante.
21. Summary Jurisdiction Act 1848, 11 & 12 Vict, c.43.

The Avoidance and Adjustment of Punishment

Penal theory at common law was very simple. For misdemeanour, the punishment was in the discretion of the justices; fines and whipping were the usual forms, penal imprisonment being a costly modern invention. For felony, the convict's person was in the king's mercy. In the earliest times this enabled some discretion to be used in ordering mutilations thought appropriate to the crime, but the common law soon fixed the sentence, with very few exceptions,[22] as death. For treason, it was a particularly cruel death; for murder and felony, death by hanging. The fixed penalty excluded undue savagery as well as undue mercy, but it introduced rather too much uniformity: the convicted murderer expected nothing worse than the accidental slayer or the petty villain who stole two shillings. Clearly this was not a tolerable state of affairs, and it survived in theory only because of the several ways which were discovered of avoiding the death penalty in practice. The effect of these evasions on the substantive law was stultifying and confusing. The common law felonies were narrowly confined, and development was left to statutes which as often as not elaborated the evasions instead of reforming the law. The three principal modes of evasion were derived from the prerogatives of the Crown and the Church respectively.

PARDONS

It seems to have been recognised from the beginning of royal intervention in the prosecution of criminals that the king enjoyed a power to grant charters of pardon to individual persons for wrongs done, as a matter of grace. This prerogative was essential to justice as regards homicide, because the early common law failed to distinguish intentional murder from accidental killing. Any man who killed another, however innocently, was a felon; but the king, out of mercy, could pardon such an offender, and by virtue of his coronation oath was morally bound to do so. Ironically, the existence of this prerogative perpetuated the barbaric rule itself, and what ought to have been a plain question of law remained for centuries at least nominally a matter of favour. What is worse, pardons were granted in many other cases for the wrong reasons. In 1328 parliament complained that pardons had been given out too freely, and enacted that in future they should only be granted where a man had killed another in self defence or by misfortune.[23] The statute did not, in fact, prevent the issue of pardons for money or through influence.

22. E.g. petty larceny (treated like a misdemeanour) and suicide (forfeiture of chattels).
23. Statute of Northampton 1328, 2 Edw III, c.2.

Pardoning contributed directly to the law of homicide, and it also contributed, though less consistently, to penal reforms. From the time of James I it was a common practice, usually on the recommendation of the trial judge, to pardon convicts on condition of transportation to some such wild and uninviting territory as Minorca or America. If the convict refused to go, or came back without licence, he could be executed on the original sentence. By the eighteenth century transportation was losing its deterrent value, and many welcomed it as offering a new start in life. The legislature then began to introduce more useful punishments, such as hard labour, and then pardoning gradually lost its value as a means of adjusting penalties.

The pardoning procedure also enabled the introduction of a system of informal appeal. If the trial judge doubted the legal propriety of a conviction upon the evidence he had heard, he referred the question to his brethren, who could recommend a pardon if they shared the doubt.[24] Not until 1848 were judges given the power to quash convictions themselves, except for errors on the face of the record. The only surviving uses of the pardon after 1848 have been where the Home Secretary entertains a doubt as to the safety of a conviction after all regular avenues of appeal have been exhausted, or where a change of circumstances after sentence is thought to warrant the exercise of compassion.

SANCTUARY

In medieval England there were a number of ecclesiastical places where the king's writ did not run. The underlying theory was that consecrated places ought not to be profaned by the use of force, but the result in practice was that thieves and murderers could take sanctuary and acquire an immunity even against the operation of criminal justice. In the case of parochial churches, the sanctuary lasted for forty days only. Before the expiration of this period, the fugitive had to choose whether to stand trial or 'abjure' the realm. If he chose abjuration, he was allowed to proceed on foot to a prescribed port and thence to leave the country, never to return. His action was tantamount to a confession, because his statement and abjuration were taken down in writing by a coroner, and his property was forfeited as upon conviction; his life only was spared, and if he ever returned to England he could be executed.

The greatest evil was the existence of private or special sanctuaries, usually in religious houses, where criminals could take permanent refuge. Without threat of expulsion, criminals in these sanctuaries

24. See p. 426, post.

could even sometimes carry on their outside activities. Some great churches, such as Durham, Beverley and Beaulieu, had substantial bodies of sanctuarymen in residence. In the great case of St John's Priory in 1516, several suggestions for restriction and reform were put forward. Fyneux CJ said that sanctuaries could not be claimed by prescription or papal grant alone without the king's consent, and that it was doubtful whether new sanctuaries could have been created after 1189; after this, proof of a sanctuary became very difficult. Henry VIII said that the old kings and popes in creating sanctuaries never intended them to become dens of thieves, and that he proposed to reform the abuses. This was agreed by the laymen present.[25] Henry later abolished most of the sanctuaries, and removed the availability of the privilege in respect of nearly all offences; the last vestiges were finally eradicated in 1623.[26]

BENEFIT OF CLERGY

Most important of all was the privilege of clergymen from temporal punishment, a privilege which became wildly extended, through fictions and legislation, as a vehicle for the avoidance of the mandatory death penalty for felony. The privilege was settled in the reign of Henry II after the conflict with Becket,[27] and the result was that a convict who could prove himself a clerk would be handed over to the ecclesiastical authorities to be dealt with according to Canon law. Many clerks convict escaped further penalty by performing compurgation; others were put in Church prisons, from which escape was notoriously easy in ordinary cases.

By the fifteenth century the benefit of clergy was being widely claimed by all manner of convicts, and the courts were in suitable cases allowing them to escape sentence of death by turning them over to the Church. This was made possible by the decision that the test of clergy should be the ability to read. When a man was convicted of felony, he could fall on his knees and 'pray the book'; he would then be tendered a passage from the psalter, called the neck-verse,[28] and if he could read or recite it his 'clergy' was taken to be proved. The decision whether the convict 'read as a clerk' was for the bishop's representative, present in court; but he was subject to the control of the judges,

---

25. *Pauncefote v Savage* (1516) KB 27/1020, m.60; Keil 188.
26. Stat 32 Hen VIII, c.12; 21 Jac I, c.28.
27. See pp. 111–112, ante.
28. At first, judges may have chosen passages at random. Later, *in favorem vitae*, it was customary to assign Psalm li, 1: *Miserere mei Deus secundum magnam misericordiam tuam; et secundum multitudinem miserationum tuarum, dele iniquitatem meam*. But some discretion was always retained: see *Crime in England 1550–1800*, p. 307, nn.150–151; 94 SS *329*.

who facilitated the extension of the benefit to all literate or hurriedly educated felons. By fiction, therefore, the judges extended clerical privilege as far as they could to laymen; but they could not extend it to persons who were incapable of being clergy. In the sixteenth and seventeenth centuries the fiction was cleared of the remaining ecclesiastical impediments, and a short term of imprisonment was substituted for delivery of the 'clerk' to the bishop. Clergy was extended to illiterate peers and women. Then in 1706 it was decided that the reading test had become of 'no use' and it became possible to claim clergy without knowing the neck-verse.[29]

The clemency of the royal judges in extending this privilege was as indiscriminate as the automatic punishment which occasioned it. It was as inconvenient that murderers and robbers should automatically escape all punishment as it was that they should inescapably suffer death. The restriction of the means of escape to those who could read was not rationally defensible, save on the social grounds that it weeded out the less intelligent criminal; but reason might equally have suggested that intelligent people were more to blame for criminal conduct than others. Some other means of control were needed. No doubt to some extent the reading test was applied with discretion, and we know that sometimes a judge heard a man read when the performance would have failed most other forms of examination. The first direct reform, in 1489, was to enact that laymen should only have clergy once; and to prevent evasion convicts who were allowed clergy were to be branded M (manslayer) or T (thief) in the brawn of the left thumb. Then the number of offences for which clergy could be allowed was reduced. Treason had never been clergiable,[30] and one early proposal—accepted in Ireland in 1494[31]—was to make murder once again a capital offence by turning it into treason. But if that could be done, parliament might as well make specific offences 'non-clergiable' without subterfuge. In 1512 clergy was temporarily removed from murder and certain forms of robbery; the experiment provoked an angry reaction from the Church,[32] but by the end of Henry VIII's reign the principle was firmly established. From 1531 until the nineteenth century most penal reforms were effected by withdrawing clergy in various circumstances and thereby reintroducing capital punishment, which in some cases was commutable to

29. Stat 1 Edw VI, c.12; 3 Will & Mar, c.9, s.6.
30. *R v Merks* (1401) 88 SS 102, 104; *Anon* (1532) Spelman Rep (93 SS) 49, pl. 15.
31. Stat 10 Hen VII (Irish), c.21. An English proposal to turn sacrilege into treason was rejected in 1467: Rot Parl, vol. V, p. 632, no. 17. Henry VIII made murder by poisoning high treason: Stat 22 Hen VIII, c.9.
32. See *Dr Standish's Case* (1515) Keil 180.

transportation. Meanwhile, the branding was used less and less. Peers were exempted from the iron after 1546, and it was usual to pardon persons of quality; the mark proved useless as a record, and it was not intended as a punishment; in many cases the iron was heated so perfunctorily that the process became 'a nice piece of absurd pageantry, tending neither to the reformation of the offender nor for example to others'.[33] When in 1779 the judges were given power to award fines or whipping instead of branding, the iron went out of use altogether. It was not until 1827 that clergy itself was abolished,[34] and the wording of penal statutes thereby released from the tortuosities of the previous three centuries.

Substantive Law of Crimes

The universality of the general issue in criminal cases prevented any legal development through the vehicle of special pleading, such as took place in private law. It has been concluded that 'nothing worthwhile was created. There is no achievement to trace . . . the only intellectual interest and the only hope for the future lie in the external investigations of the criminologist.'[35] Yet there had to be a law of crime, and it would have been a strange law if it had escaped professional discussion and development. Even if debates could not be framed upon tentative special pleas, questions of law were raised by the form of indictments, by the wording of statutes controlling the benefit of clergy or adding to the list of crimes, and (most important of all) by the evidence given at trials.

The formal way in which questions of law could be raised for determination was by removing an indictment into the King's Bench by certiorari, and taking exception to it for some defect. This procedure was common enough before Tudor times, and it enabled indictments to be quashed and convictions set aside for reasons which were recorded; but it was confined to errors on the face of the record. The King's Bench was thus enabled to set the bounds of offences, in so far as they were set out in indictments, but was unable to consider more detailed questions raised on the evidence. In practice, certiorari was chiefly employed to obtain discharges on purely technical grounds; and it is possible that, in the period before other methods of reviewing convictions were developed, technical errors were used as pretexts for quashing convictions thought unsafe for reasons not overtly given.

33. M. Foster *Crown Law* (1762), p. 372.
34. Stat 7 & 8 Geo IV, c.28. Branding: 19 Geo III, c.74, s.3.
35. Milsom HFCL, p. 353.

More detailed questions of criminal law could only arise informally at the trial, when it had to be decided whether the evidence proffered was sufficient to support the indictment. In reviewing indictments, the King's Bench could only decide whether the formalised phrases were in order; if the indictment was formally correct, it was for the trial judge to rule whether the facts proved fitted the forms. Thus, an indictment for theft would allege a taking and carrying away with force and arms; but only the trial judge could say whether a bailee or a finder who appropriated goods could be said to take with force and arms. If the trial judge directed the jury on such a question he was applying law. But whether he was making law is a different matter: his opinions were neither entered on the record nor reported, and if another judge in the next county was directing juries differently nothing could be done by way of appeal. The detailed development of the criminal law depended on the introduction of some mechanism for ensuring uniformity among judges, by providing for centralised discussion of questions of the kind which arose at trials. This type of discussion could not take place in banc, as in civil cases, because criminal cases began and ended in the county. But it could occur in other ways.

First, there was the discussion of abstract principle at readings and moots in the inns of court. Criminal law was the main subject of discussion next to the land law, in the early Tudor period (1485–1546),[36] and probably had been so before then, precisely because its principles could not easily be aired in other ways. Those who attended included most present and future justices of the peace and sometimes assize judges visiting their former inns to lend the benefit of their experience to the discussion. The inns of court probably contributed as much to the formulation of the criminal law as did any courts of law. The cessation of these discussions coincided with the emergence of a printed literature of criminal law in the shape of Fitzherbert's *New Boke of Justices of Peas* (1538) and Staunford's *Les Plees del Coron* (1557), both of which were influenced by the learning previously handed down at readings.

The second technique, which also came to the fore in the early Tudor period, was for the trial judge to adjourn a difficult case for consultation with his brethren in Serjeants' Inn or the Exchequer Chamber the following term. By 1500 there seem to have been regular meetings in Serjeants' Inn to discuss actual cases reserved from the circuits; and it was these meetings which developed over three centuries later into the Court for Crown Cases Reserved.[37] The

36. See 94 SS *347–350*.   37. See p. 120, ante.

procedure was slightly formalised in the seventeenth century by taking special verdicts for the purpose,[38] and in the eighteenth century the practice whereby the judge stated a case from his own notes—in the same way that civil cases were stated for the court in banc[39]—became an acceptable alternative. In either case, the cases were not being discussed in a court; the conclusion of the assembled judges was expressed either as advice to the trial judge or, if conviction had already occurred, as advice to the Home Secretary whether to grant a pardon. Yet these discussions, which after 1500 were sporadically reported by judges or serjeants who were present, made as real a contribution to legal development as did more formal precedents in private law.

THE MENTAL ELEMENT IN CRIME

Much of the criminal law was concerned with the definition of felonies; and, because a felony was a capital offence, the attitude of the courts tended towards restrictive rather than equitable exposition. The filling of gaps was left to parliament, which understandably shied away from broad principles of criminal liability and legislated ad hoc to counter specific evils. One pervasive question at common law, however, was the extent to which moral wickedness was a constituent element in criminal offences. The word 'felony' implies wickedness, and is the antithesis of blameless accident and misadventure. When crime and tort became separate, the essence of felony was identified as a forcible criminal act done with a guilty mind (*mens rea*). The internal element of crime, the *mens rea*, had not been an essential prerequisite for a feud or an appeal, and we have seen that it was not an element in trespass *vi et armis*.[40] It was difficult to try. Even so, the common law adopted the canonist view—which may be traced to the teachings of St Augustine—that mental guilt was the prime ingredient of criminal conduct: *reum non facit nisi mens rea*.[41]

In indictments for murder, 'malice aforethought' was laid expressly; in other indictments, the *mens rea* was held to be implicit in the word *felonicè* (feloniously). What amounted to such an intent could only arise upon the evidence, and such questions were therefore appropriate for the Serjeants' Inn procedure, of which there are several reported examples from the 1530s; for instance, whether a suicide who cut his throat and then repented and wished to live was

38. See 8 IJ 307 n.27.
39. See pp. 74, 119–120, ante.
40. See p. 341, ante.
41. Pollock & Maitland, vol. II, p. 476, n.5.

guilty of felony *de se*.[42] Most of the discussions, however, turned on the defendant's capacity to form a malicious intent.

It was settled in medieval times that a child could not be convicted of felony if he was too young to discern between right and wrong; no age was fixed, but the question of fact was left to the jury.[43] The same was true of lunatics and insane persons; and at least one fifteenth-century lawyer considered automatism to be a defence.[44] Drunkenness, however, was more an aggravation than an excuse, because the want of discretion was self-inflicted; therefore, according to the old proverb, 'he that killeth a man drunk, sober shall be hanged'. The law excused madmen if they were unable to know right from wrong, so that their actions were more like animal reflexes than the exercise of moral choice. That was the way the matter was left to jurors in medieval times and in the nineteenth century; there was no refinement in the test for six centuries. The rise of medical jurisprudence and the inevitable conflicts over the types and consequences of insanity led to popular dissatisfaction at some acquittals of the 'partially insane', even though the acquitted lunatics were locked up in Bedlam. In 1843 the House of Lords summoned the judges to answer certain abstract questions about insanity and criminal responsibility, particularly in cases of 'delusion', and the answers were the basis of subsequent development.[45] The procedure was most ill advised, and has not been followed, because the judges' opinions were given without the benefit of argument and yet were cast in a form which had all the disadvantages of legislation. The situation provides the strongest argument for those who maintain that the criminal law was unable to develop under the old procedures.

TREASON

The history of high treason, which is the most serious offence known to English law, properly belongs to constitutional history and little will be said of it here. Since felonies also were offences against the king and public order, the notion of treason as something worse than felony was inherently elastic. It is 'a crime which has a vague circumference and more than one centre'.[46] The essence of the offence was a

42. *Anon* (1533) Spelman Rep (93 SS) 68, 140. See also ibid. 58 (insanity), 72 (provocation). In the last case the question was raised by a special indictment.
43. YB Mich 3 Hen VII, 1, pl. 1; and f.12, pl. 8; 94 SS *309* n.3.
44. Cambridge Univ Lib MS Ee.5.22, f.102.
45. *The M'Naghten Rules* (1843) 10 Cl & Fin 200. For a clear specimen direction using the old test, see *R v Arnold, Arnold's Case* (1724) 16 State Tr 695 at 754, 764 per Tracy J.
46. Pollock & Maitland, vol. II, p. 503.

treacherous usurpation of or challenge to the king's authority. But the limits at common law were vague, and Hale cites a case of 1347 in which a man was indicted for imprisoning another to exact money, and thus usurping or 'accroaching' the royal power.[47] Because of the uncertainty, a statute was passed in 1351 which made treason the first major statutory offence and has served to define treason down to the present day.[48] The most heinous form is compassing the death of the sovereign and certain members of the royal family. This was at times very widely construed, and in 1615 was held to include expressions of opinion that killing the king was lawful. In most ages, however, the courts required proof of an overt act in addition to words, and this was laid down as a necessary element in 1628.[49] The most important form of treason consists in levying war against the king in his realm, or adhering to the king's enemies. The 'king' for this purpose is the de facto sovereign, and so in times of civil war allegiance was owed to the king in possession of the Crown.[50] This rule probably operated only to excuse the adherents of a de facto king, but it was wise for a victorious incoming king to pardon his own supporters. In peace time there could be a constructive levying of war if three or more 'arose' to alter the established religion or law or to effect some public purpose against all opposition.[51]

Petty treason was a lesser form of the offence, which consisted in domestic treachery by a wife, servant or monk. If a wife killed her husband, or a servant his master, or a monk his abbot, the offence was not merely murder; as a form of treason it was more severely punished and, at least after this point was clarified in 1496, was not clergiable.[52] But the offence was strictly confined; thus parricide was only treason if the child happened to perform services for the parent.[53] Petty treason was abolished, and the offence reduced to murder, in 1828. Another lesser form of treason consisted in counterfeiting the great seal or any coin of the realm; this offence was reduced to felony in 1835.

---

47. *History of Pleas of the Crown*, vol. I, p. 80. It seems, however, that accroaching the royal power was not high treason but a form of petty treason.
48. Treasons Act 1351, 25 Edw III (sess. v), c.2.
49. *R v Owen* (1615) 1 Rolle Rep 185; *R v Pine* (1628) Cro Car 117.
50. Stat 11 Hen VII, c.1, which was said to declare the common law.
51. An extreme example is *R v Bradshaw* (1597) Co Inst, vol. III, p. 10 (putting down enclosures). There a mere conspiracy was treason, because of the Stat 13 Eliz I, c.1.
52. Stat 12 Hen VII, c.7. Wives who killed their husbands suffered death by burning: e.g., *R v Ferthing* (1380) 88 SS 14. But it was not petty treason for a man to kill his wife.
53. *Anon* (1553) Dalison Rep, Brit Lib MS Harley 5141, f.17v. Cf. Co Inst, vol III, p. 20.

HOMICIDE

The early history of homicide suffered more than other crimes from the lack of any distinction, in the first place, between crime and tort. Any killing, even by accident, had sufficed to warrant a feud; and an appeal of death could be brought whenever the appellee's conduct had brought the victim nearer death and further from life. As far as the king was concerned, every death in unusual circumstances required investigation by the coroners, because any chattel which occasioned the death was forfeited as deodand.[54] The same principle was adopted when a man was indicted for killing another; if his action caused the death, he was liable to conviction. It is unlikely that accidental or justifiable killings were ever in fact intended to attract the death penalty, but the remedy lay solely in the king's grace; 'the man who commits homicide by misadventure or in self defence deserves but needs a pardon'.[55] The issue of a pardon in such cases became a matter of course, and in 1278 it was provided that the trial judge could report cases of misadventure or self defence to the king without the need for a special commission of inquiry.[56]

The law of pardons not only drew a distinction between felonious homicide and killing by misadventure, or in self defence; but it was also established that a pardon of 'all felonies' did not extend to murder.[57] Originally the word 'murder' had been used only for secret or stealthy killings, where the killer's identity was unknown; but by 1400 it denoted a malicious, premeditated or deliberate killing. The distinction between murder and other forms of felonious homicide (called 'manslaughter') was accentuated by statutes which, from 1512, removed benefit of clergy from murder done with malice aforethought.[58] The result of these various provisions was the tripartite classification of homicides: if the killing was done out of malice, it was punished by death and forfeiture; if there was no prior malice, for instance if the death arose out of a spontaneous quarrel (*chance medley*), then it was clergiable and punished only by forfeiture of chattels; while if the killing was accidental or excusable, for instance if done in self defence, there would be a pardon and the forfeiture would not be enforced.

Before long it was realised that the dichotomy of malice and chance medley—of cold and hot blood—was not very sound. Malice was not

54. See p. 322, ante.
55. Pollock & Maitland, vol II, p. 479. In the 1480s it was said that accidental killing was a 'contempt' to the king, because it deprived him of a subject: Keil 108, pl.27.
56. Statute of Gloucester 1278, c.9.
57. Stat 13 Ric II (sess. ii), c.1; 94 SS *305* n.4.
58. The earliest statutes were 4 Hen VIII, c.2; 23 Hen VIII, c.1.

easy to define, and even harder to prove; often it had to be implied from the facts surrounding the killing.[59] So long as there was a general evil intent, an intent to injure someone, there was no need to prove any intent to kill the deceased.[60] Moreover, a chance fight, if unprovoked, might itself be murderous. In a case of 1600 a shopkeeper became so incensed with a customer who had 'flirted' him on the nose and made faces at him from the street that he came out of his shop and hit him so hard that he died. He was indicted and convicted of manslaughter; but the widow brought an appeal and the judges held it to be murder, because there was insufficient cause to start a quarrel.[61] After this, the doctrine of chance medley faded away and the test of manslaughter in such a case came to be, not hot bloodedness, but the presence or absence of 'provocation'.[62] This development was facilitated by a statute of 1604 which took away benefit of clergy for killing by stabbing, where the deceased had no weapon drawn, even if at common law the killing was but manslaughter.[63]

PERSONAL INJURIES

Physical assaults which did not amount to homicide fell only partially within the common law range of felonies. A maiming, that is, a serious incapacitation or loss of limb, was the subject of the appeal of mayhem; but this form of redress gave way to the action of trespass, and mayhem did not become an indictable felony.[64] Violent assaults were therefore mere trespasses or misdemeanours until a number of offences akin to mayhem were made felonies by statute.[65] Demanding money or other valuables with menaces was not a felony until 1722.[66]

The forcible carnal knowledge of a woman against her will was the subject of an appeal of rape. The punishment was castration and blinding, or fine and imprisonment, until 1285 when rape was made a capital felony.[67] Buggery was not a felony at common law, probably because it included an element of consent inconsistent with the notion of force and arms; it became a capital felony in 1533, and it remained a

59. See *R v Yong* (1586) 4 Co Rep 40; *R v Mackalley* (1611) 9 Co Rep 68.
60. 94 SS *309–310; R v Saunders and Archer* (1573) Plowd 473.
61. *Watts v Brains* (1600) Cro Eliz 778, Noy 171, Brit Lib MS Add. 25203, f.216v. Cf. *R v Huggett* (1666) Kel 59.
62. *R v Royley* (1612) Cro Jac 296, 12 Co Rep 87, Godb 182; *R v Mawgridge* (1707) Kel 119.
63. Statute of Stabbing 1603, 1 Jac I, c.8. See *R v Lord Morly* (1666) Kel 54.
64. For a consequence in the law of defamation, see p. 369, ante.
65. The first was the Stat 5 Hen IV, c.5 (cutting out of tongues and eyes).
66. YB Trin 9 Edw IV, 26, pl. 36; Black Act 1722, 9 Geo I, c.22.
67. Statute of Westminster II, c.34.

serious felony until its scope was reduced by a permissive government in 1967.[68]

ARSON

Arson, the malicious burning of dwelling houses and barns, was the more serious of the two common law felonies concerning a man's home. The criminal misuse of fire was not only purely destructive of the victim's property, but also a serious threat to public safety in times when most houses were constructed of timber and thatch, and the means of extinguishing large fires were primitive. For these reasons, arson[69] was among the earliest pleas of the Crown and was a felony. Throughout the thirteenth century it was punished, *jure talionis*, with death by burning. Unlike murder, however, the offence always required a malicious intent, and accident was a good defence.

It is easy to see why arson was so seriously regarded, but it is astonishing that until comparatively recent times it was the only offence of causing damage to property. If a man burned property other than houses or granaries, or destroyed houses otherwise than by fire, then at common law the only remedy was a civil action of trespass. The gaps were filled piecemeal by numerous statutes which were consolidated in 1861. In 1971 the miscellaneous offences were abolished and replaced by an offence of unlawfully destroying or damaging property.[70]

BURGLARY

The criminal invasion, as opposed to the destruction, of a dwelling house was known to the English as *hamsoken* or *husbrice*. There was no appeal of felony corresponding to this offence, except where the housebreaking was aggravated with robbery. Nevertheless, before the fifteenth century housebreaking had become an indictable felony, usually called 'burglary'.[71] The older sources make no distinction between day and night, but it was settled by the 1450s that burglary was a nocturnal crime.[72] Offences committed at night were regarded more seriously than daytime offences because all decent folk were supposed to be asleep and off their guard. The limitation had the unfortunate effect, however, that housebreaking in the daytime, or

68. Stat 25 Hen VIII, c.6; Sexual Offences Act 1967 (c.60).
69. From the French *arder*, to burn.
70. Malicious Damage Act 1861, 24 & 25 Vict, c.97; Criminal Damage Act 1971 (c.48).
71. The word may originally have denoted breaking into a walled town to carry out a raid (*burgaria, burglaria*). Breaking town-walls was mentioned in some definitions of burglary as late as the time of Henry VIII: 94 SS *325* n.1.
72. This is stated by John Baldwin (d. 1469) in his reading at Gray's Inn: 94 SS *326* n.2.

while a house was uninhabited, was no felony at common law. This shortcoming was remedied by a string of statutes beginning in 1547.[73]

Having decided that burglary could only be committed at night, the judges had to define 'night'. At first it was agreed that night began at sunset and ended at sunrise, so that burglary could be committed in the twilight periods between sunset and darkness and between daybreak and sunrise; it was said to be easier to try the setting and rising of the sun than the beginning and ending of daylight.[74] But this test was later replaced by that of darkness: whether the countenance of man was discernible.[75] In 1837 an arbitrary definition of night was introduced by statute, and now the nocturnal element has disappeared from the law altogether.[76]

The indictment for burglary charged that the accused broke and entered a dwelling house by night *felonicè et burglariter*. These last words did not denote the actual commission of a felony, but only a felonious intent. Serjeant Marow (d. 1505) thought it necessary to prove either an intent to murder or the actual commission of any felony; but Fitzherbert (d. 1538) and later writers took the view that an intent to commit any felony was sufficient. It had always been necessary to show a breaking into the house, which operated as a further restriction; but the law managed to include within the definition the insertion of hooks through windows after drawing a latch, or shooting through a hole made in a wall.[77]

ROBBERY AND THEFT

Robbery was an offence against the person and also against property; manifest theft coupled with personal violence. It was a felony, subject to the appeal and the indictment. Secret theft, on the other hand, was more an offence of dishonesty than of violence and was not immediately recognised as a felony. But the king's peace was wide enough to accommodate larceny[78] in due course as an indictable felony; and in order to distinguish the felony from a mere trespass *de bonis asportatis* it was necessary to show *mens rea*, in this case an intent to steal. The distinction between theft and robbery was of particular importance

---

73. Stat 1 Edw VI, c.12, s.10 (housebreaking). It was debatable whether this introduced a new offence, or removed clergy from an offence which did not exist.
74. *Anon* (1506) Keil 75 per Frowyk CJ.
75. Co Inst, vol. III, p. 63; *Anon* (1606) Brit Lib MS Hargrave 29, f.214.
76. Stat 7 Will IV & 1 Vict., c.86, s.4; Theft Act 1968 (c.60), s.9.
77. See *Anon* (1584) 1 And 114, Sav 59, Clench MS Rep.; *Anon* (1616) 8 IJ 317.
78. This word is the French equivalent of *latrocinium*, though the classical Latin *latro* was a robber. In the common law it meant taking and carrying away goods feloniously with force and arms. But the word was not used in indictments and records, where the operative phrase was *felonicè furatus fuit*.

from the sixteenth century to the nineteenth because larceny was clergiable, whereas robbery was usually a capital offence.

Because of the death penalty, minor thefts were excluded from the capital felony of 'grand larceny'. Petty larceny, the theft of money or goods of or below the value of twelve pence, was normally punished by whipping; and benevolent prosecutors or jurors were at liberty to value stolen goods at a shilling or below, contrary to the fact, if they thought mercy was called for. Things annexed to land,[79] and objects of sport and pleasure—such as dogs, cats, singing birds, and according to one Tudor judge diamonds[80]—were not larcenable at all.

On the other hand, larceny was unduly narrowed by its trespassory character. Many forms of dishonesty could not be treated as felonious because they did not include a taking with force and arms. Thus the bailee, agent, factor or trustee who appropriated property entrusted to him could not be convicted of larceny because the owner had voluntarily parted with possession and so there was no taking *vi et armis*. If this needed a justification, it was that in all these cases the owner knew whom to call to account and could avail himself of detinue or conversion; the essence of larceny was a taking by stealth or force, against which it was more difficult to guard. Nevertheless, the requirement of a forcible taking was regarded as an inconvenient restriction, and from the fifteenth century various inroads were made on the doctrine. First, in 1473, a meeting of all the judges held that a carrier could be guilty of theft if he 'broke bulk' by opening the package consigned to him and appropriating the separate contents; and this on the rather strained reasoning that he was a bailee of the whole package only, so that he could be said to act with force and arms in respect of the contents.[81] The second extension was directed against servants. It was already law that a person having merely the temporary use of a thing was not in legal possession, so that a drinker who stole the cup served to him in a tavern was guilty of felony. Towards the end of the fifteenth century it was held that a servant attending his master likewise did not have a separate possession of goods in his keeping; a man did not part with the possession of the wine in his cellar by giving the keys to a butler. But this was as far as the common law would go in this direction. A servant sent on an errand away from the household did have possession of the goods he took with him, and could not steal them feloniously except by breaking

79. *R v Gardiner* (1533) Spelman Rep (93 SS) 99; 94 SS 317.
80. *Anon* (1553) Dalison Rep, Brit Lib MS Harley 5141, f.12 per Hales J. It was held in the 15th century that holy relics could not be stolen because they were invaluable: 94 SS *318* n.2.
81. *The Carrier's Case* (1473) 64 SS 30. For other cases, see 94 SS *319–321*.

bulk. Parliament closed this gap in 1529 by making it felony for a servant to abscond with or 'embezzle' goods worth more than forty shillings which he had received from his master to look after; but the full offence of embezzlement, the appropriation of money or goods received from third parties to the master's use, was not clearly recognised as a felony for another 170 years.[82] In the eighteenth century some bolder judicial extensions of the scope of larceny were made by narrowing in other ways the notion of legal possession. Possession ceased to be a physical fact and became an abstract legal notion in which there was a mental element. The origin of the new law was the old idea that one could hand over goods without passing possession. Possession did not pass, for example, to the drinker in a tavern, or to the customer in a shop,[83] who were merely using or handling goods which remained in the owner's immediate control. The next step was for lawyers to argue that when physical possession was handed over for a specific purpose, which the recipient had no intention of carrying out, the possession did not pass in law. Thus the hirer of a horse who rode off, never to return, and sold the horse, could be convicted of theft if he had had the intention of stealing from the moment when the horse was delivered to him.[84] This was perhaps the point at which the law began to part company with logic, because whether possession passed was made to depend not on the actual intention of the owner but on the guilty intent of the receiver; the 'taking' in such a case was constructive, or fictitious. The new idea of constructive taking, where an apparent parting with possession could be negatived, proved fertile. Now it was possible to convict of felony those who obtained possession by a trick, on the theory that if the owner did not truly consent to part with possession then it did not pass. By the early nineteenth century, even those who appropriated goods they had found[85] could be convicted of felony, on the principle that the loser remained in constructive possession. In 1873 the theory got quite out of hand, and a majority of judges held that a man who had been

82. Stat 21 Hen VIII, c.7; 39 Geo III, c.85. For attempts to deal with these situations at common law, see *R v Armysby* (1533) Spelman Rep (93 SS) 50, 94 SS 280; *R v Penley* (1542) 94 SS *320*. Defeat was admitted in *R v Bazeley* (1799) 2 Leach 835, which prompted the legislation. Trustees and bailees were not reached till 1857: Stat 20 & 21 Vict, c.54.

83. *Anon* (1616) 8 IJ 313; *R v Chisser* (1679) T Raym 275.

84. *R v Tunnard* (1729) and *R v Pear* (1779) 1 Leach 213, 2 East PC 685. The other cases are examined fully in E. H. East *Pleas of the Crown* (1803), vol. II, pp. 635–698.

85. Much confusion arose from misuse of this term. A thief will say he 'found' goods merely because they were out of the owner's sight. An intruder who takes a coin mislaid under a bed does not 'find' it. Likewise a coachman who 'finds' goods left in his coach is not truly a finder. It is easy to see how the owner's possession in such cases came to rest on intention.

overpaid by mistake could steal the surplus feloniously, even though the payer intended to pass the property and the payee practised no deceit in accepting it.[86] Meanwhile, parliament had been moving in a similar direction, by introducing various offences of dishonesty, such as embezzlement, fraudulent conversion, receiving stolen goods, obtaining property by false pretences, and obtaining credit by fraud. Stealing, in the old sense, came to be generally regarded as no less serious in its nature than the other forms of dishonest enrichment; and the idea began to take root that he who was as bad as a thief should be treated as a thief. In 1968 the traditional notion of theft, as a forcible taking of possession, was finally laid to rest, and a broad but troublesome definition of dishonesty put in its place.[87]

Further reading

Pollock & Maitland, vol. II, pp. 448–511

Plucknett CHCL, pp. 424–458

Milsom HFCL, pp. 353–374

J. H. Beale, 'The Borderland of Larceny' (1892) 6 HLR 244–256

F. B. Sayre, 'Mens Rea' (1932) 45 HLR 974–1026

J. Goebel, *Felony and Misdemeanour* (1937)

J. Scurlock, 'The Element of Trespass in Larceny at Common Law' (1948) 22 *Temple Law Qly* 12–45

L. Radzinowicz, *History of English Criminal Law from 1750* (1948–   )

T. F. T. Plucknett, *Edward I and Criminal Law* (1960)

J. M. Kaye, 'Early History of Malice Aforethought' (1967) 83 LQR 365–395, 569–601

N. Walker, *Crime and Insanity in England Volume One: the Historical Perspective* (1968)

N. D. Hurnard, *The King's Pardon for Homicide* (1970)

J. G. Bellamy, *The Law of Treason in England in the later Middle Ages* (1970); *The Tudor Law of Treason* (1979)

J. H. Baker, 'Criminal Justice at Newgate 1616–27' (1973) 8 IJ 307–322; 'Criminal Courts and Procedure at Common Law 1550–1800' in *Crime in England 1550–1800* (J. S. Cockburn, Ed, 1977), pp. 15–48; 'Pleas of the Crown' (1978) 94 SS 299–350

J. H. Langbein, *Prosecuting Crime in the Renaissance* (1974); 'The Criminal Trial before the Lawyers' (1978) 45 *Univ Chicago Law Rev* 263–316

---

86. *R v Middleton* (1873) LR 2 CCR 38.
87. Theft Act 1968 (c.60).

T. A. Green, 'The Jury and the English Law of Homicide
1200–1600' (1976) 74 *Michigan Law Rev* 414–499

G. P. Fletcher, 'The Metamorphosis of Larceny' (1976) 89 HLR
469–530

'The Making of English Criminal Law' (1977–   ) *Criminal Law Rev*
(continuing)

Appendix A
Specimen Writs

Judicial Writs

i) Common Pleas process: *capias ad respondendum*[1]

GEORGE the second, by the grace of God of Great Britain, France and Ireland king, defender of the faith, and so forth; to the sheriff of Oxfordshire, greeting. WE command you, that you take Charles Long, late of Burford, gentleman, if he may be found in your bailiwick, and him safely keep, so that you may have his body before our justices at Westminster, from the day of Easter in five weeks, to answer to William Burton, gentleman, of a plea that he render to him two hundred pounds, which he owes him and unjustly detains, as he saith: and whereupon you have returned to our justices at Westminster, that the said Charles hath nothing in your bailiwick whereby he may be distrained. And have you there then this writ. WITNESS sir John Willes,[2] knight, at Westminster, the sixteenth day of April, in the twenty-eighth year of our reign.

ii) King's Bench process: *latitat*[3]

GEORGE the second, etc., to the sheriff of Berkshire, greeting. WHEREAS we lately commanded our sheriff of Middlesex that he should take Charles Long, late of Burford in the county of Oxford, if he might be found in his bailiwick, and him safely keep, so that he might be before us at Westminster at a certain day now past, to answer unto William Burton, gentleman, of a plea of trespass; AND ALSO[4] to a bill of the said William against the said Charles, for two hundred pounds of debt, according to the custom of our court, before us to be exhibited; and our said sheriff of Middlesex at that day returned to us that the aforesaid Charles was not found in his bailiwick; whereupon on the behalf of the aforesaid William in our

1. From Bl Comm, vol. III, Appendix III (2), where all the process is set out.
2. Chief Justice of the Common Pleas.
3. From Bl Comm, vol. III, Appendix III (3), where the Bill of Middlesex is also set out.
4. The *ac etiam* clause.

court before us it is sufficiently attested, that the aforesaid Charles lurks and runs about in your county; THEREFORE we command you, that you take him, if he may be found in your bailiwick, and him safely keep, so that you may have his body before us at Westminster on Tuesday next after five weeks of Easter, to answer to the aforesaid William of the plea and bill aforesaid: and have you there then this writ. WITNESS sir Dudley Ryder, knight,[5] at Westminster, the eighteenth day of April, in the twenty-eighth year of our reign.

iii) Exchequer process: *quominus*[6]

GEORGE the second, etc., to the sheriff of Berkshire, greeting. WE command you, that you omit not by reason of any liberty of your county, but that you enter the same, and take Charles Long, late of Burford in the county of Oxford, gentleman, wheresoever he shall be found in your bailiwick, and him safely keep, so that you may have his body before the barons of our Exchequer at Westminster, on the morrow of the holy Trinity, to answer William Burton our debtor of a plea that he render to him two hundred pounds which he owes him and unjustly detains, whereby he is the less able to satisfy us the debts which he owes us at our said Exchequer, as he saith he can reasonably shew that the same he ought to render, and have you there this writ. WITNESS sir Thomas Parker, knight,[7] at Westminster, the sixth day of May, in the twenty-eighth year of our reign.

Original Writs[8]

A: PRAECIPE WRITS

i) *Writ of right patent*[9]

Henry, by the grace of God etc., to Henry Earl of Lancaster, greeting. We command you, that without delay you do full right to *A* of *B* in respect of one messuage and twenty acres of land with the appurtenances in *J* which he claims to hold of you by the free service of one penny a year for all service, of which *W* of *T* deforceth him; and unless you will do this, let the sheriff of Nottingham do it, that we may hear no more clamour thereupon for want of right. Witness etc.

5. Lord Chief Justice of the King's Bench.
6. From Bl Comm, vol. III, Appendix III (4).
7. Chief Baron of the Exchequer.
8. This very limited selection is intended only to illustrate the principal varieties of original writ.
9. Fitzherbert *Natura Brevium*, 1 G. The translation of the writs taken from Fitzherbert are based on those in the 1794 edition.

Henricus Dei gratia etc. Henrico Comiti Lancastriae salutem. Praecipimus tibi, quod sine dilatione plenum rectum teneas A de B de uno mesuagio et xx acris terrae cum pertinentiis in I, *quae clamat tenere de te per liberum servitium unius denarii per annum, pro omni servitio, quod* W *de* T *ei deforciat; et nisi feceris, Vicecomes Nottingham' faciat, ne amplius inde clamorem audiamus pro defectu recti. Teste etc.*

ii) *Praecipe in capite*[10]

The King to the sheriff of Nottinghamshire greeting. Command *A* that justly and without delay he render to *B* one messuage with the appurtenances in *D*, which he claimeth to be his right and inheritance, and to hold of us in chief, and whereof he complains that the aforesaid *A* unjustly deforceth him; and unless he will do this, and [if] the aforesaid *B* shall give you security to prosecute his claim, then summon by good summoners the aforesaid *A* that he be before our justices at Westminster on such a day to show wherefore he hath not done it. And have there the summoners and this writ. Witness etc.

Rex vicecomiti Notingham' salutem. Praecipe A *quod juste et sine dilatione reddat* B *unum mesuagium cum pertinentiis in* D, *quod clamat esse jus et haereditatem suam, et tenere de nobis in capite, et unde quaeritur quod praedictus* A *ei injuste deforciat etc. Et nisi fecerit, et praedictus* B *fecerit te securum de clamore suo prosequendo, tunc summone per bonos summonitores praedictus* A *quod sit coram justiciariis nostris apud Westmonasterium etc. ostensurus quare non fecerit. Et habeas ibi summonitores et hoc breve. Teste, etc.*

iii) *Writ of entry in the per and cui*[11]

The King to the sheriff of *N* greeting. Command *A* that justly and without delay he render to *B* one water gulf with the appurtenances in *D*, which he claimeth to be his right and inheritance and into which the same *A* hath not entry but by *C* to whom the aforesaid *B* demised it for a term which is past. And unless he will do this etc.

Rex vicecomiti N *salutem. Praecipe* A *quod juste et sine dilatione reddat* B *unum gurgitem cum pertinentiis in* D, *quod clamat esse jus et haereditatem suam et in quem idem* A *non habet ingressum nisi per* C *cui praedictus* B *illud dimisit ad terminum qui praeteriit etc. Et nisi fecerit etc.* [as above].

iv) *Writ of formedon in the descender*[12]

The King to the sheriff of *M* greeting. Command *A* that justly and without delay he render to *B* the manor of *N* with the appurtenances

10. Ibid., 5 I.
11. Ibid., 201 E.
12. Ibid., 212 D.

which *C* gave to *D* and *E* his wife, and the heirs of the bodies of the said *D* and *E* issuing, and which after the death of the aforesaid *D* and *E* ought to descend to the aforesaid *B* the son and heir of the aforesaid *D* and *E* by the form of the gift aforesaid, as he saith. And unless he will do this etc.

Rex vicecomiti M *salutem. Praecipe* A *quod juste et sine dilatione reddat* B *manerium de* N *cum pertinentiis quod* C *dedit* D *et* E *uxori ejus, et haeredibus de corporibus ipsorum* D *et* E *exeuntibus, et quod post mortem praedictorum* D *et* E *praefato* B *filio et haeredi praedictorum* D *et* E *descendere debet per formam donationis praedicti ut dicit. Et nisi fecerit etc.*

v) *Writ of covenant*[13]

The King to the sheriff of *L* greeting. Command *A* that justly and without delay he keep to *B* the covenant between them made for a certain granary to be newly constructed at *N* at the charges of him the said *B*. And unless he will do this etc.

Rex vicecomiti L *salutem. Praecipe* A *quod juste et sine dilatione teneat* B *conventionem inter eos factam de quodam granario sumptibus ipsius* B *apud* N *de novo construendo. Et nisi fecerit etc.*

vi) *Writ of debt*[14]

The King to the sheriff of *N* greeting. Command *A* that justly and without delay he render to *B* one hundred shillings, which he owes to him and unjustly detains, as he saith. And unless he will do this etc.

Rex vicecomiti N *salutem. Praecipe* A *quod juste et sine dilatione reddat* B *centum solidos quos ei debet et injuste detinet ut dicit. Et nisi fecerit etc.*

vii) *Writ of detinue of bonds*[15]

The King to the sheriff of *N* greeting. Command *A* that justly and without delay he render to *B* one box with three writings obligatory signed under the seal of the aforesaid *B*, contained in the same box, which he unjustly detains from him, as he saith. And unless he will do this etc.

Rex vicecomiti N *salutem. Praecipe* A *quod juste et sine dilatione reddat* B *unam pixidem cum tribus scriptis obligatoriis in eadem pixide contentis sub sigillo praedicti* B *consignatis, quam ei injuste detinet, ut dicit. Et nisi fecerit etc.*

viii) *Writ of quod permittat for pasture*[16]

The King to the sheriff of *M* greeting. Command *A* that justly and

13. *Registrum Omnium Brevium* (1531), f. 166a.
14. Fitz. *Nat. Brev.*, 119 L. Cf. Glanvill, x, 2.
15. Ibid., 138 B.
16. Ibid., 123 G.

without delay he permit *B* to have common of pasture in *N* and in forty acres of wood, which he ought to have, as he saith. And unless he will do this etc.

Rex vicecomiti M *salutem. Praecipe* A *quod juste et sine dilatione permittat* B *habere communiam pasturae in* N *et xl acris bosci, quam habere debet, ut dicit. Et nisi fecerit etc.*

B: POSSESSORY ASSIZES

i) *The assize of mort d'ancestor*[17]

The King to the sheriff of *S* greeting. If *A* shall make you secure to prosecute his claim, then summon by good summoners twelve free and lawful men of the neighbourhood of *N* that they be before our justices at the first assize when they shall come into those parts, ready to recognise by oath whether *W* father of the aforesaid *A* was seised in his demesne as of fee of one messuage and one yard-land with the appurtenances in *N* on the day he died, and whether he died after the coronation of the Lord King Henry, and whether the same *A* be his next heir. And in the mean time let them view the said messuage and land, and cause their names to be put in the writ, and summon by good summoners *B* who now holds the aforesaid messuage and lands, that he may be there to hear that recognition. And have there the summoners and this writ. Witness etc.

Rex vicecomiti S *salutem. Si* A *fecerit te securum de clamore suo prosequendo tunc summone per bonos summonitores xij liberos et legales homines de visneto de* N *quod sint coram justiciariis nostris ad primam assisam cum in partes illas venerint, parati sacramento recognoscere si* W *pater praedicti* A *fuit seisitus in dominico suo ut de feodo de uno mesuagio et una virgata terrae cum pertinentiis in* N *die quo obiit. Et si obiit post coronationem domini* H *Regis. Et si idem* A *propinquior haeres ejus sit. Et interim praedictum mesuagium et terram videant, et nomina eorum imbreviari facias, et summone per bonos summonitores* B *qui praedictum mesuagium et terras nunc tenet, quod sit ibi ad audiendum illam recognitionem, et habeas ibi summonitores et hoc breve. Teste etc.*

ii) *The assize of novel disseisin*[18]

The King to the sheriff of *N* greeting. *A* hath complained unto us, that *B* unjustly and without judgment hath disseised him of his freehold in *C* after the first passage of the Lord King Henry, son of King John, into Gascony; and therefore we command you that if the aforesaid *A* shall make you secure to prosecute his claim, then cause that tenement to be re-seised of the chattels which were taken in it, and the

17. Ibid., 195 E. Cf. Glanvill, xiii, 3.
18. Ibid., 177 F. Cf. Glanvill, xiii, 33.

same tenement with the chattels to be in peace until the first assize when our justices shall come into those parts, and in the mean time cause twelve free and lawful men of that neighbourhood to view that tenement, and their names to be put into the writ; and summon them by good summoners that they be before the justices aforesaid at the assize aforesaid ready to make recognition thereupon, and put by gages and safe pledges the aforesaid *B* or (if he shall not be found) his bailiff, that he may be then there to hear that recognition. And have there the summoners, the names of the pledges, and this writ.

Rex vicecomiti N salutem. Quaestus est nobis A quod B injuste et sine judicio disseisivit eum de libero tenemento suo in C post primam transfretationem Domini Henrici Regis filii Johannis in Vasconia, et ideo tibi praecipimus, quod si praedictus A fecerit te securum de clamore suo prosequendo tunc facias tenementum illud reseisiri de catallis quod in ipso capta fuerint et ipsum tenementum cum catallis esse in pace usque ad primam assisam cum Justiciarii nostri in partes illas venerint, et interim facias xii liberos et legales homines de visneto illo videre tenementum illud et nomina illorum imbreviari; et summone eos per bonos summonitores quod sint coram praefatis Justiciariis ad praefatam assisam parati inde facere recognitionem, et pone per vadios et salvos plegios praedictum B vel ballivum suum si ipse inventus non fuerit, quod tunc sit ibi ad audiendum illam recognitionem, etc. Et habeas ibi summonitores nomina plegiorum et hoc breve, etc.

C: OSTENSURUS QUARE WRITS

i) *Writ of trespass vi et armis (for battery)* [19]

The King to the sheriff of *S* greeting. If *A* shall make you secure to prosecute his claim, then put by gages and safe pledges *B* that he be before us on the octave of St. Michael, wheresoever we shall then be in England,[20] to shew wherefore with force and arms he made an assault upon him the said *A*, at *N*, and beat, wounded and ill treated him, so that his life was despaired of, and inflicted other outrages upon him, to the grave damage of him the said *A* and against our peace. And have there the names of the pledges and this writ.

Rex vicecomiti S salutem. Si A fecerit te securum de clamore suo prosequendo, tunc pone per vadios et salvos plegios B quod sit coram nobis in octavis Sancti Michaelis ubicunque fuerimus tunc in Anglia[21] *ostensurus quare vi et armis in ipsum A apud N insultum fecit, et ipsum verberavit, vulneravit et male tractavit, ita quod de vita ejus desperabatur, et alia enormia ei intulit, ad grave dampnum*

---

19. Fitz. *Nat. Brev.*, 86 I. For a specimen declaration on such a writ, see p. 448, post.
20. King's Bench. Or 'before our justices at Westminster on the octave of St. Michael' (Common Pleas).
21. Or '*coram Justiciariis nostris apud Westmonasterium in octavis Sancti Michaelis*' (see last note).

ipsius A *et contra pacem nostram. Et habeas ibi nomina plegiorum et hoc breve. Teste etc.*

ii) *Writ of ejectment*[22]

The King to the sheriff of *N* greeting. If *A* shall make you secure to prosecute his claim, then put by gages and safe pledges *B* that he be before our justices at Westminster [on such a day] to shew wherefore with force and arms he entered into the manor of *I* which *T* demised to the said *A* for a term which is not yet passed, and took and carried away the goods and chattels of him the said *A* to the value etc. found in the same manor, and ejected him the said *A* from his farm aforesaid, and inflicted other outrages upon him, to the grave damage of him the said *A* and against our peace. And have there the names of the pledges and this writ.

Rex vicecomiti N *salutem. Si* A *fecerit te securum de clamore suo prosequendo, tunc pone per vadios et salvos plegios* B *quod sit coram Justiciariis nostris apud Westmonasterium* [*tali die*] *ostensurus quare vi et armis manerium de* I, *quod* T *praefato* A *dimisit ad terminum quod nondum praeteriit, intravit, et bona et catalla ejusdem* A *ad valentiam etc. in eodem manerio inventa cepit et asportavit, et ipsum* A *a firma sua praedicta ejecit, et alia enormia ei intulit, ad grave damnum ipsius* A *et contra pacem nostram. Et habeas ibi nomina plegiorum et hoc breve.*

iii) *Writ of trespass on the case for negligence*[23]

The King to the sheriff of *L* greeting. If John *S* shall make you secure to prosecute his claim, then put by gages and safe pledges *R* that he be etc., to shew wherefore, whereas the same John had delivered a certain horse to the said *R*, at *N*, well and sufficiently to shoe, the same *R* fixed a certain nail in the quick of the foot of the aforesaid horse in such manner that the horse was in many ways made worse, to the damage of him the said John one hundred shillings, as he saith. And have there the names of the pledges and this writ.

Rex vicecomiti L *salutem. Si Johannes* S *fecerit te securum de clamore suo prosequendo, tunc pone per vadios et salvos plegios* R *quod sit etc. ostensurus quare cum idem Johannes quendam equum praefato* R *ad bene et competenter ferrandum apud* N *tradidisset: idem* R *quendam clavum in vivo pedis equi praedicti intantum infixit, quod equus ille multipliciter deterioratus fuit, ad damnum ipsius Johannis centum solidorum ut dicit. Et habeas ibi nomina plegiorum et hoc breve.*

22. Fitz. *Nat. Brev.*, 220 G. For the pleadings in such an action, in full, see Bl Comm, vol. III. Appendix II.
23. *Registrum Omnium Brevium* (1531), f. 106a.

iv) *Writ of assumpsit for negligence by a carrier*[24]

The King to the sheriff of *L* greeting. If *NA* shall make you secure to prosecute his claim, then put by gages and safe pledges *TB* that he be etc., to shew wherefore, whereas the same *T* at the town of *S* had undertaken safely and securely to carry a certain pipe of wine of him the said *N* from the [aforesaid] town of *S* to the town of *F*, the aforesaid *T* carried the pipe so negligently and carelessly that in default of him the said *T* the pipe was cracked, so that the same *N* lost the great part of the aforesaid wine, to the damage of him the said *N* ten marks, as he saith. And have there the names of the pledges and this writ.

Rex vicecomiti L *salutem. Si* NA *fecerit te securum de clamore suo prosequendo, tunc pone per vadios et salvos plegios* TB *quod sit etc. ostensurus quare cum idem* T *ad quandam pipam vini ipsius* N *a villa de* S *usque villam de* F *salvo et secure cariandam apud praedictam villam de* S *assumpsisset: praedictus* T *pipam illam tam negligenter et improvide cariavit, quod pipa illa in defectu ipsius* T *confracta fuit, sicque idem* N *magnam partem vini praedicti amisit, ad damnum ipsius* N *decem marcarum ut dicit. Et habeas ibi nomina plegiorum et hoc breve.*

v) *Writ of assumpsit for nonfeasance*[25]

The King to the sheriff of *L* greeting. If *WH* shall make you secure to prosecute his claim, then put by gages and safe pledges *JP* that he be etc., to shew wherefore, whereas the same *J*, for a certain sum of money paid to him in hand by the aforesaid *W*, had undertaken [at *R*] newly to construct a cross of stones at *R* within a certain term, the aforesaid John did not take care to construct the said cross within the aforesaid term, to the damage of him the said *W* twenty pounds, as he saith. And have there the names of the pledges and this writ.

Rex vicecomiti L *salutem. Si* WH *fecerit te securum de clamore suo prosequendo, tunc pone per vadios et salvos plegios* JP *quod sit etc. ostensurus quare cum idem* J *pro quadam pecuniae summa sibi per praefatum* W *prae manibus soluta, quandam crucem de lapidibus apud* R *infra certum terminum de novo construere ibidem assumpsisset: praedictum Johannes crucem illam infra terminum praedictum construere non curavit, ad damnum ipsius* W *viginti librarum ut dicit. Et habeas ibi nomina plegiorum et hoc breve.*

24. Ibid., f. 110a.
25. Ibid., f. 109b.

Prerogative Writs

i) *Writ of error*[26]

The King to his trusty and beloved *AB*, knight,[27] greeting. Because in the record and process, and also in the giving of judgment, of the plaint which was in our court before you and your fellows our justices of the Bench, by our writ, between *X* and *Y*, of a certain debt of two hundred pounds which the same *X* has recovered against him in our same court before you and your aforesaid fellows, manifest error hath intervened, to the great damage of him the said *Y* as we from his complaint are fully informed: We, being willing that the error, if any there be, should be corrected in due manner, and that full and speedy justice should be done to the parties aforesaid in this behalf, do command you, that if judgment thereof be given, then under your seal you do distinctly and openly send the record and process of the plaint aforesaid, with all things concerning them and this writ, so that we may have them in three weeks from the day of the Holy Trinity wheresoever we shall then be in England; that, the record and process aforesaid being inspected, we may cause to be done thereupon, for correcting that error, what of right and according to the law and custom of our realm of England ought to be done.

Rex dilecto et fideli suo AB *militi salutem. Quia in recordo et processu ac etiam in redditione judicii loquelae quae fuit in Curia nostra coram vobis et sociis vestris justiciariis nostris de Banco per breve nostrum inter* X *et* Y *de quodam debito ducentarum librarum quod idem* X *in eadem Curia nostra coram vobis et sociis vestris praedictis recuperavit versus eum error intervenit manifestum ad grave dampnum ipsius* Y *sicut ex querela sua accepimus: Nos errorem si quis fuerit modo debito corrigi et partibus praedictis plenam et celerem justiciam fieri volentes in hac parte vobis mandamus quod si judicium inde redditum sit tunc recordum et processum loquelae praedictae cum omnibus ea tangentibus nobis sub sigillo vestro distincte et aperte mittatis et hoc breve ita quod habeamus a die sanctae Trinitatis in tres septimanas ubicunque tunc fuerimus in Anglia ut inspectis recordo et processu praedictis ulterius inde pro errore illo corrigendo fieri faciamus quod de jure et secundum legem et consuetudinem regni nostri Angliae fuerit faciendum.*

ii) *Writ of certiorari to commissioners of sewers*[28]

The King to his trusty and beloved *A*, *B*, *C* and *D*, our justices

---

26. Based on Coke's *Entries*, f. 246; Bl Comm, vol. III, Appendix III(6).
27. Chief Justice of the Common Pleas. The same form *mutatis mutandis* was used for all other courts of record.
28. *Registrum Omnium Brevium* (1687), f. 287. This form is for removal into the Chancery, but a similar form was used by the King's Bench for reviewing summary convictions and justices' orders.

assigned to survey the banks, dykes, channels, sewers, bridges, causeys and weirs by the coast of the sea and marsh in the parts of *M* between the waters of *E, F, G* and *H*, in the county of *E*, and to each of them, greeting. We, being willing for certain causes to be informed concerning all and singular the presentments made or presented before yourselves, as it is said, against *JS* by whatever name he is rated: We command you that under the seals of yourselves, or of one of you, you do distinctly and openly send the tenors of the aforesaid presentments, and this writ, to us in our Chancery at such a day wheresoever it should then be.

Rex dilectis et fidelibus suis A, B, C *et* D, *justiciariis nostris ad wallias fossata gutteras seweras pontes calceta et gurgites per costeram maris et marisci in partibus de* M *inter aquas de* E, F, G·*et* H, *in comitatu* E *supervidenda assignatis et eorum cuilibet salutem. Volentes certis de causis certiorari super omnibus et singulis praesentationibus coram vobis versus* JS *quocunque nomine censeatur factis sive praesentatis ut dicitur: Vobis mandamus quod tenores praesentationum praedictorum nobis in cancellariam nostram tali die ubicunque fuerit sub sigillis vestris vel unius vestrum distincte et aperte mittatis et hoc breve.*

iii) *Writ of habeas corpus ad subjiciendum*[29]

The King to *JL*, knight, Warden of our prison of the Fleet, greeting. We command you that you do have the body of *WE*, knight, who as it is said is detained in our prison under your custody, by whatever name the aforesaid *WE* is charged, before us on such a day wheresoever we shall then be in England, together with the cause of his detention, to undergo and receive what our court should then and there happen to order concerning him in that behalf. And this in no wise omit, upon the peril incumbent, and have there this writ.

Rex JL *militi Gardiano prisonae nostrae de le Fleet salutem. Praecipimus tibi quod corpus* WE *militis in prisona nostra sub custodia tua detentum ut dicitur una cum causa detentionis suae quocunque nomine praedictus* WE *censeatur in eadem habeas coram nobis tali die ubicunque tunc fuerimus in Anglia ad subjiciendum et recipiendum ea quae curia nostra de eo adtunc et ibidem ordinare contigerit in hac parte et hoc nullatenus omittas periculo incumbente et habeas ibi hoc breve.*

Writ of Summons after 1834[30]

William the fourth by the grace of God etc. to *CD* of *Y* in the county of *Z* greeting. We command you that within eight days after the service

29. Based on 3 State Tr 11 (1628), which contains several misprints.
30. Uniformity of Process Act, 2 Will IV, c.39, Sch. I. With slight changes, the same form is still in use.

of this writ on you, inclusive of the day of such service, you do cause an appearance to be entered for you in our court of . . . in an action on promises [*or as the case may be*][31] at the suit of *AB*; and take notice, that in default of your so doing the said *AB* may cause an appearance to be entered for you and proceed therein to judgment and execution. Witness etc.

31. This statement of the cause of action was omitted after 1852. The forms of writ ordained in 1852 are set out in the Common Law Procedure Act 1852, 15 & 16 Vict, c.76, Sch. A.

Appendix B
Specimen Pleadings

Few law students will ever have occasion to consult a plea roll; but the forms of pleading used before 1852 were so different from those of today that it will be instructive to read this specimen entry, selected at random from the rolls of the King's Bench. The words have been extended from the original court-hand, and punctuation introduced.

Similar forms of pleading were in use for over five centuries. English was used from 1650 to 1660 and after 1731, but the same formulae were retained. The specimen shows an issue joined in common form upon a justification of battery in self defence. Other precedents, with Latin and English in parallel texts, will be found in the publications of the Selden Society and Ames Foundation. Examples, for instance, of actions on the case, account, debt, trespass, error, and criminal proceedings, including special pleas, demurrers, verdicts and judgments, will be found in the records belonging to Spelman's *Reports* (94 SS, 1978).

Frenche v Baker (1470)[1]

Midd' § *Johannes Baker husbondman attachiatus fuit ad respondendum Thomae French de placito transgressionis per billam. Et sunt plegii de prosequendo, scilicet Ricardus Rous et Hugo Hunt.*

[*Note of commencement:*] MIDDLESEX John Baker, husbandman, was attached to answer Thomas Frenche concerning a plea of trespass by bill. And there are pledges for prosecuting, to wit, Richard Rous and Hugh Hunt.[2]

Et unde idem Thomas, in propria persona sua, quaeritur quod praedictus Johannes, decimo septimo die Novembris anno regni regis Edwardi quarti post

1. Public Record Office, KB 27/835, membrane 22 (Hilary term, 9 Edward IV).
2. Where the bill was brought against a defendant arrested by *latitat*, the record began with a memorandum that on a certain date a bill was preferred against the defendant 'being in the custody of the marshal' and the bill was then set out. Where proceedings were originated by writ, the record would note the writ and proceed (as here) with a declaration. The pledges were taken to ensure that the plaintiff pursued the action; but by this date they were fictitious.

conquestum nono, vi et armis, videlicet gladiis, baculis, etc., domum ipsius Thomae apud Westborne in comitatu praedicto fregit et intravit et in ipsum Thomam adtunc et ibidem insultum fecit et in ipsum verberavit vulneravit et male tractavit et alia enormia ei intulit contra pacem domini Regis praedicti; unde dicit quod deterioratus est et dampnum habet ad valenciam viginti librarum. Et inde producit sectam.

[*Count, or declaration:*] And thereupon the same Thomas, in his own person,[3] complains that the aforesaid John on 17 November 1469 with force and arms—that is to say, with swords, staves, and so forth[4]—broke and entered the house of him the said Thomas at Westbourne in the aforesaid county, and then and there made assault upon him the said Thomas and beat, wounded and ill treated him, and inflicted other outrages upon him, against the peace of the lord King aforesaid; whereby he says he is the worse and has damage to the value of twenty pounds. And thereof he produces suit.[5]

Et praedictus Johannes Baker, per Thomam Luyt attornatum suum, venit et defendit vim et injuriam quando etc. Et quoad venire vi et armis, seu quicquid quod est contra pacem domini Regis, ac totam transgressionem praedictam praeter insultum praedictum, dicit quod ipse in nullo est inde culpabilis. Et de hoc ponit se super patriam. Et praedictus Thomas Frenche similiter.

Et quoad insultum illum idem Johannes Baker dicit quod praedictus Thomas Frenche actionem suam praedictam inde versus eum manutenere non debet; quia dicit quod praedictus Thomas Frenche, praedicto decimo septimo die Novembris apud Westborne praedictam, in ipsum Johannem insultum fecit et ipsum adtunc et ibidem verberasse vulnerasse et male tractasse voluerit; idemque Johannes se erga praefatum Thomam Frenche adtunc et ibidem defendebat; et malum si quod eidem Thomae adtunc et ibidem evenit, hoc fuit de insultu ipsius Thomae proprio et in defensione ipsius Johannis. Et hoc paratus est verificare, unde petit judicium si praedictus Thomas Frenche actionem suam praedictam inde versus eum manutenere debeat etc.

[*Defence:*] And the aforesaid John Baker, by Thomas Luyt his attorney, come and denies the force and wrong when [and where he ought].[6] [*Plea of not guilty as to all but the assault:*] And as to the coming with force and arms, or whatever is against the peace of the lord King, and all the aforesaid trespass except the assault aforesaid, he says that he is in no wise guilty thereof. And of this he puts himself upon the

---

3. I.e., he was not represented by attorney.
4. These words were mere form, and were used no matter how the trespass was actually inflicted. Bows and arrows were sometimes added for good measure.
5. The 'suit' were originally witnesses, but long before 1470 the words had become mere form.
6. *Defendere* here means 'deny'. The 'defence', or general denial, was not part of the plea but was the way of entering an appearance.

country. And the aforesaid Thomas Frenche likewise. [*Special plea of self defence as to the assault:*] And as to the assault, the same John Baker says that the aforesaid Thomas Frenche ought not to maintain his aforesaid action against him for that; because he says that the aforesaid Thomas Frenche, on the aforesaid 17 November at Westbourne aforesaid, made assault upon him the said John and would then and there have beaten, wounded and ill treated him; and the same John then and there defended himself against the aforesaid Thomas; and if any ill then and there came to the same Thomas, it was a result of Thomas's own assault and in defence of him the said John.[7] [*Averment:*] And this he is ready to verify. [*Conclusion si actio:*] And so he prays judgment whether the aforesaid Thomas ought to maintain his aforesaid action against him therein.

Et praedictus Thomas Frenche dicit quod ipse per aliquam praeallegationem ab actione sua praedicta de insultu praedicto versus eum habenda praecludi non debet; quia dicit quod praedictus Johannes, tempore transgressionis praedictae factae, vi et armis de injuria sua propria et absque causa per ipsum Johannem superius placitando allegata, in praedictum Thomam Frenche insultum fecit in forma qua idem Thomas superius versus eum quaeritur. Et hoc petit quod inquiratur per patriam. Et praedictus Johannes similiter.

[*Replication de injuria:*] And the aforesaid Thomas says that he ought not to be barred by anything so far alleged from having his aforesaid action against him for the assault aforesaid; because he says that the aforesaid John, at the time when the aforesaid trespass was done, of his own wrong and without the cause alleged by him the said John above in his pleading, made assault upon the aforesaid Thomas Frenche with force and arms in the way that the same Thomas above complains against him.[8] [*Joinder of issue:*] And this he prays may be inquired into by the country.[9] And the aforesaid John likewise.

Here the pleadings end, because the parties have reached issue. The next stage would have been the trial. If the case proceeded so far, the roll would record the writ of *venire facias juratores*, the *postea* clause with the verdict of the jurors, and the judgment.

---

7. As the plea depended on the notion of retaliation, the assault was said to be a result of the plaintiff's own assault: *de son assault demesne.*
8. The replication *de injuria* enabled the plaintiff to put the whole of the plea in issue, and did not drive him to take issue on any single fact alleged in the plea. See *Crogate v Marys* (1608) 8 Co Rep 66.
9. I.e., by jury. The replication *de injuria* 'concludes to the country' because no new allegations have been introduced. The plaintiff tendered issue by praying an inquiry; if the defendant tendered issue (as Baker does, ante, as to the residue), the words were *de hoc ponit se super patriam: Practice Note* (1534) YB Trin 26 Hen VIII, 3, pl. 12.

Index